Fundamentals of
Media Effects

Third Edition

Jennings Bryant
late of University of Alabama

Bruce W. Finklea
University of Montevallo

WAVELAND

PRESS, INC.
Long Grove, Illinois

For information about this book, contact:
Waveland Press, Inc.
4180 IL Route 83, Suite 101
Long Grove, IL 60047-9580
(847) 634-0081
info@waveland.com
www.waveland.com

In memory of
Dr. Jennings Bryant
1944–2020
A true scholar, mentor, and friend

About the Authors

Jennings Bryant (PhD, Indiana University, 1974) was Distinguished Professor Emeritus at The University of Alabama (UA). Prior to his retirement in 2010, he was CIS Distinguished Research Professor, holder of the Reagan Endowed Chair of Broadcasting, and Associate Dean for Graduate Studies and Research in the College of Communication and Information Sciences at UA. He received the university's Burnum Distinguished Faculty Award in 2008, the Blackmon-Moody Outstanding Professor Award for 2000, and was President of the International Communication Association (ICA) in 2002–2003. In 2006, he received a Distinguished Scholar Award from the Broadcast Education Association, was elected a Fellow of the International Communication Association, and a Research Pioneer Tribute Essay was published in his honor in the *Journal of Broadcasting & Electronic Media* ("Jennings Bryant—The 'Compleat' Scholar"). In 2011, he received the Steven Chaffee Career Productivity Award from ICA. Bryant was inducted into the University of Alabama College of Communication and Information Sciences Hall of Fame in 2018. He was Advisory Editor of the 12-volume *International Encyclopedia of Communication*. Bryant was author or editor of more than two dozen scholarly books or textbooks in communication. He also published 160 journal articles and more than 250 conference papers.

Bruce W. Finklea (PhD, University of Alabama, 2014) is an Associate Professor and Coordinator of Mass Communication at the University of Montevallo. Finklea teaches a variety of courses related to broadcast news production, media and culture, and media theory and effects. In 2021, Finklea was the recipient of the University of Montevallo National Alumni Association Outstanding Commitment to Teaching Award. He was selected for the UMNNA's 15 Within 15 Award in 2022, which recognizes 15 alumni achieving success within the first 15 years of earning their degree. Finklea's research focuses on gender portrayals in children's media, particularly in Pixar films. In addition to the second and third editions of *Fundamentals of Media Effects*, he has contributed to the *International Encyclopedia of Media Effects*, *Communication Theory and Millennial Popular Culture: Essays and Applications*, and *Race and Gender in Electronic Media: Content, Context, Culture*.

Contents

Section Two
THEORY AND CONCEPTS

Section Three
KEY AREAS OF RESEARCH

Preface

From polarized presidential elections to a global pandemic, recent years have highlighted the ever-present role of mass media in our daily lives. College students are socialized into an environment in which media permeate their lives and are so omnipresent that they are essentially invisible—like water to those proverbially oblivious fish. Moreover, today's typical undergraduate students are so routinely exposed to inaccurate hype about media effects in popular culture that setting the record straight about media effects has become an increasingly important part of a liberal arts education. Although most of today's students may not remember a time without social media and smartphones, the fact that they grew up surrounded by media technologies and messages does not mean they necessarily understand how and why mass media impact their lives.

For more than two decades, the primary goal of *Fundamentals of Media Effects* has been to represent the massive body of literature about media effects in such a way that undergraduate students can comprehend, manage, and appreciate this vitally important topic. By building a foundational understanding of prominent mass communication theories and exploring major areas of research, this book can help students develop their media literacy skills and become better media producers, consumers, and citizens.

The world has undergone significant changes since the release of the previous edition of this text. Similarly, the third edition of *Fundamentals of Media Effects* has received *significant* updates that highlight advances in communication theory, effects, and psychology.

Special Features

In order to assist instructors who teach courses in media theory and effects, we are pleased to offer several special features within the book plus supplemental instructor materials on Waveland Press's website (waveland.com).

Key Terms

In each chapter, key terms that need to be understood in order for students to fully comprehend the material are identified by bold typeface and are defined in the accompanying discussion.

Research Spotlights

Starting in Chapter 4, each chapter contains a Research Spotlight that gives students a deeper look at a key study related to the chapter. Structured similarly to research articles, Research Spotlights allow students to see the hypotheses, research questions, methods, samples, and results in greater detail.

Test Bank

Instructors can obtain a password from the publisher (see book's web page) to access numerous multiple choice and true/false questions (available in both Word and PDF formats).

PowerPoint Slides

PowerPoint slides for each chapter include summaries of chapter concepts and key figures.

Discussion Questions

The instructor resources include discussion questions for each chapter that can spark lively conversations between you and your students and encourage students to think about the roles and effects of mediated communication in their lives. The questions can work well as in-class exercises or as online assignments.

Acknowledgments

When Jennings Bryant and Susan Thompson set out to write the First Edition of this text more than 20 years ago, they were aided by the feedback and advice of numerous reviewers:

Oscar Patterson III, University of North Florida
George Comstock, Syracuse University
Daniel Riffe, Ohio University
Elizabeth Perse, University of Delaware
James Weaver, Emory University
Mary Cassata, SUNY—Buffalo
David J. Atkin, Cleveland State University
Michael Meffert, University of Maryland
Mike Basil, University of Lethbridge
John Chapin, Pennsylvania State University
Randyll Yoder, Ohio University
Donald Singleton, Salisbury State University
Diane Furno Lumade, University of New Mexico
Susanna Priest, University of Nevada, Las Vegas

As we were working on revisions for the Second Edition, we also received valuable feedback from the following First Edition adopters. Our sincere appreciation to:

William Christ, Trinity University
Aysel Morin, East Carolina University
Sriram Kalyanaraman, University of North Carolina

After Susan Thompson's retirement, Dr. Bryant and I set out to write this edition, and we were extremely appreciative of the Second Edition reviewers and early adopters who provided feedback:

Amy Damico, Endicott College
Jennifer Fogel, SUNY—Oswego
Carol Walker, East Stroudsburg University
Emily Edwards, University of North Carolina—Greensboro
Reed Smith, Georgia Southern University
James Denny, Cleveland State University
Bruce Drushel, Miami University
James Robinson, University of Dayton
Jessica Myrick, Indiana University
Glenn G. Sparks, Purdue University
Hernando Rojas, University of Wisconsin
Beth Austin, University of Wisconsin
Carol Atkinson, University of Central Missouri
Michael Throop, Benedictine College
Joe Watson, Baker University
Sophie Janicke, University of Arkansas
Daekyung Kim, Idaho State University
Clariza Ruiz De Castilla, California State University
Cecilia Uy-Tioco, California State University
Bradley Bond, University of San Diego
Patricia Hernandez, California Baptist University
Riva Tukachinsky, Chapman University
Ruth Moon, University of Washington

My deepest thanks go to Dr. Jennings Bryant. Even in retirement, he was eager to take on this project. It was such a pleasure to once again work alongside such a titan in the field. I am thankful to have known him as a mentor and friend for more than a decade. Understandably, his passing in late 2020 came as a shock. I was unsure if I could complete the monumental task of writing a new edition without him, but thanks to the encouragement of my outstanding publisher, Neil Rowe, I carried on. Rest assured, Dr. Bryant's words and (most importantly) his wisdom are still very much a part of *Fundamentals of Media Effects, Third Edition*. My hope is that this edition would make him proud.

I would also like to thank Waveland Press's dynamic duo, Neil and Carol Rowe. This book would not have been possible without their encouragement and patience. I promise that I worked as fast as I could (which, as it turns out, was pretty slow).

There are so many friends and family who have supported me throughout the years it took to complete this book. To my wife, Jackie, and daughter, Harper, thank you for putting up with me for countless evenings and weekends where I was holed up in my office writing. I look forward to enjoying much more free time with you two! Thanks to my dad, Bill, who helped proofread some of the chapters. To Justin and Jennifer Thomas and Barry and Jessica Evans, thank you for your friendship and support; it means more to me than words can express. Special thanks to my students who provided feedback on drafts of the chapters in this edition. And to my colleagues in the University of Montevallo Department of Communication, your encouragement has been instrumental in helping me finish this project. Each of you has made me a better teacher and scholar.

Lastly, thank you to all of the professors who have waited patiently for me to finish this edition. I invite you to become part of the editorial team. Please send comments and suggestions about how *Fundamentals of Media Effects* can better serve you in your classrooms as you endeavor to teach students about the effects of media on our society.

Bruce W. Finklea

Section One

OVERVIEW AND HISTORY

┌─┐
│ **1** │
└─┘

Understanding Media Effects

> Whoever controls the media, controls the mind.
>
> —Jim Morrison
> American musician, 1943–1971

In 1995, an Oklahoma couple, 18-year-olds Benjamin Darras and Sarah Edmonson, became obsessed with *Natural Born Killers,* a violent movie about a young duo who engage in a random killing spree after taking hallucinogenic drugs. Darras and Edmonson watched the video up to six times a day. They wanted to become the main characters, Mickey and Mallory, who murder innocent people for the sheer thrill of it, apparently feel no remorse, and ultimately escape punishment for their evil deeds.

One day in early March, Darras and Edmonson smoked some grass, dropped some acid, loaded some guns, and went out joy riding in search of a Grateful Dead concert. Like their heroes in the film, they also went looking for victims. They never found the concert, but they did find victims, the first of them in rural Mississippi. Darras shot a cotton gin manager named Bill Savage. The first shot grazed Savage's shoulder, but the second hit him in the face, killing him (Ahrens, 1995). The next day, after traveling to Louisiana, Edmonson put a bullet in the throat of Patsy Byers, a convenience store clerk and mother of three, and left her for dead. (Byers lived the next two years as a quadriplegic. She died in 1997, the day before she was supposed to record her testimony for Edmonson's trial [Baldwin, 2010].) During Darras and Edmonson's murderous road trip, life had unfortunately imitated "art."

Such instances of imitation are rare, but their sensational nature attracts tremendous attention from the news media. As you will learn in the chapters throughout this book, a great deal of research has revealed that people learn from mediated communication (Bandura, 1977, 1986, 1994, 2009), and numerous studies have found a causal link between the viewing of media violence and an increase in aggressive behavior (e.g., Bandura, 1978, 1979, 1982, 1986; Centerwall, 1989; Liebert & Schwartzberg, 1977; Williams, 1986). For decades, no research findings or theoretical formulations adequately explained why the great majority of people who watch violent movies seemingly exhibit no ill effects, whereas a few go out and imitate the actions they see on the screen—no matter how gruesome those actions. Our knowledge of the link between media violence and aggression is growing, however. Several different theories explaining why media violence may result in real-world violence have been proposed and tested. Recent developments in communication theory focus on why some people are more susceptible to media effects than others.

Measuring the effects of viewing screen violence represents one important facet of media effects research, but the study of media effects encompasses many other types of research as well. Social scientists are also interested in the persuasive powers of mass mediated messages (advertisements, propaganda, communication campaigns, etc.), the impact of new communication technologies, the effects of viewing sexually explicit media fare, reactions to frightening or disturbing media content, effects from political communication, and much more.

This chapter provides a foundation for the concepts, theories, and research methodologies covered throughout the remainder of the text, which is divided into three sections. In the first, we will explore the importance of media effects from a historical perspective. We will also review historical evidence for media effects (and for societal concern about them) since the dawn of mass communication. The first section concludes with a look at the history of the scientific study of media effects and some of the pioneers in the field. The next section includes several of the concepts and theories that serve as the basis for different types of media effects research. Social cognitive theory, priming, agenda setting, framing, cultivation, uses and gratifications, and various persuasion theories are covered, along with some of the relevant research in each of the areas. The final section covers key areas of media research, including the effects of media violence, sexual content, disturbing or frightening media content, political communication, health-related media messages, media stereotypes and representations of diversity, children's educational media, video games, the internet and social media, and mobile communication technologies.

Following a review of communication processes in this chapter, we turn to a brief discussion of different types of communication models. We then explore the quantitative and qualitative research methodologies social scientists use to measure media effects and the theories that inform and guide the study of media effects. The chapter concludes with a word about the importance of studying media effects in today's media-saturated society.

Processes of Communication

> Communication can be any or all of the following: an *action on* others,
> an *interaction with* others, and a *reaction to* others.
>
> —McQuail & Windahl (1993, p. 5)

Communication may take several different forms. It may be interpersonal in nature, it may involve the use of a personal communication medium, or it may be described as mass communication. When two people have a conversation, they are engaging in *interpersonal communication.* When people text each other or converse via social media or email, *media* (or *mediated) communication* occurs. When a news anchor talks to a camera and their image and voice are transmitted to a large number of viewers watching on television or news apps, *mass communication* takes place.

The act of communicating involves a *process*. In its simplest form, communication historically has been perceived as a sender delivering a message via a channel to a receiver, *usually* producing some kind of effect. For instance, we hear a joke, and we laugh. We see a sad movie, and we cry. We listen to a lecture, and we learn—or we become confused. These examples illustrate that communication may be thought of as a *cause* that produces some kind of *effect*. Another view of communication is that of *symbolic interaction*, whereby meaning is shared through the use of symbols, which can be either words or images.

We emphasize the word *usually* in the previous paragraph because not all communication produces effects. The effects of any communication are subject to the conditions under which the communication occurs: the receptivity of listeners, readers, or viewers as well as numerous other factors. Certain factors may keep us from attending to the messages as we should, thereby mitigating effects or preventing them entirely. Someone may whisper something to us and cause us to miss the punch line of a joke. We may be more interested in our date than in the movie and not pay any attention whatsoever to the actions on the screen. We may sit through a lecture with our mind on upcoming weekend plans and walk out of the classroom without a clue as to what we just heard.

Even in its most basic form, communication between even two people is rarely simple and typically takes on an *interactional* or *transactional* dimension. In an interpersonal conversation, the listener may offer immediate feedback to the initial talker. In the course of a conversation or discussion, direct or electronically mediated senders and receivers may alternate repeatedly in their respective roles.

In contrast, the process of mass communication involves a single source (usually a complex entity like a television network) reaching thousands or millions of people with the same institutionalized message. The audience members are often heterogeneous—or demographically diverse—and typically are unknown to the message source. An interpersonal relationship between a network or station and any one audience member usually does not occur, although it should be noted that program websites and, especially, interactive television and other new media technologies can offer an interpersonal dimension to mass communication. Mass communication also has been revolutionized in recent decades with the widespread adoption of the internet and mobile technology. These media have shattered some of the previous ideas held about mass communication. Rather than consuming media produced by television and film studios, today's consumer is also a mass media producer. Consider the vast quantities of information people share on social media, which Castells (2007) calls "mass self-communication." As Valkenburg (2017) explains, "Like mass communication, mass self-communication can potentially reach a global audience, but it typically focuses on personal, self-related information" (p. 6). Research in this area extends traditional media effects theories that examine effects of recipients by also looking at effects on the message creators themselves, which are known as *self-effects*.

Communication Models

To understand processes of communication and effects from communication, some scholars have developed pictorial models to explain their theories and illustrate abstract notions regarding communication behavior. These models make it easier for us to identify the similarities and differences among the various types of communication. Models also help demonstrate the different processes of communication, whether linear, interactional, or transactional in nature.

A simple search for the phrase "communication model" in an academic database results in hundreds of hits. The ubiquity of the phrase has made it something of a cliché in academia. Models of communication have been employed in disciplines from psychiatry to parapsychology and just about everything in between.

Even in the field of communication, the phrase "communication model" may be used in several different ways. In this chapter, we define the term model as a pictorial means of explaining an abstract process such as communication. (In Chapter 3 "model" is used in another sense: to describe a prevailing paradigm or overall trend in scholarly thought, such as the powerful effects model, the limited effects model, and so forth.)

The pictorial models identified in this chapter offer three major advantages: they *organize* concepts, *explain* processes, and *predict* outcomes (Deutsch, 1966). These models range from the very simple to the very complex, but all attempt to make concepts readily understandable. A familiarity with these models may prove beneficial when the various instances of media effects are described throughout this book.

In this section we will briefly examine two broad categories of pictorial models: those that describe various communication processes and those that explicate some kinds of media effects. The examples we offer represent only a few of the many different kinds of communication models that scholars have developed.

Models to Depict Communication Processes

A number of pictorial models illustrate the various processes of communication, and scholars' understanding of communication processes and the models used to depict them have evolved over time. The earliest models depicted communication as a linear process, which we will discuss in this section because of their historical significance in the field of mass communication. Over the decades, models began highlighting the interactive and transactional nature of communication.

Linear models are based on the principles of stimulus-response psychology, in which a receiver is affected (response) by a message (stimulus) that emanates from a communication source. These models depict the communication process as a series of progressive, linear steps in the transmission of ideas from one person to another.

One of the first linear models of communication, known as the **Shannon-Weaver model**, described the process of telecommunication. Claude Shannon and Warren Weaver, researchers in the Bell Telephone laboratory in the 1940s, developed a model (see Figure 1.1) that depicts a message emanating from an information source, which becomes a signal after passing through a transmitter. Depending upon the amount of noise or interference present, the signal passes through to a receiver, where it is decoded as a message.

In the 1950s, Bruce Westley and Malcolm S. MacLean, Jr., sought to expand upon the Shannon-Weaver model. They developed a sender-receiver model to explain types of communication other than telecommunication, such as interpersonal and mass mediated. The various versions of the **Westley-MacLean model** (see Figures 1.2a and 1.2b) differ from the Shannon-Weaver model in that they include mechanisms for *feedback*

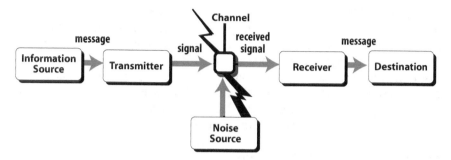

Figure 1.1   Shannon and Weaver's model describes communication as a linear, one-way process.

Source: Adapted from Shannon & Weaver, 1949, p. 7.

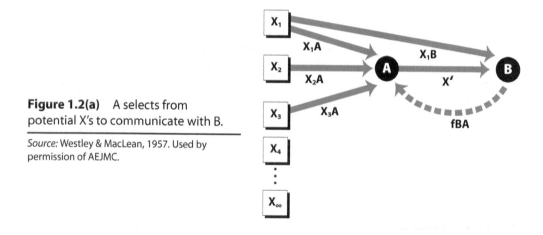

Figure 1.2(a)   A selects from potential X's to communicate with B.

Source: Westley & MacLean, 1957. Used by permission of AEJMC.

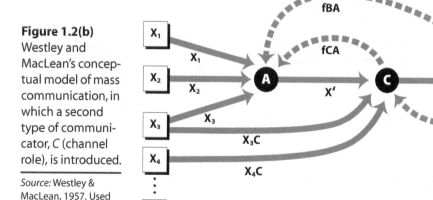

Figure 1.2(b) Westley and MacLean's conceptual model of mass communication, in which a second type of communicator, *C* (channel role), is introduced.

Source: Westley & MacLean, 1957. Used by permission of AEJMC.

(return flow of information from a receiver to the original source) and *gatekeeping* (a mechanism, usually a person, with the power to control information and even prevent it from reaching a destination). The gatekeeper was thought to be an important new dimension of communication models because it addresses the role of editors or news-cast producers, for example, who control and select the messages that ultimately get read in newspapers or watched on the news. Of course, communication is not such a simple, straightforward process. Later models of communication would highlight the increasingly complex nature of communication.

Models to Explain Media Effects

In addition to models that describe the overall processes of communication, scholars have advanced other models to depict the effects that may result whenever mediated communication occurs. Both micro- and macroanalytical models have been used to describe the different types and levels of media effects—from purely individual effects to influences on groups of people or even society at large. We will explain a few of those models in this section.

Individual Effects. One of the newest and most comprehensive media effects models is Valkenburg and Peter's (2013) **differential susceptibility to media effects model**, also known as the DSMM (see Figure 1.3). The aim of this model is "to reveal how and why specific types of media affect certain individuals; why some individuals are particularly susceptible to media effects; and how this susceptibility is enhanced or reduced" (p. 237). The DSMM identifies three types of susceptibility variables: *dispositional* (factors such as gender, personality, attitudes, moods), *developmental* (people tend to prefer content that aligns with cognitive and emotional development for their age),

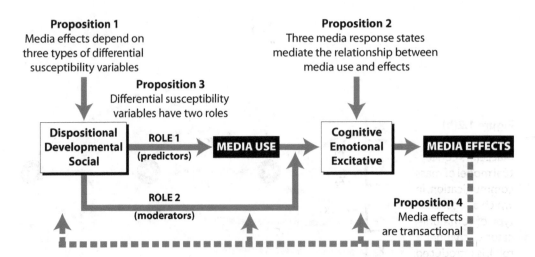

Figure 1.3 The four propositions of the Differential Susceptibility to Media Effects Model (DSMM).

Source: Adapted from Valkenburg & Peter, 2013, p. 226.

and *social* (influences such as family, friends, school; cultural norms). Furthermore, the DSMM proposes three response states to media that can mediate media effects: *cognitive* (how much attention and cognitive effort is devoted to understanding media content), *emotional* reactions to the media content (empathy and sympathy for characters), and *excitative* (the level of physiological arousal). Valkenburg and Peter use the analogy of an audio mixing console to highlight the interplay between the three response states:

> Our mixing console consists of three sliders, which represent the cognitive, emotional, and excitative response states. According to the DSMM, in some media use situations all three sliders can be high. For example, when individuals watch a soccer game of their favorite team on television, it is conceivable that their cognitive, emotional, and excitative sliders are high. A similar intensity of engagement may occur when individuals play a highly involving computer game, such as a first-person shooter (Nacke & Lindley, 2008). In other media-use situations, the cognitive and emotional sliders may be particularly high and the excitative slider relatively low, for example when one watches sad media content, which generally leads to less arousal than violent content (Davydov et al., 2011; Krahé et al., 2011). In again other situations, the excitative slider may be particularly high, for example, when males watch pornography (Murnen & Stockton, 1997).
>
> Until the evidence shows otherwise, the DSMM assumes that media effects are most evident and long lasting when the cognitive, or the cognitive and emotional or excitatory sliders, are high. (p. 229)

Social Effects. As an example of a model of media effects at the societal level, we have selected the **media system dependency model** advanced by Ball-Rokeach and DeFleur (1976). This model (see Figure 1.4) focuses on the relationships between the mass media entity (information system) and society itself (social system). It assumes that individuals in modern society become increasingly dependent upon mass media as a source of news and information. The level of the dependency relationship and the strength of the media effects hinge on the stability or instability of the society and the degree of societal importance placed upon mass media as an information source.

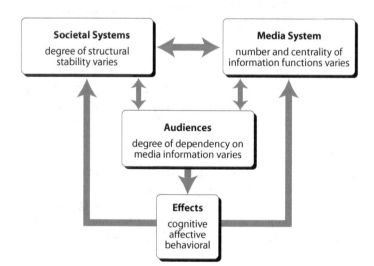

Figure 1.4
The dependency state.

Source: Adapted from Ball-Rokeach & DeFleur, 1976, p. 8.

Relationships and interactions among media, society, and audience are demonstrated, along with media effects. News in times of crisis serves as a good example of dependency theory in action. Whenever a crisis occurs (e.g., the terrorist attacks of September 11, 2001; massive wildfires burning in California; hurricanes slamming into the Gulf Coast), people turn to the news media as a source of information and even comfort. Their dependency on the media increases during times of crisis.

These examples represent only a few of the pictorial models used to illustrate communication processes and effects from media communication. With this basic foundation, we now turn specifically to the topic of media effects. In the next sections, we discuss the various means of measuring or assessing media effects and consider the social relevance of media effects research.

Measuring Media Effects

The study of media effects typically assumes a basic cause-and-effect relationship. It does not, however, completely disregard the role of chance in the unfolding of events. Social scientists employ statistical tools to account for chance while accepting the notion of causality. In fact, most contemporary communication scholars accept a view of causation that indicates that cause and effect cannot be determined exactly, only probabilistically (e.g., Born, 1949). According to Perry (1996):

> Any discussion of media effects requires a concern with causation. Before a researcher can conclude that one concept is a cause of another, the researcher must establish three things. First, the presumed cause and the presumed effect must covary, or go together. For example, people who are heavily exposed to mediated violence should tend, on the average, to be either more or less aggressive than those who are less exposed. . . . Second, the presumed cause must precede the presumed effect. Finally, a researcher must eliminate plausible rival (i.e., third variable) explanations for the observed covariation of the presumed cause and effect. (pp. 25–26)

Throughout this text, you will read about the results of many studies that have been conducted to test for evidence of media effects. Most effects research involves the use of quantitative research methods, but studies employing more qualitative measures, or some combination of the two, have also been used. In this section we examine four research methodologies that have been used to study media effects: the laboratory experiment, survey research (often called cross-sectional research), field experiments, and a form of longitudinal research known as the panel study. We also mention the importance of statistical methods in assessing the presence of media effects. Table 1.1 provides a list of terms used in the discussion of media effects.

Laboratory Experiments

By far the most popular method for measuring media effects in its most simple form, the experimental method involves having people watch, read, or listen to a certain type of media fare (violent, sexually explicit, frightening, or something else) while other people watch, read, or listen to innocuous content, then comparing any measurable changes exhibited by individuals from the two groups. The measurement tool may be either the self-reports of participants on questionnaires or automated instruments

Table 1.1   Terms Used by Social Scientists

Theory	Systematic explanations and predictions of phenomena. More formally, a theory is a systematic and plausible set of generalizations that explain some observable phenomena by linking constructs and variables in terms of organizing principles that are internally consistent.
Concept	A general idea derived from many specific particulars; for example, *social class* is a concept generalized from particulars like income, education, status, occupation, and esteem.
Hypothesis	A specific statement or proposal that can be tested by means of gathering empirical evidence.
Qualitative	Research methods that allow the investigator to describe a phenomenon without relying heavily on numbers. Qualitative methods allow the researcher to interpret a phenomenon more holistically using words rather than numbers.
Quantitative	Research methods that use numbers to describe the relative amount of something.
Triangulation	Use of multiple types of research methods to address questions of media effects.
Deductive reasoning	From the general to the particular; the process by which theory is tested. The researcher begins with a general idea or theory and asks a specific statement or hypothesis, then tests the hypothesis with the collection of data.
Inductive reasoning	From the particular to the general; the process by which theory is generated. The researcher begins with a simple research question and collects data that describe a particular case, and then develops a theory based upon findings.
Variable	Anything to which more than one value can be assigned; for example, hair color is a variable that can have values of black, brown, blond, red, and so forth.

(e.g., preference analyzers), observation of participants' actions, assessments of various activities performed by the individual, or some sort of physiological measure (e.g., blood pressure, heart rate, skin conductance) or cognitive assessment (e.g., brain waves) as the participant is viewing the content.

In more complex formulations, experiments often include control groups (e.g., people who did not read, hear, or see a media message). Complex research designs also are employed so that researchers can examine the effects of several variables simultaneously—for example, the impact of (a) frightening versus nonfrightening media content on (b) boys versus girls (c) at different ages (e.g., 3, 6, 9).

Wimmer and Dominick (1994) listed four major advantages and two disadvantages of laboratory experiments in media research. On the positive side, the experiment represents "the best social science research method for establishing causality" (p. 85). The experiment also affords the researcher much control, especially in the presentation of the variables in proper time order so that the cause is shown to precede the effect, and in the manipulation of variables. In terms of cost, experiments also involve less expense than most other research methods. Finally, the step-by-step techniques make laboratory experiments easier for others to replicate than other types of research methods. As for disadvantages, the artificial surroundings of lab experiments may affect a research participant's behavior, including the very variable that researchers are attempting to observe and measure. Another problem, experimental bias, occurs when the researcher influences the results either intentionally or unintentionally. Many researchers avoid the problem by conducting double-blind experiments, in which neither the research participants nor the researchers know which participants are part of the control group and which belong to the experimental group.

Survey Research

Another common means of measuring effects from media content uses written questionnaires, telephone interviews, face-to-face interviews, or online surveys to gauge (1) the type and extent of media exposure of an individual (e.g., number of hours the person watches violent television programs per week, or the number of pornographic websites the person visits each week), and (2) the respondent's self-reported attitudes and tendencies toward antisocial or prosocial behaviors. For the latter measure, researchers may employ any of several scales or inventories that have been refined over time. These studies often search for specific demographic or sociographic factors that might affect the relationship between variables because surveys are commonly conducted with representative samples of the population of interest.

One caveat about using survey research to determine media effects should be noted. If you recall Perry's (1996) three criteria for causation, you can see that the first criterion—that the presumed cause and the presumed effect must covary—can be readily accommodated through survey research. The third criterion—the elimination of rival causes—can also be addressed somewhat by survey research. Indeed, using a well-designed survey, a number of different potential contributors to a particular media effect can be evaluated in the same survey. For this reason, researchers conducting an experiment also frequently administer a survey to their research participants. In this way, they can use various statistical controls and partially account for rival causes at the same time as they determine cause-and-effect relationships by way of the tight research designs that experiments typically permit. However, Perry's second criterion for causation—that the presumed cause must precede the presumed effect—is the potential trouble spot in using survey research to determine media effects. The issue of time sequence or time order cannot be determined if the questionnaire or interview assesses the presumed cause (e.g., the number of hours of violent television watched) and the presumed effect (e.g., the level of fear for personal safety) at the same time. To attempt to get around the time-sequence issue, researchers often administer the same survey (or similar surveys) on multiple occasions, or they administer different portions of the instrument at different times. However, because such control typically is not considered to be as certain or as effective as that exerted by tight research designs and a properly conducted experiment, the determination of causation from such procedures is frequently called into question if surveys are the only means to assess media effects. In other words, surveys are very good for determining associations or relationships between and among variables, but they are less compelling for determining cause and effect.

Field Experiments

Experiments conducted "in the field," or in real-world settings, have not been used to study media effects to the extent that laboratory and survey research methods have been employed, but a handful of important studies have been conducted in this manner (e.g., Parke et al., 1977; Williams, 1986). Field experiments do not allow as much physical control as experiments conducted in the laboratory; however, the use of statistical controls in the field has allowed researchers to gain more control over extraneous or intervening variables. Field experiments rate high in *external validity,* or the measure of a particular study's generalizability. The attitudes or behaviors of research participants are measured in real-life settings rather than in the often sterile environment of a laboratory; therefore, the behaviors of participants are thought to be more natural. In some cases, people being studied in the field may not be aware that they are being measured and therefore may behave more naturally, although such approaches raise ethical issues. An additional advantage of the field study may be found in its expediency for studying rather complex social situations, such as the impact of television on a community receiving it for the first time.

Panel Studies

Panel studies require the researcher to interview or to send questionnaires to the same respondents at different times. This method is not employed as often in the study of media effects as other methods; however, one of the major studies in the history of media effects (Lazarsfeld et al., 1944, 1948) made use of a panel. Panel studies are inherently longitudinal in nature, meaning that the same respondents provide information at more than one point in time. This means that respondents must be recruited and retained over time, a situation that places demands on the researcher and may involve considerable expense. However, the benefits of panel studies often outweigh these human and fiscal costs.

Triangulation

Because each of these primary research methodologies for establishing media effects has limitations, researchers often try to utilize several different methodologies to address a question or issue. For example, to determine whether watching a great deal of television dramas in which the lead characters are generous and altruistic causes viewers to increase their charitable giving, it is possible to use a laboratory experiment, a field experiment, or a survey. However, it would be even better to utilize all three methodologies—a triangulation of methodologies. If the results of the three separate studies are similar, the cumulative findings are much more compelling than the findings from any of the independent investigations. Scholars who approach media effects questions utilizing complementary methodologies (or who use several different experiments or surveys to answer similar research questions) are often said to conduct *programmatic* research in media effects. This greatly increases the credibility of their findings not only among their peers but also with news reporters and policy makers.

Other Research Methodologies of Media Effects

A number of other research methodologies are also useful in understanding and predicting media effects. Two of them, content analysis and meta-analysis, are briefly profiled because of their prevalence in media effects research.

Content Analysis

Content analysis is often used to examine the presence, absence, or quantity of certain attributes of media messages that may contribute to certain types of media effects. For example, as a part of its research on the relationship between entertainment media and the public's awareness of health issues, the Kaiser Family Foundation commissioned several content analyses of sex on television, including assessments of the prevalence of sexual messages, the types of talk about sex, the types of sexual behaviors presented or discussed, and the prevalence of messages about sexual risks or responsibilities (Kunkel et al., 1999). It should be noted that the presence or absence of such message features does not provide any direct evidence of media effects on sexual behavior; instead, such content analyses can provide a valuable profile of the type of content that might be expected to lead to prosocial or antisocial media effects. Other research methodologies must be used in conjunction with content analyses to provide evidence of effects per se.

Meta-Analysis

Throughout this textbook you will find the results from various meta-analyses of media effects. Meta-analysis is an unusual methodology in media effects research in that it does not contribute any new "primary" evidence regarding media effects. Instead, a **meta-analysis** is a means of systematically integrating the extant findings from a large number of empirical studies on any given topic. Statistical methods are used to provide a "big picture" in terms of the magnitude as well as the direction of the effects attributable to the media in a particular area of inquiry (e.g., stereotyping, pornography, video games). Because the procedures employed in a meta-analysis are relatively objective and are designed to be quite comprehensive, a well-conducted meta-analysis can give an analytical interpretation of a body of media effects literature. This information can then be combined with traditional narrative literature reviews to provide further insight into the effects of media in society.

Statistical Methods

Most media effects studies make use of **statistics**, "the science that uses mathematical models to collect, organize, summarize, and analyze data" (Wimmer & Dominick, 1994, p. 205). Statistical methods may be *descriptive,* such as this sample result: "Readers of *six* or more mystery novels per month performed *three* times as well on problem-solving tasks as their peers who did not read mystery novels." However, probably the most common use of statistical tools in communication research involves the use of *inferential* statistics. The science of statistics assumes that random samples from populations take on the same distribution properties of the larger population; thus, tests conducted upon a random sample may be generalizable to the overall population within certain well-defined limits. Statistical methods are based upon laws of probability. The methods make allowances for errors in sampling, as well as provisions for chance. Errors due to chance, whether sampling errors (e.g., the chance selection or assignment of a sample that is not representative of a population) or something else, become part of the overall equation. Research designs allow investigators to isolate particular causes for media effects; statistical methods permit us to assign values to the strength of those causes.

Overview of Media Effects Theories

> There is nothing so practical as a good theory.
>
> —Kurt Lewin (1951, p. 169)

Theories are a key component of media effects research. This section—especially Table 1.2—will give you a brief introduction to some of the most prominent theories used in media effects research and how media effects theories have changed over time.

Defining Media Effects Theories

So what exactly is a media effects theory? Valkenburg and Oliver (2020) noted that few scholars have sought to develop a definition, so they put forth their own:

> We define such a theory as one that attempts to explain the uses and effects of media on individuals, groups, or societies as a whole. To be labeled a media effects theory, a theory at least needs to conceptualize media use (or exposure to specific mediated messages or stories) and the potential changes that this media use can bring about in individuals, groups, or societies (i.e., the media effect). (p. 17)

They also noted that some media effects theories are called media effects *models*, such as the differential susceptibility to media effects model discussed earlier in this chapter and the Elaboration Likelihood Model that you will read about in Chapter 10. This is because some of these theories include pictorial models to visually illustrate processes and relationships between concepts and variables. Although they do not have the word "theory" in their names, many communication models are theories nonetheless.

"Evergreen" Theories of Media Effects

Valkenburg and Oliver's (2020) analysis of bibliometric studies (i.e., studies that examine citations in academic journals) of prominent media effects theories revealed six theories that "have held up fairly well over the past decades, and so they can rightly be named 'evergreen theories'" (p. 21). These theories include:

- Cultivation theory (Gerbner, 1969),
- Agenda setting theory (McCombs & Shaw, 1972),
- Diffusion of innovations theory (Rogers, 1962),
- Uses and gratifications theory (Katz et al., 1973; Rosengren, 1974),
- Social learning/social cognitive theory (Bandura, 1986), and
- Media system dependency theory (Ball-Rokeach & DeFleur, 1976).

Throughout this book, you will see how these theories have been used to study various kinds of media content. Section 2 of this text will go into much more detail on several of the most prominent evergreen theories, including cultivation, agenda setting, uses and gratifications, and social cognitive theory.

Valkenburg and Oliver (2020) also identified other well-cited theories that you will learn about in later chapters of this book, including:

- Two-Step Flow Theory (Lazarsfeld et al., 1948),
- Knowledge Gap Theory (Tichenor et al., 1970),

- Spiral of Silence Theory (Noelle-Neumann, 1974),
- Priming Theory (Berkowitz, 1984),
- Third-Person Effects (Davison, 1983),
- The Elaboration Likelihood Model (Petty & Cacioppo, 1986),
- Framing Theory (Entman, 1993), and
- The Limited Capacity Model (Lang, 2000).

See Table 1.2 for brief descriptions of these prominent media effects theories.

Table 1.2   Prominent Theories of Media Effects

Agenda Setting Theory	This theory describes how news media's coverage of certain topics or events can influence how important audiences rate the same topics/events.
Cultivation Theory	According to this theory, people who spend a lot of time watching television develop a view of the real world that is similar to what they see on television.
Diffusion of Innovations	This theory explains how, why, and how quickly new ideas or technology spread among certain groups.
Elaboration Likelihood Model	This theory is prominent in persuasion research. Stimuli are processed by either the central or peripheral route. This processing can influence how a person's attitude is formed or changed.
Framing	This theory examines the ways in which mediated messages are constructed (i.e., frame building) and how frames of reference can impact audience perceptions (i.e., frame setting).
Knowledge Gap Theory	According to this theory, mass media can increase the gap in knowledge between people in higher or lower socioeconomic classes.
Limited Capacity Model	This theory is used to study how audiences' limited capacity for cognitive processing affects how they remember and engage with mediated content.
Media System Dependency Theory	According to this theory, the more a person depends on media to meet their needs, the more important media will become in their life. This increased importance then leads to more effects from media.
Priming	This theory is used to explain how media can activate cognitive nodes and related feelings and/or behaviors in a person's mental network.
Social Learning/ Social Cognitive Theory	These theories primarily seek to explicate how symbolic communication via mass media affects human thought, behavior, and emotions. A primary area of study is observational learning and its related mechanisms.
Spiral of Silence Theory	This theory is used to explain how people remain silent when their views are different from the majority. Research shows that mass media play a role in the development of majority views.
Third-Person Effect	According to this theory, people tend to believe that others are more affected by mediated messages than themselves.
Two-Step Flow Theory	This theory explains how media effects can be indirect rather than direct. The personal influence of so-called opinion leaders can result in a media effect for a larger group of people.
Uses and Gratifications Theory	This theory seeks to explain how and why audiences actively consume certain types of media to meet specific needs.

How Theories Change Over Time

As our understanding of media effects evolves, so do media effects theories. In fact, many once-popular theories have essentially fallen by the wayside and are mainly mentioned and taught for their historical significance. This includes the Shannon-Weaver model discussed earlier in this chapter and Marshall McLuhan's (1964) medium theory. You may be familiar with McLuhan's famous saying, "The medium is the message," which concisely summarized his theory that media channels are more powerful than the mediated messages they delivered. McLuhan's theory fell out of favor with media effects researchers because studies that used the theory often produced unconvincing results (Clark, 2012; Valkenburg et al., 2016).

A dramatic shift in media effects theories known as the "cognitive turn" took place in the 1980s and 1990s (Valkenburg & Oliver, 2020). During this time, researchers sought to better understand the cognitive processes involved in media use. Theories developed during this time (e.g., priming theory, the Elaboration Likelihood Model, and the limited capacity model) recognized that media effects are indirect, and "they argued that the cognitive mental states of the viewer act as a mediating (or intervening) variable between media use and media outcomes. Indeed, these new theories recognized that the mental states of the media users play a crucial role in explaining media effects" (Valkenburg & Oliver, 2020, p. 22). Established theories also sought to incorporate cognitive processes. For instance, Bandura (1986) modified his existing social learning theory into social cognitive theory to better illustrate the cognitive processes involved in learning.

Key Features of Modern Media Effects Theories

Valkenburg and Oliver (2020) summarized three key features that both newer media effects theories and older ones that have been recently expanded share.

- **Selectivity**   Media users rather than media sources are central to the process of media effects in that they select what media they consume. Valkenburg et al. (2016) noted that by selecting certain media, audiences are also partly responsible for shaping the media effects they may experience.
  Examples: Uses and gratifications theory (Katz et al., 1973; Rosengren, 1974) and selective exposure theory (Knobloch-Westerwick, 2014)

- **Transactionality**   Unlike early linear media effects theories, contemporary theories acknowledge media use and media outcomes are often reciprocal. For instance, these theories posit that (1) certain characteristics of the media users, such as beliefs or needs, can drive selective media consumption, (2) resulting in certain media effects. (3) Those effects can then drive further selective media use.
  Examples: Social cognitive theory (Bandura, 1986), the reinforcing spiral model (Slater, 2007), and the General Aggression Model (Anderson & Bushman, 2002, 2018)

- **Conditionality**   Essentially, this feature acknowledges that media effects are not the same for all media users. Further, media effects can depend on dispositional, situational, and social factors.
  Example: Differential susceptibility to media effects model (Valkenburg & Peter, 2013)

Furthermore, Valkenburg and Oliver (2020) noted that the inclusion of theories in communication research papers has significantly increased over the decades. Scholars have been working to develop new theories or expand old ones to better understand today's modern media landscape. One of the most important aspects of the recent evolution of media effects theories is that they "increasingly recognize the selectivity, conditionality, and transactionality of media effects" (p. 28).

Importance of Studying Media Effects

We live in a world in which we create and receive a multitude of mediated messages daily. As you will learn in the next chapter, the concern about effects from media communication, as well as evidence for effects, are as old as mass communication itself. People have always wondered how media messages are affecting them and, especially, their children. They have always been concerned for the negative effects of a particular message, or message systems, and they have been curious about the potential prosocial effects of others.

As we move further into the 21st century, the knowledge of effects from mediated communications assumes increasing importance. We have become so information oriented and information dependent that some have dubbed ours an "information society." Computers, mobile technology, and mass media are vital cogs in our societal infrastructure. With so much of what is perceived to be wrong in today's world blamed on media of some sort or another, the issue of mass media effects continues to be of paramount social relevance. But effects from mediated violence, pornography, advertising, video games, or news are but the most visible facet of this fascinating and important research domain. As we hope you will discover as you read the chapters of this text, knowledge of the power of mediated communications is important for us all. It is often said that we are the "sovereign consumers" of the information age. If our consumption is to be fruitful, we must be extremely knowledgeable about the effects of media in our lives.

Summary

Measuring the effects of viewing on-screen violence represents one important facet of media effects research, but the study of media effects encompasses many other types of research as well. Social scientists are also interested in the persuasive powers of mass mediated messages (e.g., advertisements, propaganda, communication campaigns), the impact of new communication technologies, the effects of viewing sexually explicit media fare, reactions to frightful or disturbing media content, effects from political communication, and much more.

Communication may take several different forms. It may be interpersonal in nature, it may involve the use of a personal communication medium, or it may be described as mass communication. The act of communicating via interpersonal, mediated, or mass media channels involves a process or series of stages. Even in its simplest form, communication between a source and a receiver may take on an interactional or transactional dimension. In the case of an interpersonal conversation, the receiver may offer immediate feedback to the source. In the course of a conversation or discussion, senders and receivers may alternate repeatedly in their respective roles. Mass communication involves one or more institutional sources (usually complex entities such as production houses in conjunction with a television network) reaching thousands or millions of people with the same message. The audience members are demographically diverse and unknown to the message source.

Scholars have developed models to explain their theories and illustrate abstract ideas regarding communication processes and behavior. Models may also be used to explain media effects. Models help demonstrate the different processes of communication, whether linear, interactional, or transactional in nature. Successful pictorial models offer three major advantages: (1) they organize concepts, (2) they explain processes, and (3) they predict outcomes.

The study of media effects assumes a basic cause-and-effect scenario. Social scientists employ statistical methods to account for chance as an important component of the notion of causality.

Researchers often measure media effects in laboratory settings using experimental methods. Other research methods include surveys, field experiments, and panel studies. Triangulation is the use of several research methods to address questions of media effects. Content analyses are used to examine the presence, absence, or quantity of certain attributes of media messages that allegedly contribute to certain media effects. Meta-analyses are useful for systematically integrating extant findings from a large number of empirical studies on any given topic. Most media effects studies employ statistical methods.

Theories are a key component for understanding media effects. Some media effects studies have withstood the test of time and remain highly cited. However, theories have also adapted as our understanding of media effects has evolved.

With so many of the problems in today's world being blamed on media communications, the issue of mass media effects has become one of paramount social relevance. Media effects is an important and fascinating research domain. A fundamental knowledge of media effects is a necessary criterion for excelling in the information age.

2

Historical Evidence
of Media Effects

This is Orson Welles, ladies and gentlemen, out of character to assure you that the *War of the Worlds* has no further significance than as the holiday offering it was intended to be: the Mercury Theatre's own radio version of dressing up in a sheet and jumping out of a bush and saying "Boo!"

—Orson Welles's concluding remarks at the end of his
War of the Worlds broadcast on October 30, 1938

Since Johannes Gutenberg invented the printing press in the mid-15th century, people have suggested that mass media have important effects on their audiences. Sometimes historical evidence has been utilized to chronicle pronounced changes in public opinions or behavior after widespread exposure to certain media content. At other times, media effects have been less obvious, but *concern* of the critics for media effects on others has prompted various actions against mass media. Such concerns for generalized "others" rather than oneself have been systematically explained as **third-person effects**, which are said to occur whenever individuals believe other audience members are more susceptible than they are to persuasive, violent, or objectionable media content (Davison, 1983).

This chapter examines the concern for media effects from a historical perspective and the historical evidence for actual media effects on opinions and behaviors since the invention of the printing press. The chapter also documents selected popular concerns about media effects prior to and after social scientific measurement of such effects became an area of scholarly enquiry.

The existence of media effects ultimately requires a cause-and-effect perspective, with the most common "cause" being some kind of message conveyed by way of a communication medium (i.e., message effects). When social and behavioral scientists enter their media effects laboratories, they typically exercise tight control to ensure that extraneous influences are minimized and that precise measurement of influences on individuals can be accomplished. They are thereby equipped to assess actual media effects on individuals in a variety of ways. In contrast, historians are usually limited to assessing cause-and-effect relationships involving media only when the effects, as indicated in recorded opinions and actions, seem obvious and powerful in retrospect.

Moreover, whereas social and behavioral scientists typically amass evidence for or against media effects by treating or examining individuals, often one at a time, historians sometimes examine aggregate data from public records and the like, thereby focusing on societal-level effects. It should be noted that the various historical examples we cite provide evidence for media effects among great numbers of people rather than individual and isolated cases of the "man bites dog" variety. We will emphasize major trends rather than idiosyncratic events of media impact that may be newsworthy because of their human-interest value.

Many scholars might argue that historical examples do not provide adequate, scientific evidence of a cause-and-effect relationship. As a University of Chicago social scientist once stated:

> The case method and the collection of anecdotes do not supply proof of a generalization; rather they provide illustrations, and such illustrations can be deceptive if they lead the author or others to accept them as proof. (Stouffer, 1942, p. 144)

In answer to this argument, we emphasize that historical methods are different from other research methods. A historian looks for a preponderance of evidence, usually various concurring indications of influence, that suggest cause-and-effect relationships. A book such as Harriet Beecher Stowe's *Uncle Tom's Cabin* (1852), for example, is known to have been influential because of its high sales figures and from discussions about its influence among writers and orators of the period. It should be remembered that scores of examples of null or minimal media effects may never show up on a historian's radar screen.

Examples of what certainly appear to be media effects on opinions and behavior are plentiful throughout modern history, especially when peo-

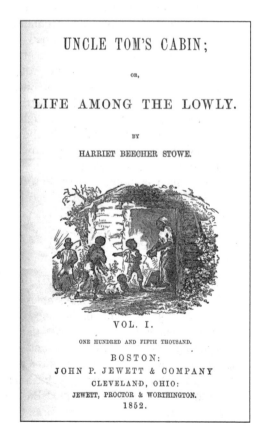

Uncle Tom's Cabin was recognized as influential in swaying public opinion toward the abolitionist cause.

ple reacted to frightful or disturbing media content and persuasive messages. Historical evidence of public concern about media effects also abounds and has manifested itself in different ways. The many instances of suppression of the press by authorities can be viewed as evidence of concern about the power of the media to affect the masses. Similarly, there are examples of individual efforts against violent or sexually explicit material because of their suspected harmful effects on the masses, especially children.

Historical Concern for Media Effects

The modern-day emphasis on quantitative, experimental measures in media effects research has obscured the obvious bond that exists between the study of media history and that of media effects. Like scientific effects researchers, many media historians also search for evidence of media effects. However, a historian's "laboratory" is the past— the centuries since humans first used mass media to communicate with each other. Therefore, a historian's participants can speak only through records that have survived.

Historical evidence reveals that, at first, only society's elite recognized potential societal influences from exposure to the printed word. Due to their fear of the effects of literacy on the masses, many leaders sought to control publications and thereby silence opposition voices. Such fear of media influences lingers today in many totalitarian societies where leaders suppress or control media to maintain their power.

In the 19th century, new technologies and increasing literacy rates made possible the development of remarkable new forms of mass communication. Since that period, concern for powerful media effects has been expressed not only by society's educated elite but also by individuals and groups from all strata of the population—from presidents to parents, from the intelligentsia to beginning students. These historical instances of the concern about detrimental societal impacts of media messages have been strong enough and loud enough to influence lawmakers, shape public policy, and attract the interest of numerous scholars.

Western history provides many examples of attempts to control the press due to the supposed power of its messages over its audience. The control has taken various forms, such as suppression or censorship of information, use of propaganda, or physical violence against editors or reporters. The agents of control have included government officials, the clergy, and others. This section offers a brief survey of some of the more memorable instances in history when concern for media effects caused actions against the press or other media.

Suppression Due to Concern for Media Effects

The most compelling examples of the concern for powerful media effects on the masses might be found in the many instances in which authorities have taken preemptive measures to suppress mass media messages. Soon after the appearance of the printing press, the ecclesiastical and governmental elite showed concern for the power of the printed word. They used the press for their own ends and attempted measures of censorship to prevent the publishing of opposition views. For example, in the mid-16th century, Catholics wanted Protestant material banned. In 1559, Pope Paul IV issued an *Index of Prohibited Books.* The list of forbidden works included Protestant books, pornography, occult books, and opposition political works. Protestant leaders such as Martin Luther defied the pope and used the printing press to spread Reformation literature to the masses throughout Europe. The repercussions against the rebels who used media without authority were extremely severe. When printers were caught spreading propaganda, they were often imprisoned or burned at the stake.

In the early 16th century, England's King Henry VIII was so concerned about the printed word that he created the Court of the Star Chamber, which prosecuted those who published material offensive to the Crown. Henry also insisted upon a system of licensing that held the English press under strict control.

In the late 1700s in the United States, Benjamin Franklin Bache's *Philadelphia Aurora* newspaper provided a leading voice for the cause of Republicanism in the United States. His inflammatory writings galvanized public opinion and produced a number of notable reactions.

> On one occasion or another, Treasury Secretary Oliver Wolcott threatened to investigate the *Aurora* for treason, Federalist Speaker of the House Jonathan Dayton barred Bache from the House floor, Federalist editors and politicians subjected him to written and verbal attacks, Federalist merchants imposed an advertising boycott on the *Aurora* and barred the paper from their establishments, the government tried Bache for sedition, and individuals and mobs physically attacked him. (Sloan, 1998, pp. 130–131)

In an effort to control opposition voices such as Bache's, the Federalists passed one of the most oppressive government measures in U.S. history, the Sedition Act of 1798. The act was passed at the time of the French Revolution in an effort to keep pro-French voices from being heard in American newspapers. "Give to any set of men the command of the press and you give them the command of the country, for you give them the command of public opinion, which commands everything," wrote Judge Alexander Addison in the *Columbian Centinel* on January 1, 1799 (Sloan, 1998, p. 119).

> Federalists by 1799 had come to realize a fact that had been at the essence of American public life almost since the first colonists had stepped ashore in the early 1600s. Public opinion was the basis for public policy, and the printing press was the means that provided a forum for it. (p. 119)

From the 1830s until the Civil War, many feared the powerful effects of abolitionist messages. Southerners objected vehemently to publication and circulation of such material because they believed it would encourage slave revolts. President Andrew Jackson urged Congress to pass a law to prevent incendiary material regarding the slavery debate from being circulated in the mail.

During World War I, Congress passed both the Espionage Act of 1917 and the Sedition Act of 1918. These acts made it illegal to publish information critical of the U.S. government or in support of any of the enemy powers. The government feared the effects of voices that opposed the war effort.

Mob Violence as Media Effect

Another historical indicator of suppression due to concern for media effects might be instances of mob violence directed against mass media offices or editors in response to the publishing or showing of incendiary material. History is filled with such outbreaks of violence directed against the press (Nerone, 1994). One of the nastiest antipress mobs in history attacked producers of Baltimore's *Federal Republican,* a radical Federalist paper that opposed American participation in the War of 1812. Several people died and at least one editor was maimed for life.

Many examples of mob actions against the expression of race-related messages abound (Grimsted, 1998). During the abolitionist movement, a pro-slavery mob attacked and killed newspaper editor Elijah Lovejoy in Illinois. Frederick Douglass, the African American editor of *The North Star,* was continually harassed and even had his house burned by those who opposed his views. During the civil rights movement of the 1950s and 1960s, Mississippi editor Hazel Brannon Smith spoke out against racial injustices against African Americans and, as a result, faced considerable opposition from local residents and local government officials alike. A white citizens' council urged local businesses to stop advertising in her paper, subscribers canceled their subscriptions, and one white official brought a libel suit against her—all in reaction to her stand against the unfair treatment of Blacks (Davies, 1998).

Frederick Douglass's role as the editor of *The North Star* made him a target for mob violence.

Not all of the mob incidents related to racial issues involved the press. At least one instance of mob action came in response to a major motion picture. In 1915, release of the film *The Birth of a Nation*—which was the first blockbuster film—caused race riots and mob actions against Blacks by arousing emotion and controversy. Directed by D. W. Griffith, the father of American filmmaking, *The Birth of a Nation* told the story of the Civil War, Reconstruction, and the rise of the Ku Klux Klan from a white supremacist perspective. Boston proved to be a key battleground for the film, where newspaper editor and civil rights activist William Monroe Trotter teamed up with the fledgling NAACP to stage nearly 20 rallies against the film, each drawing between 500 and 2,500 protesters (Lehr, 2016).

Public Concern for "Indecent" Material

The public concern for the ill effects of media violence and sexually explicit material is not exclusive to the 20th and 21st centuries. In the early 19th century, a new type of journalism emerged in England, one that would soon be copied successfully by penny dailies in the United States. In the English press, humorous reports on the activities of arrested thieves, drunks, prostitutes, and other miscreants and lowlifes of society became immensely popular among many readers but elicited severe criticisms from social critics. In the United States, the appearance of New York's *The Sun* in 1833 and its similar reports of police and courtroom activities in New York City resulted in the same mixed response: The articles made the penny sheets very popular among their devoted readers, but the emphasis on violence, sexuality, and unseemly conduct also caused many to criticize the sheets and express concern for the effects of such material on an innocent and expanding reading public.

The second successful penny paper, James Gordon Bennett's *The New York Herald*, though immensely popular, attracted controversy almost from the start due to Bennett's habit of ridiculing his competitors in print, his language (which was not always respectable by 19th-century standards), and his extensive coverage of sensational trials that involved scandal, illicit sex, and murder. Competitors and opponents thrashed him in print and in person. On several occasions angry readers physically attacked Bennett on the streets of New York. The "moral war" on Bennett is a good 19th century example of society's concern for printed material it considered indecent. Prominent citizens called for a boycott against the *Herald* and businesses that advertised in it. As a result, the *Herald* lost some of its mammoth circulation, and Bennett soon modified the tone of his paper.

The readable style of *The Sun*, the *Herald*, and the other penny dailies, as well as their sensational and sometimes titillating news stories, made them popular and profitable. Critics continued to complain about the suspected negative effects on society, especially as other newspapers began to copy the *Herald's* techniques and a new style of journalism emerged. A commentator in 1847 complained about the sorry state of the periodical press as a purveyor of immorality. The article "Pernicious Literature" called for press reforms to avoid serious effects from such "contamination."

> Among the most alarming evils of our age and country is the injurious tendency of the publications that are daily flowing from the press. The licentious and anti-social works which are so profusely scattered throughout the length and breadth of the land, in the shape of annuals, brochures, and family newspapers, are sowing a seed of corruption which will bring disgrace and wretchedness upon thousands, if not lay the foundation of that sensual and selfish spirit which will contaminate the nation at large, and threaten the downfall of its free institutions. . . . In this state of things the secular press must be reformed itself. . . . Until this be done, the spirit of our newspapers and the depravity of the popular appetite will exert a reciprocal influence—one will encourage the other, and both will combine to swell and precipitate that torrent of licentiousness which is beginning to excite the profound and just apprehensions of all good men. ("Pernicious Literature," 1847, pp. 46, 48)

After film became popular in the early 20th century, public concern for negative effects of violent and sexually explicit film presentations on youngsters prompted the Payne Fund studies. These studies examined the influence of motion pictures on juvenile delinquency, attitudes, and other factors.

In the 1950s, Fredric Wertham's *Seduction of the Innocent* (1954) expressed an anti-comic-book sentiment that resulted in the inclusion of comic book content in the meetings of the Senate Subcommittee to Investigate Juvenile Delinquency. The comic book industry began measures of self-regulation to ward off government intervention. The Comics Magazine Association of America was formed and issued the Comics Code Authority, which prohibited graphic violence and erotic depictions, among other things.

More recently, novels such as *The Catcher in the Rye,* movies like *Natural Born Killers,* musical recordings, and video games have been blamed for influencing audience members to commit horrible acts of violence or for causing "copycat crimes." The concern for the negative effects of viewing violence and sexual content on television and in movies has led to countless studies and government-sponsored inquiries. The debate over the strength of these effects continues to this day.

There has also been concern about the supernatural effects of mass mediated messages. For instance, a Catholic school in Tennessee banned the *Harry Potter* series—a frequent target for book challenges and book bans—claiming that reading the spells in the books could conjure evil spirits (Quinn, 2019).

Historical Evidence for Changes in Behavior and Opinion Due to Mass Media

Although actual media effects are impossible to demonstrate empirically in a historical context—owing to the difficulty of controlling for or eliminating rival causes, among other limitations—Western history is rich with more general, anecdotal examinations of media effects. Such effects include the social changes that occurred after the introduction of new communication technologies, the many instances when individuals and groups used mediated messages to achieve certain goals, and instances in which citizens took actions due to their fear of the power of media messages to sway audiences in some undesirable manner. Long before media effects were studied scientifically and measured analytically, they were assumed, felt, witnessed, and recorded.

Effects from the Printing Press

Through the years, historians have examined new media technologies as they developed and have uncovered what they considered to be evidence for rather powerful effects at societal and cultural levels. Many studies have explored the advent of the printing press and the many societal changes it brought about (Eisenstein, 1979, 1983; Febvre & Martin, 1984). With the introduction of the printing press, paper, and movable type, more books appeared, prices fell, and literacy spread. The societal impact was considerable. Within approximately one hundred years, the audience for books exploded from a select, elite few to masses of people. By 1500, printers throughout western Europe had established more than 250 presses that produced some 35,000 editions and from 15 to 20 million copies (Febvre & Martin, 1984). Specific historical studies on the diffusion of innovations have looked at the spread of other new media technologies, such as the telegraph and the phonograph, and have also included research examining social effects from the use of the new technology (Hyde, 1994). Other historical studies have explored dynamics and changes in social processes brought about by new media technologies (Marvin, 1988; Pool, 1977).

Media Effects on Public Opinion

The influence of the abolitionist press in the years prior to the Civil War illustrates the power of the press (in this case, an alternative press) to sway public opinion. African American newspapers such as *Freedom's Journal, The Colored American,* and *The North Star* advanced the cause of Black people, attacked slavery, and contributed to the growing abolitionist sentiment in the North. The effects of such printed material included the education, mobilization, and motivation of Black people and the cultivation of attitudes that were much less tolerant of human slavery and more sympathetic to the rights of African Americans among whites in the northern United States.

> Gunnar Myrdal, in *An American Dilemma,* called the black press the most important educational agency for blacks. One of the most powerful arenas in which political, economic, and cultural battles could be fought, it provided a way to tell the black experience: African American life, concerns, achievements. It was a forum to air blacks' views and discuss issues concerning blacks. Further, coverage of blacks' achievements instilled pride and a sense of progress, identity and hope for the future. The black press also was an educator and aid to readers' intellectual development at a time when blacks were barred from formal education, and it served a vital political function. That is, it helped blacks first understand and then find their political potential. Black editors informed, inspired, unified, and mobilized readers, directing them to act on information and how. (Dicken-Garcia, 1998, p. 154)

History provides a number of other examples of media messages that seemingly proved powerful enough to influence public opinion. In the newly formed United States, a series of articles called "The Federalist Papers" appeared in the *New York Independent Journal* and were widely reprinted. Written by Alexander Hamilton, James Madison, and John Jay, this series has been credited with garnering support for adoption of the new constitutional form of government (Bent, 1969).

Another example from the antebellum period is *Uncle Tom's Cabin,* which we mentioned previously in this chapter. Historians have generally agreed that Harriet Beecher Stowe's classic novel was instrumental in fueling the fires of the abolitionist movement in the antebellum United States and helped turn public opinion against the continuance of slavery in the South.

> Stowe's novel *Uncle Tom's* Cabin originally appeared in serialized form in 1852–1853 in the *National Era,* an abolitionist newspaper. It was the most widely read literature of the time. Within months of publication in book form, sales reached 300,000. The book was the single most important writing in increasing the demand that slavery be abolished. (Dicken-Garcia, 1998, p. 155)

Several other works published about this same time eventually had significant effects on thoughts and actions in the 19th and 20th centuries. These included Karl Marx and Friedrich Engels's *Communist Manifesto,* published in 1848, Charles Darwin's *Origin of Species,* and John Stuart Mill's essay "On Liberty," both published in 1859 (Cowley & Smith, 1939).

After the Civil War, William Tweed and his political machine, the Tammany Ring, took control of municipal government in New York City and eventually stole hundreds of millions of dollars from the city coffers. The stinging caricatures of Thomas Nast, an illustrator for the *New York Times,* were especially powerful in gaining public support that eventually brought down the party boss. The *New York Times's* successful crusade against the Tweed Ring and municipal corruption set the stage for the muckraking era in American journalism that soon followed (Bent, 1969).

The sensational yellow journalism of the newspapers owned by Joseph Pulitzer and William Randolph Hearst in the late 1800s resulted in great increases in circulation (over 1 million) for both newspapers—evidence of powerful media effectiveness if not effects per se. Some historians have claimed that Hearst's cries of Spanish atrocities in Cuba were responsible for turning public opinion and causing the Spanish-American War, especially after a mysterious explosion sank the U.S. battleship *Maine* near Havana.

> Hearst has been credited with inflaming public opinion and ultimately starting the war with jingoistic headlines such as "THE WHOLE COUNTRY THRILLS WITH THE WAR FEVER!" Whether or not he deserved such dubious credit, he certainly believed his newspaper was instrumental in the U.S. intervention and actually published the query "HOW DO YOU LIKE THE JOURNAL'S WAR?" in a box next to the masthead for two days. (Hoff, 1998, p. 247)

Two interesting instances of powerful media effects on public opinion in the 20th century involved a significant shift in the public perception of Standard Oil Company magnate John D. Rockefeller. One of these shifts was the result of work during the "muckraking"[1] years at the turn of the century—the Progressive Era—when a group of magazine journalists wrote series after series of scathing articles to expose a number of social ills. The muckraking journalist Ida Tarbell painted Rockefeller as a ruthless capitalist who used shady methods to gain advantages over his competitors. Tarbell's articles in *McClure's Magazine* soon made the ultrarich Rockefeller one of the most hated figures in America, as evidenced in disparaging news cartoons and articles from the period. Ironically, a few years later, Rockefeller hired public relations pioneer Ivy Lee to improve his public image. Lee made Rockefeller's philanthropic activities more visible to the press and public and presented him as a kindly old man—grandfatherly and fun loving—and helped change public opinion favorably toward the former robber baron. The media giveth, and the media taketh away!

Ida Tarbell's investigative reporting on the Standard Oil Company is credited with leading to the breakup of the oil monopoly and making Rockefeller one of the most despised men in the United States.

The works of other muckraking journalists during the Progressive era have been credited with arousing public opinion and forcing social changes. The articles of Lincoln Steffens led to a focus on local corruption and a demand for better city government. Leaders in the campaign against patent medicine advertisers were the *Ladies' Home Journal*, which ran strident editorials, and *Collier's Weekly*, which published in 1905 a series of exposés under the title "The Great American Fraud." These articles contributed to a "truth in advertising" campaign that resulted in the establishment of the Federal Trade Commission and better business bureaus. Upton Sinclair's exposure of the horrible conditions of the meatpacking industry in Chicago spawned a government inquiry that led to passage of the Pure Food and Drug Act of 1907, which formed the Food and Drug Administration. The orchestrated media efforts of others precipitated improved industrial relations, child labor laws, workmen's compensation laws, and general social reform measures.

Powerful Effects: Widespread Fright Reactions to Media Content

Fright reactions in the modern sense usually involve the media presentation of monsters or supernatural beings or real-world occurrences that cause fear, especially in children. As will be shown in Chapter 13 on the effects of frightful or disturbing media content, the work of Joanne Cantor is typical of modern-day studies. Her work and that of several of her prominent students have focused on measuring the fright reactions of individual children to scary movies or television programs or to disturbing news reports. These experiments have contributed much to our knowledge about the kind of program content that frightens children at different ages, and about ways for parents to reduce the effects of frightening program content on their children.

The Great Moon Hoax of 1835

The first penny newspaper, New York's *The Sun*, concocted a hoax in 1835 that proved so disturbing and entertaining to its audience that circulation for the paper increased to more than 19,000, the largest of any newspaper in the world at that time. Reporter Richard Adams Locke wrote that a British astronomer had discovered life on the moon while peering through his giant telescope. Readers requested reprints of the articles and other newspapers throughout the world republished the stories. Women in Bible societies talked about traveling to the moon to convert the lunar beings to Christianity. Edgar Allan Poe said the hoax "was, upon the whole, the greatest hit in the way of sensation—of merely popular sensation—ever made by any similar fiction either in America or Europe" (Poe, 1902, p. 134).

Media history provides numerous earlier instances of powerful effects from frightful or disturbing media content at a more societal level. *The New York Herald* on November 9, 1874, included a frightening hoax that caused audiences to react in hysteria. Reporter T. B. Connery felt that animals at the Central Park Zoo were not as secure as they should be, so he concocted a story about their escape. "The list of mutilated, trampled and injured in various ways must reach nearly two hundred persons of all ages, of which, so far as known, about sixty are very serious, and of these latter, three can hardly outlast the night," he wrote. "Twelve of the wild carnivorous beasts are still at large, their lurking places not being known for a certainty" (Hoff, 1998, p. 239). The final paragraph explained that the story was "pure fabrication" and "a huge hoax," but not everyone read the entire article. A number of people took to the streets with their guns to hunt down the killer animals.

The best known—and certainly most exaggerated—historical example of fright reaction from media content is that of the *War of the Worlds* broadcast. On the night before Halloween in 1938, Orson Welles and the Mercury Theatre on the CBS radio network presented an adaptation of H. G. Wells's science fiction thriller *The War of the Worlds*, in which aliens from Mars invade Earth, killing millions with heat rays and poison gas. Ironically, it was a plot that Welles and the other actors thought was too unbelievable to be taken seriously (Schwartz, 2015). The beginning of the radio program was structured so that a seemingly real musical performance was repeatedly interrupted by breaking news bulletins about the Martian invasion. Some listeners were enjoying another program—*The Chase & Sanborn Hour*, a popular variety show— when the *War of the Worlds* presentation began, then switched their radio dials during a musical interlude to the Mercury Theatre broadcast already in progress, missing the original announcement that the presentation was fiction. CBS made the announcement four times during the program, but these occurred

> (1) at the beginning of the broadcast (when most people were not listening), (2) before the station break, about 8:35 (by this time, most of those who panicked were no longer listening, but fleeing), (3) right after the station break, and (4) at the end of the broadcast. Moreover, the most terrifying part of the broadcast, it should be remembered, came *before* the station break. Those listeners who failed to hear the original announcement therefore had ample opportunity to become frightened. (Lowery & DeFleur, 1995, p. 51)

Orson Welles (arms raised) rehearses *War of the Worlds* with members of the Mercury Theatre. The broadcast frightened many listeners, with some even fleeing their homes to escape the Martian invasion. However, recent research indicates the panic caused by the broadcast was smaller than originally thought.

At the time, an estimated 1 million people were frightened by the broadcast (Cantril, 1940). Some of them actually panicked and left their homes in an effort to escape the sinister invaders (Cantril, 1940; Schwartz, 2015). However, more recent examinations of the incident suggest that although some listeners may have been frightened (however briefly) by the radio show, the number of listeners who panicked was much smaller than the original estimates, which were methodologically flawed (Schwartz, 2015). In fact, much of the sensationalism and hype about the panic was driven by newspapers (Pooley & Socolow, 2013).

Although the actual panic was much smaller than originally thought—and certainly smaller than what is often told in embellished retellings of the legendary event—the broadcast does indicate how familiar listening audiences already were with the workings of radio, which was then still a new form of mass media. Schwartz (2015) noted that audiences of fictional programs expected a station break at the half hour point; however, because of the show's lopsided script, the break was pushed back. People who already believed the broadcast was actual breaking news would likely be even more convinced when the station break did not occur at its usual 8:30 time.

Even if an audience member did not actually panic, enjoyment of the frightening and suspenseful broadcast hinged on audiences understanding of and familiarity with normal radio broadcasts and the urgency of breaking news updates. As Sconce (2000) explained:

> The terror could be realized only if the listener understood how electronic news gathering and dissemination operated, realized the social significance of disrupted network transmissions, and, above all else, invested in the radio's new sense of presence as both a national authority and a means of social surveillance. (p. 112)

Evidence for Effects from Persuasive Messages

Throughout history people have been convinced of the power of particular media messages to persuade others. This singular recognition has served to shape the evolution of American media systems because advertising is predicated on the assumption of media effects. Long before the first mass-circulation newspapers appeared, advertising had gained a foothold as a major revenue producer. As the years advanced, advertising profits became the lifeblood of newspapers, magazines, commercial radio, and television.

Other types of persuasive messages have proven important and effective throughout history. In Europe during the 17th century, despite tight restrictions on printing by the authorities, new ideas and renegade views found their way into print. A century later, an intellectual movement known as the Enlightenment created a revolution in thought. Restrictions on the printed word loosened somewhat. A literate middle class emerged, and the works of Voltaire, Jean-Jacques Rousseau, and others had the persuasive power to move people to seek more individual freedoms and rebel against tyranny.

In the 16th and early 17th centuries, noblemen and investors began to recognize the influential power of the printed word. Many books, pamphlets, and tracts promoting colonization in America circulated at this time and throughout the colonial years. Earlier printed works such as *Divers Voyages* (Hakluyt, 1582/1850), *A Briefe and True Report of the New Found Land of Virginia* (Hariot, 1590/1972), *Nova Britannia* (Johnson, 1609), *A Description of New England* (Smith, 1616/1986), *A Relation of Maryland* (Hall & Jameson, 1635/1910), and *Some Account of the Province of Pennsylvania* (Penn, 1681/1938) outlined the advantages of colonization and presented favorable accounts of life in America. If population growth in the New World is any indication, these promotional materials and advertisements produced powerful media effects (Thompson, 1998).

On the American frontier, editors used newspapers to promote their towns and to attract potential settlers. Throughout the 19th century, as pioneers moved west, newspapers appeared in the burgeoning towns and cities. Frontier editors became known as "town boosters" due to the promotional services they performed in an effort to increase population and economic prosperity. Their efforts proved effective. One historian called the California gold rush "one of the most effective promotional campaigns in history" (quoted in Huntzicker, 1998, p. 198). During the second half of the 19th century, the number of newspapers west of the Mississippi River increased from less than 50 to more than 650.

P. T. Barnum and promotion were synonymous in mid-19th-century America. Long before the days of the public relations pioneers Ivy Lee and Edward Bernays, Barnum mastered the art of successful publicity campaigns. Swedish singer Jenny Lind was unknown in the United States throughout most of the antebellum period, although she was famous in Europe. Before Lind traveled to North America, Barnum issued press releases, wrote letters to the editors, printed pamphlets, and even sponsored a songwriting contest. By the time Lind arrived in New York in 1850, more than 40,000 excited fans greeted her at the docks (Applegate, 1998; Hume, 1977). In another example, Barnum was so successful in publicizing his acquisition of Jumbo the Elephant that in the first week of Jumbo's display he earned back the $30,000 it cost him to buy and transport the animal from London to the United States (Applegate, 1998; James, 1982).

During the two world wars of the 20th century, the U.S. government took measures to spread propaganda in support of the war effort. In World War I, President Woodrow Wilson set up the Committee on Public Information (CPI), which engaged in propaganda and censorship activities. The CPI, under the direction of the muckraker George Creel, produced articles, advertisements, press releases, films, and hired speakers to promote the war effort throughout the country. Many of the scholars who served in a similar "public information" effort during World War II later became the founders of modern media effects research.

In the late 1930s, a number of newspapers began vigorous campaigns to encourage traffic safety; as a result, fatalities decreased substantially. An earlier newspaper campaign had successfully promoted a "safe-and-sane" Fourth of July. Newspaper editor James Keeley has been credited with initiating the crusade (Bent, 1969).

> On the evening of July 4, 1899, when he was beside a child gravely ill, the thunder of giant firecrackers outside disturbed her, and he telephoned his office to collect figures from thirty cities on fatalities and accidents that day. The figures showed that the celebration of a national holiday had cost more in suffering and life than the Spanish-American War. The next year the *Tribune*, demanding a "sane Fourth," presented a similar table of statistics, and thereafter other newspapers followed suit, until mortality and casualties were reduced by more than nine-tenths. (p. 220)

Summary

Since the invention of the printing press in the mid-15th century, people have acknowledged mass media's potential influence on audiences. The concern for powerful media effects has not been exclusive to society's elite but has been felt by all strata of society. This concern has influenced lawmakers, shaped public policy, and attracted the interest of scholars.

History is replete with examples of media effects. These include changes that occurred due to the spread of new media technologies, instances of suppression of the press by authorities, instances of public reaction against violent or sexually explicit material, reactions against producers of inflammatory material, and reactions to frightful media content. The many successful publicity and advertising campaigns throughout history attest to the power of media communications to persuade audiences.

NOTE

[1] The journalists were labeled "muckrakers" by President Theodore Roosevelt, who compared them to a character in John Bunyan's book *Pilgrim's Progress*—a man who raked muck or filth and refused to look up from his task.

3

History of the Scientific Study of Media Effects

> Tantalized fascination surrounds all efforts to study the effects of mass media.
> —Paul Lazarsfeld, 1949

The previous chapter leaves the impression that effects from mediated communication are powerful, but history is biased toward recording instances when mediated communications seem to provoke action. Major reactions that can be traced to mediated communication are easy to locate. Except for the existence of a very detailed personal diary or some other trustworthy personal account, instances of limited media effects are difficult for the historian to identify.[1]

Several studies in psychology and sociology in the late 19th century involved research on mass media and presaged the theoretical bases for more sophisticated and numerous studies in the decades to follow, media effects research emerged categorically in the 20th century. The first departments of communication were created in the late 1940s (Simonson & Park, 2015a). Since 1960, graduate programs in mass communication have sprung to life at major research universities throughout the country, and the study of media effects has quickly matured and diversified. Researchers now search for evidence of media effects in a number of distinct research branches such as persuasion, media violence, sexually explicit material, fright reactions, agenda setting, new media technologies, uses and gratifications, cultivation research, and other areas.

Several communication scholars have offered excellent historical studies of communication (Dennis & Wartella, 1996; Heath & Bryant, 2000; Rogers, 1994; Simonson & Park, 2015b). Katz (1980, 1988) examined the media effects research tradition from a conceptual standpoint, offered an interesting analysis of media effects research issues, and suggested significant points of connection among the various theories of media effects.

This chapter relates the history of media effects research and identifies some pioneering scholars who contributed significantly to our knowledge of the field. We also discuss the notions of powerful, limited, and varying effects levels. Finally, we conclude this chapter with some suggestions for advancing the knowledge of media effects in the future.

The Early Days of Media Effects Research

Several 19th- and early 20th-century studies in psychology, sociology, and social psychology involved the examination of particular mass media effects. Some studies were philosophical in nature and offered comments on the suspected influence of mediated communications on audiences and public opinion, but these studies did not isolate particular social effects on mass media audiences in a controlled design or a laboratory setting. The handful of experimental studies conducted usually focused on the measure of very specific physical or psychological effects from media exposure.

We cite these studies for two reasons. Because of their emphasis on mass media and their introduction of ideas that would later become the theoretical bases of particular media effects studies, they should be considered precursors to the mass media effects studies that would arise in the 20th century. Additionally, two of these precursory studies reveal that the models for suspected powerful and limited effects from mass media communications developed almost simultaneously.

Two articles in the *American Journal of Sociology* in the late 19th century illustrate early differing views on the power mediated communications exerted on audiences. They introduced ideas that other social scientists would explore more fully in theoretical formations and controlled experiments during the next century. It is interesting that of these two articles, the "limited effects" view preceded the "powerful effects" view. Jenks (1895) doubted the influence of newspapers of the period on the formation of public opinion, and he proposed that the individual differences of audience members modified the influential power of communications.

> One chief reason, perhaps, of the comparatively small influence of our press is that the people know the fact that the papers are run from motives of personal profits, and that the policy of the paper is largely determined by the amount to which its opinions will affect its sales and advertising. . . . [A]ll of us doubtless have our opinions formed from former prejudices, we ourselves unconsciously selecting the facts and statements that fit into these former prejudices, and thus tend to conform to our own beliefs. . . . It is probably not too much to say that not 25 percent of our adult voting population have deliberately made up an opinion on a public question after anything like a reasonably full and fair study of the facts in the case. Public opinion, then, seems to be a mixture of sense and nonsense, of sentiment, of prejudice, of more or less clearly defined feelings coming from influences of various kinds that have been brought to bear upon the citizens, these influences perhaps being mostly those of sentiment rather than those acting upon the judgment. (Jenks, 1895, p. 160)

Yarros (1899) took the opposite view by emphasizing the power of the newspaper to both shape and express public opinion; however, he bemoaned the "mendacity, sensationalism, and recklessness" (p. 374) that characterized most of the newspapers of his day. He also regretted that so many editors were so incompetent, yet wielded so much power over an unsuspecting public:

> The editor is glad to have the support of authority, but he is not daunted or dis-
> turbed at finding recognized authority against his position. The mature opinions of
> scholars and experts he treats with a flippancy and contempt which the slightest
> degree of responsibility would render impossible. But the editor is irresponsible.
> The judicious and competent few may laugh at his ignorance and presumption, but
> the cheap applause of the many who mistake smartness for wit and loud assertion
> for knowledge affords abundant compensation. Controversy with an editor is a
> blunder. He always has the last word, and his space is unlimited. He is adept at
> dust-throwing, question-begging, and confusing the issue. In private life he may be
> intellectually and morally insignificant, but his readers are imposed upon by the air
> of infallibility with which he treats all things, and the assurance with which he
> assails those who have the audacity to disagree with him. The average newspaper
> reader easily yields to iteration and bombast. He believes that which is said daily in
> print by the august and mysterious power behind the editorial "we." His senti-
> ments and notions are formed for him by that power, and he is not even conscious
> of the fact. (p. 375)

The debate about the power of newspapers to either direct or reflect public opinion (the forerunner of the mirror/lamp metaphor of the popular culture debate of the
1950s, as well as an antecedent of the modern-day argument for and against the
agenda-setting hypothesis) continues to this day. In the 20th century, articles in the
American Journal of Sociology and elsewhere kept the debate alive (Angell, 1941; Orton,
1927; Park, 1941; Shepard, 1909).

Several early experimental studies deserve mention as precursors to modern-day
media effects investigations, especially in the area of entertainment. These include a
study of the effects of music on attention (Darlington & Talbot, 1898), the effects of
music on thoracic breathing (Foster & Gamble, 1906), and a study of musical enjoyment as measured by changes in circulation and respiration (Weld, 1912). Another
early study, more theoretical than experimental, examined the nature and origin of
humor as a mental process and the functions of humor (Kline, 1907).

One of the earliest (perhaps the first) studies of the effects of consumption of
media violence on behavior was a doctoral dissertation by Frances Fenton. The partial and summary findings of her study appeared in two issues of the *American Journal
of Sociology* in November 1910 and January 1911. Fenton pointed out that the popular
notion that newspaper accounts of antisocial activities had suggestive powers on readers was well established prior to her thesis (see Fenton, 1910, pp. 345 and 350 for lists
of articles). She defined *suggestion* as

> the process by which ideas, images, impulsive tendencies, or any sort of stimulus,
> enter from without into the composition of the neural make-up or disposition and,
> at times more or less in the focus of consciousness, at other times not in the focus
> at all, are transformed into activity by the agency of a stimulus which bears an
> effective though unrecognized relation or similarity to the image or neural set, and
> in which there is in large part, or wholly, failure to anticipate the results of the sug-
> gested act. (pp. 364–365)

Fenton argued "on the basis of the psychology of suggestion" that a direct causal relationship could be assumed between reading newspaper articles on crime and on antisocial activities and subsequent criminal or antisocial acts. In her dissertation, she

identified numerous cases in which individuals were known to have committed copy-cat-type crimes or other antisocial acts after getting ideas from a newspaper article. Due to lack of available space, the journal articles included only summary headings to describe the nature of the cases, but these headings were said to represent "a mass of both direct and indirect evidence of the suggestive influence of the newspaper on antisocial activity gathered from a wide range of territory and from many different sources" (1911, pp. 557–558).

Fenton also measured the amount of such material appearing in several large-circulation newspapers of the "yellow" variety, although she emphasized that

> this was undertaken not because the actual amount of antisocial matter in a newspaper is known to bear a direct relation to the growth of crime, or because we have any evidence to show that changes in the two bear a constant relation to one another. (1911, p. 539)

The Notion of Powerful Effects

Because of the historical bias toward chronicling powerful media effects and the concern about media's impact, it should not be surprising that in the early days of scientific effects studies in the 20th century, powerful effects were assumed by many. During World War I, social scientists were concerned about propaganda spread by the military and, after the war, by corporations (in the form of advertising and public relations efforts).

People in the United States (including most social scientists) believed that mass media, especially electronic media such as film and radio, had incredible powers to influence their audiences. For instance, as radio brought popular music into living rooms across the country, there were growing concerns about its effects from parents and teachers.

> Jazz, the pop music of its day, was thought to be so sexually arousing for men that young women were cautioned not to date a jazz fan without a chaperone, and certainly never to get into a car with one. (Valkenburg & Piotrowski, 2017, p. 29)

The immense power of media messages on unsuspecting audiences was described in colorful ways: Mass media supposedly fired messages like dangerous bullets or shot messages like strong drugs pushed through hypodermic needles. These descriptions gave rise to the "bullet" (sometimes referred to as the "magic bullet") or "hypodermic needle" theory of powerful media effects.

Carey (1996) provided an eloquent summary of the bullet theory:

> As the "jazz age" turned into the Great Depression, the fears of propaganda and the media were confirmed by the mass movements in politics and culture typical of that period and by a series of specific and startling events of which Orson Welles' radio broadcast "The War of the Worlds" stood as an archetype. In the standard history, this random assortment of fears, alarms, jeremiads, political pronouncements, and a few pieces of empirical research were collapsed into the "hypodermic-needle model" or "bullet theory" or "model of unlimited effects" of the mass media, for they converged on a common conclusion: The media collectively, but in

particularly the newer, illiterate media of radio and film, possessed extraordinary power to shape the beliefs and conduct of ordinary men and women. (p. 22)

Early theorists focused on the phenomenal changes in society from the late 19th to early 20th century and the resulting influences on the masses. Blumer (1951), noting the importance of mass behavior, wrote that due to urbanization and industrialization of the early 20th century,

mass behaviour has emerged in increasing magnitude and importance. This is due primarily to the operation of factors which have detached people from their local cultures and local group settings. Migrations, changes of residence, newspapers, motion pictures, the radio, education—all have operated to detach individuals from customary moorings and thrust them into a wider world. In the face of this world, individuals have had to make adjustments on the basis of largely unaided selections. The convergence of their selection has made the mass a potent influence. At times its behaviour comes to approximate that of a crowd, especially under conditions of excitement. At such times it is likely to be influenced by excited appeals as these appear in the press or over the radio—appeals that play upon primitive impulses, antipathies and traditional hatreds.[2] (pp. 187–188)

Early books were written with an underlying acceptance of the bullet or hypodermic needle theories;[3] that is, the immense power of mass communication messages on their audiences. These included Walter Lippmann's *Public Opinion* (1922), Harold Lasswell's *Propaganda Technique in the World War* (1927), and G. G. Bruntz's *Allied Propaganda and the Collapse of the German Empire in 1918* (1938). In fact, one media historian called journalist Walter Lippmann's *Public Opinion* "the originating book in the modern history of communication research"[4] (Carey, 1996, p. 28). Another prominent media scholar viewed it as a founding work for agenda-setting research (Rogers, 1994). In this classic work, Lippmann called upon his experiences with propaganda during World War I. The book became "a key intellectual influence in creating public apprehension about the role of propaganda in a democratic society" (Rogers, 1994, p. 236). Lippmann emphasized the role of the news media in influencing the perceptions of audiences about issues of importance.

The bullet theory served as the basis for a series of studies sponsored by the Payne Fund from 1929 to 1932. These studies sought to determine the influence of motion pictures on children and found that

as an instrument of education it has unusual power to impart information, to influence specific attitudes toward objects of social value, to affect emotions either in gross or in microscopic proportions, to affect health in a minor degree through sleep disturbance, and to affect profoundly the patterns of conduct of children. (Charters, 1933, p. 43)

However, the Payne Fund studies ultimately acknowledged the conditionality of media effects from movies, rather than a universal effect on audiences:

That the movies exert an influence there can be no doubt. But it is our opinion that this influence is specific for a given child and a given movie. The same picture may influence different children in distinctly opposite directions. Thus in a general survey such as we have made, the net effect appears small. (Charters, 1933, p. 16)

The reaction of children to movies was the focus of the Payne Fund studies of the late 1920s and early 1930s.

The Notion of Limited Media Effects

The hypodermic needle theory remained dominant until after the Depression, when empirical studies began to indicate that effects from mass media were not as powerful as originally thought. This limited effects phase lasted until the end of the 1960s. Rather than a society of fragmented individuals receiving all-powerful messages from mass media, the view shifted to one of a society of individuals who interacted within groups and thus limited the effects of media messages. Studies by Paul Lazarsfeld at Columbia University's Bureau of Applied Social Research and by other social scientists such as Carl Hovland working for the U.S. War Department indicated that mass media had only limited effects on individual audience members (Carey, 1996).

> What was also discovered, in the standard rendition, was that individuals, the members of the audience, were protected from the deleterious possibilities inherent in the mass media by a group of predispositional or mediating factors. . . . Some individuals (a few) under some circumstances (rare) were directly affected by the mass media. Otherwise, media propaganda and mass culture were held at bay by an invisible shield erected by a universally resistant psyche and a universally present network of social groups. (Carey, 1996, p. 23)

The limited effects model became thoroughly established in 1960 with the publication of Joseph Klapper's *The Effects of Mass Communication*. This classic work, based on his doctoral dissertation at Columbia University, reviewed hundreds of media effects studies from the 1920s through the 1950s and attempted to make blanket generalizations on the subject of mass media effects (see the sidebar later in this chapter). Klapper called for a new approach to research in the field: a "phenomenistic approach," which emphasized particular factors that limited the effects of mass media messages on individuals.

> In a well-known line, interest shifted from what it was that the media did to people toward what it was people did with the media. This was then a shift in interest and attention from the source to the receiver and a relocation of the point of power in the process: The audience controlled the producers. Except for some special problems (violence and pornography are the best-known examples) and some special groups (principally children), interest in direct effects and propaganda withered away. (Carey, 1996, pp. 23–24)

Effects of Varying Levels

Researchers began to focus experiments on the different reactions of individuals to the same media presentations. Rather than viewing audiences as passive victims who could be manipulated by mass media messages, scholars soon realized that individual differences and environmental factors were important moderators in the process of mass media effects.

> Experiments in behaviorism, motivation, persuasion, and conditioning led researchers to examine the processes of habit formation and learning. Differences among individual personality traits and psychological organization were found to be affected by the social environment in which people were raised. Moreover, studies in human perception showed that an individual's values, needs, beliefs, and attitudes were instrumental in determining how stimuli are selected from the environment and the way meaning is attributed to those stimuli within an individual's frame of reference. (Heath & Bryant, 2000, p. 347)

Studies with theoretical bases in psychology and sociology found that audience members selectively attended to media messages, depending upon their predispositions, interests, attitudes, social category, and a number of other factors. Similar variables were found to influence an individual's perception of a media message and what the person remembered about the message. These concepts were later defined as selective exposure, selective perception, selective retention, and the social categories perspective, which posits that people with similar demographic characteristics react similarly to media messages.

In the decades following the 1960s, mass media research thrived as the field of mass communication became firmly established at research universities throughout the nation and around the world. Certain new theories and research findings did not fit neatly into the limited effects paradigm; therefore, the history was amended to include new studies that indicated moderate to powerful media effects were indeed possible (Ball-Rokeach et al., 1984a, 1984b; Blumler & McLeod, 1974; Maccoby & Farquhar, 1975; Mendelsohn, 1973; Noelle-Neumann, 1973).

Many research studies through the years have indicated different levels of media effects. As Esser (2008) noted, studies supporting strong or weak effects can be found throughout the various phases of media effects research. Without standard lines of demarcation, media effects researchers have often made qualitative judgment calls about the power of effects. Based upon these qualitative verdicts, what emerges is a history of research that states conclusively that various kinds of mass media effects do occur—but the levels of influence have been assumed to vary from limited to rather powerful, which researchers have recognized (and argued) from the beginning.

Transactional or Negotiated Effects

We are currently in a phase of research that examines transactional or negotiated media effects (McQuail, 2010). Vorderer et al. (2020) summarize the transactions between media and individuals this way:

> Media present an image of social reality but compete with other opinion-forming sources such as personal experiences or the social environment. These other sources can create resistance to the media's influence on the individual. However, the user is seen to be free to decide whether or not to adopt the views offered by the media. Instead of a direct transfer of meaning, users negotiate between what is offered by the media and what he or she is inclined to believe. This approach differs significantly from the previous ones, as it allows both the media and the users to be powerful. (p. 8)

The intense debate about the power or limits of media effects continues to this day (e.g., the effects of video game violence in Chapter 18), but knowledge in the field continues to advance. For example, as is delineated in subsequent chapters, researchers have discovered that media effects may be cognitive (affecting thoughts or learning), behavioral (affecting behavior), or affective (affecting attitudes and emotions). Effects may be either direct or indirect, and they may be short term, long term, or delayed. They may be self-contained or cumulative.

Overall, in modern media effects research, scholars are placing less emphasis on whether effects exist and more emphasis on understanding the underlying mechanisms related to media effects and identifying which people are more susceptible to them (Valkenburg & Piotrowski, 2017). Although we have learned much about individual differences, psychological factors, environmental factors, and social group characteristics that cause audience members to perceive and react to media messages in specific ways, much still remains to be discovered.

Some Pioneers in Media Effects Research

In the years following World War I, innovative scholars from various disciplines at several institutions of learning conducted pioneering studies to examine the fledgling domain of scientific research on the effects of mass communication. These scholars, who came from disciplines outside journalism or mass communication, hailed principally from the University of Chicago, Columbia University, and Yale University.

Carl Hovland

Carl Hovland studied the effects of training films on the attitudes of American soldiers during World War II (Hovland et al., 1949) and later directed experimental research that explored media effects on attitude change.[5] The tight design of the experiments conducted by Hovland became the model for much future research in media effects. Wilbur Schramm, a principle "mover and shaker" of mass communication research in the United States, said that Hovland's body of research from 1945 to 1961 constituted "the largest single contribution . . . to this field any man has made" (Schramm, 1997, p. 104).

Paul Lazarsfeld

Paul Lazarsfeld earned a PhD in mathematics, but his diverse research interests included social psychology, sociology, and mass communication. Lazarsfeld and his research institute at Columbia University pioneered research in the effects of radio and introduced the notion that interpersonal communication was an important moderating factor in certain mass media effects. In the 1940s, Lazarsfeld and his colleagues examined the influences of mass media on public opinion during a presidential campaign. They found that most people were influenced primarily through interpersonal contacts rather than by what they read in newspapers and magazines or heard on the radio, although those media were found to have some influence.[6] Particular individuals whom the researchers called "opinion leaders," who were often heavy users of mass media, were found to pass along information to others in the community who looked to them for guidance. This finding led to establishment of a two-step flow model of mass communication, in which media effects were perceived as being modified by interpersonal communication about those media messages. Subsequent research expanded the two-step flow model into one of multistep flow:

> Later studies concluded that the influence of opinion leaders was not always "downward," as in the interpretation of news events for a less informed audience. Opinion leaders were found to communicate "upward" to the media gatekeepers (i.e., newspaper editors and radio programmers) as well as share information "sideways" with other opinion leaders. Further studies of interpersonal communication showed that an individual's personal identification with an organization, religion, or other social group has a strong influence on the type of media content selected. . . . Group norms apparently provide a type of "social reality" check built on similar and shared beliefs, attitudes, opinions, and concerns that tend to form barriers against mediated messages contrary to the group's point of view. Likewise, mediated messages in agreement with the group or provided by the group are usually attended to and utilized to reinforce the status quo. (Heath & Bryant, 2000, pp. 349–350)

Harold Lasswell

Harold Lasswell made many contributions to the study of media effects, with the most notable being his five-question model—"who says what in which channel to whom with what effects?" (Lasswell, 1948). Other important contributions included his studies of propaganda and his identification of three important functions that mass communications serve in society: surveillance of the environment, correlation of society's response to events in the environment, and transmission of the cultural heritage.[7] Rogers (1994) listed five major contributions that he believed Lasswell made to communication study.

1. His five-questions model of communication led to the emphasis in communication study on determining effects. Lasswell's contemporary, Paul F. Lazarsfeld, did even more to crystallize this focus on communication effects.

2. He pioneered in content analysis methods, virtually inventing the methodology of qualitative and quantitative measurement of communication messages (propaganda messages and newspaper editorials, for example).

3. His study of political and wartime propaganda represented an important early type of communication study. The word *propaganda* later gained a negative connotation and is not used much today, although there is even more political propaganda. Propaganda analysis has been absorbed into the general body of communication research.

Harold Lasswell. *Courtesy of Hanna Holborn Gray Special Collections Research Center, University of Chicago Library*

4. He introduced Freudian psychoanalytic theory to the social sciences in America. Lasswell integrated Freudian theory with political analysis, as in his psychoanalytic study of political leaders. He applied Freud's id-ego-superego via content analysis to political science problems. In essence, he utilized intraindividual Freudian theory at the societal level.

5. He helped create the policy sciences, an interdisciplinary movement to integrate social science knowledge with public action. The social sciences, however, generally resisted this attempt at integration and application to public policy problems (pp. 232–233).

Kurt Lewin

Social psychologist Kurt Lewin instituted pioneering studies in the dynamics of group communication. While at the University of Iowa, he conducted experiments to explore the persuasive power of different group conditions on audiences. In the best known of these experiments, "the sweetbreads study," groups of housewives reluctant to serve glandular meats to their families learned about the benefits of beef hearts, thymus (sweetbreads), liver, and kidneys by either attending a lecture or a discussion group. Lewin found that the discussion group situation proved far more effective in changing the behavior of the housewives (making them more likely to serve glandular meats to their families).

Rogers (1994) noted that Lewin's "greatest academic influence was through the brilliant students whom he trained" (p. 354). One such student was Leon Festinger, who went on to advance the now famous theory of cognitive dissonance, which proposes that whenever an individual's attitudes and actions are in conflict, the person will adjust cognitions in an attempt to resolve the conflict.[8]

Samuel Stouffer. *Courtesy of Ann S. Bisconti*

Samuel Stouffer

Paul Lazarsfeld (1962) dedicated his Columbia University voting studies to Samuel Stouffer because the studies "profited from his skillful procedures of survey analysis" (p. xxxi). He also cited Stouffer's influence on Carl Hovland's studies on attitudes and communications conducted at Yale University after World War II. Stouffer pioneered the use of empirical research—especially survey research—for social enquiries and the use of precise statistical methods. He directed research for the Division of Information and Education of the United States Army during World War II.

After the war, Stouffer conducted several studies of communications media, but these studies deal more with the effectiveness of media and often are not labeled as effects studies.[9] His importance to the history of media effects research lies in his empirical expertise, his influence on early communication researchers such as Hovland and Lazarsfeld, and his insistence that communication research adhere to strict empirical standards. In a 1942 chapter called "A Sociologist Takes a Look at Communications Research," Stouffer applauded the careful methods of the investigation by Peterson and Thurstone (1933), one of the famous Payne Fund studies that examined the effects of movies on children.

> A classic example of a complete experimental study in communications research was Thurstone and Peterson's study of the effects of specific motion pictures on social attitudes. . . . Subsequently there have been several other studies more or less similar to Thurstone's and Peterson's, but it is surprising that there have not been more. . . . This experiment demonstrated that a single movie has measurable and relatively lasting effects on children—but did anybody doubt that? Why spend a lot of money and time to demonstrate the obvious? There are two answers to this. In the first place, Thurstone showed that the direction of the effect (whether toward or against a given set of values) was not always predictable on a common-sense basis. A film glorifying a gambler had the unpredicted effect of making children feel more than ever that gambling was an evil. In the second place, Thurstone and Peterson were able to prove that effects of single films lasted over a long period of time and also that certain combinations of films had mutually reinforcing effects. It is true that they left hundreds of interesting questions unanswered. What types of children were affected most? What types of scenes within a given picture had the most effect? Were there differences in the kind of effect which would require a multidimensional rather than unidimensional attitude continuum for description? Such questions call for further research, and the Thurstone-Peterson method shows a way of answering them. (pp. 138–141)

Stouffer emphasized the importance of controlling for variables such as educational status, age, or other differences among audiences that could account for differences between the groups tested—variables that might make a difference in media effects. When the researcher does not control for confounding variables, he warned, "we can only hope and pray that we are controlling all the factors which would tend to differentiate" (p. 139) the control and experimental groups.

Finally, Stouffer's empirical expertise and prescience allowed him to identify problems in 1942 that continue to plague communication researchers in the 21st century—namely, the accurate measure of cumulative effects of mass media communications.

> It is a difficult matter to design an experiment which will measure the cumulative effect of, say, a year's exposure to a given medium of communication. . . . The difficulty of evaluating cumulative effects of many small stimuli in the field of communications is all the more serious because there is good basis for the belief that it is in just this way that communications have their principal effect. One soft-drink ad may not invite the pause that refreshes, but hundreds, and even thousands of them, confronting the consumer in as many different social situations evidently help sell the product. (Stouffer, 1942, pp. 141–142)

Douglas Waples

Douglas Waples was a professor in the Graduate Library School at the University of Chicago. In 1940, at the same time that Lazarsfeld was conducting radio studies at Columbia University, Waples, Bernard Berelson, and Franklyn Bradshaw published their work on the effects of print media, *What Reading Does to People*. The work revealed much about print media effects on attitude change.

> The studies have repeatedly shown that reading can change attitudes. They have also shown that certain reader traits and certain content elements will modify the effect of the reading. For example, the effects are modified by differences in what the readers already know about the subject. The less the reader knows about the complexities of and objections to issues discussed in the text, the greater the change in attitude will be. (pp. 108–109)

More significantly, Waples offered the earliest published version of the five-question model discussed earlier. In fact, exact origins of the model—which has always been credited to Lasswell (1948)—may be lost to history. Six years before Lasswell's version of the model was published, a 1942 article by Waples in the *American Journal of Sociology* begins with the following quotation: *"Who communicates what to whom by what medium, under what conditions, and with what effects?"* (p. 907). So who really said it first? Rogers (1994) attributed the five-question model—"who says what in which channel to whom with what effect"—to Lasswell while speaking at a Rockefeller Communication Seminar in 1940, a conference also attended by Waples. However, the quotation is not recorded in the rather detailed conference papers.[10] Ultimately, it is unclear in Waples's 1942 article whether he was quoting Lasswell, himself, or someone else. To further complicate the matter for historians, neither scholar provided a citation for the words in 1942 or 1948.

The identity of the originator of the model is less important than the inclusion of the "under what conditions" phrase. This phrase—which is absent from any of the published Lasswell versions—adds a sophistication to the process that is essential to sorting out media effects at their various levels. After the quote, Waples (1942) wrote, "Reliable answers to this complex question at regular time intervals would greatly clarify the process of social change via communications and would simplify predictions of impending changes" (p. 907).

Wilbur Schramm

Wilbur Schramm. *Courtesy of the University of Illinois Archives*

Wilbur Schramm did not specialize exclusively in media effects. In fact, one of his principal areas of interest was in international communication and the role of mass communication in developing third-world nations. However, Schramm is important because of his role as consolidator and legitimizer of mass communication study—including media effects.

> Schramm was the first professor of communication so-designated; his was the first communication research institute and the first doctoral program awarding degrees in communication; and Schramm presided over the first academic unit (a "division") of communication in the world. (Rogers & Chaffee, 1997, p. 7)

While serving as director of the journalism school at the University of Iowa, Schramm initiated the first PhD program in mass communication in 1943. Three years later, he founded the Bureau of Audience Research at Iowa, one of several communication research institutes that sprang to life during the 1940s and 1950s. These institutes were patterned somewhat after Lazarsfeld's Bureau of Applied Social Research at Columbia.

Bernard Berelson

Bernard Berelson, another pioneer in media effects research, was a colleague of Waples at the University of Chicago (where Berelson served as dean of the Library School) and later a colleague of Lazarsfeld at Columbia University and the Bureau for Applied Social Research. He coauthored the classic voting study *The People's Choice* with Lazarsfeld.

Berelson (1948) was perhaps the first researcher to attempt to make umbrella generalizations about mass communication effects when he suggested the following formulation for research:

> Some kinds of *communication* on some kinds of *issues,* brought to the attention of some kinds of *people* under some kinds of *conditions,* have some kinds of *effects.* This formulation identifies five central factors (or rather groups of factors) which are involved in the process, and it is the interrelationship of these variables which represents the subject matter of theory in this field. At present, students can fill out only part of the total picture—a small part—but the development of major variables and the formulation of hypotheses and generalizations concerning them are steps in the right direction. (p. 172)

Berelson's concern was for the influence of communication effects on public opinion, rather than media effects overall, yet his formulation could be applied to other research in media effects. In 1950, he noted the many complex findings that had emerged from research studies that would have to be considered in the development of any overarching theory of mass communication effects.

The effects of communication are many and diverse. They may be short-range or long-run. They may be manifest or latent. They may be strong or weak. They may derive from any number of aspects of the communication content. They may be considered as psychological or political or economic or sociological. They may operate upon opinions, values, information levels, skills, taste, behavior. . . . Because of the variety and the complexity of the effects of communications, this topic probably represents the most neglected area in communication research. (Berelson & Janowitz, 1950, p. 395)

Joseph Klapper

In 1960, Joseph Klapper, who was one of Lazarsfeld's students, published his still valuable and classic work, *The Effects of Mass Communication*. In this book, Klapper offered several overarching generalizations "in their bare bones" (p. 7) about the effects of mass media messages. In a review of Klapper's book, Wilbur Schramm (1961) noted that the text did not include new research but instead gathered, resynthesized, and updated some of Klapper's earlier work: "The impact of the book, therefore, is not newness, but rather the weight of so much research evidence brought together, passed through a single mind, organized, and presented lucidly and reasonably" (p. 321).

Unfortunately, Klapper's ideas have been greatly reduced to a "limited effects" notion that encouraged a "phenomenistic approach" that would identify moderating factors involved in effects—even though Klapper warned repeatedly about the grave

---

Klapper's Generalizations

1. Mass communication *ordinarily* does not serve as a necessary and sufficient cause of audience effects but rather functions among and through a nexus of mediating factors and influences.

2. These mediating factors are such that they typically render mass communication a contributory agent, but not the sole cause, in a process of reinforcing the existing conditions. Regardless of the condition in question—be it the vote intentions of audience members, their tendency toward or away from delinquent behavior, or their general orientation toward life and its problems—and regardless of whether the effect in question be social or individual, the media are more likely to reinforce than to change.

3. On such occasions as mass communication does function in the service of change, one of two conditions is likely to exist. Either:

   a. The mediating factors will be found to be inoperative and the effect of the media will be found to be direct; or

   b. The mediating factors, which normally favor reinforcement, will be found to be impelling toward change.

4. There are certain residual situations in which mass communication seems to produce direct effects, or directly and of itself to serve certain psychophysical functions.

5. The efficacy of mass communication, either as a contributory agent or as an agent of direct effect, is affected by various aspects of the media and communications themselves or of the communication situation, including, for example, aspects of textual organization, the nature of the source and medium, the existing climate of public opinion, and the like.

danger in "the tendency to go overboard in blindly minimizing the effects and potentialities of mass communications" (p. 252).

Klapper's generalizations have usually been overlooked or quoted only in partial form. In most cases, only the first two generalizations have been reproduced—the two that, not surprisingly, emphasize the many studies that show limited or indirect effects of media communications. Generalizations 3, 4, and 5—those that emphasize that direct effects from media communications are indeed possible—have been ignored by the standard history.

Albert Bandura

In the 1970s, the decade following the appearance of Klapper's book, psychological theories arose that had strong implications for understanding mass media effects.

Albert Bandura. *Photo credit: Chuck Painter / Stanford News Service*

The theories of Albert Bandura (1973, 1991)—social learning theory and, later, social cognitive theory—opened up alternative lines of inquiry for communication researchers.[11] Rather than focus primarily on mass communication's effects upon attitude change, scholars in the 1970s and beyond began for the most part to examine more complex behavioral responses, changes in cognitive patterns, and media effects on learning and knowledge (Becker et al., 1975; Chaffee, 1977; Clarke & Kline, 1974). Many of the most important of these findings are discussed throughout the remainder of this text.

Social learning theory explains how viewers learn and model behaviors they see in the mass media, based upon their environmental and cognitive predispositions. It began to serve as the basis for a bevy of research that examined the effects, especially among children, of viewing violence on film and television, the latter medium fast coming into dominance.

The Legacy of the Pioneers

In the years since the 1960s, as the field of mass communication research continued to blossom and attract more scholars interested specifically in media effects, other areas of media effects research were either born or developed into maturity. These included cultivation analysis and other sociological procedures that attempt to measure the cumulative effects of mass communication, research to examine the agenda-setting hypothesis that mass media are responsible for bringing public awareness to particular issues, research to explore the reasons why audience members used particular mass media, and the many other areas of media effects.

Future of Media Effects Research

The challenges for media effects researchers of the 2020s and beyond are great, but they will eventually be met if scholars continue to approach the problems with the "tantalized fascination" mentioned by Lazarsfeld in the quotation that opened this chapter. With decades of media effects research having been conducted, Valkenburg et al. (2016) noted that recent meta-analyses have revealed that effect sizes are typically small to moderate. However, there is anecdotal and empirical evidence that some people do experience strong media effects, suggesting "that there are strong individual differences in susceptibility to media effects" (p. 317). Media effects meta-analyses typically focus on macro-level effects, which means media effects sizes appear limited in large, diverse groups, and "more subtle yet potent individual differences" may not be highlighted (p. 317). Newer theories—such as the differential susceptibility model of media effects (Valkenburg & Peter, 2013)—focus on these differences and how they can result in micro- or individual-level effects. Moreover, Vorderer et al. (2020) noted that "macro-level media effects have largely been put out of focus in communication studies, at least within the social psychology of media effects model" (p. 12), which focuses on "how media messages and processes could in some way be connected causally to particular cognitive, attitudinal, or behavioral changes—or reinforce the status quo" (p. 3).

Meanwhile, some older theories are being updated and extended, "partly due to the rapid changes in the new media landscape, which demands a rethinking of theories that originated in periods when the relation between media and audiences was predominately anonymous and one-directional" (Valkenburg & Oliver, 2020, p. 28). Modern media effects scholars are also reconceptualizing the idea of "media use," both in terms of advancements in media technologies and in media multitasking. For instance, streaming your favorite Netflix show on your smart TV may also include simultaneously posting your reactions on social media, engaging with other fans in online communities, and searching for information about the actors on imdb.com.

Media effects researchers must adapt to ever-changing technological advances. Our constant use of technology and the continual integration of mass media into our daily lives results in experiences unlike those of any previous generations. Today's media consumers are both permanently online and permanently connected (Vorderer et al., 2018).

> Media outlets and their message systems are now available everywhere, and exposure can happen anytime, with implications for both mass and (mediated) interpersonal communication. . . . As a result, media use and media effects may now materialize everywhere, anytime, and with respect to any sort of content. (Vorderer et al., 2020, p. 11)

Researchers continue to seek to understand what effects can result from being constantly connected. In fact, Vorderer et al. (2020) noted that "we are only at the beginning of media effects research in our always-on environment" (p. 12). Whereas much of the previous research relied on self-reported data to understand media effects, contemporary studies are incorporating new techniques and technologies to study media effects, including face readers, eye trackers, and functional magnetic resonance imaging (Valkenburg & Oliver, 2020). You will read about many of these studies throughout the remainder of this book.

Another newer area of study in media effects research is in the area of what is known as **self-effects** (Valkenburg, 2017)—the effects that mediated messages can have on message creators themselves. For example, expressing your opinion on Twitter or uploading a photo to Instagram not only affects others who see your content—those communicative acts can affect you, too! Furthermore,

> given individuals' tendencies to select media content that is congruent with their cognitions, beliefs, and attitudes, it is likely that messages which are self-generated and originate from its generator's own beliefs may have an even stronger effect on the message generators themselves than on their message recipients. There is an apparent need for future communication research that investigates and compares the effects and effectiveness of messages on both recipients and message generators themselves. (Valkenburg & Oliver, 2020, p. 30)

Summary

In the latter part of the 19th century, several studies in psychology and sociology involved research on mass media and presaged the theoretical bases for more sophisticated studies in the decades to follow. Media effects research emerged categorically in the 20th century.

One of the earliest studies of the effects of consumption of media violence on behavior was a doctoral dissertation by Frances Fenton. Fenton pointed out that the popular notion that newspaper accounts of antisocial activities had suggestive powers on readers was well established prior to her thesis.

During the early years of scientific effects studies in the 20th century, powerful effects were assumed by many. The impact of media messages on audiences was likened to firing a bullet or injecting a drug, which gave rise to the magic bullet theory or hypodermic needle theory of mass communication.

The hypodermic needle theory remained dominant until after the Depression, when empirical studies began to indicate that effects from mass media were not as powerful as originally thought. Rather than a society of fragmented individuals receiving all-powerful messages from mass media, the view shifted to one of a society of individuals who interacted within groups, which limited the effects of media messages. Studies by Paul Lazarsfeld and other social scientists indicated that mass media had only limited effects on individual audience members.

The limited effects model became thoroughly established in 1960 with the publication of Joseph Klapper's *The Effects of Mass Communication*. Klapper made blanket generalizations about media effects; interestingly, he mentioned only two indirect effects.

Researchers began to focus experiments on the different reactions of individuals to the same media presentations. Rather than viewing audiences as passive victims who could be manipulated by mass media messages, scholars soon realized that individual differences and environmental factors were important moderators in the process of mass media effects.

Certain new theories and research findings did not fit neatly into the limited effects paradigm; therefore, the history was amended to include new studies that indicated moderate to powerful media effects were indeed possible. From the beginning, overwhelming evidence accumulated for *significant* effects from media communications on audiences, based for the most part upon scientific methods and traditional statistical models.

Without standard lines of demarcation, media effects researchers have often made qualitative judgment calls about the power of effects. The intense debate about the power or limits of media effects still rages to this day, but knowledge in the field continues to advance.

Regarding the future of media effects, researchers will continue to explore the variables that make some people more susceptible to media effects. The field has and will continue to update older media effects theories and to develop and test new ones, especially as technology advances. Researchers will also continue to explore the self-effects that result when we create messages ourselves. Ultimately, scholarship on media effects will continue "reflecting a greater nuance of human experience and its intersection with communication technologies" (Valkenburg & Oliver, 2020, p. 30).

NOTES

[1] Difficult but not impossible: F. L. Mott (1944) conducted a historical study and found "no correlation, positive or negative, between the support of a majority of newspapers during a campaign and success at the polls" (p. 356). Another instance of limited effects that could be argued is indicated by Isaiah Thomas's *History of Printing,* which offered state-by-state counts on the number of newspapers for and against ratification of the Constitution. In some cases, newspapers seemed to have little or no effect upon the outcome of the vote. In Delaware, for example, no newspapers favored adoption and two opposed adoption, yet Delaware was the first state to adopt the Constitution—and by unanimous vote at its convention.

[2] Blumer's statement, originally written in 1939, was later called by Denis McQuail (1972/1969) "the most influential single statement of the concept of the mass, looked at from the perspective of the sociology of collective behaviour" (p. 100).

[3] None used these terms, however. Many have attributed the "hypodermic needle" phrase to Lasswell, but a rereading of Lasswell's works revealed he used no such phrase (Chaffee & Hochheimer, 1985).

[4] Carey wrote: "Lippmann, in fact, redefined the problem of the media from one of morals, politics, and freedom to one of psychology and epistemology. He established the tradition of propaganda analysis and simultaneously, by framing the problem not as one of normative political theory but as one of human psychology, opened up the tradition of effects analysis that was to dominate the literature less than two decades after the publication of *Public Opinion"* (Carey, 1996, p. 30).

[5] It should be recalled that Hovland's U.S. Army studies reportedly showed limited media effects; however, the limits of the effects extended only to attitude change—the films proved to have much stronger effects on learning; that is, the soldiers learned a great deal from the films.

[6] Other findings (Blumler & McLeod, 1974; McLeod & McDonald, 1985; Ranney, 1983) suggest that the influence of mass media may be more powerful in the political communication process than the findings of *The People's Choice* indicated.

[7] Wright (1960) added "entertainment" as another important function of mass media.

[8] Rogers (1994, p. 352) offered this example of cognitive dissonance: "One effect of dissonance is for an individual to avoid exposure to conflicting messages. For example, once an individual purchases a new car, that individual tends to avoid advertisements for competing makes of cars."

[9] One explored the different advantages of radio and newspaper as news sources and identified preferences for one or the other among various classes and groups of people. Another examined the effect that radio was having on newspaper circulation. Both were included in Lazarsfeld's *Radio and the Printed Page* (1940).

[10] The conference proceedings are included in the papers of Lyman Bryson at the Library of Congress (Rockefeller Foundation, "Needed Research in Communication," "Public Opinion and the Emergency," and "Memorandum on Communications Conference," U.S. Library of Congress: Papers of Lyman Bryson, Box 18, October 17, 1940, November 1, 1940, and January 18, 1941).

[11] Bandura began studying children and teens and the learning of antisocial behavior by viewing models' actions on films or on television during the 1960s (e.g., Bandura, 1965b; Bandura, Ross, & Ross, 1963a; Bandura & Walters, 1963).

Section Two

THEORY AND CONCEPTS

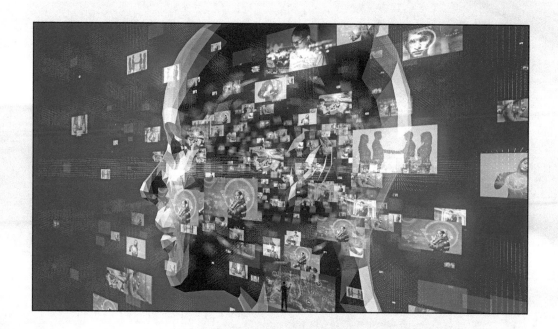

4

Social Cognitive Theory

Social cognitive theory embraces an interactional model of causation in which environmental events, personal factors, and behavior all operate as interacting determinants of each other.

—Albert Bandura, 1986

For many years, psychologists, especially social psychologists, have advanced various theories about why people behave as they do. Some say behavior is based upon a person's motivations. Others propose that behavior is a response to external stimuli and subsequent reinforcements. Still others point out that people react differently in different situations, and these scholars think that the *interaction* between a person and a situation produces a particular behavior.

It may seem strange that concepts from social and behavioral psychology would appear in a media effects textbook. As subsequent chapters will reveal, however, the study of effects of mediated communication often is a specialization in the social science research domains of communication, psychology, anthropology, and sociology. One theory undergirds a great deal of the media effects literature, including theories in the critical and highly scrutinized area of media violence. For this reason, familiarity with *social cognitive theory* is essential for a basic comprehension of media effects.

Social cognitive theory provides a framework that allows us to analyze the human cognitions (or mental functions) that produce certain behaviors. Put simply, this theory "explains how humans can learn and be motivated to perform behaviors by observing others" (Krcmar, 2020, p. 101). Social cognitive theory explains human thought and actions as a process of *triadic reciprocal causation* (Bandura, 1994, 2009; see Figure 4.1). This means that thought and behavior are determined by three different factors that interact and influence each other, with variable strength, at the same time or at different times: (1) behavior, (2) personal characteristics such as cognitive and biological qualities (e.g., IQ, gender, height, or race), and (3) environmental factors or events.

Albert Bandura's social cognitive theory of mass communication and his earlier social learning theory are the foundation for volumes of research in several areas of

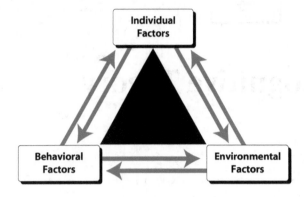

Figure 4.1   This illustration of triadic reciprocal causation highlights how personal, behavioral, and environmental factors influence each other bidirectionally to determine human thought and behavior.

Source: Adapted from Bandura, 2001, p. 266.

media effects study—including those that examine effects of violent, frightening, sexual, and persuasive forms of media. For the student of media effects, an understanding of Bandura's theory is essential because the concepts serve as a common denominator among other media effects theories and hypotheses.

Various dimensions of social cognitive theory are examined in this chapter, including the cognitive characteristics distinct to humans, the dynamics of observational learning, the effects of modeling, and the ways we learn from media content. The theory provides a framework to explain prosocial effects from mass media; social prompting or persuasion; and diffusion of an idea, message, or belief by way of symbolic modeling. The overall objective of the chapter is to provide an explanation of social cognitive theory and discuss significant studies that have drawn heavily upon the theory.

Distinctly Human Traits

A key aspect of social cognitive theory is its emphasis that people have agency. As Krcmar (2020) notes:

> We are proactive, self-regulating, self-organizing, and both purposefully and reflexively adaptive to changes in the environment. This understanding of agency is crucial.... [A]lthough our environment provided much needed input to aid in learning and behavioral processes, SCT emphasizes the vital aspect that information processing and human motivation play; that is, whereas factors external to us may influence our actions, the origins of our actions are internal. Humans are not mere imitators; we are not automatons. (p. 101)

Of course, many animals have the ability to learn, but several distinct cognitive traits set human beings apart. Social cognitive theory emphasizes the importance of these uniquely human characteristics, known as the *symbolizing, self-regulatory, self-reflective,* and *vicarious capacities* (Bandura, 1994, 2009).

Symbolizing Capacity

Human communication is based upon a system of shared meanings of various symbols known as language. These symbols occur at more than one conceptual level—

letters of the alphabet are symbols used to construct words, for example, and words serve as symbols to represent specific objects, thoughts, or ideas. The capacity to understand and use these symbols allows people to store, process, and transform observed experiences into cognitive models that guide them in future actions and decisions.

Self-Regulatory Capacity

The self-regulatory capacity includes the concepts of motivation and evaluation. People have the ability to motivate themselves to achieve certain goals. They tend to evaluate their own behavior and respond accordingly to maximize positive outcomes and minimize negative ones. In this way, behavior is *self-directed* and *self-regulated*.

For example, a young father and mother are motivated to achieve the goal of providing for the emotional and material needs of their toddler. If they find that they are not earning enough money to achieve their goal, they may evaluate the situation and decide to look for higher-paying jobs or supplemental second jobs. They may then realize that the child's emotional needs are not being fulfilled because of their absence. In this case, one of the two may decide to start a home-based business in order to spend more time with the child. In either case, the couple evaluated, regulated, and directed their behavior in response to a common motivation or goal.

Self-Reflective Capacity

The self-reflective capacity involves the process of thought verification. It is the ability of a person to perform a self-check to make sure their thinking is correct. There are four different self-reflective "modes" used in thought verification: the enactive, vicarious, social, and logical modes (Bandura, 1986, 1994, 2009).

In the *enactive* mode, a person assesses the agreement between thoughts and the results of actions. For example, a young girl may think she has the potential to be an Olympic gymnast, but when she goes for her first gymnastics lesson, she discovers that she is a hopeless klutz. The instructor encourages her to concentrate on her studies at school and forget about sports. In this case, her actions do not verify her thoughts, and she must reassess her thinking. However, if she shows incredible natural talent in the gym, the instructor might tell her that with hard work the Olympics might someday be possible. In this scenario, the girl's actions corroborate her thoughts and provide verification.

With the *vicarious* mode, observation of another's experiences and the outcomes of those experiences can confirm or refute the veracity of thoughts. Perhaps the gymnast who initially thought she had considerable talent enters the gym and sees a world-class gymnast working on routines in preparation for the Olympic Games. After joining the gym and seeing the Olympic-bound gymnast working day after day for months or years, the younger girl sees that, with talent and hard work, the realization of her big dreams are possible.

Social verification involves comparison of personal beliefs with what others believe, using that comparison to determine if thinking is correct. For example, exposure to new ways of thinking after arriving at college may cause a person to do things previously unthinkable. Consider, for example, a young woman raised in a nondrinking Baptist family who has been homeschooled until going away to college. Once on campus, she is exposed to many other young people who encourage her to change her beliefs.

The last mode of thought verification within the self-reflective capability is the *logical* mode, which involves verification by using previously acquired rules of inference. The young woman may decide that the rules that were set in her strict religious upbringing are more important to her than popularity at school. She remembers times when she strayed from those rules and regretted it later, so she chooses to avoid drinking and finds a group of friends with views similar to hers.

Numerous studies have highlighted humans' ability to learn and model behaviors from watching others, either in person or on some sort of screen. For instance, this family is learning about yoga by watching a yoga video.

Vicarious Capacity

Vicarious capacity, which is the ability to learn without direct experience, is a human characteristic that emphasizes the potential contributions of mass media messages—for better or worse. As an example of positive social impact, the vicarious capacity allows a person to learn all sorts of beneficial things by reading or watching media content that presents prosocial behaviors. On the negative side, people may witness and learn antisocial behaviors to which they might not otherwise have been exposed.

> Much social learning occurs either designedly or unintentionally from models in one's immediate environment. However, a vast amount of information about human values, styles of thinking, and behavior patterns is gained from the extensive modeling in the symbolic environment of the mass media. (Bandura, 2009, p. 98)

Observational Learning and Modeling

Social learning and social cognitive theories place much emphasis on the concept of **observational learning**. A person observes other people's actions and the consequences of those actions, learning from what has been observed. The learned behavior can then be reenacted by the observer.

Modeling

The phenomenon of behavior reenactment, called **modeling**, includes four component processes: *attention, retention, motor reproduction,* and *motivation* (Bandura, 1986, 1994, 2009). These can be explained by using a simple example of observational learning, such as learning how to swing a golf club.

The process of modeling behavior, such as learning the proper technique for swinging a golf club, involves four processes: attention, retention, motor reproduction, and motivation.

Attention.   A person must pay attention to any behavior and perceive it accurately in order to model it successfully. The beginning golfer must watch the actions of the teacher and listen carefully to instructions—in short, pay close attention to the actions that are to be modeled.

Retention.   Modeled behavior must be remembered or retained in order to be used again. The permanent memory stores the information by means of symbolic representations that subsequently can be converted into actions. The beginning golfer must understand the instructor's comments and remember them, along with demonstrations and corrections, as well as what he sees other golfers do—either in person or on television.

Motor Reproduction.   At first, motor reproduction may be difficult and even faulty, as the beginner has to "think through" all the various steps involved in making a successful swing. As the golfer practices the modeled swing, however, the cognitive process becomes less tedious. If the beginner possesses the necessary component skills, observational learning occurs at a much faster rate. In other words, the natural athletic ability or the superior motor memory of the beginner largely determines the length of time required for mastery of the modeled swing.

Motivation.   The final process of observational learning and modeling is motivation, which in this context is simply the desire to perform an observed action or behavior. Motivation becomes a major factor in the decision to use modeled behavior—and people are not always motivated to model the behaviors they learn. For instance, our beginning golfer might notice that the instructor cannot drive the ball nearly as far as professional golfer Jon Rahm can. The beginner may also notice that the two stand differently, hold the club differently, and move different parts of the body whenever they swing. In this case, the beginner may choose to model their behavior after the more successful Rahm. Another possibility is that the student golfer may realize that green fees and cart fees are too expensive and that the years it will take to master a swing like Rahm's will be hard and costly. Furthermore, motivation is influenced by **self-efficacy**, which is the belief in one's ability to perform a behavior or action. If our beginning golfer believes they have (or can develop) the skills to become one of the greats, they will be more motivated to continue playing the game.

Some instances of modeling result in behavior reenactment that has greater consequences than learning a golf swing. Different learning situations dictate the importance of the four component parts of modeling. Consider, for instance, the young medical intern learning to perform surgery or the fearful child learning to swim. Whether there's a patient lying on the operating table or the child jumps into the pool, the actual *motor reproduction* of the modeled behavior in these situations is of paramount importance. Although the surgeon and the swimmer may have paid attention and remembered what to do, being able to reproduce the learned behaviors can mean the difference between life and death. Furthermore, various situations also affect *motivation* in the learning process. Compare two situations of people learning to speak a foreign language. A student in the United States learning French for a degree requirement would not have the same motivation as a French immigrant learning English to find a job in the United States.

Three types of situations provide the incentives that motivate a person to model learned behavior: (1) positive outcomes through direct performance of the behavior, (2) observation of another's behavior and the subsequent outcomes, and (3) evaluation based upon personal values or standards of behavior (Bandura, 1989, 1994). For instance, a preschool girl who learns a song from *Blue's Clues,* then performs the song for her parents and receives much praise and encouragement, is motivated to model that learned behavior in the future. In this case, the child performed the behavior and experienced the outcome directly.

The successful Nickelodeon program *Blue's Clues*—which was relaunched in 2019 as *Blue's Clues & You!*—also serves as a good example of the more vicarious, second type of motivational situation. In every show, the human character solves a mystery message from his animated puppy Blue. As they sing and play games, three clues are discovered, then the young man sits in his chair to think through the problem and solve the mystery. The child sees that the technique is always successful; therefore, the child is likely to model such "thinking chair" behavior whenever faced with solving a mysterious problem. Social cognitive theory researchers have often studied this type of vicarious reinforcement. Seeing a character on a TV show experience positive outcomes because of their actions can motivate a viewer to model the behavior; conversely, seeing a character experience negative outcomes can motivate a viewer *not* to model the character's actions (Krcmar, 2020). However, sometimes negatively reinforced behaviors observed on TV (e.g., a character expressing regret for having a one-night stand) may still be modeled by the viewer (Nabi & Clark, 2008).

To illustrate the third motivational situation, consider a young boy who views and imitates the violence he sees in an *Avengers* film. Perhaps he is a sensitive child who does not wish to hurt anyone physically, and he has been told that violence is wrong, yet his ability to imitate Captain America impresses the other children and makes him very popular at school. One day he jumps, kicks his friend a little too hard, and knocks him onto the pavement, breaking the friend's arm. The scene is a frightful one—the bloody bone protrudes from the skin, and the arm dangles. The child who kicked his friend is devastated. He cries intermittently for a week and never again imitates Captain America. In this case, the child is motivated to avoid modeling the violent behavior because he has witnessed a horrible outcome. He reevaluated his internalized standard of conduct because of personal experience.

Abstract Modeling

Modeling observed behavior "is not merely a process of behavioral mimicry, as commonly misconstrued" (Bandura, 2009, p. 101). Rather, rules of behavior learned in the past serve as a *guide* for new life situations (Bandura, 1994). These rules often provide an abstract framework for decision making in new situations. In other words, existing standards of behavior are not perfect or constant for each new situation, and a certain level of improvisation is required. A person is merely guided by the outcomes of their past experiences or the observed experiences of other people.

Abstract modeling takes learning to a higher level than mere mimicry of observed behavior. New situations generate new behaviors based upon the rules of behavior learned previously. These behaviors are themselves learned and stored in memory for future adaptation in other situations.

The use of abstract modeling offers many practical advantages (Bandura, 1986, 1994; Rosenthal & Zimmerman, 1978). One acquires personal standards for judging one's own motivations and behavior that can also be applied to evaluating the behavior and motivations of others. Abstract modeling also boosts critical thinking, communication skills, and creativity. Consider, for example, the creativity of the Beatles or other artists. Paul McCartney often said that he and John Lennon tried to imitate the work of other musical groups or soloists but also drew from their personal knowledge, experience, and preferences to put a personal stamp on their popular music. They were performing abstract modeling.

Effects of Modeling

Sometimes a person observes behavior or receives information that conflicts in some way with that person's established pattern of behavior. Two major effects are associated with such situations—**inhibitory** and **disinhibitory effects** (Anderson et al., 2003; Bandura, 1973, 2009; Berkowitz, 1984; Malamuth & Donnerstein, 1984; Zillmann & Bryant, 1984). The inner conflict causes a person to reexamine their personal motivations to perform the established behavior.

Inhibitory Effects

Many studies on inhibitory and disinhibitory effects have examined transgressive, aggressive, or sexual behavior (e.g., Berkowitz, 1984; Liebert et al., 1982; Malamuth & Donnerstein, 1984; Zillmann & Bryant, 1984). In each case, inhibitory effects occurred whenever a person refrained from reprehensible conduct for fear of the consequences, such as formal punishment by society or self-reproach because of a guilty conscience.

Inhibitory effects occur whenever new information or the observation of new behavior *inhibits* or *restrains* a person from acting in a previously learned way. Disinhibitory effects *disinhibit* or lift previously learned internal restraints on certain behaviors. A smoker might decide to change his behavior if he sees his favorite uncle (who smoked all his life) suffer miserably and die of emphysema. He has experienced inhibitory effects. On the other hand, consider a teenage girl from a strict family where alcohol and tobacco use are taboo. She goes to college and makes friends with students who drink and smoke, which lead to her established beliefs becoming more relaxed. When she decides to try a beer for the first time, she has experienced disinhibitory effects.

For another example of inhibitory effects, imagine two friends taking an introductory communication course during their first semester at college. One watches television while studying, a habit acquired in high school; she skims over her notes during the commercials. The other student isolates herself in her room to read and study without distraction. The student who works in quiet seclusion receives an "A" on the first exam, whereas the other student gets an "F." After recovering from the initial shock, the second student decides to *inhibit* her usual behavior and to model the behavior of her friend while reading and studying.

Disinhibitory Effects

A 1963 study by Bandura and his colleagues is a classic example of disinhibitory effects. The researchers exposed nursery school children to an adult performing physically aggressive actions against an inflatable plastic clown, called a Bobo doll. The children who saw that behavior later imitated the aggressive acts. Moreover, the researchers found that the children who saw the behavior were less inhibited about performing *other* violent acts they had learned in the past—acts that were not demonstrated by the adult (Bandura et al., 1963a). The exposure had a *disinhibitory* effect upon the children who watched it. (See the Research Spotlight for a discussion of the Bobo Doll experiment.)

Disinhibitory Devices.   Many types of behavior are not socially acceptable. Murder, rape, physical violence against others, and other criminal acts serve as extreme examples of impulses that must be restrained. Other less sensational behaviors also qualify. Research has shown that people who engage in reprehensible behavior often use cognitive techniques to justify their actions to themselves. In other words, they lose their inhibitions (become disinhibited) about acting in a certain way—even if those actions conflict with their internal moral standards. Researchers have identified eight such cognitive techniques or devices: moral justification, exonerative comparison, euphemistic labeling, displacement of responsibility, diffusion of responsibility,

Imitation of Film-Mediated Aggressive Models
Albert Bandura, Dorothea Ross, and Sheila A. Ross (1963)
Journal of Abnormal and Social Psychology, 66(1), 3–11

In this classic research experiment, Bandura and his associates observed children to determine if watching aggressive actions in person or on television caused the children to imitate the behavior.

Subjects

Children ranging in age from about 3 to 5 years old (mean age of 4 years 4 months) from the Stanford University Nursery School were tested. The subjects consisted of 48 boys and 48 girls.

Procedure

Three experimental groups and one control group consisted of 24 subjects each. One group saw real-life aggressive models. A second group saw the same models portraying aggression on film. The third group watched a film with an aggressive cartoon character. The control group subjects had no exposure to aggressive models.

Two adults, a male and a female, served as models in the real-life aggression and in the filmed human aggression conditions. The children were subdivided by gender so that half of the subjects exposed to human models saw the behavior of a same-sex model and half saw the behavior of an opposite-sex models. In the cartoon condition, the female model in a black cat costume performed the physical aggression toward the Bobo doll and used a high-pitched, animated voice for the verbal aggression. This condition was included to test whether the power of example was weaker if performed by characters more remote from reality.

Subjects in the real-life aggression condition were brought individually into the experiment room. The model was in the hallway outside the room, and the experimenter invited the model to enter the room. The subject was seated in one corner of the room at a small table that contained drawing materials, stickers, and colored paper. The experimenter demonstrated to the child how to make pictures with the materials provided. The model was seated in another corner of the room at a table with a tinker toy set, a mallet, and the 5-foot inflated Bobo doll. After the model was seated, the experimenter left the room.

The model began the session by assembling the tinker toys but after about a minute turned attention to the Bobo doll and started pummeling it, sitting on it and punching it in the nose, hitting it on the head with a mallet, tossing the doll up in the air and kicking it about the room. The sequence of aggressiveness was repeated about three times. During the aggressive behavior toward the doll, the model used verbally aggressive phrases such as "Sock him in the nose" or "Hit him down" or "Kick him" or "Pow."

Subjects who saw the film of the aggressive models were also taken individually into the experiment room to the table with the materials for making pictures. They were told that while they worked on their pictures a movie would be shown on a screen about 6 feet away. The film was shown for a duration of 10 minutes while the child was alone in the room. The models used for the first condition were also used in the filmed condition. The aggressive behavior in the film was identical to the real-life aggressiveness toward the doll.

Subjects who saw the cartoon film were taken individually into the experiment room and seated at the table with the picture construction material. The experimenter walked over to a television console about 3 feet in front of the subject's table saying, "I guess I'll turn on the color TV." The cartoon began playing.

(continued)

After the exposure experience, the experimenter escorted the subject to an anteroom containing very attractive toys and said the child could play with the toys. The experiment involved frustrating the subjects to test aggressive tendencies. Once the subject was involved with the toys, the experimenter said these were the very best toys and she had decided to reserve them for some other children. She said the subject could play with any of the toys in an adjoining room (the actual test room).

The toys in that room consisted of a 3-foot Bobo doll, a mallet and peg board, two dart guns, a tether ball with a face painted on it that hung from the ceiling, and nonaggressive toys (i.e., a tea set, crayons and coloring paper, a ball, two dolls, three bears, cars and trucks, and plastic farm animals).

Each subject spent 20 minutes in the room while being observed through a one-way mirror in an adjoining room by researchers.

Aggressive behavior was scored in six categories: total aggression, imitative aggression, mallet aggression, sitting on Bobo doll (this category was not included in the total aggression score), nonimitative aggression, and aggressive gun play. (Scan the QR code to see actual footage of participants interacting with the Bobo doll.)

Results

The results showed no difference in total aggressiveness for the subjects who viewed the real-life models and the film-mediated models. All three groups were significantly more aggressive than the control subjects. The subjects in the first three groups performed considerably more imitative physical and verbal aggression than the control group. The data suggested that exposure to humans on film portraying aggression was the most influential in eliciting and shaping aggressive behavior, even more so than the real-life condition. Subjects exposed to the human and cartoon models on film showed nearly twice as much aggression as subjects in the control group.

The researchers noted that boys exhibited significantly more total aggression, imitative aggression, more aggressive gun play, and more nonimitative aggressive behavior than girls. The sex of the model was shown to have some influence in promoting social learning.

In this experiment, behavior was learned through observation without any reinforcement. Exposure to adult aggression both facilitated learning aggressive responses and weakened inhibitory responses. The results countered the prevailing school of thought at the time, which argued that watching someone else vent aggression could be cathartic for the viewer, alleviating their aggressive impulses.

distortion of the consequences of action, dehumanization, and attribution of blame (Bandura, 2009).

The first three techniques—moral justification, exonerative comparison, and euphemistic labeling—are the most powerful in terms of cognitive and moral restructuring. This means that a person may actually change or restructure the way they view the undesirable behavior. Through use of disinhibitory devices, reprehensible conduct might be seen as not only *acceptable* but actually *desirable*. As an example of such restructuring, consider the case described previously—the girl with the strict upbringing who decided to try a beer with her college friends. She may have engaged in some degree of cognitive and moral restructuring that made beer drinking seem to be a desirable behavior.

Moral justification occurs whenever a person believes their otherwise objectionable actions are serving some moral, noble, or higher purpose and are therefore justified. In such cases, inhibitive restraints on certain behaviors are released or relaxed. In the mind of the transgressor, a greater good is served. A good example of moral justification is soldiers during wartime who legitimize aggression based on the "greater good" of protecting freedoms. A more common example would be that of a mother who spanks a misbehaving child.

Exonerative comparison also involves seeing one's bad actions as serving the greater good of society. A modern-day Robin Hood-type thief would exonerate himself for stealing because he gives what he steals to the poor.

Euphemistic labeling offers not only a means of camouflaging reprehensible conduct but it may also make the conduct respectable or at least acceptable. For example, the girl who watches television while studying might euphemistically consider her viewing as an *educational* rather than a *recreational* (or mindless) experience. She convinces herself that watching television keeps her up to date on current events; therefore, it is just as important as her textbook reading assignment. The teenage girl who starts smoking cigarettes euphemistically labels the activity as "cool" or "sexy" in her mind, rather than viewing the activity as a health hazard and a nasty habit.

The Showtime series *Dexter* relies heavily on these first three moral disengagement techniques (Finklea, 2011b). The show's protagonist, Dexter Morgan, is a serial killer who only kills other serial killers. He engages in both moral justification and exonerative comparison by relying on a code that condones only murdering serial killers who somehow eluded justice. Dexter's kills serve the greater good because they prevent the other serial killers from murdering more people. Furthermore, Dexter engages in euphemistic labeling by describing murdering other serial killers as "taking out the garbage." Moral disengagement techniques used on the series not only show the audience how Dexter justifies his actions, they can also help the audience root for Dexter as the show's "good guy."

Two disinhibitory techniques or devices cause a transgressor to shift the responsibility for wrongdoing to someone else. **Displacement of responsibility** occurs when someone in authority directs a person to act in a reprehensible way, and the authority figure accepts responsibility for the actions. With **diffusion of responsibility**, a transgressor acts within a group and therefore does not feel personally responsible for the behavior. Again, soldiers at war serve as excellent examples of such devices in action.

Disregard or distortion of the consequences of action refers to situations in which a person performs an act without thinking about the harm that act may cause or with the belief that the act will cause only minimal harm (Brock & Buss, 1962, 1964). The teenager who accepts the dare of peers and throws bricks through a store window is concerned only with the thrill of the moment—the idea of "getting away with" the wrongdoing and meeting the challenge of the dare. He gives no thought to the poor store owner who must have the window replaced or the jail time he will serve if caught.

The final devices, **dehumanization** and **attribution of blame**, focus on the attitudes of transgressors toward their victims. Dehumanization occurs whenever a person is divested of human qualities and considered no better than a beast. Nazi soldiers dehumanized Jewish people during World War II; therefore, they were able to commit unspeakable atrocities without feelings of remorse. In the United States prior to the civil rights movement, many whites dehumanized Blacks and thus prevented them from voting and enjoying advantages known by white people. Belligerent whites attacked peaceful civil rights demonstrators and justified their hostilities by attributing blame to the demonstrators or the situation rather than to themselves—they blamed the demonstrators for causing trouble and "provoking" them to hostile actions.

Learning from Media Content and Modeling

When the thriller *Jaws* played in theaters in the 1970s, audiences across the country applauded after the sheriff took aim, fired, and blasted the monster shark out of the water. In the summer months that followed, newscasters reported that many people at beach resorts were afraid to set foot in the ocean because they had seen the film and feared a shark attack. Remember the end of the film *Avengers: Infinity War* when Thanos wiped out half of all life in the universe, causing many of our favorite superheroes to turn into dust and blow away? It was one of those "lump in the throat" scenes for audience members. Then, at the end of *Avengers: Endgame*, it became difficult for some moviegoers to contain their excitement when those heroes returned, only to be brought to tears when Tony Stark died.

As these examples show, whenever a person sees a character on the screen expressing some strong emotion or performing some powerful action, the viewer is affected or *aroused*. The viewer remembers similar experiences and emotions, and these thoughts and images serve as cues that trigger self-arousal (Bandura, 1992; Wilson & Cantor, 1985).

Such experiences of arousal are not always fleeting in nature. Several studies have shown that audience members sometimes develop lasting emotional reactions, attitudes, and behaviors after viewing emotional content that arouses them. Vivid memories of the killer Great White shark from *Jaws* kept many people out of the ocean for years, and many who did brave the waves were cautious and uneasy. A decade earlier, the shower scene in Alfred Hitchcock's *Psycho* made many people throw back their shower curtains and opt for a much safer bath!

Examples of such fear reactions abound, but research has shown that people also learn many other reactions from media content, some of them lasting. Coping skills portrayed on the screen help people deal with their fears and phobias by lessening them and making them more tolerable (Bandura, 1982). Audience members learn to dislike whatever screen characters dislike, and they like whatever pleases or gratifies those characters (Bandura, 1986; Duncker, 1938).

Viewing Disinhibitory Devices

Media effects scholars are also interested in what happens whenever viewers see television and film characters acting in violent ways and employing the disinhibitory devices described in the previous section. How do viewers respond? How are they affected?

Research has shown that whenever viewers see television or movie characters injuring their victims and engaging in one or more of the devices, those viewers are then more likely to inflict punishment or penalty on others. Injurious conduct on the part of the viewer is linked to the sanctioned social behavior depicted on the screen (Bandura et al., 1975).

Effects of Social Construction of Reality, Cultivation, and Stereotypes

Only a fraction of our understanding of the world around us comes from our direct experiences. In addition to our first-hand knowledge, our perception of reality comes from interactions with others—including those seen in mass media—to create a shared reality. Scholars call this the **social construction of reality.** Characters in mass media inhabit "realities" that do not always reflect the true state of affairs in the real world. Research has shown that heavy consumption of media content can shape viewers' perceptions and beliefs to align with the mediated world portrayed on screen rather than the real world. As you will learn in Chapter 8, one media research tradition associated with such effects is known as **cultivation**.

Much of this research has examined television programs. Some of the best examples of television's power to alter viewers' perceptions are revealed whenever regular television viewers are asked to estimate their chances of being aboard a plane that will crash or their chances of being a victim of a violent crime. Such events are extremely rare in the real world, whereas they occur frequently in the mediated world. Most people, especially those who are heavy viewers of particular types of television programs, grossly *overestimate* their chances of being in a plane crash or becoming a victim of a crime.

Some studies have shown that viewers tend to have misconceptions due to stereotypical portrayals on television. Social cognitive theory posits that exposure to mediated stereotypes should result in effects in line with what was observed in the content (Krcmar, 2020). For instance, Buerkel-Rothfuss and Mayes (1981) tested 290 college students who reportedly watched, on average, seven episodes of daytime soap operas each week. Students were asked to estimate the occurrence in society of certain occupations (e.g., doctor, lawyer, businessman, blue-collar worker, housewife), health concerns (e.g., nervous breakdown, major operation, abortion), and other life issues and crises (e.g., having an affair, being happily married, getting divorced). Out of groups of 10, students estimated how many women and how many men could be classified in the various categories. The researchers controlled for factors such as intelligence, sex, age, and self-concept, and they designed their investigation to ensure that any exaggerated estimates resulted from viewing only rather than demographic factors. As the researchers expected, the students who watched the most soap operas were more likely than light viewers or nonviewers to perceive the real world as similar to that of television. These students overestimated the number of doctors and lawyers, the number of extramarital affairs and divorces, the number of illegitimate births and abortions, and other events that occurred on soap operas far more frequently than in the real world.

Behm-Morawitz and Mastro (2008) performed a content analysis of teen films and portrayals of gender. The content analysis revealed that female characters were shown being more socially aggressive (e.g., bullying, spreading rumors, backstabbing, etc.). They then surveyed college students about their gender role beliefs and how often they watch teen movies. As social cognitive theory would predict, the surveys suggested that watching teen films was associated with holding negative stereotypes about gender roles and female friendships. Rousseau and Eggermont (2018) found that preadolescents who watched sexually objectifying TV shows were more likely to agree with an objectified dating script that, in turn, caused self-objectification and contributed to objectification of females in general. These findings clearly indicate modeling effects.

Effects of Viewing TV, Movie, and Video Game Violence

Through the years, many media effects studies have examined the negative effects that result from the vicarious capacity, such as learning aggressive behavior by viewing violent television shows or movies. Video game violence is another area of concern. For instance, Krcmar et al. (2010) used social cognitive theory to study the effect that realistic video games can have on aggression. Their findings showed that participants who played realistic violent games were more physically and verbally aggressive. Effects of video game violence are discussed further in Chapter 18.

Researchers point out that millions of viewers who watch violent programming or play violent games are *not* inspired to imitate such violent behavior. This suggests that individual factors such as a person's disposition (or predisposition to violent behavior), state of mind, emotional stability, and personal circumstances play a major role in determining whether that person will resort to aggression after viewing violent fare. (Recall the differential susceptibility to media effects model introduced in Chapter 1 that explores the role of individual factors in media effects.)

Social scientists often are concerned with more subtle media effects—those that they can measure through strictly controlled experiments that do not involve harm or injury to anyone. Most studies have concentrated on identifying the effects of media violence as *cognitive, affective,* or *behavioral.* Each of these will be discussed in detail in Chapter 11 on media violence.

Learning Good Things from Mass Media

A growing body of research that examines children's television programming has yielded promising findings (see Chapter 17 on educational effects). These studies have shown that many children's television shows have *prosocial* or positive learning effects. In general, research has shown that watching educational and nonviolent programs such as *Sesame Street* helps children improve literacy, science, and mathematics skills; learn positive social behaviors; enhance their imaginative powers; and develop problem-solving skills (Fisch, 2002; Fisch & Truglio, 2001).

Studies of *Sesame Street* suggest positive gains in cognitive skills and other prosocial effects for viewers compared to nonviewers, both in the United States (Wright & Huston, 1995; Wright et al., 2001) and abroad (Brederode-Santos, 1993; Ulitsa Sezam Department of Research and Content, 1998; UNICEF, 1996). Longitudinal studies have revealed that positive effects (especially in terms of academic achievement and reading skills) from viewing *Sesame Street* as preschoolers continued as children advanced to grade school (Kearney & Levine, 2019; Zill, 2001; Zill et al., 1994) and even high school (Anderson et al., 1998).

Studies have also found beneficial effects from programs such as *Barney & Friends* (Singer & Singer, 1994, 1995, 1998), *Gullah Gullah Island* and *Allegra's Window* (Bryant et al., 1997; Mulliken & Bryant, 1999), *Blue's Clues* (Anderson et al., 2000; Bryant et al., 1999), *Mister Rogers' Neighborhood* and *The Electric Company* (Ball & Bogatz, 1973; Ball et al., 1974; Rice, 1984; Rice & Haight, 1986), *Between the Lions* (Linebarger, 2000), *Reading Rainbow* (Leitner, 1991), *Square One TV* (Hall et al., 1990), and *3–2–1 Contact* (Cambre & Fernie, 1985; Johnston, 1980; Johnston & Luker, 1983; Wagner, 1985). More recently, studies have found benefits from watching *Daniel Tiger's Neighborhood* (Rasmussen et al., 2019), *PEG+CAT* (Pasnik et al., 2015), *Odd Squad* (Tiu et al., 2015), and *The Cat in the Hat Knows a Lot About That!* (Grindal et al., 2019). Positive benefits of educational programming for children are enhanced whenever parents or caregivers view programs with the children and reinforce the messages (e.g., Fisch et al., 2008; Singer & Singer, 1983; Wright et al., 1990).

In a two-year assessment of Nickelodeon programs *Gullah Gullah Island* and *Allegra's Window,* children who watched regularly were able to solve problems with greater ease and exhibit more flexible thinking skills than children who did not watch the program. In addition, regular viewers learned more about appropriate social behaviors than children of similar ages who did not watch the programs (Bryant et al., 1997) and performed better on three types of problem-solving tasks (Mulliken & Bryant, 1999).

Another two-year assessment targeted viewers of *Blue's Clues* and found effects for viewers were beneficial compared to effects for nonviewers (Anderson et al., 2000; Bryant et al., 1999). Nonverbal problem solving and non-humorous riddle solving on standardized Kaufman tests were two areas that showed statistically significant differences in favor of viewers of *Blue's Clues.*

Language development, literacy, mathematics and problem solving, science and technology, civics, and social studies are other areas that have shown positive effects for viewers of educational programming (Fisch, 2002).

Social Cognitive Theory and Health Campaigns

Another practical application of social cognitive theory is health campaigns (Krcmar, 2020). Campaigns often use modeling and vicarious reinforcement to change a person's perceptions about their self-efficacy regarding health decisions and behaviors. A campaign may feature a celebrity or actor demonstrating a positive action, like a breast self-exam (Anderson, 2000). This type of campaign message has been shown to boost a person's perceived self-efficacy (Anderson, 1995) and intention to perform the behavior (Anderson & McMillion, 1995).

Additionally, research has shown that social cognitive theory-based email interventions can help breast cancer survivors engage in physical activity (Hatchett et al., 2013). Social cognitive theory has also been used to better understand why people choose to use indoor tanning and how that information can be utilized in the development of skin cancer prevention messages (Noar et al., 2015).

Social Prompting or Persuasion

Advertising campaigns and other persuasive efforts serve as excellent examples of social prompting, another example of modeled behavior. Social prompting does not involve learning new behavior; therefore, it differs from observational learning and disinhibition. **Social prompting** implies that a person is offered an *inducement* (an incentive) to act in a particular way that has already been learned.

Most people are not inclined to try a new product unless, of course, the new product is shown to offer great benefits or inducements. Using toothpaste as an example, a viewer might be prompted to switch brands if a new, whitening toothpaste promises a beautiful smile, popularity, love, and happiness (as indicated by the actions of the attractive models in the commercial). We see this technique used far too often in the advertising of products that have few if any real advantages over other products in the same category.

Many Influences Cause Persuasion

According to social cognitive theory, many different influences of varying strengths often determine human behavior. No single pattern of influence exists to explain every instance of persuasion or modeling or adoption of a new behavior. Sometimes people are influenced by what they see on television, sometimes they are persuaded by interpersonal communication, and sometimes by a little of both. In all cases in which behavior is influenced, a combination of outside factors and personal characteristics are at work. The dynamics of those combinations differ with each person. Recall from Chapter 3 the findings by Lazarsfeld and his colleagues that media effects are modified by interpersonal communication about media messages. The limited effects hypothesis held that influential people in the community, called "opinion leaders," are influenced by mass media. These opinion leaders in turn influence others through interpersonal contact.

A substantial body of evidence debunks the idea that media can *only* reinforce changes in behavior rather than initiating them. Research has shown that in some cases media influences *do* initiate change (Bandura, 1986; Liebert et al., 1982) and have direct effects on viewers (Watt & van den Berg, 1978). Media influences vary in strength, as do influences from other sources that ultimately determine a person's behavior (Bandura, 1994).

Applying Social Cognitive Theory to New and Emerging Media

Viral challenges are a common occurrence on social media these days. Some, like the ice bucket challenge to raise money for ALS research (Sifferlin, 2014) or the Murph challenge to raise funds for the Lt. Michael P. Murphy Memorial Scholarship Foundation (Hughes, 2019), encourage people to model safe physical behaviors, like pouring a bucket of ice water over your head or exercising. However, there are some viral challenges, like the infamous Tide pod challenge (Bever, 2018), that encouraged people to perform dangerous behaviors. (Although it should go without saying, please do not eat detergent pods!)

With the proliferation of new media technologies, the impact of communication media in influencing behaviors has become even more significant. Krcmar (2020) noted that newer media, such as virtual reality, video games, social media, and other online content, offer researchers new environments to study social cognitive theory. Much of the initial research into the visual elements (i.e., photos and videos) of platforms like Instagram and Facebook result in effects similar to those caused by traditional media. Exposure to political posts on Facebook has been linked to increased political efficacy (Velasquez & LaRose, 2015). Furthermore, a study of Hispanic Americans found that observing others' behaviors and experiences, engaging in more social media use, and feeling confident about using social media for political reasons resulted in being more likely to express political opinions online and engage in offline political opportunities (Velasquez & Quenette, 2018). Seeing online messages from others about weight loss has resulted in improved self-efficacy in viewers to lose weight themselves (Sarge & Knobloch-Westerwick, 2013). Evidence of imitation and modeling have also been found in a study of adolescent girls who looked at photos on social media (Kleemans et al., 2018). Viewing the photos, especially ones that had been manipulated, increased both the girls' negative feelings about their body image and their desire to look more like the people in the photos.

Studies such as the ones mentioned in the previous paragraph indicate that social media function in similar ways to traditional media, such as television and movies. However, there is some evidence that the effects of social media may be stronger (Krcmar, 2020). To understand why effects of social media may be stronger, we need to understand how those types of communicative acts are different from traditional media. Bandura (2009) summarized the differences this way:

> On the input side, communications can now be personally tailored to factors that are causally related to the behavior of interest. Tailored communications are viewed as more relevant and credible, are better remembered and are more effective in influencing behavior than general messages (Kreuter, Strecher, & Glassman, 1999). On the behavioral guidance side, interactive technologies provide a convenient means of individualizing the type and level of behavioral guidance needed to bring desired changes to fruition (Bandura, 2004). In the population-based approaches the communications are designed to inform, enable, motivate, and guide people to effect personal and social changes. In implementing the social linking function, communications media can connect people to interactive online self-management programs that provide intensive individualized guidance in their homes when they want it. (p. 113)

Because we can choose whom to include in our online social networks—friends, family, or even our favorite celebrities—we are more likely identify with them, and Bandura (2009) noted that identification plays an important role in modeling behavior. Krcmar (2020) surmised that the self-selecting aspect of social media could possibly increase modeling outcomes; however, she noted that this idea has yet to be empirically tested.

Modeling and imitation effects have also been observed in studies of virtual reality and video games. Downs and Oliver (2016) found that playing a golfing video game affected players' golf efficacy and actual putting performance. Meanwhile, Fox and Bailenson (2009) studied immersive virtual environments and the effects of identification with a virtual avatar on health behavior change. They found that when participants watched avatars that looked like them, which was accomplished by photographing the participants and creating look-alike avatars, they were more likely to engage in voluntary exercise than those who observed avatars that looked like someone else. Participants were also more likely to exercise if they had observed their look-alike avatar running, as opposed to their avatar simply standing around. Seeing their virtual selves provided vicarious reinforcement, as discussed earlier in this chapter.

Virtual reality gives researchers a new way to study social cognitive theory and effects of modeling.

Diffusion by Way of Symbolic Modeling

One important area of media effects research involves the study of diffusion or spread of an innovation—a new technology, tool, behavior, or even farming technique—throughout a society or a large group of people. Communication scholar Everett Rogers (1983) is well known for his scholarship in this area, which is called **diffusion of innovations**.

Research has shown that successful diffusion of an innovation follows a similar pattern: an S-shaped distribution, which is the normal bell curve plotted over a period of time. (Although some research shows diffusion via heavy use of information and communication technologies can also take place along a convex r-curve [e.g., Danowski et al., 2011].)

Social cognitive theory views diffusion of innovations in terms of symbolic modeling, persuasion, social prompting, and motivation. Three major events define the diffusion process:

1. when the person learns about an innovation (a new behavior, tool, product, and so on);

2. when the person adopts the innovation or performs the new behavior; and

3. when the person interacts with others in a social network, either encouraging them to adopt the new behavior or confirming their own decision to adopt the behavior.

Diffusion of innovations research examines the different strengths of media and interpersonal influences in adoption of new behavior. The symbolic world of television is broadcast to masses of viewers at the same time. Satellite telecommunications systems and a growing number of streaming content providers carry television programs and movies to millions of viewers in different countries throughout the world. Social changes have occurred due to the influences of television on entire societies of viewers who model the various behaviors, styles, and ideas that they see and learn (Bandura, 1986; Singhal & Rogers, 1989; Winett et al., 1985).

Limitations of Social Cognitive Theory

By now, you have observed the usefulness of social cognitive theory and its broad application in studies seeking to understand the effects of mediated communication on human behavior. However, Krcmar (2020) noted the theory's broad applicability can be seen as both a strength *and* a weakness. She acknowledged that the theory can be applied to a wide variety of media technology and content and can be used to study any behavior. Additionally, many of the elements of the theory—attention, retention, motivation, modeling, identification with the model, and vicarious reinforcement—can easily be tested.

As outlined earlier in this chapter, social cognitive theory explores human behavior through the triadic reciprocal causation process, or the interaction among cognitive, behavioral, and environmental factors. Although researchers have identified many variables in the process,

> the theory itself is somewhat agnostic, or at least vague, on the exact mechanism(s) by which observed behaviors become modeled. . . . Thus, additional clarification of the mechanisms involved in moving a witnessed behavior to an enacted one would improve the precision of the theory. (Krcmar, 2020, p. 109)

Other limitations of the theory as outlined by Krcmar (2020) include a lack of specified boundaries for what the theory can and cannot explain and research that only focuses on a handful of the theory's variables (e.g., vicarious reinforcement, imitation) while largely neglecting others (e.g., identification). Krcmar called for future research to explore the ways newer variables connect to the existing theoretical model.

Summary

Albert Bandura's social cognitive theory serves not only as a major, independent theory of media effects but also as a component of many other theories of media effects. It provides a framework to analyze human cognitions that produce certain behaviors and to describe mental processes at work whenever a person learns. Social cognitive theory explains behavior by examining the triadic reciprocal causation process, or the interaction among cognitive, behavioral, and environmental factors.

Social cognitive theory emphasizes the importance of several distinct cognitive traits that set human beings apart. These include the symbolizing, self-regulatory, self-reflective, and vicarious capacities. The self-reflective capacity includes four different modes used in thought verification: the enactive, vicarious, persuasory, and logical modes.

Finklea (2017a) notes that "social cognitive theory allows us to view media as true teaching machines. Observational learning can be just as impactful as face-to-face instruction. Our media saturated world creates content for learning for audiences ranging from young children to the elderly" (p. 934). Observational learning and modeling are key elements in social cognitive theory. Whenever a person observes other people's actions and the consequences of those actions, the person may learn from what has been observed. Modeling is the reenactment of learned behavior and includes four component processes: attention, retention, motor reproduction, and motivation.

New life situations require people to apply the rules of behavior learned in the past to the new and different situations. Abstract modeling takes learning to a higher level than mere mimicry of observed behavior and therefore offers many practical advantages.

Whenever a person observes behavior or receives information that conflicts with established patterns of behavior or principles of conduct, the inner conflict causes a reexamination of motivations to perform the established behavior. Inhibitory effects occur whenever a person refrains from reprehensible conduct for fear of the consequences. Disinhibitory effects remove previously learned internal restraints on certain behaviors.

People who engage in reprehensible behaviors often use cognitive techniques or devices to justify their actions. Eight such disinhibitory devices have been identified: moral justification, exonerative comparison, euphemistic labeling, displacement of responsibility, diffusion of responsibility, distortion of the consequences of action, dehumanization, and attribution of blame.

Viewers are affected or aroused by much of what they see on the screen. Some experiences of arousal are not fleeting in nature. Fear reactions, coping skills, and likes and dislikes may all be learned—some with lasting results—from media characters.

Social cognitive theory helps explain cultivation, priming, and prosocial effects in terms of cognitions, observational learning, and modeling. The basis for many persuasion effects or social prompting from mass media can be found in social cognitive theory, which recognizes that motivations or influences to model new behavior or adopt new ideas are dynamic and usually a combination of outside factors and personal cognitions and characteristics. Additionally, researchers are exploring how social cognitive theory can be applied to the study of new and emerging media, such as social media, virtual reality, and video games.

Diffusion of innovations research also finds a conceptual basis in social cognitive theory. Diffusion of an innovation throughout a society or a large group of people is explained in terms of symbolic modeling, persuasion or social prompting, and motivation. Successful diffusion of an innovation requires three steps: learning about the innovation, adoption of the innovation, and the development of social networks after initial adoption.

Overall, social cognitive theory has become an often-used theory to better understand human behavior. Its breadth can be viewed as both a strength and a weakness. However, the weaknesses offer future researchers opportunities to explore and enhance this incredibly useful theory.

5

Priming

It is assumed that concepts that have some relation to each other are connected in some mental network, so that if one concept is activated, then concepts related to it are also activated.

—University of Alberta's Cognitive Science Dictionary, 1998

Suppose someone in your family once battled cancer and overcame it through conventional treatment. Years later, a Hollywood celebrity announces on social media that they are suffering from the same cancer that your family member had. Chances are you would be more interested in learning more about the star's plight with the disease, curious about treatment, and so forth. You would already have certain information stored in your memory about that particular kind of cancer due to personal experience with someone who battled the disease. Your old memories would be activated by the new information.

Priming is the study of this activation of related concepts archived in the mind of a media consumer. Studies of priming usually test priming activation from the introduction of information from media messages. For example, many priming studies have looked at how exposure to media content related to political issues affects presidential performance ratings or other measures of public opinion. In the case of these studies, the media are said to "prime" certain information in the minds of audience members, which can cause them to give more importance to a particular issue (i.e., agenda setting, see Chapter 6) or influence their judgments on important matters (i.e., persuasion, see Chapter 10).

Consider the example of viewing violent media content. What mental associations would you expect such content to prompt in viewers? Does media violence cause viewers to make associations with angry or critical thoughts stored in their memories? More significantly, does the viewing of mediated violence and the mental associations it arouses make viewers more likely to commit acts of violence themselves?

These types of questions lie at the heart of many social scientific investigations of media effects, as well as questions related to the psychological processes present whenever media effects occur. Cognitive research typically explores *short-term* media effects that sometimes have long-term implications. Historically, such research has employed strong experimental designs and tight controls that lend rigor and specificity to the research, although at the expense of generalizability to "real-world" media violence issues.

This chapter examines the theoretical underpinnings of network models of memory and priming. We will also review some of the important studies that have measured priming effects resulting from mediated communication. Following a description of the priming mechanism and factors that may determine its activation, the chapter provides a glimpse into the conceptual foundations for the theory and explores variables that enhance priming effects. Finally, we explore recent studies involving priming in several key areas of research.

Accessibility

Before discussing priming specifically, we want to give a brief explanation of the related concept of accessibility. In simplest terms, **accessibility** refers to how easily a concept is activated from a person's memory (Ewoldsen & Rhodes, 2020). Network models of memory—also known as models of semantic memory—illustrate concepts in someone's memory as a network of interconnected nodes, with each node representing a particular concept. For example, think back to your high school years. Your main "high school" node branches out to related nodes for classes, field trips, extracurricular activities, friends, graduation, etc. When you are not thinking about high school, that node is in a resting, inactive state. But a friend's mention of an experience from high school can activate your high school node. In this example, the accessibility of that concept would most likely be temporary, as you would soon go on to think about other things. However, for concepts that are activated more frequently, accessibility can become chronic (Wyer, 2004).

Furthermore, Ewoldsen and Rhodes (2020) noted that because nodes are interconnected, energy can spread from one node to other related nodes along associative pathways; however, the strength of these pathways can vary. For instance, stronger pathways can allow for greater energy transfer between nodes.

> The classic example is that if the "doctor" node is activated in memory, activation will travel from the "doctor" node to the "nurse" node because doctor and nurse are likely highly associated. Assuming the strength of the pathway is high, if doctor is activated (e.g., its activation threshold is met), then energy should travel to the "nurse" node, which may result in the "nurse" node becoming active or it may increase the ease by which nurse is activated because the node is closer to its activation threshold. The energy that spreads from "doctor" to "nurse" dissipates in time. Therefore, the effect of the spreading activation is to increase temporarily the accessibility of "nurse." This is commonly referred to as *priming*. (p. 84)

Network models of memory illustrate memory as web of interconnected nodes. Each node represents a different concept in a person's memory.

Activation of Priming

In the context of media effects, priming occurs when exposure to mediated communication activates related thoughts that have been stored or "archived" in the mind of a media consumer. In a network model of memory,

> the presentation of a stimulus [i.e., a mediated message] triggers an activation "wave" that sweeps along the associative pathways connected to the mental representation of the stimulus. Each episode of such "spreading activation" has the effect of reinforcing used pathways, whereas neglected links and memories continue to lie dormant and decay over time. As a consequence, nodes that happen to possess numerous and strong links with top-of-the-head constructs have a higher likelihood to be retrieved and used than less accessible nodes. (Marquis, 2016, p. 1237)

For a certain period of time after viewing such content, a person is more likely to have thoughts about the content, related thoughts, or memories. In some instances, the related thoughts or memories become permanently associated with the message content or **stimulus** (Fiske & Taylor, 1991).

For example, a network newscast that features a story on racial tensions in the United States may cause a viewer to remember their grandparents' or great-grandparents' stories of protests during the civil rights movement. Any knowledge already acquired regarding race relations would be associated with new information gathered from the newscast. The viewer's interest in the news story and reaction to it may well be affected by existing knowledge and previous experiences. If, for example, stories heard during childhood caused much anxiety, a news report of current racial tensions might cause the recollection of such feelings. In other words, the newscast *primed* a particular reaction.

> As applied to the media, priming refers to the effects of the content of the media on people's later behavior or judgments related to the content that was processed. . . . [I]t is important to understand that, with priming, the effect of the priming event is time bound. For example, in media priming focused on violence, studies often find that the priming effect fades quickly—oftentimes within the time course of the experimental setting. (Roskos-Ewoldsen et al., 2009, pp. 74–75)

The priming activation may also influence a person's behavior, causing a particular reaction, sometimes with undesirable consequences. For most people, priming effects cause only mild reactions that usually diminish rather quickly and may even pass unnoticed. Nevertheless, the overall evidence for priming has been substantial. The strength of the activation, the types of thoughts provoked, and the behavioral results of the activation depend on a number of contingent factors.

Characteristics and Boundary Conditions of Priming Effects

The vast body of research into media priming has identified three common characteristics of priming effects (Ewoldsen & Rhodes, 2020). First, priming effects dissipate over time. Recent primes have a stronger effect on behaviors and judgments than primes that happened longer ago (Higgins et al., 1985). Given enough time with no further activation, a node will return to its resting state; at that point, it is no longer primed. In general, priming effects have been found to dissipate within roughly 15 to 20 minutes of exposure to the prime. However, political priming effects can last much longer—sometimes for several weeks or months. This type of long-term priming may occur due to ongoing news coverage of politics making the primed concepts chronically accessible (Price & Tewksbury, 1997).

Second, stronger primes, such as those that involve more cognitive energy, tend to result in stronger effects on a person's behaviors and judgments (Higgins et al., 1985). According to Ewoldsen and Rhodes (2020), the strength of a prime can be manipulated by either its duration (e.g., 5 minutes of exposure to the prime compared versus 30 seconds) or frequency (e.g., being exposed to the prime once versus being exposed repeatedly in a short time frame).

> Vividness might also influence priming, with highly vivid portrayals resulting in stronger priming effects (Riddle, 2010). Importantly, a linear increase in the strength of the prime does not result in a linear increase in the priming effect. (Ewoldsen & Rhodes, 2020, p. 90)

The third characteristic of priming effects is that primes often have stronger effects when situations are ambiguous (Roskos-Ewoldsen, 1997). Arendt (2017) looked at the priming effects of racial stereotypes in crime news and subsequent judgments of strangers' facial expressions. Some participants read crime stories that primed the "dark-skinned criminal" stereotype; meanwhile, the control group read crime stories without any mention of race. Later when the participants were shown images of facial expressions of strangers, a priming effect (i.e., perceived threat from a stranger) was found for dark-skinned strangers but only when their facial expressions were ambiguous. Although unambiguous situations leave little room for various interpretations, ambiguous behavior can be interpreted in a variety of ways, and "given the ambiguity of much of social behavior, priming effects can be occurring quite frequently in our day-to-day lives" (Ewoldsen & Rhodes, 2020, p. 90).

Moy et al. (2016) outlined four "boundary conditions" for priming effects: (1) the recency and (2) repeated exposure to a prime, then the prime's (3) applicability and (4) subjective relevance. Regarding *recency*, Moy and her colleagues noted "that the accessibility of primed information in people's minds decays over time, which makes any later application of the information to the target stimulus less likely" (p. 6). *Repetition* simply refers to how often certain nodes in a person's memory are primed. The more often those nodes are activated, the more likely those same nodes will activate in response to later stimuli. Exposure to a prime must be both sufficiently recent and frequent to trigger a priming effect.

Research has shown that access to related memories provides only part of the picture—the application of related knowledge constructs also occurs (Althaus & Kim, 2006). To be *applicable* in evaluating the target stimulus, the primed concept must either overlap with or have similar features to the target stimulus (Price & Tewksbury, 1997; Tewksbury, 2020). The last condition, *subjective relevance*, is similar to applicability but highlights the subjective component of priming: "If people do not see how a primed construct relates to a given target stimulus, they will not consider it applicable to its evaluation" (Moy et al., 2016, p. 6). (These last two boundary conditions will be explained in greater detail in the next section.)

However, simply meeting these four boundary conditions does not guarantee priming effects will occur. Understandably, individual differences in perceptions cause priming activation strengths to vary considerably from person to person (Bargh & Chartrand, 2000). Other factors that can affect a media prime's influence include political involvement and attitudes, cognitive styles, and personality traits (see Moy et al., 2016, for further review).

Models of Priming

There are several models that have been developed to explain priming effects. Both the accessibility-applicability model (Price & Tewksbury, 1997; Tewksbury, 2020) and the cognitive neoassociation model (Berkowitz, 1984, 1990, 1994, 1997) are based on network models of memory, which we described earlier in this chapter. This overall network can be described as *memory*. When a person watches a movie or reads a news article online, the information being processed triggers or activates certain pathways throughout the network. Individual thoughts or feelings from past experiences are *remembered* and associated with the new information. These ideas and thoughts may stimulate other related ideas that may influence a person's actions.

Both cognitive neoassociation and the General Aggression Model (Anderson & Bushman, 2002, 2018; Anderson et al., 2007; Bushman & Anderson, 2002) are the main models used to explore the priming of aggression. The accessibility-applicability model (AAM), on the other hand, was developed to study political communication, but it can also be applied to other types of messages.

Scholars continue to put forth theoretical advances related to priming (e.g., Hoewe, 2020; Lee et al., 2020; Lee & McLeod, 2020), but we will primarily focus to the three main models of priming. Additionally, we will discuss how mental models may also play a part in priming.

Accessibility-Applicability Model

Although there are multiple models that can explain priming of aggression, Ewoldsen and Rhodes (2020) note that there is only one model of priming that has been sufficiently developed to explain political priming effects—the **accessibility-applicability model**, which was originally developed by Price and Tewksbury (1997). In addition to priming, this model has also been used to study agenda setting and framing, which you will learn more about in the next two chapters. Furthermore, the AAM can be used to study priming effects beyond the realm of politics.

In short, the AAM highlights how exposure to salient attributes of a stimulus can lead to chronic, temporary, and applicable constructs stored in a person's long-term memory being activated (or moved to short-term or working memory, also known as active thought). "At a basic level, constructs that are activated for use in interpreting and reacting to mediated stimuli are those that are most accessible and applicable to the message and task at hand" (Tewksbury, 2020, p. 5). Once in active thought, those constructs are evaluated for relevance. Those that are deemed relevant are then used in evaluations of the stimulus's salient attributes. (See Figure 5.1 for an illustration of the AAM.)

As previously discussed, priming has been explained as a network model that takes into account the accessibility or frequency of primed information from mass media in a person's memory. However, the AAM also incorporates the *applicability* of such information in the mind of the media consumer (Price & Tewksbury, 1997; see also Scheufele & Tewksbury, 2007; Tewksbury, 2020).

> Applicability refers to deliberate judgments of the relevance of information to the current situation. Clearly, if primed information is not relevant, it should not be used when making political judgments. Within Price and Tewksbury's model, constructs that are activated by the media and judged as applicable to the current situation influence how a message is framed or interpreted. On the other hand, those constructs that are activated by the media and judged as not applicable to the current situation are not brought into working memory, but the activation of these constructs by the media means that they may work as a prime. (Ewoldsen & Rhodes, 2020, p. 92)

Tewksbury (2020) offers a word of caution encouraging media scholars (and students) to note that "an active evaluation of a construct's relevance may sound similar but is different than the applicability process that leads to activation" (p. 8). Scholl et al. (2016) provide a useful explanation:

> Applicability is a very rough and simplistic matching process between the stimulus and the constructs in memory, whereas relevance judgment is more careful and conscious. For example, consider the question, "What do cows drink?" Applicability is what makes most people want to answer "milk" because of the associative connections in memory between milk and two different words in the stimulus. However, most people manage to inhibit the response milk because of relevance judgment. (p. 75)

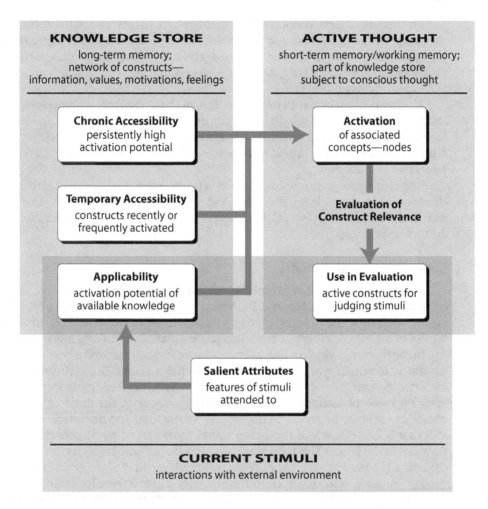

Figure 5.1   Price and Tewksbury's (1997) accessibility-applicability model.

Source: Adapted from Price & Tewksbury, 1997, p. 186.

Cognitive Neoassociation

The concept of **cognitive neoassociation** is a social psychological perspective that attempts to explain a portion of the phenomenon of memory (Anderson & Bower, 1973; Landman & Manis, 1983). Based on network models of memory, cognitive neoassociation hypothesizes that exposure to violent media content activates concepts related to hostility or aggression in a person's memory. When these concepts are activated, the likelihood increases that a person will interpret ambiguous behavior as aggressive and respond with aggressive behaviors. In other words, "people who are primed with violent media content are more likely to respond with hostility when a person provokes them after the priming event" (Ewoldsen & Rhodes, 2020, p. 90).

Furthermore, ideas connected to emotions can trigger associated feelings and responses. For example, research has shown that exposure to ideas of aggression can produce feelings of anger or even aggressive acts under some circumstances (Berkowitz & Heimer, 1989). Similarly, *thinking* depressing thoughts can actually cause *feelings* of depression (Velten, 1968).

Additionally, audience members are likely to have thoughts with meanings similar to what they are viewing. In short, the primed ideas activate *semantically* related thoughts (Collins & Loftus, 1975). For instance, watching a love scene in a movie causes audiences to remember similar moments in their own lives and recall emotions associated with the events.

Interestingly, cognitive neoassociation has also been used to explore how media effects can even extend into our dreams. Van den Bulck et al. (2016) found that people who watched violent or sexual media were more likely to have violent or sexual dreams, respectively.

General Aggression Model

The General Aggression Model (GAM) is an extensive expansion of the cognitive neoassociation model (Anderson & Bushman, 2002, 2018; Anderson et al., 2007; Bushman & Anderson, 2002). Incorporating arousal and affect into a network framework, the GAM explains priming as a three-step process that can affect aggressive behavior.

In the first step, which is largely an automatic response beyond a person's control, arousal is increased when exposure to situational variables (e.g., frustration, pain, mediated violence) primes hostile thoughts, memories, and feelings. In step two, a primary appraisal or interpretation of a situation is made in the mind of the viewer, which also tends to be an automatic process. In the third and final step, a secondary appraisal is made in which the viewer thinks more carefully and deliberately about reactions to the prime. This third stage can override the primary appraisal as a person thoughtfully considers various behaviors that can be applied to the situation.

For instance, watching a violent movie may prime aggressive thoughts in your mind, which could make you more likely to respond aggressively to a later stimulus. Imagine that after watching the movie, someone cuts you off in the movie theater parking lot. Your automatic response/primary appraisal may be to yell at the other driver; however, after your secondary appraisal, you might decide not to retaliate in a hostile manner.

Mental Models

In addition to the AAM, cognitive neoassociation, and GAM, some scholars have also proposed that mental models of memory could be used to explain priming effects, especially ones that last for longer periods of time (e.g., Roskos-Ewoldsen et al., 2009). The use of mental models to explain priming effects offers an alternative to network models of memory. To understand how mental models may play a role in priming, we first need to discuss some terminology. Throughout this section and in subsequent chapters, you will encounter references to *schemas* and *mental models*, which are two broad categories of cognitive structures that we create as we interact with our physical and social environments, including mediated environments, and that we retrieve from memory and use to interpret the people, objects, and events with experience directly and through media. (Busselle, 2017, p. 1753)

According to Roskos-Ewoldsen et al. (2009), these cognitive structures exist along a "continuum of abstractness," ranging from schemas (the most abstract) to mental models to situation models (the least abstract).

A **schema** is "a cognitive structure that represents knowledge about a concept or type of stimulus, including its attributes and the relations among those attributes" (Fiske & Taylor, 1991, p. 98). For example, a schema for a college classroom might include rows of desks, a white board, lectern, and projector. Mental scripts and stereotypes are also types of schemas (or schemata).

A **mental model** is a less abstract mental representation of an event, situation, or object (van Dijk & Kintsch, 1983). Mental models contain knowledge about how processes or objects function (Medin et al., 2001). For instance, a mental model for how the projector in your classroom works could include a computer, cables, the projector, and the images projected onto a screen. A mental model may also include information about the process of the computer sending data through the cables to the projector, which focuses an image through a lens so that it appears in focus on the screen.

Characteristics of Mental Models

- The first characteristic of mental models is that *they are mutable*. This means that the parts of a mental model are interchangeable, similar to how Lego blocks can be used to build different shapes.

  For instance, a person watching a new *Star Wars* series on Disney+ might imagine how *Star Trek's* Captain Kirk would behave in the place of a Jedi master. "The mutability of situation and mental models is critical for developing inferences about the possible outcomes of the model or for determining how the model operates, which involves 'running' simulations using dynamic mental representations" (Roskos-Ewoldsen et al., 2009, p. 86).

- The second characteristic of mental models is that *they are dynamic*, which means—in the case of media use—that the media consumer can control and manipulate them to test different scenarios, make inferences, and draw conclusions from information that may or may not be in the media content.

  For example, movie viewers may use cinematic features—editing techniques, costumes, music, dialogue, etc.—as cues to make predictions about future events and make inferences about previous events. When anomalous information is foregrounded by filmmakers, viewers attempt to find out why such information is presented. These predictions are generated through the manipulation of situation models that viewers create as they watch a film. (Roskos-Ewoldsen et al., 2009, p. 86)

- The third characteristic of mental models is that *they are contextualized*, meaning they are situated in time. After a while, the applicability of a particular mental model will fade.

  But, importantly, the time frame for the applicability of a mental model is much different than the time frame for priming the activation of a node within a network model of memory. That is, a mental model may be applied even after a few days or weeks. (Roskos-Ewoldsen et al., 2009, p. 86)

A key aspect of the mental model approach is that there is some correspondence between an external event, situation, or object and our constructed mental representation of it (Johnson-Laird, 1983, 1989; Norman, 1983). Other key characteristics of mental models is that they are mutable, dynamic, and contextualized (or time bound).

Lastly, a **situation model** is a specific type of mental model and is the least abstract cognitive structure. A person creates a situation model in memory to represent a particular story or episode viewed via mass media, whereas a person would create a mental model based on a number of related stories or episodes. "Situation models are of particular relevance to narrative processing and comprehension because they explain how audience members (readers, viewers, or listeners) represent the current, unfolding state of affairs at a given point in a story" (Busselle, 2017, p. 1757).

Mental models are time-bound, like priming activations, but exist for longer periods of time than network models of priming. Mental models therefore can explain priming effects of political communications that last weeks or even months. At some point, however, the repeated priming of concepts via mass media passes the threshold into cultivation effects rather than priming effects. (See Ewoldsen and Rhodes, 2020, for further discussion of *chronic accessibility* to mental concepts and connections to cultivation theory. Also see Busselle, 2017, for a more in-depth explanation of schemas and mental models.)

Variables That Enhance Priming Effects from Violent Content

Extensive research has been conducted on the effects of media violence on aggressive behaviors, thoughts, and emotions. Research indicates that video game and television violence may influence people's actions, especially in the short term (Huesmann et al., 2013). However, the connection between the *priming* of aggressive thoughts and the *actual display of aggression* is, generally speaking, a tenuous one. It is, however, substantially strengthened whenever certain variables are present. **Intervening variables** strengthen and serve as catalysts for the cause-effect phenomenon when they are present. They include the following:

1. the perceived meaning of the communication;
2. the perceived justifiability of the witnessed aggression;
3. the extent to which audiences identify with the characters;
4. the perceived reality of the mediated communication; and
5. the stimulus of prior experiences.

Perceived Meaning

Berkowitz and Alioto (1973) angered male participants and then showed them either a professional prizefight or a professional football game. The participants were given information that would enable them to interpret the events in one of two ways: either the athletes were intent on hurting each other or the athletes were simply performing their professional jobs without emotion. After watching the event, the participants had the opportunity to shock the person who had provoked them earlier. The men who had been led to believe that the athletes were intent upon hurting each other

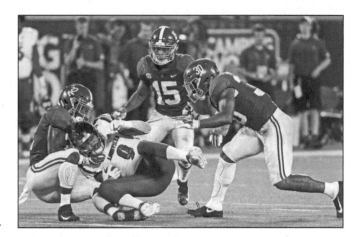

Contact sports have the potential to prime thoughts about hostile and aggressive behaviors.

showed evidence of being primed with more aggressive thoughts because they administered more punishing electrical shocks.

Perceived Justifiability

Research has shown that the actions of viewers of mediated violence are also influenced by the *outcomes* of the situations they see. Several studies have revealed that viewers believe what happens on television or in movies could also happen to them if they behave in ways similar to the characters depicted (Bandura, 1977; Comstock, 1980; Comstock et al., 1978; Huesmann, 1982). When viewers see aggressors suffering as a result of their behavior, they are less likely to imitate the aggressive behavior (Bandura, 1965b, 1977). Also, when viewers are reminded of the serious and unfortunate consequences of violence, aggression is usually restrained.

Goranson (1969) gave angry participants a chance to punish their provocateur after viewing a film in which a man received a bad beating in a prizefight. One group of participants was told the beaten man subsequently died from his injuries; the other group did not receive this information. The participants who were led to believe that the fighter died showed more restraint in punishing the provocateur than did participants in the other experimental condition.

Character Identification

Research has also shown that identification with a media character enhances priming effects. In one study, three groups of male participants were angered, then asked to watch a prizefight (Turner & Berkowitz, 1972). The members of one group were told to think of themselves as the winner. The men in the second group were told to think of themselves as the referee. The third group did not receive any instructions. In each group, half the participants were directed to think of the word "hit" each time the winner punched his opponent. After the movie, each participant had the opportunity to shock the person who had angered him. The most severe punishment was administered by the group of men who had pictured themselves as the winner and had been instructed to think "hit" with each punch.

Researchers have advanced various hypotheses to explain the strength of identification in causing priming effects. The "hit" word may have served as a cue from memory to retrieve combative experiences from the past. The inducement of such memories, along with the thoughts and feelings associated with them, might intensify aggression.

> It could be that the viewers who identify with (or think of themselves as) the movie aggressor are especially apt to have aggression-related thoughts as they watch the violent events. In their minds they strike at the film victim along with the movie aggressor so that these aggression-related thoughts then prime their aggression-associated mental networks relatively strongly. (Jo & Berkowitz, 1994, p. 54)

Perceived Reality

The perceived reality of media depictions can also intensify the strength of priming effects. Research has shown that priming effects are strongest when audiences believe they are witnessing *actual* rather than *fictional* events. In one study, angered participants saw the same war film, but only half were told it was a fictional movie (Berkowitz & Alioto, 1973). The other half were told that the film depicted actual combat. When given the opportunity afterward to punish their provocateur with electrical shocks, members of the latter group administered shocks that were longer in duration. Another study found similar results among three groups of fifth- and sixth-grade children (Atkin, 1983). The first group of children saw a fight being reported realistically on the news. The second group viewed the fight in the context of fantasy entertainment. The control group viewed an ordinary commercial. When tested, the first group scored significantly higher on an aggression index than did the other two groups.

Memories of Prior Experiences

Another factor identified with enhancing priming effects is that of *prior learning* or *remembered experiences*. As an audience member views a violent act, semantically similar thoughts or feelings from other occasions surface. The memory reactivates a neural network or a mental model and strengthens the effects of priming.

Research Has Shown . . .

Priming effects from violent media are most enhanced when audience members:

- interpret the meaning of a film or communication in a particular way;
- believe that the violent behavior they are seeing is justified for some reason;
- identify with the characters they see;
- believe they are seeing actual events rather than fiction; and
- see the portrayed violence and remember experiencing similar feelings and thoughts in the past.

Key Areas of Priming Research

Media effects scholars continue to study priming effects, especially those that result from exposure to media violence. Whereas researchers used to focus primarily on television and cinema violent content, more recent research has examined video games and avatars. Meanwhile, political priming research has shifted to investigate how movies, television, and online content prime political information. Many other studies have examined the priming of racial stereotypes in media content (Ewoldsen & Rhodes, 2020; Roskos-Ewoldsen et al., 2009).

Video Games and Avatars

Studies have shown that playing violent video games primes aggression, but on a short-term basis only (e.g., Anderson, 2004; Anderson & Dill, 2000; Anderson & Murphy, 2003; Carnagey & Anderson, 2005; Uhlmann & Swanson, 2004). Other studies have not found such a link (e.g., Cooper & Mackie, 1986; Graybill et al., 1985; Scott, 1995). Three meta-analyses found that video game violence primes aggression and aggression-related concepts in memory (Anderson & Bushman, 2001; Roskos-Ewoldsen et al., 2007; Sherry, 2001). Other researchers noted that the earliest two meta-analyses did not include longitudinal studies (Dill & Dill, 1998). (See Chapter 18 for more on the effects of playing video games.)

Another problem with the research that social scientists have identified is that there are so many different kinds of games available, and each one has potentially different effects. For example, Williams and Skoric (2005) selected the violent video game *Asheron's Call 2*, which involves repetitive killing of monsters to advance. They hypothesized that over time players would approve of aggression as a response in a social situation. However, they found that the amount of game play over a month's time did not predict increased argumentative behaviors with friends and partners during that time. "There were no strong effects associated with aggression caused by this violent video game" (p. 228).

Virtual avatars have been the subject of a growing body of research for their ability to prime users' behavior and judgment (Peña, 2011). Peña et al. (2009) found that using avatars in virtual settings can prime negative attitudes and thoughts. Their study consisted of two experiments. In the first, those using black-cloaked avatars showed more aggressive intentions and attitudes and less group cohesion than those using white-cloaked avatars. In the second experiment, the researchers had some participants use avatars dressed as Ku Klux Klan members, while others were dressed as doctors. They found that the KKK avatars primed more aggressive thoughts and could inhibit positive thoughts. Another study by Peña and his associates (2012) found that social stereotypes could be primed by avatars. In this study, they assigned some participants to use avatars that were formally dressed; others were assigned glamorously dressed avatars. They observed that the two groups used significantly different language. Those using formally dressed avatars talked more about books, numbers, and education. Meanwhile, those using glamorously dressed avatars were more likely to discuss clothes, beauty, entertainment, and sports. The study also found that labeling the formally dressed avatar as a professor and the glamorously dressed avatar as a supermodel could prime the use of stereotypical language.

Aside from research into the priming effects of video games, relatively few studies have examined the priming effects of newer communication technologies. Research has shown that pictures and text seen online can prime racial stereotypes when subsequently looking at a stranger's social media profile (Northrup & Dillman Carpentier, 2015). Other studies have found that viewing banner and sidebar ads containing sexual cues on websites primed participants' evaluations of people's sexual characteristics when viewing their social media profiles (Dillman Carpentier, Northrup, & Parrott, 2014; Dillman Carpentier, Parrott, & Northrup, 2014). Ewoldsen and Rhodes (2020) concluded that these studies "certainly demonstrated that priming can occur in rather novel ways in online environments" (p. 94).

Stereotypes

Stereotype priming continues to be a growing area of research. Numerous studies have shown that media content can prime various stereotypes, such as mental health (Holman & McKeever, 2017), gender (Hansen & Hansen, 1988), and racial stereotypes (e.g., Arendt, 2017; Dalisay & Tan, 2009; Oliver et al., 2007).

Media primes about postpartum mental illnesses can influence pregnant women's attitudes toward their own health risks (Holman & McKeever, 2017). Music videos featuring stereotypical portrayals of men and women can prime gender stereotypes, such as women being less dominant (Hansen & Hansen, 1988).

Racial stereotype priming has received significant attention from media scholars. In one study, some participants viewed video segments of three stigmatizing stereotypes of African American women: a mammy, a jezebel, or a welfare queen. Then they were asked to rate a well-groomed African American woman on a mock job interview. Those who saw the videos were more likely than those who did not see them to use stereotype-consistent adjectives to describe the interviewee (Monahan et al., 2005). For another study examining the priming of stereotypes toward Black women, see this chapter's Research Spotlight.

Dalisay and Tan (2009) examined television portrayals of Asian Americans to see if they would affect viewers' judgments of both Asian and African Americans and whether viewers were inclined to endorse affirmative action. Previous studies have shown that television portrayals usually stereotype Asian Americans as hardworking and skilled in business and technology. The study found that priming viewers with positive portrayals of Asian Americans as a so-called "model minority" resulted in more positive perceptions of them. Priming Asian American stereotypes also resulted in more negative stereotypical perceptions of African Americans, even though African Americans were not mentioned in the clip. The positive portrayal of Asian Americans was also associated with less endorsement of affirmative action.

In a political context, Valentino et al. (2017) stated, "Racial priming theory posits that subtle cues in news coverage, political advertising, or candidate speeches activate racial attitudes, boosting their impact on candidate evaluations or policy opinion" (p. 759). Domke et al. (1999) found that how immigration news stories are framed (i.e., focusing on the economic impact versus the ethical issues of immigration; also see Chapter 7) influenced whether racial stereotypes of Hispanics were primed, despite Hispanics not being mentioned in the stories. Dixon (2006) found that participants

RESEARCH SPOTLIGHT

Priming Mammies, Jezebels, and Other Controlling Images: An Examination of the Influence of Mediated Stereotypes on Perceptions of an African American Woman

Sonja M. Brown Givens and Jennifer L. Monahan (2005)
Media Psychology, 7(1), 87–106

After showing participants images of a mammy, jezebel, or nonsteretypic image of African American females on video, participants observed mock interviews with African American and white women. The African American interviewee was associated more readily with negative terms (such as "aggressive") than with positive terms (such as "sincere"). Participants who saw the jezebel stereotype video were more likely to associate the African American interviewee with jezebel-related terms (such as "sexual") than with positive, negative, or mammy-related (such as "maternal") terms.

Hypotheses

H1a: Response times will be faster to negative words and slower to positive words when evaluating an African American woman.

H1b: Response times will be faster to positive words and slower to negative words when evaluating a white woman.

H2a: Exposure to stereotypic portrayals of an African American woman will result in stereotype-consistent judgments of another African American woman.

H2b: Response times will be faster to stereotype-consistent adjectives than to stereotype-inconsistent adjectives after viewing a stereotypic image of an African American woman.

Method

Undergraduate students from introductory speech communication courses participated in the study. Of the 182 students, 70% were between the ages of 18 and 21, with 158 who classified themselves as white, 13 as Black, 2 as Hispanic, 8 as Asian, and 1 as "other." About half (48.4%) were male.

Participants viewed a 3–minute videotaped segment of a movie clip that represented either a mammy (a nurturing Black woman), a jezebel (a sexually aggressive African American woman), or a nonstereotype control condition (no references to African American women or female sexuality). The "mammy" condition was taken from the 1959 film *Imitation of Life*. The "jezebel" condition was from the 1999 biographical film of Dorothy Dandridge's life, played by Halle Berry. The control condition was a segment of the movie *Better Off Dead* showing a middle-aged white man having difficulty retrieving the morning newspaper from his lawn.

After viewing one of the tapes, participants watched one of two 3–minute mock employment interviews. The interviewees were female, either white or African American. Great care was taken so that the interviewees responded to interviewer questions in very similar ways.

A list of adjectives was developed, 40 in all, with eight being stereotypically positive (such as sincere, friendly, intelligent), nine stereotypically negative (aggressive, hostile, lazy), eight related to the mammy stereotype (maternal, loyal, devoted), and nine related to the jezebel stereotype (sexual, alluring, erotic). The remaining terms were used as fillers (shy, fun, organized, etc.).

Participants were asked whether the character traits fit the person they observed on the interview tape. The speed at which they responded with each adjective was timed and recorded in milliseconds. Participants also responded to 40 items that indicated the suitability of the African American or white woman for the position of sales representative.

(continued)

Results

Participants who viewed the African American female interviewee responded significantly faster to negative adjectives than positive ones, and those who viewed the white female interviewee responded significantly faster to positive adjectives than negatives ones. Hypotheses 1a and 1b were supported.

Hypothesis 2a was not supported by the evidence, but Hypothesis 2b received partial support. Participants who saw the jezebel prime responded significantly faster to jezebel-related terms than to mammy terms when evaluating the African American interviewee. Those who viewed the mammy prime responded faster to mammy-related terms than to jezebel-related terms, but the difference was not statistically significant.

who watched a newscast with Black suspects showed stronger support for the death penalty when compared to those who watched a newscast that covered the same crimes but did not mention race. Dixon (2007) also found that when the race of an officer and a criminal are not revealed in a crime news story, heavy viewers of news were more likely than light news viewers to think of the arresting officer as white and the criminal as Black.

Priming researchers have also sought to understand if a person's already highly accessible racial stereotypes can be further primed. Bargh et al. (1986) found that chronically accessible constructs can be primed to make them even more accessible in a person's memory, but that was in a laboratory setting. Ewoldsen and Rhodes (2020) noted,

> The question is whether such an effect—which is by its nature subtle—can be demonstrated in a media context. Specifically, for Caucasians in the United States, racial attitudes of African Americans tend to be highly accessible from memory. Can these already chronically racial stereotypes be primed? (p. 93)

Research suggests that politicians attempt to prime highly accessible racial stereotypes in their campaigns. Messing et al. (2015) analyzed photos of Barack Obama used during the 2008 presidential race by the McCain campaign. Their content analysis found that McCain's campaign used photos showing Obama with a darker skin tone, especially when talking about Obama and crime issues. But can media actually prime racist attitudes? Studies suggest that, through priming, media can increase the accessibility of those chronic attitudes (Luttig & Callaghan, 2016; Messing et al., 2015).

Valentino et al. (2017) summarized previous research into racial stereotyping that predicted that subtle racial cues would prime racial attitudes but that those attitudes would be suppressed when people were confronted with racist arguments for or against a given political candidate or policy. However, Valentino et al. found that that key assumption no longer holds, highlighting a shift in the norms of racial political rhetoric. Their findings revealed

> that invocations of racial conflict and even explicit derogation of African Americans did not reduce the power of racial attitudes to predict evaluations of policies and politicians, as previous studies had found. . . . Many of our subjects simply did not reject political arguments that explicitly derogate black Americans. . . . Many whites now view themselves as an embattled and even disadvantaged group, and this has led to both strong in-group identity and a greater tolerance for expressions of hostility toward out-groups. (p. 768)

Political Information

In the area of political news coverage, studies have usually focused on media coverage of particular issues and subsequent presidential performance ratings among audiences. The studies investigate whether the media primed the audiences to make certain judgments. In one famous priming study, researchers examined people's opinions of President Ronald Reagan before and after the Iran-Contra scandal of 1986. (The scandal involved the United States selling weapons to Iran and giving the profits to the Contras in Central America.) Before the event, the overall evaluations of Reagan were predicted by domestic issues, but after the Iran-Contra affair, people based their evaluation of Reagan on foreign affairs issues, particularly those in Central America (Krosnick & Kinder, 1990). A study in 2008 involved a telephone survey prior to the presidential primary election. Respondents were primed to think about the war in Iraq and then-President Bush, who was near the end of his second term before they were asked to express their candidate choice. The priming more than doubled the support for Barack Obama and hurt support for the Republican front-runner (Cassino & Erisen, 2010). A study from South Korea also found that television news coverage affected evaluations of their president, but the researchers pointed out that the priming was largely due to the recency rather than the frequency of the coverage (Kim et al., 2010).

More recently, "fake news" became a ubiquitous phrase in politics leading up to and after the 2016 presidential race between Donald Trump and Hillary Clinton. Although Trump often labeled true stories that he thought cast him in a negative light as fake news, active disinformation campaigns did fill social media with literal fake news (i.e., stories that are blatantly false, written with the intention of misleading the reader). Discussions about fake news were common occurrences online, in person, and in the news media. Researchers found that people who were primed with tweets from political leaders, journalists, and activists about fake news subsequently showed lower trust in news media and were less accurate at identifying real news stories compared to participants who were not primed (Van Duyn & Collier, 2018).

Further research into the 2016 presidential campaign found that norms of political correctness could serve as a prime that boosted support for then-candidate Trump, whose brash and often politically incorrect style of communication became a hallmark of his campaign and subsequent presidency. Conway et al. (2017) found that

Research shows that priming people with norms of political correctness resulted in greater support for Donald Trump. Research has also shown that priming people with tweets about so-called "fake news" results in lower trust in the news media and less accuracy in identifying real news stories.

when people were primed to think about political correctness, their support for Trump significantly increased, while the opposite was true for Clinton. Furthermore, those who reacted more negatively to political correctness norms also showed more support for Trump, even when controlling for their political ideology. Conway and his colleagues concluded that "norms that are designed to increase the overall amount of positive communication can actually backfire by increasing support for a politician who uses extremely negative language that explicitly violates the norm" (p. 244).

Entertainment media as well as news media can serve as primes for political concerns. In particular, viewing of primetime crime dramas is a significant indicator of people's concerns about crime in the real world, and those primes caused people to judge the president based on how they addressed crime (Holbrook & Hill, 2005).

A study of the documentary film *Fahrenheit 9-11* showed that viewing the movie had significant effects on people's evaluations of President George W. Bush (Holbert & Hansen, 2006). This study found that ambivalence—the presence of both positive and negative evaluations—sometimes exists in the minds of the electorate, especially those who identify as politically independent. When presented with the strong anti-Bush message of the movie, those identifying themselves as Republicans, Democrats, or politically independent reacted in different ways. Democrats and independents decreased in ambivalence and had more negative attitudes toward Bush than did Republicans, who increased in ambivalence.

In addition to movies and crime dramas, late-night talk shows are a source for political priming. Moy et al. (2006) investigated whether appearances by candidates on the shows served as a prime for viewers' evaluations. They found that viewers of *The Late Show with David Letterman* were more likely than nonviewers to base their evaluations of George W. Bush on character traits after he appeared on the show.

Voters' existing political knowledge and involvement also affects media priming. Moy et al. (2016) summarized this body of research:

> In general, political involvement tends to diminish citizens' susceptibility to political priming effects. Strong knowledge and intense discussion of politics appears to put them in a position where they deliberately resist received primes and stick with their default evaluative standards. Priming effects are generally smaller among those with greater general interest in politics. However, effects can become more complex, given how political involvement interacts with other characteristics. When coupled with high levels of trust in the media sources that provide priming information, political knowledge leads to *stronger* priming effects, because people will be willing to trust the source of the prime and will be able to integrate the primed concept with their existing beliefs and attitudes. (p. 6)

Summary

Priming theory has become a viable theoretical basis for the explanation of the effects of content on later attitudes, behaviors, and judgments. Priming helps explain the effects of media violence, the influence of political coverage on evaluations of candidates, stereotyped portrayals of minorities, and more.

Priming explores the cognitive components of information processing, and it occurs when exposure to mediated communication activates related thoughts in the mind of an audience member. In other words, media content triggers concepts, learning, or knowledge acquired in the past that is related to the prime. For a certain period of time after being subjected to the prime, a person is more likely to think about the content and to review memories of similar thoughts than a person who does not experience the prime. For most people, priming effects cause mild reactions that diminish in time or may pass unnoticed. The priming effects from media violence often pass very quickly, whereas political priming effects can last for weeks or even months.

Scholars have identified three primary characteristics of priming effects. First, they fade over time. Second, stronger primes—such as those that require more mental energy—result in stronger effects. Third, primes have strong effects when people make judgments about ambiguous situations or behaviors.

Most studies investigating the priming of media violence have been based on one of two models: cognitive neoassociation or the General Aggression Model. Political priming has additionally been explained by the accessibility-applicability model (AAM) that takes into account the accessibility or frequency of primed information from mass media, along with the applicability of such information in the mind of the viewer.

The use of mental models to explain priming effects offers an alternative to network models of memory. Mental models are time-bound, like priming activations, but exist for longer periods of time than do network models of priming. Mental models therefore can explain priming effects of political messages that last weeks or even months. At some yet undefined point, however, the repeated priming of concepts via mass media passes the threshold into cultivation effects rather than priming effects.

Media effects studies have shown strong evidence for priming, especially for the priming of ideas related to aggression; however, the connection between the priming of aggressive thoughts and the actual display of aggression is not particularly strong unless certain variables are present. These include (1) the perceived meaning of the communication, (2) the perceived justifiability of the witnessed aggression, (3) the extent to which audiences identify with the characters, (4) the perceived reality of the mediated communication, and (5) memories of prior experiences.

In recent years, media effects scholars have continued to study priming effects, especially those that result from exposure to media violence, but the scope has expanded from television and movies to include the impact of video games, avatars, and social media. Many studies in recent years have examined the priming of racial stereotypes in media content. Political priming examines how news coverage can impact subsequent appraisals of a political figures. More recent research has also looked into how social media and norms of political correctness can prime voters.

6

Agenda Setting

A handful of us determine what will be on the evening news broadcasts, or, for that matter, in the *New York Times* or *Washington Post* or *Wall Street Journal*. Indeed it is a handful of us with this awesome power. . . . And those [news stories] available to us already have been culled and re-culled by persons far outside our control.

—Walter Cronkite
Anchor of the *CBS Evening News* from 1962 to 1981

Does the news media tell us what to think? Or, in an oft-quoted remark by communication scholar Bernard Cohen (1963), is it "stunningly successful" at telling us "what to think about" (p. 13)? The strong link between the importance that news media place on particular issues and the importance that the public places on those same issues demonstrates a type of communication effect called **agenda setting**. As you will learn in this chapter, agenda-setting research explains how news media can tell us what to think about, how to think about it, and how to associate news items.

For more than 50 years, numerous studies have shown that news media do set the public agenda, and media effects researchers have been able to solve earlier empirical problems that had made it difficult for them to address agenda-setting issues in compelling ways. For years, critics of agenda setting pointed out that the methods employed in agenda-setting research only indicated that a relationship existed between the media agenda and the public agenda. The causal direction, they said, could not be established.

Using precise statistical methods, causal directions can now be determined. Agenda-setting effects are clearly indicated only when researchers are able to measure public opinion before and after media coverage of specific issues and to control or account for additional factors. For this reason, election campaigns have been popular among researchers because of their periodicity and other characteristics that make them suitable for agenda-setting research designs.

Initially, agenda-setting research examined in fairly global terms the influence of news media in shaping people's perceptions of varied issues and events. Since the seminal study of public issues in the 1968 presidential campaign (McCombs & Shaw, 1972), studies have confirmed the strong correspondence between the amount of coverage issues receive in the news and the salience of those issues to the public. This is known as the first level of agenda setting. Scholars have since then identified additional levels of agenda setting, which will be discussed in detail in this chapter.

Over the decades, there has also been ongoing research into who sets the agenda. Each day, countless news stories occur around the world, throughout the nation, in individual regions and states, and at local levels. News professionals cannot possibly examine, organize, and report to the public *all* the news of the day. Space, time, and resource limitations preclude doing that. Instead, journalists must decide which stories to cover, which to run, and which to ignore. In making such decisions, news professionals invariably *set the agenda* for news consumers. They gauge the value of news on the basis of their perceptions of its importance to their audiences.

Control over the flow of news information by media professionals is an important and powerful function called **gatekeeping**, which is highlighted in this chapter's opening quote from legendary news anchor Walter Cronkite. Simply put, journalists, editors, and broadcasters allow a certain amount of news to "pass through" to the public each day, but time and space constraints force them to shut the gates and stop the flow of most information to news consumers.

In addition to studying how journalists set the agenda, there is also research that explores how news consumers may actually play a role in setting the agenda and how they combine various agendas through a process known as *agenda melding*. Researchers have also studied the concept of *intermedia agenda setting*, where a particular news outlet can set the agenda for other news outlets.

One of the most recent issues facing agenda-setting research is the growing number of news sources and the increasing role of selectivity on behalf of the consumer. Put simply, can the media set the agenda for the public when the public has so many media options from which to choose? In the early days of agenda-setting research, there were only a handful of television stations, and many people still read newspapers. Today there are an ever-growing number of news outlets ranging from traditional television networks (e.g., ABC, CBS, NBC) and newspapers (e.g., *The New York Times* and *The Washington Post*), cable news channels (e.g., MSNBC, CNN, Fox News), and online news outlets (e.g., Huffington Post and Buzzfeed News). Streaming news outlets, such as Newsy and NBC News Now, and news-related podcasts have also entered the mix. Furthermore, social media also increases engagement with news (Oeldorf-Hirsch, 2018), and researchers are actively examining the intersections of online platforms and agenda-setting effects (e.g., Conway-Silva et al., 2018; Feezell, 2017; McCombs et al., 2014; Ragas et al., 2014; Valenzuela et al., 2017).

This chapter begins by identifying the conceptual foundations of agenda setting and provides a brief history of the agenda-setting research tradition. It also takes a look at other areas of agenda-setting research, such as attribute agenda setting and the more recent network agenda setting model, and studies that examine who sets the media agenda, including intermedia agenda setting. We will also explore our growing understanding of the psychology behind agenda setting. The chapter concludes with a look at agenda setting in our modern media landscape.

Conceptual Roots

Bernard Cohen (1963) was not the first to describe the role of the press in setting the public agenda. The concept can be traced to Walter Lippmann, a famous newspaper columnist and social commentator of the early 20th century. Lippmann's *Public Opinion* (1922) has been called the most influential, non-scholarly work in the history of the academic study of mass communication (Carey, 1996). In the book, Lippmann wrote about how the news media are responsible for shaping the public's perception of the world. He emphasized that the pictures of reality created by the news media were merely *reflections* of actual reality and therefore were sometimes distorted. Lippmann said that the news media projections of the world create a **pseudo-environment** for each news consumer. The pseudo-environment exists in addition to the *actual* environment, and people react to this pseudo-environment that media create. "For the real environment is altogether too big, too complex, and too fleeting for a direct acquaintance" (p. 16).

Other scholars also described the concept of agenda setting in their writings prior to empirical assessment of the concept in the early 1970s. In 1958, Norton Long wrote:

> In a sense, the newspaper is the prime mover in setting the territorial agenda. It has a great part in determining what most people will be talking about, what most people will think the facts are, and what most people will regard as the way problems are to be dealt with. (p. 260)

The following year, Kurt and Gladys Lang (1959) wrote: "The mass media force attention to certain issues. They build up public images of political figures. They are constantly presenting objects suggesting what individuals in the mass should think about, know about, have feelings about" (p. 232).

The Cognitive Paradigm

During the 1960s and 1970s, researchers rejected using the persuasion paradigm to explain agenda-setting effects, and they began taking notice of the emerging cognitive paradigm. According to Kosicki (1993):

> Agenda setting, with its apparently simple, easy-to-explain, and intuitively appealing hypothesis, seemed right for the time. On its face it is a rejection of persuasion, a "reframing" of the basic research question from "telling people what to think" to "telling them what to think about" (Cohen, 1963). This seemingly small, but clever, twist of phrase focuses attention away from persuasion and onto something new. The freshness of the model has obvious appeal. It signals not only a move away from persuasion toward other cognitive factors (Becker & Kosicki, 1991), but a move toward a particular kind of cognitive factor: an agenda of issues. (p. 231)

In the cognitive paradigm, three primary factors influence each other bidirectionally: a person's behavior, a person's cognitive abilities, and environmental events to which a person is exposed. "Reciprocal causation provides people with opportunities to exercise some control over events in their lives, as well as set limits of self-direction. Because of the bidirectionality of influence, people are both products and producers of their environment" (Bandura, 1994, p. 61).

More recently, scholars have returned their attention to understanding the psychology of agenda-setting effects. This includes the role of **need for orientation (NFO)**, which is based on the idea of cognitive mapping. A person's NFO is determined by whether they consider an issue to be relevant and what their degree of uncertainty about that issue is.

For instance, if you are highly involved on your campus, you would probably consider an upcoming student government association (SGA) election highly relevant to you, but you may not have a lot of information about the candidates running for SGA president (i.e., high uncertainly). In this case, you would have high NFO. As a result, you would probably be more inclined to read about the candidates in your college newspaper or watch stories about them on your campus newscast. The higher the NFO, the more likely a person will turn to mass media. If agenda setting occurs, the person will place similar importance on the issues and attributes found in media coverage and be primed to evaluate the candidates using that information (McCombs & Valenzuela, 2021). NFO will be discussed in greater detail later in this chapter.

Priming

Priming is connected to the agenda-setting phenomenon, as it is considered by researchers to be one of the outcomes of agenda setting (Chernov & McCombs, 2019). Moy et al. (2016) explain the connection this way: "By making some issues more salient in people's minds (agenda setting), the mass media can shape the considerations that people take into account when making judgments about political candidates or other issues (priming)" (p. 5–6). Furthermore, McCombs and Valenzuela (2021) note, "The link between agenda-setting effects, which result in the salience of issues or other elements among the public, and the subsequent expression of *opinions* about specific public figures is called media priming" (p. 138).

Priming is significant because people cannot pay attention to everything. In making judgments, people frequently use intuitive shortcuts rather than a comprehensive analysis of their store of information.

> Citizens rely upon the agenda of salient objects and attributes in their minds, the agenda that is set to a considerable degree by the news media. This agenda determines the criteria—sometimes the single criterion—on which an opinion is based. (McCombs & Valenzuela, 2021, p. 138).

Research Tradition

The first empirical test of Lippmann's ideas about agenda setting was published in 1972 by two University of North Carolina researchers, Maxwell McCombs and Donald Shaw, in what came to be known as the Chapel Hill study.

In 1968 the Vietnam conflict raged, African Americans struggled for civil rights, Dr. Martin Luther King, Jr. was shot to death at the Lorraine Motel in Memphis, the country's youth rebelled against authority, and drug abuse became a serious problem.

Robert F. Kennedy's bid for the presidency ended tragically when an assassin gunned him down in California. Hubert Humphrey emerged as the Democratic nominee instead, challenging Republican Richard Nixon and the independent candidate, George Wallace.

In that tempestuous social climate as the nation prepared to select a new chief executive, McCombs and Shaw (1972) designed a study to test the influence of campaign coverage on public perceptions of the importance of issues. The study compared what voters said were the key issues of the campaign with the actual content of the mass media used by respondents. Prior to the 1968 presidential election, the researchers asked Chapel Hill voters who had not yet committed to a candidate to outline the key issues regardless of what candidates were saying. The issues that respondents identified—foreign policy, law and order, fiscal policy, civil rights, and public welfare—were ranked according to the percentage of respondents identifying them.

The actual content of local news media served as a measured independent variable in the Chapel Hill study, and the dependent variable—*issue salience*—was compared to topic coverage. The researchers analyzed the contents of local newspapers, television, and radio for three weeks during the campaign to identify issues that were

The first agenda-setting study was conducted before the 1968 presidential election that would send Republican nominee Richard Nixon, seen here during a campaign parade in Chicago, to the White House.

receiving the most media attention. When McCombs and Shaw compared the media content to the concerns identified by the respondents, they found almost identical agendas. There was a very strong relationship between the emphasis placed on issues by the media and the judgments of voters regarding the salience of topics.

After this groundbreaking study, it might be said that agenda-setting research caught fire among communication investigators, with hundreds of studies being conducted throughout the ensuing decades. In fact, agenda setting has been cited more than 10,100 times, according to Google citations (Valkenburg & Oliver, 2020). McCombs and Shaw (1993) reviewed the abundant research findings and identified four phases of growth in agenda-setting research: (1) publication of their original study in 1972, (2) replication and examination of contingent conditions, (3) an expansion of the original idea of agenda setting into the areas of candidate characteristics and other political aspects, and (4) a focus on the sources of the media agenda. A fifth phase began in the early 2000s as researchers focused on examining the psychological processes of information processing that result in agenda-setting effects, which will be discussed later in this chapter (also see McCombs & Stroud, 2014, for review).

G. Ray Funkhouser (1973) replicated the Chapel Hill study and identified a strong correspondence between public opinion trends in the 1960s and coverage of issues in the news media during that period. Funkhouser assessed public opinion using answers to a Gallup Poll question regarding the most significant problem in the nation. He analyzed the content of issues of *Time, Newsweek,* and *U.S. News and World Report* to determine the media agenda. He then compared these findings with official statistics (e.g., the actual number of U.S. soldiers in Vietnam, number of demonstrations on campus or on behalf of civil rights) to gauge congruence between *actual* reality and *perceptions* of reality on the part of the public and the media. He found a strong correlation between the amount of media coverage of an issue and the public's perceived importance of that issue; moreover, he also found that media coverage did not always represent the actual reality of issues and situations.

McCombs and Shaw's second study examined the causal directions for agenda-setting effects and contingent conditions for such effects during the 1972 presidential election campaign (Shaw & McCombs, 1977). Voters in Charlotte, North Carolina, were surveyed before and after the election to reveal short-term agenda-setting effects. The researchers found that voters with a greater need for orientation to their world and voters who used the mass media more frequently than others were more likely to have agendas that corresponded to the news media agenda. As for causation, the researchers claimed to find evidence to support the agenda-setting influence of the press, but the evidence was not overwhelming.

In an attempt to provide stronger evidence for causal direction, the next major study of agenda setting was conducted in a laboratory setting where the researchers manipulated videotaped network television newscasts to vary the placement and emphasis given to the stories (Iyengar et al., 1982). Each day for a week, research participants viewed the altered newscasts, which were presented to them as actual and unaltered. Participants were divided into two groups. One group was shown newscasts that emphasized the weak nature of U.S. military defenses; the other group saw newscasts that did not contain these particular stories. The researchers surveyed participants before and after the weeklong experiment and found statistically significant agenda-setting effects. At the end of the week, the group that had seen the "weak defense" stories rated the issue of military defense significantly higher than the group that had not been shown the stories. Follow-up experiments provided additional empirical evidence for the agenda-setting effects of mass media (Iyengar & Kinder, 1987; Wanta, 1988).

The third phase of agenda-setting research began during the 1976 presidential campaign when the agenda of candidate characteristics and the alternative agenda of political interest were examined (Weaver et al., 1981). The researchers analyzed the dynamics of how voters perceived candidate characteristics and the images of candidates portrayed in the media (McCombs, 1992). Voters in six locations—three sites in the Northeast and three in the Midwest—participated in the longitudinal study to assess contingent factors at work in the agenda-setting process. The voters' occupations, education levels, and geographic locations were found to affect the degree to which the media were responsible for setting their issue agendas at various times during the election campaign.

The fourth phase began in the 1980s when researchers began investigating sources of the media agenda. A number of influences that create the media agenda each day were identified (Shoemaker & Reese, 1991, 1996, 2014). These included sociological factors related to the news organization and external organizations, the routine of media work, ideological concerns, and individual differences between reporters and editors. This phase, as well as the fifth phase focusing on the psychology of agenda-setting effects, will be discussed in greater detail later in this chapter.

Second- and Third-Level Agenda Setting and Beyond

McCombs and Shaw's (1972) Chapel Hill study illuminated the first level of agenda-setting effects where audiences' perceptions of issue salience mirror the importance placed on those issues by news outlets. In the decades since the Chapel Hill study, agenda-setting research has expanded, and media effects researchers have identified various levels of agenda-setting effects.

Second-Level Agenda-Setting Effects

Second-level agenda setting, also known as **attribute agenda setting**, explains how salience of specific attributes of an object or issue are transferred from media sources to the public. As McCombs (2014) simply stated, "Attributes that are prominent in the mass media also tend to become prominent in the public mind" (p. 62). Attribute agenda setting strongly resembles framing research in many ways (see Chapter 7). Researchers study the attributes of different elements related to media stories—such as the attributes of issue coverage or of candidates and/or their images. Studies have shown that people tend to attribute to candidates that which the press tells them to attribute (e.g., Becker & McCombs, 1978; Kim & McCombs, 2007; King, 1997; McCombs et al., 2000). The way the news media covers attributes of issues has also been found to influence voters (e.g., Takeshita & Mikami, 1995).

An attribute agenda setting study conducted by Kim and McCombs (2007) found that media portrayals of candidates' attributes (e.g., positions on specific issues, biographical information, and personal qualifications and character) had a strong influence on voters in the 2002 elections for Texas governor and U.S. senator. The researchers analyzed the content of a daily newspaper in Austin, Texas. They identified attributes that were strongly covered in the press, including "general political descriptions, specific issue positions, personal qualifications and character, biographical information, campaign conduct, and support and endorsements" (p. 303). Then they conducted telephone interviews of a sample of residents in the area. Those people who read the newspaper were found to be more likely to have their judgments affected by what they read in the press regarding the attributes of the candidates. Additionally, Wu and Coleman (2009) found that the attributes describing then-President George W. Bush and his Democratic opponent John Kerry during the 2004 presidential election had a strong influence on voter perceptions of the candidates and actually predicted people's voting intentions. The study also confirmed that negative media coverage of a candidate's image influences the public more than positive coverage.

Partisan media and attribute agenda-setting effects have also been studied. As McCombs and Stroud (2014) noted, "Partisan media may be particularly influential at the second level of agenda setting. Partisan outlets may cover similar issues (first-level) but offer substantially different takes on those issues (second-level)" (p. 83). For instance, Feldman et al. (2012) studied the differences in coverage of climate change on MSNBC, CNN, and Fox News and found that audience members' attitudes about the issue aligned with which cable news channel they watched (i.e., watching MSNBC or CNN was associated with greater acceptance of global warming, while the opposite was true for those who watched Fox News). Muddiman et al. (2014) also observed attribute agenda-setting effects in their study of cable news and the war in Iraq. Meanwhile, Camaj (2014) conducted a study that integrated need for orientation, selective exposure (i.e., choosing politically like-minded news sources), and attribute agenda-setting effects. Her findings show that those with clear party affiliations and greater interest in politics are more likely to seek out ideologically similar news sources, particularly on television and radio, and adopt their attribute agendas. Furthermore, the salience of attributes in those agendas is more likely to reinforce preexisting attitudes.

Third-Level Agenda-Setting Effects

Third level agenda-setting effects, also known as the **network agenda setting model**, investigates how news media transfer a network of objects or attributes—or a combination of the two—to the public (Guo, 2012, 2013; Guo et al., 2012). Wanta and Alkazemi (2017) describe how the third level of agenda-setting effects builds on the first two:

> Thus, the first level of agenda-setting—the agenda of objects—presupposed that the media tell news consumers what to think *about*. Meanwhile, the second level of agenda-setting—the agenda of attributes—presupposes the media can tell news consumers *how* to think about the news. Finally, the third level of agenda-setting tells news consumers how to *associate* news items. (p. 21)

Furthermore, McCombs et al. (2014) note that the first two levels of agenda setting

> treat objects and their attributes as separate and distinct disaggregated elements. Of course, in reality objects and their attributes are bundled together in media messages and in public thought and conversation. Lippmann's concept of "the pictures

in our heads" raises the question: To what extent are the media able to transfer the salience of an integrated picture? (p. 792)

Whereas previous agenda-setting research focused on rank-ordered lists of objects or attributes, the network agenda setting model illustrates "that the news media can actually bundle different objects and attributes and make these bundles of elements salient in the public's mind simultaneously" (Guo et al., 2012, p. 55). Furthermore, this model hypothesizes that the more news media mention certain elements together, the more likely audiences will perceive the elements are interconnected.

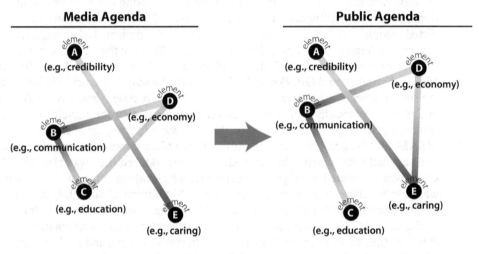

Figure 6.1   Network agenda setting model.

Adapted from Guo, 2012, p. 619.

Guo and McCombs (2011) first studied this third level of agenda setting by reanalyzing data collected for Kim and McCombs's 2007 study on Texas elections discussed in the previous section. Guo and McCombs conducted a social network analysis of both the media and the public's agendas of candidates' attributes. Their findings showed a significant correlation between the media and public's network agendas.

Vargo et al. (2014) studied mainstream and niche news outlets' network agendas on Twitter with the network agendas of supporters of then-President Barack Obama and Mitt Romney, his Republican challenger during the 2012 presidential election. After analyzing 38 million public tweets, they found that the ways news media associated various election issues when discussing Obama and Romney positively correlated with how their supporters talked about them. Research has also shown that both news media and political campaign messaging can transfer network agendas that establish "ownership" of campaign issues to the public (Guo & Vargo, 2015).

Attributes play a key role in both second and third level agenda setting. Attributes can be *cognitive* in nature, meaning that the media user thinks about the issues or candidates and their attributes, or attributes can be *affective* in nature, meaning that the media user notices the tone in which the attributes are portrayed. If the media portray candidates or issues in negative or positive tones, they can influence how voters think, rather than simply what they think about. This makes framing of a news story very important. Journalists can use particular viewpoints from various sources or even particular word choices to "frame" a story in a particular light. Frames "invite people to think about an issue in a particular way" (Tewksbury & Scheufele, 2009, p. 19). We will discuss framing in more detail in Chapter 7.

Agenda Setting: Three Levels at a Glance

First-Level Agenda Setting *(Traditional Agenda Setting)*
The more an issue is covered in the news, the more important audiences will think the issue is. At this level, news media tell audiences *what to think about.*

Second-Level Agenda Setting *(Attribute Agenda Setting)*
Media outlets transfer an attribute about a specific issue or object to the public. At this level, news outlets tell audiences *how to think about an issue.*

Third-Level Agenda Setting *(Network Agenda Setting)*
Whereas attribute agenda setting transfers salience about one specific issue or object, network agenda setting transfers salience of a "bundle" of objects and attributes. At this level, the media tells audiences *how to associate news items.*

Agenda Melding

More than 50 years after McCombs and Shaw's seminal Chapel Hill study, there continues to be great interest in the study of agenda setting, and scholars continue to explore new ways to expand the theory (Vargo, 2018). One of those ways considers the role that audiences play in choosing which media agendas they consume. This is known as **agenda melding**, which McCombs et al. (2014) defined as "the social process by which we meld agendas from various sources, including other people, to create pictures of the world that fit our experiences and preferences" (p. 794). In their 2014 study of agenda melding, Shaw and Weaver dubbed traditional mainstream news outlets "vertical media," which transmit information to the largest audiences possible; conversely, niche media were dubbed "horizontal media," which reach out to specific, smaller audiences. For instance, you may combine agendas from traditional media (such as *NBC Nightly News* and *USA Today*) with agendas from niche media outlets (such as blogs, cable news programs, and podcasts) that fit your personal interests. McCombs et al. describe the process of agenda melding as "so intimate and personal that we are not aware we are doing it" (p. 794).

Studies have shown that political affiliation can affect how people meld agendas. A study of the 2012 presidential election found Democrats and Republicans meld agendas differently (Vargo et al., 2014). The results found Democrats melded agendas from vertical media sources, while Republicans melded agendas from horizontal sources. There are also differences in agenda melding for influential political journalists and bloggers on Twitter, depending on their political affiliation (Hedding & Ripka, 2018).

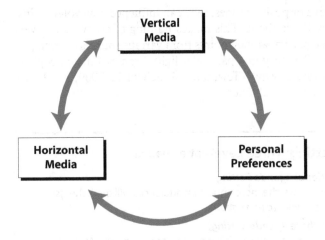

Figure 6.2
Model of agenda melding.

Adapted from McCombs et al., 2014, p. 795.

The Psychology of Agenda Setting

Although researchers have identified multiple moderating variables for agenda setting (e.g., media trust and need for cognition), one of the most important underlying concepts is **need for orientation (NFO)**, which "provides a psychological explanation for the transfer of salience from the media agenda to the public agenda" (McCombs & Valenzuela, 2021, p. 74). In general terms, NFO explains how people strive to orient themselves whenever they find themselves in unfamiliar settings. In agenda-setting research, NFO "is defined by a combination of *uncertainty* about a topic in the news and how *relevant* people find the news about that topic to be." (McCombs & Stroud, 2014, p. 70). Relevance is the first factor taken into consideration when determining a person's NFO. If someone does not view a particular issue as relevant to them, then their NFO is low. However, if the issue is perceived as relevant, then the level of uncertainty must be examined.

"High relevance and high uncertainty define a high need for orientation, the theoretical condition under which the highest degree of correspondence is predicted between the media agenda and the public agenda (McCombs & Valenzuela, 2021, p. 78). When people believe they have sufficient information about a topic, their uncertainty is low. For issues relevant to the public but for which public opinion is stable, people monitor the news to detect any significant changes. "Under these conditions of high relevance and low uncertainty, the need for orientation is moderate" (p. 75). For example, the complexity and significance of health care reform resulted in high relevance and high uncertainty for many people. "In theoretical terms, those citizens had a high need for orientation" (p. 76).

Importantly, NFO research highlights the fact that issue salience is not simply the result of issues being more accessible in the minds of news consumers because of the frequency of coverage. "An individual's cognitive involvement with an issue, specifically each individual's perception of the issue's relevance and desire for additional information about the issue, moderates the strength of the media's agenda-setting effect" (McCombs & Stroud, 2014, p. 73).

Dual Path Models of Agenda-Setting Effects

For several decades, the underlying mechanism used to explain agenda-setting effects was cognitive accessibility, meaning that judgments about an issue were the result of constructs in a person's memory recently activated by the media (see our discussion in Chapter 5). However, more recent research showed that accessibility did not play a key role in agenda setting. In addition to research into NFO, scholars have developed dual-process approaches to understanding agenda-setting effects (see Stoycheff et al., 2018, for a review).

Peripheral and Central Agenda Setting.   As we know, audiences are made up of unique individuals, and each person can respond to news stories in a variety of ways. How and if a person responds to various issues is determined by their personal situation (McCombs, 1999). Therefore, agenda-setting effects can occur either peripherally or centrally. (These routes of cognitive processing stem from the Elaboration Likelihood Model, which is discussed further in Chapter 10.) The key to understanding which of these two paths is activated is *personal relevance*. As Bulkow et al. (2013) explained, "Since not every issue has equal personal meaning for all audience members, it will be processed more peripherally by some and more centrally by others" (p. 5).

Bulkow et al.'s (2013) study involved examining how participants interacted with a news website created for their experiment; they also surveyed the participants to measure their personal involvement with issues in the news and their judgments about the importance of issues covered in the news over time. They found that people who view an issue as irrelevant rely more on peripheral cues (e.g., where an article is placed on a website, how often an issue is reported on, scanning news stories for key words) to form an opinion. The effects of automatic or peripheral agenda setting are less persistent and more unstable. Conversely, if people view an issue as relevant, they invest more cognitive effort (e.g., reading stories more closely and subsequently reading additional stories about the issue) to learn more information. The effects of deliberative or central agenda setting are more stable and persistent over time. Lee's (2021) results also showed a stronger agenda-setting effect for those who used the deliberative path.

Regardless of whether information was processed peripherally or centrally, Bulkow et al. (2013) noted that the resulting agenda-setting effect can be the same.

> Our findings show that less involved persons, who initially did not assign much importance to an issue and did not pay much attention to the issue-related coverage, estimated the issue as important as the high-involved, prejudiced, and attentive persons, if the media emphasis placed on the issue was strong enough.
>
> From this perspective agenda-setting, as it originally was devised, homogenizes the public opinion by bringing in line the judgments of involved and uninvolved persons for issues, which are regarded as important by the media at a certain point of time. Thus, it widens the view of audience members beyond their personal life for problems in the society as a whole. (p. 17)

Agenda Cueing and Agenda Reasoning.   Pingree and Stoycheff (2013) developed another dual-processing model for understanding agenda-setting effects. The two key mechanisms of their model are **agenda cueing** and **agenda reasoning**. Pingree and Stoycheff define agenda cueing as "the use of the perceived news agenda as a cognitive shortcut in the agenda response. By taking the agenda cue, audience members effectively delegate the difficult task of prioritizing problems to journalists" (p. 853). Agenda cueing, they argue, is rooted in **gatekeeping trust**, which McCombs and Stroud (2014) defined as "the perception that journalists have done the 'heavy lifting' to determine the importance of issues and that their news judgments are useful cognitive shortcuts to use in determining the importance of an issue" (p. 78). People with high gatekeeping trust believe that the news media carefully weigh issue importance, thus providing reliable cognitive shortcuts (McCombs & Valenzuela, 2021). Meanwhile, individuals using agenda reasoning examine the specific content of the news to judge the importance of an issue. Agenda reasoning "involves effortful cognitive processing of reasons recalled from memory that are seen as relevant to deciding the relative importance of problems" (Pingree & Stoycheff, 2013, p. 856).

To isolate exposure to agenda cues from agenda reasons that may be present in the content of news stories, Pingree and Stoycheff (2013) used summarized reports of news coverage from the previous week—not the actual stories. The reports indicated how much coverage each topic received. Researchers manipulated which issue was the top story, either unemployment or national debt, but in each condition, the top story was said to have made up 23% of all news coverage for the week. To test agenda reasoning, the same summarized reports of coverage were used, but researchers also included a few paragraphs of information that gave reasons supporting why either national debt or unemployment was the top story. Their results showed significant agenda-setting effects for participants only exposed to the agenda cue, especially for those with high gatekeeping trust. Conversely, for those with low gatekeeping trust, agenda-setting effects were strengthened when agenda reasons were present.

More recent research compared the influence of agenda cues from traditional news and Twitter (Stoycheff et al., 2018). Like the previous study, this experiment used reports that were labeled as summaries of stories from mainstream media or summaries of popular topics on Twitter. They found that both news and Twitter cues resulted in significant agenda-setting effects without any exposure to actual content. This study also found that one-time exposure to agenda cues resulted in effects 78% as strong as classic agenda-setting experiments where participants were exposed to a week's worth of manipulated news content. Based on these findings, Stoycheff et al. (2018) concluded,

> Agenda cueing may be the dominant mechanism at work in this [agenda setting] process. In other words, the mere perception that media has focused on issues may be what drives the majority of agenda-setting effects, with the content of that coverage only playing a supporting role. (p. 197)

Regardless of how agenda-setting effects are generated, McCombs (2014) reminds us that "the core theoretical idea is that elements prominent in the media pictures not only become prominent in the public's pictures, but also come to be regarded as especially important" (p. 39).

Aggregate Effects vs. Individual Effects

You may have noticed by now that agenda-setting effects are talked about in terms of how the public is affected. In these studies "'the public' is conceptualized as an aggregate whole . . . treating all members of the public as a homogenous unit" (Guo, 2017, p. 27). But what about measuring effects at an individual level?

McCombs and Stroud (2014) argued that "a focus on the psychology of agenda setting begs us to focus on individual-level effects. At the individual level, even if an individual pursues her own interests when making information selections, agenda setting *still can occur*" (p. 81). There have been a few attempts to study agenda setting at the individual level. Guo (2017) summarized those studies as having "produced varying and even opposing results. It remains controversial whether the news media can exert an agenda-setting influence at individual levels in this new media environment" (pp. 34–35).

Agenda Setting in the Modern Media Landscape

The media landscape has changed drastically since the Chapel Hill study. With the explosion of cable news channels, online news outlets, social media, and more, is agenda setting still applicable in today's fragmented media landscape? Numerous studies show that it is. The internet and social media have received much scholarly attention since the turn of the century, and these studies are important to our current understanding of **agenda building**, which examines how news agendas are formed, and **intermedia agenda setting**, which looks at how media outlets influence other outlet's news coverage.

Agenda Setting in Online Environments

For more than 20 years, agenda-setting researchers have explored the various effects of online news coverage. Wang (2000) conducted an experiment in which certain groups were shown an online newspaper containing articles on racism, and other groups were shown online newspapers not containing the racism articles. The groups who read the racism articles subsequently identified racism as an important public issue. Althaus and Tewksbury (2002) compared readers of the online version of *The New York Times* to those who read the print edition. For 5 days, some readers examined the print version of the newspaper and others examined the online version. Both groups experienced agenda-setting effects, but their perceptions of important issues were different, corresponding to the differing issues of importance in the print and online versions.

More recently, scholars have turned their attention to social media to study agenda-setting effects. As previously discussed, Stoycheff et al. (2018) found that exposure to agenda-setting cues on Twitter can result in strong effects. Cowart's (2020) study of agenda setting on Facebook found that the more posts someone sees about an issue, the more likely they are to consider it important. (See the Research Spotlight for an in-depth look at this study.) Feezell (2018) also found that agenda-setting effects can occur when exposed to political content on Facebook. Effects were strongest for those with low levels of political interest.

What to Think About:
The Applicability of Agenda-Settings in a Social Media Context
Holly Cowart (2020)
The Agenda Setting Journal, 4(2), 195–218

In this study, Cowart examined how agenda setting affects Facebook users in the United States. Study participants viewed mock Facebook feeds and then answered questions about the importance of certain issues.

The Hypotheses

H1: Issues presented repeatedly in news stories in a social media news feed will be identified as being of greater importance than issues presented less frequently in that news feed.

H2: The order in which issues appear in a news feed will impact perceived issue importance.

H3: Issues in posts that include more endorsements (likes) will be perceived as more important than issues in posts with fewer endorsements.

Method

The study had 379 participants who were recruited from both a large public university in the southern United States and a national professional sample from Qualtrics. Participants received $5 in compensation for taking part in the study.

A pilot test was conducted to determine which two news issues and which news sources would be used in the actual study. The pilot test also identified how many "likes" a Facebook post would need to be considered highly endorsed. Results of this pilot test were not included in the study's overall findings.

The main experiment used a 3 x 2 x 2 design. The independent variables tested were repetition, story order, and endorsement. Issue importance was the dependent variable. The two news topics chosen from the pilot data were baby powder's link to cancer and the war in Aleppo. Cowart then created 12 posts for each topic to make it appear as if they were published by one of the 12 news outlets identified in the pilot.

Those posts were used to create 12 mock Facebook feeds with three levels of repetition (low, medium, or high), two different story orders, and two levels of endorsement. News posts were mixed with non-news posts to create a more realistic Facebook experience. Posts in the high endorsement category were given a random number of "likes" between 218 and 550, and those in the low endorsement category were randomly given between 0 and 217. The posts did not include comments (which would have introduced another variable), and participants could not comment on the posts. Additionally, links were disabled, meaning participants were only able to view the post on Facebook.

Measures

Participants were randomly assigned and viewed one of the 12 mock Facebook news feeds for three minutes. They ranked their responses to questions about baby powder's link to cancer and the war in Aleppo on a 7-point Likert scale (which measures a person's level of agreement or disagreement). Questions asked if a specific topic was "an important story," "not an important story," and "an issue the public should care about."

Results

Of the 379 participants who completed the study, 11 were removed from data analysis for failing an attention-check question. Therefore, 368 responses were included in the final analysis. Demographic data showed 94% of the sample was between 18 and 23 years old. The other 6% were between 24 and 35 years old. The sample was predominantly female (73%) and white (75%).

Hypothesis 1 was confirmed. Results showed statistical significance between those in the low repetition category and those in the medium and high repetition categories for both issues.

Hypothesis 2 was not confirmed. Data showed no statistical significance of story order on perceived issue importance. Similarly, Hypothesis 3 also was not supported. Data showed no statistical significance in perceived issue importance between the high and low endorsement categories for either issue.

Analysis of demographic data showed gender was a significant factor in ranking story importance for the Aleppo issue but not for baby powder's link to cancer. Men ranked Aleppo about a third of a point higher on the Likert scale than did women. Cancer rankings were more similar between men and women. Furthermore, ethnicity influenced the relationship between repetition and issue importance for the cancer story.

Overall, this study found that "repetition of content influences how important a social media user considers a topic to be. . . . This study's findings regarding repetition therefore support agenda-setting theory" (p. 213). Regarding the lack of support for Hypothesis 2, Cowart concluded that the rules of "visual hierarchy" for both print and online news "simply do not translate into social media. The idea that the most important news items appear above the fold in newspapers, at the top of a broadcast, or even the top of a web page does not have a social media equivalent" (p. 212). As for Hypothesis 3, Cowart suggested several factors that could have impacted results, such as "likes" being less visually prominent than repetition or story order and the possibility that participants may not have noticed the differences because of how they interacted with the content during the experiment.

Agenda Building

Investigation of news sources that may set the media agenda has continued to interest scholars (Vargo, 2018; Wanta et al., 1989). Agenda-setting researchers have often used the metaphor of peeling an onion to describe the process of setting the media agenda (e.g., McCombs, 2014; McCombs & Valenzuela, 2021; Ragas & Tran, 2019).

> The concentric layers of the onion represent the numerous influences at play in the shaping of the media agenda, which is the core of the onion. This metaphor also illustrates the sequential nature of this process in which the influence of an outer layer is, in turn, affected by layers more proximate to the core of the onion. (McCombs & Valenzuela, 2021, p. 111)

Shoemaker and Reese's (1996, 2014) hierarchy of influences model identifies five distinct levels that shape news coverage. They include, from smallest to largest, individual characteristics of journalists themselves, routines of media work, concerns at the organizational level, "extramedia" forces (such as public relations, powerful sources, or audiences), and larger social systems. It should be noted that Reese and Shoemaker (2016) refined the concept of "extramedia" forces as "social institutions," noting the "interplay of economic, political, and cultural factors" that function at a level between the organization and society as a whole (p. 402).

Several studies have focused on the influence of U.S. presidents on the news media agenda. In particular, these studies have identified issues covered prominently in the news media a month before and after the President's State of the Union Address to determine any influence the speech may have had.

Wanta and Foote (1994) examined presidential documents related to various issues, employing a time-series analysis to compare news coverage of those issues on three national TV networks. The researchers identified 16 issues that they categorized into four groups: international problems, the economy, social problems, and social issues. They found significant correlations between media coverage and presidential emphasis on the issues in all categories except that of the economy. Another important finding of the study was that the president's issue agenda strongly influenced the media agenda, while the news media influenced the president on only 3 of the 16 issues examined: East-West relations, crime and drugs, and environmental concerns.

A recent study by Yao et al. (2020) examined decades of presidential and public opinions, news coverage, and policy making regarding environmental issues. They found that the president's environmental agenda led the media's agenda, which then set the public agenda. They found no evidence that the public agenda influenced the president's agenda. Other research found that presidential influence on media coverage was greater when the president's party "owns" a particular issue; however, strong public concern about an issue lessens the president's influence (Boydstun et al., 2017).

There are other influences on the media agenda. Public relations news releases, political advertisements, and websites play a role in setting the agenda for other news outlets (Boyle, 2001). For instance, Ku et al. (2003) found evidence of agenda-setting effects from political campaign websites. Lee and Riffe (2017) found that press releases influenced coverage in *The New York Times* and *The Wall Street Journal*. Furthermore, real-world issues, like the price of oil, can affect the news agenda (Alkazemi & Wanta, 2018).

A growing body of research explores the role of news audiences in agenda building. Searles and Smith (2017) found a reciprocal influence between the public's agenda and cable news coverage of the 2008 economic collapse in the United States. Other studies of audience behaviors found that online searches (Ragas et al., 2014) and online audience feedback (Lee & Tandoc, 2017) can influence news coverage.

Studies have also examined how social media impacts agenda building. Parmelee's (2014) study of political reporters found they use tweets from political leaders to generate story ideas, find out about stories, get quotes, access a wider range of sources with diverse viewpoints, discover background information, and double-check information. Bane (2019) compared how traditional print outlets (i.e., *The New York Times* and *The Washington Post*) and alternative web-only outlets (i.e., Buzzfeed News and Huffington Post) utilize tweets in their reporting. The results showed that although the overwhelming majority of tweets quoted in both print and online stories were opinion- or reaction-based, online-only publications were more likely than print publications to use tweets to gather facts. Buzzfeed News and Huffington Post also quoted tweets in a higher proportion of their stories than did the newspapers, and stories that used quotes from Twitter contained twice as many tweets as print stories. Another difference between the two types of publications was that a majority of tweets used by print media were from official sources, while online outlets quoted more non-officials. These findings suggest that not only do non-officials on Twitter have a strong voice in alternative web-only publications but also "official sources may no longer be the primary agenda-builders across all mediums" (p. 203).

Intermedia Agenda Setting.   One of the most-studied aspects of agenda building is the role that media outlets play in setting the agenda for other news sources. For instance, earlier research found *The New York Times* to be a key influencer in setting the agendas for other newspapers and television newscasts (Gilbert et al., 1980; Golan, 2006; Reese & Danielian, 1989; Shaw & Sparrow, 1999). Current scholars studying intermedia agenda setting tend to focus on effects between traditional media and online media.

Communication researchers have examined how presidential candidates use Twitter to influence media and public agendas. Researchers looked at the 2016 presidential election. Findings showed that Donald Trump's use of Twitter influenced both the media and public agendas (Lee & Xu, 2018; Wells et al., 2016). It is also important to remember that because tweets are available to the general public, not just journalists, they "have the opportunity to influence the public directly as well as through the media" (Parmelee, 2014, p. 446).

Overall, numerous studies have found strong evidence of reciprocal, dynamic intermedia agenda-setting relationships between traditional media and social media (e.g., Conway et al., 2015; Conway-Silva et al., 2018; Neuman et al., 2014; Valenzuela et al., 2017). For example, studies of newspaper coverage and Twitter content during presidential primaries found what researchers called a "symbiotic relationship" between the two (Conway et al., 2015; Conway-Silva et al., 2018). However multiple studies have found that traditional media still exert a stronger agenda-setting influence (Conway et al., 2015; Conway-Silva et al., 2018; Guo & Vargo, 2015; Stoycheff et al., 2018). It should be noted that some studies have presented evidence to the contrary (e.g., Valenzuela et al., 2017).

Researchers have also examined intermedia agenda setting effects in online news from traditional, partisan, and emerging media outlets. Vargo and Guo (2017) observed reciprocal relationships among various outlets. Despite the increasing number of media choices, agendas across outlets were similar, suggesting "that there is still a consensus among various media organizations as to what issues remain the most important and central in society today" (p. 1047). However, their findings showed online partisan media played a larger role in setting the overall media agenda than did traditional outlets. Although traditional media (i.e., *The New York Times* and *The Washington Post*) did not play a leading role in overall intermedia agenda-setting effects, they did set the agenda for other outlets on the topic of health care. Vargo and Guo noted the Affordable Care Act continued to generate headlines during the time of their study, and most other media outlets followed the *Times* and *Post*'s coverage of the law and its implications. This finding supports Vargo et al.'s (2015) stance that traditional media generate greater agenda-setting effects for stories with ongoing news coverage. Additionally, recent research by Stern et al. (2020) examined how sentiment about a specific topic propagates throughout media networks over time. They found that traditional mainstream news sources are more likely to be identified as "bellwethers" of sentiment, influencing how other outlets report a story.

Considering how the modern media landscape is constantly evolving, communication and media researchers will continue to study the implications for agenda setting in online environments and agenda building. Furthermore, scholars are beginning to develop new frameworks for understanding the public agenda in our high-choice digital world (Bentivegna & Artieri, 2020).

Summary

Walter Lippmann (1922) was the first to describe the agenda-setting process. He wrote about the news media's responsibility for shaping the public's perception of the world and creating a pseudo-environment for each news consumer—the so-called "pictures in our heads." The first empirical test of Lippmann's ideas about agenda-setting was Maxwell McCombs and Donald Shaw's Chapel Hill study (1972), which tested the influence of campaign coverage on public perceptions of issue importance.

Hundreds of agenda-setting studies were conducted in the years following the Chapel Hill study, and it continues to be a popular area of research today. Traditional agenda setting is often described in terms of Cohen's memorable characterization of the press as stunningly successful in telling people what to think *about*. Research has identified second-level agenda-setting effects that reveal mass media are also successful in telling people *how* to think by increasing the salience of a particular attribute. Meanwhile, the third-level of agenda setting examines how salience of "bundles" of objects and attributes seen in news coverage can be transferred to the public; thus telling audiences how to *associate* news items.

Initially, agenda-setting research examined the influence of news media in shaping people's perceptions of the world. Later, agenda-setting research expanded to ask the question, "Who sets the media agenda?" Control over the flow of news information by media professionals is an important function called gatekeeping. Researchers began a new phase of inquiry in the 2000s investigating the psychology behind agenda setting, and various teams of researchers have put forth new dual-path models to explain agenda setting. Other areas expanding agenda-setting theory include agenda building, intermedia agenda setting, and agenda melding.

With all of these new developments regarding agenda setting, the core axiom remains the transfer of salience among agendas (McCombs & Valenzuela, 2021).

> From a parsimonious hypothesis about the effects of the news media on the public's attention to social and political issues during election campaigns, agenda setting has expanded to include propositions about the psychological process for these effects, the influences that shape communication agendas, the impact of specific elements in their messages, and a variety of consequences of this agenda-setting process. Expanding beyond the traditional news media, agenda-setting theory has become a detailed map of the effects of the flow of information about public affairs through a growing plethora of communication channels. (p. xiv)

7

Framing

> The social world is . . . a kaleidoscope of potential realities, any of which can be readily evoked by altering the ways in which observations are framed and categorized.
>
> —Murray Edelman, 1993

News consumers are bombarded daily with stories from news media, and we form attitudes and opinions and make judgments based in part on the information we read, watch, and hear. In the previous chapter on agenda setting, we learned that mass media have the power to set our issue agendas (i.e., tell us what to think about). They also decide how to present that information, which can affect the way we think.

Media effects researchers have examined the ways that journalists put together news stories and the effects of their choices on media consumers. You will recall from the agenda-setting chapter that attribute agenda setting focuses on the media not only telling viewers *what* to think about but also *how* to think about it. Research on this process has developed into a field of study called **framing**. Some media effects scholars believe framing should be distinguished from agenda-setting research and priming research both theoretically and experimentally, and thus it receives its own chapter in this book.

This chapter examines the theory of framing, the effects of framing, frame-building and frame-setting approaches, and types of frames. Then we take a look at relevant recent research and future directions for the study of framing.

Foundations of Framing Theory

Framing theory finds its roots in the fields of psychology and sociology. Psychologically oriented research typically has featured micro-level studies of individuals, whereas sociologically oriented research has generated macro-level studies of society.

According to Tewksbury and Scheufele (2020), the psychological perspective of framing comes from Sherif's (1967) work on "frames of reference" and from prospect theory (Kahneman, 2003; Kahneman & Tversky, 1979, 1984). Individuals make judgments and perceive the world within certain frames of reference, and these frames of reference can be set up in such a way to impact individual judgments and perceptions. **Prospect theory** expands this idea by noting that perceptions depend on the point of reference of the information that is being given. In other words, framing a message in different ways will result in different interpretations.

The sociological approaches to framing are drawn from attribution theory (Heider, 1959; Heider & Simmel, 1944) and frame analysis (Goffman, 1974). **Attribution theory** states that people simplify their perceptions of social reality by making judgments about what causes others to act in particular ways. They attribute the actions they observe to either personal, social, or environmental factors (Tewksbury & Scheufele, 2020). In **frame analysis theory**, people not only attribute the cause of actions but they also rely on socially shared meanings to categorize information into schemas in their minds called "primary frameworks" (Goffman, 1974, p. 24). "Primary frameworks are often described as relatively stable socially shared category systems that human beings use to classify new information" (Tewksbury & Scheufele, 2020, p. 52). These primary frameworks serve as important tools for information processing in society; both societal and media messages often employ specific frameworks to influence audiences' interpretations.

What Is a News Frame?

"A frame can be a phrase, image, analogy, or metaphor that a journalist uses to communicate the essence of an issue or event. Frames simplify the story-writing process for journalists and help audiences make sense of what they encounter in the news" (Moy et al., 2016, p. 7).

Tewksbury and Riles (2018) note that "a frame's primary function is to provide a comprehensible structure of interpretation" (p. 142).

Distinguishing Framing from Similar Concepts

The core idea of framing research is that news frames suggest how audiences can interpret issues and events. "At their most powerful, frames invite people to think about an issue in particular ways" (Tewksbury & Scheufele, 2009, p. 19). Furthermore, news frames can substantially influence audiences' attitudes, beliefs, and behaviors (Tewksbury & Scheufele, 2020). Other processes of news consumption and information processing (i.e., information effects, agenda setting, and persuasion) "bear at least passing resemblance to framing effects and very likely occur in parallel to framing" (p. 53). The discussion below distinguishes framing from these other concepts.

Information Effects

If a news story contains information on an issue that has never been covered before, people will learn about that issue from the presentation. The learned information can be facts, figures, images, etc. The frame unifies that information, building associations among concepts that can influence audiences. If people already have set ideas about a particular issue covered by the news media, the manner in which a story is framed may cause them to rethink that issue or react in some way to the information that is being presented. Other times, if audiences already have an available frame, the mere presence of a frame in a news story can affect the audience. Tewksbury and Scheufele (2020) explained that "a very effective frame needs no supporting arguments to give it meaning within some text. Frame effects can rely upon culture-based meanings, norms, and values" (p. 53).

For example, Simon and Jerit (2007) found that people exposed to a news story about a new abortion procedure were affected by the way the story was framed by only changing the words "baby" and "fetus." When presented with the version of the news story that referred to a "baby," people were more likely to support regulation of the new abortion procedure. Those presented with an article that used the terms "fetus" and "baby" equally in the story also experienced these framing effects. However, audiences who read the "fetus"-only version of the story were significantly more likely *not* to express support for regulation of the procedure. This example highlights the fact that a single word can function as a frame that affects people's thoughts and attitudes about a complex topic (Tewksbury & Scheufele, 2020).

Tewksbury and Scheufele (2020) summarized the differences between information effects and framing effects this way:

> Information effects result from a process in which people acquire beliefs and impressions of an issue and its context. A framing effect occurs when a phrase, image, or statement links issues to particular beliefs that carry with them concepts for interpreting the origins, implications, and treatment of the issue. It is very likely that news stories frequently have both framing and information effects, but a story could presumably have one effect and not the other, as the Simon and Jerit (2007) study illustrates. (p. 53)

Agenda-Setting Effects

In the agenda-setting chapter, we learned that coverage of certain issues by news media set the agenda for the public or made those issues salient in the minds of the audiences. Framing is often compared to second-level (or attribute) agenda setting. Weaver (2007) wrote that although both agenda setting and framing focus on ways of thinking, "framing does seem to include a broader range of cognitive processes—such as moral evaluations, causal reasoning, appeals to principles, and recommendations for treatment of problems—than does second-level agenda setting (the salience of attributes of an object)" (p. 146). However, there are still some that argue for framing to be subsumed into agenda setting (McCombs, 2014).

Framing theorists distinguish framing effects from agenda-setting effects by pointing out that framing goes beyond the mere *accessibility* of particular issues in the news by inviting audience members to apply the information or ideas in particular ways. As Tewksbury and Scheufele (2020) note, framing researchers

> suggest that the primary effect of a frame is to render specific information, images, or ideas *applicable* to an issue. The basis of a psychological difference between

agenda setting and framing, therefore, lies in this accessibility/applicability distinction. Brewer, Graf, and Willnat (2003) demonstrated that information primes that merely raised the accessibility of potentially relevant concepts failed to prompt audiences to use those considerations in their judgments. Rather, frame-suggested links between issues and concepts seemed to exert substantial influence on audience members. This result supports the primacy of applicability in understanding framing effects.

Perhaps ironically, the best way to conceive of the difference between framing and agenda setting is to recognize that accessibility and applicability go hand-in-hand in everyday information processing. . . . All else being equal, the accessibility of a construct is positively associated with the likelihood that it will be used to interpret some political issue. Likewise, the more applicable a construct is to an issue, the more likely people are to use it when thinking about the issue. Naturally, then, a construct that is both accessible and applicable is all that much more likely to be used (whether the relationship between these two processes is additive or interactive in this situation is unclear). (pp. 54–55)

Persuasion Effects

Framing researchers also distinguish framing studies from persuasion studies because some framing studies focus on the origin or evolution of news frames. Persuasion studies involve the presentation of persuasive information that audiences usually recognize as having persuasive appeal and intent. In contrast, news frames are built from journalists' choices of what words, details, images, etc. to include in their reports, and research suggests that news consumers are unaware of both the presence and influence of news frames (e.g., Tewksbury et al., 2000). "As a result, the message processing that persuasion and frame audiences are undergoing is likely very different" (Tewskbury & Scheufele, 2020, p. 54).

Another important difference between persuasion research and framing research is the effects that are measured. Persuasion researchers try to measure changes in *attitudes* and message adoption due to exposure to persuasive messages. Framing researchers, on the other hand, seek to discover audience *interpretations* of news information (Tewksbury et al., 2000).

In summary, perhaps the best way to consider the relationship between information, persuasion, agenda setting, and framing effects is to observe that all four effects can result from exposure to a news message. They are distinct processes and very likely operate in tandem, together determining the ultimate outcome of exposure to the news. (Tewksbury & Scheufele, 2020, p. 55)

Frame Building and Frame Setting

Framing studies generally come in two types. The first includes studies that examine the way frames are put together by news professionals and are included under the heading of **frame building**. The second type is comprised of studies that examine the effects on audiences from news frames, known as **frame setting**.

Frame Building

Studies that examine frame building focus on the way frames are constructed—by journalists, by politicians, and by culture. Issues come to be framed in a particular manner because of the way elites present the information or by the way the media present the information in line with events and popular culture (Scheufele & Nisbet, 2007).

Research on new reporting processes has identified five factors that can influence how journalists cover stories, including the ways they frame the information they present. Journalists may be influenced by

- societal norms and values;
- the pressure and constraint of news organizations;
- pressures from interest groups or policy makers;
- their professional routines; and
- each journalist's own political orientation or ideology (Shoemaker & Reese, 1996, 2014; Tuchman, 1978).

The elite in society—interest groups, politicians, government agencies—routinely attempt to frame issues that the media cover (Gamson & Modigliani, 1987; Miller et al., 1998; Nisbet et al., 2003; Nisbet & Huge, 2006; Scheufele, 1999). Research has shown that the elite are sometimes successful (e.g., Andsager, 2000) but at other times are not (e.g., Miller et al., 1998) in influencing journalists on the way issues are framed. For instance, earlier research into frame building in political candidates' press releases and subsequent news coverage found that candidates were only moderately successful at getting journalists to use the same frames (Miller et al., 1998). More recent research into frame-building efforts by political candidates has looked at the use of social media during their campaigns and the effects on their followers' engagement with posts (e.g., Sahly et al., 2019).

The surrounding culture also plays a part in the way journalists frame issues. Journalists are a part of the culture in which they work, and their stories reflect that culture. Because of this, frames "often are unnoticed and implicit, their impact is by stealth" (Van Gorp, 2007, p. 63). For example, the cultural movement to separate church and state matters in the United States has been taken seriously by journalists, who do not frame stories from a religious standpoint.

Lastly, figurative language (e.g., similes, metaphors, and analogies) can contribute to frame building (Burgers et al., 2016). Metaphors equip "people with a means of connecting political issues to their own experiences" (Brugman et al., 2017, p. 183). Tewksbury and Scheufele (2020) note that figurative language can be used to summarize background concepts applicable to an issue; it can also suggest new ways for audiences to think about an issue. "Most importantly for the study of news framing, figurative language can influence audience interpretations of an issue without explicitly presenting new information and arguments concerning the issue. That is, such frames influence applicability without creating information effects" (Tewksbury & Scheufele, 2020, p. 57). Examples of these types of frames include the use of a "Frankenfood" metaphor to frame the origins and implications of genetically modified foods (Hellsten, 2003). More recently, the "war" metaphor was heavily used in coverage of the COVID-19 pandemic by using words like "front line," "combat," "fight," and "defeat" (Wicke & Bolognesi, 2020; Zheng, 2020).

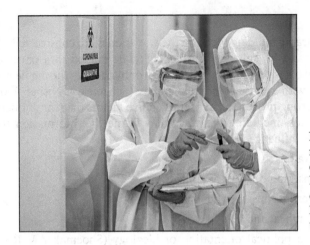

News media often used a "war" metaphor to frame their reporting during the COVID-19 pandemic. Doctors and nurses were often described as being on the "front lines" of the "fight" against the virus.

Frame Setting

Frames can influence individuals to make connections in their minds that can result in four outcomes—defining the issue, determining the causes for an issue, noting the implications for an issue, and the treatment of an issue (Entman, 1993; Tewksbury & Scheufele, 2009).

A frame can wield its influence cognitively (i.e., the way the individual *thinks* about an issue) or affectively (i.e., the way the person *feels* about an issue). It all depends on the way a story is constructed—whether it focuses on conflicts among elite policy makers, the results of certain policy changes on individuals, or a human-interest angle that stirs the emotions of individuals (Price et al., 1997).

In one study, researchers presented participants with two identical stories, except the stories had different lead (beginning) sentences and different headlines. One story's headline and lead paragraph favored the economic benefits of large farms that raised hogs, whereas the other story pointed out serious environmental concerns with such farms. Participants who read about the economic benefits of the farms showed support for the farms, and those who read about the environmental problems associated with the farms were significantly less likely to support them. Not only did the way the story was framed significantly affect individual opinions on large hog farms but the effect also persisted for several weeks after the people read the stories (Tewksbury et al., 2000).

Such research makes it clear that journalists need to take seriously their duty to present all sides of an issue and not focus on only one aspect. It also demonstrates the power that reporters have to influence the public in the way they frame stories.

Another study tested tolerance for a Ku Klux Klan rally by presenting individuals with stories framed in different ways. The people who read articles that framed the rally in terms of free speech were significantly more tolerant when asked about Klan speeches and rallies than were those who read articles that framed the rally in terms of public order (Nelson et al., 1997).

Studies also have shown that individual differences among audience members affect the power of the framed information. People with particular beliefs and attitudes—or *schemas*—about a topic tend to accept new information on the topic more than those without such existing schemas (Rhee, 1997; Shen, 2004). People react differently to news stories, depending upon their personal knowledge, experiences, and attitudes. For example, someone who has lived with Type 1 diabetes for many years would accept information about new treatment options for the condition. They would attend to the information and possibly store the information based on their existing schema for the autoimmune disorder.

Research has shown that frames can have effects on attitudes—either formation of attitudes or change of attitudes (Brewer, 2002; Nelson & Oxley, 1999)—and sometimes on behaviors (e.g., Borah, 2014; Boyle et al., 2006; Valentino et al., 2001).

Most studies of framing effects have focused on short-term evaluations; for that reason, they resemble priming studies. Framing theorists point out that the best way to show that people apply the information they learn in frames is through longitudinal research (Price & Tewksbury, 1997; Tewksbury & Scheufele, 2009). These studies test for applicability of the frame weeks or months after exposure, which differs from priming studies.

A model of frame setting put forth by Baden and Lecheler (2012) suggests that knowledge is the most influential moderator on how long framing effects last. Essentially, people with enough knowledge to process new information and applicability beliefs—but not dense enough knowledge that the frame presents no new concepts—are the most likely to experience persistent frame-setting effects. What this model predicts could be thought of as a so-called "Goldilocks zone" for lasting framing effects: Too little or too much knowledge will not lead to a persistent effect, but a medium level of knowledge is just right. Subsequent research by Lecheler et al. (2015) into the effects of repetitive exposure to frames supported the model.

Research in Framing

Numerous framing researchers have noted the dramatic increase in framing studies in recent decades. Obviously, we cannot review all of that research here, but we want to provide an overview of a few areas that receive a great deal of attention from framing researchers.

Framing and War

Framing of war has been a popular area of research, and many studies have examined frame building and the Iraq War. Leading up to the war, Fox News and CNN were more likely to use pro-war frames and less likely to use antiwar frames when compared to ABC, CBS, NBC, CNBC, and public radio and television; overall, all of the news outlets studies used frames that aligned with the Bush administration's framing (Harmon & Muenchen, 2009). Another frame-building study examined *The Washington Post*'s coverage of the Abu Ghraib prison incident that involved abuse of Iraqi prisoners by U.S. military personnel. Previous studies (Bennett et al., 2006, 2007) had suggested that the newspaper accepted the Bush administration's framing of the incident as an isolated instance of wrongdoing perpetrated by a few bad individuals—the "a few bad apples" frame—and did not suggest that administration policy had anything to do with the scandal. In a content analysis of the *Post*, Porpora et al. (2010) found evidence to the contrary. They said that the newspaper did engage in counter-framing measures. The researchers concluded that the earlier research, which had coded for instances of the words *abuse* and *torture*, had not delved deeply enough into the content of *The Washington Post* during the period of investigation. More recently, Speer (2017) also found that *The New York Times* avoided the White House's preferred frame of "War on Terror," preferring to use the military's "insurgency" frame.

Framing of the Iraq War was also different from country to country. While online news sources from Coalition countries (i.e., the United States and United Kingdom) preferred the "rebuilding of Iraq" frame, Arab outlets in Egypt and Qatar emphasized "military conflict" and "violence of war" frames (Dimitrova & Connolly-Ahern, 2007). Schwalbe and her colleagues have examined how the war was framed through visual media. *TIME, Newsweek*, and *U.S. News & World Report* framed the war from an American-centered perspective by focusing on conflict, politicians, and human interest, while generally avoiding images of antiwar protests, destruction, and the Iraqi military (Schwalbe, 2013). "What readers do not see can be as revealing as what they do see. Not showing the harsh realities of war can give readers a lopsided, sanitized view that dehumanizes both enemy troops and noncombatants" (Schwalbe, 2013, p. 254). Earlier work on visual framing at the onset of the war revealed how visual frames changed from week to week, moving sequentially through five categories: shock and awe, conquering troops, heroes, victory, and control (Schwalbe et al., 2008). For more on the effects of visual framing, see this chapter's Research Spotlight.

Framing and Politics

Politics is another popular topic for framing researchers. Research shows that exposure to partisan conflict frames in news can polarize the audience along partisan lines (Han & Yzer, 2020). Scholars have also looked at both how media outlets frame political candidates and how candidates' campaigns engage in frame building. Entman (2010) studied news frames of Sarah Palin during the 2008 presidential election campaign. He found evidence of slanted framing and expanded framing theory to include systematic studies of bias in news reporting. "Slanted framing results from the interaction of real-world developments, cultural norms, and journalistic decision rules with the sometimes proficient and other times maladroit efforts of competing elites to manage the news" (p. 389).

A study of how news media framed Hillary Clinton after she had an emotional moment during the 2008 primary found that she was framed both as a strategist appealing to female voters and as someone unable to withstand the pressures of a national campaign (Curnalia & Mermer, 2014). The authors noted that "frames reveal the gender double bind that female candidates face, as it suggests that women have to be feminine in order to win, but that very display of femininity is also evidence that they are not viable candidates" (p. 26). A more recent framing study examined memes of Clinton during the 2016 presidential election; gendered frames were used to portray her as weak, ill, dishonest, untrustworthy, and unqualified (Nee & De Maio, 2019).

Researchers also studied the frame-setting effects when Kamala Harris was tapped to be Joe Biden's running mate and after she was inaugurated as vice president. Harris made history as the first woman and first Black and Asian American elected as vice

Identity frames of gender and ethnicity had little impact on voters after Kamala Harris's nomination as Joe Biden's running mate, but they increased support for both Vice President Harris and President Biden after their inauguration.

president of the United States. Much of the news coverage highlighted her gender and multiethnic background. Interestingly, those identity frames had little effect on attitudes toward the Biden-Harris ticket following her nomination. However, after Harris was sworn in, headlines framing her as a woman (gender only) or a Black woman (race and gender) boosted support for both her and President Biden (Clayton et al., 2022).

Sahly et al. (2019) examined how both Donald Trump and Hillary Clinton engaged in frame building on social media during the 2016 election and what effects it had on audience engagement. There were differences in framing between Trump's Twitter and Facebook content. On Twitter, Trump frequently used morality and responsibility frames when attacking his opponents; he also used more negative emotional frames than Clinton. However, Trump's Facebook posts shifted to more positive frames. Meanwhile, Clinton's Twitter and Facebook content was similar, focusing on conflict and positive emotional frames. Regarding audience engagement, use of conflict and morality frames resulted in more retweets for both candidates. The use of emotional frames increased favoriting tweets but decreased commenting on Facebook. Sahly and his colleagues said these findings make sense because

> favoriting is an instantaneous activity that expresses how audiences "feel," whereas commenting is a deliberative activity that articulates how audiences "think." The results suggest that emotional frames might be effective in soliciting immediate engagement but could be counterproductive if a campaigner intends to mobilize discursive, deliberative participation. This suggests that campaign strategists should consider the anticipated mode of audience engagement when building emotional framing. (p. 10)

Framing and Social Issues

Many framing scholars have examined framing of social issues like race relations and immigration. In 2014, Michael Brown, a Black teen, was fatally shot by Officer Darren Wilson in Ferguson, Missouri. Protests after Brown's death received extensive media coverage. News outlets framed protestors as troublemakers, and journalists continued to rely on police and local leaders as official sources of information, in spite of both being under heavy criticism at the time (Blackstone et al., 2017). "However, in framing the information, ten percent of tweets from news organizations studied presented the information as potentially unreliable or suspect" (p. 610). Meanwhile, online news sources targeted toward African American audiences utilized racial injustice frames, whereas online outlets targeting general audiences used conflict frames to highlight tensions between protestors and police (Riddle et al., 2020).

Immigration is another social issue that has received a lot of attention in framing research. Recent research shows that the conflict frame is the most dominant in reporting on immigration, and stories that used a human-interest frame were more likely to have a pro-immigration tone (Kim & Wanta, 2018). In a study of visual framing of immigration, political frames (i.e., photos showing politicians) increased negative emotions, which led to negative attitudes (Parrott et al., 2019). Meanwhile, human-interest visual frames (i.e., photos showing immigrants and refugees as regular people) increased positive emotions and enhanced positive attitudes toward immigration. (See this chapter's Research Spotlight for more on this study.)

Researchers have also investigated how framing may impact someone's willingness to help after learning about a social issue. Kogen and Dilliplane (2019) found that framing an issue (i.e., malaria in Africa) as unsolvable increased sympathy, which promoted a willingness to help address the problem. Conversely, framing the issue as solvable increased perceived efficacy, which also increased willingness to help. Powell et al. (2018) examined multimodal framing effects between text-based articles and news videos about the European refugee crisis. Regardless of the frames used (i.e., refugees as victims versus refugees as intruders), the articles resulted in stronger intentions to help (i.e., donating money, sharing a story, and signing a petition) than the news videos.

RESEARCH SPOTLIGHT

Portrayals of Immigrants and Refugees in U.S. News Media: Visual Framing and its Effect on Emotions and Attitudes
Scott Parrott, Jennifer Hoewe, Minghui Fan, and Keith Huffman (2019)
Journal of Broadcasting & Electronic Media, 63(4), 677–697

In this study, researchers examined news photographs of immigrants and refugees shared on Twitter by news outlets in all 50 states to determine the predominant visual frames used in reporting on immigration. Parrott and his colleagues then conducted an experiment to see what effects the images had on people's emotions and attitudes about immigrants and refugees.

Research Questions and Hypotheses

RQ1: What frames appear in the photographs that news outlets use to communicate information about immigrants and refugees through the social media platform Twitter?

H1a: Individuals who encounter a human-interest visual frame in regard to immigrants and refugees will demonstrate a more positive emotional response, compared to people who encounter a political visual frame.

H1b: Individuals who encounter a political visual frame in regard to immigrants and refugees will demonstrate a more negative emotional response, compared to people who encounter a human-interest visual frame.

H2a: Negative emotions will lead to (1) increased perceptions of threat from immigrants and refugees; and (2) a decreased willingness to allow immigrants and refugees to live in the United States.

H2b: Positive emotions will lead to (1) reduced perceptions of threat from immigrants and refugees; and (2) an increased willingness to allow immigrants and refugees to live in the United States.

RQ2: Will a human-interest frame or a political frame have any direct effect on perceptions of threat or willingness to allow immigrants and refugees to live in the United States?

Study 1

The researchers first compiled a list of the Twitter handles for the largest regional news outlet in each state based on circulation and number of Twitter followers. Twitter's advanced search function was then used to find any tweets from the outlets using "immigrant" or "refugee." Results showed 5,833 tweets with the search terms. Of those, 1,791 tweets contained photos. For the overall analysis, 802 randomly selected photos from the sample were examined.

Results

Descriptive statistics were used to answer RQ1. Politicians were shown in 317 (40%) of the photos, followed by immigrants or refugees depicted as everyday people in 243 photos (30%). Photos of political rallies appeared 90 times (11%). Images of law enforcement and immigrants or refugees under arrest rarely appeared.

Study 2

Three hundred participants were recruited via Mechanical Turk. A majority (54%) were women. Ages ranged from 18 to 72 years old. All participants were U.S. based. Regarding race, 242 (80.7%) identified as white, 16 (5.3%) as African American, 16 (5.3%) as Hispanic, 15 (5%) as Asian/Pacific Islander, four (1.3%) as Native American, and one (0.3%) selected some other race/ethnicity. Out of all participants, 12 (4%) indicated they were either an immigrant or refugee.

Method

Participants were randomly assigned to evaluate three tweets that included photos of politicians or of immigrants or refugees as regular people. Aside from the photos, all other tweet content was the same (i.e., news organization, text in the tweet, number of likes and retweets). Each tweet was about immigrants or refugees either seeking or being given permission to resettle in the United States.

Participants answered questions to measure positive and negative emotions, attitudes toward U.S. immigration policies, perceptions of threats from refugees or immigrants, and political ideology. Data from three participants were removed after they failed a manipulation check. Participants' responses were analyzed in SPSS.

Results

Results indicated that participants who were exposed to human interest frames were significantly more likely to have more positive emotions and less negative emotions than participants who saw tweets with political frames, thus supporting H1a. Negative emotions predicted a drop in desire for more refugees and immigrants to be allowed into the United States and an increase in the perception of threat, which supported H2a. Conversely, positive emotions predicted a higher desire to allow more immigrants and refugees into the country and a decreased perception of threat, thus supporting H2b. As for RQ2, the direct effects on policy attitudes and threat perceptions did not reach significance.

> Taken together, these studies demonstrate that the way journalists cover migration, specifically the information they highlight through photographs, does indeed carry consequences for audience members' interpretation of these issues. (p. 691)

Interestingly, Taylor and Gunby (2016) suggested that negative framing for social movements may not be a bad thing. Instead, negatively framed stories are more likely to include in-depth reporting about the movement.

The Future of Framing Research

Despite several decades of framing research, there are still many questions to be answered. This includes questions about different types of frames, issues regarding frame distribution and frame selection in today's media landscape, isolating framing effects from information effects, and refining terminology in framing research.

Types of Frames

Researchers have studied the effects of specific types of frames on audience reactions. These include frames like gains vs. losses, episodic vs. thematic (*episodic* involves reporting in terms of a specific event or person; *thematic* frames give a story more general context, presenting broader patterns, trends, and/or issues), strategy vs. issue, or human interest, conflict, and economic consequences frames (see Tewksbury & Scheufele, 2020, for a review).

Tewksbury and Scheufele (2020) pointed out that the common inductive approach to framing research often identifies unique frames in each study. They argue that this has a limiting effect on framing research, in that it ignores the possibility of **master frames** (Snow & Benford, 1992) or frames that might exist in the culture that could apply across issues. Benford (2013) gave an example of "equal rights and opportunity" master frame that was successfully used during the civil rights movement in the United States. Later movements were able to adapt the frame to their campaigns.

Frame Distribution

As described earlier, framing studies typically fall into either the frame-building or frame-setting category; however, technological advancements in news dissemination have opened up a potential third area of framing research: **frame distribution** (Tewksbury & Riles, 2018). Falling between frame building and frame setting, frame distribution describes the numerous ways in which frames from stories reported by journalists reach audiences, who can then appropriate and incorporate elements of the frame into new messages (Moy et al., 2016; Tewksbury & Riles, 2018; Tewksbury & Scheufele, 2020).

Commenting on news stories and sharing stories on social media allow audience members opportunities to share the original frame intended by journalists or issue advocates; however, it also gives audience members the chance to reframe information in a new way. For example, Holton et al. (2014) studied framing in online health articles and comments made by readers, finding that readers' comments did not echo frames used in the stories.

Furthermore, Tewksbury and Riles (2018) suggested that social media platforms could reshape the balance of power in society: "The people with the largest social networks or those at the hubs of large intersecting networks can exert more influence over the framing process. They have newfound power to select and disseminate the frames they prefer" (p. 157). Hashtags on social media can also be framing-distribution devices and give audiences the opportunity to take part in the framing process (see Borah, 2018, for a review). However, there are still many questions about how frames shift from news stories to personal communication in social media environments (Tewksbury & Scheufele, 2020).

Frame Selection

As we have discussed in various other chapters, audiences play an active role in their media consumption. In regard to framing, only limited research has examined how selective exposure affects whether someone is exposed to a specific frame in news coverage (Tewksbury & Riles, 2018). Audience members have more power than ever before to choose what media they want to consume, and previous research has shown people will choose some news outlets over others because of political beliefs (e.g., Iyengar & Hahn, 2009). Trussler and Soroka (2014) found that politically interested readers are more likely to select stories that are framed negatively and include strategic political frames (e.g., frames focusing on the "horse race" and conflict-driven aspects of politics). Earlier research into framing and online news selection suggested that frames used in article headlines influenced readers' choices (Zillmann et al., 2004). In that study, participants spent more time reading stories with headlines utilizing conflict and agony frames, which the researchers attributed to the compelling nature of those specific frames.

Tewksbury and Scheufele (2020) caution that audiences' growing selectivity could result in fewer frames used in discussions about politics, problems, and policies: "If audience members are likely to choose stories that feature a relatively narrow range of frames, both advocates and journalists will have fewer tools at their disposal, resulting in a narrow range of policy options and actions" (p. 63).

Detangling Framing Effects from Information Effects

Throughout the expansive body of literature on framing, many studies fail to clearly differentiate framing effects from information effects (Cacciatore et al., 2016). Part of this issue has to do with **external validity** (i.e., how well a study's findings can be generalized to the real world) and **internal validity** (i.e., how confident researchers are that the causal relationship being studied is not influenced by other variables).

In the real world, framing and content go hand-in-hand, but this confounds framing effects and information effects in terms of research (Tewksbury & Scheufele, 2020). When studies include both frame and informational content manipulations, they have high external validity but limited internal validity. Unfortunately, these studies also have limited ability to ensure framing effects were not contaminated by information effects. For instance, imagine a study of media coverage about NASA's plans for a manned mission to Mars that compared stories on the scientific gains of such an endeavor against stories about the high cost and risk of the mission. The stories would contain different facts and arguments, which means this study would have more to do with presentation of the information and less to do with framing.

On the other hand, studies that contain frame manipulation but not content manipulation have limited external validity but high internal validity. This type of study would be able to isolate a "pure" framing effect. To study this type of effect, researchers would have to ensure that stories contained all the same information with only the frames altered. Being able to differentiate between framing and information effects is key to the future of framing research (Tewksbury & Scheufele, 2020).

More Precise Framing Terminology

Earlier in this chapter, we compared framing to similar concepts. There has been an ongoing debate among mass communication scholars about the similarities and differences of agenda setting, framing, and priming. Some say framing and priming should be included as subcategories of agenda setting (e.g., Ghanem, 1997; McCombs, 2014). Others argue that these three areas of research should be distinct from one another (e.g., Chernov & McCombs, 2019; Scheufele, 2000, 2004; Scheufele & Tewksbury, 2007).

Semantics contributes to the difficulty of distinguishing framing from priming and agenda setting. Priming and agenda setting are phrases that denote active influence of one thing on another—a media effect. *Framing* is the activity of putting something in a particular light or saying it in a particular way. It does not imply an effect of any kind, even though most framing studies test for effects of the news frame. In other words, people can be "primed" and their agendas can be "set" by mass media, but a mass media consumer cannot be "framed" (except for a crime). The term refers only to a preliminary activity—not an effect.

According to Cacciatore et al. (2016), one way to delineate more effectively between framing and information effects would be to use more precise terminology in framing research. They suggest abandoning "framing" as a general term. Furthermore, they recommend refocusing framing research on **equivalence framing** (which examines differences in the presentation of equivalent information) and moving away from **emphasis framing** (which examines how certain aspects of an issue may or may not be emphasized). Equivalency frames manipulate the presentation of logically equivalent phrases (e.g., 5% unemployment or 95% employment) while emphasis frames manipulate the content of a communication. Emphasis frames are not logically identical; they present different—but potentially relevant—considerations. For example, depending on which emphasis frame is used (e.g., law and order, police brutality, or race), news stories can include—or exclude—different information, which can lead to different interpretations among news consumers (Fridkin et al., 2017).

McCombs (2014) argues that emphasis framing is synonymous with attribute agenda setting but that equivalence framing is unique to framing research. McCombs uses the term "rhetorical frames" to describe equivalence frames.

> A classic example of equivalence/rhetorical frames is "the glass is half full" versus "the glass is half empty." As an attribute in agenda setting, these two frames are identical, both describing the amount in the glass as 50%. As rhetorical frames, they are very different. (Chernov & McCombs, 2019, pp. 74–75)

Although a narrower definition of framing is becoming more acceptable, Chernov and McCombs (2019) note that framing theory's diverse roots "may not allow scholars to reconcile parallel conceptualizations and methodologies that are currently in the field" (p. 75).

Summary

Framing theory is rooted in the fields of psychology (micro-level studies of individuals) and sociology (macro-level studies of society). For many years, media effects researchers have focused attention on the power involved in framing information and the effects that framing can have on the minds of media consumers. Though there may be come conceptual overlap, framing research can be distinguished from agenda-setting research and priming research both theoretically and experimentally.

Framing can result in several types of effects, including knowledge, persuasion, or agenda setting. Framing studies usually deal with news stories created by journalists who are supposed to be objective in their presentations, and audiences usually do not suspect that the information may be persuading them or at least influencing the way they perceive certain issues.

Generally, framing studies come in two types. The first type, frame building, examines the way frames are put together by news professionals. The second type, frame setting, examines the effects of news frames on audiences.

As framing researchers look to the future, they continue to identify types of frames and how frames are distributed and selected in the ever-changing media environment. Some scholars are also calling for a return to a narrower definition of framing and for more precise terminology within the field.

8

Cultivation

> Where people see a possible relationship between exposure to stories and to beliefs about the world, they see the possibility of cultivation.
> —Michael Morgan, James Shanahan, & Nancy Signorielli, 2017

Do you watch a lot of television? Cultivation research has shown that if you do, then chances are high that if someone asked you to estimate crime rates in the United States you would grossly overestimate the frequency of crime in the real world. You would probably be more fearful of falling victim to a crime than a person who does not watch much television.

Since the dawn of mass mediated entertainment, people have feared powerful and harmful media effects, especially on that segment of the population considered most vulnerable—the nation's children. As a result, the media effects tradition has been one of the most prolific, socially important, and highly scrutinized areas of mass communication research.

In the 1920s and 1930s, before television became a household fixture, feature films thrilled millions of moviegoers across the country; however, those same films raised public concerns because of their violent and sometimes sexually explicit content. The Payne Fund studies brought together a group of social scientists who examined the effects of movies on the nation's youth. They found that some children could experience negative effects from movies filled with violence and booze.

Once television became entrenched in daily routines, apprehension about negative media effects assumed a dominating presence on the public and political agenda. In the 1960s and 1970s, U.S. presidents appointed commissions and charged them with studying television violence and assessing its effects on young people.

Through the years the research findings have varied, but many studies have shown that the connection between viewing television and developing a distorted image of reality—closer to what is depicted on television—often occurs.

The Cultural Indicators Project

Cultivation theory developed as one attempt to explain the influence of television on its viewers. The cultivation tradition grew out of a media violence research project called the Cultural Indicators Project, headed in the 1960s by George Gerbner (1919–2005), a University of Pennsylvania (and later Temple University) communication scholar. The Cultural Indicators Project conducted research in three areas to explain the effects that media messages had on society. The first was **institutional process analysis**, which examined the production, management, and distribution of media messages. The second was **message system analysis**, which investigated images in media content, such as gender roles, portrayal of minorities, and the way certain occupations are depicted. Finally, **cultivation analysis** examined "the impact these messages and this message system had on society by analyzing the relationship between television viewing and reality perception" (Busselle & Van den Bulck, 2020, p. 69).

Simply stated, **cultivation theory** proposes that over time heavy viewers of television develop—or cultivate—views of the world similar to what they see on television. (We will discuss how cultivation theory applies to other forms of media later in this chapter.) The first major cultivation study published found that heavier viewers were more likely to see reality as a "mean" world filled with violence and crime (Gerbner & Gross, 1976). Cultivation researchers call this the **mean world syndrome**.

People who watch a lot of television tend to overestimate the frequency of crime in the real world and tend to view the world as a more dangerous place than those who watch less television.

Since the early days of the project, cultivation research has expanded to encompass many topics in addition to media violence. Investigators now explore the relationship of long-term television viewing with the ingraining of various perceptions, values, and beliefs on audiences.

Cultivation research has typically involved two research methods: content analyses of television programs and survey methods to assess viewer perceptions of the world. In measuring cultivation effects related to violence, researchers developed the Mean World Index, a tool for measuring perceptions of the prevalence of violence and danger in the world (Signorielli, 1990). Among various demographic groups, heavy viewers of television score consistently higher on the Mean World Index than do light viewers.

The "symbolic world" of television is very different from objective reality, and this disparity has been a major point of interest for cultivation researchers. Examples of the distorted realities presented on television abound. For instance, analyses of network television programs have revealed that most TV characters are young, energetic, and appealing. Few shows feature elderly people (age 65 or older) in starring or important roles. When older people are used as characters, they often portray sick or dying people. Television does not accurately reflect the true proportions, conditions, or health status of the elderly population in U.S. society today.

Violent crime serves as the most obvious example of television's distortion of reality. With all the gun battles, fist fights, karate chops, and high-speed chases that occur as standard fare on most programs, it should come as no surprise that in a given week, more than half of all the leading characters on television are involved in some kind of violent act. Actual crime statistics from the FBI tell a much different story. In a single year, less than 1% of the population in the United States actually fall victim to criminal acts.

Research has shown that among certain groups of people, heavy viewers of television tend to cultivate the same distorted pictures of reality that they see on television. Using the examples of the condition of the elderly and the frequency of criminal acts, heavy viewers tend to *underestimate* the number of elderly people in the U.S. population as well as their health status. In addition, heavy viewers consistently *overestimate* real-world crime statistics.

Since the Cultural Indicators Project began, most studies have revealed only low-level statistical evidence of a cultivation effect, but the consistency of such findings offered credence to the theory. Gerbner and his associates insisted that cultivation has considerable implications for society, despite low-level statistical correlations and effect sizes. They often made the analogy between cultivation effects upon society and global temperature changes upon the climate—a variance of only a few degrees in temperature would result in another ice age, they say (Morgan et al., 2009).

The Cultural Indicators Project

- Initiated in 1967 by George Gerbner.
- First study conducted for President Johnson's National Commission on the Causes and Prevention of Violence.
- Introduced the Mean World Index, an instrument used to measure people's perceptions about violence and aggression in the world.
- Performed content analysis of televised violence each year.
- Focused on content of network television, both primetime dramas during the week and daytime programming on weekends.
- Investigated the cultivation effect on audiences due to television portrayals with regard to issues of gender, age-role stereotypes, the family, and so forth.

Cultivation used to be described as a *hypothesis* rather than a formal media effects *theory* due to a lack of theoretical and supporting empirical evidence to explain how the cultivation process occurs. In particular, early studies did not reveal the psychological dimensions of cultivation—how television viewers learn to construct their views of social reality.

Through the years, most explanations of media effects have been firmly grounded in theories of cognitive psychology. Media effects scholars trained in this tradition criticized the work of Gerbner and his associates for their lack of emphasis on cognitive processes (Bryant, 1986; Hawkins & Pingree, 1990; Potter, 1994). Much of the criticism was constructive, leading Gerbner and other cultivation researchers to make revisions and improvements in their explanation of cultivation (see Morgan et al., 2017, for a review). Later studies began to fill this void and answer the critics. Shrum (1995, 1999, 2007) and others have done much to explore the psychological dimensions of cultivation and the mediating factors present. Research that explores the cognitive dimensions of cultivation continues.

Studies have shown that certain characteristics among audiences tend to make cultivation effects more or less pronounced; for example, educational level has been shown to affect cultivation effects. Among heavy viewers of television, those with higher levels of education are less likely to have their views of the world influenced by television. Age has been shown to be another mediating factor, as has need for cognition.

In this rest of this chapter, we delve into the research domain of cultivation analysis, including the concepts and criticisms associated with cultivation and models that help us understand different levels of cultivation effects. We close with some of the most recent studies in cultivation research, including studies of genre-specific effects.

Concepts and Criticisms

Cultivation adherents argue that television, as a "wholesale distributor of images," is different from other mass media (Morgan & Signorielli, 1990, p. 13). It serves as the *great storyteller* of our age. Programs are produced to appeal to millions of viewers. Even very young viewers find it easy to become enthralled by an entertaining television show.

According to these researchers, the diverse publics that make up the United States—the poor children living in a housing project in Georgia, the wealthy families living in an exclusive neighborhood in New York, the farm families in middle America, the sorority sisters on a West Coast campus, and retirees living along Florida's sunny shores—all tend to think more alike when watching television because they all receive similar messages. All television programs, from entertaining action programs to news programs, possess similar, repetitive patterns, sometimes called myths, "facts," or ideologies. These patterns are thought to influence viewers' perceptions of the world. Long-term exposure to these overall patterns of television programming is most likely to result in "the steady entrenchment of mainstream orientations for most viewers" (Gerbner et al., 1994, p. 25).

Mainstreaming and *resonance* are two of the principal concepts that underlie cultivation analysis. The concept of **mainstreaming** assumes that dominant sets of attitudes, beliefs, values, and practices exist within cultures and that "TV viewing tends to draw disparate audiences together" (Morgan et al., 2017, p. 311). Patterns emerge across the spectrum of television programming—patterns regarding outcomes to various situations, gender roles, minority representations, and so forth. These patterns result in a "mainstream" set of attitudes, beliefs, and values that are repetitively presented on television. Heavy television viewers tend to cultivate similar mainstream views; mainstreaming acts as a homogenizing agent across segments of society. Cultivation researchers Nancy Signorielli and Michael Morgan (1996) defined the concept in this way:

> Mainstreaming means that heavy viewing may absorb or override differences in perspectives and behavior which ordinarily stem from other factors and influences. In other words, differences found in the responses of different groups of viewers, differences that usually are associated with the varied cultural, social, and political characteristics of these groups, are diminished or even absent from the responses of heavy viewers in these same groups. (p. 117)

Resonance occurs when real-world events support the image of reality shown on television. Whenever direct experience is consistent with mediated messages from television, the messages are reinforced—they *resonate*—and the cultivation effect is amplified. For example, research has shown that the heavy television viewers who are most likely to fear crime are those who live in inner-city areas where crime rates are high (Morgan, 1983).

Cultivation researchers stress that the concept of cultivation assumes that television and its viewers *interact* in a dynamic process. The extent to which a person cultivates the messages seen on television depends upon a number of factors. Some people are more susceptible to cultivation influence due to personality traits, social background, cultural customs, and even their past television viewing experiences. Gerbner et al. (1994) explained the interaction process in this way:

> Although a viewer's gender, or age, or class makes a difference in perspective, television viewing can make a similar and interacting difference. Viewing may help define what it means, for example, to be an adolescent female member of a given social class. The interaction is a continuous process (as is cultivation) beginning with infancy and going on from cradle to grave. (p. 23)

Cultivation scholars define television exposure in terms of time. They assume that television messages are relatively *uniform* in nature and that viewing of television is *nonselective*. In other words, the narrative structure of various types of programs—cartoons, dramatic movies, crime shows—often resemble each other in terms of casting, action, and other factors. In this sense, scholars say, the messages are uniform. The concept of nonselective viewing is based on the idea of *ritualized viewing* or habitual viewing—watching television at certain times and being confined to whatever programs are offered for viewing at those times. Some networks actively promote habitual viewing, like NBC's long-running shows that were once dubbed "Must See TV." Of course, DVRs and streaming services (like Netflix, Hulu, and Paramount+) are making ritualized viewing increasingly uncommon.

As mentioned previously, many have argued that complex psychological processes form the basis for cultivation effects, but most early studies were criticized

---

Key Concepts of Cultivation

- Television serves as the great storyteller—the wholesale distributor of images—with programs designed to appeal to the entire population
- Mainstreaming
- Resonance
- Interaction
- Complex psychological processes

---

because they were not directed toward identifying the cognitive components that would *explain* cultivation effects rather than *merely showing* the connection between television viewing and beliefs about social reality (Hawkins & Pingree, 1990; Potter, 1993). The ways in which cognitive mechanisms involved in cultivation resemble those of social learning theory needed to be examined, critics said (Bryant, 1986). A number of scholars expressed concerns about statistical controls and interpretation of cultivation findings (Hirsch, 1980; Hughes, 1980; Wober, 1978). Still others questioned the causal order of effects in cultivation research and objected to certain theoretical formulations (Doob & MacDonald, 1979; Zillmann, 1980).

Shrum (2017) concluded that cultivation theory "persists despite the early criticisms, and its longevity and ubiquity are arguably strong testaments to its validity. Tests of the theory have been approached from various theoretical perspectives (cultural, social, psychological) and the convergent findings suggest cultivation rests on strong theoretical ground" (p. 304).

Many procedural crime dramas on television feature violent crimes, such as murder and sexual assault. Most episodes of shows in the *NCIS* franchise (such as *NCIS: New Orleans* pictured here) depict grisly crime scenes, which could contribute to the cultivation of ideas about real-world violence.

Theoretical Bases for Cultivation

Cultivation assumes that television has become a primary source of shared meanings and messages for people in the United States and throughout the world. It has evolved into a medium with many functions for people in modern society. According to Signorielli and Morgan (1996):

> Television has thus become our nation's (and increasingly the world's) most common and constant learning environment. It both mirrors and leads society. It serves, however, first and foremost as our storyteller; it has become the wholesale distributor of images which form the mainstream of our popular culture. The world of television shows and tells us about life—people, places, striving, power, and fate. It presents the good and bad, the happy and sad, the powerful and the weak, and lets us know who or what is successful or a failure. (p. 114)

In the words of Morgan and Signorielli (1990), cultivation analysis "is designed to understand gradual, long-term shifts and transformations in the way generations are socialized (not short-term, dramatic changes in individuals' beliefs or behaviors)" (p. 19).

Gerbner and colleagues (1994) elaborated on the differences in theoretical bases for cultivation and other types of media effects research:

> Traditional effects research is based on evaluating specific informational, educational, political, or marketing efforts in terms of selective exposure and measurable differences between those exposed and others. Scholars steeped in those traditions find it difficult to accept the emphasis of cultivation analysis on total immersion rather than selective viewing and on the spread of stable similarities of outlook rather than on the remaining sources of cultural differentiation and change. . . . Cultivation theory is based on the results of research finding a persistent and pervasive pull of the television mainstream on a great variety of conceptual currents and countercurrents. The focus on broad commonalities of perspective among heavy viewers of otherwise varied backgrounds requires a theoretical and methodological approach different from traditional media effects research and appropriate to the distinct dynamics of television. (pp. 20–21)

First- and Second-Order Judgments

Other researchers insist that psychological processes underlie the cultivation process, and therefore the *cognitive paradigm* should serve as the theoretical base. A major breakthrough in our understanding of how cultivation works came with Hawkins and Pingree's (1981, 1990) introduction of first- and second-order cultivation effects, which are based upon first- and second-order judgments. **First-order judgments** measure quantifiable concepts related to frequency, such as the percentage of people who will be victims of crimes or the percentage of the workforce who are police officers, doctors, or lawyers. Busselle and Van den Bulck (2020) explained how researchers quantify first-order judgments:

> First, respondents in surveys or participants in experiments can be asked to give an actual numerical estimate of what they believe the real world looks like. Second, using content analysis, it is possible to quantify the extent to which the same con-

cepts are a part of television's reality, as Gerbner did when developing violence pro-files that charted the demography of TV violence. Third, researchers can attempt to determine the actual demography in the real world. With first-order judgments, then, it is possible to compare television to the real world and to examine the extent to which viewers' perceptions resemble either version of reality. (p. 73)

Second-order judgments, on the other hand, refer to attitudes and beliefs, such as the belief that the world is a mean and violent place or attitudes about whether other people can be trusted.

Hawkins and Pingree (1982) theorized that the cultivation process involves *learning* and *construction*. The viewer learns by watching television, perceiving, and remembering the contents. The viewer constructs an outlook regarding the real world based upon television viewing. The researchers assumed that first-order judgments were stored in a person's memory and then used to make second-order judgments (Hawkins & Pingree, 1981), but little evidence was found at the time to support this learning model (Shrum, 2017). However, some research has provided support (see Schnauber & Meltzer, 2016).

The Accessibility Model of Cultivation Effects

Shrum is credited with solving "the first and second-order puzzle by looking at processes that explain the role of memory in judgment formation" (Busselle & Van den Bulck, 2020, p. 74). Shrum's (1995, 2009) accessibility model of cultivation effects has two general propositions:

- First, watching TV results in increased accessibility, or ease of recall, of constructs and exemplars often seen on television programs.
- Second, judgments of social reality, which are typically thought to be both difficult to answer accurately and are rarely of importance to study participants, are made via heuristic processing.

Shrum (1995, 1999, 2007) determined that televised images and messages remembered by audience members are readily available when asked an impromptu question. These memories operate under an **availability heuristic**, meaning they provide a cognitive shortcut for audience members. In various studies, Shrum found that heavy viewers of television tended to give quick responses to questions about social reality, and this indicated that an answer was more readily accessible to them. As Busselle and Van den Bulck (2020) summarized:

> Most of us do not have a ready-made judgment about the proportion of medical doctors who are female or other typical *first-order* estimates. This means that when cultivation researchers ask study participants to report their estimates, the respondent or participant does not *recall* an estimate but will have to *produce* one. . . . Shrum argued that heavy viewers would be able to recall or imagine certain events more easily if they have seen many television portrayals of them. (p. 74)

Additional research has revealed that people who view more crime dramas or other TV genres are more likely to store in their memories scenes and messages from those particular genres, and those memories are accessible to them when they make judgments about the social world around them (Shrum, 2002).

Furthermore, viewers typically do not think about the source of their memories. As a result, they fail to automatically filter out memories of content watched on television. However, when people are prompted to process information more carefully or to think about the source of recalled information, the first-order cultivation effect is eliminated (Shrum, 1997, 2001; Shrum et al., 1998).

Bradley (2007) found support for Shrum's heuristic model of cultivation effects and that the ability to process information systematically can make cultivation effects disappear. For example, priming people with non-TV examples and asking them to think carefully before answering the questions posed by cultivation researchers and to attempt to answer correctly, greatly diminishes any cultivation effects—even among heavy viewers of television. Additionally, people tend to think more carefully about questions cultivation researchers ask when responding to mail surveys rather than telephone inquiries (Shrum, 2007). Cultivation effects were strongest among those who responded to telephone surveys.

The Online Processing Model of Cultivation Effects

Although the accessibility model helps us understand memory-based judgments (i.e., estimates about crime or demographics of the workforce), it does not explain judgments of attitudes, beliefs, or values. Rather than being held in memory like first-order judgments, second-order judgments develop via *online processing*—meaning in real time, not on the internet—while people are consuming media content. Shrum (2017) explains the process this way:

> Online judgments are made when information being processed in real time is used to spontaneously construct new judgments (e.g., form a new attitude) or update existing ones (e.g., change an attitude). This general process is consistent with the process of cultivation: As people watch television and encounter specific information as well as the overall "message" of the program content, they may construct or update their beliefs, attitudes, and values in ways that reflect the TV message. As such, this resembles a typical persuasion process. The persuasive communication (TV message) effectively changes attitudes. (pp. 303–304)

Furthermore, Shrum (2004) said cultivation effects on attitudes and beliefs can result from one of two routes to persuasion—the *central* and *peripheral* routes (see our explanation of the Elaboration Likelihood Model in Chapter 10). According to Shrum, "When motivation or ability to process information *during viewing* is high, the cultivation effect is *increased*" (p. 337). Several studies by Shrum and his colleagues provide support for this model of TV viewing influencing second-order judgements through online processing (Shrum, 2017). For example, the amount of TV viewing has been shown to correlate with materialistic values (Shrum et al., 2005). The effects were stronger for participants with greater motivation and ability to process while watching, which aligns with ELM persuasion research. A later study replicated those findings experimentally, confirming that levels of materialism increased after viewing materialistic programs (compared to nonmaterialistic ones) and that the effect was stronger for participants who were more immersed in the shows (Shrum et al., 2011).

Other Areas of Cultivation Research

Cultivation researchers continue to answer their critics and to collect evidence for cultivation effects. Researchers have expanded their domain to include countries throughout the world. Additionally, scholars continue to explore how cultivation can take place in today's evolving media landscape, including studying cultivation effects in specific genres of television programming and from binge watching.

Studies of Cultivation Around the World

Studies have examined cultivation effects in foreign countries that import considerable television programming from the United States. Findings have varied, but most indicate interactions between television viewing and cultural contexts. Most reveal a cultivation of attitudes toward violence, values, social stereotypes, and other areas of interest similar to the distorted pictures of reality shown on television. Sweden (Reimer & Rosengren, 1990), Argentina (Morgan & Shanahan, 1995), and Japan (Saito, 2007) are among the several countries that have been the focus of such cultivation analyses.

In Australia, Pingree and Hawkins (1981) found that students with high levels of exposure to television programming from the United States were more likely to rate Australia as a dangerous place to live.

In a study conducted in South Korea, women with high levels of exposure to U.S. television programs were more likely to have liberal views regarding marriage, clothing, and music, but Korean males who were heavy viewers of U.S. programming supported traditional Korean cultural values and expressed hostility toward the United States (Kang & Morgan, 1988). Another Korean study examined the cultivation effect of viewing particular television dramas and people's perceptions about the number of single adults and the number of children in married families. Heavy viewers of dramas that positively depicted the life of singles and families with fewer children tended to cultivate overrated perceptions about the number of unmarried Koreans and the number of Korean married couples having no children (Jin & Jeong, 2010).

In Japan, heavy viewers of television demonstrated traditional views about gender in society, except among the most conservative viewers (Saito, 2007). Conversely, heavy viewers in Korea cultivated more liberal ideas about family values and women in society (Kang & Morgan, 1988).

Researchers found that heavy viewing of exported U.S. television programs in the countries of South Korea and India resulted in feelings of deprivation (Yang et al., 2008). Heavy viewers among South Koreans reported more dissatisfaction with their own society, as did heavy viewers in India, who also reported dissatisfaction with their personal lives.

In Israel, heavy viewers of U.S. programming tended to estimate the number of occupations in the United States in accordance with what they viewed on television, whereas viewers of Israeli programs did not (Hestroni, 2008; Hestroni et al., 2007).

As mentioned earlier, findings from studies around the globe have had mixed results when it comes to cultivation effects. For instance, a recent study of people in Trinidad found no relationship between fiction, news, and reality shows and fear of real-world crime (Chadee et al., 2019).

Cultivation Effects in TV Genres

Cultivation research began at a time where there were only a few television channels on the airwaves. The world of television has changed drastically since that time with the explosion of cable and satellite services throughout the 1980s and 1990s and the current boom of streaming services, such as Netflix, Peacock, and Disney+. This plethora of options "created the opportunity both for greater delivery and availability of content in the most popular genres and for viewers to concentrate their consumption within a favorite genre" (Busselle & Van den Bulck, 2020, p. 75). Furthermore, some researchers argue that genre-specific cultivation research is important because of the differences across genres (Bilandzic & Busselle, 2008; Bilandzic & Rössler, 2004).

Researchers have studied a wide variety of genres, including daytime talk shows (Woo & Dominick, 2001), reality TV (Jahng, 2019; Riddle & De Simone, 2013), television news (Lee & Niederdeppe, 2011), romantic shows and movies (Lippman et al., 2014; Timmermans et al., 2019), medical dramas (Cho et al., 2011; Chung, 2014; Quick, 2009), and crime-related shows (Ceonen & Van den Bulck, 2016), just to name a few.

Scharrer and Blackburn (2018a) studied exposure to genre-specific programs and audience's perceptions of masculinity. For viewers of sports, reality TV, and police/detective shows, genre viewing rather than the amount of viewing was more strongly associated with endorsement of traditional and stereotypical masculine gender roles by both men and women. In contrast, there were differences among men and women who were heavy viewers of sitcoms. Women were less likely to endorse traditional masculinity, whereas men were more likely to endorse traditional masculine gender norms, particularly regarding the importance of sex and avoiding femininity.

Cultivation effects have also been found in research into the reality TV subgenre of "docusoaps" or "surveillance" programs, such as *16 and Pregnant, Teen Mom, Jersey Shore, Keeping up with the Kardashians,* and the *Real Housewives* and *Real World* franchises. Watching docusoaps predicted approval of both verbal and physical aggression (Scharrer & Blackburn, 2018b). Furthermore, heavy viewers of these types of shows were also more likely to think real-world women engage in bad behaviors like gossiping and arguing more than real-world men (Riddle & De Simone, 2013). Heavy viewers were also more likely to overestimate the prevalence of affairs and divorces and the emphasis on sex in romantic relationships (e.g., having sex on a first date, having multiple sex partners).

High exposure to television news cultivated perceptions among heavy viewers that juvenile crime was on the increase (Goidel et al., 2006). Those who watched reality crime shows expressed perceptions that crime overall was increasing and also perceived that more juveniles were imprisoned for violent crimes than was actually the case.

Other research on the heavy viewing of crime dramas indicated that it leads to concern about crime in society (Busselle, 2003; Holbrook & Hill, 2005). Heavy viewing of crime shows on television was associated with support for the death penalty (Holbert et al., 2004). Vivid portrayals of crime on crime-related dramas were connected with viewers' tendencies to give a higher estimate of crime's prevalence in the real world (Riddle, 2010). Researchers have explored differences in television genres.

Exposure to televised nonfiction (news and reality cop shows) provided more evidence of a cultivation effect of fear of falling victim to an actual crime than did the viewing of crime dramas (Grabe & Drew, 2007).

Studies of medical dramas (e.g., *Grey's Anatomy*, *ER*, *House*) found that heavy viewers are more likely to underestimate the seriousness of chronic illnesses like cardiovascular disease and cancer and minimize the importance of treatment (Chung, 2014). Perceiving *Grey's Anatomy* as realistic or credible mediated the relationship between how often someone watched the show and how courageous they believed real-world doctors to be (Quick, 2009; for more on this study, see this chapter's Research Spotlight). In general, perceived realism is related to greater cultivation effects (see Busselle & Van den Bulck, 2020, for a review).

Grey's Anatomy, the longest-running medical drama on television, has been included in several cultivation studies to explore effects on audiences' perceptions of health issues. Because of the show's emphasis on the love lives of the doctors, it has also been studied for cultivation effects stemming from romantic media.

RESEARCH SPOTLIGHT

The Effects of Viewing *Grey's Anatomy* on Perceptions of Doctors and Patient Satisfaction
Brian L. Quick (2009)
Journal of Broadcasting & Electronic Media, 53(1), 38–55

This study examined the effect that watching *Grey's Anatomy* could have on viewers' attitudes and beliefs about their real-world doctors. Cultivation theory has been used primarily in a broad context (i.e., overall television consumption); however, Quick examined the cultivation effects of watching a single series. Because TV doctors are often seen performing risky operations and choosing unconventional treatments, Quick noted that television doctors are often seen as courageous. But do those feelings about TV doctors carry over to one's own real-life doctor? Citing research that found cultivation effects were greater after watching programs with which the audience had little personal experience (e.g., the daily activities of a hospital emergency room), Quick formulated the following hypotheses and research question.

(continued)

Hypotheses and Research Question

H1: The viewing of *Grey's Anatomy* is positively associated with perceived credibility of this program.

H2: Perceived credibility of *Grey's Anatomy* is positively associated with perceived courageousness of real-world doctors.

H3: The viewing of *Grey's Anatomy* is positively associated with perceived courageousness of real-world doctors.

RQ1: Does perceived credibility of *Grey's Anatomy* mediate the relationship between *Grey's Anatomy* viewing and perceived courageousness of real-world doctors?

H4: Perceived courageousness of real-world doctors is positively associated with patient satisfaction with their real-world doctors.

Method

Grey's Anatomy was selected to be the focus of this study due to its popularity. During the 2005–2006 season, the show averaged 19.9 million weekly viewers, making it the fifth most-watched series of the season.

Two hundred sixty-nine participants took part in a paper-and-pencil survey regarding their television viewing habits—particularly of the second season and first five episodes from season three of *Grey's Anatomy*—and their beliefs about doctors. Participants were asked how many of the 32 episodes in the sample they watched.

To measure credibility (whether the program was perceived as realistic), the survey asked participants to complete the following sentence: "In general, images and story lines communicated in medical dramas like *Grey's Anatomy* are _____." Participants then used a 5-point scale to rate realism, credibility, and believability. Courageousness was measured with questions asking participants to rate doctors on a scale of one to five for characteristics like heroism, bravery, courageousness, cleverness, and brilliance. Lastly, to measure patient satisfaction, participants responded to two questions: (a) "In general, I am satisfied with my physician," and (b) "On average, my physician meets my health needs." These questions were also answered using a 5-point scale.

Results

On average, participants reported watching almost 13 episodes of *Grey's Anatomy* during the second and third seasons. Seventy-eight participants had watched all 32 episodes; on the other hand, 95 never saw the show.

Analyses showed support for Hypothesis 1; viewing *Grey's Anatomy* was associated with stronger perceptions about the show's credibility. Secondly, Hypothesis 2 was also supported. The belief that the show was credible was positively related to the perception that real-world doctors are courageous. However, Hypothesis 3 was not supported; simply being a heavy viewer of *Grey's Anatomy* did not positively relate to perceptions of real-world courageousness. Regarding Research Question 1, perceived credibility did appear to be a key factor for cultivating ideas about real-world doctors' courageousness. Lastly, Hypothesis 4 was supported; the more courageous participants perceived their real-world doctors to be, the more satisfied they were with them.

Overall, the findings support cultivation theory. The study contributed to the cultivation research by highlighting the importance of perceived credibility in promoting cultivation effects. It also demonstrated that cultivation effects can be created by watching a single series.

Timmermans et al. (2019) studied the exposure of 18- to 25-year-olds to romantic media (e.g., *Friends, New Girl, How I Met Your Mother, Gossip Girl, Sex and the City*, and the often-studied *Grey's Anatomy*) and real-world fear of being single. Although the overall analysis of the cross-sectional sample did not show any significant relationship between watching romantic media and fear of being single, there was a significant relationship for women who were single.

> Being in a relationship appeared to "protect" women from being more vulnerable than men to cultivation effects of romantic media content exposure on self-reported fear of being single. . . . The moderation results reported in this study appear to make sense from the perspective of psychological processing approaches to cultivation research: the relationships are greatest for people who are likely to identify with single characters and process information about singlehood to a greater extent because of its personal relevance. (p. 166)

These findings support the concept of *resonance* in cultivation research discussed earlier in this chapter.

Cultivation in the Evolving Media Environment

Cultivation research in the 2020s and beyond will need to consider the growing popularity of streaming services, especially as a growing number of households continue to cut the cord on their cable or satellite subscriptions. In fact, the way we watch television has changed dramatically over the last few decades. From VCRs to DVRs and DVDs to streaming, the way we watch TV is very different than it was a few years ago. In fact, many of us "watch TV" on our phones, tablets, and laptops rather than on actual televisions, which could pose methodological challenges for future cultivation researchers. After all, "the word 'television' meant different things for Gerbner and his research subjects than it might for today's researchers and study participants" (Busselle & Van den Bulck, 2020, p. 77).

In addition to technological changes in television viewing, binge watching has become more prevalent in recent years. In a recent study of popular binge-watched shows on Netflix, exposure to those shows was positively related to an increase in "mean world" perceptions and to a decrease in beliefs that other people will be altruistic (Krongard & Tsay-Vogel, 2020).

Video games are another area for cultivation researchers to explore. Players of *Asheron's Call 2* experienced significant cultivation effects (Williams, 2006). Study participants who played the game were more likely than those in a non-playing control group to overestimate real-world tendencies for armed robbery. Players of *Grand Theft Auto IV* were more likely to give higher estimates of people dying in car accidents and from drug overdoses than were people who did not play the game, thus providing evidence of first-order cultivation effects (Chong et al., 2012). However, there was little support for second-order effects. In fact, researchers found counter-cultivation effects: people who played *GTA IV* were more likely than those in the control group to think stealing cars in the real world was difficult, despite its prevalence in the video game. Other research in this area has examined hostile sexism, interpersonal aggression, and rape myth acceptance (Fox & Potocki, 2016).

Researchers are also examining the potential for cultivation on the internet. In one study, there was little support for cultivation for those who consumed news online compared to those who watched news on television (Roche et al., 2016). However, research into social media has had more promising results for cultivation researchers. Tsay-Vogel et al. (2018) studied Facebook use over a 5-year period and found that using the site cultivated more relaxed attitudes about privacy, which subsequently increased users' self-disclosure both online and offline. More recently, Stein et al. (2021) incorporated cultivation theory along with social comparison theory into a study of Instagram use and body image. Their findings revealed that viewing public content (i.e., not posts from friends or family) correlated to stricter judgments about strangers' weight (especially among women) and an increased risk of eating disorders (among both men and women). Interestingly, heavier Instagram browsing of public content was not linked to higher dissatisfaction with one's own body. The researchers speculate that this could be because young social media users "prefer the profiles of their friends and colleagues as a resource for their self-evaluation, whereas browsing public Instagram profiles might serve to modify future impressions of others" (p. 94).

From streaming TV to video games to social media, these studies highlight the fact that much of our media consumption takes place on a screen—even if it is not on a traditional television. Despite these evolutions in media consumption from when cultivation was initially studied,

> one must assume that, at least for important developmental periods of their lives, significant numbers of citizens today are enveloped in mediated environments that provide common messages on screens that vary in shape and size and are ubiquitous. Further, those messages, while distributed across thousands of different channels may be relatively homogenous with respect to important aspects of social reality. (Busselle & Van den Bulck, 2020, p. 77)

Cultivation researchers point out that concentration of ownership will continue to produce similarities across media and channels, despite the diversity of choices available to today's media consumers. Nonetheless, cultivation research should continue expanding its horizons to include investigations into the impact of messages from these new media technologies.

Summary

Simply stated, *cultivation* proposes that over time heavy viewers of television develop views of the world similar to what they see on television—generally a "mean" world filled with violence and crime. (Although, researchers have also found cultivation effects from consuming other forms of media and studying different variables.) Cultivation research has typically involved two research methods: content analysis of television programs and survey methods to assess viewer perceptions of the world. The "symbolic world" of television is very different from objective reality, and this disparity has been a major point of interest for cultivation researchers. Violent crime serves as the most obvious example of television's distortion of reality. Research has shown that among certain groups of people, heavy viewers of television tend to cultivate the same distorted pictures of reality that they see on television.

Since the Cultural Indicators Project began, most studies have revealed only low-level statistical evidence of a cultivation effect, but the consistency of such findings offered credence to the theory. *Mainstreaming* is one of the principal concepts that underlie cultivation analysis; another is *resonance*.

Through the years, most explanations of media effects have been firmly grounded in theories of cognitive psychology. Media effects scholars trained in this tradition often criticized cultivation researchers for not explaining the underlying processes at work, but cultivation scholars began to explore these processes in terms of cognitive psychology and persuasion. Studies have explored the cognitive processing involved in cultivation, including models that explain first- and second-order judgments.

Researchers have examined cultivation effects in foreign countries that import considerable television programming from the United States. Findings have varied, but most indicate interactions between television viewing and cultural contexts.

More recent research has explored the heavy exposure to specific television genres, such as crime or medical dramas and reality programs. Cultivation researchers are also finding new ways to study cultivation on social media, video games, and other forms of media.

9

Uses and Gratifications

Television: Teacher! Mother! Secret lover.

—Homer Simpson, *The Simpsons*

In the checkout line at the grocery store, a young woman reaches for the latest copy of *Cosmo* because she is interested in the new fashion trends that are going to be popular that year. Another woman, much older and a gardening enthusiast, picks up the current issue of *Better Homes and Gardens* to get the latest tips on spring planting arrangements. The woman's 13-year-old granddaughter begs for the latest copy of her favorite teen magazine with a pop music singer on the cover.

In front of the television one evening, a couple and their children are arguing over which program to watch. The father wants to watch *Jeopardy!* to show off his trivia knowledge (and because he hopes his kids will learn something while watching). The mother wants to watch a home renovation show on HGTV to get ideas for remodeling the kitchen. One sibling wants to watch *SpongeBob SquarePants* to help them forget about a bad day at school. The other is anxious to stream the latest episode of a new Star Wars series on Disney+ for an evening of sci-fi adventure.

These examples demonstrate how people use media content to satisfy a variety of very personal needs. Their behavior is often goal-oriented when they select media fare, and their selections are based on the satisfaction they anticipate they will receive by viewing a certain program, reading a certain magazine, or visiting a particular website.

The uses and gratifications approach assumes that individual differences among audience members cause each person to seek out different messages, use those messages differently, and respond to them uniquely. Many social or psychological factors cause audience members to select different media fare as well as to experience divergent if not idiosyncratic media effects. The approach assumes that a person's social and psychological makeup is as responsible for media uses and effects as are the media messages themselves.

Rather than focusing on the direct effects from mass media on audience members, **uses and gratifications** (U&G) research examines the motivations and behavior

144

of viewers—*how* and *why* they use media. It assumes that viewers actively choose programs or other media content to gratify their individual needs.

This chapter examines the U&G approach to media effects. After a brief look at the functions of mass media in society, we then trace U&G research historically. We discuss several basic assumptions and criticisms of U&G and the communication models used to explain uses and effects. We will also explore a few areas of U&G research, such as social media, podcasts, and parasocial phenomena.

Societal-Level Functions of the Mass Media

To understand why individuals use media, it may be helpful to examine the reasons why societies use media. Lasswell (1948) identified three major functions that media serve in a society. First, media keep viewers aware of what is going on in the world around them by *surveying the environment* to distribute information. The second function, *correlation of environmental parts,* provides an interpretation of how various components of the environment operate, allowing audience members to form a more accurate and perhaps holistic view of the world around them. Finally, media messages *transmit social norms and customs* to new generations of audiences. Transmission of the social heritage is a powerful and controversial function. For example, people in countries throughout the world who receive programs produced in the United States have complained of Western cultural imperialism, or the imposition of Western social norms and values on citizens with very different cultural norms.

Researchers have identified several other functions of mass media in society. Wright (1960) added *entertainment,* which we will discuss in greater detail later in this chapter. This important function recognizes that many people use mass media for personal enjoyment. Another function is *parasocial interaction* (Horton & Wohl, 1956), which describes the phenomenon that occurs when viewers feel as though they have a personal connection with television personalities (e.g., talk show hosts Jimmy Kimmel and Kelly Clarkson or news anchors Hoda Kotb and Lester Holt) and film because they see and hear them so often. *Escapism,* another function, assumes that television entertainment allows viewers to escape from real-life problems (Pearlin, 1959). Other related functions that have been identified include *anxiety reduction* (Mendelsohn, 1963) and *play* (Stephenson, 1967), two escapist functions that allow audience members to put aside the pressures and tensions of real life and experience enjoyment while being entertained with fantasy.

U&G Research: A Brief History

Most research activity in the area of U&G looks at why people choose to consume certain forms of media. Instead of focusing on what the media do to people, these studies ask the question: What do people do with the media? (Klapper, 1963; Rubin, 2009).

A series of studies in the 1940s examined people's motives for listening to certain radio programs and for reading the newspaper. Some scholars conducted their studies before the phrase "uses and gratifications" appeared (Berelson, 1949; Herzog, 1940, 1944; Lazarsfeld, 1940), typically using the labels "functionalism" or "functional analysis" for this early empirical research. These researchers were more interested in the motives of audience members than the effects of the media content, and their findings were quite revealing. Their studies examined (1) radio quiz shows to determine their various appeals among audiences, (2) daytime serials to find out what gratifications women received from listening to them, and (3) newspaper readership to determine motives for reading or subscribing. The results indicated listeners enjoyed the media selected for various reasons—from the educational appeal of quiz shows to the emotional release provided by daytime serials.

By the 1970s, researchers had begun to categorize the various motives for media use (Katz et al., 1973). Needs were related to social and psychological factors. Viewers used the media to help them gain more understanding of themselves, the people close to them, or society at large. In addition, people used media to increase personal status and to strengthen relationships.

Other researchers developed their own typology for audience gratifications (McQuail et al., 1972). They found that people use television to be diverted, to fulfill the need for personal relationships, to reinforce personal identity, and to keep abreast of happenings in the world around them.

Rosengren and Windahl (1972) were among the first to suggest that media uses and effects should be linked. Research should inquire into the effects of particular gratifications or the effects of particular uses of the media. People depend on the media to fulfill certain needs—vicarious experience and escapism or involvement or interaction—and explored how these needs lead to particular effects. Other researchers have suggested that a synthesis of the two research realms would be logical and beneficial. These research domains have some obvious similarities in that each examines the consequences of mass communication from an individual or societal level—changes in attitudes, perceptions, or behavior.

Since the mid-1970s, research has provided a greater understanding of the uses and effects of mass media. For example, studies by Greenberg (1974) and Rubin (1979) found that motives for viewing changed with a person's age. Most habitual viewers liked watching comedies rather than news. Most viewers seeking excitement tended to watch action/adventure programs. Based on the work of these two researchers and to answer criticisms regarding lack of uniformity, uses and effects researchers have adapted similar measures for viewer motives. Most U&G scholars recognize the following motives for media use among audience members: learning, habit, companionship, arousal, relaxation, escapism, or a way to pass time (Rubin, 1994).

Assumptions of U&G

Several basic assumptions lie at the heart of the U&G perspective. Scholars identified most of these assumptions in 1974. Since then, others (e.g., Palmgreen, 1984; Palmgreen et al., 1985; Rubin, 1986, 2002; Rubin & Windahl, 1986) have learned more about media audiences and have expanded the list of assumptions inherent in U&G. Rubin (2009) provided a concise list of these assumptions.

The Active Audience

U&G research assumes that media users are active participants in the communication process and that audience activity varies. The communication behavior of audience members is motivated, purposive, and goal directed. Audiences make media selections based on personal motivations, goals, and needs; these same factors influence what they actually see and hear.

Additional research has attempted to explore audience involvement with the media (Rubin & Perse, 1987). Studies have found that individual audience members experience variability in their media activity levels, involvement, and reasons for viewing at various times. For example, viewers motivated by diversion are not particularly active when they seek programs, but those viewers do actively seek out information when they watch news programs (Levy & Windahl, 1984).

The U&G approach assumes media users are active, selecting media content based on personal motivations and needs. It also assumes that media content competes with other forms of communication for selection, attention, and use.

Media Use for Gratifications

This perspective emphasizes that viewers use the media for a variety of reasons—sometimes to obtain information about something that interests or troubles them or sometimes for entertainment. The purpose of the media use or selection is always to gratify the needs or wants of the audience member.

Finn (1992) described the motives for media use as falling under one of two headings: proactive or passive. Examples of proactive media use are watching a TV show to learn more about a subject of interest, watching a movie for the express purpose of being entertained, or using the internet to find information for a project at school or work. In other words, the media user actively seeks something from the media based upon their wants, needs, and motives. As the name suggests, passive motives describe the use of media in a lackadaisical (passive) sense, what we could consider "mindless consumption." For example, sometimes we turn on the television simply because it is there, just to "see what's on." We are not actively seeking information, entertainment, or anything in particular. This does not mean that we will not be entertained or learn something—we very well might. Passive motives denote only that we did not begin the viewing experience with a particular, proactive motive in mind.

Media use orientations can be described as either ritualized or instrumental (Rubin, 1984). **Ritualized use** describes habitual use of the media to pass time or to divert one's attention from real-life concerns. **Instrumental use** characterizes active and goal-oriented use of the media. Watching news programs or a particular documentary because of a desire for news and information is an example of instrumental media use; listening to favorite music to calm one's nerves before playing a big game is another.

Social and Psychological Factors

A host of social and psychological factors mediate people's communication behavior. When someone watches a newscast or dramatic program, their reaction to the information depends upon individual personality, social circumstances, psychological disposition, and so forth. For example, people who are not particularly mobile and those who are lonely rely heavily on media use (Perse & Rubin, 1990; Rubin & Rubin, 1982).

Competition, Mediation, and Moderation

Media compete with other forms of communication (such as interpersonal interactions or even other forms of media) for selection, attention, and use to gratify our needs or wants. A viewer must pay attention to media messages in order to be influenced or affected by them. Personal choices and individual differences are strong influences that mitigate media effects. A person's motives mediate patterns and consequences of media use. For example, if you plan on auditioning for the next season of *American Idol*, it is likely that you will watch every episode of this and related television talent shows (e.g., *The Voice, America's Got Talent*) this season. Lack of sufficient individual initiative results in stronger influences from media messages.

Furthermore, media use motives can also moderate effects. For example, motives of entertainment and passing time can predict affinity for reality television (Papacharissi & Medelson, 2007), and a motive of voyeurism was related to more enjoyment of reality shows (Nabi et al., 2006). Xie and Lee (2008) found that arousal motives were related to greater enjoyment of arousing movie trailers. As Krcmar (2017) concluded, "a motive can mediate an effect but, in turn, be enhanced by it" (p. 2001).

Five Key Assumptions of U&G

Rubin (2009) laid out the five key assumptions that ground U&G research:

- Selection and use of media is motivated, purposive, and goal-directed.
- Audience members are active participants in initiating the selection and use of media to satisfy needs and desires.
- Social and psychological factors guide behavior.
- The media compete with other forms of communication for selection, attention, and use
- People are usually more influential than the media in this process—but not always.

Criticisms of U&G

Rubin (1994) reviewed the literature on uses and gratifications and identified several major criticisms of the approach. Some of the criticisms were aimed at the results of early research. Additional research has answered the critics on several issues.

Too Individualistic

An early criticism of U&G research was that the focus on individual differences made the findings difficult to extend to other people or to society as a whole (Carey & Kreiling, 1974; Elliott, 1974; McQuail, 1979). However, the consistency of findings in replicated studies (including standardization of measures in terms of viewer motives) has contributed to the generalization of results.

Lack of Synthesis of Research Findings

The various typologies that have been developed to describe audience uses and gratifications had initially been criticized as difficult to synthesize (Anderson & Meyer, 1975; Swanson, 1979). Since the 1970s, the efforts toward consistency in typologies have produced more systematic categorizations, although differences still exist. Haridakis and Humphries (2019) argue that the multitude of typologies "has proven to be a strength of the perspective and has extended our understanding of how and why various media are selected and used," noting that "it would strain credulity to expect that people would have precisely the same motives for watching TV and for using social media with different functions and attributes, or for watching news and watching situation comedies or graphic horror movies" (p. 141).

Krcmar (2017) warns that "while it is certainly true that different media have different motivations for use, generating typologies with little attempt to integrate them at a broader level may do little to forward uses and gratifications as a meaningful approach" (p. 1999).

Differences in the Meaning of Key Concepts

Some researchers have argued that key concepts such as needs, motives, behavior, and so forth have not been clearly explicated (Anderson & Meyer, 1975; Blumler, 1979; Elliott, 1974). Since the 1970s these concepts have been studied and described more explicitly, but the criticism still has some validity.

Other critics have pointed out that researchers have offered different definitions for various concepts such as motives, uses, and gratifications (Elliott, 1974; Swanson, 1977, 1979). Comparisons between studies become difficult when one investigator defines a key concept in one way and another defines it in a different way. "Thus, without clear conceptual work, integration across studies is difficult" (Krcmar, 2017, p. 2000).

The Active Audience and Use of Self-Reporting

U&G typically assumes "that audiences not only are active and motivated users of a medium but also have access to those motives" (Krcmar, 2017, p. 2000). These two related notions have been criticized for a perceived lack of accuracy and consistency (Elliott, 1974; Strizhakova & Krcmar, 2003; Swanson, 1977, 1979). For the most part, studies have answered the criticisms by using validating scales (Rubin, 1979, 1981), experimental methods (Bryant & Zillmann, 1984), and other means.

Other critics have pointed out that self-reports might be affected by individual interpretations and perceptions (Babrow, 1988). Furthermore, users may not be able to identify their motives for using media. Strizhakova and Krcmar (2003) argue that our behaviors are motivated by both conscious and nonconscious factors, which means our motives for media use may not be known to us. Together, assumptions about the active audience and self-reported measures remain criticisms of U&G research (Krcmar, 2017).

Models to Explain Uses and Effects

In response to the numerous criticisms, researchers continued to refine U&G's conceptual foundation. Several models that attempt to explain individual-level media uses and effects have been incorporated into U&G research (Papacharissi, 2009), including the gratification seeking and audience activity model (Rubin & Perse, 1987), the expectancy-value model (Palmgreen & Rayburn, 1982), and the uses and dependency model (Rubin & Windahl, 1986).

Expectancy-Value Model

The expectancy-value model examines the use of the media in terms of the gratifications sought and obtained in addition to the outcomes that are expected at the onset. Palmgreen and Rayburn (1982) proposed the model to explain a person's behavior, intentions, and attitudes as a function of two separate components: expectancy and evaluation. They defined *expectancy* as "the probability that an attitude possesses a particular attribute or that a behavior will have a particular consequence" and *evaluation* as "the degree of affect, positive or negative, toward an attitude or behavioral outcome" (pp. 562–563). For example, people might watch a presidential debate expecting their favorite candidate to win—and then witness the opposing candidate do a much better job. Viewers may or may not change their attitude toward their favorite candidate, but their evaluation of the candidates' performances might well affect their subsequent political behaviors.

As that example illustrates, the gratifications that a person expects to get out of media use are not always the gratifications that are obtained. For instance, research has shown that people who watch television with social motives sometimes end up feeling lonelier after watching TV, which is the opposite of what they had hoped for (Perse & Rubin, 1990). Therefore, U&G research makes a distinction between **gratifications sought** (i.e., viewing motives) and **gratifications obtained** (i.e., viewing outcomes):

> Gratifications sought are those that we bring to a media use situation: we want to pass time, we want to feel a sense of social companionship, we want to learn something. Gratifications obtained are those that result from a media use situation: we experienced physiological arousal, we alleviated boredom, or we exacerbated it. (Krcmar, 2017, p. 1999)

Previous research noted that gratifications obtained—a term that implies that media use is in some way gratifying—may not necessarily be enjoyable or rewarding for users (Nabi et al., 2006). Krcmar (2017) suggests that a "a more precise conceptualization may be that gratifications *sought* and *obtained* should be thought of as merely *needs* and *outcomes*" (p. 1999). (No doubt U&G critics would appreciate that distinction.)

Viewers who watch a presidential debate have an opportunity to evaluate the performance of each candidate. Those evaluations may or may not be in line with viewers' original expectations.

Gratification-Seeking and Audience Activity Model

In the gratification-seeking and audience activity model, many different factors and elements affect the uses and effects process. Particular kinds of gratifications sought by the viewer, as well as the viewer's attitude, determine the viewer's attention to the content of media messages. Effects on viewers' thoughts, emotions, or behavior depend on their degree of involvement with the message and the behavioral intentions of the viewer (Rubin & Perse, 1987). For example, a person with asthma would pay more attention to a commercial for an asthma medication than would a person who does not have asthma.

Uses and Dependency Model

Research has shown that dependency on a medium is the result of two major factors: user motives for obtaining gratifications and the availability of media alternatives. Each of these factors may be affected by any number of social or psychological characteristics. For example, a person with poor health and limited mobility would be more likely to be dependent upon a medium such as television for entertainment and diversion than would a healthy person who enjoys many different types of activities. Furthermore, the person with limited mobility would be more likely to become dependent upon a medium such as television if they did not have access to other media options—such as a laptop, tablet, video games, and so forth—in the home. Conversely, "people who possess a wide variety of communication channels, and are willing to use them, should be less dependent on a particular channel" (Papacharissi, 2009, p. 139).

The **uses and dependency model** (Rubin & Windahl, 1986) proposes that certain elements in a media system (e.g., the system itself, the structure of society, individual differences that result in highly personal motives) cause people to use and depend upon the media. Dependency upon the media may lead to effects in itself. For example, such dependence could produce an attitude change and thus affect the other elements in the model.

The greater the dependency upon a medium, the more likely that medium will have effects upon the viewer. For example, Miller and Reese (1982) studied the political effects of exposure to newspapers or television news and expressions of reliance on one medium or the other. Political efficacy and activity effects were more likely to occur from exposure to a relied-upon medium.

Media Use for Entertainment

Obviously, we often use media for entertainment, and the scientific study of media entertainment has grown substantially in recent decades (Raney & Bryant, 2020). Studies of people's motives for using entertaining media have largely been explored through U&G and selective exposure. Together, these two research traditions provide insight into our needs for entertainment and enjoyment.

According to Raney and Bryant (2020), motives for selecting media for entertainment can fall into two categories: foundational needs and situational needs. **Foundational needs** are tied to basic human needs stemming from evolutionary, biological, and psychological processes. These include the need for "play," life balance, autonomy, competence, and relatedness. Raney and Bryant explain that human evolution allows us to engage in safe imaginative play in "secondary realities" (p. 325).

> That is, media entertainment facilitates temporary shifts in our perceptions of reality during which we access narrative worlds filled with jubilant, disappointing, suspenseful, challenging, and rewarding situations. By "playing" in these safe and controlled secondary environments, we learn how to cope with and compensate for our material and existential problems and shortcomings. (Raney & Bryant, 2020, pp. 325–326)

Furthermore, selecting media entertainment can help us achieve better life balance by allowing us to alter our environment to foster more positive thoughts and feelings (Vorderer & Hartmann, 2009). Consuming entertaining media also satisfies our needs for autonomy (being free to select which content to encounter), competence (comprehending the content), and relatedness (relating to characters).

In addition to foundational needs, Raney and Bryant (2020) also outline various **situational needs**, including mood regulation, escape, recovery, learning, and social utility. We all experience bad moods from time to time, and **mood management theory** (Zillmann, 1988b) explains how we often choose certain media content to alleviate our bad moods and prolong positive moods. The theory also explains that we learn which content will affect our moods in certain ways. For instance, athletes may have a special playlist of high-energy songs to hype them up before a game. Or a student who is stressed about a class project may take a break to watch their favorite sitcom in an effort to take their mind off their worries.

We may also use media to escape, either *from* something we wish to avoid or *to* a desired media world. Henning and Vorderer (2001) identified three motivations for escape: sociological motives such as stress from work or problems with work-life balance; social-psychological motives caused by negative social situations; and individual-psychological motives (those not caused by social situations) like "having nothing to do."

Recovery is another motive for media use, allowing us to detach from causes of stress, relax, be in control of our actions, and build internal resources (Raney & Bryant, 2020). We also use media entertainment to learn. For example, children watch entertaining shows, like *Sesame Street*, to have fun and simultaneously learn letters, numbers, and a wide variety of other concepts. Anecdotally, we sometimes see contestants on game shows like *Jeopardy!* or *Wheel of Fortune* admit to the host that they learned English by watching the show as a child.

Lastly, we consume entertainment content for social utility. Raney and Bryant (2020) note that media often focuses on characters' social lives and inner thoughts. "Because of this, audiences encounter an unending stream of social information. At times, we are specifically motivated to consume entertainment to wade through that stream" (Raney & Bryant, 2020, p. 328). Our choices for entertainment selection can also be driven by many other needs related to ourselves and to others. Raney and Bryant listed several examples of these needs, such as binging reality television to boost self-esteem, watching a popular show to be prepared to talk about it with coworkers the next day, or watching a drama program to help cope with a loved one's cancer diagnosis.

Much of the research into media use for entertainment focused on **hedonic (pleasure-based) motivations** and the enjoyment that results from it, but scholars have started to explore outcomes involving connectedness, meaningfulness, and well-being, which are known as **eudaimonic motivations** (see Raney et al., 2020, for a review).

U&G Research in the 21st Century

Since the turn of the century, there have been calls for U&G research to adapt to new media. For instance, Sundar and Limperos (2013) suggested that technological innovations change the way we interact with media (e.g., online virtual tours), "which in turn have cultivated in users new needs that they seek to gratify from their media usage" (p. 521). Whereas U&G research often looked at social and psychological needs, the researchers argue that they should be triangulated with technology-driven needs. Using what is called the MAIN model (Sundar, 2008), U&G researchers advise that the common technological affordances of modality, agency, interactivity, and navigation can result in new gratifications that are distinctive to new media (Rathnayake & Winter, 2018; Sundar & Limperos, 2013). For example, Oeldorf-Hirsch and Sundar (2016) found that people are motivated to share photos online in part due to technical affordances of websites, such as being able to edit photos and upload them quickly.

In recent years, more U&G research has focused on internet-based media use (Lev-On, 2017). A great deal of research has looked at social media, but there have also been studies of many other forms of media use, such as binge-watching television and listening to podcasts, just to name a few. Some studies have involved expansion of U&G into other domains, such as third-person effects, cultivation, and parasocial interaction.

Numerous studies focus on uses and gratifications of social media use. Motivations for using various social media apps include entertainment, self-expression, social interaction, and passing time, just to name a few.

Internet and Social Media

In a study of U&G and internet use, Ko et al. (2005) discovered that people with strong motives to seek information are more likely to interact with others via a website than those who had strong motives for social interaction, who were more likely to prefer face-to-face contact. In another study, people who were motivated to use the internet experienced more dependency than others and that internet dependency and motivation were mediated by how cognitively and affectively they were involved (Sun et al., 2008).

In 2008, U&G research began to focus on social networking sites, primarily Facebook (Lev-On, 2017). Looking specifically at college students, Park and Lee (2014) identified four motivations for Facebook use: entertainment, relationship maintenance, self-expression, and communication. Impression management (the ability to control your online persona so others form positive impressions of you) was also a significant predictor of Facebook use. Ferris and Hollenbaugh (2018) examined U&G and Facebook dependency. People who were motivated by virtual community (the need to develop new relationships with people online) were most dependent on Facebook.

Ozanne et al. (2017) found that the action of clicking "Like" on a Facebook post can be driven by numerous motivations of entertainment, bonding, self-identification, and information/discovery. Facebook users are sometimes motivated to "Like" a post rather than hit "Share" as a form of self-protection. For instance, if sharing the post to their own profile may have negative consequences, a user may opt to "Like" the post instead.

Alhabash and Ma (2017) examined college students' motivations for using Instagram, Snapchat, Facebook, and Twitter. The top motivators for social network site use across the four platforms were entertainment and convenience. Other motivators included self-documentation, social interaction, medium appeal, and information sharing. Additional research into Instagram identified other motives for use: surveillance/

knowledge about others, documentation, coolness, and creativity (Sheldon & Bryant, 2016). Another motivator researchers have examined in relation to Instagram use is the fear of missing out (FOMO). Barry et al. (2019) found that FOMO was linked to higher levels of engagement on the app. Additionally, those who experienced higher levels of FOMO had more connections on Instagram and used more hashtags, which the authors said could be done in an effort to make more connections with other Instagram users.

Television

Technological advancements (e.g., smart TVs and streaming services) have changed the way many of us consume television content. Lotz (2014) says television is now in the "post-network" era, meaning "viewers now increasingly select what, when, and where to view from abundant options" (p. 28) Tefertiller and Sheehan (2019) identified five motivators for watching TV (either streaming or traditional) in the post-network era: stress management, habitual viewing, information seeking, social interaction, and (most notably) the need for relaxing entertainment. This study supported Rubin's (1984) concepts of instrumental and ritualized viewing and noted the emergence of two distinct viewing patterns.

> Instrumental viewers, best identified by television use for relaxing entertainment, increased selectivity and attention, and streaming technology use, differ from ritualistic viewers, who watch television habitually and—to a lesser degree—to reduce stress. Ritualistic viewers are younger and pay less attention while watching, while instrumental viewers are more likely to use streaming technology to find scripted entertainment. Streaming technology is associated with finding specific programming for entertainment purposes, suggesting the technology itself has implications for audience activity and gratification seeking processes. (Tefertiller & Sheehan, 2019, p. 611)

Researchers have also explored motivations for binge-watching. Light binge watchers were motivated by a need for entertainment, while heavy binge watchers were motivated by entertainment and passing time (Sung et al., 2018; see this chapter's Research Spotlight for an in-depth look at this study). Riddle et al. (2018) used the differential susceptibility to media effects model (DSMM, see Chapter 1) along with sensitivity theory and U&G to study the addictive potential of binge-watching. Young adults engage in both intentional and unintentional binges. Impulsivity was related to heavier unintentional binging, which correlated with symptoms of addiction.

Focus groups were used to determine college students' uses and gratifications from watching reality television programs (Lundy et al., 2008). Students were, for the most part, embarrassed by the amount of time they spent watching reality programming. The students noted that viewing such programs provided an excellent means to escape from the pressures of life and live vicariously through the lives of people featured in the programs. They said that reality television did not require their full attention; therefore, the convenience of watching such programs while multitasking was determined to be a major gratification from viewing. Students reported enjoying watching such programs in the presence of other students and talking about the programs afterward. Another focus-group study (Barton, 2009) examined competition reality programs and suggested that people watch the shows to be gratified on an individual rather than social level.

RESEARCH SPOTLIGHT

Why Do We Indulge?
Exploring Motivations for Binge Watching
Yoon Hi Sung, Eun Yeon Kang, and Wei-Na Lee (2018)
Journal of Broadcasting & Electronic Media, 62(3), 408–526

Noting the increase in binge-watching in recent years, the researchers conducted this exploratory study to provide insights into binge-watching behavior, identify the factors that motivate people to binge-watch, and learn about how those factors influence the viewing experience.

After reviewing relevant research on extreme media use and television viewing, they noted, "People may binge watch programs in order to break away from the daily grind, to enhance enjoyment, and/or reinforce social interaction. These motivations overlap with motivations of general TV watching identified in past literature. However, additional empirical evidence is needed to confirm these observations for binge watching" (p. 412). Therefore, the researchers put forth two research questions.

Research Questions
RQ1: What motivational factors are significantly related to binge-watching behavior?
RQ2: Do motivations differ depending on the level of binge-watching?

Method
Researchers conducted an online survey using participants from a university in the southwestern United States. The survey included three major parts:

1. *General TV-watching behavior.* This measured how much time participants spent watching TV on an average weekday.

2. *Binge-watching-specific behavior.* This section included questions about how many episodes of a show participants watched in one sitting, how long people binged (in hours), and how often they binged a month. This section also measured media transportation by having participants express their agreement to statements like "The program captured my attention," "My mind was only on the program and not on other things," and "Watching the program was relaxing," just to name a few. Binge watchers also answered questions about what platforms they often used to binge-watch (such as websites or streaming services), days of the week they binge-watch, their favorite types of shows to binge, and a TV show that they recently binge-watched.

3. *Motivations to binge watch.* The researchers adapted motivation scales for television watching. Seven motivations were included in this study: passing time, habit, relaxation, information/learning, entertainment/enjoyment, escape, and social interaction.

After removing incomplete survey responses, the resulting sample (*n* = 292) was mostly female (76.4%), and nearly all of the sample was either 19 or younger (50%) or in their 20s (48.3%). The majority of respondents were white (59.4%), followed by Asian/Pacific Islander (18.2%), Hispanic/Latino (17.8%), African American (1.7%), and "other" (2.7%).

Results
Results of binge-watching behavior showed that 24.3% of study participants only watched one episode during a single sitting, 58.6% watched two to three episodes, 13.7% watched four to five episodes, and 3.4% watched more than six episodes. In terms of time spent binge-watching, the overwhelming majority (76.5%) watched for one to three hours, while only 11.8% watched for three to five hours. The analysis of how often people binge-watch revealed that 37.6% binge-

watched two to three times a month, 28.5% binge-watched once a month, 18.6% binged four to five times, and 15.4% binged more than six times a month.

Most people binge-watched on weekends (56%), and an overwhelming number binge-watched alone (83.3%). Further analysis showed streaming services like Netflix and Hulu were the most popular ways to binge-watch (91.9%), and all of the top ten binge-watched shows were season-based dramas (e.g., *Grey's Anatomy, Orange is the New Black, Breaking Bad*). The researchers noted that the ongoing story lines from episode to episode and season to season can encourage audience members to continue to watch.

Using a definition of watching more than two episodes of a show in a single sitting, the researchers classified 75.8% of the participants as binge watchers. Results also showed that the more episodes a person watches, the more frequently they binge-watch and the more they experienced engagement with the show.

Regarding RQ1, only entertainment of the seven motivations studied was a significant predictor of binge-watching behavior, meaning the desire to be entertained was what motivated participants to binge-watch.

The researchers then grouped participants into either low or high binge-watching categories based on their responses about the number of episodes, amount of time, frequency, and engagement they experience while binging and then analyzed the motives for binging for each group. RQ2 inquired whether motivations differed depending on the level of binge-watching. Entertainment remained the only significant motivator for those in the low binge-watching category. However, for those in the high binge-watching group, entertainment and passing time were significant motivators.

Other Media Use

U&G researchers have also investigated other forms of media use, including playing augmented reality video games, reading live blogs, and listening to podcasts.

Numerous studies have used U&G to explore why people played the location-based augmented reality game *Pokémon Go* (see Hamari et al., 2019, for a review). Overall, research has shown that challenge, competition, socializing, outdoor activity, and nostalgia are strong gratifications sought and obtained from playing the game. In-app purchase intentions for *Pokémon Go* are motivated by similar gratifications, plus intentions to reuse (or continue playing) the game.

Many people turn to live blogs for news coverage, and Pantic (2020) conducted a study to understand what motivates people to read them. The results identified two contemporary gratifications—immediacy and convenience—as the main motivations for reading live blogs. Information seeking, which is a traditional motivation in U&G research, came in third.

Research has also studied U&G for audio-based media. Perks and Turner (2019) used focus groups to explore the U&G of podcast consumption. Their results identified both emerging typologies (e.g., customizable experiences and multitasking) and expanded existing ones (e.g., parasocial interaction and social gratifications). Perks et al. (2019) developed a scale to better understand motivations for listening to podcasts. They identified four overarching factors for listening to podcasts: controlling edutainment, storytelling transportation, social engagement, and multitasking. In short, these motivations show that podcast listeners want both educational and entertaining content and control of that content. They desire engaging narratives that make time pass more quickly, and they hope to share what they have heard with others. Lastly, they want podcast listening "to effortlessly overlap with and easily nest into the time-crunched, media rich lives we lead today" (Perks et al., 2019, p. 628).

Connecting U&G to Other Theories & Effects

U&G has been studied alongside several other mass media theories and concepts. Researchers have examined third-person effects from the U&G perspective. **Third-person effects** occur when media consumers perceive that media content affects others more than it affects them personally. (For example, when asked if watching a violent movie might cause you to act aggressively, you would probably say "no," but when asked if the same movie might cause others to act aggressively, you are more likely to say "yes.") Continued exposure to a public safety campaign resulted in a third-person effect (Banning, 2007). Haridakis and Rubin (2005) also connected U&G with third-person effects.

Another area of expansion has been with **parasocial interaction**. As mentioned at the beginning of the chapter, parasocial phenomena occur when media consumers feel that they are personally connected with media characters, either fictional or non-fictional. In one study, talk-radio listeners parasocially interacted with the host of the program, and this behavior predicted the frequency with which they listened to the show and whether or not they made plans to listen (Rubin & Step, 2000). Listeners viewed the host as an influential opinion leader. Parasocial interaction has also been shown to correlate with greater relaxation and decreases in emotional stress (Madison & Porter, 2015). See "Parasocial Phenomena" sidebar to learn more about this concept.

Parasocial Phenomena

Part of human nature is forming social connections with other people. This can also happen with people we see on television. These attachments are known as *parasocial interactions* (PSIs) or *parasocial relationships* (PSRs).

One aspect of television that can foster these types of attachments is that sometimes it appears as if people on TV are talking directly to us, such as news anchors and talk show hosts. Sometimes fictional characters speak to or acknowledge the camera (known as breaking the "fourth wall"). This is commonly seen on "mockumentary" style comedies, such as *The Office*, *Parks and Recreation*, and *Abbott Elementary*. Other times, we can form attachments to fictional characters that never appear to interact with us.

Researchers have investigated parasocial attachments for more than 60 years, but Dibble et al. (2016) noted that researchers sometimes fail to clearly distinguish between PSI and PSR phenomena: "Parasocial interaction refers to a faux sense of mutual awareness that can only occur during viewing. In contrast, parasocial relationship refers to a longer-term association that may begin to develop during viewing, but also extends beyond the media exposure situation" (p. 25).

Another parasocial phenomenon that researchers have studied is what happens when the relationship ends. This is known as a *parasocial breakup* (PSBU). This often happens when a character on a TV show dies or a series ends. Research shows that PSBUs can generate the same negative emotions that we feel with real-world interpersonal or romantic breakups.

Parasocial attachments formed over multiple exposures are known as *parasocial relationships*. Parasocial relationships have helped people deal with grief and the loss of a loved one (Stever, 2016). If you are thinking that parasocial attachment to media characters sounds abnormal and unhealthy, do not worry. Evolutionary theory and decades of research show us that it is both normal and to be expected (Stever, 2016). (See Liebers & Schramm, 2019, for more about research into parasocial attachment.)

Other researchers have linked U&G with cultivation (Bilandzic & Rössler, 2004), information processing (Eveland, 2004), an integrated model of active audience exposure to television (Cooper & Tang, 2009), and social capital theory (Phua & Kim, 2017).

Summary

Uses and gratifications research examines the motivations and behaviors of viewers—how and why they use the media. Communication scholars have developed several different models that attempt to explain media uses and effects. These include the gratification-seeking and audience-activity model, the expectancy-value model, and the uses and dependency model.

Several basic assumptions lie at the heart of the U&G perspective. It assumes that viewers actively choose which programs or other media content they will use to gratify their individual needs. U&G also assumes the audience is a variably active one, that they seek out media use for specific gratifications, and that audience or user reactions depend on social and psychological factors or needs.

Several components and characteristics of uses and gratifications research have been criticized through the years. The more substantial criticisms include the following: findings that are too individualistic and not easily generalized, lack of synthesis among research findings, lack of clarity among key concepts, the notion of the active audience, and the perceived lack of accuracy of self-reporting measures. In answer to criticisms about the lack of uniformity, most U&G research now recognizes the following motives for media use among audience members: learning, habit, companionship, arousal, relaxation, escapism, and a way to pass time. However, researchers have also found new motives and gratifications related to new media.

In recent decades, researchers have extensively explored media use for entertainment, noting differences between foundational and situational needs. A great deal of research has looked at social media, and there have been studies of binge-watching television, listening to podcasts, and reading blogs. Researchers have examined third-person effects and parasocial attachments from the U&G perspective. Studies involving new communication technologies also have been abundant in recent years. The agency, interactivity, and navigation possible with new technologies result in new motives and gratifications in our evolving media landscape.

10

Persuasion

> The real persuaders are our appetites, our fears and above all our vanity.
> The skillful propagandist stirs and coaches these internal persuaders.
>
> —Eric Hoffer, 1955

Persuasion research in mass communication examines the process of attitude formation and change in audience members and the modification of behavior based upon attitude change. Its roots are in antiquity, and it remains one of the most prolific realms of modern communication scholarship.

Any individual or group that has some stake in influencing mass audiences stands to benefit from this particular arm of communication research. Advertising agents, consumer product manufacturers, politicians, and public service organizations are a few of the groups that use research findings to their practical advantage. Knowledge of persuasive influences is also important for consumers, voters, and other audience members who wish to protect themselves from being manipulated.

Persuasion research differs in an important way from most other areas of media effects research. Most persuasive messages are intentional; that is, they are designed to have an *intended effect*. For instance, Ha (2020) described advertising as a "deliberate attempt at persuasion" (p. 275). Media effects in other realms of effects research (e.g., aggressive behavior after viewing violent content) are usually *unintended*. (The exceptions to this would be some instances of fright reactions in horror films and certain gratifications obtained from media use.)

Persuasion involves certain processes of attitude change. Psychologists Richard Petty and John Cacioppo created a popular model to explain the processes that audience members experience as they are persuaded. Their Elaboration Likelihood Model (ELM) of persuasion identifies two separate "routes to persuasion"—or one of two bridges that must be crossed before persuasion can occur (Petty & Cacioppo, 1981, 1986b; Petty & Wegener, 1999; Petty et al., 2009).

Following a review of the research tradition associated with studies of persuasion, we discuss the importance of attitudes, emotions, and behavior in the persuasion pro-

From television commercials to glossy magazine layouts to the digital billboards in Times Square, the goal of advertising is persuasion.

cess. We then take a look at various models of persuasion, including models that link attitudes and actions. Finally, we examine recent trends in persuasion research.

Research Tradition

When radio became popular in the early 20th century, psychologists and sociologists began investigating the persuasive power of mass media. As discussed in chapter 3, respected social scientist Harold Lasswell (1927) found that propaganda messages had had *powerful* effects upon audiences during World War I.

In the years between the world wars, several events provided additional evidence of the power of the media to influence the masses. In 1929, news of the crash on Wall Street brought nationwide panic. In 1938, Orson Welles's *War of the Worlds* broadcast (detailed in Chapter 2) resulted in cases of hysteria that received much publicity. Finally, Adolf Hitler's rise to power in Germany underscored the frightening potential for the power of mass persuasion.

During World War II, researcher Carl Hovland continued to investigate the effects of persuasive messages on attitude change (see Chapter 3). His study of soldiers who viewed military training films demonstrated that they learned new information from the

Carl Hovland. *Courtesy of Katharine Walvick*

films, but the persuasive power of the films in effecting changes in attitudes and behavior was limited. Persuasion was contingent on a number of variables that moderated the effects (Hovland et al., 1949).

After the war, Hovland continued his research on persuasion at Yale University. His research priority became the identification of the moderating variables that acted upon the persuasive process. Successful persuasion involved a process of three important steps: (1) listeners must pay attention to a message, (2) they must comprehend the message, and (3) they must accept the message. He identified a number of variables that affected the power of a persuasive message. These included the credibility of the message source, the type of message appeal (e.g., fear arousing or motivational), the order of the arguments presented, identification of audience members with certain groups, and specific personality characteristics of audience members.

Much of the evidence for powerful and direct media effects during the early years was not based on effective research designs. For example, little effort was expended toward measuring people's attitudes *prior to* receiving the propaganda messages—a crucial factor in proving that attitude change had actually occurred due to the propaganda message.

Social scientists continued to study the effects of persuasive messages in the 1940s and 1950s, using more rigorous empirical methods. To be successful in changing attitudes, persuasive messages had to overcome certain psychological barriers (Hyman & Sheatsley, 1947). Persuasive campaign messages from the media had little effect on changing people's preferences for candidates in the 1940 presidential election (Lazarsfeld et al., 1948).

Paul Lazarsfeld.

Paul Lazarsfeld and his colleagues determined that media messages served primarily to reinforce existing attitudes rather than to change anyone's opinion. As discussed in Chapter 3, media messages did seem to influence certain members of the community who were respected for their knowledge of current affairs. These **opinion leaders**, as the researchers called them, had the personal influence to change the attitudes of others in the community. Thus, media influence was described as a **two-step flow** or **indirect effects** situation in which media messages influenced opinion leaders who, in turn, influenced others in the community via interpersonal communication (Katz & Lazarsfeld, 1955).

Through the years, communication scholars have debated the extent to which mass mediated messages have the power to persuade audiences. Most recent research has shown that persuasion is not simply a stimulus-and-response-type situation, but a more complicated process that emphasizes the *receptivity* of the receiver—their willingness to receive the message.

Attitude, Emotions, Behavior, and Persuasion

To understand the persuasion process, one must first understand the concept of **attitude**. A person's attitude can be defined broadly as that person's "abstract evaluation of an object" (Chaiken et al., 1996, p. 702). Others have defined attitudes as "a learned predisposition to respond in a consistently favorable or unfavorable manner with respect to an object (Fishbein & Ajzen, 1975). A similar definition is "people's general predispositions to evaluate other people, objects, and issues favorably or unfavorably" (Petty et al., 2009, p. 127). Attitudes have flexible stability; they are consistent but not rigid (Dillard, 1993). They can adapt to accommodate changes.

Most contemporary research involving persuasive effects places much importance on the critical role of attitudes in the persuasion process. Attitude is viewed as the all-important mediator that stands between the acquisition of new persuasive information and subsequent behavioral change. If the new information changes a person's attitude, then behavioral change is more likely.

What actually causes a change in attitude? What internal processes come into play? Are people motivated to change their attitudes and behavior to gain rewards or avoid punishment, or do they make the change due to some other reason?

One explanation of this complex process is the **theory of cognitive dissonance** (Festinger, 1957). The best way to understand this theory is to define each of its components. We have already learned that the term "cognitive" is used to describe mental processes or thoughts. "Dissonance" in this case refers to something being *inconsistent*. Cognitive dissonance occurs when attitude and action become inconsistent with one another. For example, someone who is forced to make major dietary changes for health reasons would also have to make significant adjustments in their attitude, especially if the old way of eating was believed to be a "healthy" diet. According to Festinger's theory of cognitive dissonance, this inconsistency causes the person anxiety that must be resolved. The way it is resolved is to bring the attitude in line with the actions. The new diet is soon believed to be healthier than the old one.

For example, consider the person who has negative attitudes toward immigrants. Perhaps the person has carried strong prejudices toward immigrants for many years, even cracking jokes about immigrants and using derisive names. Such behaviors would not be tolerated in the person's workplace where coworkers, clients, or subordinates might be from different countries. The person may even come to like and respect some coworkers who have immigrated to the United States, adding to the dissonance between attitude and behavior. Rather than continue with intolerance, the person might ease cognitive dissonance by changing attitudes toward immigrants.

Many social scientists emphasize the connection between the affective components of attitude and emotion. Persuasive messages that contain emotional appeals can be powerful. Studies have found that emotions are very important in the formation and change of attitudes (Jorgensen, 1998). For instance, a happy or sad state of mind can determine how confident one is in one's attitudes and therefore affect persuasive processes (Briñol et al., 2007; DeSteno et al., 2000; DeSteno et al., 2004).

A range of emotions (e.g., pride, hope, anger, guilt, amusement) have been studied for their persuasive influence, but the majority of the research into emotions and persuasion has looked at the influence of fear appeals (Nabi, 2020). According to Nabi (2020), researchers are still investigating the process of how fear affects decision-making, and to date, "no model of fear appeals has been endorsed as accurately capturing the process. . . . Regardless, evidence does support a positive linear relationship between fear and attitude, behavioral intention, and behavior change" (p. 168).

Persuasion Models and Theories

Through the years, a number of researchers have developed various models to explain the persuasion process. Special emphasis is given to the Elaboration Likelihood Model (ELM), which provides one of the most comprehensive explanations for persuasive processes in terms of mediated communications. However, ELM is just one method of understanding persuasion; we will also examine other theories that contribute to our understanding of how we are influenced by mediated messages.

McGuire's Communication/Persuasion Matrix Model

McGuire (1985, 1989, 2013) introduced a model to explain persuasion effects by identifying *inputs* and *outputs*. Inputs, or independent variables, include the source, the message, the channel, the receiver, and the destination. As Atkin and Freimuth (2013) noted in their discussion of guidelines for public communication campaigns, the first three inputs (i.e., source, message, channel) are variables controlled by the person or group attempting to persuade or influence audience members. Although characteristics of the receiver cannot be manipulated, "sensitivity to the background attributes, abilities, and predispositions of individuals enhances the effectiveness" of persuasive messages (p. 55). Destination is the last input variable. It refers to the types of impacts persuasive messages seek to produce, such as prevention versus cessation or immediate versus long-term change.

Outputs are dependent variables controlled by the audience members. The variables include (1) exposure to the information; (2) attention to the information; (3) liking or maintaining interest in and (4) comprehending the message; (5) generating related cognitions and (6) acquiring new skills; (7) agreeing with the message and changing one's attitude; (8) storing the information and new attitude in memory and (9) retrieving the information when needed; (10) deciding to act according to the new attitude; (11) acting on it; (12) post-action cognitive integration of the behavior; and (13) proselytizing (telling others to behave similarly).

In one study, researchers used McGuire's matrix model as a framework to develop a marketing campaign targeting non-adjudicated and untreated substance-using men who abused their partners (Mbilinyi et al., 2008). The goal of the campaign was to persuade the men to talk about their actions, learn about treatment options, and voluntarily start treatment.

McGuire's model has several shortcomings (Petty & Priester, 1994). The first is its lack of detail regarding the process of yielding to a new attitude. Second, the model assumes that the input and output variables are sequential; that is, they must

> ### McGuire's Matrix Model
>
> **Variables that Affect the Persuasive Power of a Communication Message**
>
> **Input Variables (Controlled by Communicator)**
>
> Source   Channel   Message   Recipient   Destination
>
> **Output Variables (Controlled by Receiver)**
>
> | | | | |
> |---|---|---|---|
> | Exposure | Attention | Interest | Comprehension |
> | Generation | Acquisition | Agreement | Memory |
> | Retrieval | Decision | Action | Integration |
> | Proselytizing | | | |

occur in the order listed (from left to right in the sidebar) to have persuasive effects. However, subsequent research has shown that the variables do not need to be sequential for persuasion to occur. Acquisition (or learning) and remembering of new information are independent of each other and even unnecessary steps in the persuasion process (Greenwald, 1968; McGuire, 1985; Petty & Cacioppo, 1981). For example, a person might acquire and learn new information but refuse to change their attitude, or a person might conceivably misunderstand the information, learn it wrong, but still change their attitude in the intended way.

Cognitive Response Theory

In an attempt to overcome the shortcomings of the matrix model, several researchers developed the **theory of cognitive response** (Greenwald, 1968; Petty, Ostrom, & Brock, 1981). According to this theory, an audience member does not yield to a new attitude after simply learning a new message. Yielding depends upon cognitive responses to the message—or what they *think* about the message. The memory of what is thought about a message is much more important than a memory of the message itself. In other words, favorable thoughts toward a persuasive message produce agreement with the appeal, but when a message elicits unfavorable thoughts toward the recommendation, it is not effective at changing the recipient's attitude.

Scholars later argued that simply "generating thoughts is not sufficient for them to have an impact on judgments. Rather, one must also have confidence in them" (Briñol & Petty, 2009). **Self-validation theory** (Petty et al., 2002) posits that persuasion depends on the amount of *confidence* (ranging from extreme certainty to extreme doubt) people have in their thinking about a persuasive message. When peoples' thoughts about a persuasive message are favorable, increasing confidence in the validity of their thoughts causes persuasion to increase, while increasing doubt about the validity causes persuasion to decrease. Conversely, when people think unfavorably about a persuasive message, increasing confidence of the validity of their thoughts causes persuasion to decrease, while increasing doubt about the validity increases persuasion (Briñol & Petty, 2004; Petty et al., 2002).

In some cases, however, persuasion occurs even when an audience member does not think carefully about the content of a message. Cognitive response theory could not explain such instances (Petty, Cacioppo, & Goldman, 1981).

The Elaboration Likelihood Model

Petty and Cacioppo (1981, 1986a, 1986b) extended the theory of cognitive response and developed a theoretical model to explain the processes that occur when a person yields to a persuasive message. Their **Elaboration Likelihood Model (ELM)** explains the process of persuasion by identifying the likelihood of a person to elaborate cognitively—or think very carefully—about a persuasive message.

This dual-process model proposes two distinct routes that may be taken in order for persuasion to result: central and peripheral. The **central route** to persuasion requires much cognitive effort on the part of the audience member in order to judge the merit of the advocated position or persuasive message. The message recipient listens closely to what is said and then evaluates the information in light of past experiences and previous knowledge. During this process, the person forms opinions about the message—either favorable or unfavorable—and these play a major part in determining the success

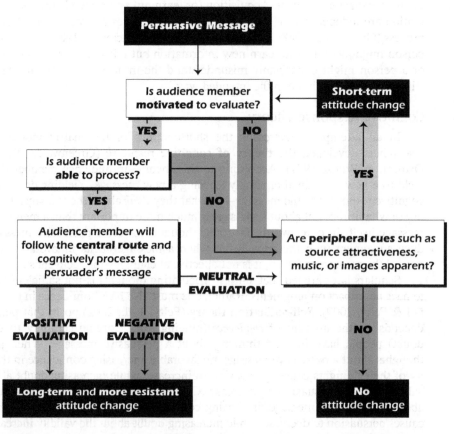

Figure 10.1   Elaboration Likelihood Model.

Adapted from R. E. Petty and J. T. Cacioppo, *Communication and persuasion: Central and peripheral routes to attitude change*, 1986.

of the persuasive message. For example, news reports about important national and international issues usually require a great deal of cognitive processing on the part of the viewer or reader. Persuasion usually depends on whether or not the reader or viewer uses the central route to process the information.

As mentioned, the central route necessitates considerable cognitive effort on the part of the audience member. As a result, attitude changes resulting from the central route have shown several common characteristics, including: (1) accessibility, (2) persistency, (3) predictability of behavior, and (4) resistance to change (Petty & Priester, 1994). In other words, persuasion by way of the central route has been shown to be more successful in long-term attitude change.

The **peripheral route** to persuasion may occur in any number of ways, none of which involves considerable cognitive effort. *Simple cues* in the context of the message are more responsible for the change in attitude than a purposeful effort to process and understand information. For example, a relaxing scene by a calm, crystal-blue mountain lake in a TV commercial might cause the viewer to experience a nice, contented mood that becomes associated with the mountain-fresh scented detergent that is being pitched. The viewer is persuaded to try the detergent because the commercial has conditioned a certain affective response—the nice, contented mood—that is associated with the product.

The *use of experts* to pitch particular products is another example of the peripheral route to persuasion. "More doctors use this pain reliever" . . . "More hospitals use this brand" . . . "More dentists recommend this toothpaste"—are all examples of cues used to effectively shortcut the route to persuasion. The viewer infers that experts are supposed to be correct; therefore, the message is judged as truthful, and the viewer is persuaded to use the product (Chaiken, 1987).

Another example of the peripheral route, the *bandwagon effect,* was identified by researchers for the Institute for Propaganda Analysis in the 1930s (Lee & Lee, 1939). Audience members were made to believe that many other people already supported the position of a speaker. They inferred that with so many people in agreement, the speaker's message must be true. Such an inference served as a cue that the message of the speaker was valid, and the bandwagon effect occurred (Axsom et al., 1987).

Peripheral route persuasion has been shown to be successful in the short run, but the strength of the peripheral cues weakens over a period of time. A person's mood and feelings may change, for example, or cues are no longer associated with certain messages. Attitude changes that occurred through the peripheral route were much weaker than those that occurred through the central route in terms of resistance to attack and durability (Petty & Cacioppo, 1986a).

The amount of cognitive effort someone is willing to put forth determines whether the central or peripheral route is more influential in the persuasion process. The amount of thinking can vary from high to low along a *continuum of elaboration.* As someone moves along this continuum, there is a trade-off between the influence of the central and peripheral routes (Petty & Wegener, 1999). As the likelihood of mental elaboration (careful processing of a persuasive message) increases, the central route to persuasion is dominant and has a greater impact. Conversely, as the likelihood of mental elaboration decreases, the peripheral route becomes more important in the persuasion process. (It should be noted that although Petty and Wegener, 1999,

---

Predictions of the Elaboration Likelihood Model

When the likelihood for elaboration is high (e.g., when the message has personal relevance for the audience member, when there are few distractions), a person is motivated to listen to the message, mentally process, and evaluate the information. Peripheral cue variables are likely to have less impact in such a situation.

When the likelihood for elaboration is low (e.g., when the message has low personal relevance or there are many distractions), the importance of peripheral variables increases significantly. Under such circumstances, the audience member is not likely to be motivated or able to process the message with careful thought.

When the likelihood for elaboration is moderate (e.g., when the audience member has some knowledge of the issue but uncertainty about its personal relevance), the recipient may evaluate the context of the message to determine whether the message should be processed. A contextual component would be, for example, the credibility or the attractiveness of a source.

The use of an attractive spokesperson in a commercial or advertisement can influence a message's persuasive appeal by serving as a peripheral cue.

acknowledge that the central and peripheral processes occur simultaneously at most points along the continuum and jointly influence judgments, they place more emphasis on the relative impact of the two distinct routes.)

Variables that Motivate.   The strength of the central route to persuasion has led researchers to examine the variables that motivate a person to think carefully about a message. One of the most important of these variables is that of *personal relevance* of the message (Brickner et al., 1986; Leippe & Elkin, 1987; Petty et al., 1992).

Whenever information is perceived as personally relevant, people process the information more carefully. When this happens, strong arguments become more persuasive, and weak arguments become less persuasive (Petty & Cacioppo, 1979). In one study, personal relevance was increased by using the second-person pronoun "you" rather than the third-person pronouns "he" or "she." Participants who received messages containing "you" listened and processed information more carefully. Those who processed the information more carefully were more persuaded by strong arguments and less persuaded by weak arguments (Burnkrant & Unnava, 1989). A study of health-related messages about breast cancer screenings found that tailored messages were more effective than generic ones because the tailored messages increased the perceived personal relevance of the message (Jensen et al., 2012).

Researchers have identified other variables that provide the necessary motivation for a receiver to think carefully about a message. One of these involves formulating a question rather than making an assertion in a message to provoke more thought processing on the part of the receiver (Howard, 1990; Petty, Cacioppo, & Heesacker, 1981; Swasy & Munch, 1985). For example, rather than say "Vote for John Doe" at the end of a campaign commercial, it is more effective to present arguments and say "Shouldn't you vote for John Doe?"

Another way to increase the personal relevance of the message is to frame it to align with a person's values or self-perceptions (Petty & Wegener, 1998; see Petty et al., 2000, for review). In one study, students were given a test to determine if they had outgoing or shy personalities. The introverts were shown ads for a VCR that promised "you can have all the luxuries of a movie theater without having to deal with the crowds" while the extroverts were shown ads that promised "you'll be the life of the party, whether the party's in your home or out of it" (Wheeler et al., 2005, p. 789). By matching the persuasive message content with the individual's self-perception, persuasion was enhanced or reduced, depending upon the quality of the argument.

"Peripheral Cue" Variables.   A number of variables have been shown to affect the persuasion process by means of the peripheral route. According to researchers, a **peripheral cue** can be defined as "a feature of the persuasion context that allows favorable or unfavorable attitude formation even in the absence of an effortful consideration of the true merits of the object or issue" (Petty et al., 2009, p. 141). As the likelihood of mental elaboration (careful cognitive processing of a message) decreases, peripheral cues become more potent. Petty and Priester (1994) identified several variables that serve as simple cues. These included:

1. The likability or attractiveness of the message source.
2. The credibility of the source.

3. The number of arguments the message contained.

4. How long the arguments were.

5. How many other people were perceived by the viewer to agree with the position, also known as the bandwagon effect.

The Role of Variables.   For persuasion to occur, three factors must be present. A *source* must deliver a persuasive *message* to a *recipient.* Variables that affect the persuasion process may take on different roles and impact any of the three factors.

Source factor variables would include characteristics such as the attractiveness or credibility of the source. Research has shown that such variables serve as peripheral cues when the likelihood of elaboration is low, but they are not as important as the quality of the argument itself when the likelihood of elaboration is high (Petty, Cacioppo, & Goldman, 1981). Such variables either enhance or weaken the likelihood for persuasion, depending upon the strength of the argument (e.g., Heesacker et al., 1983; Moore et al., 1986; Puckett et al., 1983). An attractive or expert source made a strong argument stronger and more persuasive, but the same type of source made a weak argument weaker and even less persuasive.

In one study of source credibility, people were presented either strong or weak arguments for a new pain relief medicine. After the presentation of the persuasive messages, audience members were told that the source of the information was either (1) a federal agency that does research on such products or, (2) a 14-year-old student's class report. Those who believed the message came from the highly credible source showed more favorable attitudes and evidence of persuasion—when the arguments of the message were strong. Less favorable attitudes and less likelihood of persuasion occurred when they were presented with weak arguments from the credible source (Tormala et al., 2006).

According to the ELM, persuasion variables can influence either the central or peripheral routes for different reasons and under different conditions. Therefore, a particular variable is not necessarily exclusively tied to either route. This is known as the **multiple roles postulate** (Dillard, 2020; Petty & Weneger, 1999). As Xu (2017) noted, "an expert source could serve as a cue to activate the *expert is correct* heuristic under peripheral processing. It may also elicit more in-depth processing because the expert source may lead individuals to pay more attention to the message" (p. 421).

Variables that could be considered message factors would include all the informational items included in a message. When the likelihood for elaboration is low, the informational items in the message serve as peripheral cues. When the likelihood for elaboration is high, the items are processed carefully and are not merely peripheral cues. Research has shown that the addition of weak arguments in support of a position for each of the low and high ELM conditions results in a different outcome. When informational items are peripheral cues, the addition of weak supporting arguments makes persuasion more likely, but when informational items are evaluated cogently as arguments themselves, weak additional arguments are less likely to affect persuasion (Alba & Marmorstein, 1987; Petty & Cacioppo, 1986a).

An example of a recipient factor would be a person's mood at the time the message is received. An experiment by Petty, Schumann, et al. (1993) revealed several ways in which the recipient's mood influenced the persuasion process. Participants saw a product advertisement while watching one of two television programs, either a pleasant sitcom or a neutral documentary. In the high involvement (or high elaboration likelihood) condition, participants were told they could select a free gift afterward from several brands of the product in the commercial. In the low involvement or low elaboration likelihood condition, participants could select from several brands of products other than what was depicted in the commercial. The study revealed that viewing the pleasant program not only made people evaluate their own moods more positively but also made them evaluate the commercial product more positively. This was true for both the high- and low-involvement conditions, though it must be pointed out that more positive thoughts about the product were generated when the elaboration likelihood was high rather than low. Generally speaking, mood tended to affect a person's attitude directly when involvement (elaboration likelihood) was low, but when involvement was high, the effect of mood upon attitude depended upon the number of positive thoughts generated.

The Heuristic-Systematic Model

Another dual-process model that helps us understand how people process persuasive messages and information is the **heuristic-systematic model** or **HSM** (Chaiken, 1980, 1987; Chen & Chaiken, 1999). Much like the ELM, the HSM proposes two modes of cognitive processing: heuristic mode and systematic mode. **Systematic processing** is similar to the ELM's central route of persuasion, requiring thought, analysis, and greater cognitive effort. **Heuristic processing** is less analytical and uses less cognitive effort. In this mode, cognitive heuristics (or mental shortcuts) are activated from memory. These heuristics allow people to make judgments quickly without much cognitive effort. "For example, the length of a persuasive message could serve as a cue to trigger the heuristic of *length implies strength* and lead to a favorable attitude when a person is not motivated to engage in in-depth processing" (Xu, 2017, p. 422). These processing modes are not mutually exclusive, and a fundamental assumption of the HSM is that both the heuristic and systematic processes occur simultaneously.

Another aspect of the HSM worth noting is the **information sufficiency principle**, which explains why and to what degree message processing occurs when making a judgment. Essentially, the principle describes the motivational balancing act between wanting to put forth a minimal amount of cognitive effort and the desire to be correct in one's judgment. Dillard (2020) summarized it this way: "The sufficiency threshold is the point at which one's desire for accuracy is balanced by the countervailing desire for cognitive economy. In other words, it is the point of *good enough* [emphasis added]" (p. 116). For instance, when someone's actual confidence in their judgment is lower than their desired confidence, they are more likely to engage in systematic processing in hopes of closing that gap and arriving at more confident judgments. On the other hand, when a person's actual confidence is equal to or higher than their desired confidence in a judgment, they will engage in heuristic processing. There is no need to put forth extra mental effort because they are at (or past) the "point of good enough."

Comparing the Elaboration Likelihood Model and Heuristic-Systematic Model

The ELM and HSM may seem very similar, and in many ways they are. However, there are also major differences between the two models. Xu (2017) provides a summary of those similarities and differences.

Similarities

1. "Both models maintain that persuasion can be achieved through two qualitatively different modes of information processing . . . [and] one mode is more effortful, involves more deliberation, and consumes more cognitive resources than the other" (p. 425).

2. Both models "consider desire to be accurate as one significant motivation that influences information processing in persuasion settings" (p. 425). This motivation involves being open-minded and treating persuasive information in a relatively fair manner.

3. "Both models contend that people are economically minded even though they may desire to be correct about judgments. They will tend to try and use a minimal amount of cognitive effort to process information and make judgments as efficiently as possible" (p. 425).

4. Both models acknowledge that a person's motivation and ability to process "are the key determinants of which processing mode a person will rely on" (pp. 425–426).

Differences

1. The HSM assumes the systematic and heuristic processes may happen simultaneously. Although the ELM acknowledges the two processes can co-occur, it argues that there is a trade-off between the central and peripheral routes along the elaboration continuum, but "it does not imply that one processing mode is more or less likely to occur than the other when elaboration likelihood varies" (p. 426).

2. "Another major difference between the ELM and the HSM lies in the distinctions between peripheral processing and heuristic processing" (p. 426). The HSM's heuristic processing involves cognitive shortcuts (heuristics) stored in memory when people are not motivated to systematically process information. In the ELM, the use of heuristics is just one of several types of less effortful processes in the peripheral route, such as mere exposure, classical conditioning, and self-perception.

3. Although both models acknowledge accuracy as a major motivation in information processing, they differ in their assumptions about overriding motivations. The ELM assumes accuracy is the default motivation for information processing in persuasion settings. The HSM, on the other hand, does not propose an overarching motive, arguing that accuracy, defense (i.e., protecting one's personal values and beliefs), and impression (i.e., satisfying social goals and experiencing positive interpersonal outcomes) motivations influence information processing.

Social Judgment Theory

Although **social judgment theory** is viewed as a "historical relic" (O'Keefe, 2009, p. 277), its contributions to our understanding of persuasion make it worthy of discussing here. One of the main factors in social judgment theory is the idea that people make various judgments about the differing views that could be held about a particular issue (Sherif et al., 1965).

Take the issue of abortion, for example. Although a person most likely has a certain belief about abortion, they may view other positions as acceptable, others as unacceptable, and still some may be viewed neutrally. These various mind-sets "represent the person's latitudes of acceptance, rejection, and noncommitment" (O'Keefe, 2009, p. 276) about the issue. The latitude we give to various viewpoints is influenced by the degree to which our identity is tied to a viewpoint on a particular issue. The stronger the connection between our belief about an issue and our self-identity, the more likely we are to reject differing viewpoints.

Models Linking Beliefs, Attitudes, and Actions

A large body of persuasion research has addressed the connection between beliefs and attitudes and actions or behavior. According to Yzer (2017), "attitude is shaped by specific beliefs that people hold about the likelihood of particular outcomes of performing the behavior and people's evaluations of those outcomes" (p. 1956). Whether or not a person changes their behavior to align with a change in attitude depends upon a number of factors. Most of these factors are related to particular situations or the person's disposition (Ajzen, 1988).

Scholars have developed several general purpose models that explain the processes that link a new or changed attitude with corresponding action or behavior. Multiple models detail how behavior is a result of thoughtful reasoning, but we will also discuss how a behavior linked to an attitude could happen automatically without much thought.

Theories of Reasoned Action and Planned Behavior

Both the theory of reasoned action and theory of planned behavior are cornerstones of what is known as the **reasoned action approach** of understanding how to predict and change human behavior (Fishbein & Ajzen, 2010). Despite the fact that the TRA and TPB are not technically theories of persuasion (Dillard, 2020) and that they were not designed with the intention of explaining media effects, both persuasion scholars and professionals have embraced the theories "in large part because they recognize that, the better one knows which factors guide people's behavior, the better able one is to design messages that can improve those factors. . . . As a result, reasoned action has had a strong presence in persuasion domains such as consumer behavior, health communication, innovation adoption, and environmental behavior" (Yzer, 2017, p. 1959).

Fishbein and Ajzen (1975) introduced the **theory of reasoned action (TRA)** with the assumption that "people consider the implications of their actions before they decide to engage or not engage in a given behavior" (p. 5). The model hypothesizes that people make the decision to behave or not to behave in a certain way based upon two criteria: (1) the person's attitude toward the behavior and (2) the person's perceptions about how others will view the behavior. Essentially, "the TRA depicts behavioral intentions as potentially shaped by both personal (attitudinal) and social (normative) influences" (O'Keefe, 2009, p. 273). These personal and social factors allow persuaders to better tailor their messages to audiences depending on which factors influence the audiences' intentions to do something (e.g., vote for a particular candidate, buy a certain brand of car). Before the person engages in a particular behavior, they carefully weigh the personal advantages or disadvantages of doing so. If engaging in the behavior comes at a cost, that cost is considered and carefully weighed against the perceived benefits of engaging in that behavior.

Ajzen (1991) revised the TRA to include the **theory of planned behavior (TPB)**. In addition to basing intentions for action upon attitudes and the behavioral norms of others, the expanded model reveals that intentions to act are also based upon the perceived *control* the person has over the behavior. This factor essentially examines whether a person thinks the action is easy or difficult to perform.

It is easy to see how the TRA and TPB work when we look at health-related behaviors, such as dieting or exercise. An overweight person would probably think that dieting is desirable (which is a positive attitude toward the behavior) and that person's friends and family would also think it is a good idea (which means there is a positive social norm); however, the overweight person may believe that they are not able to go on a diet—healthy food is often more expensive, healthy food takes too long to prepare, they do not like the taste of broccoli and squash, and so on (the overweight person believes the change is too difficult to perform).

In these types of situations, creators of persuasive messages need to work on finding ways to change a person's perceptions about their behavioral control, rather than focusing on the benefits of changing their behavior (because the people already have a positive attitude toward the behavior). Imagine a mattress company trying to persuade people to buy a new mattress. Audiences and society at large have positive attitudes about getting a good night's sleep, but audience and society members also believe that they cannot personally achieve this benefit because quality mattresses are too expensive. The mattress company should focus its persuasive message on the cost factor, showing audiences that they can, in fact, afford the mattress.

By using the three factors (personal attitude, societal or subjective norms, and perceived behavioral control) associated with the reasoned action approach, persuaders can tailor their messages to influence their audiences more effectively.

Factors that Determine Behavioral Intentions

According to the reasoned action approach, three factors influence a person's behavioral intentions:

1. *Attitude toward the behavior:* Weighing the pros/cons or risks/rewards of engaging in a particular behavior
2. *Subjective norms:* Social pressure from family, friends, media, etc.
3. *Perceived behavioral control:* A person's perception about their ability to perform the behavior

---

Protection Motivation Theory

Similar to TRA and TPB, **protection motivation theory (PMT)** was developed to better understand what influences people to engage in protective behaviors, such as practicing safe sex, taking measures to prevent skin cancer, and ceasing to smoke

(Rogers, 1975; Rogers & Prentice-Dunn, 1997). Recent examples of PMT studies examined protective behaviors during the COVID-19 pandemic (Bashirian et al., 2020; Ezati Rad et al., 2021). Two main factors are examined when looking at PMT: (1) threat appraisal (what a person thinks about the threat) and (2) coping appraisal (what a person thinks about the protective behavior).

Two sub-factors of threat appraisal include perceptions about how serious the threat is (e.g., breast cancer, obesity-related illnesses) and how likely one is to suffer from the threat (e.g., family history of cancer or obesity). The coping appraisal is also made up of two sub-factors: perceptions of how effective the protective behavior is (e.g., chemotherapy and radiation, diet and exercise) and how capable one believes oneself to be to perform the protective behavior (e.g., undergoing chemo treatments, the ability to lose weight).

Research has shown that when a threat is seen as more severe or when a protective behavior is seen as more effective, people are more likely to engage in the protective action (e.g., Floyd et al., 2000; Witte & Allen, 2000).

Stage Models

Persuading someone to change a behavior is not as simple as flipping a switch. In fact, behavior change is often thought of as a process in which a person passes through several distinct stages. The **transtheoretical model of health behavior change (TTM)** identifies these stages as precontemplation, contemplation, preparation, action, and maintenance (Prochaska, 1994; Prochaska et al., 2002).

Let us use the example of running for exercise to illustrate the progression through the stages in this model. Your friend Justin wants to get in better shape, but in the *precontemplation* stage he is not even thinking about starting to run. When he starts seriously thinking about running—researching the best brand of running shoes and thinking about where he could run—he is in the *contemplation* stage. Then Justin actually buys the running shoes and maps out his route, entering the *preparation* stage. After lacing up his shoes and hitting the pavement, Justin enters the *action* stage, where he is actually running. Lastly, as he continues to go for daily runs for several months, he enters the *maintenance* stage.

In a review of the TTM, Noar (2017) notes:

Once jogging becomes routine, joggers are in the maintenance stage of the transtheoretical model of health behavior change.

> People do not progress through these stages in purely a linear fashion, however. Rather, the TTM posited the change process as dynamic, cyclical, and nonlinear, and research indicates that individuals may move forward through the stages, backslide, and then continue cycling and recycling through the stages as they attempt to change (Prochaska, Velicer, Guadagnoli, Rossi, & DiClemente, 1991). In fact, relapsing to unhealthy behaviors is not viewed as failure (as it previously often was) but rather as a natural part of the change process. (para. 6)

With this model, every stage is influenced by different considerations. To persuade someone to move from the precontemplation stage to the contemplation stage, a persuader must increase awareness of a problem (Slater, 1999). To move from contemplation to preparation there must be a change in relevant beliefs. Moving from the preparation to action stage involves increased self-efficacy and accessibility of supportive attitudes. Moving from action to maintenance involves reinforcement of intentions and increased certainty. When designing a campaign, matching messages to relevant variables and desired outcomes for a particular stage was more successful than when they were mismatched.

Automatic Activation

The **automatic activation model** proposes that behavior follows automatically whenever an attitude comes to mind. The process is spontaneous and does not involve any extended reflection or reasoning on the part of the individual. Fazio (1990), the originator of the model, offered two contingent circumstances that allow attitudes to guide behavior automatically: (1) if there is spontaneous access to the attitude whenever the object of the attitude is present, and (2) if the object is perceived according to the attitude (if the attitude is favorable, it is perceived favorably; if unfavorable, it is perceived unfavorably).

Researchers have developed measures to study the availability of automatic attitudes (Fazio et al., 1995; Greenwald et al., 1998; Petty et al., 2008; Wittenbrink & Schwarz, 2007). At first, researchers thought that automatic attitudes might show more resistance to change, but studies have shown that even long-held attitudes can be subject to change via classical conditioning and exposure to the new information and the processing of it (Briñol et al., 2008; Fazio & Olson, 2003). The new information can be presented in the form of advertisements, mass mediated campaigns, or other means of verbal communication (Briñol et al., 2008; Czyzewska & Ginsburg, 2007; Gawronski & Bodenhausen, 2006; Maio et al., 2008; Park et al., 2007). For example, Park and associates (2007) used implicit measures to determine that people held automatic attitudes toward Arab-Muslims, in that they associated them with terrorism. When presented with positive information about Arab-Muslims, the attitudes were moderated.

Research has also shown that people sometimes need time to adjust to their new attitudes, to become more confident in them (Rucker & Petty, 2006), or to rehearse the new attitude in new situations until it replaces the old attitude (Petty, Gleicher, & Jarvis, 1993; Wilson et al., 2000).

Recent Research

Persuasion research continues to evolve in the 21st century, and we close this chapter by taking at brief look at some (but certainly not all) areas of study. Researchers continue to explore the impact of certain variables, such as gender, on persuasion effects. Technological advances, like virtual reality, also give researchers new areas in which to investigate persuasion effects.

Gender's Influence on Persuasion

Gender differences and their influence in the persuasion process continue to interest researchers. Earlier research by Burgoon and Klingle (1998) suggested that, generally, men are more persuasive and women are more persuadable, but the gender of the communicator and the strategies of the persuasive message are important determinants. More recently, researchers have investigated gender differences among millennials exposed to cause-related marketing (CRM) messages (Vilela & Nelson, 2016). (This study used a CRM example of purchases of Cheerios cereal benefiting Big Brothers Big Sisters.) Results showed that women responded more favorably to CRM compared to men. Women were also more likely to buy the product after being exposed to the CRM message, whereas men's purchase intention decreased after exposure but increased after a two-week delay.

Another study examined gender differences and the persuasiveness of advertising (Papyrina, 2019). In line with previous research, this study found that men were persuaded more by the quantity of product assertions in a message (relying on a *more equals better* heuristic), whereas women tended to engage in more effortful elaboration of ad content and were persuaded by the quality of the message. (For more on this study, see this chapter's Research Spotlight.)

RESEARCH SPOTLIGHT

The Trade-Off Between Quantity and Quality of Information in Gender Responses to Advertising
Veronika Papyrina (2019)
Journal of Promotion Management, 25(1), 1–19

The goal of this study was to explore differences between how males and females process informational content (i.e., product features) in advertisements. Previous studies have shown that males are more likely to engage in heuristic processing, whereas females are more likely to engage in more effortful cognitive processing.

Rather than listing explicit hypotheses, Papyrina put forth a "main proposition" of this research: "Males and females will employ their preferred cognitive strategies in processing informational ads, and that these strategies will interact with the quantity of arguments conveyed in the message to determine its persuasiveness" (p. 4).

Papyrina conducted three experiments to study the main proposition.

(continued)

Study 1

This study used a 2 (gender) by 2 (four- vs. six-argument ad) between-subjects design. Participants viewed a print ad for light bulbs that contained a color photo of the product as well as either four or six claims about the products, such as "Last up to 10 times longer than traditional bulbs," "Use 50–80% less energy than traditional bulbs," "Can be used both indoors and outdoors," etc. Participants then answered a questionnaire about the persuasiveness of the ad they viewed.

Results showed that males were more persuaded by the six-argument ad than the four-argument ad. However, there was no difference in persuasiveness between the two ads for females.

Study 2

Study 2 sought to find boundary conditions for product claims and persuasiveness. This study used a 2 (gender) by 3 (two- vs. four- vs. six-argument ad) between-subjects design. The product used for this study was mosquito repellent. Examples of product claims included "Provides long-lasting protection—up to 8 hours per application," "No need to wash it off when you come back indoors," "Feels light and clean on the skin," etc.

Analysis showed that there was a positive linear effect of argument quantity on persuasiveness for males. Males found the six-argument ad more persuasive than the four-argument ad, and the four-argument ad was rated more persuasive than the two-argument ad. Females were also more persuaded by the four-argument ad than the two-argument ad, but when all six message claims were included, the ad's effectiveness leveled off. Although females rated the six-claim ad as more persuasive than the two-claim ad, there was no statistical difference between the four- and six-argument ads.

Study 3

This experiment included the quality of the arguments. Research has shown that women engage in more cognitive elaboration than do men. Thus, the strength of the claims made about a product could be an important predictor of advertising persuasiveness for females. This experiment used a 2 (gender) by 2 (three-argument vs. five-argument ad) by 2 (weak vs. strong argument) between-subjects design. The product used for this experiment was printer paper and included product claims like "Can be used in all printers, copiers and fax machines," "Delivers razor sharp images and outstanding color replication," "Can be used for all types of documents," "Easy to recycle," etc.

Like the first two studies, males reported being more persuaded by the ad with five attributes than the one with three. The quantitative effect of weak claims was similar to the effect of strong arguments. This means that even when the features highlighted on the ad were relatively unimportant, males continued to rate five-argument ads as more persuasive than three-argument ads.

Interestingly, males were more persuaded by ads with three strong arguments than with three weak ones. However, the difference between ads with five strong claims and five weak claims was not significant. Papyrina concluded that males did discriminate between strong and weak arguments when the cognitive demands were low (evaluating three claims), but when the cognitive demands increased (evaluating five claims), males resorted to heuristic processing.

Meanwhile, female participants were more persuaded by strong arguments and less persuaded by weak ones, no matter how many arguments were presented in the ad.

Overall Results

Together, these experiments show that increasing the number of claims about a product is an effective tool for increasing the persuasiveness of an ad for males. Conversely, citing numerous product features will have a limited effect on females, and weak claims can undermine an ad's effectiveness. Therefore, advertisers should focus more on the strength—not the number—of an ad's arguments to persuade females.

Interactive Technology and Persuasion

Persuasion researchers are interested in technologies that can motivate and persuade users. Of particular interest to these researchers as well as human-computer interaction researchers is interactive computer technology. "Computers can not only help users achieve their goals, but also motivate and even persuade them to change the way the users think and behave" (Sundar & Oh, 2020, p. 359). Interactivity is the key feature that can lead to changes in beliefs and behaviors.

Virtual reality is a fertile area for persuasion research, especially because the technology allows users to experience accelerated futures of certain actions and behaviors (Kalyanaraman & Bailenson, 2020). Whether it is planting a tree, stopping smoking, or eating a healthier diet, "VR allows the user to experience the long-term consequences of their actions immediately after they are initiated" (p. 411). For example, researchers can use VR to allow participants to visualize the negative health consequences of excess sugar consumption. One obstacle in trying to convince someone to eat less sugar is that the long-term damaging effects may not be seen and felt for many years. The consequences are "out of sight, out of mind," so to speak. However, accelerated futures in VR may be able to persuade people to change because "a 'sugar body' in VR could portray the short-term (one month, six months, one year) and long-term (five years, ten years) effects of excess sugar consumption" (p. 412).

Other health-related VR research indicated that using an avatar representing a person's weight-reduced body resulted in healthier dietary choices in a later task (Kuo et al., 2016). Kalyanaraman and Bailenson (2020) noted that although the dietary decisions did not impact the virtual avatars in Kuo et al.'s study, "leveraging this accelerated framework is a logical progression" (p. 411).

Summary

Persuasion research in mass communication examines the process of attitude change in audience members and the modification of behavior based on attitude change. Persuasion is an *intentional* process.

Research on the persuasive power of mass media began in the 1920s and 1930s when radio and films were popular. More recent research has shown that persuasion is not simply a stimulus-and-response-type situation; it is a more complicated process that emphasizes the receptivity of the receiver. Contemporary research places considerable importance on the critical role of attitudes in the persuasion process. Attitudes can be defined as general predispositions to evaluate issues, objects, or people favorably or unfavorably. Attitude is the mediator between the acquisition of persuasive information and behavioral change.

Numerous models and theories of persuasion have been put forth over the years. McGuire's Communication/Persuasion Matrix Model explained persuasion effects by identifying inputs (variables controlled by the persuasive source) and outputs (variables controlled by audience members).

Cognitive response theory holds that yielding to persuasive messages depends upon audience members' cognitive responses to the messages. Self-validation theory expands on cognitive response theory to include a person's confidence in their thoughts about a persuasive message.

The Elaboration Likelihood Model (ELM) further extends the theory of cognitive response and explains the processes that occur whenever a person encounters a persuasive message. It identifies the likelihood of a person to elaborate cognitively about a persuasive message. The ELM proposes two distinct routes to persuasion—central and peripheral. The central route requires much cognitive effort. When persuasion occurs by means of the peripheral route, simple cues in the context of the message, the use of experts to pitch products, and the bandwagon effect are more responsible for attitude change than any considerable cognitive effort. As the likelihood of mental elaboration (careful processing of a persuasive message) increases, the central route to persuasion is dominant. As the likelihood of mental elaboration decreases, the peripheral route to persuasion becomes more important in the persuasion process.

The heuristic-systematic model (HSM) also proposes two routes similar to the ELM. The heuristic route relies on cognitive shortcuts, whereas the systematic route involves more cognitive effort.

There are also numerous models and theories linking beliefs, attitudes, and behaviors. Many of these models are often employed in health communication campaigns. The theory of reasoned action (TRA) hypothesizes that people make the decision to behave or not to behave in a certain way based upon two criteria: (1) the person's attitude toward the behavior itself and (2) the person's perceptions about how others will view the behavior. The theory of planned behavior (TPB) expands TRA to include intentions to act based on the perceived *control* the person has over the behavior. This factor essentially examines whether a person thinks the action is easy or difficult to perform.

Similar to TRA and TPB, protection motivation theory (PMT) was developed to better understand what influences people to engage in protective behaviors like practicing safe sex, taking steps to prevent skin cancer, quitting smoking, and wearing a mask during a pandemic.

The transtheoretical model of health behavior change outlines five stages people go through to adopt a behavior: precontemplation, contemplation, preparation, action, and maintenance. However, people do not always go through the stages in a purely linear fashion. Research has shown that the process is often dynamic and cyclical.

Another model linking attitudes with behavior is the automatic activation model. It proposes that when an attitude comes to mind there is a spontaneous process in which behavior follows automatically without the need for reflection or reasoning.

Recent persuasion research continues to explore long-studied variables like gender plus new interactive technologies. Virtual reality can be an interesting tool for persuasion because it allows people to see the accelerated consequences of their actions, which otherwise could not be observed for months or years.

Section Three

KEY AREAS OF RESEARCH

11

Effects of Media Violence

> I have no problem with screen violence at all, but I have a big problem with real-life violence.
>
> —Quentin Tarantino, 1994

From bloody battles on *The Witcher* to gruesome murders on *American Horror Story* to homicidal superheroes on *The Boys*, our screens are often filled with violence. For generations, audiences watching *Tom & Jerry* have laughed when Jerry whacks Tom so hard that the cartoon feline's teeth fall out. Cheers erupted in theaters when Thor beheaded Thanos in *Avengers: Endgame*. Graphic violence is a hallmark of many movie directors, like Quentin Tarantino. Furthermore, advances in technology allow for the blood and gore in first-person shooter games to look incredibly realistic.

Violence is part of our media experience from a very young age. In fact, by the time a child turns 18, they have seen more than 200,000 acts of violence on TV, including 16,000 murders (The Effect of Television Violence on Children, 2004). One of the most important social issues of our time has been public concern for the negative effects of exposure to media violence, especially among children.

For decades, there has been concern about the violence on our screens translating to the real world. Columbine. Virginia Tech. The Century 16 movie theater in Aurora, Colorado. Sandy Hook Elementary School. Pulse nightclub. Marjory Stoneman Douglas High School. Robb Elementary School. For countless people, simply reading those words are enough to summon vivid images of the horrific shooting massacres that took place in those locations. The debate about the effects of violent media on real-world aggression "rears its ugly head" each time this type of real-world violence occurs (Piotrowski & Fikkers, 2020, p. 211).

Through the years, many studies have revealed that viewing mediated violence leads to or causes aggressive thoughts, feelings, and behaviors. Despite the findings, critics of these studies and the research methods they employ abound. Due to the implications for society as a whole, the media violence issue has been a major concern for public policy makers over the years. This chapter will review the important studies and critical voices from a public policy standpoint. We will take a brief look at the theories and research methods used to study the effects from mediated violence. Then we turn to the various types of effects from consuming mediated violence, including behavioral, emotional, and cognitive effects. We also discuss the enjoyment of violent media content. This chapter concludes by looking at the debate over whether we should be concerned about the effects of violent media.

Media Violence Research and Public Policy: History and Future

Through the years, numerous studies of media effects have examined the negative effects on behavior that result from consuming media violence, whether reading, viewing, or listening to it. Since the beginning of radio, movies, and television, concern about media violence has been a major force in public policy making. The struggle for lawmakers has always been maintaining balance between First Amendment rights in a free society and concern for the public welfare.

Social scientists coordinated their efforts in the 1920s and 1930s to investigate the behavioral and social influences of viewing motion pictures. The Payne Fund studies are considered by many scholars as "the formal beginning of scientific inquiry into the study of media violence" (Sparks et al., 2009). The studies found that the violent and sexual content of movies did not match conventional social mores, but the research evidence did not provide any wholesale support for popular public contentions of detrimental effects on the social standards of adult movie audiences. However, the findings did suggest that particularly "vulnerable" children who were prone to juvenile delinquency were influenced by violent and criminal behavior they watched on the screen (Blumer & Hauser, 1933; Dysinger & Ruckmick, 1933).

The next major study to gain public attention appeared in the mid-1950s. This time, the comic book industry came under intense scrutiny. *The Seduction of the Innocent*, a book by psychiatrist Fredric Wertham (1954), contended that comic books offered children a distorted picture of reality and were responsible for problems with reading and even instances of juvenile delinquency. The author's methods and interpretations were questioned by the social scientific community, but his work captured the attention of the general public and the press, leading to an anti-comics movement (see Chapter 2). To prevent the government from regulating the content and sale of comic books, the Comics Magazine Association of America adopted the Comics Code of 1954—"one of the most restrictive examples of industry self-censorship in mass media history" (Campbell et al., 2019, p. 301). For instance, the code prohibited showing gruesome crimes and scenes of excessive violence. Scenes depicting excessive bloodshed, torture, zombies, vampires, ghosts, and werewolves were also banned.

In the 1950s and early 1960s, when television became a popular medium for entertainment, communication researchers in the United States and Great Britain became curious about the effects of exposure to the new medium, especially among young audiences. In their studies, researchers in the United States found a connection between viewing televised violence and aggressive behavior among youngsters (Schramm et al., 1961), whereas a British group did not find evidence of such a causal relationship and contended that such a link would be difficult to prove (Himmelweit et al., 1958).

Later, in the socially turbulent and violent 1960s, two more important reports again produced findings that conflicted with one another. First, President Lyndon Johnson's National Commission on the Causes and Prevention of Violence (1969) studied the issue and concluded that television could not be implicated as a primary cause for violence in society. Soon thereafter, the U.S. Surgeon General's Scientific Advisory Committee on Television and Social Behavior (1971) issued its five-volume report. According to the Surgeon General's committee, the evidence indicated that viewing violence on television *did* increase a viewer's tendencies to behave aggressively.

Throughout the 1980s, the Federal Communications Commission loosened earlier restrictions that had been placed on broadcasters to operate "in the public interest." Although the relaxing of restrictions signified a victory for broadcasters' First Amendment rights, the resulting changes in programming caused considerable public concern. Many children's programs disappeared, for example, and those that remained were more violent or highly commercial. A 1982 report from the National Institute of Mental Health called *Television and Behavior* fueled more public controversy. Congress reacted to the lowering of program standards by passing the Children's Television Act of 1990, which required broadcasters to air a certain amount of educational programming suitable for young viewers. It also placed time limits on the number of commercials shown on children's programs.

Three years later, Congress began hearings to explore the subject of media violence and its effects on children. Due to increased public awareness and concern over the issue, the television networks decided to begin labeling programs to warn parents about violent and unsuitable content. This led to the suggestion for some device that would permit parents to control access to televised programs. The Telecommunications Act of 1996 made installation of the V-chip mandatory on new televisions. This device allows parents to block programming containing violence, sex, or strong language from being received in their homes. The act also required the television industry to rate programs based upon suitability for certain age levels (see Figure 11.1).

Many saw these developments as positive steps, but others pointed to problems inherent in attempts to limit or prohibit children's exposure to undesirable programming (Potter & Warren, 1996). According to some, advisory warnings and blocking devices created a "forbidden fruit" effect, causing children to be extremely interested in seeing the very programs their parents were trying to block (Christenson, 1992).

The National Television Violence Study (NTVS) conducted by researchers at several leading universities began in 1994. The three-year project examined 10,000 hours of programs on 23 of the most frequently viewed broadcast and cable television channels. Researchers found that the *way violence was portrayed* on primetime network and cable shows encouraged children to imitate the behavior they saw. In addition, age-based ratings did not indicate the amount of violent content in a program (Federman, 1998).

> More important than the simple prevalence of violent content, however, is the consistent finding that when violence does occur, it is portrayed all too often in ways that a body of research suggests will increase the likelihood of negative consequences to viewers. . . . Roughly three-quarters of all violent scenes show no remorse, criticism, or penalty for violence; violence is associated with humor about 40% of the time; over half of all violent interactions show no pain. . . . Cartoons contain high rates of violence portrayed in ways that many existing studies agree

will increase the probability of harmful effects. Children under 7 years are particularly at risk because of limited ability to distinguish fantasy from reality. (p. 14)

The context in which most violence is presented on television poses risks for viewers. According to Strasburger and Wilson (2014), the NTVS found that violence on television was frequently glamorized (perpetrated by good characters who could be viewed as role models), sanitized (the pain of victims was not depicted and rarely were there negative consequences for violence), and trivialized (many violent scenes included some form of humor).

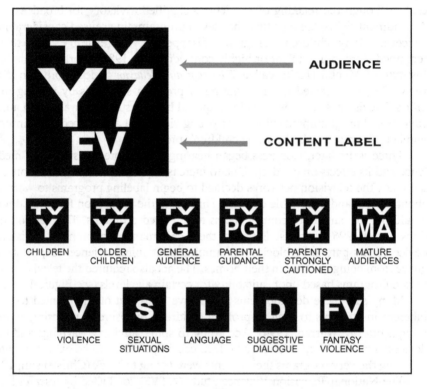

Figure 11.1   The Federal Communications Commission's *TV Parental Guidelines.*

After the Columbine High School shootings in Littleton, Colorado, in April 1999, the perceived link between media violence and murderous behavior thrust itself squarely into the public eye once again. The reactions of horror to the senseless slayings resulted in congressional actions and a subsequent report on violence from the U.S. Surgeon General ordered by President Clinton. *Youth Violence: A Report of the Surgeon General* found a strong relationship between consumption of media violence and short-term aggression, but the aggressive behavior that typically resulted stopped far short of breaking limbs or committing murder.

The American Academy of Pediatrics, American Academy of Child and Adolescent Psychiatry, American Psychological Association, American Medical Association, American Academy of Family Physicians, and American Psychiatric Association (2000) issued a Joint Statement on the Impact of Entertainment Violence on Children. It pointed to 30 years of research that had suggested that viewing violent media content could lead to aggression, especially among children, but it qualified its stance on the issue by pointing out that other important factors contribute to youth aggression, such as the influence of peers, the situation at home, and the easy availability of weapons in this country. Similarly, the NTVS advised that "peer influences, family role models, social and economic status, educational level, and the availability of weapons can each significantly alter the likelihood of a particular reaction to viewing violence on television (Federman, 1998, p. 5).

Despite the enormous number of studies linking mediated violence to aggression, critics point to statistical problems within the studies that have to do with effects sizes, which tend to be small to moderate. Researchers usually respond by pointing out that even small effects sizes could be detrimental when considering that mass media audiences number in the millions.

Other critics point to the nature of the experiments in an artificial setting and the use of college students as subjects, as well as the short-term nature of the effects usually measured. Zillmann and Weaver (1999) answered some of these criticisms:

> It seems that critics of media-violence research could only be satisfied with longitudinal experimental studies in which, within gender and a multitude of personality variables, random assignment is honored and exposure to violent fare is rigorously controlled—that is, with research that in a free society simply cannot be conducted. (p. 147)

Although some critics of media violence research acknowledge the connection between violent media consumption and increases in aggressive thoughts, feelings, and behaviors, they caution against generalizing laboratory and survey results to severe acts of violence in the real world, such as homicide and assault. Whereas lawmakers, popular media, and even some researchers try to link violent media to severe real-world violence, the vast majority of studies on mediated violence do not make such a leap. Instead, most studies only point to aggressive predispositions and tendencies being measured after viewing mediated violence—and aggressive tendencies *do not* equal criminal behavior.

Savage (2004) conducted a methodological review of the literature on media violence and concluded that a clear causal relationship between viewing violence and subsequent criminal behavior does not exist (see also Grimes & Bergen, 2008; Savage, 2008). Furthermore, a meta-analysis of 26 independent samples of subjects also found no positive association between media violence and criminal behavior (Savage & Yancey, 2008). More recently, a study looked at popular violent video games and violent crimes and found no evidence that the games were positively related to severe real-world violence in the United States (Markey, Markey, & French, 2015). Ferguson (2015) found that as consumption of violent video games increased, youth violence actually decreased. Similarly, a pair of studies analyzed decades of data on movie violence and real-world violence, particularly homicides. Both concluded that violent content in films did not contribute to societal violence (Ferguson, 2015; Markey, French, & Markey, 2015).

> However, we would note that just because violent media does not appear to con-
> tribute to trends in violent crime, this does not imply that previous research exam-
> ining violent media is unimportant. There is ample evidence that violent media
> can increase aggressive cognitions, aggressive affect, and some minor aggressive
> behaviors. Although watching a violent film does not seem to be related to shifts in
> homicide or aggravated assault rates, such exposure may affect other types of less
> severe aggressive behaviors such as bullying, spreading gossip, minor fights at
> school, pushing and shoving, or hurling insults. (Markey, French, & Markey, 2015,
> pp. 168–169)

Key Theories Used to Study Media Violence Effects

A number of theories help us understand the effects of consuming violent media, many of which have been discussed in previous chapters, such as social cognitive the-ory, priming, and cultivation (see Chapters 4, 5, and 8, respectively). Scholars also use the General Aggression Model (GAM; Anderson & Bushman, 2002, 2018) and the differential susceptibility to media effects model (DSMM; Valkenburg & Peter, 2013) introduced in Chapters 5 and 1, respectively.

We will provide a review of previously discussed theories and take a more in-depth look at both the GAM and DSMM.

Social Cognitive Theory

Albert Bandura's social cognitive theory is "among the most heavily cited when it comes to explaining how violent media content may induce aggressive behavior" (Piotrowski & Fikkers, 2020, p. 213). As we discussed in Chapter 4, the theory posits that we learn behavior either by direct experience or by observing others, which can include "family members, peers, teachers, and characters portrayed in movies, TV shows, and video games" (Prot et al., 2017, p. 260).

Learning behaviors, including aggressive ones, is a three-step process: (1) observ-ing certain behaviors, (2) acting out those behaviors for ourselves, and (3) relying on social cues to either encourage or dissuade us from continuing those behaviors (Ban-dura, 2009).

One of the major concerns in research into effects of violent media is how long the effects may last. Observational learning is key to both short- and long-term effects that violent media can have on aggression. In the short-term, exposure can lead to mimicry (which is discussed in more detail later in this chapter), whereas repeated exposure plays a role in long-term increases in aggression (Anderson et al. 2003; Anderson & Carnagey, 2014).

Whether someone imitates an observed aggressive action also hinges on the observed consequences. For instance, if the aggressive actions seen on a movie, show, or video game are rewarded, children are more likely to emulate those actions, but if the observed actions are punished, children are less likely to imitate them (Prot et al., 2017).

Cartoons and movies made for children contain numerous acts of violence. Generations of kids have been entertained by Tom and Jerry's violent game of cat-and-mouse (pun intended) for almost a century.

Desensitization Theory

The concept of **desensitization** is a simple one: the more we see or experience something, the more accustomed we become to it and the less we react to it. We can become desensitized through consuming violent media—repeated exposure to violence that initially made us anxious or fearful reduces our emotional response. Desensitization can occur from short-term exposure to violent media content (such as playing violent video games or watching violent films) resulting in decreased empathy for victims of violence and decreased helping (Anderson et al., 2003, 2010; Bushman & Anderson, 2009; Greitemeyer & Mügge, 2014). However, this theory primarily focuses on long-term effects of exposure:

> Over time and with increased exposure, audience members become more accustomed to aggressive behavior, which then impacts moral judgments and behaviors. In particular, it is anticipated that audiences will find violent content less ethically problematic and eventually become indifferent to enacting and observing aggressive behavior in their daily life. (Piotrowski & Fikkers, 2020, p. 214)

As Prot et al. (2017) note, desensitization is one of the "key mediating mechanisms of media violence effects on aggression and related variables" (p. 261). Not all desensitization is bad—for instance, surgeons becoming desensitized to the sight of blood. However, in the context of media violence, desensitization leads to mostly harmful effects, such as disinhibition (which will be discussed later in this chapter) and reducing the likelihood of helping victims of violent acts (Anderson & Carnagey, 2014).

Priming Theory

In contrast to desensitization theory's focus on long-term effects, priming helps explain short-term effects from media exposure (Piotrowski & Fikkers, 2020). Recall from Chapter 5 that a person's memory can be thought of as a complex network of interlinked nodes. The nodes represent certain concepts or schemas (mental frameworks we use to better understand the world), and the links represent associations among them. Exposure to a stimulus can activate—or *prime*—related concepts and schemata, temporarily making them more accessible. Numerous researchers argue that violent media consumption can prime violent schemas and activate other related schemas in our cognitive network.

Priming can also activate behavioral *scripts* (sets of "rules" for how to process and respond to particular situations). Scripts not only guide our interpretation of events but also influence our behaviors. We can learn aggressive scripts by observing violent behavior in the media. For example, seeing characters on a TV show or movie use a gun to resolve an argument could help viewers learn a "conflict → use gun → resolution" script that could have real-world consequences (Anderson & Carnagey, 2014).

Excitation Transfer Theory

Whereas priming argues that activation of interconnected nodes in a person's neural network can trigger aggressive thoughts and behaviors, some scholars suggest the relationship is explained by a physical response: arousal. **Excitation transfer theory** says people experience physical arousal while consuming certain media content. However, once the media exposure ends, arousal does not automatically switch off, rather it dissipates slowly (Zillmann, 1971, 1978, 1979, 1982b). During this time, arousal can transfer to behaviors performed after consuming media content, resulting in those experiences seeming more arousing (i.e., misattribution; Zillmann, 1978).

For example, if you are frustrated (e.g., your professor assigns a group project that you must work on over Spring Break) and then you experience something that makes you angry (e.g., someone bumps into you in the hallway, causing you to drop your phone on the floor, cracking the screen), then the residual arousal from the first event (frustration) will be added to the arousal response from the second event (anger). This results in you experiencing the second event more intensely than you would have otherwise (Piotrowski & Fikkers, 2020).

If a person consumes violent media content prior to a situation that makes them angry, their anger may be intensified—increasing the likelihood that they will behave aggressively. Furthermore, Anderson and Bushman (2001) proposed that heightened arousal from consuming violent media content energizes a person's action tendencies immediately after exposure. "Individuals may feel more aroused after consuming violent media and then opt for action-based activities afterwards, which may be more aggressive in nature than had they consumed less violent media content" (Piotrowski & Fikkers, 2020, p. 216). If a person experiencing heightened arousal is provoked, they are more likely to have an aggressive response (Ireland et al., 2018).

Cultivation Theory

As we discussed in Chapter 8, cultivation theory proposes that over time, heavy viewers of television develop—or *cultivate*—views of the world similar to what they see on television. We also know that heavy viewers overestimate crime in the real world and see reality as a "mean" world full of violence and crime (Gerbner & Gross, 1976).

Bushman's (2016) meta-analysis of 37 studies with a total more than 10,000 participants found that violent media exposure was linked to hostile worldviews. Although cultivation research has generally revealed relatively small effect sizes, the theory has received consistent empirical support. Cultivation can help to explain long-term effects. Anderson and Bushman (2018) note, "It is the cumulative effects of violent media exposure that pose the greatest risks to increasing aggressive and violent behavior" (p. 398).

General Aggression Model

Anderson and Bushman (2002, 2018) integrated the theories reviewed above to create the **General Aggression Model** (GAM) to explain aggressive behavior. The GAM was not designed specifically to explain media violence effects, nor is it solely a mass communication theory. Instead, it provides a "general bio-social-cognitive model of how various complex processes combine to influence the likelihood that aggressive behavior will be enacted (Anderson & Bushman, 2018, pp. 387–388).

As you can see in Figure 11.2, *personality development* and *social encounters* are the two major components of the model. Personality development includes biological

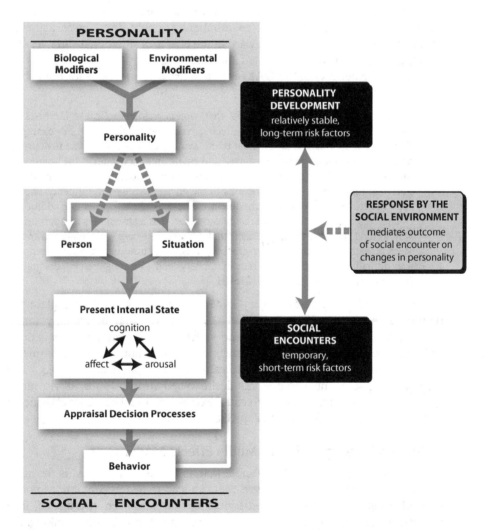

Figure 11.2   Anderson and Bushman revised the GAM in 2018 to highlight the importance of the response from the social environment on a person's behavior.

Adapted from Anderson & Bushman, 2018, p. 389.

modifiers (e.g., ADD/ADHD, impulsivity deficits, low serotonin, etc.) and environmental modifiers (e.g., cultural norms, difficult life conditions, exposure to violent media, antisocial peers, etc.). These are "relatively stable distal long-term risk factors and processes" (Anderson & Bushman, 2018, p. 390). Social encounters, which are also sometimes referred to as *episodes*, contain short-term proximal risk factors and processes. These include relatively stable personality traits, beliefs, and attitudes (e.g., aggression scripts, attitudes toward violence, narcissism, self-image, etc.) and situational factors related to the situation at hand (e.g., bad moods, pain/discomfort, social exclusion, social stress, violent media, uncomfortable temperatures, etc.).

Personality development influences social encounters, which in turn influence personality development. The latter is mediated by the response of the social environment. For instance, if the social environment strongly discourages aggression by actively punishing it or failing to reward it, the effects of situational variables that tend to trigger aggression can be mitigated and vice versa.

One of the benefits of the GAM is that is explains processes for both short- and long-term effects:

> In the short term, the model posits that violent media can cause increases in aggression via a person's cognitive, affective, and physiological state. For example, Bushman and Anderson (2002) note that playing a violent video game may prime aggressive cognitions, increase arousal, and create an angry state. In the long-term, the GAM specifies that learning processes—namely, learning how to perceive, interpret, judge, and respond to events in the environment—will influence knowledge structures. In this way, each violent media episode is seen as one additional trial to "learn that the world is a dangerous place, that aggression is an appropriate way to deal with conflict and anger, that aggression works" (p. 1680) and more. With repeated exposure, these hostile knowledge structures become more complex and difficult to change, which may ultimately lead to an aggressive personality. (Piotrowski & Fikkers, 2020, pp. 216–217)

In addition to aggression, the GAM has also been used to explain violence (DeWall & Anderson, 2011; DeWall et al., 2011). You may be asking yourself what the difference is between aggression and violence. In general, *aggression* is defined as any behaviors that intend to harm someone who does not want to be harmed, while *violence* is any behavior that intends to cause extreme physical harm (e.g., injury or even death) to someone who does not desire to be harmed. "Thus, all violent acts are aggressive, but only acts intended to cause extreme physical harm are classified as violent" (Anderson & Bushman, 2018, p. 388).

Differential Susceptibility to Media Effects Model

Piotrowski and Fikkers (2020) note that as useful as the GAM is for helping us understand risk factors and processes that can lead to aggression, it does not encompass other outcomes related to media violence that have been investigated, including prosocial behavior, empathy, criminal violence, and ethical decision-making. Furthermore, researchers also face the challenge of identifying which competing media effects theories are the best for explaining the relationship between media violence and the observed outcome. This is where the **differential susceptibility to media**

effects model (DSMM) developed by Valkenburg and Peter (2013) is a valuable tool for understanding media effects.

Recall from Chapter 1 that the goal of the DSMM is "to reveal how and why specific types of media affect certain individuals; why some individuals are particularly susceptible to media effects; and how this susceptibility is enhanced or reduced" (Valkenburg & Peter, 2013, p. 237). The model identifies three types of susceptibility variables: dispositional (e.g., gender, personality, attitudes, moods), developmental (i.e., people tend to prefer content that aligns with cognitive and emotional development for their age), and social (i.e., influences such as family, friends, school; cultural norms). The DSMM also proposes three response states to media that can mediate media effects: cognitive (i.e., how much attention and cognitive effort is devoted to understanding media content), emotional (i.e., reactions to the media content; empathy and sympathy for characters), and excitative (i.e., the level of physiological arousal).

Piotrowski and Fikkers (2020) acknowledge that although the DSMM has only been applied to a handful of media violence studies, "the evidence—both using and related to the DSMM—suggests that the model deserves special consideration. . . . In many cases, effect sizes reported in media violence studies are relatively small, while in other cases there seem to be reasonably robust effects for certain groups of the population" (pp. 217–218).

Furthermore, the vast body of research on media violence is consistent with the DSMM's predictions of the relationship between susceptibility variables (i.e., dispositional, developmental, and social factors) and subsequent media effects (Valkenburg & Piotrowski, 2017). For instance, people with an aggressive temperament or a strong need for sensation (dispositional factors) seem to be more susceptible to the effects of violent media. Similarly with regards to development, most researchers agree that children are especially at risk for negative effects due to violence in children's media and the fact that children's emotional and cognitive capacities are not fully formed.

Some research into social contexts was inspired by cultivation theory and the concept of resonance (see Chapter 8). Researchers looked at whether living in an environment that endorses aggressive actions had an impact on media violence effects in teens. Teens who grew up in households with increased family conflict were particularly aroused by violent media and were more likely to subsequently demonstrate aggression (Fikkers, Piotrowski, & Valkenburg, 2016; Fikkers et al., 2013). In addition, teens were more aggressive after consuming violent media if they thought their friends were likely to behave similarly (Fikkers, Piotrowski, Lugtig, & Valkenburg, 2016).

Lastly, the DSMM acknowledges that the content itself matters, particularly the ways in which it is shaped, contextualized, and delivered (Piotrowski & Fikkers, 2020). Despite the terms "violent media" or "media violence" often being used as though all violent content were the same, we know that it can be very different contextually.

> A documentary containing violent scenes that is meant to inform viewers cannot be compared with a movie in which a character attacks his enemies with a chainsaw. In other words, it is not difficult to predict that the effects of viewing *Schindler's List* will differ from those of *Terminator Genisys*. (Valkenburg & Piotrowski, 2017, p. 111)

Despite individual differences among viewers, research indicates that people often experience similar, harmful effects after viewing particular types of violence portrayed in certain contexts (e.g., Anderson et al., 2010; Bandura, 1986; Federman, 1998; Krcmar & Valkenburg, 1999; Paik & Comstock, 1994). Researchers have identified five key contextual elements that make people susceptible to negative effects.

1. The perpetrator is an appealing role model.
2. Violence is rewarded.
3. Violence is justified.
4. Violence has no consequences.
5. Violence is arousing.

Research has shown that many television programs include these "high risk" contexts. Children, especially, are at high risk for learning aggressive behaviors from portrayals that feature all five of the contexts. Researchers from the University of California at Santa Barbara working on the National Television Violence Study found that most violence on the screen is initiated by the "good guys," the screen characters that are most likely to serve as role models. Moreover, only about 15% of primetime programs revealed the long-term, negative consequences of violent behavior. Approximately three out of four violent acts were performed without remorse or penalty, and the "bad guys" went unpunished in about 4 of 10 programs (Federman, 1998).

Media Violence Research Methods

When carried to perhaps its worst extreme, the modeling or imitation of screen violence has been linked to violent and brutal "copycat" crimes—including rapes and murders. As we discussed in Chapter 1, violent copycat crimes are among the most disturbing examples of imitative behavior. The sensational nature of copycat crimes attracts the notice of the news media; therefore, examples of such crimes are prevalent in the public's memory (see Chapter 7 in Valkenburg & Piotrowski, 2017, for a review). In reality, however, copycat crimes are *extremely* rare. Millions of other people who watch the same movie or show or play the same video game are *not* inspired to imitate such extreme violent behavior. As we just discussed with the DSMM, this suggests that individual factors—such as a person's disposition (or predisposition to violent behavior), state of mind, emotional stability, and personal circumstances—play a major role in determining whether a person will behave aggressively after exposure to violent content.

Social scientists attempt to record more subtle media effects—those that they can measure through strictly controlled experiments and studies, which do not involve actual harm or injury to anyone. Researchers concentrate their efforts on several major issues related to media violence. Many studies are designed to measure the *amount* of violence that occurs on various media. Other studies explore the *contexts* in which the violence occurs, as research has demonstrated that such contexts are very important in determining the extent of harmful effects. Most importantly, these and other studies examine viewers' exposure to such violence and attempt to answer the difficult question: What effect does media violence have on those who consume it?

Research studies on the effects of viewing violent media fare have employed a number of different methodologies. This methodological diversity in the literature is seen as one of the greatest strengths of media violence research (Prot et al., 2017).

Laboratory Experiments

Strictly controlled experiments in a laboratory setting have provided compelling evidence that watching media violence may cause a viewer to behave more aggressively. Such experiments are constructed to show a *causal relationship* between viewing film, TV, and video game violence and behaving aggressively. Critics point to the unnatural circumstances surrounding the viewing in such experiments and question whether the results have any meaning in the real world.

One experiment tested the role of song lyrics, video clips, and musical tone on aggressive tendencies. Individuals exposed to violent lyrics, whether or not violent images accompanied the music, showed the highest level of aggression (Brummert et al., 2011).

A three-part experiment by Anderson and Carnagey (2009) looked at the effects of playing a violent video game versus a nonviolent video game on players' aggressive cognitions, affect, and behavior immediately after gameplay. In each of the experiments, participants were randomly assigned to play a violent sports video game (MLB Slugfest Baseball or NFL Blitz Football) or a nonviolent video game (MVP Baseball 2004 or Madden Football) for 20 minutes. Study 1 found that those who played a violent game were quicker to identify aggressive words and showed an increase in aggressive thoughts compared to those who played the nonviolent games. Study 2 found that those in the violent game condition scored higher on a questionnaire designed to mea-

---

Advances in Brain Science

Incorporation of neuroscience into media violence studies gives researchers a look into people's brains as they consume violent media. In fact, Anderson and Bushman's (2018) update to the GAM added "brain structure and function" as an influential factor in the formation of an aggressive personality.

Some media violence research studies have used Magnetic Resonance Imaging (MRI) to examine the brain as it is exposed to violent content. One study found differences in brain activity among children who viewed violence as opposed to children who did not view violence (Murray et al., 2006). In another study, 13 males were scanned with MRI while playing a violent video game. The images showed low activity in the areas of the brain related to affect or emotion (Weber et al., 2006).

A study by Gentile et al. (2016) used functional MRI (fMRI) to study differences between habitual violent and nonviolent video game players. The nonviolent gamers showed increases in the brain's emotional response regions while playing violent games; meanwhile, violent game players showed active suppression in those same areas. Furthermore, participants who did not normally play violent games showed increases in regions for spatial attention and navigation when playing a violent game, but participants who normally played violent games did not. Overall, their findings provided support for "both the 'positive' effects of violent games on visual/spatial processing, and the 'negative' effects of violent games on desensitization" (p. 49).

More recently, Hummer et al. (2019) utilized fMRI and found that playing a violent video game reduced activity in the prefrontal cortex, which they say could impair someone's ability to control aggressive behavior over the long term. Cognitive functions controlled by the prefrontal cortex are linked to less aggression (Bartholow, 2018).

For an extended look at the use of neuroscience in media effects research, see Bolls et al. (2020).

sure aggressive affect. The survey included items like "I feel like I'm about to explode" and "I feel furious." Study 3 showed increases in aggressive behavior for those in the violent game condition. All participants were given the opportunity to blast a supposed opponent with an uncomfortable noise. Those who played one of the violent video games selected over 76% more high-intensity noise blasts compared to those in the nonviolent game condition. Importantly, these aggressive effects occurred even when controlling for perceived competitiveness in the video games, meaning that the effects were the result of the violent content and not of the competitive nature of the games.

Field Experiments

Most field experiments have taken place among children in an institutional setting, such as a nursery school. Prior to viewing violence, the children are randomly assigned to groups (one group views violence and another sees nonviolent programming). Their levels of natural aggressiveness and attitudes are measured and then compared to measures taken *after* viewing violent content. Field experiments avoid the problem of unnaturalness associated with laboratory experiments.

One field study worth noting provided strong evidence for the connection between viewing violent content and behaving aggressively (Williams, 1986). Three communities in Canada were selected for the study. When the research began, there was no television in one community; the second received only one channel; and the third had access to several channels. The study showed that the children from the community without television showed significant increases in aggressive behavior over a two-year period after TV was introduced. The aggressiveness of children in the other two communities did not change over the same period.

In addition to studying effects on aggression, some studies look at effects of media violence on prosocial behavior. In a quasi-experiment outside a movie theater by Bushman and Anderson (2009, Study 2), a young woman with her ankle wrapped dropped her crutches and had difficulty picking them up. She performed this behavior before and after a violent or a nonviolent movie played inside. There was no difference in bystanders' willingness to help the woman before they watched one of the movies. However, after watching a violent movie, viewers took longer to help the woman compared to those who watched the nonviolent movie or had not yet watched any movie.

Correlational Surveys

In these cross-sectional studies, typically viewers are asked to read a list of program titles and select the ones that they watch regularly. Researchers rely on content analyses of the amount of violence in potential programs to develop a measure of the amount of violent programming exposure per viewer. Viewers are also asked about their attitudes and behavior in order to gauge some measure of aggressiveness or hostility. The two measures are then correlated to ascertain any relationship between the viewing of violence and subsequent aggressive behavior or attitudes. The major problem with such studies is that they are ultimately unable to demonstrate a causal relationship with any degree of certainty. There have been findings of statistically significant correlations between consumption of violent media and aggressive or hostile behaviors and attitudes, but most of those associations have been relatively weak.

One study made use of survey research in a short-term longitudinal design. Third and fourth graders, their peers, and teachers were surveyed twice in the school year to determine if various forms of aggression might be predicted by violent media exposure. "Children's consumption of media violence early in the school year predicted higher verbally aggressive behavior, higher relationally aggressive behavior, higher physically aggressive behavior, and less prosocial behavior later in the school year" (Gentile et al., 2011, p. 193).

Longitudinal Studies

These studies attempt to identify relationships that may develop over a period of time between consumption of violent fare and antisocial attitudes and behaviors. According to Gunter (1994), such studies "represent perhaps the best kind of studies of TV effects. They can test causal hypotheses and they usually employ sound sampling methods" (p. 174). Researchers remain in contact with participants and test them at various intervals to determine whether consumption of media violence is affecting them. Longitudinal studies investigate the assumption that exposure to media violence has a *cumulative* effect; in other words, does repeated exposure to media violence over time have an increasing effect on aggressive behavior or attitudes?

In particular, children who have consumed a heavy diet of media violence in their most formative years are more likely than their peers to behave aggressively as adolescents and adults. In one extensive longitudinal investigation, children who watched a lot of violent media at ages 8 to 10 were significantly more aggressive 15 years later when they were adults (Huesmann et al., 2003). After conducting interviews with the participants and their spouses and friends, results showed that children who had watched more violent TV exhibited significantly more aggressive behaviors in their mid-20s. Males who watched more violent TV during childhood were nearly twice as likely to have assaulted their spouses as an adult. They were also 18% more likely to have threatened someone with a gun or knife. It is important to note that violent TV consumption as a child was still a significant predictor of aggressive behavior as an adult, even after controlling for effects of intellectual ability, socioeconomic status, and parenting factors.

Intervention Studies

Just as vaccinations are used to inoculate people to protect them from dangerous or deadly diseases, intervention studies are designed to *intervene* and inoculate viewers against the harmful effects of viewing televised violence. With these studies, the harmful effects of viewing violence are assumed to be prevalent in the population; researchers then attempt to alleviate the negative effects through some intervention strategy. Some intervention studies have indicated that increased media literacy (critical understanding of media content and production methods) may reduce the negative effects of mediated violence (e.g., Krahé & Busching, 2015; Webb et al., 2010).

Meta-Analyses

The technique of meta-analysis allows media effects researchers to combine the large number of studies that have been done on media violence and its effects in a statistical study that measures overall effects sizes (Sparks et al., 2009). A number of meta-analyses have confirmed that exposure to mediated violence and subsequent aggression are indeed related (Anderson et al., 2010; Christensen & Wood, 2007; Greitemeyer & Mügge, 2014; Hearold, 1986; Paik & Comstock, 1994; Prescott et al., 2018; Sherry, 2001; Wood et al., 1991).

For instance, Anderson and his colleagues (2010) conducted a meta-analytic review of the effects of violent video games on aggression, empathy, and prosocial behavior. "The evidence strongly suggests that exposure to violent video games is a causal risk factor for increased aggressive behavior, aggressive cognition, and aggressive affect and for decreased empathy and prosocial behavior" (p. 151). A later meta-analysis obtained similar results (Greitemeyer & Mügge, 2014). The researchers also studied the effects of prosocial games, finding that those games fostered prosocial outcomes and reduced antisocial ones.

The Psychological Impact of Media Violence

Communication scholars have identified three different levels of psychological impact that violent media content may have on viewers. These levels—behavioral, affective, and cognitive—refer to the different types of effects from consuming violent media. In this section, studies from the various methodologies described earlier will be used to illustrate what happens at each of the levels.

Behavioral Effects

When a 4-year-old boy watches an old episode of the *Power Rangers*, then pretends he is the Red Ranger while kicking and hitting "the villain" (his 2-year-old brother), that child is exhibiting a *behavioral effect* from viewing televised violence. Specifically, the child is using the mechanism of *imitation*, one of five major mechanisms through which behavioral effects may occur that we will discuss in this section. The other important mechanisms include *arousal, disinhibition, desensitization*, and *catharsis.*

Arousal.   The behavioral effect of this mechanism is that of excitement or, as the name says, arousal. Whenever a viewer watches a violent scene (or a particularly funny or sexually explicit scene), they become excited or emotionally aroused, and this arousal can be measured physiologically. Viewers usually do not attribute their elevated arousal to what they are viewing. Recall our earlier discussion of excitation transfer theory: If a teenage boy who is already mad about something is watching a violent program, he interprets his heightened arousal, which is in part due to excitation from the television program, as intense anger. He may therefore respond more aggressively than he would if he had not watched the violent program, particularly if an opportunity to become aggressive occurs shortly after viewing (Tannenbaum & Zillmann, 1975; Zillmann, 1988a, 2000).

Disinhibition.   The disinhibition mechanism operates under the assumption that as viewers grow more accustomed to seeing violent media content, especially when violence is justified by the situation or is socially sanctioned, they become less inhibited by social sanctions against committing violent acts.

Psychological Effects from Exposure to TV Violence

Behavioral

Watching TV violence influences a person's behavior. Five major categories of behavioral effects:

• Arousal • Disinhibition • Imitation • Desensitization • Catharsis

Affective (Emotional)

Watching TV violence causes an immediate or long-term emotional reaction.

Cognitive

Watching TV violence influences a viewer's beliefs about the real world.

In one group of laboratory studies, a confederate angered research participants who then watched a clip from a violent film (usually a boxing match, which is a socially sanctioned form of violence). The same participants were then allowed to administer electric shocks to the person who had angered them. Other research participants were angered and shown a nonviolent film, while a third group of participants assigned to a control group were not angered. Participants who saw the violent clip delivered harsher shocks than those who had not viewed violence; those who had been angered beforehand and viewed the sanctioned violence were the most aggressive of all. The investigators interpreted these results as providing evidence that watching sanctioned violence in the film clips removed some inhibitions, therefore permitting the research participants to be more aggressive (Berkowitz & Alioto, 1973; Berkowitz et al., 1963; Berkowitz & Geen, 1966; Berkowitz & Rawlings, 1963). Other research also found that viewers behaved more aggressively after watching a program presenting sanctioned violence, especially if they were angry when they began watching (Berkowitz, 1962, 1965, 1974); however, more specialized investigations are required to indicate whether these results are due to disinhibition.

Longitudinal studies have provided evidence for the disinhibition mechanism. One example is the 15-year study discussed earlier in this chapter in which participants who had watched more violent TV as children exhibited significantly more aggressive behaviors in their mid-20s (Huesmann et al., 2003). In another such study conducted decades earlier, researchers collected data from about 800 8-year-olds regarding their TV viewing habits and their levels of aggressiveness. Ten years later, the researchers located about half of the original group and collected the same data. There was a strong positive correlation between viewing televised violence when young and measures of aggression at age 18 (Eron et al., 1972).

Imitation.   This mechanism assumes that viewers learn from what they see on television and sometimes try to mimic the actions themselves. This is especially true for young children who identify with the characters they see on television and try to imitate them. (Chapter 4 discusses the concept of *observational learning,* the essence of the imitation mechanism.)

Recall from Chapter 4 that the laboratory experiments of Albert Bandura (1965a, 1978, 1979, 1982, 1986) and Bandura, Ross, and Ross (1963a, 1963b) found that children imitated the aggressive behaviors they witnessed on the screen. The children who had seen films of the Bobo doll being battered were not only more aggressive toward the Bobo doll than were other children but they also copied the violent behaviors they had witnessed in the film. Bandura attributed the copycat behavior in part to the disinhibition mechanism and in part to observational learning or the imitation mechanism.

Several intervention studies with children have attempted to mitigate the imitation effect. These studies have revealed that making children aware that viewing violence may have harmful effects on them and teaching them critical viewing skills may reduce future aggressive tendencies (Huesmann & Eron, 1986; Singer & Singer, 1983). Some significant research has focused on reducing the negative consequences of consuming mediated violence. Nathanson (1999) found that parental involvement—whether limiting the type and amount of programs viewed, talking to their children about the violence they see, or teaching them critical viewing skills (such as recognizing exaggeration or distortion or determining the consequences if the violence were real)—reduces aggressive effects.

Desensitization. As we discussed earlier, repeatedly witnessing violent acts on the screen has cumulative effects. As exposure over the years increases, viewers become less and less sensitive to seeing violence, less sympathetic to the victims of violence (Linz et al., 1988), and more likely to accept real-life violence. Children who viewed a violent program beforehand were less likely to go for adult help when they witnessed a playroom fight between two other children (Drabman & Thomas, 1974; Thomas et al., 1977). In another study, children who watched 25 or more hours of television per week experienced less physiological arousal when viewing TV violence than children who watched less than four hours per week (Cline et al., 1973). People who consumed more violent media content were less likely to experience arousal from a violent film clip and were more likely to access aggressive thoughts after the viewing (Krahé et al., 2011).

Similar desensitization effects have been observed among children who play a lot of violent video games. In particular, playing violent video games seems to have a pronounced effect on diminishing the empathy players feel for victims of violence (e.g., Bushman & Anderson, 2009; Funk et al., 2004).

Catharsis. The catharsis mechanism purportedly allows viewers to vent their aggressive impulses harmlessly. In the 1950s and 1960s, Feshbach (1955, 1961) reported the existence of a cathartic effect when participants in his experiments were able to release aggressive urges nonviolently by viewing acts of televised violence or by fantasizing about violence. In 1971, Feshbach and Singer observed teenage boys in natural settings—residential schools and homes—for six weeks. During the experimental period, the researchers controlled the boys' exposure to televised violence. Boys who had watched mostly nonviolent television behaved *more aggressively* toward their peers than the boys who had watched violent programming, thus presumably indicating a catharsis effect.

It should be noted that very few of the hundreds of experimental studies have replicated Feshbach's findings or have supported the catharsis mechanism. Despite this weak body of scientific evidence, a substantial portion of the public believes that catharsis occurs through watching mediated violence. Media industry spokespeople happily remind the public and its elected representatives of the alleged benefits of catharsis every time a public investigation of the effects of media violence is undertaken.

Violent Media Content and Empathy

In addition to aggression, researchers have studied the effects of habitual use of violent media on empathy. For example, one study looked at more than 1,200 seventh- and eighth-grade German students and measured their media use, aggression, and empathy (Krahé & Möller, 2010). The researchers found that use of violent media led to higher levels of physical aggression and lower empathy.

Conversely, other research has shown that people with low levels of empathy tend to consume more violent media content (Sigurdsson et al., 2006).

Affective (or Emotional) Effects

Research indicates that everyone, regardless of age, experiences an emotional reaction when viewing violent media content. Studies have examined reactions to programs that depict violence, defined as either physical injury or threat of bodily harm. The emotional effects from watching such violence may be immediate (e.g., fright, anxiety) or long term (e.g., persistent fear of becoming a victim of crime).

Palazzolo and Roberto (2011) showed study participants media news messages about intimate partner violence "containing information designed to increase or decrease attributions of responsibility both toward the perpetrator and toward the victim" (p. 1). The viewers experienced many emotions, but only certain emotions (i.e., anger or sympathy) were triggered related to whether or not the viewers saw the perpetrator or the victim as being responsible for the violence.

The reactions of children have been of particular interest to social scientists involved in this realm of media effects research. Studies have revealed that children become very frightened when viewing certain kinds of programs. These fright reactions, which are sometimes very intense, have been observed by a number of researchers (see Blumer & Hauser, 1933; Himmelweit et al., 1958; Preston, 1941; Schramm et al., 1961). The reactions range from loss of control over their feelings (Blumer & Hauser, 1933) to horrible nightmares (Singer, 1975).

Research has also revealed that children experience fright reactions to television news as well as to fictional drama. In a survey, Cantor and Nathanson (1996) surveyed parents and found that almost 40% of their children had been frightened or upset by something seen on newscasts. The most fear-producing stories were those that involved violence among strangers, wars and famines abroad, and natural disasters. Younger children tended to react emotionally to upsetting images such as weapons and people dying, whereas older children were more troubled by abstract issues—fears of nuclear wars, bombing, and the reality of death. We will explore the effects of frightening media further in Chapter 13.

Cognitive Effects

When viewing mediated violence influences a viewer's beliefs about the real world, that viewer has experienced a *cognitive* effect. Indeed, many of the affective fright reactions just discussed may have become cognitive effects over time. The most extensive research on such cognitive effects has been performed by George Gerbner and his associates.

In the 1970s, Gerbner and his colleagues analyzed data from national public opinion surveys to gauge some of the cognitive effects of television viewing. The surveys contained a large amount of useful information from each of the participants, such as how much time they spent watching television and their perceptions about the world in which they lived. The researchers found a positive correlation between the amount of time spent watching television and the prevalence of certain beliefs about the world. Those who watched the most television perceived the world as a more dangerous place than light viewers did (Gerbner, 1972; Gerbner & Gross, 1976; Gerbner et al., 1977; Gerbner et al., 1978; Gerbner et al., 1980). This is called *cultivation analysis*.

Through analysis of the content of network television programs, Gerbner and his associates showed the primetime dramatic world of television to be an exceedingly violent place. They hypothesized that regular exposure to mediated violence made viewers develop an exaggerated view of real-life dangers in society. (See Chapter 8 for our full discussion about cultivation.)

The strength of television's influence on viewers' perceptions of the world can be mitigated by many factors. Gunter (1987) identified four leading categories of these factors, which he called **levels of judgment**: program specificity, viewer perceptions or interpretations, personal judgments about crime, and situation specificity.

Program specificity means simply that television's influence on perceptions about the real world may have more to do with the types of programs watched rather than the total time spent viewing. For example, two people might watch the same amount of television each week, but one may view only violent programs, while the other watches nonviolent educational shows. The perceptions of real-world crime on the part of the two viewers might be vastly different, even though both watch the same amount of TV (Weaver & Wakshlag, 1986).

The influence of television also may depend on how viewers perceive what they are viewing and their interpretations of what they have seen (e.g., Collins, 1973; Pingree, 1983; Teevan & Hartnagel, 1976). *Viewer perceptions and interpretations* may conceivably render even the most violent programs rather innocuous in their effects.

Personal judgments about crime may also modify television's influence on viewers of violent programming. Examples of such judgments would be beliefs about the prevalence of crime in society or beliefs about one's own chances of becoming a victim of crime. Tyler (1980, 1984; Tyler & Cook, 1984) found that such judgments often were not connected to viewing behavior at all but rather to a person's particular personal encounters with crime.

Situation specificity means that television's influence on personal perceptions about crime may also be moderated by the person's individual situation or setting. For example, those who live in urban areas tend to fear crime more than those who live in rural, low-crime areas (Tamborini et al., 1984).

Researchers have turned their attention to video games and the internet as sources of mediated violence to investigate. The evidence suggests that those who play violent video games are more likely to have aggressive thoughts and behaviors afterward (e.g., Anderson, 2004; Anderson et al., 2004; Anderson & Dill, 2000; Bartholow

With a mix of gratuitous violence and wisecracking humor, *Deadpool* and its sequel smashed box office records. The movies hold two of the top three spots for highest-grossing R-rated films of all time.

& Anderson, 2002; Bushman & Anderson, 2009; Irwin & Gross, 1995). Repeated exposure can cause desensitization to violence (e.g., Bartholow et al., 2006). We will have in-depth discussion of the effects of violent video games in Chapter 18.

Enjoyment of Media Violence

Raney and Bryant (2020) note that media production and distribution outlets have long been criticized for content with excessive violence. "The typical industry defense for the preponderance of violence has been that they just give people what they want" (p. 331). After all, audiences have tuned in for decades to shows that feature violent content, like *Law & Order: SVU*, *The Walking Dead* (and its spin-offs), *The Boys*, *Westworld*, and *Dexter*. Violent films like *Deadpool*, *Logan*, and *Joker* (the highest-grossing R-rated film of all time) shattered box office records. And consumers spend billions of dollars a year on video games, many of which are violent. Clearly, there is both demand and desire for violent content.

One meta-analysis on the enjoyment of media violence found that males tended to enjoy violence more than females, and viewers who measured high on sensation seeking and exhibited a low measure of empathy also enjoyed violence more (Hoffner & Levine, 2005). A recent study revealed that movies, TV shows, and video games that pair humor and media violence are most enjoyed by males with so-called "dark personalities" (especially with traits of sadism, moral disengagement, and getting pleasure from another person's misfortune) and a history of consuming violent media (Allen et al., 2022). "Overall, findings suggest that those laughing the hardest at violent media may also have the darkest personalities" (p. 45).

Another study revealed little support for violent media being enjoyed more than programs that do not contain violence (Sparks & Sparks, 2002). Sparks et al. (2005) showed some participants an unedited version of *The Fugitive*; other participants watched the movie with violence edited out. Removing the violence had no effect on the enjoyment of the movie—those who saw the edited version enjoyed the movie just as much as those who saw the violent version. (For more on this study, see this chapter's Research Spotlight.)

Weaver and his colleagues (2011) manipulated violence and action in slapstick cartoons using animation software. Elementary school children in various groups watched the programs; violence did not have a direct effect on whether the children liked the cartoon.

RESEARCH SPOTLIGHT

The Appeal of Media Violence in a Full-Length Motion Picture:
An Experimental Investigation
Glenn G. Sparks, John Sherry, and Graig Lubsen (2005)
Communication Reports, 18(1), 21–30

For this study, researchers edited out all the violence in a full-length motion picture to see if students would enjoy the film as much as students who saw the unedited version.

Participants

A total of 134 undergraduate students at a large midwestern university (41 males, 93 females) served as participants. Most of the participants were white and ranged in age from 18 to 22 years.

Method

Participants saw one of two versions of a full-length Hollywood film, *The Fugitive*. One version was the original movie; the other version was edited to remove violence. After watching the film, respondents rated the film on a variety of questions that were converted to scales, including overall enjoyment, desire to see the movie again, degree of entertainment, how much fun it was to watch, and other measures of the perceived quality of the movie and perceived violence.

Participants were randomly assigned to view one of the two versions. The original film version was viewed by 15 males and 51 females. The edited version was viewed by 26 males and 42 females.

The original film ran for 2 hours, 11 minutes, and 5 seconds; there were 104 separate acts of physical violence. The edited version without the violent scenes lasted 2 hours, 0 minutes, and 49 seconds. Participants saw the films at the same time in different rooms and were asked to avoid talking during the film.

In order to disguise the purpose of the experiment, researchers asked the respondents to guess the hypothesis. Seven participants indicated that they thought the experiment involved some sort of editing of the film to test differences in perceptions of the movie. Those seven were eliminated from subsequent analysis. The final design of the study included 64 participants who watched the original movie (15 males and 49 females) and 63 participants who watched the edited version (24 males and 39 females).

Results

Using analysis of variance (ANOVA), no significant differences emerged on any of the enjoyment measures by version or by gender. Results were also analyzed for ratings of suspense. There were no significant differences for the version viewed, but women found the film significantly more suspenseful than men did.

The results showed that the violent version of the movie was no more enjoyable than the nonviolent version. Although supporting the null hypothesis leaves open a wider range of interpretations than might be desirable, the results raise questions about the media industry's frequent claims that violence is a critical ingredient of audience enjoyment.

Should We Be Concerned About Media Violence?

On the gratuitously violent HBO series *Westworld*, various characters often quote a line from Shakespeare's *Romeo and Juliet*: "These violent delights have violent ends." But is it true in reality?

Over the last century, there have been hundreds of studies about the effects of media violence, especially on aggression. As we have noted throughout this chapter and as multiple meta-analyses have shown (see Piotrowski & Fikkers, 2020, for a review), the effect sizes in media violence studies tend to be small to moderate—meaning there is a small to moderate chance that consuming violent media will result in aggressive behavior. "So, the question becomes, is a small or moderate chance of media violence effects sufficient to warrant concern?" (Piotrowski & Fikkers, 2020, p. 220).

Rather than focusing on size of the effects, some suggest that we should consider whether the effect is *meaningful* (Valkenburg & Piotrowski, 2017). Some scholars argue that the effects are absolutely meaningful and should be taken seriously (e.g., Anderson & Bushman, 2001; Bushman et al., 2010). Others argue that the effects are statistically so small that they do not rise to the threshold of a public health concern and that the focus should be turned to other risk factors, such as harsh family environments and aggressive temperament (e.g., Ferguson & Kilburn, 2009, 2010). Still others acknowledge the small percentage of people particularly susceptible to violent media effects but point out that mass media content reaches very large audiences—so we could be talking about *millions* of people experiencing these effects (Valkenburg & Piotrowski, 2017).

> So, where does this leave us? In this hotly contested debate, it almost feels as though there are two "camps": one that acknowledges the existence of effects, the other rejecting them. Both are working with the same data, the same articles, the same results, and drawing entirely different interpretations. (Piotrowski & Fikkers, 2020, p. 220).

Which camp is right? What we do know is that "some media violence affects some individuals in some situations" (p. 221). Rather than viewing effects as meaningful only if they hold for all people, the key to future research is focusing on the complex relationships between violent media consumption and individual difference variables (Fikkers & Piotrowski, 2019).

Summary

Public concern for the negative effects of exposure to media violence has been one of the most important, ongoing social issues of the 20th and 21st centuries. Through the years, many studies have established a causal link between viewing media violence and subsequent aggressive behavior or attitudes. Concern about media violence has always been a major issue for public policy makers. Despite the great number of studies that suggest a link between viewing mediated violence and subsequent aggression, critics point to statistical problems within the studies.

There are a number of theories that researchers use to understand the effects of violent media, including social cognitive theory, desensitization, priming, excitation transfer, cultivation, the GAM, and DSMM. Content analyses (the focus of the National Television Violence Study) indicate that primetime TV shows contain a great deal of violent content, as do nonfictional programs. Content analyses provide a system for coding and describing content; they do not measure audience perceptions. Contextual content analyses examine the situations surrounding the portrayals of violence. Research has shown that contextual features are most important in determining what effects violence will have upon audience members.

One strength of this area of study is that researchers have employed many different methods for studying the effects of exposure to media violence, including laboratory experiments, field experiments, correlational surveys, longitudinal panel studies, intervention studies and meta-analyses. Meta-analyses use statistical methods to combine a great number of different research studies to find overall indications of effects and general trends. Meta-analyses that examine media violence have consistently found a causal link between viewing violence and aggressive behavior, though effect sizes tend to be small to moderate. The major effects have been imitative behavior, fear, and desensitization.

Violent media content may affect audiences at three different psychological levels: behavioral, affective (emotional), and cognitive. Behavioral effects may be exhibited through one of five different mechanisms: imitation, catharsis, arousal, disinhibition, and desensitization. Emotional effects may be immediate or extended, long-term reactions. Fright reactions of children are one example of emotional effects. Cognitive effects occur whenever viewing violent content influences a person's beliefs about the real world. The approach of cultivation analysis examines such cognitive effects.

Television's influence on viewers' perceptions can be mitigated. Four leading mitigating factors, called levels of judgment, include program specificity, viewer perceptions or interpretations, personal judgments about crime, and situation specificity.

Scholars have also studied the enjoyment audiences and users get from consuming violent media. Several studies have indicated that removing violence from content does not have a negative impact on overall enjoyment.

Lastly, the debate continues about the meaningfulness of the small to moderate effect sizes related to violent media exposure. Although some argue that the effects are meaningful, others say they are too small to warrant public concern.

12

Effects of Sexual Media Content

> Sex is more exciting on the screen and between the pages than between the sheets.
>
> —Andy Warhol, 1975

Whatever the medium—television, movies, magazines, music videos, the internet—media users, including children, are inundated daily with sexual messages and images. These messages range from the mildly suggestive to various levels of the **sexually explicit**, a term used to describe media depictions of individuals engaging in various kinds of sexual activities.

In Chapter 11, we explored the issue of media violence and discovered that links exist between the viewing of violence and subsequent acts of aggression. Sexual content in mass media also has important implications because of its perceived connection with serious social concerns, such as teenage pregnancy and the numbers of people contracting sexually transmitted diseases.

The Centers for Disease Control (CDC) reports on teenage sexual activity at various intervals. Percentages of teenagers who have ever had sexual intercourse have declined for decades—from 51% for female teenagers in 1988 to 42% for the years 2011–2015; for male teenagers, the decline was from 60% to 44% (Abma & Martinez, 2017). The most recent CDC figures (2015–2017) show the same percentage for females with an additional decline for males to 38% (Martinez & Abma, 2020). Interestingly enough, a longitudinal meta-analytic review revealed that sexual content on network television declined from 1975 to 2004, except for homosexual content, which increased from the 1980s (Hestroni, 2007). A 2010 study on homosexual activity among teens showed that just over 9% of teenagers—nearly one in 10—reported having sex with someone of the same sex, double the number reported in 2002 (Pathela & Schillinger, 2010). Between 2015 and 2019, the percentage of 15- to 17-year-olds who identified as lesbian, gay, or bisexual increased from 8.3% to 11.7% (Johns et al., 2020).

Juxtaposing statistics and studies such as these amounts to anecdotal evidence in the eyes of scholars and other critics because no causal relationship can be established. However, many studies on sexually explicit content have documented causal evidence for harmful effects.

This chapter looks at the nature and extent of sexual content in mainstream and sexually explicit media. We also present a model for understanding the effects from media exposure. Next, we review results from studies that examine effects from exposure to sexual content in mainstream media, social media, sexually explicit material and sexually violent media. We also discuss the growing body of research into factors that mediate and moderate effects from consuming sexual media content.

The Nature of Sexual Content

Whenever you use the word "sexual" to describe media content, you must clearly define what it means, as it occurs at many levels of intensity. In its broadest sense, it includes *all* types of media products that either show or imply sexual acts or make sexual references or innuendoes, whether in humorous or dramatic contexts—from X-rated materials to general-audience sitcoms. Sexual content may range from rather mild sexual comments on network television to unabashedly blatant XXX videos.

The degree of sexual explicitness in media content usually depends upon how much is left to the imagination. Highly explicit materials such as NC-17, X-rated,[1] or XXX movies and videos leave nothing to the viewer's imagination. R-rated movies contain nudity and a moderate degree of explicitness, but sexual activities are less explicit than those depicted in adult films. Frontal nudity does not appear on broadcast network television in the United States; therefore, the sexual explicitness of network programs is rather tame when compared to R- and NC-17-rated movies. However, the sizzling sex scenes on daytime soap operas, primetime serial programming, and reality shows should leave no doubt in anyone's mind that television contains an abundance of sexual content. Moreover, premium cable and streaming series (e.g., Starz's *Outlander*, HBO's *Game of Thrones*, *Girls*, and *Euphoria*, Showtime's *Masters of Sex* and *Shameless*, Netflix's *Bridgerton*, *Sex Education*, and *Sex/Life*) often contain explicit sex scenes that can range anywhere from sensual to sadistic, often with full frontal nudity of both male and female characters.

Surveys and studies reveal the pervasiveness of mass media as a source of sexual information, especially for adolescents and teenagers. Half of 13- to 18-year-olds actively sought sexual content, including online pornography, when choosing what media to consume (Bleakley et al., 2011). Furthermore, 30% of 16- to 17-year-olds identified pornography as their primary source for learning about sex, followed by parents/guardians (21%), siblings/peers (16%), school/teachers (11%), nonsexually explicit TV/movies (10%), doctors (9%), and other (3%) (Rothman & Adhia, 2016). Of heterosexual youth, 19% turn to the internet for sexual health information; for LGBTQ youth, the percentage jumps to 78% (Mitchell et al., 2014).

In any discussion of sexual content in mass media, particular terms appear from time to time and need explication. *Pornography* and *obscenity* are two such terms.

Pornography

The extreme class of sexually explicit materials is commonly referred to as erotica or **pornography**, which Cline (1994) defined as "the graphic and explicit depictions of sexual activity" (p. 229). However, there are inconsistent definitions of pornography in the literature (see Busby et al., 2017, and Kohut et al., 2020, for a review), and discussions about the definition of pornography are ongoing (see McKee et al., 2020).

Today, most pornographic content is consumed online (Herbenick, 2020). Peter and Valkenburg (2011) define sexually explicit internet material (SEIM) as "professionally produced or user-generated (audio) visual material on or from the Internet that typically intends to arouse the viewer and depicts sexual activities and (aroused) genitals in unconcealed ways, usually with close-ups on oral, anal, and vaginal penetration" (p. 751). Ortiz and Thompson (2017) argue that this definition of SEIM is the most comprehensive definition of pornography. See Kohut et al. (2020) for suggested definitions of the conceptualization and use of pornography.

Ultimately, the term "pornography" is difficult to define in a standard way. Each person's definition may be different, depending upon their values. For example, some people do not consider nudity to be pornographic. Others may not consider consensual and nonviolent intercourse to be pornographic. See Busby et al. (2017) for more on the multidimensionality of pornography.

The pervasiveness of pornography is indisputable. Grubbs et al. (2019) note that consuming online pornography "is a common activity for many adults and adolescents worldwide, with a frequency that is unprecedented by previous forms of erotic media" (p. 117). Consider these statistics from Pornhub (2019), just one of *many* online pornography websites, about what happened on the site during *every minute* of 2019:

- 80,032 people visited the site.
- 14 videos were uploaded.
- 77,861 searches were made.
- 219,985 videos were viewed.
- 12,550 gigabytes of data were transferred.

In 2019, Pornhub had an average of 115 million visitors a day. By 2021, 130 million people were logging onto the site each day (Pornhub, 2021).

Peter and Valkenburg (2016) reviewed 20 years of research from 1995 to 2015 that examined adolescents and pornography. Looking at data from around the world about adolescents' pornography use, they found diverging results among studies that did not distinguish between intentional and unintentional exposure. However, they concluded that "the studies suggest that at least a sizeable minority of all adolescents use pornography, but exact aggregate figures about adolescents' pornography use seem difficult to derive from the literature" (p. 515). A recent study indicated that the average age at which boys in the United States are first exposed to pornography is 13 (Herbenick et al., 2020). The average age of first exposure for girls is 17.

Obscenity

Pornographic material is not always considered obscene. The term **obscenity** is a legal one that has been defined by the U.S. Supreme Court. The *Miller v. California* case in 1973 set the criteria for proclaiming material legally "obscene." Three criteria, as judged by a jury representative of the community, must be present. These include (1) the material appeals to a prurient (shameful, sick, morbid, or lustful) interest in sex, (2)

Findings from 20 Years of Research into Adolescents and Pornography

Peter and Valkenburg (2016) conducted a review of 75 studies across two decades of research (1995–2015) into the prevalence, predictors, and implications of pornography use by 10- to 17-year-olds. Here are some of the key findings from their review.

- At least a sizable minority of adolescents use pornography, but prevalence rates vary greatly from study to study.
- The typical adolescent porn user is a *male* at a *more advanced stage of puberty* who is a *sensation-seeker* with *weak or troubled family relationships*.
- Pornography use is associated with less strict sexual attitudes and some sexual behaviors (e.g., occurrence of sexual intercourse, more experience with casual sex); however, causal directions are unclear.

---

the material is patently offensive or beyond the contemporary community standards regarding depictions of sexual content or activity, and (3) the material as a whole lacks "serious literary, artistic, political, or scientific value" (Cline, 1994, p. 230).

The Extent of Sexual Content in the Media

Researchers have studied the extent and the explicitness of sexual content in mass media for decades. Many of these studies have been content analyses that focus on various types of sexual media fare that children and teens are likely to see, such as websites, R-rated movies, sex magazines, and, especially, network television programming.

Harris and Barlett (2009) observed that sex magazines had been declining in circulation since the 1990s. By 2020, consumption of print pornography was uncommon, with most porn consumers watching free online content on their smartphone (Herbenick et al., 2020). Over the years, other media stepped up to make sexual content even more pervasive in our society. The sale and rental of videos and films, whether X-rated or R-rated or highly suggestive music videos; the proliferation of cable, pay-per-view, and streaming services; the explosion of free online pornography; and sexting—all have contributed to a sexually charged media environment over the years.

> Sex in media is not limited to explicit portrayals of intercourse or nudity, however, but may include any representation that portrays or implies sexual behavior, interest, or motivation. Sex also occurs in many other places besides explicitly sexual materials. Many news stories, including reports of sex crimes, sex scandals, celebrity starlet social gossip, or tragic excesses like the Abu Ghraib prison abuses, involve sexual content. Sex is rampant in advertising, particularly for products like perfume, cologne, and aftershave, but also for tires, automobiles, and kitchen sinks. (Harris & Barlett, 2009, p. 305)

A number of content analyses have identified that, aside from explicit sexual portrayals, *talk about sex* has been on the increase, especially on network television, and the effects of this can be equally as harmful (Hestroni, 2007; Kunkel et al., 2003).

There has also been growth in gay- and lesbian-oriented (GLO) media content. Bond's (2015) analysis of GLO TV shows, movies, and music (e.g., *RuPaul's Drag Race*, *Queer as Folk*, *Milk*, *Brokeback Mountain*, Lady Gaga's songs "Bad Romance" or "Telephone") noted that (not surprisingly) GLO media includes significantly more LGBTQ sexual depictions than heterosexual depictions, and gay men are depicted significantly more often than lesbian women or bisexual people. Furthermore, Bond's analysis suggested that gay, lesbian, and bisexual people are portrayed in more realistic sexual situations and in more validating contexts in GLO rather than mainstream media.

Of course, the amount of sexual content and the degree of explicitness varies considerably among different types of mass media (Greenberg, 1994). In the following sections, we will explore sexual content in music videos, mainstream TV and movies, and X-rated videos.

Music Videos

You do not have to look far to find examples of sexual music videos. Consider Cardi B and Megan Thee Stallion's hypersexual video for "WAP" (an acronym for "wet-ass pussy") or Lil Nas X's controversial video for "Montero (Call Me By Your Name)," where his character slides down a stripper pole into hell to give the devil a lap dance. Both of these songs and their videos caused quite a stir when they were released.

For example, after Cardi B and Megan Thee Stallion performed a *heavily* edited version of "WAP" at the Grammys in 2021, the Federal Communications Commission (FCC) received more than 1,000 emails complaining about the "raunchy performance" where "both rappers and their backup crew masqueraded as strippers under a giant stiletto heel" (Schaffer, 2021, para. 2).

Numerous content analyses have measured the amount of sexual content contained in music videos. Two major studies in the 1980s examined MTV and televised music programs that aired on other networks; the majority of music videos contained sexual content (Baxter et al., 1985; Sherman & Dominick, 1986). A summary of two decades of research into music videos indicated three main ways in which sexual messages are conveyed to audiences: sexual innuendo, sexy clothing (or lack thereof), and stereotypes (Andsager & Roe, 2003).

Rapper Cardi B is known for her sexually provocative songs and risqué on-stage performances.

Turner (2011) conducted two content analyses of music videos. In his first analysis, music videos by Black artists airing on MTV, MTV2, VH-1, BET, and CMT were significantly more likely to show sexual content and feature female characters in provocative clothing; 59% of the 407 videos contained some type of sexual content. By genre, videos mixing rap and R&B had the most sexual content (83%), while country videos had the least (36%). In Turner's second content analysis, 95% of the videos shown on *BET Un:Cut* included sexual content. Furthermore, those videos featured seven times as many sexual acts and significantly more discouraged sexual behaviors (such as prostitution, exhibitionism, and aggressive sex) compared to videos aired at earlier times of day on the other music channels and on BET.

A study of 405 music videos airing on television during G and PG-rated time slots in Australia found that 55% contained sexual content (Ey, 2016). Of 34 additional music videos that children named as popular (but had not aired on the TV programs sampled), 77% included sexual content. R&B (88%), hip hop (82%), dance (75%), and pop (68%) video genres had both the highest number and greater duration of sexualized content. Those four genres also contained the greatest number of videos preferred by kids in the study.

Television

R-rated movies, music videos, and the internet contain far more explicit sexual content than network television, but many drama series often contain sex scenes, many of which continue to push the envelope for network TV. *Grey's Anatomy* and its spin-off *Station 19* often portray their main characters in passionate love scenes or talking about sex. And *Law & Order: SVU*, the longest-running primetime scripted drama series in TV history, has been entertaining audiences for more than 20 years with plotlines featuring sexual assault, rape, and murder. Furthermore, sexual comments and overtures are numerous and frequent on network programming (Dillman Carpentier et al., 2017; Greenberg et al., 1993; Greenberg & Hofschire, 2000; Kunkel et al., 1999, 2003, 2007). Most of the sexual innuendoes on TV occur in humorous scenes.

Kunkel and his colleagues (1999, 2003, 2007) conducted multiple content analyses of sexual content on network and cable television in the late 1990s and early 2000s. From the 1997–1998 television season to the 2001–2002 season, programs with sexual content increased from 56% to 64%. During that same time span, talk about sex increased from 54% to 61%, sexual behaviors increased from 23% to 32%, and instances of sexual intercourse doubled from 7% to 14%.

A more recent analysis by Dillman Carpentier et al. (2017) revealed that nearly half of television content from 25 popular network and cable shows (e.g., *Grey's Anatomy, The Big Bang Theory, Doctor Who, NCIS, American Horror Story, Gossip Girl*, just to name a few) contained sexual talk, behavior, or jokes/puns. The researchers summarized the sexual content this way:

> Overall, the sexual content on television appeared to be more suggestive than overt—perhaps a function of many of the shows airing on network television. Based on this analysis, one can readily expect kissing, flirting, talk about liking or loving someone, and talk about relationships and sexual interests from popular television. However, active pursuit of sex (i.e., talk toward sex) and implied or real-

ized depictions of sexual intercourse might be rarely encountered in these types of programs. (p. 704)

Timmermans and Van den Bulck (2018) conducted a content analysis of casual sex depicted on nine internationally popular U.S. television shows from 2000 to 2015 known for their depictions of sex (i.e., sitcoms: *Friends, The Big Bang Theory, New Girl*; dramas: *Grey's Anatomy, Gossip Girl, Orange is the New Black*; comedy dramas: *Sex and the City, Californication, Girls*). Although casual sex was depicted almost as frequently as sex in committed relationships, instances of casual sex were more likely to depict explicit scenes of sexual intercourse. Sexual behaviors in committed relationships were limited to passionate kissing. Furthermore, casual sex was most often seen in dramas (40%) compared to comedy dramas (34%) and sitcoms (19%). One-fifth of characters cheated on their significant others by engaging in casual sex. The majority of casual hookups (57%) did not lead to any relationship between the characters involved. The researchers argue that casual sex seen on television can influence the sexual scripts people use in real life.

Lampman et al. (2002) and Taylor et al. (2016) found that sexual talk and behaviors are extremely common in television workplaces, especially on sitcoms. However, characters rarely experience any negative consequences for their sexual talk or behavior in the office (Taylor et al., 2016). For instance, NBC's popular sitcom *The Office* contains many examples of sexual innuendo (and sometimes sex itself, such as when Dwight and Angela repeatedly have sex in the warehouse). Michael Scott continually uses the sexual innuendo "That's what she said!" despite being told by the Dunder Mifflin legal team not to say the phrase in the workplace (Meier & Medjesky, 2018). He suffers no negative consequences.

Other studies have looked at the consequences of characters having sex on teen dramas (e.g., Aubrey, 2004; Ortiz & Brooks, 2014). In those types of programs, emotional and social consequences of sex (e.g., guilt/anxiety, disappointment, rejection, increases in self-esteem or relationship satisfaction) outnumber physical consequences (e.g., unwanted pregnancy, contracting a sexually transmitted disease, physical abuse), and negative consequences outnumber positive ones. In Aubrey's (2004) study, negative consequences were more common when female characters initiated sexual activities. Ortiz and Brooks (2014), however, found that both male and female characters were equally likely to experience both positive and negative consequences from sexual activities.

Mainstream Movies

From the *American Pie* to *Magic Mike* to *Fifty Shades* film franchises, sexual content is common in mainstream movies. A content analysis of the 855 top-grossing U.S. films from 1950 to 2006 revealed that 82% depicted some sort of sexual content (Bleakley et al., 2012). Additionally, female characters, despite being underrepresented in the films, were twice as likely to be involved in sexual content compared to male characters. Starting in the mid-1960s and early 1970s, female characters were increasingly more likely to be seen in explicit sexual content.

When looking at race, a greater proportion of Black characters engaged in sex than white characters in films from 2013 and 2014 (Ellithorpe et al., 2017). Black characters were also more likely than white characters to engage in risky health behaviors combining sex and alcohol use, both within scenes and throughout films as a whole.

Alexopoulos and Taylor (2020) studied sexual messages seen in the comedy sub-genre of "teen sex romps." They conducted a quantitative content analysis of the 38 top-grossing teen sex comedy films. Nudity, sexual behavior, and conversations about sex were extremely common. In fact, more than half of the movies depicted sexual behavior or explicit content in the first five minutes of the film. However, messages about sexual risk and responsibility were rare. Messages about sexual precautions were only seen once in every 10 occurrences of sexual behavior, and mentions of birth control happened only once in every 17 conversations about sex.

Recent studies about sexual consent in mainstream movies found that the most common consent cues were nonverbal and implicit (Jozkowski et al., 2019; Willis et al., 2020). A majority of sex scenes showed consent immediately before characters engaged in sexual activity, and nonverbal cues were used more often by characters in established relationships than by those in new relationships (Jozkowski et al., 2019). R-rated films portrayed sexual behaviors without any consent cues more frequently than did PG-13 films (Willis et al., 2020).

X-Rated Videos

Technology has changed how people access X-rated videos. VHS and DVD sales and rentals have given way to online porn. No matter the medium, the content of these videos has been of interest to researchers for decades. In an early content analysis of sexual activities in 45 X-rated videos, there were almost 450 sexually explicit scenes (Cowan et al., 1988). Overall, the scenes depicted one of four major themes: reciprocity, domination, exploitation, or autoeroticism. Scenes featuring satisfying and consensual sex (*reciprocity*) were the most numerous of the four types, occurring in 37% of the 450 scenes; however, the themes of either domination or exploitation (mostly men over women) appeared in more than half of those scenes. *Domination,* or sexual control by one person over another, occurred in 28% of all scenes. *Exploitation,* where one person coerced another or used status to get what they wanted, was present in 26% of all scenes. *Autoeroticism,* which means some form of self-stimulation, was the least frequent theme, occurring in only 9% of the scenes studied.

More recently, Klaassen and Peter (2015) examined gender differences in the 400 most viewed pornographic videos on Pornhub, RedTube, YouPorn, and xHamster. Sex scenes employed significantly more close-up shots of women's genitals, buttocks, and/or breasts (61%) compared to close-ups of men's body parts (19%). Men were more likely than women to receive oral sex and to experience orgasms. Men and women initiated sex almost equally (36% to 32%, respectively). In almost half of the sex scenes, dominance and submission between partners was either not shown or was equally portrayed. When characters did display dominance, they were significantly more likely to be male. Instances of characters being manipulated into sex were rare, but when it happened, women were more likely to be coerced into having sex than men. Furthermore, females in amateur porn videos experience more gender inequality than do females in professional porn videos.

Why Do People Watch Porn?

According to Bőthe et al. (2021), the most common motivations for pornography use are:

- Sexual Pleasure
- Sexual Curiosity
- Stress Reduction
- Fantasy
- Boredom Avoidance
- Lack of Sexual Satisfaction
- Self-Exploration
- Emotional Distraction/Suppression

Men scored higher than women on all motivations, except sexual curiosity and self-exploration.

Rasmussen et al. (2019) found that women are more likely than men to engage in infidelity than men in online porn videos. On-screen committed relationships were only seen in 8% of videos, but infidelity occurred in 25% of pornographic videos.

Researchers have often looked at aggressive acts depicted in porn videos. In a recent content analysis of more than 4,000 heterosexual scenes from Pornhub and Xvideos, at least one act of physical aggression was portrayed in 45% of scenes from Pornhub and 35% of scenes from Xvideos (Fritz et al., 2020). Spanking and gagging are two of the most common acts of aggression seen in online porn (Fritz et al., 2020; Klaassen & Peter, 2015). Other aggressive acts include slapping, hair pulling, and choking. Women are overwhelmingly the targets of aggressive behaviors (Bridges et al., 2010). For instance, Fritz et al. (2020) found that women were the targets of aggression 97% of the time. Reactions to aggressive acts are mostly neutral or positive, while negative reactions are seen only seen between 2–7% of the time, depending on the study.

Shor and Seida (2021) conducted an analysis comparing aggression in gay, lesbian, and heterosexual videos on Pornhub. Gay and lesbian videos were more likely to depict visible aggression (26% and 24%, respectively) compared to heterosexual videos (13%):

> Videos featuring two men contained the highest amount of both visible and nonconsensual aggression, while f/f clips had the highest amount of verbal aggression, as well as various forms of physical aggression, such as spanking and choking. These findings therefore challenge the proposition that pornography is primarily about the aggression of men toward women. (p. 101)

Many critics and scholars argue that porn becomes increasingly aggressive year after year and that viewers respond favorably to more aggressive pornography. However, recent research looking at popular videos uploaded to Pornhub over the last decade did not find support for either of those claims (Shor & Seida, 2019, 2021). In fact, segments showing aggression have become shorter over time. Furthermore, videos depicting aggressive behaviors received less views, were ranked less favorably by viewers, and were not sought out by a majority (almost 80%) of people who watch online porn.

In another content analysis, Cowan and Campbell (1994) examined interracial X-rated pornography and coded 476 characters in sexually explicit scenes in 54 videos. Black women were the targets of more acts of aggression than white women, and

Black men displayed fewer intimate behaviors than white men. Further, interracial sexual interactions contained more aggression than same-race sexual interactions. A recent content analysis by Fritz et al. (2021) confirms most of these findings. Black women are still more likely than white women to be the targets of aggression. Black men are seen more often as perpetrators of aggression against women and are significantly less intimate with their partners compared to white men. Notably, scenes with Black couples featured the most aggression compared to other racial pairings, including interracial sexual encounters.

However, there have been conflicting results regarding race and targets of aggression in pornographic videos in recent research. Shor and Golriz (2019) found that videos with Black women were *less* likely to contain aggression than those with white women; meanwhile, videos featuring Latina or Asian women were *more* likely to include aggression than those with Black or white women. As acknowledged by Fritz et al. (2021), differing results could be explained by how aggression was coded in the studies. Shor and Golriz included "forceful penetration" in their definition of aggression. Fritz et al. did not include that category in their analysis due to difficulty achieving reliability among coders, and they admit this could have led to their study *underestimating* instances of aggression.

Regardless of these different results, the words of Cowan and Campbell (1994) are still true today: "These findings suggest that pornography is racist as well as sexist" (p. 323).

Effects of Exposure to Sexual Content in Mainstream Media

Although the study of effects of pornography dates back several decades, the study of effects from sexual content in mainstream media is much newer, but it is now common and crosses disciplinary and global boundaries (Wright, 2020a). Much of this research focuses on the effects on teens. Of course, mass media is just one of many factors that contribute to the development of sexual attitudes, beliefs, and behaviors, but exposure to sexual content has been specifically "linked with shifts in attitudes about sex and gender, earlier progression to sexual activity, pregnancy, and sexually transmitted infection among adolescents" (Collins et al., 2017, p. S162).

Changes in Attitudes

Consuming more mainstream media has been linked to more positive or permissive attitudes toward one-night stands, sex in public, casual oral sex, maintaining sexual relationships with more than one partner at a time, sex outside of marriage, and sex as part of quid pro quo (e.g., Chia, 2006). In a study of college males in the United States, magazine and television use predicted more positive attitudes toward casual, uncommitted sex (or "hooking up") eight months later (Aubrey & Smith, 2016). Galdi et al. (2014) found that Italian men's favorable attitudes toward nonrelational sex increased after watching sexual content on television. In another study, the exposure of 14- to 16-year-olds to TV sitcoms made them think more positively about having sex, whereas watching dramas made them think more negatively (Gottfried et al., 2013).

Seeing negative consequences of unintended pregnancies on TV shows led to more positive attitudes for some U.S. college students about the use of condoms and intentions to avoid having risky sex (Finnerty-Myers, 2011). In another study, exposure to mainstream TV and movies that portrayed a combination of alcohol use and sexual behavior played a role in influencing both Black and white teens' attitudes and intentions to do the same in the real world, with the effect being significantly stronger for white teens (Bleakley, Ellithorpe, Hennessy, Khurana, et al., 2017).

Some studies have found correlations between exposure to homosexual television characters and positive attitudes about homosexuality, increased acceptance of same-sex sex, and willingness to interact with gay men (e.g., McLaughlin & Rodriguez, 2017). Chinese college students who saw sympathetic portrayals of gay and lesbian characters in entertainment media had more positive attitudes toward same-sex sex and a stronger belief that a person's sexual orientation is innate (Zhang & Min, 2013).

Changes in Beliefs

Mainstream media consumption is associated with the beliefs that men are driven by sex, women are sexual objects, and dating is a "battle of the sexes" (e.g., Ferris et al., 2007). Media use has correlated with higher estimates of teenage pregnancy, sex in public, extramarital sex, sex with multiple partners, and frequency of sex (e.g., Woo & Dominick, 2001).

Numerous beliefs about sexual risk have correlated with greater use of mainstream media, including reduced perceptions of the risk of pregnancy, lower intentions to not have sex if protection is not available, and unrealistically optimistic beliefs about lifestyles and finances after an unintended pregnancy (e.g., Martins & Jensen, 2014).

Changes in Behaviors

A number of sexual behaviors (including intercourse initiation and frequency, one-night stands, and having multiple sexual partnerships) are correlated with increased mainstream media use (e.g., Ybarra et al., 2014). A longitudinal study by Brown et al. (2006) found that mainstream media use predicted intercourse initiation two years later for white adolescents in the United States.

The amount of sexual content that 12- to 17-year-olds watch on television (whether viewing physically sexual scenes or hearing talk about sex) may cause them to begin engag-

Outlander often depicts passionate sex scenes between the main characters, Jamie (Sam Heughan) and Claire (Caitriona Balfe), but the popular Starz show also depicts graphic scenes of sexual assault and rape.

ing in sex sooner (Collins et al., 2004). However, reducing the amount of sexual content in entertainment programs, increasing references to and depictions of negative consequences of sexual activity, and parents watching shows with their teenaged children and discussing their beliefs about sex and what is being portrayed mitigated the impact of watching sexual content on television (see also Kim et al., 2006). Other studies have confirmed that the more sexual content exposure among adolescents, the more likely they are to experiment with sexual activity (Bleakley et al., 2008; Bryant & Rockwell, 1994; Collins et al., 2004; Fisher et al., 2009).

Interestingly, the relationship between teens' exposure to sexual media and their sexual behaviors works both ways: Those who are exposed to more sexual content are more likely to engage in sexual behaviors, and those who engage in sexual activity are more likely to seek out media with sexual content (Bleakley et al., 2008).

However, not all scholars agree on the influence of media content (sexual or otherwise) on teens' sexual behavior. A meta-analysis of 22 papers published between 2005 and 2015 found no correlation between general media use and teens' sexual behaviors (Ferguson et al., 2017). Furthermore, sexual media only weakly correlated with teens' sexual behaviors. Ferguson and colleagues (2017) acknowledged that sexual media content may influence people's sexual attitudes, but they concluded that "evidence for an association between media and sexual behavior is minimal" (p. 355).

Effects of Exposure to Sexual Content on Social Media

Compared to the body of research into the effects of sexual content in mainstream media, research into the effects of sexual content on social media is in its infancy. Although the research in this area is sparse, commonalities can already be seen (Wright, 2020a). First, these studies most often focus on teens and young adults. Second, studies suggest that posting and/or seeing sexual posts may increase the likelihood of some risky sexual beliefs and behaviors (e.g., Eleuteri et al., 2017; van Oosten et al., 2015).

Young adults also discuss a variety of sexual health issues with romantic partners via private social media messages (Tannenbaum, 2018). Various social media platforms and apps also facilitate sharing of explicit photos, such as "dick pics," which can result in varied reactions from the receiver, ranging from disgust to desire (Paasonen et al., 2019).

The primary focus of much of this growing body of research is sexual objectification (Wright, 2020a). Research reveals that using social media is associated with girls' and young women's self-sexualization (e.g., engaging in activities to appear sexually appealing; treating oneself as a sexual object), objectified body-consciousness (i.e., assuming and internalizing an outside observer's view of one's physical self, which could lead to the development of one's identity being defined by physical appearance), and lower sexual assertiveness (e.g., Boursier et al., 2020; Manago et al., 2015). The more women and girls use social media, the more they may compare themselves to self-sexualized others; they may also feel as if they should also self-sexualize (Fardouly et al., 2015). However, there is no convincing evidence that posting sexy photos online either increases or is the result of offline sexual agency (Ramsey & Horan, 2018).

Using a sexualized profile photo on Facebook could have relational costs for female users. Daniels and Zurbriggen (2016) found that females using a sexualized profile photo were rated by female teens and young women as less physically and socially attractive and less competent to complete tasks compared to users with non-sexualized profile photos.

Of course, much of our social media use happens on our phones, and sexting has become more prevalent in recent years. See Chapter 20 for our discussion about sexting and the effects of mobile communication.

Effects of Exposure to Highly Explicit Sexual Content

Findings from several decades of research show that highly explicit sexual content may affect media users in several ways. One type of effect is sexual arousal. Other effects include changes in attitudes, values, and behaviors. Each of these areas has been studied extensively, especially the behavioral changes that result from viewing pornography (e.g., Gunter, 2002; Huston et al., 1998; Linz & Malamuth, 1993; Malamuth, 1993; Malamuth & Impett, 2001; Mundorf et al., 2007; Oddone-Paolucci et al., 2000; Pollard, 1995). More recent meta-analyses of studies of pornography give us a broader view of the effects of explicit sexual content (e.g., Hald et al., 2010; Smith et al., 2016; Tokunaga et al., 2019; Wright et al., 2016b).

As Wright (2020a) summarizes, "pornography researchers have hypothesized that exposure to sexually explicit media increases the likelihood of sexual attitudes and behaviors that are more unrestricted, risky, and gendered" (p. 233).

Sexual Arousal

A number of studies have demonstrated that sexually oriented media content does tend to sexually arouse the viewer or user (e.g., Abramson et al., 1981; Eccles et al., 1988; Elsey et al., 2019; Malamuth & Check, 1980; Schaefer & Colgan, 1977; Sintchak & Geer, 1975; Wright et al., 2021). These studies have used different types of measures. In some cases, viewers were asked to rate their level of sexual arousal after seeing sexually explicit material. In other instances, researchers used physiological measures to determine arousal, such as the measurement of penile tumescence or vaginal changes. Thermography has also been used.

There are usually gender differences in terms of usage of sexually explicit materials and arousal. Drinking alcohol and exposure to violent pornography depicting victims experiencing pleasure can lead to greater arousal for men than for women (Davis et al., 2006). Evidence suggests that men are more intentional seekers of sexually explicit content, and they tend to be more aroused by it (Allen et al., 2007; Malamuth, 1996), especially depictions of sexual violence or dehumanization (Murnen & Stockton, 1997).

Results of a recent study indicated that compared to men, "women were more likely to find at least some forms of aggression in pornography arousing (nearly two-thirds of the women we interviewed), and many of them also reported that they found harder forms of aggression arousing (almost 40% of the women)" (Shor & Seida,

2021, p. 127). However, "both men and women who sometimes found aggression in pornography arousing often emphasized that they would not want to experience such acts in their own sex lives" (p. 90).

Men are significantly more likely than women to have watched an X-rated film in the last year (35% to 16%, respectively) (Frutos & Merrill, 2017), and the porn industry largely caters to male consumers. Women react more positively to sexually explicit material written and directed by women, especially when themes are romantic (Mosher & Maclan, 1994; Quackenbush et al., 1995) and when the content is more female-centric (e.g., pornography portraying genuine female pleasure, mutual enjoyment of sex, natural bodies, respect between characters, etc.) (French & Hamilton, 2018). There have also been a growing number of women watching porn in recent years (see Shor & Seida, 2021, for a review).

Researchers have also studied the relationship between the explicitness of sexual content and the extent of sexual arousal. Less explicit materials are sometimes *more* arousing than highly explicit ones (Bancroft & Mathews, 1971). Scenes that leave much to the viewer's imagination may arouse the viewer more than those that leave no questions unanswered.

Different individuals are "turned on" by different sexual stimuli. While there are many individual differences in arousal, classic conditioning studies demonstrated that sexual arousal can sometimes be *learned.* In the 1960s researchers showed heterosexual men photos of nude women paired with boots and taught the men to be aroused by only the sight of women's boots (Rachman, 1966; Rachman & Hodgson, 1968).

Studies have also revealed that viewers of common pornography (nonviolent sex between a man and woman) become habituated over time and seek more uncommon porn (e.g., bondage, sadomasochism, bestiality) in order to find stimulation (Zillmann & Bryant, 1986). Also, heavy consumption of pornography over time causes viewers to assign increased importance to sex without emotional involvement and to report less sexual satisfaction with their intimate partners, specifically their sexual skill and adventurousness (Zillmann & Bryant, 1988).

Some studies reported positive or no effects on satisfaction in the relationships of pornography users (e.g., Kohut et al., 2017). However, after reviewing the literature, Wright et al. (2021) note, "It is difficult to dispute the conclusion that if there is an association between pornography use and satisfaction for the average person in a coupled relationship, it is negative rather than positive" (p. 204). The researchers tested and found support for a path model illustrating the mechanisms through which pornography use impacts sexual and relational satisfaction (or lack thereof). This model fit data from men and women equally well. (For more on this study, see this chapter's Research Spotlight.)

The study of virtual reality (VR) pornography is an emerging field (Ortiz & Thompson, 2017). Although there is not currently much research available about VR porn, one study compared VR and traditional 2D pornography (Elsey et al., 2019). First-person scenes were more arousing than voyeuristic scenes in both VR and 2D. VR pornography was more arousing than 2D pornography for men but not for women. Virtual reality also resulted in a greater sense of presence than 2D content, and presence positively correlated with arousal.

Pornography and Sexual Dissatisfaction:
The Role of Pornographic Arousal, Upward Pornographic Comparisons, and Preference for Pornographic Masturbation

Paul J. Wright, Bryant Paul, Debby Herbenick, and Robert S. Tokunaga (2021)
Human Communication Research, 47(2), 192–214

This study sought to evaluate the underlying mechanisms for the relationship between pornography use and decreased sexual satisfaction. Based on a variety of theoretical assumptions about pornography use, the researchers developed and tested a model to better understand the process.

Theoretical Background

The researchers summarized a wide body of research into the effects of pornography, including pornography use resulting in sexual arousal, comparing one's own sex life to what is seen in pornographic media leading to lower sexual/relational satisfaction, and repeated use of pornography resulting in real-world sex with a partner being less appealing.

The Proposed Model

Based on this body of research, Wright and colleagues proposed the following conceptual model:

> (a) recurrently consuming pornography conditions the user's arousal template to be particularly responsive to pornographic depictions, (b) this increased arousal to pornography increases both (c) upward comparisons between one's own sex life and sex as it is shown in pornography and (d) a preference for masturbation to pornography over partnered sex, which in turn (e) diminish perceptions of how satisfying it is to have sex with one's partner, and ultimately (f) lowers perceptions of how satisfying one's relationship is with one's partner. (p. 194)

Participants

This study included 811 men and 818 women who were either dating or married. Participants were recruited from all 50 states and ranged in age from 18 to 60 with an average age of 40. Regarding sexuality, 93% identified as heterosexual, and 7% identified as homosexual, bisexual, asexual, or something else. The majority of the sample was white and had not graduated from college (65% for both measures).

Measures

Data were collected from the National Survey of Porn Use, Relationships, and Sexual Socialization. Survey questions asked participants how often they used porn (never, once or twice per year, once or twice per month, once or twice per week, every day). Participants were asked to rate statements about arousal from porn use (ranging from "does not describe me at all" to "describes me exactly") and to rate agreement with the statement "I am disappointed that my sex life isn't as good as what I see in porn" (ranging from "strongly disagree" to "strongly agree"). Participants were also asked to evaluate whether masturbating to porn was more enjoyable than having sex with their partner (ratings ranged from "strongly disagree" to "strongly agree"). Lastly, they were asked to rate their overall happiness with their relationship (ranging from "unhappy" to "perfect").

(continued)

Findings
Statistical analysis showed that the "serial mediation from pornography consumption to relational satisfaction was significant" (p. 203). Furthermore, the model fit data from men and women equally well.

Regarding the components of the originally proposed model, the authors suggest that both preference for masturbating to pornography and upward pornographic comparisons can be combined into a single construct: preference for pornography over partner.

Changes in Attitudes

Researchers have studied the effects of pornography on attitudes for many decades. Early studies revealed that exposure to sexually explicit materials produces significant changes in attitudes (Zillmann & Bryant, 1982, 1984). For six weeks, one group of participants saw sexually explicit films; a second group saw nonexplicit films. When tested, the first group overestimated the popularity of the sexual activities they had viewed in the movies (e.g., fellatio, cunnilingus, anal intercourse, sadomasochism, and bestiality). The estimates of the second group were much more conservative.

Later, Zillmann and Bryant (1988) used similar methods to determine if the viewing of such films caused changes in attitudes toward sexual partners or changes in basic values, such as a desire for marriage, monogamy, children, and so forth. Changes did occur. For instance, those who saw the explicit films reported less satisfaction with their real-life partners than those in the control group. In addition to rating their partners lower in terms of physical appearance and sexual performance, the group that viewed explicit films was more accepting of premarital sex and extramarital sex. They reported less of a desire for marriage, monogamy, and children than the control group. The researchers explained these findings as follows:

> Only pornography shows men and women to experience the greatest sexual pleasures from coition with many partners, one after the other, or from sexual activities with several partners at the same time. . . . And only this genre provides specifics such as fellatio in which women make entire male organs vanish or coition in which penises of extreme proportion cause women to scream in apparent painful ecstasy. The sexual experience of normals must pale by comparison. Partners must seem prudish, insensitive, inhibited, frigid . . . and deficient in endowment and skill. And who, confronted with the bounty of readily attainable sexual joys that are continually presented in pornography and nowhere else, could consider his or her sexual life fulfilled? (p. 452)

Repeated exposure to explicit sexual materials usually results in desensitization of a person's attitudes and values. **Desensitization** is a change in values or attitudes that occurs over time as a previously taboo behavior is gradually accepted because of repeated exposure to mass media. For example, if a man watches a number of X-rated movies that depict women enjoying being raped, he may change his perceptions about the frequency of rape in the real world, his attitude about the amount of social and psychological harm rape causes, and even his beliefs about the likelihood that he would commit such a crime. The consumption of sexually explicit material leads to attitude changes regarding extramarital sex, sexual objectification of women, and sexist attitudes. For instance, a study of married U.S. adults revealed that watching porn correlated with more positive attitudes to sex outside of marriage (Wright et al., 2014a).

The effects of pornography consumption on sexist attitudes is another area that has received a lot of attention from researchers. Ortiz and Thompson (2017) note studies reveal that the more porn a person consumes, the greater their likelihood of having sexist attitudes toward women; conversely, the more someone reports having harmful sexist attitudes toward women, the more likely they are to frequently consume pornography. Notably, "the direction of causality between pornography consumption and sexist attitudes is not always clear; however, some experimental and longitudinal studies do provide insights into how these relationships may work" (p. 249).

For instance, Hald and Malamuth (2015) found that men and women who rated lower in agreeableness and higher past pornography use predicted significantly higher attitudes about sexual violence against women. However, when analyzing the effect of exposure to pornography in a laboratory setting on sexist attitudes, a significant effect was only observed for men low in agreeableness. Furthermore, this effect was mediated by arousal—the more the participants said they were sexually aroused by pornographic video, the more likely they were to report having sexist attitudes.

Peter and Valkenburg's (2009) longitudinal survey study of Dutch children found that earlier consumption of online porn predicted attitudes of viewing women as sex objects in both boys and girls; however, perceiving women as sex objects only predicted greater pornography consumption for boys. In a later study, both online and offline pornography use were associated with stronger perceptions of women as sex objects (Omori et al., 2011).

Not all of the attitude changes linked to pornography use are bad. Studies show that watching porn can lead to greater acceptance of traditionally stigmatized sexual relationships, such as same-sex couples. Results of these studies suggest pornography consumption can make someone more likely to develop more liberal attitudes toward nontraditional sex roles and relationships (Wright & Bae, 2013; Wright & Randall, 2014; Wright et al., 2014b).

Changes in Behavior

Behavioral effects from the consumption of sexually explicit media content may occur at several levels. For better or worse, people often *learn* when they consume sexual content. The learning may be highly constructive (as in a couple undergoing sexual therapy) or it may be extremely destructive (as in copycat sexual offenses that involve violence).

Disinhibition causes changes in behavior in much the same way that desensitization causes changes in attitudes and values. After seeing an R-rated movie or an X-rated video, a person becomes less inhibited about performing the sexual behaviors witnessed—behaviors that were previously taboo or risky, such as unprotected sex. Ortiz and Thompson (2017) explain pornography's potential effects on condom use this way:

> Pornography is arguably a source of sexual scripts and information, such that the activities portrayed can function as a frame of reference for how to engage in sex. . . . Frequent exposure to pornography without condoms may normalize lack

of use in the consumer's own life and thus potentially increase the incidence of sexually transmitted infections. (p. 251)

Condom use is the most-studied sexual risk behavior, and studies have looked at both the general population and gay men (Wright, 2020a). There have been mixed results from research into the general population, pornography use, and condomless sex. Some studies show a relationship between consuming porn and having unprotected sex, but others do not. Recent research suggests that the effects may be seen only with heterosexual individuals not in monogamous relationships (Wright et al., 2018, 2019). Moreover, it is the combination of porn consumption frequency *and* the belief that porn is a source of sex information that is more likely to result in having sex without a condom. Additionally, because gay pornography generally depicts more condom use, associations between watching porn and having condomless sex in the real world may only be seen among gay men who prefer watching videos of men having sex without condoms (Rosser et al., 2013).

Pornography researchers have also studied unrestricted sexual behaviors, such as recreational or casual sex. For example, a meta-analysis of over 70 studies spanning more than 40 years revealed that watching pornography predicted an impersonal approach to sex (Tokunaga et al., 2019). This relationship held for men, women, adolescents, and adults. It was also seen across countries, time, and research methods. Importantly, "exposure to pornography leads to more positive attitudes toward impersonal sex, which in turn increases the likelihood of engaging in impersonal sex behavior" (p. 27).

A longitudinal study by Lin et al. (2020) followed Taiwanese middle school children into their early twenties. Early exposure to sexually explicit media in middle school was strongly related to three risky sexual behaviors: early sexual debut, multiple sexual partners, and unsafe sex. The relationship between consuming sexually explicit content and risky sexual behavior was even stronger for those who consumed pornography using multiple modalities (e.g., websites, movies, magazines, novels, etc.).

Herbenick et al. (2020) studied pornography use and sexual behaviors in a nationally representative probability sample of more than 2,200 Americans between 18 and 60 years old. Frequent pornography use in the past year and greater lifetime range of pornography use were significantly associated with engaging in dominant and target sexual behaviors among all study participants. Men were significantly more likely than women to engage in at least one dominant sexual behavior, which included spanking (77%), choking (20%), name calling (23%), and pressuring someone to do something sexually that they did not want to do (15%). Additionally, more than a third of men (36%) had aggressively thrust their penis in and out of someone's mouth (i.e., "face-fucking"), and nearly half of men (48%) had ejaculated on someone's face. Conversely, women were more likely to report target sexual behaviors, with the exception of target behaviors experienced by men who have sex with men. Examples of target sexual behaviors include having been choked (21% of women), having their face ejaculated on (32% of women, 53% of men who have sex with men), and aggressive fellatio (34% of women, 54% of men who have sex with men). Three times as many women had been sexually pressured compared to men (37% to 12%, respectively), and 27% of women and 31% of men who have sex with men reported having had a male partner attempt anal sex with them without asking or discussing it.

This has implications for sexual assault and coercion as well as risk of sexually transmitted infections, since one cannot negotiate condom use if one has not first been given the opportunity to consent or to express interest in a sexual behavior. (p. 630)

Effects of Pornography on Aggression

Concerns about the use of pornography and its effects on sexual and nonsexual aggression date back many decades. However, research on the effects of general use of mainstream pornography on sexual aggression has produced inconclusive results (Shor & Seida, 2021). According to some studies, watching pornography has little or no effect on sexual aggression. Ferguson and Hartley (2022) conducted a meta-analysis of roughly 50 years of research on pornography (both violent and nonviolent) and sexual aggression. Their analysis showed no association between nonviolent pornography consumption and sexual aggression and only a weak correlation between violent porn and sexual aggression.

A recent longitudinal study by Kohut and colleagues (2021) of Croatian adolescents concluded that "pornography use, when considered on its own, but also in confluence with other risk factors for sexual aggression, was not substantially associated either with contemporaneously measured sexual aggression or changes in the probability of subsequent sexual aggression" (p. 661). Similarly, Hatch et al. (2020) found no connection between pornography consumption and intimate partner violence.

On the other hand, Wright et al.'s (2016b) meta-analysis revealed a significant association between consuming pornography and committing real-world acts of verbal and physical sexual aggression. Results did not vary between men and women and were similar in both U.S. and international samples. Associations of pornography use with both verbal and physical sexual aggression were significant; notably, there was a stronger effect for verbal sexual aggression than for physical sexual aggression. Both violent and nonviolent pornography were associated with sexual aggression.

Myth vs. Reality: Aggression and Pornography

In *Aggression in Pornography: Myths and Realities*, Shor and Seida (2021) detail findings of their research, which combines content analyses and in-depth interviews with people who consume pornography. You have read about several of their studies in this chapter. A concise list of what they call "nine of the most interesting and surprising findings" (pp. 122–130) appears below.

- Most pornography viewers separate fantasies from behavior.
- Viewers emphasize consent and mutual pleasure when reflecting on aggression.
- Most videos *do not* contain aggression.
- Mainstream pornography is *not* becoming increasingly aggressive.
- Most viewers prefer to watch less aggression.
- Women, not men, are relatively more likely to express interest in aggression.
- Viewers overwhelmingly prefer videos in which female performers express pleasure.
- Popular same-sex videos contain more aggression than popular heterosexual videos.
- Videos featuring women of color do not always contain more aggression.

Shor and Seida (2021) note that more conclusive results have been found for studies that examine effects of exposure to pornography that features aggression. Results show that increased exposure to aggressive sexual acts in porn has been linked to more permissive attitudes toward coercion, aggression, sexual violence targeting women, and a greater inclination to commit sexual assault. Furthermore, a person's individual characteristics (e.g., aggressive or antisocial tendencies) can moderate the effects of pornography consumption and aggression.

Impact of Exposure to Sexually Violent Material

It is common for entertainment media to portray sex in combination with violent acts. Popular shows like *Outlander, American Horror Story,* and *Law & Order: SVU* graphically depict sexual assaults, including rape.

Should we be concerned about this tendency to mix sex with violence? Again, findings over the decades are mixed. Early studies comparing rapists to non-rapists revealed that the mixture of sex and violence had potentially harmful effects. Convicted rapists were aroused by viewing both rape and consenting sex; however, non-rapists were aroused only by depictions of consenting sex (Abel et al., 1977; Barbaree et al., 1979). A study of college students showed that depictions of rape where the victim has an involuntary orgasm could result in levels of arousal that were comparable to arousal resulting from depictions of consensual sex (Malamuth et al., 1980). Male students were most aroused by depictions of rape if the victim appeared to experience both an involuntary orgasm and pain. Females, on the other hand, were most aroused when the victim had an involuntary orgasm but did not experience pain.

Experimental studies in the 1980s indicated that exposure to violent pornography contributed to increases in men's fantasies about rape, beliefs that women enjoy being raped, and acceptance of violence toward women (Fisher et al., 2013). Laboratory experiments found that men who had been angered by a woman and who had watched sexually violent content would then engage in greater aggression toward female targets. However, other experiments failed to replicate those key findings, and there is criticism that the negative effects observed from exposure to sexually violent content may be unique to laboratory settings and not generalizable to the real world. (Recall the 2022 meta-analysis findings by Ferguson and Hartley of only a weak correlation between violent pornography use and aggression.)

A review of 43 studies with teen and young adult samples found that exposure to sexually explicit and sexually violent media was positively related to dating violence and sexual violence myths; more accepting attitudes toward dating and sexual violence; and anticipated or actual dating or sexual violence victimization, perpetration, and not intervening as a bystander (Rodenhizer & Edwards, 2019). Sexually explicit and sexually violent media content more strongly affected men's dating violence and sexual violence attitudes and behaviors.

Kohut et al. (2020) offer the following summary of the effects of violent pornography:

> Some research indicates support for the notion that exposure to sexually violent pornography is more strongly associated with rape-supportive attitudes (Garcia, 1986; Hald, Malamuth, & Yuen, 2010) and self-reported sexual aggression (Ybarra

et al., 2011; Ybarra & Thompson, 2018) than is exposure to nonviolent pornography, though causal direction is not always easy to infer from this literature. (p. 14)

Sexual Violence in Slasher Films

Slasher films, a sub-genre of horror films, have received attention from scholars for their depiction of violence and sexualization of female characters. The highly popular, R-rated slasher movies contain a great deal of violence, which occurs during or soon after an erotic scene (Linz et al., 1988; Weaver & Tamborini, 1996). According to Harris (1994):

> The main concern with such films is the juxtaposition of erotic sex and violence. For example, one scene from *Toolbox Murders* opens with a beautiful woman disrobing and getting into her bath, with the very romantic music "Pretty Baby" playing in the background. For several minutes she is shown fondling herself and masturbating in a very erotic manner. Suddenly the camera cuts to the scene of an intruder breaking into her apartment, with loud, fast-paced suspenseful music in the background. The camera and sound track cut back and forth several times between these two characters until he finally encounters the woman. He attacks her with electric tools, chasing her around the apartment, finally shooting her several times in the head with a nail gun. The scene closes after seeing her bleed profusely, finally lying on the bed to die with the sound track again playing the erotic "Pretty Baby." (pp. 261–262)

There are disagreements among scholars about whether there is a relationship between sex and violence in slasher films. For instance, Ménard et al. (2019) analyzed male and female characters in 30 of the highest-grossing slasher films in the 1980s, 1990s, and 2000s (10 from each decade). Characters were more likely to be killed if they appeared nude on screen, dressed provocatively, failed to fight against the films' antagonists, and exhibited fewer prosocial behaviors. Their analysis found no relationship between characters engaging in sexual behaviors and dying. These findings support earlier research that found no significant connection between sex and violence, presumably because violent behaviors occur much more often than sexual behaviors throughout slasher films (Sapolsky et al., 2003). Interestingly, slasher films are "significantly less sexy than their reputations would suggest" (Ménard et al., 2019, p. 634). Out of the 30 films in their study, there were only 10 full sex scenes, 11 partial or interrupted sex scenes, and six where sex was implied but not seen.

Other researchers have identified significant links between sexual and violent content in slasher films. Wellman et al. (2021) studied female characters in 48 influential slasher films from the 1960s through the 2010s, such as *Psycho*, *Texas Chainsaw Massacre* (both the 1974 and 2003 versions), *Halloween*, *Friday the 13th*, and *Scream*. In line with previous studies (e.g., Cowan & O'Brien, 1990; Welsh, 2010), female characters' sexuality and sexualized behaviors were directly linked to higher levels of brutalization and higher risk of dying. "Slasher films disseminate messages that equate femininity with purity and female sexuality with sin that is punishable with horrific violence" (p. 676).

Researchers have also studied slasher movies for the effects of the sexual violence on young audiences. Men become desensitized when they repeatedly watch slasher films (Linz et al., 1984), but women do not (Krafka, 1985). Watching slasher films over an extended period of time resulted in men finding the movies to be more enjoyable, less degrading to women, less offensive, and less violent.

Sexual Script Acquisition, Activation, Application Model

Many scholars use social cognitive theory (see Chapter 4) as a theoretical framework for studying the effects of sexual media content. Put simply, the theory posits that people can learn observationally and that rewarded behaviors are more likely to be copied by the observer than unrewarded behaviors. As discussed previously, pornographic videos and mainstream media rarely depict negative consequences of sexual behaviors, so it is possible that viewers would be more likely to model behaviors they have seen on the screen.

Of course, social cognitive theory was not developed specifically to study sexual media content. Wright (2011) designed the **sexual script acquisition, activation, application model ($_3$AM)** to explain the effects of media on sexual behavior and other outcomes. Integrating theories related to behavior, mass communication, and information processing, the $_3$AM "posits a multipart sequence for socialization effects due to media exposure, a variety of pathways through which effects can result, and a large number of moderating factors at each step of the model" (Wright, 2020a, p. 227).

Importantly, the $_3$AM acknowledges that mediating and moderating factors operate simultaneously. Regarding mediation, the model suggests that effects of sexual media content occur through the acquisition, activation, and application of **sexual scripts**—symbolic guidelines for sexual behavior and activity. According to the $_3$AM, being exposed to sexual media can lead to someone learning a new sexual script (acquisition), priming an existing sexual script (activation), and using sexual scripts to guide their own actions or judgments about the actions of others (application). Regarding moderation, the model includes a number of factors that either increase or decrease the likelihood of acquiring, activating, and applying sexual scripts from the media.

> These include *content factors* such as model attractiveness, behavioral rewards, and punishments, and depiction prevalence; *audience factors* such as existing sexual scripts, personal motivations, psychological involvement, identification, perceptions of norms and risk, evaluations of functionality and realism, moral views, and efficacy; and *situational factors* such as script-situation correspondence, time pressure, and sexual arousal. Additionally, *accessibility* moderators are specified for the stage of sexual script activation (e.g., recency, frequency, and duration of exposure, message vividness). (Wright, 2020a, p. 228)

Furthermore, the $_3$AM acknowledges that several moderation variables can also act as mediators, depending on the person and circumstances. For example, although people may react differently to the same sexual content due to differences in sexual attitudes and norms (moderation), it is possible that some sexual content could lead to shifts in certain sexual attitudes that could result in influencing other sexual thoughts behaviors (mediation) (Wright, 2020b; Wright et al., 2016a).

> ### Sexual Scripts on Broadcast, Cable, and Streaming TV
>
> Aubrey et al. (2020) conducted a content analysis of TV shows airing on broadcast, cable, and streaming television to examine the heterosexual scripts in programs for preteens, teens, and young adults. The researchers identified the following three most common scripts.
>
> 1. Sex is equated with masculinity.
> 2. Men value sex over commitment.
> 3. Women's virtue is tied to their sexuality (the "good girls" script).

Mediating and Moderating the Effects of Sexual Media Content

Mediating variables explain the *how* or *why*—or reason—an observed relationship exists between independent (predictor) and dependent (outcome) variables. Meanwhile, moderating variables influence the *strength* and *direction* of the relationship.

Factors that Mediate Effects of Sexual Media Content

Examples of potential mediators include self-efficacy, normative perceptions (also referred to as perceived norms), perception of risk, sensation-seeking, sexual expectations and attitudes, and arousal.

Martino et al.'s (2005) longitudinal study of adolescents in the United States demonstrated that mainstream TV exposure predicted greater sexual *self-efficacy*, such as a belief in the ability to talk with a potential partner about sex-related topics, which then predicted a greater likelihood of initiating sexual intercourse. College students who watched a soap opera that featured a conversation about sexual health were more likely to engage in sexual health discussions two week later, thanks in part to an increase in self-efficacy regarding their ability to have a discussion about sexual health (Moyer-Gusé et al., 2011). Another study examined the association between gay men's consumption of pornographic videos that depicted condom use and decreases in STI-risk behavior, finding that it was mediated by self-efficacy regarding condom use and being able to negotiate condom use with a sexual partner (Traeen et al., 2014).

Repeated depictions of sexual viewpoints or practices have the potential to "influence viewers' normative perceptions and result in corresponding adjustments to their sexual judgments and behaviors" (Wright, 2020a, p. 230). For example, the association between college students' porn use and condomless sex was mediated by *perceived norms* that fewer of their peers were using condoms (Wright et al., 2016a). A two-wave study of U.S. teens revealed that watching sitcoms in an earlier wave of the study predicted sexual initiation at a later wave (Gottfried et al., 2013). This was attributed in part to teens' normative perceptions that their friends were having sex. Our understanding of the role of perceived norms is preliminary because measures, samples, and results have differed among studies (Wright, 2020a).

Gottfried et al.'s study also highlighted another mediating factor: *perception of risk*. Sitcoms have far fewer messages about sexual risk and responsibility compared to dramas, and watching comedies was related to intercourse initiation, in part because of lower perceptions of harm from having sex.

Sensation-seeking is another potential mediator of particular interest to researchers because it is often conceptualized as a stable personality trait. In one study, watching movies led to heightened sensation-seeking later, which in turn led to having sex at an earlier age and increases in risky sexual behaviors (O'Hara et al., 2012).

Multiple studies have examined the mediating influence of *sexual expectations*. For example, watching porn can lead people to having sex outside of a committed relationship because of expectations that they should have multiple options for sex partners, as is often seen in pornographic videos (Gwinn et al., 2013). Videos depicting sex with strangers or people saying "no" to sex when they really mean "yes"—both of which are known risk factors for sexual aggression in men—can foster expectations that those things are common in the real world. D'Abreu and Krahé (2014) found that the association between previous pornography use and later sexual aggression was partially mediated by expectations of taking part in real-world sexual encounters where those risk factors are present.

Sexual attitudes can also serve as a mediator between pornography use and real-world sexual behaviors. Because pornographic content overwhelmingly portrays sexual behaviors as pleasurable with no negative consequences, it is possible that "such portrayals may produce or reinforce more positive attitudes toward those behaviors among consumers, leading to an increased likelihood of engaging in those behaviors if given the chance" (Wright, 2020a, p. 235).

Although *arousal* was discussed earlier as an effect of sexually explicit content, it can also mediate the cognitive effects of pornography for three reasons:

> First, higher arousal should reduce the motivation and ability to engage in an effortful and deliberate search for the most applicable sexual script, increasing the likelihood that the most accessible script will be applied (Wright, 2011). Second, if arousal was present when the script was encoded, later arousal should increase the likelihood the script will be reactivated (Hald & Malamuth, 2015; Wright, 2011). Third, in order to reclaim cognitive balance during or after being aroused by a particular pornographic depiction, the consumer may adjust their attitudes to be more accepting of the type of sex depicted (Peter & Valkenburg, 2009). (Wright, 2020a, p. 235)

Factors that Moderate Effects of Sexual Media Content

Moderating factors include (but are not limited to) parental behaviors, perceived media realism, perceived similarities with media characters, gender, ethnicity, confidence in the media, the compatibility of messages about sex with one's personal beliefs, and education.

A central focus of research into *parental behaviors* involves investigating intervention strategies, such as parents talking with their children about the media they consume or setting limits on media use, which evidence indicates is a significant factor in countering potential effects from sexual media content (e.g., Fisher et al., 2009). In one longitudinal study, frequent TV watching combined with no content restrictions from parents resulted in the highest rates of adolescents having sex (Ashby et al., 2006). Conversely, the lowest rates of adolescent sex were among teens who watched less TV and had content restrictions in place.

However, research shows that parental intervention is not always a consistent or relevant moderator. "It may be that parental behaviors more core to the formation of sexual scripts, such as engaging in direct and candid discussions about sex, are more important buffers than behaviors specific to media alone" (Wright, 2020a, p. 231). For example, research by Bryant and Rockwell (1994) found that family environments that promote and engage in open discussions about issues and families having a clear, well-defined value system can help mitigate effects of teens' exposure to sexual mainstream content. Wright et al. (2013) studied the effects of parental involvement on female college students in the United States who watched MTV's *16 and Pregnant* and *Teen Mom.* Watching those programs predicted greater pregnancy-risk behavior for those whose fathers had not talked with them about sex during their adolescent years; conversely, there was a lower likelihood of pregnancy-risk behavior among viewers of the programs if their fathers had communicated often with them about sex.

Perceived media realism can moderate effects of both mainstream and explicit sexual content. For instance, perceived realism has been found to moderate the effects of consuming sexual media content on permissive sexual attitudes, meaning greater permissive attitudes toward sex are generally seen only in those who perceive sexual content to be more realistic (Baams et al., 2015; Taylor, 2005). Furthermore, overly optimistic perceptions about finances and lifestyles on teen mom reality shows were strongest for those who thought the reality TV genre was realistic (Martins & Jensen, 2014). Notably, perceptions about the realism of pornography have also been shown to have a significant direct effect on sexual aggression perpetration; however, the effect of perceived realism on sexual aggression can also be mediated by sexual scripts, sexual behavior, and acceptance of sexual coercion (Krahé et al., 2022).

Perceived similarity with media characters can also serve as a moderator. For instance, in Moyer-Gusé's (2011b) soap opera study mentioned earlier, identification with the characters was related to greater intentions to have discussions about sexual health. Another study of MTV's *16 and Pregnant* provides more direct evidence of the moderating role of identification. Increased positive attitudes about becoming a teen mom happened only when participants perceived high levels of similarity with the people they watched on the show (Behm-Morawitz et al., 2019). However, identification did not moderate effects of other outcomes, such as belief in teen pregnancy myths. Wright (2020a) cautions that further study of both media realism and character identification are needed because only a few studies have examined these factors as moderators, and results have been inconsistent.

There are numerous other potential moderators that have been studied over the years, such as *age, media multitasking, previous sexual experience,* and *recency of exposure to sexual content,* to name a few. Two of the most frequently studied are *ethnicity* and *gender.* However, in studies of both mainstream and explicit sexual media, Wright (2020a) notes that these factors produce inconsistent results, and there is no convincing explanation for that inconsistency. Wright does not argue that ethnicity and gender should not be studied for their moderating potential, but he suggests that assessing individual psychographic differences (e.g., values, opinions, etc.) may better inform our understanding of moderation effects.

For instance, people with greater *confidence in the utility and veracity of media* as a whole—and specifically pornographic content—are more likely to be affected. Higher confidence in media institutions moderates associations between pornography use and attitudes about extramarital sex (Wright, 2013) and having multiple sex partners (Wright & Arroyo, 2013). The correlation between higher pornography use by German adults and less frequent condom use was greatest for those who most strongly thought of porn as a source of sexual information (Wright et al., 2018).

Compatibility between a person's beliefs and media messages can moderate effects. For instance, studies of U.S. adults have found that they are less likely to be affected if their existing sexual scripts, morals, and values are more incompatible with pornographic depictions of sex. Associations between pornography consumption and attitudes toward unrestricted sex or multiple sexual partners are weaker for people who are more politically conservative, religious, and oriented toward moral absolutes and moral uniformity (see Frutos & Merrill, 2017; Wright, 2013, 2018; Wright & Bae, 2015; Wright et al., 2014b).

Furthermore, a person's *education*, both in general and specifically about pornography, "may decrease the likelihood that consumers incorporate information from pornography into their own sexual scripts" (Wright, 2020a, p. 236). Associations between pornography consumption and various sexual attitudes of men and women in the United States were weaker for those with more years of education (Wright, 2013; Wright & Randall, 2014).

Vandenbosch and van Oosten (2017) studied the impact of porn literacy education in schools on students' views of women as sex objects. There was no relationship between online pornography and perceptions of women as sex objects among students who learned from the porn literacy presentations. However, a relationship did appear for students who reported learning little to nothing. These results are in line with earlier work by Allen and his colleagues (1996, 1999) on the use of educational briefings to mitigate the harmful effects of sexually explicit material. Effects from exposure to violent pornography could be reduced by messages either before or after exposure explaining that pornography is fiction and fantasy. On a similar note, recent research using in-depth qualitative interviews with pornography consumers found that they have a "tendency to bracket pornography's scripts and norms as 'fantasy,' thus reducing their impact on the real world of sexual interactions" (Shor & Seida, 2021, p. 55).

Of course, the moderators outlined here are not all that have been studied. Many others have been explored in at least one study (e.g., *age of first exposure to porn, life satisfaction, relationship status, explicitness of imagery,* etc.). Wright (2018) recommends that researchers continue to study moderating factors and that researchers link them to established theoretical models.

Areas of Concern Regarding Pornography Research

To close this chapter, we want to briefly mention two areas of concern regarding pornography research: (1) addiction and problematic pornography use and (2) overall conceptual and methodological concerns about pornography research.

Problematic Pornography Use

Whether someone can be addicted to porn is mainly a debate for mental health professionals, clinical psychologists, and neuroscientists, not communication scholars (Ortiz & Thompson, 2017; Wright, 2020a). However, media research does suggest that some people can have difficulties controlling their use of pornographic content (Ortiz & Thompson, 2017).

In a survey of almost 500 adults, approximately 30% were categorized as having problematic use of online pornography (Wetterneck et al., 2012). Of the problematic users, 46% agreed with the statement "I have wanted to stop looking at Internet pornography and have not been able to," and 42% agreed with the statement "I feel like my use of Internet pornography is putting my relationship(s), job, or reputation at risk." Men were significantly more likely than women to report problematic use.

Pornography Research: "A Castle Built on Sand"

In their review of pornography research literature, Grubbs et al. (2019) concluded that this area of research is "plagued by a preponderance of causal speculations and inferences based on cross-sectional and retrospective reports" and that online pornography research "is in need of diverse methods, experimental paradigms, and longitudinal studies" (p. 144).

Kohut and his colleagues (2020) wrote a scathing critique of the field in their article titled "Surveying Pornography Use: A Shaky Science Resting on Poor Measurement Foundations." The article opened with the observation that across various studies, estimates of pornography use vary considerably.

> It is remarkable that despite five decades of empirical research, we still do not know how many people use pornography, or how much they use it. . . . If such basic issues around measurement remain unresolved, how confident can we be about the reported impact of pornography? (p. 722)

The researchers outlined other issues within pornography research, including confusion and lack of consistency regarding terminology and unclear examples of coding instruments. Furthermore, nearly 60% of the studies they examined utilized measures of pornography use not found in other published research. They point out the lack validity in asking participants to self-report their pornography use, noting that research into internet and smartphone use have found self-reports to be surprisingly inaccurate. "Taken together, the widespread use of idiosyncratic measures of self-reported pornography use that have been inadequately validated suggests to us that this field of research is a castle built on sand" (p. 727).

Kohut et al. (2020) offered numerous recommendations to shore up the field's conceptual and methodological foundations, including better understandings of differences in pornographic content, a thorough conceptual definition of pornography use for researchers, and a clearer definition of pornography to be given to study participants when self-reporting their pornography use.

Summary

Mainstream music videos, television shows, movies, and social media contain an abundance of sexual messages, ranging from the mildly suggestive to various levels of the sexually explicit. In addition to mainstream sexual content, pornography is the extreme class of sexually explicit material that is intended for adult audiences only.

Sexual media content has important implications due to its perceived connection with serious social concerns. The availability of television to all ages makes that medium a particularly dangerous one when considering the damaging social effects that result from the consumption of sexual content. Researchers are in the early stages of furthering our understanding of exposure to sexual content on social media. The internet is overwhelmingly the preferred way to access porn in the 21st century, and most recent research is in that domain.

Seeing sexual content can affect viewers' attitudes, beliefs, and behaviors. The sexual script acquisition, activation, application model ($_3$AM) helps explain the effects of media exposure on sexual behavior. A number of factors mediate how media exposure affects individuals (e.g., self-efficacy, perception of risk, arousal). Multiple factors moderate the strength of the effects (e.g., parental behaviors, perceived realism, education).

Media content continues to depict sexual situations in combination with violent acts, such as in slasher films. A recent review of the literature found that although exposure to violent pornography is generally associated with more rape-supportive attitudes and sexual aggression, causal directions are not clear.

Lastly, there is concern about pornography addiction, but that debate is largely outside the realm of mass communication research. There are also substantial concerns about how research into the effects of pornography is conducted. Suggestions of how to shore up the science behind the study of effects from sexual media exposure have been offered, but it is too early to report if or how those suggestions are being implemented. There is no doubt, however, that as mainstream media continues to push the envelope with racier content and technological advances such as virtual reality open new possibilities for hard-core content, there is a need for more research.

NOTE

[1] Technically, the X-rating has not been used since 1990, when the Motion Picture Association (MPA) began using the less sensational NC-17 rating. However, the X-rating has become synonymous with pornographic films and videos, but they are not rated by the MPA.

13

Effects of Frightening or Disturbing Media Content

> You know as well as I do that fear only exists for one purpose: to be conquered.
> —Captain Kathryn Janeway, *Star Trek: Voyager*

In 1975, the hit movie *Jaws* appeared in theaters across the United States. That summer, the press reported that the movie caused many people to fear swimming in the ocean or even in lakes. From coast to coast, beachgoers avoided stepping too far into the water—afraid of ravenous Great Whites threatening swimmers.

The emotional response that many moviegoers experienced after seeing *Jaws* is a good example of a **reaction of fright or anxiety** to media content. Other anecdotal examples of fright reactions to feature films abound. In 1974, *The Exorcist* triggered intense responses among audiences of all ages. Other films, such as *Poltergeist, Indiana Jones and the Temple of Doom, Invasion of the Body Snatchers*, and *Gremlins,* contained content that was especially disturbing to children.

Indeed, the Motion Picture Association of America implemented the PG-13 rating in the 1980s to alert parents that a film might be inappropriate for children younger than 13 (Zoglin, 1984). *Indiana Jones* director Steven Spielberg is often credited with spearheading the effort for an intermediate rating between PG and R because a scene "featuring a realistic, still-beating heart ripped from the chest of a human sacrifice angered many parents who had not expected such frightening content in a PG film" (MPAA, 2018, p. 12). Not only did the PG-13 rating establish a middle ground between movies appropriate for children of all ages and those suitable for older children and teens, it was also "an attempt to renegotiate the boundaries of the horror genre, bringing it below the R frontier" (Antunes, 2017, p. 38).

Since the mid-1970s, Hollywood has continued to produce thrillers that contain graphic and intense content. The proliferation of cable and satellite television in the 1980s and 1990s brought many of these thrillers, such as *The X-Files* and *Buffy the Vampire Slayer*, directly into the homes of millions of U.S. families. Today, countless

235

The summer blockbuster *Jaws* caused swimmers to clear the surf in 1975.

people stream frightening shows such as FX's *American Horror Story* and Netflix's *Stranger Things* and *Squid Game*.

Media effects researchers have learned a great deal about fright reactions to media content, including the reasons for it and ways to control it. This chapter will identify some of the more important findings from fright-reaction studies that have been conducted through the years. Children especially have been the focus of much of this research, but adults have not been ignored. For both age groups, many studies have explored fright as an immediate response that is rather short lived, but research has also documented long-term emotional responses that continue for hours, days, or even years.

Throughout this chapter, we will refer to the substantial work done by media effects researcher Joanne Cantor and her associates. For the past few decades, Cantor's studies have appeared in numerous journals and books, and most of what we know about fright reactions to media content comes from her work. She is considered the leading expert on the subject of fright reactions to mass media. The definition she uses for **fear** comes from the writings of Izard (1977). "Fear is generally conceived of as an emotional response of negative hedonic tone related to avoidance or escape, due to the perception of real or imagined threat" (Cantor, 2009, p. 290). (Hedonics is the branch of psychology that deals with the pleasant or unpleasant states of consciousness.)

Following a brief historical look at the study of frightening media content, we turn to the different ways in which fright is measured. Then we focus on the reasons for fright reactions to media content. We assess the importance of individual differences (e.g., age, gender, sensation seeking) in both consuming scary media content and gauging fear reactions. We close with research-directed strategies for coping with fear.

The Study of Fright

Fright reactions have been measured for many years. In the 1930s and 1940s, several studies examined reactions of fear among mass media audiences, especially children (Dysinger & Ruckmick, 1933; Eisenberg, 1936; Preston, 1941). Recall from earlier chapters that the Payne Fund studies of the late 1920s and early 1930s examined the effects of motion pictures on young people. One of the experimenters, Herbert Blumer (1933), discovered that 93% of the children in his study reported being frightened by a film.

The modern horror genre developed throughout the 20th century. Classic films such as *Dracula* and *Frankenstein* appeared in 1931. As discussed in Chapter 2, the most famous incident of media-induced fright occurred on October 30, 1938, when thousands of people panicked during the dramatic *War of the Worlds* radio broadcast. The radio drama, set up as a series of breaking news announcements that interrupted "regular" programming, alarmed Depression-era listeners by reporting an invasion from the planet Mars. Cantril (1940) studied the reactions of people throughout the country and could not pinpoint a single variable that caused the fear reaction, but he noted that a lack of critical ability on the part of listeners did seem to contribute to the fear. Cantril discovered that personality influences and other psychological differences influenced whether listeners believed what they were hearing was an actual news broadcast.

Most studies in the 1950s and early 1960s followed the lead of earlier studies by focusing on the content of movies and television shows and their effects upon viewers (Himmelweit et al., 1958; Schramm et al., 1961; Wall & Simson, 1950). One famous study, however, broke with tradition and examined the harmful effects of comic books on American youth (Wertham, 1954). In the 1950s, comic books took on a more frightful aspect, and scary stories such as those from the *Tales from the Crypt* series entertained a generation of young boys. In the 1950s and 1960s, horror films such as Alfred Hitchcock's *Psycho* were immensely popular among audiences.

Throughout the remainder of the 1960s, 1970s, and 1980s, researchers often concentrated their efforts on the *long-term effects* of mass media rather than short-term emotional effects. Enduring fright reactions—the kind that cause nightmares or long-term effects—became the focus of surveys and experiments. In interviews with parents, three out of four said their children sometimes reacted with nightmares after viewing disturbing programs on television (Hess & Goldman, 1962). Singer (1975) also found that children were in danger of having terrifying nightmares after watching disturbing media content. Years after seeing a frightening movie, children may experience such night terrors or, at the least, have strange or weird fantasies. Sarafino (1986) argued that frightening media content not only caused fear reactions in children but also threatened to impair psychological development.

Much research in the 1970s and 1980s underscored the prevalence of media fright reactions among children. Almost 50% of the first graders in one study reported having been sometimes or often frightened by television programs (Lyle & Hoffman, 1972). In a national survey, one in four children said television depictions of shootings and violent fights had frightened them (Zill, 1977). In the 1980s, two studies indicated that three out of four preschoolers and elementary school children were frightened by something they witnessed on television or in a movie (Hoffner & Cantor, 1985; Wilson et al., 1987).

Since the 1990s, a number of different types of studies have offered compelling evidence for problems associated with media-induced fright among children, including lasting, detrimental effects (Cantor, 1998, 1999; Harrison & Cantor, 1999; Hoekstra et al., 1999).

Singer and colleagues (1998) conducted a survey of more than 2,000 Ohio children in the third through eighth grades. Students who watched more hours of television each day reported more symptoms of anxiety, depression, and post-traumatic stress. In another survey, parents reported that the more television a child watched, the more likely the child was to have a sleep disturbance (Owens et al., 1999). Children with TVs in their bedrooms were significantly more likely to experience sleep disturbances and other problems than children without TVs in their bedrooms (Cantor et al., 2010; Helm & Spencer, 2019). About one-third of a sample of 13-year-olds in Belgium reported having nightmares at least once a week after watching frightening or disturbing media content (Van den Bulck, 2004).

In another study, children exposed to a destructive and deadly house fire in an episode of *Little House on the Prairie* were less likely to want to learn about building a fire in a fireplace than children who had not watched the episode (Cantor & Omdahl, 1991). In a similar study, children who watched a scene involving a drowning were more concerned about water accidents and were less likely to want to learn about canoeing than children not exposed to the scene (Cantor & Omdahl, 1999). The researchers took care in the later study to debrief the children and teach them water safety guidelines so that effects would not be long lasting.

A more recent meta-analysis found support for the impact of scary television on children's internalized reactions such as anxiety, depression, fear, PTSD, and sleep problems (Pearce & Field, 2016). Although the average age of children in the analysis was not a significant predictor of effect sizes, children under 10 were particularly vulnerable to frightening TV content. The researchers noted that some studies show extreme reactions in a substantial minority of children, but they say more work needs to be done to better understand what makes some children more vulnerable to frightening TV content. Overall, they concluded that "based on the first 25 years or so of research there is little to suggest that, at the group level, scary TV has a *severe* impact on children's mental health" (p. 114).

Many researchers have documented the effects of frightening films through the years. Buzzuto (1975) recorded incidents of neurosis following viewing of *The Exorcist*. Mathai (1983) noted an acute state of anxiety in an adolescent who viewed *Invasion of the Body Snatchers*. In 1994, Simons and Silveira reported evidence of posttraumatic stress disorder in viewers of a television program in Britain called *Ghostwatch*. For a review of such studies and others, see Cantor (2009).

In the 1990s, researchers began to investigate fright reactions, especially among children, to news broadcasts (e.g., Cantor et al., 1993; Cantor & Nathanson, 1996). Riddle et al. (2012) focused on fright reactions to everyday news exposure in a study of more than 200 kindergarten through 6th grade children. Even in the absence of major events or crises, 35% of children said they had been frightened by something they had seen on TV news. Children mentioned most frequently being frightened by natural disasters (25%), kidnappings (10%), war (8%), and burglaries (8%). Some children were able to recall vivid details about stories they saw on the news, including how many times a person was shot, where they were shot, and who shot them. In a recent survey-based study, parents reported that a majority of their children were frightened, disturbed, or upset by news coverage of the COVID-19 pandemic (Cantor & Harrison, 2022).

Recent years have brought more graphic depictions—more blood, gore, and realism—to the screen, and audiences seem to love it. Box office classics such as *Friday the 13th, Halloween, Nightmare on Elm Street*, and *Scream* continue to thrill audiences in sequels and remakes as do more current hits such as *Get Out* and *Us* plus the *IT, A Quiet Place*, and *The Conjuring* movie franchises. Advances in the art of special effects have enhanced the graphic and realistic

FX's *American Horror Story* has terrified audiences with monsters, ghosts, and witches. Perhaps one of the scariest characters was Twisty the killer clown from season 4, *AHS: Freak Show.*

nature of horrifying scenes in these popular films. Even on television and streaming services, special effects create frightening content on hits such as *American Horror Story, Stranger Things, The Walking Dead* (and its spin-offs), and *The Haunting of Hill House.*

Of course, movies and TV are not the only sources for horror and frightening media content. In recent years, horror has become a popular podcast genre (Hancock & McMurty, 2017). Researchers are also investigating the effects of horror in other forms of popular media, including video games and virtual reality (e.g., Lin, 2017; Lin et al., 2017; Lynch & Martins, 2015). Some are also examining how technology—such as chairs that provide vibrotactile stimulation—can enhance viewers' emotional response to horror films (Branje et al., 2014).

In addition to studying effects of recently viewed films or television programs, researchers have also investigated fright reactions that linger and are recalled years later by older children and adults (e.g., Cantor, 1998, 2004; Hoekstra et al., 1999; Johnson, 1980). The researchers examine self-reports by participants in studies to determine the severity and duration of fright reactions. Using a methodology called "recollective or retrospective reports," or "autobiographical memory," two independent teams of investigators found that 90%–100% of undergraduates reported having vivid memories of media-related fright reactions as children or adolescents or more recently (Harrison & Cantor, 1999; Hoekstra et al., 1999). In one of the studies, more than 25% of college students still had residual anxiety from their childhood exposure to frightening media content (Harrison & Cantor, 1999).

> In summary, research shows that children often experience anxiety and distress while watching mass media presentations and that these feelings, in varying intensities, often linger on after exposure. Recent surveys demonstrate that media-induced fears often interfere with children's sleep, and retrospective reports suggest that the negative effects of scary media can endure for years, even into adulthood. (Cantor, 2009, p. 300)

Examples of Long-Lasting Effects from Horror Movies

In her 2004 article "'I'll Never Have a Clown in My House'—Why Movie Horror Lives On," Joanne Cantor analyzed papers written by college students describing frightening effects from watching scary movies. She focused her analysis on the four most-cited movies: *Jaws*, *Poltergeist*, *The Blair Witch Project*, and *Scream*. Here are some examples of the lingering—and often irrational—fright reactions described by the students:

Jaws

- "I regularly went swimming in a lake by my house, and even though I knew it wasn't possible, I would be afraid when I was in the water and thought about *Jaws*."
- "I know that sharks are not found in lakes and pools. Yet, whenever I am in the deep end at a pool, I swim really fast to get to the edge (always looking behind me)."

Poltergeist

- "To this day I am scared of clowns and will never have one in my house, even when I have children."
- "Even now, I certainly don't leave my TV on after the station goes off the air, and I still always make sure that my closet door is closed before I go to sleep."

The Blair Witch Project

- "After I watched the movie and even a while after the true facts about *The Blair Witch Project* became public knowledge, I found myself really scared anytime that I was around woods or near a bunch of trees when any wind would pick up."
- "I swore I would never go camping again."

Scream

- "That mask was so incredibly creepy that even now when I see it in costume shops my stomach gets a little queasy."
- "For two years, every time I was home alone I felt uneasy. . . . Even though I am not as bad as I was, there are still times that being home alone is extremely scary for me."

Explanations for the Appeal of Fright

Horror has been described as stories "characterized by fear of some uncertain threat to existential nature and by disgust over its potential aftermath . . . perhaps the source of threat is supernatural in its composition" (Tamborini & Weaver, 1996). In other words, horror stories cause extreme fear. A monster or some other terrible source threatens lives, and the manner of death or the aftermath of death causes disgust.

Despite the feelings of fear and disgust, audiences are entertained—they actually seek out such experiences. This fright-as-entertainment paradoxical phenomenon has piqued the interest of several communication researchers who have attempted to explain the complexities that make unpleasant and horrible stories entertaining. Scientists have advanced a number of theories to explain the appeal of frightening stories.

Over the years, a popular view has been that of **catharsis**. This view holds that when audience members witness graphic violence on the screen or read about it in books, they purge or rid themselves of their own violent tendencies or inclinations. Some have argued that such purging is enjoyable (Clarens, 1967). Some have extended the notion of catharsis to include the purging of personal fears and anxieties (Douglas, 1966; Tudor, 1989). Also, the transformations that monsters, such as humans changing into werewolves, undergo in many horror films supposedly provide cathartic relief for teens who are experiencing physical changes as they mature sexually (Evans, 1984).

Researchers sometimes use terms like "identification" or "vicarious experience" to explain cathartic effects from horror. Some say that viewers are able to gain sadistic pleasure by identifying with the monsters and killers (King, 1981). Viewers are able to enjoy certain taboo experiences in a vicarious manner (Wood, 1984). Deep anxieties about certain acts (especially sexual acts that frequently occur in horror films) find expression and even resolution through the entertaining horror book or movie (Derry, 1987).

However, more recent research by Clasen et al. (2020) found no support for the horror-as-catharsis argument. In fact, a majority of people (52%) who consumed scary media content were *more* scared and anxious after exposure. Only 6% were less scared. (The remaining 42% reported no change after exposure.)

Another suggestion about the appeal of horror comes from Berlyne (1967, 1971), who believed that horror serves as a necessary, noxious experience that provides the viewer with feelings of gratified relief once it is finished. Of this view, Zillmann and Gibson (1996) wrote, "It is the *termination* of this aversive state that is expected to prompt pleasurable relief. In this view, the enjoyment of horror is akin to the pleasures of the sudden end to a bad toothache" (p. 26).

Rosenbaum (1979) provided an explanation with distinctly religious overtones: People enjoy horror because it encourages a belief in a superior spiritual being capable of destroying evil forces. Ultimately, they experience feelings of "spiritual safety" (Zillmann & Gibson, 1996, p. 27).

Zillmann (1991a, 1991b) described horror as frightening because viewers empathetically identify with the victims and experience their terror vicariously. Horror also frightens viewers because of their apprehensions—they fear being victims themselves. Finally, horror usually features a satisfying ending that viewers enjoy.

Combining affective disposition theory and excitation transfer theory—now the most commonly used theory to explain why people enjoy suspenseful entertainment (Raney & Bryant, 2020)—Zillmann (1996) also outlined a model of suspense involving arousal and threat resolutions. In short, audiences are aroused by suspense and feel greater negative emotions (e.g., fear) when a liked character is threatened. When that character has a happy ending or overcomes the threat, audiences feel positive emotions, and the arousal that has built up transfers to intensify their enjoyment. If the threat resolution is unresolved or unsatisfying, arousal transfers over to increase disappointment and dissatisfaction (Zillmann, 1980).

Over the years, this model of suspense has received mixed support. In particular, the positive relationship between negative emotions and enjoyment is not necessarily influenced by a film's resolution. J.-H. T. Lin and her colleagues (2017) studied horror-themed virtual reality games. They argue that "'resolution of horror' is not limited to the *'end results'* in the video game context and can be viewed as the perception of whether one can cope with the challenges *during* game play" (p. 17). This perception of a person's ability to cope with mediated fright during exposure is known as **horror self-efficacy**. Enjoyment was significantly affected by a three-way interaction between physiological arousal, fear, and horror self-efficacy. For those with high fear, greater horror self-efficacy led to significantly greater enjoyment than for those with lower horror self-efficacy. The researchers also "position fear as a factor that influences enjoyment, with self-efficacy moderating the relationship" (p. 17); however, this association only occurred in players with high arousal. For instance, high-arousal players with lower efficacy and high fear reported the least enjoyment, "suggesting that the play was 'overwhelming' and exceeded their optimized level of comfort in confronting mediated fright in VR games" (p. 15).

Zillmann (1991a, 1991b) also proposed what he called a "gender-socialization approach" for the enjoyment of horror. This explanation differed considerably from previous views. Zillmann noticed that males and females reacted very differently to horror films, and part of the enjoyment obtained from watching the film had to do with acting or reacting in those predictable ways. Zillmann and Gibson (1996) wrote:

> The precept for boys and men stipulates that exposure to horror be nondistressing. Their show of mastery of distress in the face of terror should please them and favorably impress others. Gratification is thus self-generated and of a social nature. The precept for girls and women, in contrast, stipulates that exposure to horror be distressing and duly expressed as such. Their show of appropriate sensitivity—dismay, disgust, and contempt—should give them pleasure and favorably impress others. Gratification is again self-generated and social in kind. (p. 28)

However, Hoffner and Levine's (2005) meta-analysis found little direct evidence for this approach. However, the researchers noted that earlier work by Zillmann and his colleagues (1986) suggested that people enjoyed watching a horror film more when another viewer of the opposite gender displayed "gender-appropriate" reactions to the movie. In more recent work by Lin and Xu (2017), gender was not a significant predictor of enjoying horror content on TV.

Other social approaches to understanding the appeal of fright have also been proposed, such as watching horror films "rite of passage" from childhood to adulthood or as a means for teens to bond with friends (for a review, see Oliver & Sanders, 2004).

Recent research offers another explanation for the appeal of frightening media:

Zillmann's "gender-socialization approach" for explaining the appeal of watching frightening content posited expectations for boys and men to exhibit emotional mastery and girls and women to react emotionally.

consumption of horror media is a form of **benign masochism** (deriving pleasure from pain) that allows us to experience simulated threat situations (Clasen et al., 2020). Benign masochism posits that "initially aversive activities may through hedonic reversal become pleasurable" (p. 214). Examples of benign masochism include activities like eating hot chili peppers, listening to sad music, or skydiving, where the consumer must first overcome their initial negative reactions (e.g., disgust, fear, or pain) in order to experience pleasure (Pinker, 2011).

> In the case of horror media, we argue that the attraction of horror is explicable in terms of an evolved pleasure response to threat simulations. Horror media tend to imaginatively transport consumers into fictional universes that brim with danger, for example, in the form of simulated monsters or fictional villains. Through such imaginative absorption, people get to experience strong, predominately negative emotions within a safe context. This experience, which serves as a way of preparing for real-world threat situations, may be biologically adaptive in terms of improving the odds of survival in a potentially hostile world. (Clasen et al., 2020, pp. 214–215)

Measuring Fright

Social scientists use a variety of research methods to measure responses of fear or anxiety when a person is viewing media content. Several physiological responses have been used to measure fright reactions. Among adults, the most common have been measures of heart rate and palmar skin conductance (e.g., Falkowski & Steptoe, 1983; Koriat et al., 1972). Surveys or retrospective recollections are also common in studies that utilize self-reported measures. For instance, studies have asked adults to recall media content that frightened them as children (e.g., Harrison & Cantor, 1999; Hoekstra et al., 1999) or to report on fright reactions of their children to mediated content (Cantor & Sparks, 1984; Sparks, 1986). Cantor (2017) notes that these methods "permit researchers to explore the potentially harmful effects of scary media by studying the impact of programs and movies that most people see in their everyday lives but that it might be considered unethical to inflict on research subjects, especially children, in the laboratory" (p. 653).

However, surveys and retrospective methods do not give researchers the same control as laboratory-based experiments (Cantor, 2017). In lab experiments, adult participants watch frightening or disturbing content and are then asked to select words or phrases that best describe their reactions to the content. Adults, for example, are asked to report levels of anxiety or states of anxiety they experienced (Lazarus et al., 1962). Other descriptors such as the amount of tension or emotional arousal provide additional information. The self-reports for children must be more simply stated. Usually, researchers ask the children to express reactions in varying degrees—for instance, how scared or upset they felt after viewing the disturbing scene or content (e.g., Sparks & Cantor, 1986).

Several other methods are used to measure fright reactions in experiments with children. For example, the experiments of Cantor and associates have usually involved 3- to 11-year-olds who are randomly assigned to various groups. The children in the control group view a violent or frightening scene. The other groups of children receive strategies to help them cope with the content before viewing the scene.

In all the studies, fright reactions are measured using one or more of four different methods. Immediately after exposure to a scene, children are asked to assess the extent of their fright by choosing one of four responses ranging from "not at all scared" to "very, very scared." The researchers also record and code fright reactions by evaluating the child's facial expression from a video recording of the child watching the program. As another supplementary measure, small sensors are attached to the child's fingers and physiological data are collected, such as heart rate and skin temperature (e.g., Wilson & Cantor, 1985; Zillmann et al., 1975). Finally, some studies use behavioral measures of fear. Wilson and Cantor (1987), for example, measured fear by a child's willingness to see a live snake after watching the snake scene from *Raiders of the Lost Ark.*

Reasons for Fear Reactions to Media Content

Media effects researchers have debated the reasons for fear reactions among audiences, especially those that have the age and developmental capacity to understand that what they are witnessing is not really happening. Fright occurs despite the fact that the viewer is not in danger and understands that they are not in danger. Why is this? Most social scientists explain the reaction in terms of classical conditioning (Pavlov, 1960). According to classical conditioning, certain stimuli cause certain responses, and similar stimuli evoke similar, albeit less intense, responses.

Fear-Producing Stimuli

According to Cantor (2009), three categories of stimuli that recur in media content usually result in fear responses in real life. These include (1) dangers and injuries, (2) distortions of natural forms, and (3) the experience of endangerment and fear by others.

Dangers and Injuries.   Many different kinds of events that threaten harm occur repeatedly in scary or suspenseful media content. These might include natural disasters (e.g., earthquakes, volcanic eruptions, tsunamis, and tornadoes), violent confrontations between people (such as interpersonal conflicts or large-scale warfare), animal attacks, or major accidents (Cantor, 2009).

Depictions of dangerous stimuli in mass media have produced measurable fright reactions in a number of experimental and survey research studies (e.g., Cantor, 1998; Harrison & Cantor, 1999). Although anecdotal, many people still mention feeling anxious and fearful when sharing the road with a loaded-down log truck because of *Final Destination 2*'s deadly log truck scene—even decades after the film was released (Frew, 2021; Stopera, 2020).

Distortions of Natural Forms.   Another type of stimulus capable of producing a fear response is the distortion of a familiar sight or organism through a deformity or mutilation. Monsters, mutants, aliens, and vampires also fall into this category.

Cantor (2009) notes "in scary movies, monstrous and distorted characters are typically, but not universally, depicted as evil and dangerous" (p. 292). Throughout the research literature, monstrous characters are frequently mentioned as causing fear in children. Surveys and reports have revealed such fears in children (Cantor, 1998; Cantor & Sparks, 1984).

Endangerment and Fear by Others.   Dramatic movies, television shows, video games, and other forms of scary media content are designed to involve the audience in the plight of characters responding to frightful situations. Audience members are thus drawn into the plot and establish *empathy* with the characters with whom they identify. Empathy is one of two primary mechanisms in this final category of fear-producing stimuli—the only one that involves an *indirect* response. In other words, fear is produced when audience members see characters experiencing fear while in scary situations.

Laboratory research studies indicate that empathy is something that must be developed with age and is associated with the acquisition of role-play skills (Feshbach, 1982; Selman & Byrne, 1974). For example, preschool children are often more scared of the actual frightening stimulus than by observing a character's expression of fear. Meanwhile, older children (ages 9 to 11) experience fear simply by seeing a character's fearful expression and without witnessing the frightening stimulus itself (Wilson & Cantor, 1985).

The other mechanism that produces an indirect response of fear is that of *vicarious involvement*. This mechanism explains the fear of audiences in situations in which characters are unafraid because they are unaware that any danger is impending. Suspenseful dramas rely on audience tensions and worries that something terrible might happen to characters with whom the audience identifies or develops an emotional attachment (Cantor, 1998; Cantor & Omdahl, 1991). Examples of this include when moviegoers talk to the characters on the screen, saying things like, "Don't go upstairs!" or "Look behind the door!"

Emotional Response Factors

Cantor (2009) also identified three important factors that cause viewers to react emotionally whenever they see fearful situations on the screen: (1) realism of depiction, (2) motivations of the viewer, (3) and other factors that affect a viewer's emotionality, such as music and foreshadowing.

Realism of Depiction.   Whenever viewers witness highly realistic, scary action on the screen, their fright responses tend to be intensely emotional. This is known as **stimulus generalization**. This concept refers to the similarity between stimuli from real life and what is seen on the screen. The greater the similarity between real life and screen drama, the stronger the mediated stimulus will be, enhancing the fearful or emotional response to that stimulus. Stimulus generalization explains why people react more intensely to violent scenes that involve live action or real-life depictions, rather than, for example, violence in cartoons or between puppets (Gunter & Furnham, 1984; Osborn & Endsley, 1971).

Particular fears of individuals in the audience also affect the intensity of emotional responses that screen depictions evoke. Children, for instance, are more frightened by screen incidents with which they can identify—those that are similar to their personal experiences. Experimental research has confirmed that individual fears and associated real-life experiences cause individuals to react more intensely when viewing recognizable incidents on the screen (e.g., Hare & Bevings, 1975; Sapolsky & Zillmann, 1978; Weiss et al., 1968).

A process called **stimulus discrimination** also affects the emotional reactions of audience members. This process refers to the ability of audience members at various ages to be able to (or not be able to) distinguish screen events from real-life occurrences. In young children who lack developmental maturity, for example, realizing that a TV or movie monster is not actually real or that a brutal shooting on a dramatic thriller is not indeed taking place can be very difficult and emotionally disturbing (Door, 1980). Young children lack the developmental capacity to understand that the mediated world is a distinctly different place from the real world (Cantor & Hoffner, 1990; Cantor & Wilson, 1984). However, stimulus discrimination is not entirely supported by research evidence because many adults exhibit fear after viewing media portrayals despite their understanding that the material is fictional (Johnson, 1980). Even habitual viewing of frightening material among adults does not necessarily lessen fright responses (e.g., Cantor & Reilly, 1982; Sapolsky & Zillmann, 1978).

Motivations of the Viewer.   Researchers have argued that the mature adult viewer possesses a fair amount of control over responses to media content. Certain cognitive schemas can enhance or minimize fright responses (Zillmann, 1978, 1982a). For example, viewers who want to be entertained and aroused by a screen drama might purposely "forget" that the events are being staged. On the other hand, viewers who want to keep fright reactions to a minimum might remind themselves continuously that the actions are dramatized—they are not real. Young children rarely are capable of these cognitive activities (Cantor & Wilson, 1984).

Lin and Xu (2017) studied viewers' motives for watching horror-themed TV shows, including *American Horror Story, Supernatural, Teen Wolf, The Vampire Diaries*, and *The Walking Dead*. They employed a uses and gratifications (U&G; see Chapter 9) approach to explore relationships between viewers' motivations for watching (i.e., entertainment, escape, passing time, and relaxation) and their emotional and cognitive involvement. Motives for viewing significantly influenced how people responded both cognitively and emotionally to TV shows with horror content. For more about these findings, see this chapter's Research Spotlight.

Another motivation for viewing is information acquisition. Audience members motivated to watch for this reason tend to pay more attention to the content and thus may become more aroused by what they see. Considerable research has involved documentaries as stimulus films because portrayals of violence that actually happened are significantly more arousing than programs that are known by the viewers to be purely fictional (Geen, 1975; Geen & Rakosky, 1973). Children who saw something frightening in a movie—something that could affect them in their own environment—were more frightened than children who did not think what they saw could happen in their lives (Cantor & Hoffner, 1990).

RESEARCH SPOTLIGHT

Motivations for Viewing TV Shows with Horror Content and Their Impact on Cognitive and Emotional Involvement
Carolyn A. Lin and Zhan Xu (2017)
Journal of Broadcasting & Electronic Media, 61(4), 638–657

This study examined the relationships among motivations, cognitive and affective involvement, and enjoyment for watching horror-themed TV shows. Lin and Xu found that participants' motivations for viewing significantly predicted their cognitive and emotional involvement with the shows. The researchers identified the following motivations.

Entertainment

The entertainment motive was not only a significant predictor of greater viewing enjoyment and viewing frequency but also a significant predictor of stronger positive and negative affective (emotional) involvement. This suggests that people who want to be entertained by scary TV dramas may also have greater emotional attachment to the shows.

Escape

The escape motivation is a significant predictor of a greater level of positive cognitive involvement and negative emotional involvement. Lin and Xu posit that people who watch to escape from reality may be more immersed in the fictional content while also experiencing negative emotions from the horror elements in the shows. "As negative affect is unrelated to viewing enjoyment, participants may still obtain viewing enjoyment—through the indirect effect between escape motivation and viewing enjoyment—as mediated by cognitive involvement" (p. 652).

Relaxation

The relaxation motive for watching TV shows with horror content was a predictor of stronger positive and neutral emotional states and a lower negative emotional state. People who watch horror shows for relaxation "may maintain greater neutrality and suppress their negative feelings toward the horror content, while they enjoy a positive emotional connection with the characters. These findings are particularly noteworthy, since they are the first empirical evidence that links a viewing motive to a neutral affect via exposure to media with horror content" (p. 652).

Passing Time

People who reported passing time as their motive for watching horror shows reported a lower (but still positive) emotional response. They did not experience neutral or negative emotions. "This implies that when killing time is the objective for watching these TV series, viewers may respond with a more marginal but positive affective involvement to stay engaged and perhaps to avoid experiencing negative emotions" (p. 652).

Conclusions

When viewed together, these findings indicate a "co-activation of positive and negative feelings, when the audience is exposed to adverse events such as those depicted in the horror media. . . . As the relaxation viewing motivation is the only significant predictor of neutral affective response, this implies that viewers may also co-activate a detached emotional state—to mitigate the negative affect and maintain the positive affect—that they experience concurrently" (pp. 652–653).

Cognitive involvement is a significant predictor of positive and negative emotional responses to TV shows with horror content. Lin and Xu suggest that viewers who dedicate more mental energy to watching horror-themed shows are also more likely to experience stronger positive or negative emotions in response to the frequent presence of fright, violence, and suspense in those types of shows.

Factors Affecting Viewers' Emotional Responses.   Audience members who are previously aroused before viewing an exciting or disturbing scene retain some "arousal residue," which combines with new responses to film scenes to produce more intense emotional reactions. Recall that the theory that explains this phenomenon is called *excitation transfer* (Cantor et al., 1975; Zillmann, 1978; Zillmann et al., 1974). The arousing incidents may or may not be related to one another, and may or may not occur simultaneously, but excitation transfer happens unless other factors distract the viewer or otherwise prevent the process from occurring (Girodo & Pellegrini, 1976; Schachter & Singer, 1962).

The techniques that movie producers and directors use to enhance suspense provide a good example of excitation transfer. Sound effects, for instance, are very important. Various types of music can create different moods and different degrees of arousal, thus affecting the emotional impact of a film (Thayer & Levenson, 1983). Take the foreboding themes from *Jaws* or *Halloween*, both of which have become engrained in pop culture and can send a chill down audience members' spines decades later.

Foreshadowing is another important device to enhance fright effects and fear responses. Adults become more upset when a distressing event occurs if the movie forewarned them (Cantor et al., 1984; Nomikos et al., 1968), and children experience more fear in anticipation of a forewarned scene (Hoffner & Cantor, 1990). On the other hand, a recent study found that spoilers for horror films had little to no effect on enjoyment or suspense (Johnson et al., 2020).

Neurophysiology and Fear

People often have lingering irrational fear or discomfort after exposure to frightening media content, such as a real-world dislike of clowns after watching *IT* or *Poltergeist* or a fear of a shark appearing in a swimming pool after watching *Jaws* (see Cantor, 2004). As Cantor (2017) notes, "These reactions present a paradox because they are experienced by adults who know at some conscious level that they are not in danger" (p. 655). Understanding how different parts of our brains react to and process fear help us to make sense of this paradox.

The hippocampus mediates explicit, conscious memories of fear. These types of memories are "quite malleable, and so our thoughts about the frightening stimulus can become much more reasonable over time (e.g., 'that was really just a dumb, mechanical shark,' 'that could never happen')" (Cantor, 2017, p. 656). On the other hand, the amygdala mediates implicit emotional memories that we are not necessarily conscious of and stores them for the long term. The evolutionary nature of fear helps to keep living organisms safe from predators:

> Moreover, the amygdala's role is to create a "fight or flight" response—those physiological reactions like increased heart rate, quickened breathing, and higher blood pressure that prepare the body to fight off the threat or to escape; and these reactions amplify fearful feelings. Therefore, when a person is reminded of a traumatic experience that happened in the past, the mind may be thinking, "don't worry, you're safe," but the body is feeling as though in grave danger. (Cantor, 2017, p. 656)

The fact that the amygdala controls how our bodies physically respond to fear helps us understand why so many people's retrospective recollections of watching scary media involve bodily reactions, such as spine-tingling sensations or feelings of warmth as increased blood flow causes face flushing (Cantor, 2017).

Individual Factors that Influence Fright Reactions and Enjoyment

Numerous factors can influence preference for and reactions to frightening content. These include sensation seeking, empathy, aggressiveness, negative emotions, intellect/imagination, paranormal beliefs, and gender.

Sensation seeking is "the most widely studied trait in the research on horror" (Martin, 2019, p. 7). This concept refers to the desire for new, intense, and exciting experiences (Zuckerman, 1994). Studies have repeatedly shown a strong relationship between greater sensation seeking and increased enjoyment of horror-themed media (e.g., Cantor & Sparks, 1984; Clasen et al., 2020; Hoffner & Levine, 2005; Martin, 2019). For instance, Lynch and Martins (2015) found a positive correlation between sensation seeking and enjoyment of horror video games. J.-H. T. Lin's (2017) study of sensation seeking and horror-themed VR gaming showed that high sensation seekers expressed fright less frequently while playing. Conversely, people with low sensation-seeking tendencies reported more fear from playing the game.

Empathy is another factor that influences the enjoyment of horror. A meta-analysis indicated that individuals who rated lower in empathy reported more enjoyment of horror and violent content (Hoffner & Levine, 2005). More recently, Martin (2019) notes that studies have consistently found a relationship between low empathy and greater enjoyment of horror films.

Empathy can also affect how we enjoy certain aspects of horror content. For example, empathic concern was associated with more enjoyment of excitement, danger, and happy endings in scary movies, but it was associated with less enjoyment of suffering and injury (Hoffner, 2009). People with greater empathy were more cognitively engaged with horror-themed TV series (Lin & Xu, 2017). They were also more motivated to watch the shows for entertainment and to pass the time. Lynch and Martins (2015) found that people with lower empathy played a greater number of scary video games and enjoyed them more than people with higher levels of empathy. However, there was only a marginal difference in how often high and low empathizers experienced fright. "In sum, our findings suggest that empathy may lead individuals to select frightening media but may not be a useful predictor of individuals' experience" (p. 314).

Studies have confirmed that aggressive people both prefer and enjoy violent media content (e.g., Hoffner, 2009; Hoffner & Levine, 2005), and they watch more horror and violent movies (e.g., Greene & Krcmar, 2005). *Aggressiveness* was a weak predictor for positive emotions while viewing horror TV series, and it was not related to cognitive involvement (Lin & Xu, 2017). "This suggests that more aggressive individuals may respond to the graphic horror content more positively without engaging in cognitive elaboration nor experiencing a negative emotional state" (p. 651).

Hoffner and Levine's (2005) meta-analysis found that *negative emotions* during viewing (e.g., anxiety, disgust, and fear) were associated with greater enjoyment of frightening and violent media content. However, in C. A. Lin and Xu's (2017) study focusing specifically on television horror, there was no relationship between negative emotions and enjoyment. The researchers suggest that there may be a "fundamental difference" between how audiences respond to horror on TV shows versus horror in movies in that TV viewers may enjoy these ongoing series through cognitive and affective involvement with characters, while people who watch horror movies may experience more enjoyment by focusing on fright and gore.

"*Intellect/imagination*" was the strongest predictor for consuming horror content among the Big Five personality traits (i.e., extraversion, agreeableness, conscientiousness, emotional stability, intellect/imagination) (Clasen et al., 2020). There were significant correlations between intellect/imagination and enjoyment of horror, easily being scared, frequency of horror use, and preference for more frightening content.

Similarly, *belief in the paranormal* influences the type of horror content people consume and their reactions to it. There are differences between supernatural horror (a horror subgenre that involves metaphysical forces, ghosts, and implausible monsters) and natural or psychological horror (a subgenre that focuses on psychological behaviors, such as those of serial killers). People who prefer supernatural horror scored higher on measures of paranormal beliefs (Clasen et al., 2020). There was also a significant correlation between greater paranormal beliefs and preferences for supernatural horror as well as being more scared by supernatural horror than natural horror. Conversely, people with weaker beliefs in the paranormal prefer horror media with more natural content, which the researchers say suggests that people may seek out horror media where the threats appear more plausible.

Another important factor that affects a viewer's reactions to frightening media fare is *gender*. Overall, numerous meta-analyses and literature reviews have shown that males have both a greater preference for horror media and enjoy consuming it more than do females (Clasen et al., 2020; Hoffner & Levine, 2005; Martin, 2019). Meanwhile, females are both more easily scared by horror-themed media and tend to be more frightened after using scary media than are males (Clasen et al., 2020; Peck, 1999). In another study, females exhibited greater empathy while watching horror TV series; males were more emotionally disengaged but cognitively engaged with the content in the shows (Lin & Xu, 2017).

Despite an extensive body of research demonstrating the existence of different reactions to horror content based on gender, researchers still do not fully understand why the differences exist (Oliver & Sanders, 2004). As noted previously, gender differences may have resulted from social pressures to conform to gender-specific behavior (e.g., girls who scream at horror shows, boys who demonstrate self-controlled mastery of the disturbing content). Others propose the differences may be the result of evolution, levels of sensation seeking, or differences in empathy, anxiety proneness, and disgust sensitivity (for further review, see Clasen et al., 2020, and Martin, 2019).

Many studies of fright have examined children and adolescents (see the next section), but relatively little research has looked at how age impacts adults' preference and enjoyment of frightening media. The research that exists indicates that interest in horror media declines as adults age (Mares et al., 2016; also see Clasen et al., 2020; Martin, 2019).

Fright Reactions in Children

Children can be frightened by both fictional content and by news broadcasts (Custers & Van den Bulck, 2012; Walma van der Molen & Bushman, 2008). Age is the most important determining factor of fright reactions in children because of developmental differences, especially as children learn to distinguish fantasy from reality. Gender differences among children have been less pronounced, despite the stereotypical images of girls being more easily frightened than boys (Birnbaum & Croll, 1984) and more emotional (Fabes & Martin, 1991; Grossman & Wood, 1993).

Cantor and her associates have identified various types of stimuli that frighten children at different ages, as well as strategies that help reduce fear responses in children. Monsters, ghosts, supernatural creatures, the dark, animals, strange-looking creatures, and fast-moving creatures tend to scare young children from ages 3 to 8. Slightly older children (9- to 12-year-olds) are more frightened by threats of injury or destruction to themselves or their loved ones. While children older than 12 are afraid of personal injury, they also face social and peer pressures and accompanying fears and are concerned about politics, the economy, and the environment (Cantor, 1994, 2009; Cantor et al., 1986).

The difference between the fears of very young children and those of older children can be stated plainly: Younger children fear the stimulus itself, no matter how unreal or fantastic it is; whereas older children are more afraid of what might happen to them, rather than simply the danger itself. Even older children fear more abstract concepts and issues that threaten *psychological* harm in addition to or instead of *physical* harm.

The reason for these differences has to do with children's cognitive development. Until about age seven, children remember and sort items in terms of salient attributes they perceive. After age seven, this type of organization is replaced by one based on *concepts or functions* of the items involved rather than physical characteristics alone (Birch & Bortner, 1966; Melkman et al., 1981). Thus, as children grow older, they respond more intensely to media depictions that are based more on reality than fantasy or the unrealistic (Cantor & Sparks, 1984; Flavell, 1963; Kelly, 1981; Morison & Gardner, 1978).

A study that involved *The Incredible Hulk* television show is a good example of the differences in cognitive development and the fear responses produced. Sparks and Cantor (1986) found that preschoolers became intensely frightened whenever the normal-looking hero turned into the Hulk. Older children did not fear the transformation because they understood that the creature used his powers for the forces of good.

Another excellent example is a study conducted after a showing of the televised movie *The Day After* in the 1980s. The movie depicted a community in Kansas under nuclear attack and the devastating aftermath (although depictions of injuries were rather mild in comparison to other television programs). Cantor et al. (1986) surveyed viewers by telephone the night after the movie played. Young children were least affected by the film, while children older than 12 (due to cognitive development) were highly disturbed, and their parents were even more disturbed.

Strategies for Coping with Fear

Coping strategies have been effective in reducing or even preventing fears that are induced by mass media content. As would be expected, the same developmental and gender differences that cause children of various ages to fear different types of frightening media content also affect coping strategies, although gender differences play a much smaller role in determining effective coping mechanisms.

Coping strategies fall into one of two categories: noncognitive and cognitive (Cantor, 2009). **Noncognitive strategies** are those that do not require the viewer to process verbal information; these work well with young children. **Cognitive strategies**, on the other hand, are those that require the activation of cognitive processes (e.g., talking about the fear). Cognitive strategies work well with children of elementary school age and older, although noncognitive strategies can also be useful. Adolescent girls report using more noncognitive coping strategies than do boys, but gender differences could not be measured in the use of cognitive coping strategies (Hoffner, 1995; Valkenburg et al., 2000).

Noncognitive Strategies

Several types of noncognitive strategies have been used to help young children cope with media-induced fear. *Visual desensitization* allows children to be gradually exposed to disturbing content. In one study, children were shown a rubber tarantula in order to prepare them for a scene that featured the large spiders (Wilson, 1987). Cantor et al. (1988) used behind-the-scenes video of the application of makeup to actor Lou Ferrigno in *The Incredible Hulk* as a method of visual desensitization; fear reactions to the Hulk were reduced for those who saw the behind-the-scenes footage.

Physical activity serves as another type of noncognitive coping strategy. Clinging to an emotional-support object (e.g., a blanket or stuffed animal) is an example of this strategy. Eating or drinking while viewing a scary scene reduces fears, but some

Covering your eyes is an example of a noncognitive strategy to reduce fear. The strategy effectively reduces fear for young children.

researchers argued that this takes place only because the child has been distracted from the program (Manis et al., 1980). Covering the eyes is another example (Wilson, 1989). Only younger children used this strategy as a means of reducing fear; older children actually became *more* frightened when they covered their eyes, mainly because they could still hear what was going on and understood it. Similarly, parents telling children to look away from the TV when violent images appear on the news does *not* help alleviate fear (De Cock, 2012).

Even young adults sometimes employ noncognitive strategies to reduce fear. Some people playing a virtual reality video game where players had to defend themselves from attacking zombies sometimes closed their eyes or distracted themselves to alleviate fear while playing (Lin, 2017).

Cognitive Strategies

As mentioned previously, cognitive strategies are typically more appropriate for older children because of their level of development. When children are told to remember that a program is not real, they are less likely to be frightened by it. For example, Cantor and Wilson (1984) examined the reactions of young and older children while watching *The Wizard of Oz*. Some of the children were told beforehand that the wicked witch was "just a regular person dressed up in a costume," and they were also reminded that the story was "make believe." Other children were not given such coping strategies. Older children were able to use the coping strategy to reduce their fears, and they were significantly less frightened by the witch than other older children who had not received any explanations. On the other hand, the coping strategy did not work so well with the younger children. The scary witch frightened those who had received the fear-reducing strategy (the explanation) as much as those who had not. The researchers attributed the results to developmental differences in children of different ages.

When media presentations depict highly realistic threats, one of the most effective cognitive coping strategies is that of offering reassuring information about the minimal danger of the depicted threat. In the VR video game study mentioned earlier, some players engaged in cognitive strategies of reminding themselves that the zombies were not real (Lin, 2017). Some players also experienced relief from fear by talking to themselves, screaming, or swearing while playing the game.

Regarding fear from news programming, De Cock (2012) studied the effectiveness of parental intervention on children's fear and sadness responses to everyday news coverage in Belgium. Simply talking to their children about the news did not reduce the children's fears.

> Some well-intentioned explanations may broaden the child's comprehension of the news event but do not necessarily help mitigate feelings of fear or may even magnify scary details. For parents to stress children should "avoid strange people" is an understandable suggestion when crime cases are shown on television but it does not necessarily reassure a frightened child. (p. 498)

In addition, the more children mentioned that their parents talked to them about TV news stories, the more they exhibited intense feelings of sadness. Although other research indicates parental guidance strategies are successful in reducing children's fear from general television viewing, De Cock says it may be harder for parents to comfort children who are frightened by the news because parents can't simply say "You don't have be scared. It's not real."

Prevention Strategies

Cantor (2017) notes that although the coping strategies we just covered have been effective in laboratory settings, almost any parent can tell you that once a child is frightened by media content, it can be very difficult to calm them down. As a result, certain strategies have been employed to prevent children from seeing disturbing content in the first place. However, Cantor admits that in today's media environment, it is impossible for parents to shield their children from all of this content.

Cantor (2017) outlines several prevention strategies, including closely monitoring and cutting down on overall media exposure, recording and watching questionable shows or movies in advance before allowing children to watch, and using online resources to find out more information about media content.

TV and movie ratings are another tool parents can use when making decisions about what to allow children to watch. However, these ratings may not give parents a clear picture about the frightening aspects of the content, and they can lead to a false sense of reassurance:

> For example, many "general" (G)-rated movies—animated features like *Bambi*, *The Lion King*, and *Dumbo*—involve extremely disturbing issues (e.g., the loss of a parent, bullying, and childlike characters in severe peril), and these movies are cited frequently in retrospective reports of intense fear (see Cantor, 1998). In addition, two of the offenders most frequently cited in retrospective reports, *Jaws* and *Poltergeist*, are rated PG, which implies that they are relatively mild. (Cantor, 2017, p. 661)

In one study, more than a third of elementary school children reported fearful reactions to G or PG movies (Cantor et al., 2010).

Summary

For nearly a century, researchers have examined the fright reactions that audiences experience from mass media consumption. In the early 1930s and 1940s, the Payne Fund studies and the *War of the Worlds* study examined fright reactions among movie and radio audiences. In the 1950s and 1960s, studies focused upon the content of motion pictures and television and their long-term effects upon viewers. More recent research has examined the effects of TV news and frightening video games and VR experiences. Self-reported measures and physiological responses are two methods often used in these studies.

Most fright reactions are usually transitory, but some may endure for an extended period of time. Fright reactions are debilitating in only a few cases. To an extent, people enjoy being frightened by mass media content. Over the decades, numerous explanations for the paradoxical appeal of frightening content have been put forth, including catharsis (though there is little evidence to support it), excitation transfer, and the benign masochism of simulated threat situations.

Fright occurs despite viewers' understanding that they are not in danger. According to classical conditioning, certain stimuli cause certain responses, and similar stimuli evoke similar, albeit less intense, responses. Three categories of stimuli that recur in media content usually result in fear responses in real life: (1) dangers and injuries, (2) distortions of natural forms, and (3) the experience of endangerment and fear by others. Three additional factors cause viewers to react emotionally whenever they see fearful situations on the screen: (1) realism of the depiction, (2) motivations of the viewer, and (3) other factors that affect a viewer's emotionality, such as sound effects and foreshadowing. Individual factors that influence the appeal of and reaction to frightening media include sensation seeking, empathy, and belief in the paranormal (to name only a few).

The type of fright reaction experienced depends heavily on the age of the viewer because of differences in cognitive development. These differences affect a child's ability to distinguish fantasy from reality. Very young children (ages 3 to 8) fear the stimulus itself, no matter how unreal or fantastic it may be. Older children (ages 9 to 12) are more afraid of what might occur to them, rather than simply the danger itself. Children older than 12 fear more abstract concepts and issues that threaten psychological harm in addition to or instead of physical harm.

Strategies for coping with media-induced fears include cognitive and noncognitive techniques. Cognitive strategies require the activation of cognitive processes such as talking about the fear. These strategies tend to work well with children in elementary school or beyond, although noncognitive strategies are also useful. Visual desensitization and physical activity are types of noncognitive strategies, which usually work well with younger children.

14

Effects of Political Communication

> I doubt I would be here if it weren't for social media, to be honest with you.
>
> —Donald Trump, 45th President of the United States, 2017

The opening quotation from then-President Donald Trump in 2017 crediting social media for his election to the White House highlights the dramatic change in the relationship between the worlds of mass media and politics in recent years. Labeling most media outlets as the "lamestream media" and their products as "fake news," Trump bypassed traditional routes of political communication (e.g., newspapers and TV broadcasts) in favor of the digital megaphone of social media, where he could communicate directly with his millions of followers.

Throughout the history of the study of media effects, researchers have been interested in the effects of political communication, particularly political news. In fact, "the world of news and politics is one of the most-studied contexts in media effects research" (Tsfati & Walter, 2020, p. 36). As you have learned in earlier chapters, findings on the power of mass-mediated effects have varied through the years, and political communication effects are no exception.

Studies of voting behavior in the 1940s and 1950s indicated that mass-mediated political communication effects were rather limited (Berelson et al., 1954; Lazarsfeld et al., 1948). In these well-known studies, mass media influenced opinion leaders, who in turn influenced others through interpersonal communication. Later studies questioned the limited effects model by presenting findings of more direct and powerful media influence on voters from political campaign messages (Blumler & McLeod, 1974; Chaffee & Hochheimer, 1985; Gitlin, 1978; Iyengar & Simon, 2000; Noelle-Neumann, 1984). Endorsement of more powerful media effects in the realm of political communication continued through the end of the 20th century, but the media and political landscapes of the 21st century have proven to be vastly different.

Over the past two decades, changes in media technology, in the ecology of media, and in the political environment defied many of the assumptions that laid at the core of political effects research a generation ago in a way that challenges the paradigm of media effects as previously understood. (Tsfati & Walter, 2020, p. 36)

In this chapter we will provide a snapshot of what studies had revealed about political effects of mass media up to the end of the last century. We will then turn our discussion to the major changes in the 21st century that upended much of the media and political communication ecosystems, particularly the rise and influence of social media in the political process. We begin with a look mass media's role in a democracy.

Functions of Mass Media in a Democracy

Mass media attempt to provide a number of special functions in democratic societies of the world. Gurevitch and Blumler (1990) identified eight such functions, which McLeod et al. (1994) paraphrased as follows.

1. Surveillance of contemporary events that are likely to impinge, positively or negatively, upon the welfare of citizens.
2. Identification of key sociopolitical issues including their origins and possibilities for resolution.
3. Provision of platforms for advocacy by spokespersons for causes and interests.
4. Transmission of diverse content across the various dimensions and factions of political discourse, as well as bidirectionally between potential power holders and mass publics.
5. Scrutiny of government officials, their institutions, and other agencies of power by holding them accountable for their actions and policies.
6. Incentives and information to allow citizens to become active, informed participants rather than spectators in the political process.
7. Principled resistance to external forces attempting to subvert media autonomy.
8. Respectful consideration of the audience as potentially concerned, sense-making, and efficacious citizens. (p. 126)

According to Gurevitch and Blumler (1990), these special functions are actually *goals* or *standards* that mass media should try to attain in a democratic society. In reality, because of the fundamental nature of mass media as money-making, profits-dominated entities or any number of constraints, news media sometimes fall measurably short of the standards. For example, news media sometimes cover pseudo-events or other irrelevant but entertaining stories in their quest for higher audience numbers.

The tendency of the news media to cover *events* rather than *issues* represents another stumbling block in the path of the designated goals. When issues are addressed, they are often presented from the standpoint of the news network's institutional agenda (McLeod et al., 1994). Additionally, the media frequently dramatize their coverage of political campaigns and present the event as they would a horse race: candidates neck and neck in the polls, or a dark horse candidate gaining ground, or a front-runner pulling away.

Understanding of Political Media Effects in the 20th Century

Early voting research by Lazarsfeld and his colleagues (1948) found only a limited amount of influence from mass media on the political opinions of audiences. Later studies indicated that political media messages produced much stronger effects than previously thought (Blumler & McLeod, 1974; Iyengar & Simon, 2000; McLeod & McDonald, 1985; Ranney, 1983).

Models of persuasion, such as Petty and Cacioppo's (1986a) Elaboration Likelihood Model and Fishbein and Ajzen's (1975) reasoned action model (see Chapter 10) were applied to the study of political communication effects. Several research studies used these persuasion models as a basis for understanding campaign effects (Fazio & Williams, 1986; Granberg & Brown, 1989; Krosnick, 1988; O'Keefe, 1985; Rice & Atkin, 2000). As Shah et al. (2007) noted, the study of political advertising effects has also drawn from models of persuasion.

Tsfati and Walter (2020) summarize the political effects of mass media through the end of the 20th century in two main points:

1. Previous conceptions of minimal or limited media effects, on the one hand, and of an omnipotent media, on the other, were both considered inaccurate. Research demonstrated noticeable effects of media on political life, and while these tended to be moderate at best (in terms of effect sizes), they potentially carried rather substantive political consequences.

2. Given that most people's political preferences tended to be strikingly stable, and thus not easily malleable by news and campaign information, voting—seen as "the ultimate criterion variable" of earlier studies (Chaffee & Hochheimer, 1985, p. 82)—was no longer considered an extremely useful dependent variable in political media effects studies. Rather than shaping voting directly, the media were widely believed to affect politics through their effects on other relevant attitudes and perceptions. (p. 37)

Effects of Cognitive Processes

From the 1970s through the end of the 1990s, five areas of research "predominated this 'return to powerful media' tradition" (Tsfati & Walter, 2020, p. 37). Those lines of research included agenda setting, spiral of silence, framing, priming, and cultivation. Rather than focusing on voting as the primary outcome of political communication, all of these areas of research also examined how news media *indirectly* impact individuals' personal thoughts (Tsfati & Walter, 2020).

You will recall that **agenda setting theory** (see Chapter 6) states that the news media determine prominent issues by expanded coverage of particular topics, and these issues are considered important by the public (McCombs & Shaw, 1972). Research supports the hypothesis that the issues that receive the most coverage are the very issues that the public perceives as important (e.g., Funkhouser, 1973; Iyengar & Kinder, 1987; MacKuen, 1981; McCombs, 2004).

Spiral of silence theory (Noelle-Neumann, 1984) focuses on what people perceive about public opinion—particularly what opinion they perceive to be dominant and held by a majority of people. This theory suggests powerful effects result whenever people who do not hold the dominant opinion fear social alienation or isolation and ultimately refuse to speak up, preferring instead to spiral into silence.

Priming, as you may recall from Chapter 5, occurs when exposure to a mediated message activates related thoughts in the mind of the audience member for a limited time period. Issues that received prominent media coverage primed audiences in their evaluations of presidential performance (Iyengar & Kinder, 1987). Studies have demonstrated that presidential handling of high-coverage issues disproportionately influences the overall performance rating for that president in the eyes of an audience member (McGraw & Ling, 2003; Pan & Kosicki, 1997).

Framing research (see Chapter 7) examines the effects of how a story is presented (framed) on the way audiences process and interpret the information—in other words, how they think about issues, including political ones. For in-

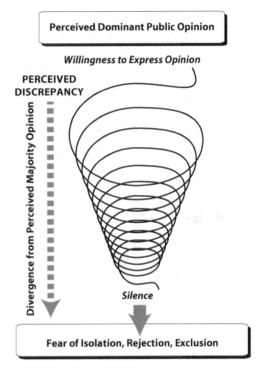

Figure 14.1   According to spiral of silence theory, people who believe they hold a minority opinion are less willing to speak out because they fear isolation.

stance, studies indicate that media coverage, especially on television, may cause voters to perceive that individuals, rather than society at large, are responsible for particular social problems such as poverty or crime (Sotirovic, 2003). The type of frame in a news story can influence whether audiences view social problems as the responsibility of the government or of individuals (Iyengar, 1991). When thematic frames (which approach an issue from a more abstract or general perspective) were used, audiences associated social problems with societal and government responsibility. However, when stories utilized episodic framing (which uses case study examples or reports of concrete events), the perceptions of system-level responsibility decreased.

Cultivation research, although originally applied to entertainment media (see Chapter 8), has found effects resulting from news consumption (Romer et al., 2003). For instance, high exposure to TV news cultivated perceptions among those viewers that juvenile crime was on the rise (Goidel et al., 2006).

Aside from the five research traditions we just outlined, other studies have examined other outcomes from political communication. Research has revealed that although audiences may or may not be persuaded by mediated political communication, they often *learn* from such messages. News reports about campaign issues and candidates, political debates, and conventions have all been responsible for various amounts of knowledge gain among audiences (Eveland et al., 2005; Grabe et al., 2009; Jerit et al., 2006; McLeod et al., 1979). Researchers also examined how the content and style of TV news coverage of politics results in "video-malaise" that fosters political apathy and mistrust while also decreasing political participation (Mutz & Reeves, 2005; Norris, 2000).

Shared Assumptions Among the Research Traditions

Beyond the aforementioned research traditions sharing the beliefs that (1) news media indirectly shape political life by influencing certain individual-level thoughts and that (2) those effects are not inconsequential, they also shared several other implicit assumptions (Tsfati & Walter, 2020). The first of these assumptions is that different news outlets reported political news in a similar way. This concept is known as **consonance**.

> Because of similarity in sources, journalists' professional values, and production routines and practices, different news outlets were presumed to have similar news agendas, tended to describe political events using similar frames, to present the same climate of opinion, and to describe politicians and politics negatively. (Tsfati & Walter, 2020, p. 38)

The assumption of consonance in political news coverage was responsible for researchers largely ignoring the role of audience selectivity in the media influence process. Prominent media scholars argued that television gave viewers limited choices and that it was "designed to be wanted in a non-selective fashion" (Gerbner et al., 2002, p. 45). The role of audience selectivity was either ignored or dismissed by framing and spiral of silence researchers (e.g., Edy & Meirick, 2007; Noelle-Neumann & Mathes, 1987). Furthermore, due to intermedia agenda setting, researchers also assumed that there were no alternate agendas to counter those of mainstream news outlets (Dearing & Rogers, 1996).

Moderating Variables for Political News Effects

Despite scholars assuming that political news content was consonant and disregarding the role of audience selectivity, they did not assume that all news audiences experienced the same effects (Tsfati & Walter, 2020). Because of various moderating variables, different audiences were affected more than others. For instance, trust in news media moderated priming (Miller & Krosnick, 2000), agenda setting (Iyengar & Kinder, 1985), and political knowledge effects (Ladd, 2012). In short, audiences with greater trust were more affected by news media than those with lower trust. According to media dependency theory, effects of media are more powerful with people do not have alternative non-mediated sources of information and weaker for those who are less media dependent (Ball-Rokeach & DeFleur, 1976).

External factors also moderated effects of political news. For instance, when one candidate received more media attention than others, the effects on political decision-making were stronger than when candidates receive more balanced coverage (Zaller, 1996).

Lastly, the strength of influence on voting behavior attributed to interpersonal communication rather than (or in addition to) mass communication has varied through the years. Lazarsfeld and his colleagues (1948) were the first to identify the influence of interpersonal communication on voters, finding that many people received information about the candidates or the election from other people rather than from news media reports. Later studies showed that conversations with others tend to work in conjunction with or to complement news reports (Chaffee, 1982) and that media reports spur interest in a campaign, leading to more interpersonal discussions (McLeod et al., 1979). Toward the end of the last century and in the early 2000s, a few studies found that the "discussion network" of people surrounding a person can have an effect on civic participation (Huckfeldt & Sprague, 1995; McLeod et al., 1996; Scheufele et al., 2006) and that the frequency of the discussions is an important consideration (Kwak et al., 2005). However, interpersonal communication primarily was viewed as unimportant in the process of news effects during the late 20th century, "despite the fact it was common knowledge that audiences did (and still do) not consume news in isolation" (Tsfati & Walter, 2020, p. 39).

> To sum up, political communication research at the end of the 1990s conceived news content to be consonant across media outlets and perceived audiences as consuming news in isolation without receiving information of feedback from other audiences. In addition, political effects were perceived to be small to moderate in size (but at times still highly politically consequential), and to affect political decision-making via their influence on mediating cognitions. (Tsfati & Walter, 2020, p. 39)

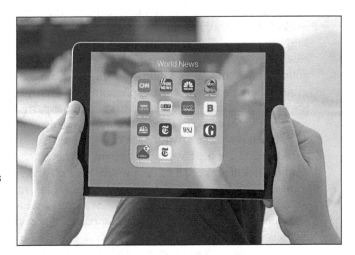

A wide variety of political news is available today—coverage ranges from the extreme left to the far right and everything in between.

Political Communication Effects in the Modern Media Landscape

The first two decades of the 21st century saw major shifts in communication technologies and both the media and political environments, shaking assumptions that had been at the core of political communication effects research for decades (Tsfati &

Walter, 2020). These shifts can be summarized into five main categories: the proliferation of news outlets and return of partisan media, polarization of the political environment, the growing popularity of political entertainment and satire, the spread of "fake news" and misinformation, and the rise and growth of social media.

Proliferation of News Outlets and the Return of Partisan Media

Since the birth of cable news in the 1980s, there has been tremendous growth in the number of choices television audiences now have for news. With so many alternative choices available, gaps in political knowledge and involvement increased (Prior, 2007). Furthermore, the explosive growth in news outlets in recent decades has challenged the once widely held assumption of news consonance. "By the early 2000s, scholars could no longer assume a homogeneous presentation of important problems, a uniform presentation of the climate of opinion, and a consonant set of homogeneous frames" (Tsfati & Walter, 2020, p. 39). Additionally, research began to document audience selectivity in consuming news from partisan news channels and blogs (e.g., Iyengar & Hahn, 2009).

> Given the intensification of partisan animus, it is not surprising that media choices increasingly reflect partisan considerations. People who feel strongly about the correctness of their cause or policy preferences are more likely to seek out information they believe is consistent with their preferences. But while as recently as 25 years ago, these partisans would have been hard pressed to find overtly partisan sources of information, today the task is a relatively simple one. (Bennett & Iyengar, 2008, p. 720)

Consider the current news landscape: in addition to the "Big Four" broadcast networks (i.e., ABC, CBS, NBC, and Fox), millions of people watch Fox News Channel, MSNBC, and CNN on cable every day. More recently, outlets like Newsy, OAN, Newsmax, and News Nation have been added to the mix of sources, in addition to political talk radio and countless websites and blogs.

Partisan media is not a new phenomenon. Many early newspapers in North America were subsidized by political parties, and the partisan press continued into the 19th century. But for much of the 20th century, finding news sources that catered to particular partisan preferences was relatively difficult (Bennett & Iyengar, 2008). Fast forward to today, and people have more options for news than ever before, and those options span the political spectrum. As a result, Bennett and Iyengar (2008) called for political communication researchers to revisit and reevaluate media effects theories to see if any needed to be adapted or abandoned. They viewed the return and rise of partisan media as a catalyst for a new era of minimal media effects confined to reinforcing and polarizing existing political attitudes, concluding that "the end result will be a less informed and more polarized electorate, with the political communication game aimed at those who have largely tuned out" (p. 724; for an alternative view, see Holbert et al., 2010.)

Several studies have examined how long-standing effects theories fare in the new era of political media, and some counter the idea of a new era of minimal effects. For instance, Shehata and Strömbäck (2013) examined agenda-setting effects in Sweden. Although mainstream media could still shape the agenda, individual-level effects were weaker for those who got more news online and did not depend on mainstream outlets. Left-wing voters perceived left-wing issues as more important, and right-wing voters perceived right-wing issues as more important. Partisan effects were primarily for issues with low salience. Traditional media effects occurred for issues more heavily emphasized in mainstream media's agenda. In another Swedish study, "the classic agenda-setting effect on public opinion remains significant despite the abundance of media choices available to citizen" (Djerf-Pierre & Shehata, 2017). Both Sweden and the United States have undergone the transition from a low-choice to high-choice media environment; however, the authors acknowledge that differences between the two countries' media systems—such as Sweden having a high newspaper circulation and few partisan media outlets—could make Sweden "a 'most likely' case for finding agenda setting effects even in today's high-choice media environment" (p. 752).

Partisan news consumption can impact how people think about certain topics. For instance, one study found that people who listened to Rush Limbaugh, a staunchly conservative talk radio host (now deceased), were more likely to agree with his framing of political issues, but conservatives who did not listen to Limbaugh did

---

Mainstream Media and Political Polarization

The Pew Research Center has conducted a great deal of research into how Americans consume news. Some of their recent work has examined partisanship in relation to evaluating and selecting news sources.

- In general, Americans agree that large newspapers and major cable networks are part of the mainstream media, including ABC News (87%), CNN (87%), *The New York Times* (79%), MSNBC (78%), Fox News (73%), and *The Wall Street Journal* (71%) (Shearer & Mitchell, 2021).

- Democrats and Republicans generally agree on which news outlets are part of mainstream media. For instance, 89% of Democrats and Democratic-leaning independents and 88% of Republicans and Republican-leaning independents identified ABC News as part of the mainstream media (Shearer & Mitchell, 2021).

- Partisan lines are also drawn along Americans' main sources for political news. Of those who named Fox News as their main source, 93% were Republican or right-leaning independents, 6% were Democrats or left-leaning independents, and 1% refused to answer or did not lean one way or the other. Conversely, of those who cited MSNBC as their primary political news source, 95% were Democrats or left-leaning independents, 5% were Republicans or right-leaning independents, and 1% either refused to answer or did not lean to either side (Greico, 2020).

- Democrats and left-leaning independents got news from a larger number of sources, including CNN, ABC, NBC, CBS, and MSNBC, compared to Republicans and right-leaning independents, whose main source was Fox News (Jurkowitz et al., 2020).

- Democrats also express more trust in news sources than Republicans. For instance, of 30 sources asked about on a recent Pew Research Center survey, Democrats expressed more trust than distrust for 22 of the sources. However, Republicans distrusted more than trusted 20 of the sources.

  Moreover, evidence suggests that partisan polarization in the use and trust of media sources has widened in the past five years. A comparison to a similar study by the Center of web-using U.S. adults in 2014 finds that Republicans have grown increasingly alienated from most of the more established sources, while Democrats' confidence in them remains stable, and in some cases, has strengthened. (Jurkowitz et al., 2020, p. 4)

not share his interpretations (Jamieson & Cappella, 2008). In research on opinion climates and partisan news exposure, people who watched left-wing media perceived a more left-wing opinion climate while people who watched right-wing outlets perceived a right-wing opinion climate (Tsfati et al., 2014).

Polarization of the Political Environment

Tsfati and Walter (2020) note that "the most studied effect of exposure to ideological media is by far its effect on political polarization" (p. 40), with most of research conducted from a communication standpoint focusing on affective (or emotional) polarization, which is conceptualized as negative feelings—ranging from dislike to loathing—toward political opponents (Iyengar et al., 2012).

Research has repeatedly found an association between exposure to like-minded partisan media and emotional polarization (Garrett et al., 2014). Studies have shown that the direction of at least part of this relationship is from exposure to polarization (e.g., Arceneaux & Johnson, 2013; Stroud, 2010). Although it is possible for researchers to manipulate whether participants are exposed to either conservative or liberal media in different experimental conditions, introducing selective exposure—allowing participants to choose whether they see like-minded media content—into a study means that researchers cannot conclude whether participants' exposure actually caused a change "because they were not randomly assigned to the liberal or conservative content (but rather selected it)" (Tsfati & Walter, 2020, p. 40).

Theories of motivated processing help explain selective exposure to like-minded partisan media and its effects (Levendusky, 2013; Taber & Lodge, 2006). According to these theories, people exposed to information that does not align with their worldview are motivated to disparage the message source, discount the quality of the arguments, or question the accuracy of the message. Conversely, when the information aligns with a person's beliefs, it is often accepted at face value, even when authority figures and experts question the validity of the information (Chang, 2015). People hold evidence and arguments that they disagree with to a higher standard than they do arguments that align with their attitudes and beliefs (Taber et al., 2009).

The typical outcomes of motivated processing are the selection of news sources, political knowledge, ability to recall information, and both attitude reinforcement and polarization (Nisbet et al., 2015). Taber et al. (2009) note that the extent of polarization is contingent on how biased a person's information processing is, which is a "direct consequence of motivated reasoning" (p. 154). Furthermore, people's biases activate automatically when someone evaluates political messages, essentially negating any process that would cause someone to update their attitudes. "Built into our cognitive and emotional processing systems are mechanisms that motivate and enable political action. The irony of motivated reasoning is that these same mechanisms undermine our ability to rationally respond to new and challenging information" (p. 154). Tsfati and Walter (2020) summarize the effects of motivated processing:

> Contrary to the common belief that quality information in the public domain has the potential to bring people together and encourage prosocial behavior, these studies demonstrate that in a news environment governed by motivated processing, even exposure to accurate information has the potential to polarize the public. (p. 40)

Researchers have identified several other mechanisms that can mediate the relationship between **selective exposure** and polarization. For instance, Tsfati et al. (2014) studied perceptions about the opinion climate and polarization effects. Democrats watching MSNBC perceive society to be more liberal, while Republicans watching Fox News view it as more conservative. These perceived norms can lead to polarization. Liberals and conservatives accept frames of liberal and conservative media outlets, respectively, which can polarize opinions (Tsfati & Nir, 2017). Activation of one's partisan identity can also lead to polarization in that one's identity can result in positive in-group evaluations and negative out-group evaluations (Garrett et al., 2014). Lastly, research has suggested that polarization may result from selective exposure because people elaborate on and remember ideologically congruent messages (Dvir Gvirsman, 2014). In other words, "when exposed to partisan media, partisans more thoroughly process and internalize the like-minded arguments they read or hear, perhaps due to increased trust in the sources of these arguments" (Tsfati & Walter, 2020, p. 41).

Fox News: Five Facts at a Glance

Since its launch in 1996, Fox News has become a cable news giant, and it "holds a unique place in the American media landscape, particularly for those on the ideological right" (Gramlich, 2020, para. 1). The Pew Research Center offers five facts about Fox News.

- Out of all adults in the United States, 43% say they trust Fox news for political and election news. However, roughly the same amount of U.S. adults (40%) say they distrust Fox News.

- A majority of Republicans and Republican-leaning independents (65%) trust Fox news more than any other news outlet. No more than a third say they trust other mainstream outlets, such as ABC News (33%), NBC News (30%), and CBS News (30%).

- On an ideological spectrum, the average Fox News audience member is to the right of an average U.S. adult, but they are not as far to the right as audiences for other sources, such as Breitbart or Sean Hannity.

- Of those who say Fox News is their primary source of political news, 37% are age 65 and older (compared with 21% of all adults), and 87% identify as white (compared to 65% of all adults).

- People who say Fox News is their main source for political news stand out in their views on key political issues. For instance, 63% of them said President Trump did an excellent job responding to the COVID-19 outbreak, compared to 23% of all U.S. adults and just 7% for those whose main source of political news was CNN.

Popularity of Political Entertainment

Even if people want to avoid politics on the news, they are still likely to encounter political messages to varying degrees in entertainment media (see Holbert, 2005). Meanwhile, there has also been growth in a wide variety of entertaining media that focus on politics. Although programs like *Last Week Tonight with John Oliver*, *Late Night with Seth Meyers*, and *The Daily Show* may have the primary intention to entertain audiences rather than becoming an alternative source for news, these types of shows can result in political effects traditionally seen from hard news (Holbert et al., 2010). In fact, survey data from the Pew Research Center revealed that U.S. adults were almost just as likely to learn about the 2016 presidential election from late night comedy (25%) as from a national newspaper (23%) (Gottfried et al., 2016), and politicians' appearances on late-night talk shows, such as *The Late Show* and *The Tonight Show,* can also influence voters' perceptions (Moy et al., 2006).

Younger audiences view political satire as fun and unbiased (Young, 2013). In part, this results from audiences interpreting the messages for themselves. In other research examining younger viewers, there was an association between exposure to political humor and greater knowledge gains, political efficacy, and trust in government (Feldman, 2013). However, the literature on the effects of political humor highlights that many factors come into play to impact the effects of comedic messages, Furthermore, a recent meta-analysis by Walter et al. (2018) of 21 studies found no direct effects of humor on political attitudes.

Tsfati and Walter (2020) note that political satire's limited effects could be due to the fact that it is often open to interpretation, and audiences can selectively process the messages. For instance, they point to a study of *The Colbert Report,* in which conservatives were more likely to believe that Stephen Colbert (the liberal host of the show who portrayed a caricature of a right-wing pundit) was actually against liberalism. They also highlight research into the CBS sitcom *All in the Family,* which aired throughout the 1970s. "Bigoted viewers identified with Archie Bunker (a working-class chauvinistic and conservative bigot) and saw nothing wrong with his use of racial and ethnic slurs, whereas liberal viewers identified with his well-educated and progressive son-in-law Mike (nicknamed 'Meathead')" (p. 45).

In addition to political comedy and satire, there have also been a number of popular political-themed drama series in recent years, such as *Scandal, The Good Wife* (and its spin-off *The Good Fight*), *Madam Secretary,* and *Designated Survivor.* Recent research into these types of entertainment programs has revealed interesting political effects. For instance, regular viewers of *Madam Secretary, The Good Wife,* and *Scandal* developed parasocial relationships with the main characters, who were strong women in positions of political leadership and power (Hoewe & Sherrill, 2019). The parasocial relationships led to greater political interest and self-efficacy. Furthermore, political interest predicted political participation in the real world. Another study by Hoewe et al. (2019) examined *Madam Secretary* and *Designated Survivor* and discovered

> causal evidence when the gender identity of the viewer matches that of the main character in a politically-driven TV show, more feminine individuals take inspiration from the female lead character, sparking future political engagement. Therefore, the creation of more shows like *Madam Secretary* could inspire a greater number of women, girls, and feminine individuals to become more politically engaged. (pp. 688–689)

The Spread of "Fake News" and Misinformation

Fake news is not a new phenomenon, but it did become a political buzzword during the 2016 U.S. presidential campaign. As mentioned at the start of this chapter,

Donald Trump often labeled stories as "fake news." However, many of those were actually true stories with which he disagreed. For instance, Sullivan (2020) notes, "The history of the Trump administration has shown that the loudest cries of 'fake news' accompany the most damning journalism. Coming from him, the phrase now dependably has another meaning: 'all-too-accurate reporting that damages my reputation'" (para. 14).

Our discussion in this chapter about information labeled as "fake news" does not focus on stories that someone simply does not like. Tandoc et al. (2018) explain actual fake news this way: "Fake news hides under a veneer of legitimacy as it takes on some form of credibility by trying to appear like real news" (p. 147). Or as Amazeen and Bucy (2019) plainly stated: "'fake news' is *not* news" (p. 416).

You may often see or hear the terms **misinformation** and **disinformation** in discussions about fake news. But what exactly do these terms mean? Lazer et al. (2018) offer this definition of all three terms.

> We define "fake news" to be fabricated information that mimics news media content in form but not in organizational process or intent. Fake news outlets, in turn, lack the news media's editorial norms and processes for ensuring the accuracy and credibility of information. Fake news overlaps with other information disorders, such as misinformation (false or misleading information) and disinformation (false information that is purposefully spread to deceive people). (p. 1094)

This type of content is created and used by those in the political world to arm their agendas, and fake news and misinformation sometimes get reported as actual news by mainstream outlets (Bennett & Livingstone, 2018; Pickard, 2016). In the three months leading up to the 2016 election, the top fake news stories generated more overall engagement on Facebook than the top election stories from 19 major news outlets (such as *The New York Times*, *Washington Post*, and NBC News) *combined* (Silverman, 2016). Despite the fact that 84% of Americans are at least somewhat confident that they can identify fake news (Barthel et al., 2016), a large-scale survey of American adults found that they were fooled by fake news headlines 75% of the time (Silverman & Singer-Vine, 2016). As you will see in this chapter's Research Spotlight, **confirmation bias** is strong when people see news headlines online—people are more likely to believe headlines that are congruent with their own political beliefs, while largely ignoring those that challenge their opinions (Moravec et al., 2019).

So what can be done to help people navigate the minefield of misinformation and fake news? On the audience side of the equation, greater levels of procedural news knowledge (i.e., an understanding of how mainstream news outlets operate) can inoculate news consumers against disinformation (by being able to identify fabricated news stories) and covert persuasion (Amazeen & Bucy, 2019). On the journalistic side, two common approaches that news outlets use to set the record straight about political mediated messages are ad watches and fact-checking (Tsfati & Walter, 2020). **Ad watches** provide analyses, interpretations, and evaluations of the veracity of campaign ads (Kaid, 1996); they have become important dimensions in election campaign coverage (Kaid et al., 1993; West, 1993). Ad watches influence voters' reactions to the candidates and to the ads themselves (Cappella & Jamieson, 1994; Pfau & Louden, 1994).

Pfau and Louden's (1994) early work into ad watch reporting revealed surprising results: the journalistic scrutiny of negative political ads sometimes enhanced the credibility of the attacking party and reinforced a negative ad's message. How did analyzing the accuracy and fairness of a negative ad end up reinforcing its message? Research has identified two factors:

1. When an ad watch simply corrects a false statement, viewers may remember the core message of the ad and forget the correction (Nyhan & Reifler, 2012).

2. Repeating the false statements from ads word-for-word has the unintended effect of increasing audiences' familiarity with the false claim, which then becomes a mental shortcut to remember the inaccurate claim (Schwarz, 2015).

Other research into ad watches demonstrated that when they are produced in a way that minimizes audiences' exposure to the ad being critiqued and maximizes exposure to the correct information presented by journalists, there is no boomerang effect of reinforcing deceptive campaign ads (Cappella & Jamieson, 1994).

Fact-checking is one of the most popular journalistic innovations in recent years; it involves "evaluating the accuracy of claims made by politicians and correcting them" (Tsfati & Walter, 2020, p. 44). Fact-checking has become a "mainstay of modern political campaigns" (Fridkin et al., 2015, p. 128). For instance, Amazeen (2013) found that fact-checking in newspapers jumped by more than 900% since 2001, and it is even more popular on broadcast news, where it increased 2,000% in that same time span. It is now common to see media outlets and other organizations performing "real time" fact-checking during candidates' townhall appearances, debates, and speeches, as well as during and immediately after presidential State of the Union addresses.

So far, there is only limited evidence of the effects of nonpartisan fact-checking. Fact-checks influence people's assessments of the tone, accuracy, and usefulness of negative political ads, with those who are more politically sophisticated and those with lower tolerance for negative campaigning being the most responsive to fact-checking (Fridkin et al., 2015). Furthermore, "the fact-checks also sway citizens' likelihood of accepting the claims made in the advertisements. Fact-checks challenging the truthfulness of the claims of the negative commercial are more powerful than fact-checks authenticating the assertions made in the negative advertisement" (p. 146).

However, negative political information can continue to influence people's beliefs—even after being discredited by objective fact-checking (Thorson, 2016). Partisanship plays a role in the diffusion of fact-checking information shared on social media. In a study of the 2012 U.S. presidential election, social media users tended to selectively share fact-checking messages that put their preferred candidate in a positive light and the opposing party's candidate in a negative one (Shin & Thorson, 2017).

The rise in fact-checking in recent decades also appears to influence the actual content in political campaign ads. For instance, research suggests that political ads are more accurate when campaigns are aware that their ads may be fact-checked (Nyhan & Reifler, 2015; see also Meirick et al., 2017).

Given the billions of dollars spent on campaign ads and the growth in ad watches and fact-checking in recent decades, you may be thinking that ads are incredibly effective at persuading voters and getting them to actually vote. However, research shows that is not necessarily the case. "Advertising can and sometimes does have a positive effect on voter turnout, but by no means is that effect large, universal, or consistent across election years" (Franz et al., 2008, p. 267).

For instance, a recent meta-analysis of 59 unique experiments that examined the influence of 49 political ads from the 2016 U.S. presidential race on 34,000 participants found that effects of those ads were small for Democrats, Republicans, and independents—regardless of whether they aired during the primary or general election, in a battleground state, or were sponsored by PACs or the candidates themselves (Coppock et al., 2020). Furthermore, the effectiveness of attack ads was about the same as positive ads at achieving their goals. On average, ads resulted in moving target candidate favorability 0.049 points on a 1 to 5 scale in the intended direction. (This finding, though small, was statistically significant due to the study's large size.) The effect on which candidate a person intended to vote for was even smaller at 0.007 of a point on a 1 to 5 scale, which was statistically insignificant. Despite the fact that these effects are very small, the researchers note that they could make the difference between winning or losing an extremely close election.

The use of ad watches and fact-checking has grown tremendously in recent decades. For instance, *USA Today* has a dedicated fact-checking section on their app and website.

Meanwhile, another recent study found an ad's tone can affect voter turnout in presidential elections (Gordon et al., 2022). These findings indicate that the use of positive ads can increase voter turnout. On the other hand, negative ads can suppress turnout—but result in a higher share of votes for the attacking candidate. The researchers conclude that the tone of ads could impact the results of a close election, but tone is unlikely to change the results of a less competitive race.

The Rise and Growth of Social Media

The explosive growth of social media in recent decades presents many challenges and new opportunities to study how traditional media effects theories—particularly agenda setting and spiral of silence—fare in online contexts. For example, scholars have questioned the validity of agenda setting theory in a media environment that is decentralized and diversified compared to what existed in the 20th century (Tewksbury & Rittenburg, 2012).

Numerous studies have examined the influence of social media and mainstream media on agenda setting, with varying results. In some, such as Towner and Muñoz's

(2020) study of Instagram and mainstream U.S. newspapers, there is little evidence of agenda setting. In others, there is strong evidence of reciprocal, dynamic intermedia agenda-setting relationships between traditional and social media (e.g., Conway et al., 2015; Conway-Silva et al., 2018; Neuman et al., 2014; Valenzuela et al., 2017).

Conway et al. (2015) examined articles published in the top U.S. newspapers and the Twitter feeds of the 2012 presidential primary candidates and the Democratic and Republican parties. The researchers concluded that the papers *followed* rather than led the political agenda for most issues analyzed in the study (i.e., taxes, health care, economy, energy, employment, and foreign policy). However, this study and multiple others propose that traditional media exert a stronger agenda-setting influence than does social media (Conway-Silva et al., 2018; Guo & Vargo, 2015; Stoycheff et al., 2018). Other studies have presented evidence to the contrary (e.g., Valenzuela et al., 2017).

Individuals can also experience an agenda-setting effect from exposure to news content on Facebook. For instance, increased repetition of a news story in a Facebook feed influenced study participants' perceptions that the story topic was important (Cowart, 2020; see the Research Spotlight in Chapter 6 for an in-depth look at Cowart's study.). The effect is stronger for those who have low interest in politics and are more likely to avoid sources of political information (Feezell, 2018).

Researchers are also exploring the application of spiral of silence theory to social media, and there are two parts to this area of research (Tsfati & Walter, 2020). The first part involves the effect that social media has on users' perceptions about public opinion. In addition to seeing stories shared on social media, public opinion can also be inferred by features highlighting a post's popularity, such as retweets and likes (Kim, 2018) and comments by other users (Lee, 2012). The second part involves the effect between what social media users perceive the majority opinion to be and the expression of their own opinion. Studies have found a negative relationship between a person's perceptions of the opinion climate and their willingness to share their opinions on social media (e.g., Gearhart & Zhang, 2014; Kushin et al., 2019). This effect can also spill over into the real world: people who are less willing to talk about controversial issues on social media are also less likely to talk about them face-to-face (Hampton et al., 2014; Kushin et al., 2019).

Kushin and colleagues (2019) studied the spiral of silence and the mediating role of fear of isolation on both online and offline interactions during the 2016 U.S. presidential election. People who perceived that their opinions about Donald Trump and Hillary Clinton, respectively, were in the majority on Facebook reported lower fear of isolation and greater willingness to express their support for their preferred candidate face-to-face and on Facebook. For anonymous online settings, the association between fear of isolation and expressing support for a candidate was weaker but still significant. At the societal level, people who believed their views about Clinton were in the majority had lower fear of isolation. However, fear of isolation was not related to opinion congruency for Trump in society.

> This implies that those strongly in favor of, or against, Trump were not necessarily afraid of how society would think about them, even if they felt a societal majority opposed Trump (for Trump supporters) or a societal majority supported him (for Trump opponents). (Kushin et al., 2019, p. 8)

Tsfati and Walter (2020) explain that although the theories agenda setting and spiral of silence emphasize that social dynamics on social media can trigger political effects, "both theories (and other theories of the 'return to powerful media' tradition) share a blind spot, as they under-theorize a central component of social media: interpersonal influence" (p. 42).

Recall from Chapters 3 and 10 Katz and Lazarsfeld's (1955) two-step flow model of communication, which suggests that messages from mass media flow to opinion leaders, who then spread the information to wider audiences. Some scholars have argued that modern audience selectivity bypasses opinion leaders in the current media environment (e.g., Bennett & Manheim, 2006). However, Feezell (2018) explains the application of the model to social media:

> In the social media environment, political information is shared socially by members of a network who impart salience and relevance to these stories—similar to how Katz and Lazarsfeld described the role of "opinion leaders" in the traditional broadcast environment. While one-step flow—from news source directly to recipient—may be more likely today than it was twenty years ago, in a social media setting, the two-step social sharing of information is alive and well. (p. 491)

A study by Weeks et al. (2017) found support of social media opinion leaders as sources of political information for others. Not only do these highly active users recognize their role as influencers and opinion leaders, but they *actively try* to educate and influence their followers. In addition to spreading information through social networks, social media opinion leaders' recommendations can also increase the level of trust people have in news media and make them want to get more news from those outlets (Turcotte et al., 2015).

Tsfati and Walker (2020) offer a warning regarding this area of research: "Indeed, either online or offline, opinion leaders are only as good as the information they share; hence more dystopian scenarios of misinformation spread and cynicism toward mainstream media should not be discounted" (p. 43).

Summarizing the Impacts of These Five Major Shifts

Tsfati and Walter (2020) conclude that "some of the core assumptions underlying theories of the 'return to the powerful media' tradition (such as agenda setting, priming, and the spiral of silence) now seem outdated" (p. 45). The political and media ecosystems are no longer the same as they were when those theories were developed. No longer can we assume that news reporting is consonant. With the multitude of media choices available, it is easier than ever to consume only like-minded political messages, limit exposure to political media content, or avoid it altogether.

Despite the shift away from limited media choices and the days of mass audiences, some of the predictions appear to remain accurate at the individual level, as demonstrated by many of the studies we have discussed. However, given the growing number of news outlets and the further fracturing of mass audiences, "society no longer has a shared set of important problems, opinion climate perceptions, and homogeneous interpretations of current events" (Tsfati & Walter, 2020, p. 45).

RESEARCH SPOTLIGHT

Fake News on Social Media:
People Believe What They Want to Believe When It Makes No Sense at All
Patricia L. Moravec, Randall K. Minas, and Alan R. Dennis (2019)
MIS Quarterly, 43(4), 1343–1360

This study used EEG data combined with self-reported data to better understand how people process news headlines they see on social media. The study also examined whether people could detect fake news headlines on social media and if a flag on the post labeling it as fake news impacted participants' cognitions and judgments.

After summarizing findings on confirmation bias (i.e., people prefer information that aligns with their beliefs) and cognitive dissonance (i.e., when two pieces of information are in conflict and cannot be reconciled), the researchers proposed a number of hypotheses.

Hypotheses

H1a: Social media users will exhibit increased cognitive activity in brain regions associated with deliberative, conscious thought when seeing a fake news flag on a headline aligned with their beliefs.

H1b: Social media users will spend more time considering the headlines when seeing a fake news flag on a headline aligned with their beliefs.

H2: Social media users will perceive headlines aligned with their beliefs that are flagged as fake as being less credible.

Method

Researchers recruited 83 undergraduate students to participate in this study. They had an average age of 19.5 years, and 39% were female. A majority (53%) self-reported as Democrats and 47% as Republicans. Three left-handed participants were excluded from the EEG analyses because some left-handed people have different brain structures.

The participants read 50 headlines on a simulated Facebook newsfeed that covered 10 political topics (e.g., student loans, legalization of marijuana, gun law changes, etc.). Of the 50 posts, 40 were designed to be possibly true or false, but were verifiably one or the other (e.g., Pell Grants discontinued to provide more money to build wall; Trump to enable concealed carry nationwide; Review finds that habitual smoking of weed is more dangerous than alcohol). The control group was comprised of 10 headlines designed to be more clearly true (e.g., Trump won't like newest poll showing approval ratings; More celebrities oppose Trump; Disillusioned Democrats turn to Obama for guidance).

For the experiment, a flag that matched the one used by Facebook for identifying fake news was randomly placed on 20 of the 40 headlines not in the control group, including some headlines that were actually true. Participants could not like, share, or comment on the posts.

Behavior-dependent variables that were measured included credibility of the headline (rated on three 7-point scales for believability, credibility, and convincingness), how long it took participants to determine a headline's credibility, and whether the headline aligned with the participant's political ideology.

Changes in cognition were measured by analyzing EEG data collected by a 14-channel wireless EEG device.

Results

Both Hypothesis H1a and H1b were supported; however, H2 was not. Analysis of EEG data suggested that participants experienced cognitive dissonance when a headline matching the participant's political beliefs was flagged as false and that people paid more attention to those headlines. When a headline was flagged as false, participants spent 1.4 seconds longer thinking about a headline. They spent an additional 1.9 seconds considering a headline with the fake news flag that aligned with their political beliefs. However, the presence of the fake news flag did not reduce credibility ratings for headlines that matched with their beliefs.

Moravec and colleagues summarized their findings this way:

> First, our research shows that the fake news flag triggered more cognitive activity and caused users to spend more time when the flag was placed on headlines they wanted to believe.... Second, despite the increased cognition triggered by the fake news flag, it did not change users' beliefs.... Third, we found that confirmation bias is a significant problem on social media. It persists even in the face of design features intended to combat it. Users read and think about headlines confirming their beliefs, and ignore headlines that challenge them; confirmation bias is so strong that users simply do not think about information they do not like. (p. 1355)

The Internet and Social Media as Political Information Sources

Although we just covered some of the political effects of social media, the shift toward the internet and social media as sources of political information sources warrants further discussion.

More Americans continue to turn to the internet and social media for news. Although television is still the preferred medium for news consumption (Mitchell, 2018), the number of Americans who often get news from news websites and social media is growing. More people now say they get news from social media than they do from print newspapers (Shearer, 2018). In general, internet use increased young voters' sense of political efficacy—their beliefs about their power to influence the political system (Tedesco, 2011). In other research into Facebook and voting behaviors, learning that a person's friends and even friends of friends had voted increased the likelihood of voting (Bond et al., 2012). However, while the overwhelming majority of Americans (71%) say using the internet can help them better understand politics, only 41% say it can give them more influence over government officials (World Internet Project, 2018).

The Impact of Second Screening

Researchers have paid considerable attention to the effects that second screening (i.e., simultaneously using a smartphone, tablet, or laptop while watching television) can have on political knowledge. Using a second screen to access or engage with political content online while also watching election news on television can increase factual political knowledge; however, non-relevant second screening, such as listening to music or surfing the internet, can result in less political knowledge (Ran & Yamamoto, 2019). Using social media to gather news can increase political knowledge for both the general public and those with higher levels of political interest and internal political efficacy (Park & Kaye, 2019).

Second screening can also make people more open to changing their political beliefs (Barnidge et al., 2017). This is especially true for people who frequently interact with others on social media or use social media platforms for news. However, second screen interactions on Twitter often take place in echo chambers, with little crossover between conservative and liberal groups (Hayat & Samuel-Azran, 2017). At a time when political debates online seem especially contentious, Hayat and Samuel-Azran (2017) concluded that

> although second screeners are, by definition, active seekers of information about the television contents they consume, their heightened interest and participation in related social networks (as posters or followers) does not translate into democratically healthier political exchanges, and instead strengthen echo chambers. (p. 305)

Second screening during 2016 political debates weakened the direct effects of the televised debates on people's perceptions of Trump and Clinton (Camaj & Northup, 2019). The researchers suggested this could be because second screening diverted viewers' attention away from the candidates' actual debate performance. Regarding the 2016 election, second screening during televised news led to decreased political participation, both online and offline, for people who held negative views toward Trump (McGregor & Mourão, 2017).

Motivations for Following Political Figures on Social Media

A growing number of Americans cited finding out about political news before other people and believing that information on social media is more reliable than traditional news organizations as major reasons for following political figures on social media (Smith, 2014). More than a third said it made them feel more personally connected to political candidates or groups.

A content analysis of Twitter usage by members of the United States Congress found that Twitter facilitates direct communication between constituents and their representatives (Golbeck et al., 2010). The vast majority of Instagram users (80%) follow current elected officials on the platform (Parmelee & Roman, 2019). The top motivators for following political figures on Instagram are information/guidance (i.e., helping users decide about an issue or how to vote), social utility (i.e., using information from the posts in both online and offline social interactions), entertainment, convenience, and self-expression.

What Types of Content Do Political Figures Post?

Overall, congressional members post in more conservative ways on social media. Early research on congressional Twitter use indicated that most tweets were informational in nature—providing facts, opinions, or positions on issues—whereas only 4% of tweets were personal messages (Golbeck et al. 2010). In a more recent analysis of Instagram posts by members of the 115th Congress, only 8% contained personal content, compared to almost 70% that highlighted activities related to their job (O'Connell, 2018).

On Instagram, women and senators are more likely to post than are men and members of the U.S. House of Representatives (O'Connell, 2018). These findings aligned with previous research about the activity of political figures on other social media platforms (e.g., Evans et al., 2014; Lassen & Brown, 2011). Democrats and Republicans are equally likely to have an Instagram account, and they post with the same frequency (O'Connell, 2018). However, Democrats tend to post longer captions that contain more political messaging.

Age had a significant effect on what type of content congressional members posted. Younger members posted far more personal content, including selfies, personal and family photos, pictures taken at home, and photos with their pets. For instance, Representative Alexandria Ocasio-Cortez (a Democrat from New York elected to the 116th Congress in 2018) has amassed millions followers on Instagram. She has used her account (@aoc) to give followers a glimpse into her personal life, such as livestreaming herself cooking at home and behind-the-scenes looks at her time on Capitol Hill (Gypson, 2019).

U.S. Representative Alexandria Ocasio-Cortez (left) with fellow representatives in the 116th Congress; Ocasio-Cortez has utilized social media to communicate directly with millions of her followers.

O'Connell (2018) concluded that age-related differences in Instagram use could point toward future changes in representation.

> Younger members better understand and make use of Instagram . . . offering their constituents the kind of access they have never before had—the ability to experience, in real time, a member's meal, or workout, or family gathering. This access may therefore strengthen the trust between a member and their constituents. (p. 15)

O'Connell (2018) also noted that younger members had wider social networks which could consist of many people who do not live in their states or districts. This could be because people simply enjoy the type of content the congressional member is posting; however, these members could "feel obligations to that dispersed online constituency that may pull them in different directions, and ultimately even impact their behavior in office" (p. 15). This feeling of accountability is known as **surrogate representation** (Mansbridge, 2003).

No political figure has had a more noticeable and influential presence on social media—particularly Twitter—than the 45th president of the United States, Donald Trump. Preferring to use his personal Twitter handle (@realDonaldTrump) rather than the official @POTUS account, Trump garnered more than 88 million followers before Twitter banned his account in January 2021 after his supporters stormed the U.S. Capitol in an attempt to overthrow the results of the 2020 presidential election.

Since joining the platform in March 2009, Trump tweeted tens of thousands of times, and his use of Twitter and other social media platforms during the 2016 election was unprecedented, bucking the norms of political and deliberative discourse. An analysis of more than 30,000 of Trump's tweets from 2009 to 2017 demonstrated his use of Twitter as a tool for both attack and defense, often angrily refuting what others were saying about him or reacting to perceived slights (Pain & Chen, 2019). The analysis also revealed three main themes in his tweets.

> These were the outsider who will make America great, which focuses on Trump's populist promises to restore the nation to an imagined former glory and give the country back to the people; racism, misogyny, and hate, which exposes the acerbic underbelly of his discourse; fake news, which includes his attacks on the news media and foreign policy by Twitter, which comprised his beliefs about Russia and North Korea. (p. 6)

Other Political Effects of Internet and Social Media Use

In an analysis of Facebook and Twitter users in the 2016 presidential election, following political candidates on social media was associated with enthusiasm for the favored candidate and anger at the opposing candidate (Weeks et al., 2019). That enthusiasm and anger were related to hostile media perceptions—that is, the perception of an unfair media bias against one's candidate of choice. "If an individual is very enthusiastic about their favored politician, they are more likely to think the media are treating that politician unfairly" (p. 388).

Additionally, when Republicans and Democrats followed their parties' candidate on social media in 2016, they were more likely to believe their candidate would win, which resulted in an increased intention to vote for their parties' candidate (Macafee et al., 2019). This effect is largely attributed to the fact that candidates can carefully craft messages and narratives on social media and that voters "interpret and process political messages in ways consistent with their party affiliation" (p. 7). In other words, Republicans who saw Trump's social media posts saying that he could win the 2016 election—despite what was being reported by the news media at the time—were more likely to believe that he would win and were then more likely to vote for him.

Furthermore, the divisive nature of the 2016 election was reflected in online comments on news websites. A study of comments on *USA Today*, *The New York Times*, and Fox News websites found that almost a third contained impoliteness, which was defined as name-calling, profanity, or yelling (i.e., typing in all capital letters), with the most occurring on the *USA Today* site (Masullo Chen et al., 2019). Impolite comments mirrored many of Trump's talking points and language during the campaign, such as challenging the legitimacy of the election and using sexist, racist, and homophobic speech. However, the researchers noted that the majority of comments on the stories conformed to democratic norms of speech (e.g., asking legitimate questions; using evidence to back up a viewpoint). They concluded "that some political speech, even if tainted by impoliteness, might be better for democracy than no speech at all" (p. 10).

Since the 2016 and 2020 presidential elections, the United States has become noticeably more politically divided. It is not uncommon to see people bickering back and forth about politics on social media. Regarding Twitter, it is also important to keep in mind that a small number of very active users drive the majority of conversations on the site. In a study of how partisans behave on the platform, just 10% of Twitter users generated *92%* of all tweets sent by U.S. adults between November 2019 and September 2020 (Smith & Grant, 2020). Of that top 10% of Twitter users, 69% were Democrats, and 26% identified as Republican.

The nature of social media sites themselves may be figuratively driving a wedge between us, specifically when it comes to politics. In general, social media adds more negative emotions into our social networks, and because we post so much about ourselves on social media, others can become more aware of our differences, which can increase perceived political disagreements (Barnidge, 2018).

Summary

Findings on the power of mass-mediated political effects have varied through the years. Studies of voting behavior in the 1940s and 1950s indicated limited effects from mass media, but later studies suggested more direct and powerful media influences on voters. Toward the end of the 20th century, political communication effects were found to be small to moderate—but still potentially highly consequential at times.

Many theories were used to study political communication effects in the latter part of the 20th century, including agenda setting, priming, framing, cultivation, and spiral of silence. During this time, researchers also shared some basic assumptions about political media effects. They assumed that news content was largely the same from outlet to outlet, and they ignored the role of audience selectivity.

However, the media and political landscapes of the 21st century are *vastly* different from when those theories were developed. Five major shifts highlight the differences between then and now: the proliferation of news outlets and return of partisan media, polarization of the political environment, the growing popularity of political entertainment, the spread of fake news and misinformation, and the rise and growth of social media.

In today's high-choice media environment, we know that news content is no longer consonant, and the role of audience selectivity is no longer ignored by researchers. Furthermore, although the aggregate-level predictions of many previous theories about the effects of political communication may no longer hold, current studies support many of the individual-level effects. The ever-increasing role of social media in political communication is a fruitful area for researchers to continue exploring throughout the 2020s and beyond.

15

Effects of Mass Media on Health

> Mass communication using various channels has helped increase
> public awareness, knowledge, attitudes, and behaviors on a multitude
> of health topics.
>
> —Kreslake et al., 2019, p. 1

- After seeing a story about Chadwick Boseman's battle with colon cancer, a man calls his doctor to make an appointment for a check-up.
- A health communication campaign highlighting the dangers of tobacco use results in a decrease in tobacco sales.
- In the grocery store, a child begs her mother for a box of sweetened cereal that she has seen advertised while watching cartoons.

Mass media messages often have considerable impact on personal and public health. Mass media have served as essential components in a number of important health communication campaigns (Rice & Atkin, 2009). Communication campaigns attempt (often with successful results) to change or initiate attitudes and behaviors. The goal of a media health communication campaign is to convey specific messages, designed by health and communication experts, that have intentional, positive, health-related effects on audiences.

Media campaigns are but one type of health communication available via media. Audiences are inundated with a wide variety of health-related messages from the internet, news reports, primetime entertainment programs, daytime soaps, and countless advertisements. The effects from such messages are not always positive in nature. Americans have long obtained much of their health-related information from mass media (Sandman, 1976), and this creates a problem when one considers that much of that health information—and many of the health behaviors presented to audiences—result in negative (albeit many times unintended) effects on their health.

If we step back and look at the general picture of health provided in these most pervasive of media, we find a world in which people eat, drink, and have sex with abandonment but seldom suffer the consequences. Research shows that the audience does learn from these images and that, in general, what they learn is not good for their health. (Brown & Walsh-Childers, 1994, p. 409)

As with other types of media content, effects from health-related messages may be positive or negative and intended or unintended in nature. This chapter will examine some of the research findings for effects from cigarette, alcohol, prescription drug, and food advertisements. This chapter also explores the effects of entertainment portrayals, the nature of health news coverage, and the importance of the internet in providing health-related information to millions. We will also discuss health campaigns and other educational strategies designed to bring about individual health improvements or to prompt positive changes at the policy level.

Research Findings

Many of the studies that have examined the effects of media messages on health have concentrated on advertisements, entertainment portrayals, news reports, and online health information. Some of these messages were intentionally designed to promote healthier lifestyles; others have had unintentional positive or negative impacts on media consumers. Regardless of intent, "the media do shape individuals' health-related beliefs and behaviors" (Walsh-Childers & Brown, 2009, p. 469).

Effects of Advertisements, Media Usage, and Entertainment Portrayals on Health

Research on the effects of commercial product advertising, media usage, and entertainment portrayals has focused primarily upon the health of individuals who use the products. We will review the literature on the mediated health effects from four types of products: tobacco, alcohol, prescription drugs, and foods.

Tobacco. According to the Centers for Disease Control and Prevention (CDC), more than 50.6 million U.S. adults—roughly one in five—use tobacco products, with cigarettes being the most commonly used (Cornelius et al., 2020). Cigarette advertisements have been banned from broadcast media in the United States since 1971, but the ban did not stop tobacco companies from using other means to advertise their products—including print media, billboards, and sponsorship of sporting events. These forums kept cigarette ads in clear view of the public for decades despite the broadcast ban.

Nunez-Smith et al. (2010) reviewed dozens of quantitative studies on the connection between media usage and abuse of tobacco, alcohol, and drugs. In 83% of the studies, there was a causal relationship between media exposure and smoking initiation and use of alcohol and illicit drugs; the evidence was strongest for the association between media use and tobacco use. Sargent (2009) found that receptivity to tobacco ads and exposure to characters in movies engaging in smoking were associated with smoking among 10- to 14-year-old children. (The effects of exposure to smoking in movies will be discussed in more detail later in this chapter.)

The overwhelming majority of people who smoke started smoking during adolescence (U.S. Department of Health and Human Services [USDHHS], 2012). For example, when smokers in their 30s were asked about their first time smoking a cigarette, 82% who had ever tried a cigarette said they had done so by the age of 18. Another 17% had done so by the age of 26. Out of adults who had ever been daily smokers, 88% had tried their first cigarette by the age of 18, with another 11% having had their first cigarette by 26. These findings led the U.S. Surgeon General's Office to conclude that "virtually *no* initiation of cigarette smoking (<1–2%) and few transitions to daily smoking (<4%) actually occur in adulthood after 26 years of age. Moreover, it is important to note that the initiation of cigarette smoking can often occur quite early in adolescence, before 18 years of age" (p. 134).

Through the years, numerous studies have examined the effects of various cigarette advertising or promotional appeals. Even though tobacco company executives argue that their marketing efforts do not influence young people to use tobacco and that they do not direct their ads to children or adolescents, research has shown that youngsters recognize the symbols and slogans of various cigarettes (Aitken et al., 1985; Aitken et al., 1986). After Joe Camel ("Old Joe") appeared as the trademark for Camel cigarettes, the desire for Camel cigarettes increased from 0.5% to 32% among young smokers in a three-year period (DiFranza et al., 1991). Fischer and colleagues (1991) highlighted the pervasiveness of cigarette marketing on children's awareness. In their study, 30% of 3-year-olds and 91% of 6-year-olds correctly matched an image of Joe Camel with a picture of a cigarette. The latter finding matched the percentage of 6-year-old children who correctly matched Mickey Mouse to the Disney Channel. This similar high level of awareness is remarkable when you consider that Joe Camel could not be seen on TV, unlike Mickey Mouse. (The 1998 Master Settlement Agreement later banned cartoons in tobacco advertising in the United States.)

The higher the ad recognition, the more likely one is to smoke (e.g., Goldstein et al., 1987). Exposure to print, radio, and online cigarette ads along with ownership of hats or lighters that have cigarette brand logos on them were all related to an increase in tobacco use among the young (Biener & Siegel, 2000). Research has also shown an association between cigarette use among adolescents and watching stock car racing where tobacco products were heavily advertised (Bloom et al., 1997). Eventually, tobacco advertising was banned in NASCAR and Formula One racing. However, both IndyCar and NASCAR recently began allowing racing teams to promote e-cigarette brands (Silverman, 2020).

The U.S. Surgeon General reported in 2012 that many tobacco ads focus on imagery that contains little factual information about the product. Rather, they target the "aspirations of young people by effectively using themes of independence, liberation, attractiveness, adventurousness, sophistication, glamour, athleticism, social acceptability and inclusion, sexual attractiveness, thinness, popularity, rebelliousness, and being 'cool'" (USDHHS, 2012, p. 519). Furthermore, "evidence is sufficient to conclude that there is a causal relationship between advertising and promotional efforts of the tobacco companies and the initiation and progression of tobacco use among young people" (p. 10).

Other studies have explored various issues related to the warning labels on tobacco product advertisements. One study tracked the eye movements of adolescents

Since 1971, cigarette advertising was banned from broadcast media. Sponsorship of sporting events and racing teams kept tobacco products in public view.

who viewed tobacco ads in magazines; almost half the children did not read the warning at all (Fischer et al., 1989). Those who did look at the warning did so only briefly. In another study, the warning notices for tobacco ads on billboards and on taxis were very hard to read—but the brand name of the cigarette was clearly visible (Davis & Kendrick, 1989). The Master Settlement Agreement in 1998 would later ban tobacco ads on billboards and public transit (Truth Initiative, 2017). In 2020, the U.S. Food and Drug Administration (FDA, 2021) finalized new required warnings for both cigarette packages and advertisements. The warnings include text and color images highlighting 11 health risks of smoking.

The Federal Trade Commission (2021a) reported that major tobacco companies spent $7.6 billion on cigarette advertising and promotions in 2019 in the United States alone, down from $8.4 billion in 2018. (The overwhelming majority of that money went to price discounts and promotional allowances to retailers and wholesalers.) Another $576.1 million was spent on advertising and promoting smokeless tobacco (FTC, 2021b). In 2019, tobacco companies spent more advertising and marketing dollars ($63 million) at the point of purchase than on all other advertising outlets *combined*—including outdoor signage, magazines, direct mail, and company websites (FTC, 2021a). (These point-of-sale materials include ads posted *inside* retail locations, but not outdoor ads on the retailer's property.)

Tobacco companies tend to advertise in convenience stores that are near schools and in neighborhoods that have high numbers of teens and younger children (Pucci et al., 1998; Woodruff et al., 1995). (The Family Smoking Prevention and Tobacco Control Act, which was signed into law into law in 2009 by President Barack Obama, banned *outdoor* advertising within 1,000 feet of playgrounds and schools.) Ads inside convenience stores make youngsters more aware that tobacco is available and make

As of 2023, the FDA requires that warnings be prominently displayed on the top half of the front and back of cigarette packages—and occupy at least 20% of the space at the top of advertisements.

them perceive that it is popular, and these perceptions make them more likely to start smoking (Henriksen & Flora, 2001).

Even the packaging of tobacco products plays a key role in point-of-sale advertising. In fact, "advertising bans have prompted many companies to redesign their packages to maximize their impact at the point of sale" (USDHHS, 2012, p. 534). Highly visible "power wall" displays can contain dozens of different brands of cigarettes and other tobacco products. "Locating tobacco power walls conspicuously behind the cash register increases the likelihood of consumers being repeatedly exposed to positive tobacco messages. These exposures are thought to normalize tobacco use, increase brand recognition and increase positive brand user imagery" (Shadel et al., 2016). Experiments have incorporated a life-sized replica of a convenience store to study the effects of power walls on teens and pre-teens. There was a significant positive correlation between looking at the power wall for two seconds or more and future smoking susceptibility compared to those who looked at the wall for less than two seconds (Martino et al., 2019). Hiding the power wall—for instance, simply closing the doors on the display—significantly reduced adolescents' future susceptibility to using cigarettes compared to leaving the power wall exposed (Shadel et al., 2016).

Effects of E-Cigarette Advertising

E-cigarette advertising, which is not subject to the same regulations as traditional cigarettes, has seen explosive growth in recent years. For instance, e-cigarette companies spent $6.4 million dollars on advertising in 2011; by 2014, the dollar amount had skyrocketed to $115 million (CDC, 2016). However, more recent ad spending in the United States has fluctuated, dropping to $48 million in 2017 and then rebounding to $110 million in 2018 (Ali et al., 2020).

A majority of middle and high school students (about 69%) have seen ads for e-cigs in retail stores, online, in magazines/newspapers, or on TV/movies (CDC, 2016). (Roughly 15% reported seeing ads for e-cigs from all four sources.) Ads for e-cigs frequently include themes and content (e.g., happiness, friendship, success, and sex) that may be attractive to young people (Nicksic et al., 2019; Padon et al., 2017).

Roughly one in five high schoolers use e-cigs (Wang et al., 2020). Fewer middle school students—about one in 20—use e-cigs. Looking at the U.S. adult population, almost 11 million use e-cigarettes, and e-cig use was highest for the 18- to 24-year-old age group (Cornelius et al., 2020).

Of course, e-cigarettes have been advertised as a healthier alternative to traditional cigarettes and as a tool to help cigarette smokers kick the habit (Collins et al., 2019), but research shows e-cigs can be harmful to a user's heart and lungs and just as addictive as traditional cigarettes (Blaha, n.d.). In a review of more than 120 peer-reviewed publications, Collins et al. (2019) found that numerous studies show an association between exposure to e-cig marketing materials and perceptions about the addictiveness and harm of e-cigs, intentions to use e-cigs, and actual use of e-cigs. (However, many studies utilize a cross-sectional design, meaning that causality cannot be inferred.)

Kim et al. (2019) studied the effects of e-cig advertisements on teens' perceptions of cigarettes. Their experiment revealed that teens who did not smoke reported significantly lower perceived risks from smoking traditional cigarettes after being exposed to e-cig ads compared to those in the control group.

> While the advertisements included messages about cigarettes' problems, proposing e-cigarettes as a solution may have decreased perceived risks of smoking. It is possible that adolescents, especially those who have never smoked cigarettes and thus have no direct experience with the addictiveness of cigarettes, interpreted e-cigarette advertisements as portraying an easy solution to cigarette-related problems and thus believed it was less risky to smoke cigarettes. (p. 294)

Alcohol.   Alcohol consumption has been known to result in battered spouses and children, rapes, and even murders (e.g., Fals-Stewart, 2003; Grant, 2000). "Alcohol abuse is the second most common form of substance abuse in the United States, after tobacco addiction," (Harvard Medical School, n.d., para. 1). A number of other studies have focused on the effects of alcohol use on the young. For example, the earlier a person starts drinking, the more dire the effects on health, both short-term and long-term (Grube, 2004).

Binge drinking is also an area of concern. According to data from a survey by the National Institute on Alcohol Abuse and Alcoholism (2021), 26% of U.S. adults 18

Smoking and Drinking in Video Games

- Forsyth and Malone (2016) found that 42% of 118 video games released between 1994 and 2015 contained tobacco content, but only 8% of the games were given tobacco-related content descriptors by the Entertainment Software Review Board (ESRB).

- A study of the top 20 best-selling video games in the United States during 2018 revealed that seven of the games (35%) contained tobacco imagery (Forsyth & McDaniel, 2021). Five types of tobacco imagery were seen in the games: visible tobacco paraphernalia, use of tobacco products to further game play, background characters using tobacco products, and both playable and nonplayable main characters using tobacco products. Visible paraphernalia was the most common type of tobacco imagery seen in the games.

- An analysis of five popular video games (*Call of Duty: Black Ops II, Grand Theft Auto V, Call of Duty: Modern Warfare 3, Grand Theft Auto IV*, and *Assassin's Creed III*) found that alcohol and tobacco appeared in all five games (Cranwell, Whittamore, et al., 2016). *Grand Theft Auto V* contained the most alcohol and tobacco content. Young gamers (11- to 17-year-olds) exposed to the content in video games were more than twice as likely to have used alcohol or tobacco.

---

and older reported binge drinking in the last month. Roughly 11% of 12- to 20-year-olds said they engaged in binge drinking in the last month. (The NIAAA defines binge drinking as a pattern of alcohol consumption that brings blood-alcohol levels to 0.08g/dL or higher, which they say happens after a man consumes five drinks or a woman consumes four in roughly two hours.)

Alcohol advertising is big business. Ad spending is projected to increase to $7.7 billion in 2023, up from $6.7 billion in 2020 (Zenith, 2021). Nearly half of alcohol advertisement dollars in 2020 went toward television. Research on the effects of alcohol advertising on personal and public health has generally focused on (1) whether such ads entice adolescents to start drinking, or (2) whether such ads cause increased alcohol consumption and, perhaps, drunk driving among established drinkers. With regard to the first of these issues, Atkin and his associates (1984) surveyed a group of adolescents and found that their likelihood to drink either beer or liquor was directly related to their exposure to TV alcohol ads. Moreover, other factors such as age, sex, social status, or parental influence were not as strong predictors of drinking behavior as was exposure to the TV ads. However, 13- to 17-year-olds in more recent surveys say their parents are the strongest influence on whether to drink (71%), compared to advertisements (1%) (GfK Roper Youth Report, 2016). In another survey of 10- to 18-year-olds, 64% said their parents are the main influence on their decision to drink—or not drink—alcohol (Foundation for Advancing Alcohol Responsibility, 2016).

Despite the results of those surveys, multiple studies repeatedly indicate a relationship between exposure to ads and other marketing materials for alcohol and later drinking behavior (e.g., Ellickson et al., 2005; Jernigan et al., 2017; Smith & Foxcroft, 2009). In an earlier study, the exposure of adolescents to football and basketball events where alcohol was promoted was linked to subsequent use of beer (Bloom et al., 1997). Researchers have studied the effects of brand-specific alcohol advertising on 13- to 20-year-old drinkers, finding a strong relationship between exposure to brand-specific ads and consumption of those brands (Ross et al., 2014) and the quantity consumed (Naimi et al., 2016) in the past 30 days. "In addition, there was a stronger association between advertising and consumption at higher levels of exposure" (Naimi et al., 2016, p. 728).

Unlike the tobacco industry, the alcohol industry has voluntary advertising guidelines that "nominally prohibit content that *primarily* appeals to youth, yet the guidelines only weakly define such content. This leaves some marketers unsure how to comply, as evidenced by the fact that alcohol ads have been found to use content features that appeal to youth" (Padon, Rimal, Siegel, et al., 2018, p. 22). Some alcohol brands associate alcohol use with fun, feature outdoor activities in their ads, and use animals like the Budweiser Clydesdales—all these features have strong appeal among youngsters (Collins et al., 2007; Zwarun & Farrar, 2005). Other features of ads that appeal to youth include sound effects and illustration; youthful, attractive, or famous actors; and the promise of positive outcomes in life (for further review, see Padon, Rimal, DeJong, et al., 2018). When young people see desirable models in alcohol ads and identify with them, they are more likely to think that drinking is going to be a positive experience and are therefore more likely to engage in drinking (Austin & Knaus, 2000). Alcohol brands whose ads contain more content that appeals to youth are more likely to be consumed by 13- to 20-year-olds than adults, and "the fact that adult brand consumption is not associated with these features, whereas youth consumption is, suggests that the industry codes are deficient" (Padon, Rimal, Siegel, et al., 2018, p. 25).

Some alcohol brands associate their products with animals and other appealing features with which young people identify.

With the rise of social media, alcohol brands have substantially increased their budgets for digital advertising. The COVID-19 pandemic forced brands to focus more on their digital advertising efforts, as most sporting events were canceled and bars shut down throughout much of 2020. Digital ads are projected to make up 30% of alcohol ad spending in 2023, up from 21% in 2019 (Zenith, 2021).

In an analysis of alcohol advertisements on Instagram, character appeals (e.g., famous people, animals, or cartoons) and youth-oriented themes (e.g., fantasy, violence, or humor) were rare (Barry et al., 2018). The majority of posts (70%) included product appeals (e.g., focusing on taste, quality, or cost)—which prior studies found resulted in lower purchase intent and less ad liking among youth—and promises of satisfaction and refreshment resulting from drinking (48%). Instagram ads also emphasized the following themes: positive emotional experiences (46%), achievement (29%), individuality (34%), and camaraderie (17%).

Parents can lessen the harmful effects of alcohol ads on youth by talking to their children and using proper guidance (Austin et al., 2006). Recall that recent surveys of U.S. teens revealed parents were the strongest influence on their intentions regarding alcohol consumption.

Prescription Drugs.   As you flip through a magazine or watch primetime TV, you will likely see an ad for a prescription drug. Pharmaceutical companies have employed print media, such as magazines (Curry et al., 2005), to market directly to consumers for years. In 1997, the FDA decided to allow prescription drug manufacturers to advertise their drugs directly to consumers via television (Brownfield et al., 2004; Frosch et al., 2007). Direct-to-consumer pharmaceutical advertising is not allowed in most countries. In fact, the United States and New Zealand are the only countries in the world where drug makers can market directly to consumers, and prescription drug advertising is a growing, multi-billion-dollar enterprise (Harvard Medical School, 2017). Spending on direct-to-consumer advertising in the United States went from $2.1 billion in 1997 to $9.6 billion in 2016 (Schwartz & Woloshin, 2019). While spending on prescription drug ads has increased, the information about biological factors of health conditions, risk factors, and which populations are at risk has substantially decreased since the early 2000s (Applequist & Ball, 2018).

According to the FDA (2019), ads for prescription drugs fall into three primary categories: product claim, reminder, and help-seeking. *Product claim ads*—which are the most common form of prescription drug advertising—name the drug, the condition it treats, and make claims about the benefits and risks. A *reminder ad* names the drug but not what it treats. *Help-seeking ads* do not mention any specific drug; instead, they describe medical symptoms or conditions and encourage people to contact their doctor. Interestingly, a recent content analysis of television drug ads found that "ads do not challenge the doctor's expert status; however, it is also not highly emphasized and promoted" (Adams & Harder, 2019, p. 31).

Adams and Harder (2019) categorized TV commercials for prescription drugs into "medical needs" and "lifestyle" ads. Ads in the first category depict health risks that are serious, life threatening, and require immediate medical attention. Ads about severe allergic reactions, chronic obstructive pulmonary disease (COPD), and diabetes fall into the medical needs category. Ads in lifestyle category do not heavily emphasize health risks (mainly because they are not life threatening); rather they focus on risks to one's lifestyle and identity. Ads for treatment of acne, erectile dysfunction, and birth control fall into this category. In lifestyle drug ads, "doctors are virtually absent. These ads place the choice almost entirely on the patient, who is in complete control of whether she or he will pursue treatment, while the doctor's only responsibility is to prescribe the drug" (p. 29).

There is also concern that direct-to-consumer prescription drug ads, particularly those for lifestyle conditions, contribute to the so-called "pharmaceuticalisation" of our society. Adams and Harder (2019) note that, overall, "marketers portray the use of drugs as an easy solution to one's health and life problems compared to managing those problems in the absence of drugs" (p. 30). The Harvard Medical School (2017) summarized prescription drug ads this way: "The most important issue that consumers need to realize with drug ads is that they are just that—advertisements. Their primary goal is not to help the consumer, but to sell the product" (para. 13).

Ads for prescription drugs have multiple influences on people's behaviors. In one study, 6% of those surveyed talked to their doctor about the advertised drug, and about 30% of the people who discussed the drug with their doctors were prescribed the medication (Murray et al., 2004). Another 11.5% were prescribed the drug—even though their doctors did not think it would help them. Reviews of research literature indicate that prescription drug ads resulted in increases in patient demand and prescriptions being written for advertised drugs (Gilbody et al., 2005; Mintzes, 2012). However, there is no evidence that advertising directly to consumers provides them with any health benefits.

Food.   A large amount of research on the effects of food advertisements on consumer health has focused on children. Food commercials can have positive or negative effects, depending on the nutritional value of the food advertised. Researchers studying food and drink advertisements on children's websites discovered that 3.4 *billion* ads appeared on the sites over the course of a year (Ustjanauskas et al., 2013). Fast food and breakfast cereals were the most advertised food products, and 84% of food products shown in the ads were high in fat, sodium, and/or sugar. "Food advertising is prevalent, it promotes largely energy dense, nutrient poor foods, and even short-term exposure results in children increasing their food consumption" (Boyland et al., 2015, p. 331).

Obesity in children and teens has been a primary concern for researchers (e.g., James et al., 2001; Ogden et al., 2002; Wang et al., 2002), and many research findings indicate that watching food ads on television is strongly related to childhood obesity (Committee on Food Marketing, 2006). Zimmerman and Bell (2010) found that evidence did not support the argument that watching TV contributes to obesity because it is a sedentary activity—the so-called "couch potato" argument. Instead, statistical analysis revealed a causal association between TV ads and obesity.

TV food ads influence the short-term and long-term food preferences of children (Goldberg et al., 1978). Given the vast number of ads for food items that have low nutritional value, such findings suggest negative health consequences from food advertising. However, Goldberg et al.'s study found that parental eating habits were much more influential than the commercials in determining a child's diet. More recent experiments revealed that the influence of ads and parents changes as children age (Ferguson et al., 2014). For instances, both advertisements and cartoons influenced food preferences among young children between the ages of 3 and 5. However, children between the ages of 6 and 8 were more influenced by their parents; meanwhile, older children (9- to 12-year-olds) were not influenced by either media or their parents. Other recent research has shown that parental interventions can moderate the effects that food advertisements on social media can have on children (Al Abbas, 2018).

Not all food advertisements lead to negative effects on consumers. For instance, Kellogg's campaign for All-Bran cereal during the 1980s incorporated information from the National Cancer Institute to stress the healthy (anticancer) benefits of a diet high in fiber and low in fat. As a result of this campaign, more people started eating high-fiber, low-fat foods (such as All-Bran) and more people became aware of the importance of nutrition in preventing particular types of cancer (Freimuth et al., 1988; Levy & Stokes, 1987).

Television Shows and Health

For decades, smoking and drinking or references to drinking have been common in television programs. A report released at the turn of the century examined depictions of illicit drugs, tobacco, and alcohol in popular primetime sitcom and drama series (Christenson et al., 2000). Illicit drugs were seen or mentioned in 20% of the episodes analyzed. Tobacco appeared in 19% of episodes, and alcohol was consumed in 71% of the episodes. Alcohol use and references appeared not only in adult programming but also on programs targeting teens. Tobacco and especially alcohol are often seen on reality TV shows (Barker et al., 2020). Workplace-related drama series often show or refer to alcohol, conveying the idea that drinking in the workplace is common, socially accepted, and largely free of consequences (Mayrhofer & Matthes, 2018).

Researchers analyzed programs popular with 11- to 16-year-old boys (e.g., *The Office, The Walking Dead, SpongeBob SquarePants, Family Guy, South Park,* just to name a few) for the presence of alcohol and tobacco (Keller Hamilton et al., 2018). Shows rated TV-14 exposed audiences to approximately one tobacco portrayal every two hours and 10 portrayals of alcohol every hour. Most portrayals of tobacco and alcohol were visual. Of those, 89% showed a character using tobacco, while 56% showed characters interacting with alcohol but not actually consuming it. Other researchers found that higher exposure to alcohol brands on TV shows was associated with youth drinking (Gabrielli et al., 2021).

Popular sitcoms present issues of excessive drinking, stereotypes of alcoholics, and negative consequences of drinking in humorous ways (Mayrhofer & Matthes, 2021). The authors conclude that "comedy series may trivialize negative aspects of alcohol consumption and encourage the image of a 'fun' heavy drinker personality" (p. 59).

Other research indicates that tobacco imagery has increased on television in recent years. An analysis of Netflix and broadcast/cable TV programs popular with 15- to 24-year-olds revealed that 92% of the shows included tobacco (Truth Initiative,

2019). Netflix contained far more depictions of tobacco compared to broadcast or cable. In fact, 100% of the episodes of *Stranger Things* examined in the study included tobacco. In response to this study, Netflix issued a statement saying, "Going forward, all new projects that we commission with ratings of TV-14 or below for series or PG-13 or below for films, will be smoking and e-cigarette free—except for reasons of historical or factual accuracy" (Nedelman, 2019, para. 2).

In addition to alcohol and tobacco, numerous content analyses have examined body types seen on TV. In one study, almost half (49%) of female television characters were underweight—an increase of 18% since the turn of century—while the number of average or healthy weight women has decreased by 9% (Mastro & Figueroa-Caballero, 2018). Three-fourths of male characters were an average or healthy weight. Moreover, there was a significant relationship between thinness and perceived attractiveness.

Another issue studied is the link between viewing television programs with predominantly thin characters and the effects on viewers' body image. In fact, the "slim standard" in the United States and its resulting health problems have spread to remote corners of the globe. An article in *Newsweek* (1999) noted that teenage girls in the South Pacific island of Fiji (traditionally a culture with a full-figure ideal body type) began exhibiting signs of serious eating disorders after Western programs with their pencil-thin actresses arrived in 1995. Researchers were reluctant to attribute all the blame to television alone, but it seemed to be a central factor. In other studies, Fiji girls who watched the most television were precisely the ones who considered themselves too fat; of those, two-thirds had resorted to dieting to lose the unwanted pounds (Becker, 2004; Becker et al., 2003). Moreover, 15% of those studied vomited as a way of controlling their weight.

The results of a number of studies indicate that time spent watching television is a good predictor of weight problems in children and adolescents (e.g., Berkey et al., 2000; Braithwaite et al., 2013; Dennison et al., 2002; Dietz, 1990; Dietz & Gortmaker, 1985; Saelens et al., 2002; Zhang et al., 2016). A study in the 1970s established that children who are heavy TV watchers eat more snacks between meals than do light viewers (Clancy-Hepburn et al., 1974), which was confirmed by other studies (Coon et al., 2001; Matheson et al., 2004).

Another important intersection of health and media effects is sexual activity. Sexual content has become increasingly abundant and explicit on television in recent years. A content analysis of the HBO series *Girls*, which aired from 2012 to 2017, revealed that nearly one-fifth of all scenes depicted some sort of sexual behavior, and there was sexual talk in almost a third of scenes analyzed (Stevens & Garrett, 2016). Reality shows can also impact sexual behavior. For instance, watching MTV's *16 and Pregnant* series resulted in a decrease in teen births and increased interest in birth control and abortion (Kearney & Levine, 2015). See Chapter 12 for our in-depth exploration of media's effects on sexual attitudes and behaviors.

Mental health has become a common issue on both daytime and primetime television—one that generally involves negative stereotypes. Characters living with mental illness "may be shown engaging in criminal activity; presented as unattractive in appearance; referred to as different, loony, or psycho; and accompanied by production techniques, such as music, lighting, and setting, that enhance such depictions"

(Albada, 2014, p. 816). Recently there have been more positive portrayals of mental illness on television, but generally, "Research on the outcomes of the portrayals [of mental illness] points to stigmatization. For example, people who cited media as their primary source of information held less tolerant attitudes toward those with mental illness" (p. 817).

Films and Health

Most movies regularly feature characters using alcohol and tobacco products (Roberts & Christenson, 2000). Even G-rated movies and three out of four Disney animated classics were not alcohol and tobacco-free (Ryan & Hoerrner, 2004; Thompson & Yokota, 2001; also see this chapter's Research Spotlight).

Cruella De Vil, the villain in Disney's 1961 animated classic *101 Dalmatians*, was often shown with a cigarette in her hand.

In 2015, the Walt Disney Company banned smoking in all Disney, Pixar, Marvel, and Lucasfilm movies marketed to youth (except for a few limited circumstances, such as historical accuracy or presenting the habit in a negative light). As a result, Emma Stone's live-action *Cruella* could not be shown smoking in 2021, despite cigarettes being an iconic accessory for the animated version of the character in the 1960s. Paramount, Sony, Universal, and Warner Bros. all have policies in place to limit smoking seen in films (Erbland, 2019). Despite these policies, more than half of the top-grossing U.S. films released since 2002 include smoking—and tobacco incidents in PG and PG-13 films increased by 63% since 2015 (Polansky & Glantz, 2020). In another study, 51% of the top-grossing films in 2019 included depictions of tobacco (Polansky et al., 2020). When broken down by ratings, tobacco appeared in 23% of G/PG films, 43% of PG-13 films, and 76% of R-rated films.

Good characters as well as bad characters smoke and/or drink in movies (Goldstein et al., 1999). In one study, the use of illegal drugs in movies did not occur as often as smoking and drinking, the ill effects of drug use were often displayed, and drug addicts were usually portrayed as evil (Roberts & Christenson, 2000).

Let Your Conscience Be Your Guide:
Smoking and Drinking in Disney's Animated Classics
Erin L. Ryan and Keisha L. Hoerrner (2004)
Mass Communication & Society, 7(3), 261–278

In a content analysis of 24 Disney G-rated, animated, feature-length motion pictures from 1937 to 2000, researchers looked for instances of tobacco and alcohol use. They found 381 instances of substance use with no anti-use messages in the films.

Research Questions

RQ1: Are tobacco and alcohol products present in G-rated, feature-length, animated Disney films released between 1937 and 2000?

RQ2: If so, what is the context surrounding the use of such products?

RQ3: Do such occurrences decrease over time?

Operational Definitions

An incident of exposure to tobacco and alcohol products was defined as each instance of continuous display of a tobacco or alcohol product on the screen. Whenever a character was shown holding or using an alcohol or tobacco product, the elapsed time of the incident was recorded and timed with a stopwatch. Personified alcohol or tobacco products were also included in the analysis.

Researchers also coded the context surrounding the presence of tobacco and alcohol in the films, whether "shown only on screen," or if the character responded to the product by accepting or rejecting it. Also, if characters reacted positively to the use of the product, or encouraged the use of it, or were attempting to make the viewers laugh, it was coded as accepted. Negative reactions were coded as rejected.

Characters were classified as adult, teenager, or child. Protagonists, antagonists, and supporting characters were also coded. Personified products were coded as supporting characters.

Sample

The animated Disney classics included the following:

Snow White and the Seven Dwarfs (1937)	*Beauty and the Beast* (1991)
Pinocchio (1940)	*Aladdin* (1992)
Dumbo (1941)	*Pocahontas* (1995)
Cinderella (1950)	*The Hunchback of Notre Dame* (1996)
Alice in Wonderland (1951)	*The Rescuers* (1977)
Peter Pan (1953)	*The Fox and the Hound* (1981)
Lady and the Tramp (1955)	*Oliver and Company* (1988)
Sleeping Beauty (1959)	*The Little Mermaid* (1989)
101 Dalmatians (1961)	*Hercules* (1997)
The Sword in the Stone (1963)	*Mulan* (1998)
The Jungle Book (1967)	*Tarzan* (1999)
The Aristocats (1970)	*The Emperor's New Groove* (2000)

(continued)

Results

The researchers coded 381 incidents of alcohol and tobacco exposure (106 tobacco and 275 alcohol) within the 24 films. The answer to RQ1 was yes. Only three of the films contained no alcohol or tobacco: *The Jungle Book, The Fox and the Hound,* and *Mulan.*

Eighteen films contained at least one tobacco exposure; and 18 contained at least one alcohol exposure. The pipe was the most frequently depicted tobacco product, followed by cigars and cigarettes. Beer, followed by wine, champagne, and spirits were the most frequently shown alcohol products. Only nine of the films did not have any cigar exposure, 10 did not have pipe exposure, and only six did not contain wine exposure.

Films were divided into decades (the 1937 film was included in the 1940s group) and a chi square was performed between release date by decade and type of exposure. Over time, tobacco exposure declined, but alcohol exposure increased.

In terms of context and RQ2, 91% of exposures to the products were accepted, and only 4% were rejected. Only four films contained rejections: *Pinocchio, Peter Pan, 101 Dalmatians,* and *The Sword in the Stone.* Only one film, *Pinocchio,* depicted rejection of alcohol products.

Three films had scenes with children using alcohol or tobacco products: *Pinocchio, Peter Pan,* and *Oliver and Company.* Teen consumption of either alcohol or tobacco was present in *Peter Pan, The Little Mermaid,* and *Aladdin.* Of all instances of cigar use in the films, children accounted for 22%. Anti-use sentiment was almost completely absent from all the films.

RQ3 could be answered in the affirmative for tobacco but not for alcohol.

Sargent et al. (2005) surveyed adolescents aged 10 to 14 years and identified a causal link between exposure to movie smoking and the onset of smoking among adolescents. Exposure to movie smoking was the greatest single risk factor determining smoking initiation among U.S. youths. Sargent et al. (2012) found that smoking in PG-13 and R-rated films—but not G and PG films—led to smoking initiation for young people. The researchers concluded that if all films in which smoking occurred were given a R rating, the onset of adolescent smoking could be reduced by 18%.

Furthermore, the U.S. Surgeon General's report states that "evidence is sufficient to conclude there is a causal relationship between depictions of smoking in the movies and the initiation of smoking among young people" (USDHHS, 2012, p. 10). As Polansky et al. (2020) note, almost 90% of young people who start smoking because of on-screen exposure begin before age 18; furthermore, "two million of them will ultimately die from tobacco-induced diseases, including heart disease, lung cancer, and emphysema" (p. 4).

Watching movie characters use alcohol is associated with early-onset of drinking among 10- to 14-year-olds (Sargent et al., 2006). A longitudinal study of adolescents in six European countries who were considered to have a low affinity for alcohol (i.e., they had never had a drink and did not intend to drink) examined the effects of seeing alcohol consumption in movies. After controlling for numerous variables (e.g., gender, family affluence, personality characteristics, and drinking behavior of peers, just to name a few), 40% of the participants tried alcohol and 6% had taken part in binge drinking after seeing alcohol consumption in movies (Hanewinkel et al., 2014).

Smoking and Drinking in Song Lyrics and Music Videos

- Siegel et al. (2013) studied popular music in the United States; 23% of the most popular songs contained references to alcohol. Nearly 40% of songs in the urban genre (made up of R&B and hip-hop) contained alcohol references, followed by 22% of country songs, 15% of pop songs, and 7% of rock songs. When specific brands of alcohol were mentioned, they were overwhelmingly associated with positive contexts.

- Knutzen et al. (2018) found that between 2013 and 2017, 40.2% to 50.7% of hip-hop music videos contained either combustible or electronic smoking, smoke, or vapor. Furthermore, main or featured musical artists accounted for nearly 60% of combustible use and 30% of electronic use. They noted that videos' popularity, the appeal of the hip-hop genre, and use of branded smoking products by prominent musicians may contribute to ongoing public health concerns about tobacco and marijuana use.

- Cranwell, Opazo-Breton, and Britton (2016) analyzed music videos on YouTube in Great Britain; popular videos delivered millions of impressions of both tobacco and alcohol content to viewers. Adolescents were exposed to this content much more than adults, and girls were exposed to the content more than boys. The number of impressions for alcohol was almost five times higher than for tobacco.

Effects of Health News

Research on the effects of health-related news indicates that people pay most attention to stories about public health issues among all health-related stories, but they also pay attention to public health policy stories and stories about specific diseases (Brodie et al., 2003).

Many studies of health-related news include measures of behavioral effects experienced after seeing certain news stories. For example, news coverage of the dangers of smoking can have a significant effect on the number of people who decide to kick the habit (Pierce & Gilpin, 2001). The use of marijuana among teens, as well as their attitudes about marijuana, can be affected by news coverage (Stryker, 2003). However, when confronted with contradictory health information in new reports, audiences can experience increased confusion and negative attitudes toward health recommendations and dietary science (Clark et al., 2019). News stories about suicides can result in copycat suicides, but news outlets can mitigate negative effects by not revealing all the details of the death (Stack, 2005).

Recently, researchers across the globe studied news coverage of the COVID-19 pandemic and related health effects. In an Italian study, the type of information presented in the news influenced health-related behaviors during the pandemic (Scopelliti et al., 2021). "Calming information" (e.g., the majority of people with COVID experienced no symptoms) positively correlated with healthy behaviors. Interestingly, alarming information (e.g., rising death tolls, the ease of virus transmission) did not increase healthy behaviors. In a Belgian study, people's perceived vulnerability to COVID-19 and feelings of loneliness and solidarity were determined by the overall frequency of media exposure (Frissen et al., 2020). Meanwhile, self-reported health behaviors and support of government measures to fight the pandemic were mostly determined by the type of news media consumed. In a Chinese study of health news effects, consumption of COVID-19 news could result in vicarious trauma and anxiety (Liu & Liu, 2020).

News stories can also have effects on public health policy. The way a health story is framed can have an impact on how the public and policy makers view the problem (Dorfman & Wallack, 2007), with some framing creating a polarizing effect along political lines (e.g., Gollust et al., 2009). News reports can also affect public support for health-related policies (Coleman et al., 2011). Intense media scrutiny on a particular health problem (Reese & Danielian, 1989; Shoemaker, Wanta, & Leggett, 1989) or controversial treatment (Benelli, 2003) can also cause governing officials to act, sometimes prematurely.

Health-related news had its greatest impact on public policy when health experts were in agreement on how to solve health problems, when the change occurred at the state or local level, and when news coverage supported the efforts of either private groups or public officials trying to bring about change (Walsh-Childers, 1994a, 1994b).

Online Health Information

The majority of internet users—70% to 80% of them—search online for health-related information, and such searches are among the most common personal uses of the internet (Greenberg et al., 2004). Almost three-quarters (72%) of internet users report looking for some sort of health information online, ranging from general information to details about both minor and serious medical conditions (Fox & Duggan, 2013).

LaValley et al. (2017) found that when turning to online resources for medical and health information, most users (71.8%) turn to commercial websites (e.g., WebMD—the most commonly named site in the study), followed by search engines (11.6%), sites for academic or research institutions such as the Mayo Clinic (11.1%), and government websites (5.5%). According to the CDC, women are more likely than men to look up health information online (Cohen & Adams, 2011). In addition to women, other demographic groups more likely to seek online health information include those who are younger, white, live in households earning more than $75,000 a year, and/or have a college or other advanced degree (Fox & Duggan, 2013).

Many people search for health topics on the internet, and the amount of information can overwhelm and confuse them (Fox, 2006; Kean, 2014). People who seek information about their illnesses on the internet are more likely to use the information to formulate questions for their physicians during doctor visits (Bass et al., 2006). In another survey, 53% of people who sought online information talked with a medical professional about what they discovered, and 41% had that online diagnosis confirmed by a doctor (Fox & Duggan, 2013). In a Taiwanese study, there was a significant relationship between searching for health information online to solve a medical problem and changing a person's medical decisions (Chen et al., 2018). "The more online health information patients searched for solving their medical problems, the more likely their medical decision was changed based on the online health information they had gathered" (p. 6).

Of course, online health information cannot always be taken at face value. Websites can contain inaccuracies, and the quality of information is sometimes substandard (Eysenbach et al., 2002; Kean, 2014; Powell et al., 2005). Most people who get health information online do not check the validity of the information or other measures of information quality, such as the date of the material (Eysenbach & Köhler, 2002; Fox, 2006). Evaluation of online information is a complex process influenced by both peripheral cues and numerous contextual factors, such as information needs and personal beliefs; there can be a disconnect between what medical experts and consumers consider to be quality online health information (Sun et al., 2019). Chen et al. (2018) concluded that the credibility of health information online plays an important role in medical decision making.

> Present health care professionals have a responsibility to acknowledge that, regardless of the credibility of online health information, patients' medical decision making may be changed following the health information reported on the internet. Health care professionals should assist patients' medical decision making by initiating as much dialogue with patients as possible, providing credible and convincing health information to patients, and guiding patients where to look for accurate, comprehensive, and understandable online health information. (p. 8)

Another common source of online health information is social media. Online communities facilitate patients and caregivers sharing critical health information with others (Fox, 2014). In addition to helping people access health information, social media can provide both social and emotional support for health consumers; however, those benefits are tempered by concerns about the quality of the information (Zhao & Zhang, 2017). For instance, in a recent review of antivaccine content on social media, researchers noted that the messages "describe vaccines as harmful, highlight their side effects, and undermine the effectiveness of the protection they offer. To support these statements, they use false information and conspiracy theories, and gloss over or omit the data about vaccine benefits" (Wawrzuta et al., 2021, p. 10).

In addition to the quality of health information on social media, there is also great concern about how quickly information can spread. Unsubstantiated medial information can (and does) go viral, which can result in serious health consequences for society (Chrousos & Mentis, 2020). As we saw with the COVID-19 pandemic,

> mass media and social media might play important positive roles in helping estimate the magnitude of an epidemic/pandemic and in promoting public health protective measures against the spread of the infection, [but] they can also cause social anxiety and confusion of a potentially higher ultimate cost for the society. (Chrousos & Mentis, 2020, p. 2).

Effects of Health Communication Campaigns

Health campaigns involve the purposive use of mass media for health education and behavioral change. A comprehensive review of mass media health campaigns concluded that these campaigns can result in positive health-related behavioral changes and prevent negative behavior changes in large populations (Wakefield et al., 2010). As Zhao (2020) notes, "Health communication campaigns have made important contributions to the advancement of public health globally and are often considered critical components of broad intervention efforts, such as cancer and tobacco control" (p. S11).

The effects of mediated health communication campaigns vary significantly depending on the type of health behavior. For instance, one meta-analysis revealed larger effect sizes for behaviors such as seat belt use and oral health than getting a mammogram or behaviors related to sexual health (Snyder et al., 2004). Wakefield et al. (2010) reviewed mediated health campaigns and found stronger effectiveness for behaviors like road safety and tobacco control, moderate effectiveness for behaviors related to nutrition and physical activity, and weak or nonexistent effectiveness for behaviors like breastfeeding and alcohol consumption. The likelihood of success increased substantially when people were exposed to multiple interventions and when the desired target behavior is a "one-off or episodic" action (e.g., getting a vaccination or health screening) instead of ongoing or habitual (e.g., physical activity, food choices, sun exposure). For example, a mass media campaign encouraging college students to get a flu shot resulted in a nearly 30% increase in students getting a vaccine from one year to the next (Shropshire et al., 2013).

Overall, reviews and meta-analyses of health communication campaign effects have found that the ability of a campaign to change a person's health behaviors is modest; however, "even a modest effect size for a large-scale campaign can still translate into thousands or even millions of people changing their behaviors for the better" (Zhao, 2020, p. S13).

The vast body of literature about media health campaigns reveals that their results are not always predictable. Some campaigns have produced long-term behavioral changes, but others have not. Some have produced positive, intended effects, whereas others have produced negative, unintended effects. Still others have produced a variety of effects. For example, a North Dakota media campaign to promote mammography screening seemed to adversely affect women who had never had a mammogram but encouraged women who had already been screened to have another screening (McCaul et al., 1998).

The public health campaigns in the 1980s that were designed to raise AIDS awareness and change at-risk behaviors succeeded in raising the awareness of the general public, but they also increased anxieties about the disease. Moreover, these campaigns failed to reach high-risk audiences such as drug users in both Great Britain and the United States (Department of Health and Social Security and the Welsh Office, 1987; Snyder et al., 1989).

Between 1998 and 2004, the National Youth Anti-Drug Media Campaign utilized advertising on TV, radio, websites, magazines, and movie theaters in an effort to lower drug use among youth in the United States. In fact, a significant portion of the campaign's nearly $1 billion budget was spent on the media buy. But the campaign did not have the intended outcome. Instead of curtailing drug use, exposure to the campaign was associated with both greater pro-marijuana social norms and greater intention to use marijuana in the future (for a review, see Zhao, 2020).

Myrick (2020) notes that a potential cause of unintended negative effects resulting from health messages could be from a misspecification or lack of theory: "Increased critical application of theory could help health communication scholars better explain the role of media and audience factors in shaping health outcomes. Moreover, theory could help prevent the dissemination of messages that inadvertently harm public health" (p. 315).

Subsequent research revealed that sometimes media interventions *are* consumed by at-risk audiences and *do* result in the desired effects—in this case more positive behavioral change (e.g., Elwood & Ataabadi, 1996; Guenther-Grey et al., 1995). The sidebar "Risk Learning and Stereotype Priming Models" offers two models aimed at persuading people to engage in healthy and risk-free behaviors.

An example of a successful health communication intervention is the U.S. Food and Drug Administration's The Real Cost campaign launched in 2014 (for a review, see Zhao, 2020). Initially focused on preventing youth from smoking cigarettes, the campaign has expanded to include e-cigs and smokeless tobacco. The campaign messages are seen on a variety of media, such as TV, radio, the internet, social media,

---

Risk Learning and Stereotype Priming Models

Pechmann (2001) offered descriptions of two types of complementary models aimed at persuading people to engage in more healthy behaviors and to avoid health risks. **Risk-learning models** operate with the goal of relating "new information about health risks and the behaviors that will minimize those risks," while **stereotype priming models** attempt to use "salient preexisting social stereotypes about people who do or do not behave as advocated" (p. 189) for the purpose of persuading people to avoid behaviors that cause health risks.

Risk-learning models are based on protection motivation theory, which means they work to motivate behaviors that promote and protect good health. Four types of messages increase a person's likelihood to engage in protective behavior:

- Messages presenting the severe disease consequences of engaging in risky behavior (risk severity)
- Messages revealing how easy it is to contract the disease (risk vulnerability)
- Messages displaying how protective behaviors reduce chances for or prevent/ cure the disease (response efficacy)
- Messages exhibiting effectiveness when engaging in protective behavior (self-efficacy)

The stereotype priming model depends upon a priming stimulus and preexisting links between a particular social group and particular behavior traits. For example, in a campaign that discourages smoking, cigarette smokers might be presented negatively (e.g., having yellow teeth or smelling like tobacco), while nonsmokers would be shown positively (e.g., enjoying good health).

> Risk-learning models do not require message recipients to have any prior knowledge of the substantive message content. The main goal is, in fact, to impart knowledge where it is lacking. By comparison, the stereotype priming model requires the use of messages that reflect people's prior stereotypes. In other words, the prime must mirror or correspond to a belief that already resides in long-term memory. Priming merely serves to bring a preexisting stereotype to the forefront of memory. (p. 195)

mobile games. (Some of the campaign's public service announcements can be watched on their YouTube channel: https://www.youtube.com/c/TheRealCost). The Real Cost focuses on two target audiences: nonsmokers who are at risk of starting to smoke and youth who experiment with smoking but are not habitual smokers. Studies evaluating the effectiveness of The Real Cost campaign have found that it has successfully prevented hundreds of thousands of young Americans between the ages of 11 and 19 from smoking (Duke et al., 2019). Furthermore, by reducing the number of young smokers, the campaign dramatically reduces tobacco-related financial burdens to individuals, their families, and society as a whole (MacMonegle et al., 2018).

The FDA's The Real Cost campaign has successfully helped prevent hundreds of thousands of preteens and teenagers from using tobacco.

Public health campaigns often rely heavily on emotional appeals to influence health behaviors (Myrick, 2020). One health campaign approach that has regained attention in recent years is the fear appeal. In short, "fear appeals attempt to change people's behavior by telling them the dangers posed by a particular behavior. The hope is that making people aware of the danger will raise fear levels and convince them to avoid the threat by taking protective action" (Basil & Witte, 2014, p. 498). Fear appeals have been used successfully in campaigns focusing on smoking, drinking, drunk driving, and high blood pressure (for review, see Simpson, 2017).

Witte's (1992) **extended parallel process model (EPPM)** helps explain how people respond to fear appeals. Whereas earlier models focused on cognitive responses to fear, the EPPM includes fear as an emotion (Myrick, 2020). Basil and Witte (2014) summarize the EPPM this way:

> This model suggests that whether people engage in danger control or fear control depends on the ratio of the perceived threat (the cognitive correlate to the feeling of fear) to efficacy. When the perceived threat looms larger than their sense of efficacy, individuals engage in fear control and avoid thinking about the danger. . . . . Faced with a relevant and serious threat but few means to effectively avoid it, people will find ways to control their fear instead of the threat. When their feeling of efficacy is high, however, they are more likely to take protective action and control the risk. (p. 499)

Although numerous studies show that fear appeals are effective tools of persuasion (e.g., Hale & Dillard, 1995; Mongeau, 1998; Sutton, 1982; Tannenbaum et al., 2015), researchers are continuing to develop a clearer understanding of how fear appeals work. "Researchers still do not fully understand the moderators or boundary conditions as to when and for whom fear-arousing messages lead to attitude and behavior change" (Myrick, 2020, p. 315). Furthermore,

> messages that merely generate fear can often be limited in effectiveness because they simply cause people to be afraid. Solely trying to scare people is often ineffective and may even have negative long-term effects. However, these appeals can be effective when doable behaviors that work to prevent a threat are presented. (Basil & Witte, 2014, p. 499)

Lastly, fear appeals in mediated health messages raise ethical concerns for medical professionals and communication researchers alike.

> Even if fear is positively related to persuasion, ethical concerns arise when using scare tactics to persuade audiences to change their health behaviors, especially when targeting high-risk populations who may not have the resources to effectively deal with the fear aroused by a health message (Hastings, Stead, & Webb, 2004). If fear causes distrust of a message source or if audiences become desensitized to fear-arousing messages, then fear appeals could easily backfire and cause more harm than good. (Myrick, 2020, p. 315)

Some media health campaigns have also been criticized for their "victim blaming" approaches. These campaigns offer individuals information that will allow them to take responsibility for their health by changing their lifestyles or going for health screenings. Critics have argued for decades that victims cannot take full blame for their actions when they have been bombarded since childhood with advertisements or media portrayals that feature unhealthy products such as cigarettes or alcoholic beverages (e.g., Wallack, 1989).

Overall, there is still much work to be done in the area of mediated health communication research.

> If societies want to use media to combat growing health crises related to poor diets, lack of clean water, increased stress levels, infectious diseases, and other serious threats to health and well-being, then improved application of theory and advances in methodology, as well as creative integrations of the two, are needed to continue to advance health-related media effects research. (Myrick, 2020, p. 318)

Summary

Mass media messages often have considerable impact on personal and public health. As with other types of media content, effects from health-related messages may be positive or negative, and they can be intended or unintended in nature. The goal of mediated health communication campaigns is to present specific messages that will have intentional, positive effects on the health behaviors of audiences. Other sources of health-related messages in mass media—news reports, entertainment media, and advertisements—do not always produce positive results.

Research on the effects of commercial product advertising has focused primarily on the health of individuals who use the products. Health effects from tobacco, alcohol, prescription drug, and food ads have been the focus of numerous studies; most have found that such ads are linked with negative effects on individual and public health.

Entertainment portrayals can have rather powerful effects on the health of audience members. Most studies in this area have concentrated on television programs, films, music videos, and video games, establishing links between entertainment depictions and nutrition, smoking, drinking, drug abuse, and sexual activity.

People obtain much of their health-related information from news media. News coverage of health matters has the potential to shape the impressions of both average citizens and policy makers. Some news coverage utilizes frames that seemingly place responsibility for health problems solely on individuals.

Although many campaigns are successful, there are also numerous examples of mediated health campaigns that result in negative or unintended outcomes. The appeal to fear has persuasive power in communication campaigns. However, there are conditions in which fear appeals may backfire, so message creators must carefully construct messages for these types of appeals to result in the desired outcome. The ethical concerns of using fear appeals must also be considered.

16

Effects of Media Stereotyping

We all know what it's like to be told that there is not a place for you to be featured. Yet you are young, gifted, and Black.

We know what it's like to be told there's not a screen for you to be featured on, a stage for you to be featured on. We know what it's like to be the tail and not the head. We know what it's like to be beneath and not above.

And that is what we went to work with every day because we knew—not that we would be around during awards season or that it would make a billion dollars—but we knew that we had something special that we wanted to give the world. That we could be full human beings in the roles that we were playing. That we could create a world that exemplified a world that we wanted to see.

—Chadwick Boseman speaking about *Black Panther* at the 25th Annual SAG Awards in 2019

The theatrical release of *Black Panther* in 2018 was celebrated as a watershed moment for diversity and representation in mainstream popular cultural. *Black Panther* was the first Marvel movie focusing on the story of a Black superhero, and it was the first to have a Black director. Critics and audiences alike praised the film for its depiction of African culture in the fictional nation of Wakanda. Not only did the film go on to shatter many box office records but also many long-standing media stereotypes about Black people.

For more than 50 years, communication researchers have studied issues of diversity and representation in mass media and their effects upon audiences' attitudes, values, and behaviors.

Numerous media stereotyping studies were conducted throughout the 1970s and 1980s. In the 1990s, Black people achieved very positive gains in both the number and the nature of their portrayals in entertainment programs, but other minorities did not fare so well. Latinx, Asian American, Native American groups, and women continued to be underrepresented in mass media—sometimes to the point of exclusion. When members of these minority groups were depicted, it was sometimes in stereotypical or demeaning ways (Greenberg et al., 2002; Mastro, 2009; Smith & Granados, 2009).

Billings and Parrott (2020a) define media stereotypes as "mediated messages that communicate overgeneralized information about social groups, associating positive and negative characteristics, attributes, and/or behavior with the social group" (p. 3). In recent years, the number of scholars studying media stereotyping effects has grown, as has scholars' recognition of the power of stereotypes to influence audiences (Dixon, 2020).

Media industries have also faced a reckoning for an overwhelming lack of diversity in recent years. April Reign created the #OscarsSoWhite hashtag in 2015 after learning all 20 Oscar nominees in the acting categories were white. When the same thing happened again in 2016, she said, "One time you could call a fluke, two times feels like a pattern" (Ugwu, 2020). Reign's 2015 tweet became a viral call to action that turned into a social justice campaign. Although there have been some improvements in diversity and inclusion in the Academy of Motion Picture Arts and Sciences since then, there is still much room for improvement.

Previous chapters have revealed the power of mass media to affect the cognitions or mental processes of media users. We learned that media messages are sometimes responsible for changing a person's attitudes and values. For better or worse, these changes may also alter a person's behavior. This chapter explores the nature of media portrayals of racial, ethnic, and gender stereotypes and their effects upon audiences. Of course, there are *far* more groups that are stereotyped in the media than we have space to cover in this chapter. For an in-depth examination of media stereotyping, we recommend Billings and Parrott's (2020b) award-winning book *Media Stereotypes: From Ageism to Xenophobia*.

You will recall from Chapter 8 on cultivation research that the real world is often very different from the world seen in mass media. Research analyses of media content have examined whether or not minority characters are present, how they compare to other characters, the significance of the minority characters, and the interaction of minority characters with others. Other studies have explored the preferences of minority and majority viewers for content and characters.

First, we take a look back at how media entertainment programs, news reports, and advertisements have presented minorities in the past and then at how the media convey social information to audiences today. We examine the current state of media minority portrayals, the characteristics of minority audiences, and the effects of media on racial, ethnic, and gender stereotyping.

Minority Portrayals in Media: A Look Back

Television

We begin our look back with an incredibly successful sitcom that featured the marriage of a white woman and a Cuban man—highly unusual in the 1950s and for decades to follow. *I Love Lucy* ran from 1951 to 1957 as television emerged as an influential mass medium. Millions of people tuned in to watch the comedic presentation of the everyday life of a married couple. The show challenged "gender stereotypes against the backdrop of the standard image of White, heterosexual couples within the American Dream mythology" (Ramasubramanian et al., 2020, p. 261).

Starting in the 1970s, researchers began counting the number of minority characters seen on the screen. Two major head count studies found the proportion of minority characters on television during the 1970s fell far below their real world societal percentages (Gerbner & Signorielli, 1979; Seggar et al., 1981). Throughout that decade, the percentage of white characters increased beyond their actual percentage in the population (slightly more than 87%). The percentage of Black characters increased slightly but remained below their societal percentages. Black actors and actresses were rarely cast in leading or supporting roles during this time. For instance, Seggar et al. (1981) observed that Black men accounted for 9% of leading male roles and 12% of supporting roles in 1975. By 1980, both categories had dropped to only 4.5%. Meanwhile, Black women were seen in less than 3% of leading and supporting roles in 1980. Hispanics were cast in only 2.5% of major roles (Gerbner & Signorielli, 1979).

I Love Lucy featured an interracial marriage, starring actors who were married in real life.

The number of Black characters on television fluctuated from the late 1980s into the 1990s. Black characters made up 21.6% of roles from 1987 to 1989 and 16.8% from 1991 to 1993 (Tukachinsky et al., 2015). Researchers credit these percentages to popular comedies that featured predominately Black casts, such as *Amen* and *The Cosby Show* in the late 1980s and *Hangin' with Mr. Cooper* and *The Fresh Prince of Bel-Air* in the early 1990s.

In the late 1990s, the television networks responded to demands from minority activist groups by featuring more Black characters on primetime shows, but similar increases were not experienced by other racial and ethnic minorities (Greenberg et al., 2002; Tukachinsky et al., 2015). Minority groups remained underrepresented in major network programming in the 1990s as they were 20 years earlier (Greenberg et al., 2002; Mastro & Greenberg, 2000). Underrepresentation continued well into the first decade of the 21st century. A content analysis of more than 2,500 characters from popular shows from 1987 to 2009 confirmed that "ethnic minorities are largely excluded from primetime television. Most strikingly, Native Americans are almost entirely absent" (Tukachinsky et al., 2015, p. 25).

Motion Pictures

Historically, Black and other minority actors and actresses were cast in movie roles that specifically called for a minority character. That began to change in the

1990s. Film star Halle Berry felt that her supporting role in the 1994 live-action version of *The Flintstones* was a breakthrough because "it was a part that could've gone to anybody. It could've gone to a White actress. But it went to me" (Ivry, 1998, p. 3G). Will Smith's portrayal of James West in the 1999 action-adventure movie *Wild Wild West* represented another instance when a leading role could have gone to anyone but went to a Black actor. Other examples include Denzel Washington's role in 1993's *The Pelican Brief* and Morgan Freeman's role as the President of the United States in 1998's *Deep Impact*.

Many films in the 1990s broke new ground by featuring Blacks actors and actresses in starring roles. These stars have also proven that they can attract audiences of different races to a variety of different film genres.

> Some are known for their big-budget, action-packed summer films, others for their comedic talents, and some are known for the interesting character pieces they choose. For many of Hollywood's most famous actors and actresses, the brightness of their star power outshines the color of their skin. (Zhou et al., 2010, p. 11)

Advertising

Like TV and movie characters, advertising images historically have been mostly white (Coltrane & Messineo, 2000; Wilson & Gutierrez, 1995). From the 1940s to the 1960s, Black people appeared in only about 3% of ads in national magazines, usually in one of three categories: well-known entertainers, famous athletes, or unknowns depicted as servants (Colfax & Steinberg, 1972; Kassarjian, 1969; Stempel, 1971). Analyses of magazine ads from the 1970s found even fewer Black people were represented (e.g., Bush et al., 1980; Reid & Vanden Bergh, 1980).

The situation did not change significantly in the 1980s. Jackson and Ervin (1991) examined almost a thousand ads from 1986 to 1988 that appeared in *Cosmopolitan, Glamour,* and *Vogue.* Only 2.4% of the ads featured Black women models; of those, 83% portrayed the Black woman from a distance. At that time, Black women accounted for more than 12% of the female population of the United States and 15% of the subscribers to the magazines examined.

Several studies in the 1970s and 1980s indicated that white magazine readers did not respond negatively to the use of Black models in ads (Block, 1972; Schlinger & Plummer, 1972; Soley, 1983). One of these studies measured the actual readership of ads featuring Black models; the race of the model did not affect ad readership (Soley, 1983).

On television, more and more Black and Asian people started appearing in commercials in the 1990s. In fact, both minority groups went from virtual nonexistence in advertising to being *overrepresented*. By 1994, Blacks appeared in more than 31% of all commercial advertisements featuring models (Taylor & Stern, 1997), while making up 12% of the U.S. population (U.S. Department of Commerce, 1993). Asian Americans appeared in more than 8% of all commercial ads featuring models, despite making up only 3.6% of the U.S. population at the time. Meanwhile, Native Americans and people with disabilities were largely absent in media portrayals (Greenberg et al., 2002; Wilson & Gutierrez, 1995).

Boldly Going Where No Black Woman Had Gone Before

In the 1960s, Gene Roddenberry had an idea for a television show set in outer space: *Star Trek*. He wanted *Star Trek* to portray a future where people of all races (as well as aliens) coexist peacefully. The bridge of the *U.S.S. Enterprise* was truly a racial melting pot. As the Asian Mr. Sulu and Russian Ensign Chekov piloted the ship to uncharted expanses of the galaxy, Scottish engineer Montgomery Scott worked hard to ensure the warp core and transporters stayed online. The Vulcan-human hybrid Mr. Spock was busy checking sensor readings and offering counsel to the white Captain Kirk and Dr. McCoy. But the *Enterprise* crew was not an all-boys club. Lieutenant Uhura, the ship's Black communications officer, was busy making sure the *Enterprise* was in contact with Earth and with aliens from unknown worlds. Uhura (played by Nichelle Nichols) was one of the first Black female characters on television who was not a maid or nanny. She was seen as an equal among her male peers.

Nichols planned to leave after the first season to pursue other career options. Soon after telling Roddenberry that she wanted to leave *Star Trek*, Nichols attended an NAACP dinner. There, she had a chance encounter with Dr. Martin Luther King, Jr.—who professed to be one of her biggest fans. When Nichols told Dr. King that she was leaving the show, he told her that she could not beam off the *Enterprise*. "For the first time, we [African Americans] are being seen the world over . . . as we should be seen," he told her, adding that Uhura was a crucial character in breaking down the racial stereotypes that prevailed at the time. At Dr. King's urging, Nichols asked Roddenberry for her job back, and Lieutenant Uhura continued to warp around the galaxy for the rest of the show's run and the subsequent series of movies.

Nichelle Nichols as Lt. Uhura.

Nichols's character was not only instrumental in depicting Blacks in non-stereotypical roles, she also took part in the first interracial kiss on American television. In the episode titled "Plato's Stepchildren," Lieutenant Uhura shared a kiss with William Shatner's Captain Kirk. Although Uhura and Kirk's lip lock was controversial at the time, interracial relationships have now become commonplace on television.

For more than half a century, the *Star Trek* franchise has presented a future where racial (and alien) equality prevails. On the numerous *Star Trek* spin-offs, we have seen interracial and interspecies romances. On *Star Trek: Deep Space Nine*, the Klingon warrior Worf (played by Black actor Michael Dorn) married the Trill scientist Dax (played by white actress Terry Farrell). Moreover, *Star Trek: Deep Space Nine* and *Star Trek: Voyager* featured a Black man (Captain Benjamin Sisko played by Avery Brooks) and a white woman (Captain Kathryn Janeway played by Kate Mulgrew) as commanding officers, respectively, further shattering predominant racial and gender stereotypes seen on television, especially in the 1990s.

More recently, *Star Trek: Discovery* has continued the franchise's legacy of showcasing diversity. When it premiered in 2017, *Discovery* became the first series in the franchise to feature a Black woman as the lead (Commander Michael Burnham played by Sonequa Martin-Green). Additionally, *Discovery* includes the franchise's first openly gay characters and relationship. The show's third season introduced the franchise's first regular transgender and non-binary characters—who are played by transgender and non-binary actors, respectively.

Media as Conveyors of Social Information: The Current Picture

In recent years, awareness about diversity (or lack thereof) in media has moved beyond academic research and into mainstream discourse. Head counts remain crucial to understanding what progress (or, again, lack thereof) has been made in terms of representation. However, studies of minorities in mass media now generally focus on stereotypical depictions of minorities and the effects those portrayals have on both minority and majority audiences. These studies have been important in determining the social information conveyed by various media about minorities. This research recognizes that television, film, videos, and other media—through entertainment, advertisements, news reports, and children's programming—send influential messages about minorities, especially for young people.

Television

Minority representation on television increased substantially from the 2011–2012 season to the 2018–2019 season. In head count research examining the number of lead characters on broadcast comedies and dramas during the 2011–2012 television season, only 5.1% were minorities; the rest (94.9%) were white (Hunt et al., 2014). Minorities fared better on cable series, where they made up 14.1% of lead characters. During the 2018–2019 season, minorities made up 24% of lead characters on scripted broadcast shows, 35% on scripted cable series, and 24.1% on programs airing on streaming digital platforms like Hulu, Netflix, and Amazon Prime Video (Hunt & Ramón, 2020b).

Moreover, when looking at overall cast diversity and not just lead roles, minorities made up 41.3% of all roles on broadcast, 36.4% of all roles on cable, and 33.4% of roles on digital (Hunt & Ramón, 2020b). People of color make up roughly 40% of the U.S. population, which is almost on par with the number of minority roles seen on TV. Actual time on the screen, however, has a lower percentage—26.7% (Nielsen, 2020a). Overall, out of the 300 most-watched shows on broadcast, cable, and streaming in 2019, 92% included some type of diversity (i.e., women, people of color, or LGBTQ representation) among recurring cast members (Nielsen, 2020a). For example, programs like NBC's *This Is Us*, FOX's *9-1-1*, and ABC's *Grey's Anatomy* and *Station 19* are just a few of the offerings that prominently feature women, people of color, and LGBTQ characters. Streaming shows like Netflix's *Bridgerton*, *Never Have I Ever*, and *Sex Education* have been praised for their diverse casting. On cable, Comedy Central's *Awkwafina is Nora From Queens* and FX's *Pose* have also provided minority representation on television.

Black Americans.   Although minorities have gained more prominence on television, how does the world seen on television compare to reality? According to population data from the U.S. Census Bureau (n.d.), Black people made up 13.4% of the population in 2019. Hunt and Ramón (2020b) found that Black characters made up 18.2% of overall characters on both broadcast and cable and 11.9% of characters on digital shows during the 2018–2019 season. Black characters have the highest share of screen time among minorities, with 18% (Nielsen, 2020a).

Shows like Netflix's *Bridgerton* have been praised for their representations of diversity.

Blacks are generally portrayed in sitcoms (that usually feature an all-Black cast) or crime dramas (Mastro & Behm-Morawitz, 2005; Mastro & Greenberg, 2000). Recent examples of these trends include the comedy series *Black-ish*, Shemar Moore's roles as an FBI agent on *Criminal Minds* and a team leader on *S.W.A.T.*, and Ice-T's role as a police sergeant on *Law & Order: SVU*. Because Black characters most often appear in sitcoms, research "suggests Black characters often assume satirical roles, limiting Black character respectability" (Weeks et al., 2020, p. 94). Furthermore, the TV landscape has changed in recent years, with many networks opting to produce reality shows over sitcoms. "As the number of situation comedies has declined, so has the number of African American characters" (Dixon, 2020, p. 245). When Black characters appear in drama or reality shows, they often appear in smaller numbers as part of racially diverse casts instead of casts that are predominately Black (Dixon, 2020).

Nielsen (2020a) found that both Black males and females are included above parity in the action/adventure, comedy, and drama genres (with Black males having greater representation in each). Meanwhile, Black males are also included at rates far above parity in LGBTQ and news/weather genres, whereas Black females are greatly underrepresented. The only category where Black females are represented above both parity is in the reality genre, which is also the only genre where Black males are represented below parity.

The quality of depictions of Black characters on TV has been described as a "mixed bag" (Dixon, 2020), but their portrayals on primetime TV have generally improved over time (Weeks et al., 2020). Black characters routinely appear as good and likable, and their social and professional status has improved since the late 1980s (Tukachinsky et al., 2015). However, some research indicates that Black characters are presented as immoral and more despicable than white characters (Monk-Turner et al., 2010).

Researchers also examine diversity and representation in television news. In terms of Black anchors and weather forecasters on national news, Black men are overrepresented with a 15.26% share of screen time; however, Black women are severely underrepresented with just 0.12% of screen time (Nielsen, 2020a). Black men have a significantly greater share of screen time than Black women, despite the fact that women make up a majority of the Black population.

Black people are often negatively characterized in news coverage. Blacks are far more likely to be depicted than whites in stories about crime (Dixon & Linz, 2000a).

Compared to real world crime statistics, Blacks are overrepresented as criminals on news programs and underrepresented in sympathetic roles, like being victims of crime (Dixon et al., 2003; Dixon & Linz, 2000a, 2000b). News reports also connect Black families to crime. Dixon (2017) found that Black family members are overrepresented as criminal suspects when compared to crime data. "The study suggests news sources depict Black families as sources of social instability and White families as sources of social stability. In other words, while White families appear to meet social ideals, Black families appear to fit the broken home stereotype" (Weeks et al., 2020, p. 97). Black families are also overrepresented as welfare recipients in both news and commentary/opinion content, especially during times of economic stability (Gilens, 1999; van Doorn, 2015).

Furthermore, news reporting often casts Black athletes in a negative light. For instance, the criminal activity of Black athletes is emphasized on the news more often than the criminal activity of white athletes (Mastro et al., 2011). Both sports news and commentary often frame Black athletes as unintelligent but naturally gifted athletes (Angelini et al., 2014; Rada & Wulfemeyer, 2005). Notably, those same sports media outlets depict white athletes as intelligent but less athletic.

Hispanic and Latinx Americans. Hispanic and Latinx people made up 18.5% of the population in the United States in 2019 (U.S. Census Bureau, n.d.), but they were grossly underrepresented in scripted shows across broadcast (5.3%), cable (6.3%), and digital (5.7%) during the 2018–2019 television season (Hunt & Ramón, 2020b). The percentage of Latinx characters in lead roles averages 6% across broadcast, cable, and digital. Furthermore, Latinx people are vastly underrepresented in all TV genres (Nielsen, 2020a).

Although Latinx characters have been seen in more multidimensional roles on entertainment media, there is continued use of long-held stereotypes (Mastro & Do, 2020). These include the "Latin lover" and Latinas employed as maids/housekeepers. Many Latinx characters occupy jobs with lower professional status and are hypersexualized on primetime television (Tukachinsky et al., 2015). In fact, almost one in four Latinx characters were very sexual (24.1%), compared to only 7.6% for Blacks and 11.8% for Asians. Latinx characters also are generally represented as less intelligent, less articulate, and lazier than other characters (Mastro & Behm-Morawitz, 2005).

Quantitative analyses of network and cable news coverage reveals that Latinx people are grossly *overrepresented* as both immigrants and undocumented crime suspects, compared to data from the U.S. government. Latinxs are seldom seen as authorities or experts (see Mastro & Do, 2020, for a review). Earlier research found Latinx people were underrepresented in news as perpetrators, victims, and police officers (Dixon & Linz, 2000a, 2000b). In a more recent duplication of those earlier studies, representations were still the same for victims and officers, but the number of perpetrators was correctly represented (Dixon, 2017b).

Asian Americans. Regarding Asian representation on television, Asian characters made up 5.6% of roles on broadcast, 2.5% on cable, and 4.8% on digital during the 2018–2019 season (Hunt & Ramón, 2020b). In reality, they make up almost 6% of the population in the United States (U.S. Census Bureau, n.d.).

In the 1987–1989 and 1991–1993 TV seasons, there were no recurring Asian characters on the most-watched primetime shows (Tukachinsky et al., 2015). Today, only about 2% of lead characters on broadcast, cable, and digital programs are of Asian descent (Hunt & Ramón, 2020b). Asian characters have representation above parity in both sci-fi and drama series and less on comedy and reality shows (Nielsen, 2020).

Native and Multiracial Representation. Native people are virtually absent on television. In Hunt and Ramón's (2020b) recent head count study (which defined Native people as Native Americans, Native Hawaiians, and Native New Zealanders), Native people made up 0.5% or less of characters seen on television. From 2017 to 2019, no lead characters on scripted broadcast, cable, or digital shows were Native. In an earlier study of more than 2,300 regular television characters across 12 seasons between 1987 and 2009, there were only three Native American characters (Tukachinsky et al., 2015). Although still underrepresented, Native American males had the most on-screen visibility in TV shows on streaming platforms in 2019 (Nielsen, 2020a). And there is hope for more representation in coming television seasons as more offerings are being developed with Native American characters (Oliver, 2021). Roughly 9% of characters fell into the multiracial category during the 2018–2019 season (Hunt & Ramón, 2020b). According to U.S. census data, only 2.8% of the population identified as multiracial in 2019.

Film

From 2011 to 2019, the overall racial and ethnic diversity in films increased (Hunt & Ramón, 2020a). Notably, there has been a drastic decline—from 51.2% in 2011 to 15.9% in 2019—in the least diverse films (those with less than 11% minorities). Smith et al. (2020) examined more than 3,800 speaking or named roles in the top 100 films from 2019. White characters made up the largest percentage (65.7%), followed by Black (15.7%), Asian (7.2%), Latinx (4.9%), multiracial/multiethnic (4.4%), and Middle Eastern/North African (1.6%) characters. American Indian/Alaskan Natives and Native Hawaiian/Pacific Islanders each made up less than 1%. In 15 of the movies, there were no Black speaking characters. Latinx and Asian speaking characters were left out of even more films (44 and 36, respectively).

A recent study looked at the representation of Asian and Pacific Islanders (API) in 1,300 popular films from 2007 to 2019 (Yuen et al., 2021). Only 44 (3.4%) had an API lead or co-lead—and nearly a third of those roles were played by Dwayne Johnson. Of the 79 primary or secondary API characters in the top 100 films of 2019, 67% were depicted stereotypically, including being a "perpetual foreigner," emasculated, or the target of a racist or sexist slur. Furthermore, a quarter of those API characters died by the end of the film, and all but one of the deaths was coded as violent.

Dwayne Johnson starred in almost a third of the limited number of films in which the lead character was Asian or Pacific Islander.

In recent years, there have been several high-profile films that have featured predominately minority casts: the Marvel superhero blockbusters *Black Panther* and *Shang-Chi and the Legend of the Ten Rings* and Best Picture Oscar winners *Moonlight* and *Parasite*. Disney's 60th animated feature film, *Encanto*, celebrates the culture of Colombia. "The fact that it was an all-Latinx Disney movie . . . I never thought I'd see this in my lifetime," said actor John Leguizamo (Song, 2021, para. 4). However, some films with minority casts are still criticized for how they represent minorities. For instance, *Crazy Rich Asians* and *In the Heights* were criticized for not being diverse enough in their depictions of Asian and Afro-Latinx characters, respectively (Shafer, 2021; Tseng-Putterman, 2018).

Diversity on the Cover of *Sports Illustrated Swimsuit* Issues

Naomi Osaka was one of three groundbreaking models on the covers of *SI Swimsuit* in 2021, marking the first time that a Black athlete appeared on the cover.

During the 1990s, a number of Black women achieved the status of supermodel and now enjoy enormous visibility. For instance, Tyra Banks broke the *Sports Illustrated* color barrier by being the first Black woman to make the cover of the swimsuit issue in 1996; however, she shared the cover with a white model. The following year, Tyra was the solo model on the cover. A decade later, Beyoncé became the second Black woman to grace the cover when she was chosen for the 2007 edition.

In recent years, *Sports Illustrated Swimsuit* has included more diverse women on its covers, and the magazine now prints multiple covers for its annual swimsuit issue. For instance, 2021 marked the first time for a Black athlete (Naomi Osaka, whose father is Haitian and mother is Japanese), rapper (Megan Thee Stallion), and transgender woman (Leyna Bloom) to appear on covers of *SI Swimsuit* (Lippe-McGraw, 2021). Bloom was also the first trans woman of color to be included in a swimsuit issue.

Advertising

Diversity continues to be an area of concern in advertising. A majority of American adults (61%) say diversity is important in advertising, and 38% of consumers reported being more likely to trust brands that include more diversity in their advertising (Adobe, 2019). However, 66% of Black Americans and 53% of Latinx Americans reported that their ethnic identities are often portrayed in stereotypical ways in advertising. Advertisers are also paying attention to diverse representation on TV shows before buying ad time. For instance, more than 80% of the top advertisers in 2019 purchased ad time on programs that were inclusive for both Black women and LGBTQ talent (Nielsen, 2020a).

Much of the research in this area has focused on representation in magazines. The use of Black models increased in major magazines toward the end of the 20th century; however, Hispanic and Asian models still rarely appeared (Bowen & Schmid, 1997). Blacks were usually depicted as athletes or musicians. Later studies found that representations of Black women were becoming increasingly diverse (Baker, 2005; Covert & Dixon, 2008). However, when Black women appear in ads targeting both Black and mainstream consumers, they tend to have Eurocentric features rather than Afrocentric ones (Baker, 2005). Black men were often characterized as either athletic or unemployed (Bailey, 2006).

An analysis of ads from 10 popular U.S. magazines from 1994 to 2004 (e.g., *Reader's Digest, Better Homes & Gardens*, and *People*) found that Blacks, Hispanics, and Asians were overrepresented when compared to the population (Peterson, 2007). The majority of models were white, but their percentage decreased over time. Although Asians were overrepresented, they were still far less likely to be seen compared to models of other races. A later study of popular men's and women's magazines from the early 2010s revealed that white models were still much more likely to be seen than minorities, with Asians still being the least likely to be pictured (Schug et al., 2017). Overall, Asians accounted for only 2% of the models seen in ads—less than half of their percentage of the U.S. population at the time. When Blacks or Asians were shown, Black women and Asian men were underrepresented relative to Black men and Asian women. The researchers said these findings support the argument "that stereotypes about race are gendered, with Asians stereotyped as more feminine and Blacks as masculine" (p. 229). Gender stereotypes will be discussed later in this chapter.

Harrison et al. (2017) studied representations of multiracial female models in ads in eight popular U.S. magazines (i.e., *Ebony, Time, Cosmopolitan, Ladies' Home Journal, GQ, People, Vogue*, and *Rolling Stone*); mixed-race women were virtually absent in prominent social roles at work or home. In fact, only one out of the 61 ads analyzed presented a mixed-race woman in a professional setting, and only two pictured them as wives, mothers, or in a family setting. Mixed-race female models were seen in six ads depicting public life, but they were primarily members of a group of friends, with a white woman typically the focus of the ad. The researchers also noted that "most of the depictions are objectifying in nature, focusing on the women as presented objects or fun accomplices, as opposed to women engaged in more active social roles" (p. 511).

Television advertising has traditionally underrepresented both Hispanic and Asian Americans (Coltrane & Messineo, 2000; Mastro & Stern, 2003). Asian Americans were usually presented as passive in nature and placed most often in ads for technology products and services (Mastro & Stern, 2003). Other research has found that Asian models often interacted with new technology on video game ads and covers (Burgess et al., 2011). When Hispanics do appear in TV advertisements, they are more likely than other characters to be provocatively dressed and sexualized (Mastro & Stern, 2003). A more recent analysis indicated that Latinx people are still significantly underrepresented in TV advertising (Brooks et al., 2016). A study of commercials airing on Nickelodeon revealed that, compared to U.S. census data, Blacks and

Asians were overrepresented, Latinx people were severely underrepresented, and Native and Indigenous people were absent (Peruta & Powers, 2017). Notably, this study found that presenters in the commercials, no matter their race or ethnicity, were depicted favorably without stereotypical characteristics.

RESEARCH SPOTLIGHT

Television Viewing and Ethnic Stereotypes: Do College Students Form Stereotypical Perceptions of Ethnic Groups as a Result of Heavy Television Consumption?

Moon J. Lee, Shannon L. Bichard, Meagan S. Irey, Heather M. Walt, and Alana J. Carlson (2009)
The Howard Journal of Communication, 20, 95–110

In this study, the researchers examined the relationship between television viewing and whether a viewer held stereotypical beliefs about different ethnic groups, particularly Caucasians, African Americans, Asians, Latino/Hispanics, and Native Americans. Previous research had identified common stereotypes associated with each of those ethnic groups, with Caucasians perceived as being intelligent, pleasant, and friendly, whereas African Americans were perceived as inferior, dishonest, and lazy. Asians were believed to be highly educated and soft-spoken, while Latinos were thought of as hard workers, antagonistic, and unlikely to go to college. Native Americans were generally thought to be lazy, uneducated, out of work, and on welfare.

Research Questions

Based on social cognitive and cultivation theories that explain how people's thoughts and perceptions can be influenced by the images they see, the researchers formulated five questions to explore in relation to television viewing: Do heavy viewers of television hold primarily positive or negative perceptions (stereotypes) of (1) Caucasians, (2) Asians, (3) African Americans, (4) Latino/Hispanics, and (5) Native Americans?

Method

A total of 450 participants successfully took part in the study. Each participant completed a survey that assessed television consumption (independent variable) and its effect on ethnic stereotyping (dependent variable). Participants responded to questions about what type of television shows they watched (i.e., entertainment, drama, educational, informational, sports, reality, and soap operas) in addition to indicating how many hours of television they watched. Based on viewing hours per week, participants were divided into light viewer (14 or less hours a week) or heavy viewer (15 or more hours a week) categories.

To measure participants' stereotypes, personal beliefs about different ethnic groups were rated on a bi-polar adjectives scale. This scale featured 10 pairs of descriptors—shy and outgoing, lazy and hardworking, vengeful and forgiving, and so forth. Participants rated members of each ethnic group on a seven-point scale, aligning them closer to one of the adjectives in each pairing.

Results

Viewers overwhelmingly reported positive perceptions of Caucasians. Heavy viewers rated Caucasians as more dependable, stable, and less angry.

When examining stereotypes about Asians, heavy television viewers appeared to hold more negative perceptions of Asians than did light viewers. Overall, heavy viewers rated Asians as being less warm, less responsible, and more nervous than did light viewers. (The researchers noted that perhaps Asians' quiet demeanor conveys a lack of warmth and cooperation.)

Heavy television viewers, especially of entertainment shows, rated African Americans as less agreeable and less extroverted than did light viewers. However, heavy viewers of informational programming and reality television rated African Americans as more open and less neurotic, respectively. The researchers said these findings indicate that entertainment programs may present African Americans more negatively, whereas more realistic or informational programs may try to portray them more positively.

Regarding Latinos, there was little variation in responses from heavy and light viewers. The only significant difference was that heavy viewers of sports programs rated Latinos as more agreeable (i.e., cooperative and fair) but less extroverted and less assertive than did light viewers.

For Native American stereotypes, heavy television viewers reported a significant increase in negative characteristics (i.e., less open, less conscientious, and less extroverted) than did light viewers. Ultimately, heavy viewers held mainly negative stereotypes of Native Americans.

Discussion

Overall, heavy viewers of television reported holding more negative stereotypes for every ethnicity. Asians and Native Americans were perceived the most negatively, with heavy viewers associating them with only negative stereotypes.

Heavy viewers of entertainment, educational, and sports programming held more negative stereotypes overall, while heavy viewers of information programming tended to have more positive perceptions.

Although this study does not establish a causal link between television viewing and holding ethnic stereotypes, it does indicate a relationship between the amount of television watched (both in terms of hours and programming type) and whether a viewer holds stereotypical ethnic views.

In line with social cognitive theory and cultivation, heavy television viewing does appear to relate directly to holding prejudicial stereotypes.

Characteristics of Minority Audiences

In addition to studying ethnic and racial representations in media, researchers continue to study how various demographic groups consume media, even in today's highly fragmented media environment. Audiences respond positively to diversity on screen. For instance, films with more diverse casts outperformed films with the least diverse casts at the global box office (Hunt & Ramón, 2020a). In 2019, the majority of movie tickets for eight of the top 10 films were purchased by people of color. In 2020, minorities purchased just over half (51%) of all movie tickets sold in North America (Motion Picture Association [MPA], 2021). On television, the trend of diverse audiences preferring diverse television content continues (Hunt & Ramón, 2020b). In this section, we will examine Black and Latinx audience characteristics, as well as review the limited data available for other minority audiences.

The Black Audience

Nielsen data reveal that Black people are among the heaviest viewers of television (Nielsen, 1998, 2019a). They watch considerably more television each week (50 hours and 38 minutes) compared to the total population (39 hours and 6 minutes). Earlier research found that television use in Black households can have implications for effects on children and adolescents (Botta, 2000; Brown et al., 1986; Greenberg & Linsangan, 1993). For example, Black children would be more vulnerable to negative effects from mass media in many ways if not properly supervised while viewing.

Studies through the years indicate that Black audiences enjoy watching Black characters on television (Eastman & Liss, 1980; Nielsen, 1998; Poindexter & Stroman, 1981). For instance, Rachel Lindsay's season of ABC's *The Bachelorette*, the first to focus on a Black person's search for love, sparked a 72% increase in Black viewership (Levin, 2017). Blacks make up much larger percentages of the viewing audience for many shows that feature Black casts, such as *Love and Hip Hop* (81%), *The Haves and Have Nots* (88%), and *Real Housewives of Atlanta* (61%). Research also highlights that Black audiences tend to select programs or avoid them based on the ethnicity of characters and to fulfill their needs for racial identity (Abrams & Giles, 2007).

At the U.S. box office, Black audiences see more movies per capita in theaters than white audiences, but fewer than Hispanic/Latinx and Asian audiences (MPA, 2020, 2021). Black moviegoers purchased 14% of tickets sold in the United States and Canada in 2020, up from 11% in 2019.

The Latinx Audience

Latinx consumers spend 29 hours and 28 minutes watching TV each week (Nielsen, 2019b). Compared to the U.S. population, Latinx media consumers are more likely to use their smartphones to access video content. For instance, "Latinx consumers were 59% more likely than the total population to have watched/downloaded a movie on their smartphone, 43% more likely to have used it to watch free TV shows, and 42% more likely to have watched subscription service content on it" (Nielsen, 2019b, p. 16).

The top TV genres for all Latinx age groups are participation variety (which includes reality shows), award ceremonies, and talk shows (Nielsen, 2019b). Daytime dramas, many of which are telenovelas, are popular with both younger and older Latinx viewers (Nielsen, 2019b). Latinx TV audiences, particularly Spanish speakers, like to share their live TV experiences in real time on social media, talking about both programming content and product placement.

At the theater, Hispanic/Latinx moviegoers see more movies per capita than any other racial or ethnic group in North America, and this was true both before and during the COVID-19 pandemic (MPA, 2020, 2021). They purchased 29% percent of movie tickets sold in 2020, up from 25% the year before.

Other Minority Audiences

Limited research has been done on the characteristics of other minority viewers. According to Nielsen (2020a), more Asian Americans (88%) subscribe to a streaming service compared to the total U.S. population (72%). Asian American moviegoers are second to Hispanic/Latinx audiences in movie attendance per capita (MPA, 2020, 2021). Asian Americans purchased 6% of movie tickets in 2020, down 1% from 2019.

As for Native Americans, because they lag behind the total population when it comes to adopting internet-connected devices (41% to 53%, respectively), both live TV and smartphones remain "critical gateways to content" (Nielsen, 2020b).

Gender Stereotyping

Where gender is concerned, gender schema theory is used (in addition to social cognitive theory and social identity theory) to explain media content effects. Recall from Chapter 5 that Fiske and Taylor (1991) defined a schema as "a cognitive structure that represents knowledge about a concept or type of stimulus, including its attributes and the relations among those attributes" (p. 98). Schemata about gender can affect the way people (especially children) process information in the real world and from the world of mass media.

Representations of Men and Women in Media

In an early study that examined 20 years of primetime television portrayals, women made up only 31.5% of all characters (Gerbner, 1997). Women have made gains since that study, but they are still underrepresented on television. Despite making up slightly more than half of the U.S. population, women made up 43.7% of all roles on broadcast, 45% of roles on cable, and 47.5% of roles on streaming scripted shows in the 2018–2019 season (Hunt & Ramón, 2020b). Women are also underrepresented in lead roles. Women only get 38% of screen time compared to 62% for men (Nielsen, 2020c). For women over 50, representation is even worse. Although they make up 20% of the population, they get only 8% of screen time.

Women have also historically been underrepresented in films—a trend which continues to this day. In one study that examined characters in movies released between 1990 and 2006, 73% of all characters were male (Smith & Cook, 2008). Women have made significant strides in lead roles—but have yet to reach parity with real world census data—going from 25.6% in 2011 to 44.1% in 2019 (Hunt & Ramón, 2020a). During 2019, women were vastly underrepresented in speaking roles in movies in the action/adventure (27.9%), animation (33.3%, and comedy (38.7%) genres (Smith et al., 2020). Male characters in films popular around the world spoke twice as much as female characters (Geena Davis Institute on Gender in Media, 2019).

Of course, women are also significantly underrepresented behind the camera. Of 1,300 films released between 2007 and 2019, only 57 had female directors, including Ava DuVernay, Greta Gerwig, Nancy Meyers, and Patty Jenkins (Smith et al., 2020). Some actresses have also transitioned into the director's chair, such as Angelina Jolie, Olivia Wilde, Roxann Dawson, and Jodie Foster. Looking specifically at films from 2019, women made up 10.7% of directors, 19.4% of writers, 24.3% of producers, and only 5.2% of composers.

Although women are greatly underrepresented in film and television, they have greater representation in advertising. In early research, women represented about 45% to 49% of the people seen in commercials (Coltrane & Messineo, 2000; Ganahl et al., 2003). The number women cast in lead roles in commercials has climbed—sometimes as high as 70% to almost 80% (Fowler & Thomas, 2015).

Sexuality & Romance

"One of the most consistent themes in Western media is that women are valued primarily for their bodies, primarily existing as sexual objects for others' sexual use"

(Aubrey & Yan, 2020, p. 82). When women appear in films, even G-rated ones, they are usually young and hypersexual (Bazzini et al., 1997; Herbozo et al., 2004). They are often scantily clad and featured as sex objects (Smith & Granados, 2009). Female characters in film and television are far more likely than male characters to be thin, wearing sexy clothing, exposing skin, and verbally or nonverbally labeled by another character as physically attractive or desirable (Smith et al., 2012).

You are no doubt familiar with the adage "sex sells." For many years, that was readily apparent in advertising with women far more likely to be sexualized than men (Ganahl et al., 2003; Stern & Mastro, 2004). A study of Spanish- and English-language ads found that women were often dressed revealingly, whereas men were usually fully dressed (Prieler, 2016). However, some longitudinal research suggests a decline in sexualized depictions of women in television advertising (Fowler & Thomas, 2015).

On the other hand, sexualization of women in music videos shows no signs of decreasing. One longitudinal study analyzed sexualization of women in music videos between 1995 and 2016, finding that sexualized poses, gestures, and facial expressions increased during those years (Karsay et al., 2019). Other content analyses of music videos have revealed that women are more likely than men to be more sexualized and objectified, to display more body parts, to dress more provocatively, and to engage in sexual dancing (Aubry & Frisby, 2011; Frisby & Aubrey, 2012; Turner, 2011).

Female characters in movies are more likely than male characters to be involved in romantic relationships (Smith et al., 2016; Xu et al., 2019) and be depicted as parents (Smith et al., 2020).

Occupational Status

Gendered portrayals of occupations play a role in creating stereotypes about what types of jobs are "appropriate" for men and women. "These stereotypes are especially salient for children and adolescents as they start to imagine themselves in the workforce. As young as fifth and sixth grade, media exposure seems to guide occupational preferences" (Aubrey & Yan, 2020, p. 80).

Advertising is more likely to feature women as homemakers and men as professionals (Furnham & Lay, 2019). Movies and primetime television also overrepresent women as homemakers (Sink & Mastro, 2017; Smith et al., 2010). In an analysis of the top films from 20 countries around the world, 42% of male characters were leaders compared to 27% of female characters (Geena Davis Institute, 2019). Female leaders were more likely than their male counterparts to be characterized as hard working and intelligent. However, they were also more likely than male leaders to wear provocative clothing, appear partially or completely nude, be objectified through the use of camera angles, experience verbal objectification by other characters, and be sexually harassed.

Female characters in family films (those rated G, PG, and PG-13) are rarely seen in powerful positions, such as CEOs, high level politicians, or financial investors (Smith et al., 2012). Moreover, older characters are more likely to be depicted as having powerful careers and as accomplished role models; however, older women are seen in films far less often than men (Smith et al., 2016). For instance, females in 2015 represented only 24.6% of adult characters age 40 or older. "Based on sheer frequency, viewers have far fewer chances to see talented women in influential occupations on screen" (Smith et al., 2016, p. 10).

Primetime television has been more successful at presenting women in positions of power (Smith et al., 2012). Examples of female characters in powerful leadership positions include Captain Olivia Benson on *Law & Order: SVU*, Dr. Meredith Grey and Dr. Miranda Bailey on *Grey's Anatomy*, Sergeant Athena Grant on *9-1-1*, and Captain Michael Burnham on *Star Trek: Discovery.*

Not only does the hit Fox series *9-1-1* feature a diverse cast but also the lead actress Angela Bassett's character, Sergeant Athena Grant, is a leader.

Effects of Gender Stereotypes

Viewing stereotypical depictions based on gender can have an effect on choice of occupation and attitudes toward particular occupations. Movies that expose children to "happily ever after" romantic scenarios may affect their relationships and expectations in life, and the "thin ideal" that is usually depicted in mass media can cause eating disorders, especially among females (Smith & Granados, 2009).

When characters are portrayed in counter-stereotypical ways, gender effects are diminished (e.g., Davidson et al., 1979; Davies et al., 2002; Flerx et al., 1976; Geis et al., 1984; Johnston & Ettema, 1982; Wroblewski & Huston, 1987). Children may be the most vulnerable to learning about sex role stereotypes. Parental or caregiver supervision can mitigate those negative effects (Smith & Granados, 2009).

Disney and Pixar Animating Gender

Many of the concerns about gender stereotyping involve children's media, and much of the scholarly attention is focused on Disney. Due to its global dominance, Disney has been the cornerstone of children's entertainment for decades. Gender stereotypes concern many researchers because "much of what children learn about the world outside of their immediate family and community comes from the media" (Bryant & Bryant, 2003, p. 204). In a review of the impact of entertainment media on children, Bryant and Bryant (2003) stated that media function as "potent agents of socialization" (p. 204), meaning that children tend to view reality according to what they see on television and movie screens.

Much of the research has focused on the types of stereotypes presented in Disney's classic animated films, and the presence of these stereotypes is not a coincidence. "Disney animation is not an innocent art form: nothing accidental or serendipitous occurs in animation as each *second* of action on screen is rendered in twenty-four different still paintings" (Bell, 1995, p. 108).

(continued)

A content analysis of 16 classic Disney films found that male characters outnumbered female characters 199 to 83, females performed more in-home labor than males, and males performed a much wider range of out-of-home jobs and held more positions of power than women (Wiersma, 2001). Characters also tended to align with commonly held ideas about femininity (i.e., women are passive, dependent, romantic, and emotional) and masculinity (i.e., men are aggressive, independent, unromantic, and unemotional).

Towbin et al. (2003) conducted a thematic analysis of 26 feature-length Disney films and identified the following themes about what it means to be a boy/man or girl/woman:

> (a) Men primarily use physical means to express their emotions or show no emotions; (b) men are not in control of their sexuality; (c) men are naturally strong and heroic; (d) men have nondomestic jobs; and (e) overweight men have negative characteristics. (p. 28)

> (a) A woman's appearance is valued more than her intellect; (b) women are helpless and in need of protection; (c) women are domestic and likely to marry; (d) overweight women are ugly, unpleasant, and unmarried. (p. 30)

Disney's role as a "cultural narrator" (Brydon, 2009, p. 143) expands beyond its own film catalog. Disney's prominence and dominance in the entertainment industry sets the standard for other animation studios. "The work of the Disney studios defines the gender norm for the rest of the cartoon world" (Abel, 1995, p. 185). After partnering with Disney in 1991 (and later being bought by Disney in 2006), Pixar was essentially able to use the Disney brand as a "stamp of approval, signifying that this new form of animation met the same standards of excellence and wholesomeness in family entertainment associated with Disney" (Brookey & Westerfelhaus, 2005).

Despite Pixar's dominance in children's animation, far less research has focused on Pixar and the possible gender stereotypes in its movies compared to the vast body of literature exploring Disney films. Much of the research that has been done has examined male characters, because until 2012's *Brave*, all of Pixar's films featured male protagonists. Gillam and Wooden (2008) noted a common narrative thread for male protagonists in Pixar's *Toy Story*, *The Incredibles*, and *Cars*, where alpha-male characters are emasculated, giving them the opportunity to learn what it means to be a kinder, gentler man. The characters in the three films (e.g., Woody, Buzz Lightyear, Mr. Incredible, and Lightning McQueen) are examples of the "New Man."

Finklea (2011a) examined themes of masculinity in the first three *Toy Story* films; Pixar's "New Man" narrative had crossed over into the *Toy Story* sequels. Finklea (2014) then expanded his analysis to include the first 13 feature-length Pixar films, finding six major themes about masculinities:

> (1) Males are successful when taking part in teamwork, (2) males are naturally brave, (3) male romantic interest manifests as heterosexual desire, (4) males desire to be loved and/or needed, (5) males who are fathers or paternal figures express fears about the future, and (6) male bosses are predominantly shown as greedy and driven solely by profit. (pp. 68–69)

Ultimately, these films are moving away from traditional gender stereotypes; however, there is still room for improvement. This is especially true for depictions of female characters (Finklea, 2017b; Finklea & Hardig, 2016), although there have been some promising characterizations in films like *Inside Out*, *Incredibles 2*, and *Toy Story 4*. And even when non-stereotypical male protagonists (e.g., Flik the ant from *A Bug's Life* and WALL-E the lonely robotic trash compactor) are depicted as subservient to female characters, they still exert a great deal of influence over females in positions of power (Finklea, 2017b). Perhaps the most non-stereotypical male in a Pixar film is Ken in *Toy Story 3*, but his notably feminine portrayal of masculinity is ultimately criticized and rejected as abnormal in the film's final moments (Finklea, 2011a, 2014).

Effects of Media Stereotypes

The studies that describe mass media content provide interesting data and take a step toward answering the questions: Are minority portrayals sending accurate and fair pictures to the American public? Are interactions among minority and majority characters promoting pictures of racial harmony or of racial conflict? Such studies, however, do very little to answer other important questions. For example: What effects do stereotypical minority portrayals have on minority and majority audiences? What effects do such portrayals have on children of all colors? As Ramasubramanian (2010) notes, "The presence of negative images of racial/ethnic outgroups in the media is certainly disturbing, but the ways in which these depictions influence viewers' real-life attitudes toward racial/ethnic outgroups is far more significant" (p. 106).

Scientific understanding of the effects of media stereotypes has increased significantly in recent decades (Dixon, 2020). You will recall that in previous chapters we discussed social cognitive theory, priming, and cultivation and their underlying importance in understanding much of the research on media effects. These theories lie at the heart of research that examines the effects of minority portrayals in mass media. Social learning theory posits that individuals learn from what they see in the media. Children especially are likely to pick up attitudes and behaviors by viewing situations, actions, and interactions on television and in other media. Minority portrayals have the potential to educate children about race relations, for better or for worse.

Priming Studies

Many priming studies have examined how exposure to minority stereotypes (such as thinking that Blacks are criminals and Hispanics/Latinxs are sensual) can have a short-term effect on audiences, especially majority audiences, and their evaluations of minorities in the real world (Dixon, 2006, 2007; Givens & Monahan, 2005). Other priming studies have found that stereotypical portrayals in mass media cause white audience members to respond to those stereotypes in their evaluations of minorities (Gilliam & Iyengar, 2000; Mendelberg, 1997). Even a single exposure to a mediated stereotype is enough to activate mental connections between a particular group and stereotyped characteristics and traits (Dixon, 2007; Gilliam et al., 1996; Peffley et al., 1996).

Whenever stereotypes are primed in depictions of crime, majority audiences blamed dispositional factors—such as being more prone to criminality—as the reason that Black perpetrators committed a crime—but for white perpetrators, they blamed situational aspects (Johnson et al., 1997). Whenever racial cues are implied in news stories visually, white audiences are reminded of racial stereotypes (Abraham & Appiah, 2006). When (mostly white) audiences are exposed to "the Black criminal" stereotype, they then make harsher judgments against other criminal suspects and increase their support for conservative policies (Dixon, 2006; Gilliam & Iyengar, 2000; Hurley et al., 2015).

In one study when white audiences were presented with a dark-skinned Black perpetrator, they expressed more sympathy for the victim of the crime (Dixon & Maddox, 2005). Another study indicated that news stories about crime and welfare are expected to involve race, and coverage of these areas causes stereotypes to be activated in the mind of the viewer (Valentino, 1999).

Other research has examined the effects of priming people with the "Black female jezebel" stereotype, which resulted in lower support for a subsequent hypothetical Black female job applicant or welfare recipient (Givens & Monahan, 2005; Monahan et al., 2005; also see Chapter 5's Research Spotlight). Priming the "model minority" stereotype for Asian Americans resulted in white audiences having more positive perceptions of them, while generating negative stereotypical perceptions of African Americans (Dalisay & Tan, 2009).

Other studies reveal that whenever mass media news stories contain positive information about minorities and present counter-stereotypical behavior, whites respond with more positive judgments about race and increased perception of discriminatory practices (Bodenhausen et al., 1995; Power et al., 1996).

Although priming studies tell us much about what thoughts are prompted in the short term, researchers are also interested in long-term effects of media stereotypes. Long-term exposure to stereotypical portrayals of Blacks results in subtle discriminatory thoughts among whites (Gorham, 2006). In other words, when Blacks are repeatedly depicted as criminals on news reports, whites are repeatedly primed to think of "them" as criminals. The accessibility of these constructs in memory results in strengthening the stereotypical image (Dixon & Azocar, 2007).

Cultivation Studies

Cultivation studies have been conducted in the area of stereotyping among white audiences. Recall that cultivation looks at long-term effects of repeated exposure to media content. As we discussed in Chapter 8, repeated exposure to certain mediated messages—in this case, stereotypes—can result in chronic accessibility of those stereotypes. In several studies, whites who are heavy consumers of television news tend to stereotype Blacks as being lower in socioeconomic status because of lack of initiative rather than lack of opportunity (e.g., Armstrong et al., 1992; Busselle & Crandall, 2002). Long-term exposure to news content among mostly white audiences leads to greater support for conservative policies on crime (Dixon, 2008a, 2008b; Gilliam & Iyengar, 2000). Stereotypical information about a shooting affects how blame is attributed (Dukes & Gaither, 2017). If the victim is presented in a negative light, not only will there be less sympathy for the victim but also an increased assessment of some responsibility for the crime. Other recent research suggests that daily TV viewing for largely white audiences cultivates anxiety toward Asian people (Atwell Seate et al., 2018).

One cultivation study found that white audiences who were heavy viewers of television cultivated attitudes in line with stereotypical portrayals of Hispanics (Mastro et al., 2007). Interestingly, real-world contact with Hispanics tended to lessen the cultivation effects. In other words, those who had contact with Hispanics in the real world were less likely to have stereotypical views of Hispanics than those exposed only to portrayals of Hispanics on television.

Heavy viewing of stereotypical portrayals of minorities on television can influence white viewers' voting and public policy decisions (Mendelberg, 1997; Valentino, 1999). Whites who were heavy viewers of stereotypical televised portrayals of minorities were impacted negatively, and their views caused them to be less supportive of affirmative action or other policies to address discrimination (Mastro & Kopacz, 2006; Ramasubramanian, 2011; Tan et al., 2000).

Social Categorization Theory and Social Identity Theory

A growing body of research indicates that a person's group identity can not only determine their media consumption but also what potential effects they may experience (Atwell Seate et al., 2012; Fujioka, 2005; Harwood, 1997; Mastro, 2003). Some audience members might be more vulnerable to media effects than others.

For instance, social categorization theory "argues that the higher the salience (e.g., importance) of a particular category to an individual, the greater the ingroup favoritism he or she will demonstrate" (Dixon, 2020, p. 249). Individuals who identify highly with their race or ethnic group tend to form more stereotypical attitudes toward those outside of their group, and they feel more favorably toward those in their group (Mastro, 2003). Meanwhile, "social identity theory suggests that the desire to maintain group dominance is at the heart of misrepresentations of outgroup members in popular culture" (Ramasubramanian, 2010, p. 104).

Effects on White Media Consumers.   Mastro and her associates have conducted much of the research examining effects of media stereotyping—a fact substantiated by the high number of citations for Mastro throughout this chapter. In her 2017 study with Atwell Seate, they found that when people who identify strongly with their ingroup were exposed to stories about immigrant threats, they expressed both active and passive harming behaviors toward immigrants through feelings of contempt. Dixon (2020) summarized their findings: "These authors used social identity/social categorization theory to advance the notion of intergroup emotions that might result from such media exposure. This notion states that group members with high group identification levels will experience the same emotions" (p. 250). If mediated depictions of minorities repeatedly elicit negative emotions (e.g., anger, fear, dislike, nervousness), "such feelings become strongly entrenched in the memory structure, making them accessible when evaluating feelings toward these racial outgroups in the real world" (Ramasubramanian, 2010, p. 116).

In an earlier study, white viewers exposed to Latino criminals in a fictitious TV show reported greater self-esteem (Mastro, 2003). When they were exposed to a white criminal, they offered more justifications for the criminal's behavior. Other research has also explored the role of social identity and racial stereotypes. For instance, Ramasubramanian (2010) studied the effects of Black and Latino stereotypes on white TV viewers and their attitudes toward affirmative action policies. White viewers associated both African Americans and Latino Americans on television with themes of criminality and laziness. Furthermore, "as perceived negative televised stereotyping of outgroups increased, negative real-world stereotypical beliefs increased, feelings of hostility increased, and support for affirmative action decreased" (p. 115).

White audiences' attitudes toward Black and Latinx TV characters are affected by both the quantity and *quality* of minority representation (Tukachinsky et al., 2015). The presence of hyper-sexualized Black and Latinx characters was associated with negative attitudes about Black and Latinx people in the United States. However, when Blacks and Latinx characters were depicted as having high professional and social status, white audiences tended to have more favorable views toward them. "The results illuminate the importance of improving the quality of representations of ethnic minorities, rather than merely increasing the sheer number of these characters in the media" (p. 33).

Effects on Minority Media Consumers.   Most of the research on stereotyping has studied how white media consumers react to minority portrayals, but a growing number of studies have helped answer the question of how minorities themselves react to stereotyped portrayals of their own groups. As discussed earlier in this chapter, both Black and Latinx people are heavy media consumers. When exposed to negative portrayals of Blacks on primetime TV, Black audiences' favorable characterizations and warm feelings toward Black people decreased (Tukachinsky et al., 2017).

Media that targets racial or ethnic groups can strongly influence audiences of color. For instance, when Black adolescents watch films with mostly Black casts, they report more aggression, sexual activity, and alcohol use compared to those who saw mainstream movies (Bleakley, Ellithorpe, Hennessy, Jamieson, et al., 2017). Consuming mainstream television reduced adolescents' support of mainstream gender roles, specifically for boys (Anyiwo et al., 2018). Black-oriented shows resulted in greater endorsement of the strong Black woman role (i.e., a Black woman who is independent, emotionally strong, and self-sacrificing). As Weeks et al. (2020) conclude, "While mainstream media affect perceptions about ingroup attitudes, Black-oriented media relate to Black behavioral learning" (p. 104).

Ethnicity can be an important variable in understanding the potential effects that rap music can have on Black audiences. "For instance, Black women with strong ethnic identification (e.g., the belief that Black women are beautiful) showed fewer negative effects (e.g., body dissatisfaction) after viewing thin models in music videos compared to Black women with weak ethnic identification" (Dixon, 2020, p. 250).

Researchers have theorized that exposure to stereotypic portrayals would cause lessening of self-esteem among minority audiences, but results have been mixed. Fryberg (2003) did find that Native Americans reacted to stereotypical portrayals of Native Americans on television with decreased self-esteem. Subervi-Vélez and Necochea (1990) studied Hispanic elementary children and found that their self-esteem measures were not affected by viewing either English-speaking or Spanish-speaking television. Rivadeneyra et al. (2007) conducted two studies to see if media exposure affected Latinx high school and college students' self-esteem. Greater exposure to specific TV genres and other forms of media (e.g., magazines, movies, music) were associated with lower self-esteem. For instance, there were consistent negative correlations with self-esteem for Latina college students with active media use and exposure to popular primetime shows.

> In addition, frequent exposure to popular magazines and English-language soaps was each associated with significantly lower social self-esteem. Among the men, only two significant correlations emerged. Here, frequent movie viewing was associated with lower social self-esteem, and stronger identification with popular TV characters was associated with lower appearance self-esteem. (p. 279)

These effects may be particularly detrimental to students who strongly identify with their Latinx heritage.

Summary

Since the 1960s, portrayals of minority characters in mass media, particularly on television and in film, have reflected societal changes. These changes in portrayals and, especially, their effects upon audiences' attitudes, values, and behaviors, are of particular interest to communication researchers.

Studies of the 1990s showed that Blacks achieved very positive gains in both the number and the nature of their portrayals in entertainment programs, but other minorities did not fare so well. Latinxs, Asian Americans, Native Americans, and women were underrepresented in mass media, sometimes to the point of exclusion. When these groups were depicted, it was sometimes in stereotypical or demeaning ways.

Across all types of media, whites have made up the largest percentage of characters and models. However, there has been some progress in racial and ethnic diversity in media content; although some groups, particularly Native Americans, continue to be almost entirely absent from mass media. Women have become more prominent in media, particularly film and television, but remain underrepresented compared to the percentage of women in the real world.

The evidence for the effects of minority portrayals on both majority and minority audiences reveals that some audience members might be more vulnerable to media effects than others. Individuals who identify highly with their race or ethnic group tend to form more stereotypical attitudes toward those outside of their group, and they feel more favorably toward those in their group.

Racial, ethnic, and gender stereotypes color media presentations, despite signs of progress. Much work remains to ensure that the media world to which audiences are exposed more accurately reflects the increasingly diverse world in which we live.

17

Effects of Children's Educational Media

> Television is teaching all the time. It does more educating than the schools and all the institutions of higher learning.
>
> —Marshall McLuhan

Many of you, no doubt, grew up watching countless hours of *Sesame Street*, *Dora the Explorer*, *Blue's Clues*, *Barney & Friends*, and any of the other numerous shows marketed to children and their parents as "educational television" or "edutainment." Often when discussing the effects of television on children, critics and parenting groups focus on the negative effects of viewing; however, many of these so-called effects— such as shorter attention spans, apathy toward school, and the fear of children becoming mindless "zombie viewers" (e.g., Healy, 1990; Postman, 1985; Winn, 1977)—are seldom backed by scientific evidence (Fisch, 2009). In an examination of attention and television watching, Newman (2010) highlighted a paradox commonly voiced by critics—television holds attention so well that it destroys the ability to pay attention. Even if media consumption was able to turn children into zombie viewers, Newman commented that at least they will be "zombies who count and spell" (p. 589).

There is, in fact, a large body of research that highlights the positive effects of children's educational media, which we will explore in this chapter. We also examine the big business of infant-targeted media, such as *Baby Einstein* and *Brainy Baby*, and the research that tries to determine what—if anything—these very young children learn from such media. Today's children are growing up in homes that have more screens than ever before, and we review the research conducted on the effects of print versus e-books and interactive versus passive media.

Educational Television

Research examining educational television has primarily focused on two key areas: (1) preschool programming's impact on school readiness, and (2) school-age programming's effects on literacy, math and problem solving, science, and social studies.

School Readiness

When talking about school readiness, we need to keep in mind that the term is not limited solely to knowledge and learning skills (Fisch, 2009). According to the Early Childhood Learning and Knowledge Center (2020), "Physical, cognitive, social, and emotional development are all essential ingredients of school readiness" (para. 1). For more than 50 years, one of the most influential shows that promotes both academic and interpersonal skills is *Sesame Street*. In fact, "the most frequently researched television program in the world has been *Sesame Street* (and its international co-productions), which in the United States targets children ages two to five" (Jordan & Vaala, 2020, p. 292).

Since 1969, *Sesame Street* has provided families with high-quality educational content that covers a variety of topics. A lot of research and planning went into the creation of the program. Both academic researchers and television producers worked together to create a curriculum that would emphasize cognitive development through short segments and skits, songs, and "Muppet-filled fun" (Akerman et al., 2011, p. 208). Shortly after the show debuted, researchers began to investigate Big Bird, Mr. Snuffleupagus, and Count von Count's ability to teach young children.

A pair of studies conducted in the early 1970s tested children's knowledge before watching *Sesame Street* (a **pretest**) and again after watching the show (a **posttest**) (Ball & Bogatz, 1970; Bogatz & Ball, 1971). The control group of children did not watch the program at all. Children who watched more *Sesame Street* content exhibited significantly higher knowledge gains for several academic skills, such as identifying numbers, letters, shapes, and body parts. Similar positive effects have also been seen in children watching international versions of *Sesame Street* in countries like Mexico, Russia, Portugal, and Turkey (Fisch, 2009).

A stage show featuring some Muppet "residents" of *Sesame Street* helps young children learn about and deal with the challenges of military life.

Whereas these studies indicate knowledge gains over a relatively short time period, what about the long-term effects of *Sesame Street* viewing? Part of Bogatz and Ball's 1971 study was to perform a follow-up on some of the children from the first study (i.e., Ball & Bogatz, 1970). The researchers had teachers rate their students on several school readiness skills, including language and math, attitude about school, and how they interacted with their classmates. The teachers, who did not know which children had watched *Sesame Street* most frequently, rated the heavier viewers as more prepared for school compared to the lighter viewers. Studies conducted decades later had similar results, with teachers rating *Sesame Street* viewers as better prepared for school (Wright & Huston, 1995; Wright et al., 2001). A correlational analysis of data collected from approximately 10,000 children by the U.S. Department of Education's National Household Survey found that preschool-aged *Sesame Street* viewers performed better at recognizing letters of the alphabet and telling coherent stories while pretending to read; meanwhile, first and second graders who viewed *Sesame Street* as preschoolers were more apt to read books on their own and less likely to need remedial reading help (Zill, 2001; Zill et al., 1994).

A 2013 meta-analysis synthesized the results of 24 studies of *Sesame Street*. Combined, the studies included more than 10,000 children in 15 countries. There were significant effects related to exposure to *Sesame Street* programming across a variety of learning outcomes. "The significant, positive effects on cognitive, learning, and socio-emotional outcomes observed in the current meta-analysis represent real educational benefits for the millions of preschool-age children around the world who visit *Sesame Street* via their televisions" (Mares & Pan, 2013, p. 149).

The effects of *Sesame Street* go far beyond the first years of elementary school. In fact, *Sesame Street* viewing as a preschooler impacts a student's performance in *high school*! Students in grades 9 through 12 who watched more *Sesame Street* as a child had higher grades and academic self-esteem, exhibited a higher drive to perform well in class, and read more books than did nonviewers (Anderson et al., 1998; Huston et al., 2001).

Of course, *Sesame Street* is not the only show that helps promote school readiness in preschoolers. *Barney & Friends*, *Dragon Tales*, and *Blue's Clues* impact important aspects of school readiness: knowledge, flexible thinking, willingness to pursue challenges, initiating play with others, and problem-solving skills (Fisch, 2009). Watching *Daniel Tiger's Neighborhood*, a spin-off of *Mr. Rogers' Neighborhood*, can be beneficial for preschoolers' social and emotional development (Rasmussen et al., 2016). When viewing *Daniel Tiger's Neighborhood* was accompanied by frequent active mediation (i.e., conversations between parents and children specifically about media content), preschoolers displayed higher levels of empathy, emotion recognition, and self-efficacy. This effect was especially seen in younger preschool children and in those from low-income families.

Although many of you may cringe when you think of Barney singing the theme song to the show ("I love you. You love me. We're a happy family . . ."), the big purple dinosaur's sing-song approach to teaching did help some children (mostly white, middle-class 3- and 4-year-olds) improve their ability to count and identify colors, while also improving their vocabulary knowledge about places in their neighborhood (Singer & Singer, 1994). However, it did not improve scores for identifying shapes or understanding emotions. When the study was replicated with a diverse sample that included more minorities and working-class children, the researchers observed only a very small benefit to watching *Barney* (Singer & Singer, 1995). However, there were additional benefits if the children were presented with follow-up lessons about the material seen in the 10 episodes that were part of the study.

Watching PBS's *Dragon Tales* (an animated series about two siblings who help a group of dragons) improved children's interpersonal skills. Viewers were more likely to ask others to engage in organized play and to choose challenging tasks (Rust, 2001). Viewers of *Dragon Tales* also exhibited more spontaneity and goal-oriented play.

Other shows, especially older series that were once staples in Nickelodeon's "Nick Jr." program schedule, improve children's problem-solving skills, allowing them to better "think outside the box." Children who watched *Allegra's Window* and *Gullah Gullah Island* performed significantly better on hands-on problem-solving tasks than did nonviewers (Mulliken & Bryant, 1999), and caregivers rated children as having greater flexible thinking skills (e.g., looking at a problem from different points of view, being curious) and problem-solving abilities (e.g., using different methods to solve a problem, focusing on the task at hand, not giving up) (Bryant et al., 1997).

One of the most enduring Nick Jr. shows that has had a positive impact on children is *Blue's Clues*. Each episode features the animated female dog Blue and her live-action human companion solving a simple three-part puzzle. They find clues marked with Blue's paw print and write the clues down in their "handy, dandy notebook." Characters speak directly to viewers, asking them to participate by helping to spot Blue's clues and trying to solve the puzzle. The show's

> "think along, play along style" encouraged preschoolers to use higher order cognitive skills . . . [such as] sorting; categorizing and classifying; differentiating and discriminating; predicting and anticipating; what happened and why; ordering and sequencing; patterning; matching; inferential problem solving; associating; analogies; and relational concepts. (Akerman et al., 2011, p. 212)

The catchy sing-along segments of *Blue's Clues* and its audience interactions entertain children while building their self-esteem.

Bryant et al. (1999) and Anderson et al. (2000) researched the effectiveness of *Blue's Clues*. When presented with puzzles identical to the ones in specific episodes of the show, children who watched *Blue's Clues* gave a significantly higher number of correct answers compared to children who did not watch the show. In addition to solving show-specific puzzles, *Blue's Clues* viewers were able to correctly solve simple riddles not related to the show at a significantly higher rate compared to nonviewers, demonstrating an improvement in problem-solving skills.

Nickelodeon revived *Blue's Clues* in 2019 and introduced Josh Dela Cruz as Blue's new human caretaker.

Dora the Explorer is one of the most recognizable children's show characters in recent decades.

Yet another mainstay in the educational television world is *Dora the Explorer*, featuring the first Latina lead character in preschool programming (Ryan, 2010). *Dora*'s format differs from that of *Sesame Street* and *Blue's Clues* by using a structured linear narrative to present "high-stakes adventure wherein the solution of problems *requires* the participation of viewers—Dora could not do it without them" (Akerman et al., 2011, p. 210). *Dora*'s repeated use of the word "we" throughout her adventures implies that the audience is a part of the story, helping preschoolers believe that they are instrumental in solving the problems she faces in each episode (Ryan, 2010). Thus, "the interactive style which *Sesame Street* utilized and *Blue's Clues* revolutionized, *Dora the Explorer* formalized" (Akerman et al., 2011, p. 211). Similar to *Blue's Clues*, *Dora the Explorer* has the potential to boost the self-esteem and self-confidence of viewers (Ryan, 2010). One unique feature of *Dora the Explorer* is the focus on bilingualism and language development.

Language and Vocabulary Development

Many children's shows place a heavy emphasis on vocabulary acquisition. In the mid-1980s, researchers examined the language used in *Sesame Street, Mister Rogers' Neighborhood*, and *The Electric Company* and compared it to the language patterns parents use when interacting with their young children (Rice, 1984; Rice & Haight, 1986). Educational programming utilized many of the same verbal features that are believed to help children acquire language skills. Some of these features include short, simplified segments of speech, frequent use of repetition, and language that is based on things children see on the screen. The presence of these elements illustrated that "the potential existed for such television series to contribute to language development" (Fisch, 2009, p. 406).

Many studies—though not all (e.g., Bryant et al., 1999)—demonstrated that children learn new vocabulary words from television (e.g., Linebarger & Piotrowski, 2010; Rice et al., 1990; Rice & Woodsmall, 1988; Singer & Singer, 1994). In addition, some research indicated that additional viewing results in more learning. Rice and colleagues (1990) observed that children between the ages of 3 and 5 who watched more hours of *Sesame Street* had higher vocabulary gains than did those who watched fewer hours. (The researchers found that vocabulary gains from watching *Sesame Street* essentially stopped after the age of 5. By that age, children have acquired the available vocabulary from *Sesame Street*, which was designed for preschoolers.)

Vocabulary gains have also been observed with *Dora the Explorer*, which incorporates Spanish words as part of its vocabulary curriculum. For every 14 episodes watched, 4-year-old English-speaking children learned one new Spanish word (Linebarger, 2001). Meanwhile, 3-year-olds picked up one Spanish word for every 58 episodes watched.

Although children can learn new words from television, they learn little about correct usage and grammar (see Naigles & Mayeux, 2001, for a review). This could be due to the fact that televised communication is one-way—from the screen to the viewer. Children most likely learn grammar from social interactions involving two-way communication with parents and other caregivers (Naigles & Mayeux, 2001).

Literacy Development and Reading Comprehension

One of the most prominent children's programs that focused on literacy was PBS's *Between the Lions*, which targeted 3- to 7-year-olds (Jennings et al., 2009). Airing from 2000 to 2010, *Between the Lions* shared several characteristics with *Sesame Street*, including its magazine format, animation, and combination of puppetry and live action. The show took place in a library, and the main characters were two lion librarians, Theo and Cleo, and their two children. Preschoolers who watched *Between the Lions* learned to recognize the sounds of words more quickly than their non-watching peers (Prince et al., 2001). In another study, viewers also showed significant advances in sound awareness and sound blending, both of which are key elements used to predict reading achievement later in childhood (Linebarger, 2006).

Children who watched *Super Why!* (another literacy-based PBS program targeting 3- to 6-year-olds airing from 2007 to 2016) performed better on early literacy skills assessments than children in the control group, especially in the areas of letter knowledge and phonological and phonemic awareness skills (Linebarger, 2015). The effects were particularly powerful for children from lower socioeconomic households. Meaningful change could occur after viewing fewer than 20 episodes of *Super Why!*

Reading Rainbow (which targeted 5- to 8-year-olds and aired from 1983 to 2006) presented audiences with specific books narrated on air, accompanied by illustrations from the book pages. Hosted by LeVar Burton, *Reading Rainbow* included segments related to each episode's featured book (such as songs, interviews with children, and documentaries) with the primary goal of "encouraging independent reading for enjoyment and interest" (Liggett, 2005, p. 834). A content analysis identified four literacy strategies included in *Reading Rainbow* episodes: (1) activating and building upon children's background knowledge; (2) developing vocabulary; (3) relating content to children's personal lives; and (4) monitoring comprehension and summarizing main ideas, concepts, and themes (Wood & Duke, 1997).

Mathematics

Although many children's shows incorporate some type of content or characters to promote math skills (e.g., *Sesame Street*'s Count von Count), a few series aimed at older children and preteens have focused solely on mathematics.

Cyberchase, a math-based animated series about three preteens who use mathematics to defeat an online villain, aims to teach children that "math is everywhere and

[is] a useful tool for solving problems" (PBS.org, 2011). Fisch (2003, 2005) found that watching the series significantly impacted students' math skills in three areas: direct learning (i.e., solving the same problems featured on the show), near transfer (solving problems similar to those on the program), and far transfer (solving problems different than those on the show, but using similar mathematic skills). Although the show began in the late 1990s, children in the 2020s can still watch *Cyberchase* (and many other past and current educational shows) on pbskids.org, which also includes interactive games and hands-on activities.

Peg + Cat is an animated series to teach fundamental math concepts and skills to 3- to 5-year-olds. A 12-week intervention with transmedia content (i.e., full episodes, video clips, a tablet-based app, online games, and print activities) resulted in statistically significant improvements in certain math skills, such as ordinal numbers, spatial relationships, and 3-dimensional shapes (Pasnik et al., 2015). Similarly, in a study of first grade students consuming transmedia content related to the PBS series *Odd Squad* at both school and home, there were significant increases in mathematic knowledge, especially for pattern recognition, skip counting, and basic addition and subtraction (Tiu, 2015).

Science

Children's science programming began in 1951 with the premiere of *Mr. Wizard*, and the tradition has continued with shows such as *Bill Nye the Science Guy, Beakman's World,* and *The Magic School Bus* (Fisch, 2009). Newer shows, such as the PBS series *The Cat in the Hat Knows a Lot About That!* and Netflix's *The Magic School Bus Rides Again,* continue to educate children about science. The National Science Foundation funds many science-based children's series that have been or are currently seen on PBS.

By the mid-1990s, many parents and teachers were concerned that girls and minority students were losing interest in science by the time they entered middle school (Clarke, 2005). As a result, Scholastic developed a television series, *The Magic School Bus,* based on its popular books about an eccentric teacher and her shape-shifting bus. Ms. Frizzle and her fantastic field trips originally aired on PBS. Although it received little scholarly research attention, the show proved to be a hit with audiences, easily becoming one of PBS's highest-rated series for school-age children ("Scholastic Productions," 1997). Children who watched the original series comprehended and could articulate scientific facts and ideas that were (1) repeated frequently during the episode, (2) explained via dialog and visual/dramatic elements of the show, (3) limited to three or fewer details to remember, and (4) directly related to their own lives (The Magic School Bus TV Project, 1997). Netflix released a sequel series, *The Magic School Bus Rides Again,* in 2017.

Another extremely popular series in the 1990s was *Bill Nye the Science Guy,* which featured scientist/comedian Bill Nye (in his signature bow tie and lab coat) as he performed a variety of demonstrations and experiments. (Many clips and full episodes of this show are still available on YouTube, and Nye currently uses social media to continue to teach the public about science.) Watching the show not only encouraged children's scientific exploration—resulting in more complex thinking processes and solutions—but also increased the rate at which children were able to successfully identify and explain scientific phenomena (Rockman et al., 1996).

The PBS series *SciGirls* targeted older elementary and middle school girls with the goal of helping them improve and retain interest and self-efficacy in science, technology, engineering, and math (STEM). Watching the show motivates girls to conduct their own scientific investigations with friends and helps them understand the steps of scientific inquiry (Flagg, 2012).

More recently, researchers studied the effects of *The Cat in the Hat Knows a Lot About That!* on 4- and 5-year-old children from low-income families. The study included watching videos of the show, interacting with a show-related app, and engaging in printed activities. After eight weeks, the content increased children's excitement about science compared to the control group. Furthermore, there was "suggestive evidence that the *Cat in the Hat* resources improved children's broader physical science and engineering knowledge and practices" in some areas (Grindal et al., 2019).

History and Social Studies

When many of you hear the words *Schoolhouse Rock*, you probably start thinking of some of the show's most famous segments, like "Conjunction Junction, What's Your Function?" or "I'm Just a Bill." The latter example, which described the steps through which a bill must go to become a law, and "The Shot Heard Round the World," which tells the story of the American Revolution, were the subjects of a series of studies testing children's comprehension (Calvert, 1995; Calvert & Pfordresher, 1994; Calvert et al., 1991; Calvert & Tart, 1993). These studies found that although the songs improved verbatim recall of the lyrics, they did not improve comprehension of the subject matter.

Young Minds and Media: Recommendations for Screen Time

The American Academy of Pediatrics (2016) issued the following recommendations about the amount of screen time children should have and the type of media content children at certain ages should consume.

- Children younger than 18 to 24 months should avoid digital media, except for video calls.

- If parents/caregivers choose to introduce digital media to 18- to 24-month-olds, they should pick high-quality content and watch it together with their child. Solo media use should be avoided for this age group.

- Children between 2 and 5 years old should be limited to one hour of screen time a day. Parents/caregivers should continue to pick high-quality content and watch it with the child to help children understand what they are seeing on the screen and how to apply it to the real world.

- Avoid apps with distracting content, content that includes any violence, and fast-paced shows. Children have difficulty understanding fast-paced programs.

- Children should have no screen time in the hour before bedtime, and devices should be removed from children's bedrooms.

Key Questions about Learning from Children's Media

Since the late 1990s, there has been a strong cultural focus on the importance of development in the first three years of a child's life (Lapierre & Vaala, 2015). Countless DVDs and media products, such as *Baby Einstein*, *Brainy Baby*, and *Baby Genius*, were promoted for infants and toddlers. The BabyFirst channel on television provides round-the-clock programs for children too young to use the TV remote. Parents notice infants exhibiting interest in television at around 9 months of age (Linebarger & Walker, 2005).

Lapierre and Vaala (2015) studied factors that can predict ownership of baby DVD/video products in the United States, concluding that society's "stronger focus on early childhood education may encourage parents to purchase more baby videos/DVDs marketed as educational and to be more satisfied with these products, despite the fact that existing research does not support their educational value for infants and toddlers" (p. 226). More recently, we have seen the rise of apps and other interactive media content targeting young children. Many parents hoping to give their little ones a head start on learning spend millions of dollars on these products each year. However, the American Academy of Pediatrics (2016) recommends that children younger than 18 to 24 months not have screen time, except for video-chatting. (See the sidebar "Young Minds and Media" for more of the AAP's guidelines.)

According to Jordan & Vaala (2020), three key questions about children's media use have emerged: "(1) How does development impact children's learning from media? (2) What factors impact children's learning from media? (3) Are interactive media better at teaching than passive media?" (p. 291). This next section explores these topics.

Development (Age) and Impacts on Learning from Children's Media

Children's learning from TV and other video content has been researched more extensively than children's learning from newer forms of digital media (Jordan & Vaala, 2020). Most research indicates that children get very few—if any—educational benefits from consuming media before they are 18 to 24 months old. According to the American Academy of Pediatrics (2016),

> Children younger than 2 years need hands-on exploration and social interaction with trusted caregivers to develop their cognitive, language, motor, and social-emotional skills. Because of their immature symbolic, memory, and attentional skills, infants and toddlers cannot learn from traditional digital media as they do from interactions with caregivers, and they have difficulty transferring that knowledge to their 3-dimensional experience. (p. 1)

In fact, infants do not appear to begin comprehending video until they are 18 months old. Researchers manipulated episodes of *Teletubbies* so that shots were out of order and the dialog was played in reverse (Pempek et al., 2010). Babies between 6 and 12 months old did not react differently toward the manipulated stimuli; however, babies began to exhibit increased attention (i.e., longer looks at the screen) around the 18-month mark. Furthermore, children younger than 18–24 months are not capable of understanding how what they see in media (such as a photo or video of a toy) relates to real life (such as seeing the same toy in person). Toddlers over the age of 18 months have demonstrated more ability to imitate and learn from screen-based media compared to younger children, and those skills continue to improve over the next 12 months (Barr & Hayne, 1999; Courage & Howe, 2010).

Researchers have focused on two areas when studying infants, toddlers, and television: (1) learning new words from television and (2) imitating what is seen on television (Krcmar, 2011). Children in the early stages of language acquisition do not learn vocabulary quickly (also known as *fast-mapping*) from TV until they are approximately 22 months old; however, children as young as 15 months were able to learn novel words if taught by a live adult (Krcmar et al., 2007). In another study involving three conditions (action from a parent live, action from a parent on video, and action from a stranger on video), 6- to 24-month-olds did not learn words from a video, even if the person on the video was their own parent (Krcmar, 2011). Other researchers found that 12- to 15-month-olds did not learn words after repeated exposure to a *Baby Wordsworth* DVD (Robb et al., 2009). Watching one hour of *Baby Einstein* a day was linked to a 17-point *drop* in language scores for 8- to 16-month-olds, but there was no negative effect for 17- to 24-month-old toddlers (Zimmerman et al., 2007).

An example of research into whether a child can imitate what they see on a screen involves a child watching an adult on television or in person hide a toy in another room; then the child is put in the room and told to find the toy (Schmitt & Anderson, 2002; Troseth, 2003; Troseth & DeLoache, 1998). Children between the ages of 24 and 30 months performed worse at finding the toy if they had watched the video. Children aged 36 months performed equally well whether in the television or live condition; however, those in the live condition located the toy faster.

These find-the-toy studies indicate a phenomenon that researchers have dubbed the **video deficit**, meaning that younger children appear not to be able to connect what they see on a video to the real world (see Krcmar, 2010, for a review). The video deficit is usually observed between 15 and 30 months of age, and it is part of a larger concept called the **transfer deficit**, which highlights young children's struggle with the "generalization of information from one context to another, regardless of the direction of transfer (e.g., from two-dimensional to three-dimensional or vice versa)" (Kirkorian et al., 2017, para. 1). This transfer deficit has been observed with children consuming content in picture books, television, and touchscreens. However, the deficit can be reduced with repeated exposure to content and the inclusion of age-appropriate verbal and visual cues (see Barr, 2013, for further review).

Factors that Impact Learning from Children's Media

Even in a group of developmentally similar children, the rate and nature of how they learn from media will not be the same (Jordan & Vaala, 2020). These differences can be attributed to the child, the content, and the context (Guernsey, 2007).

Child. Studies have repeatedly demonstrated that children learn best from media content when it relates to their existing knowledge or interests and when they perceive both the medium and the content as challenging. **Schema theory** (see sidebar) illustrates that when media content builds on information children already know and the topics are about things that already interest them, it "is more easily integrated into the mental representations those children already possess" (Jordan & Vaala, 2020, p. 293). Additionally, when children are both engaged with content and expect it to be demanding, they pay more attention to the content, invest greater mental effort toward it, and learn more from it, compared to when they expect content to be easy" (Salomon & Leigh, 1984).

Schema Theory and the Capacity Model

Schema theory (see Collins et al., 1978) and the capacity model (Fisch, 2000) have been used to explain how and why children can learn—or do not learn—from educational media.

Schema Theory

Luke (1985) defines schemas as "conceptual structures stored in memory that represent our knowledge, our interpretation of what we have experienced and learned" (p. 95). As children continue to grow and experience the world around them—which includes consumption of mass media—they will use various schemas stored in their memory to make sense of content (Jordan & Vaala, 2020).

How content is presented and whether the educational lesson is a central part of a show's plot (or narrative schema) can influence children's understanding (Jordan & Vaala, 2020). For instance, one study examined kindergartners' understanding of an episode of *Clifford the Big Red Dog* that contained a lesson encouraging tolerance toward those who are different (Mares & Acosta, 2008). In one condition, characters were portrayed reacting with fear toward a "different" character (i.e., a three-legged dog). When the kindergartners watched this presentation of the content, they were significantly less likely to correctly identify the pro-tolerance message compared to when the presentation did not include fear reactions. When young children focused on salient content (fear, in this instance), they were less likely to remember the show's main message.

Familiarity with media content can facilitate comprehension. In a study of *The Cat in the Hat Knows A Lot about That!*, prior knowledge related to the narrative and educational content were significant predictors of both narrative and educational comprehension (Aladé & Nathanson, 2016).

> Rather than learning completely novel concepts, which might require repeated exposure, children who had some prior knowledge related to the program were better able to retain the concepts and information, even in a one-time exposure situation, because they had a pre-existing mental structure for storing the new information. (p. 423)

Capacity Model

This model posits that viewer characteristics such as short-term memory and verbal ability influence comprehension of both narrative and educational content (Fisch, 2000). Jordan and Vaala (2020) provide this concise summary of the capacity model:

> Given the limited cognitive resources children have available at a given time to process media, this theory contends that children's understanding of the narrative (storyline) and educational components of the content will benefit when the educational content is tightly woven within the narrative. In instances where the educational content is more distinct from the narrative, cognitive process priority tends to favor the narrative over the educational. (p. 298)

In addition to highlighting aspects of schema theory, the study by Aladé and Nathanson (2016) discussed above provided empirical support for the capacity model. In another study, preschoolers exhibited greater learning from educational media when they were already familiar with it (Piotrowski, 2014). "Ostensibly, program familiarity relieves the cognitive demands needed to process the narrative, leaving sufficient resources for comprehending the educational content" (Jordan & Vaala, 2020, p. 298).

Content.   As we mentioned at the beginning of this chapter, many critics have expressed fears that TV viewing will turn children into mindless "zombie viewers." However, studies have revealed that media consumption is not a passive activity; instead, children actively pay attention to cues about the comprehensibility of what they are watching. In other words, they will not watch content that does not make sense to them. In early research, preschoolers looked away from the TV when scenes from a show were presented in a random order or when the sound track was played backwards or dubbed in a different language (Anderson et al., 1981). (Recall that children younger than 18 months, however, did not react to manipulated video.) As mentioned earlier, children also learn the most from mediated content when it is challenging to them but still within their ability to comprehend—content that is moderately complex and novel (Rice et al., 1982). Furthermore, strategic use of media production techniques (e.g., visual transitions and cuts, sound effects, and movement on the screen) can help draw attention to educational content (Kirkorian et al., 2008; Rice et al., 1982).

Generally, the greatest learning from media content comes from high-quality programs that are "designed around a specific educational curriculum and include formative and evaluative research testing" (Jordan & Vaala, 2020, p. 294). One feature of educational content that can foster children's learning is the use of language and social cues that simulate real-life conversation. For example, toddlers and preschoolers can learn from embedded social relevance cues, "such as onscreen characters talking directly to the viewer and modeling conversational turn-taking" (p. 294). These types of cues are common on shows like *Dora the Explorer, Blue's Clues & You!*, and *Mickey Mouse Clubhouse.*

Participatory cues in *Dora the Explorer* can support comprehension of educational content—but only when children are already familiar with the cues (Piotrowski, 2014). Essentially, children who were not already familiar with the show and its format had to devote more of their working memory to understanding the features of the program, which left less mental capacity for comprehending the educational content. However, once they understand the features, children can allocate more of their working memory for processing the actual content.

> It seems reasonable to assert that, for children who had little familiarity with *Dora the Explorer* and were viewing the program with participatory cues, some of their cognitive effort was allocated to learning how to use this formal feature. On the other hand, children who were highly familiar with *Dora the Explorer* and who viewed the program with cues did not have to differentially allocate cognitive effort to learn this feature, and as a result, their comprehension of the educational content within the show improved. The data thus suggest that children must learn the convention of participatory cues before they are able to efficiently process and comprehend the content of the shows in which they are embedded. (pp. 325–326)

The narrative structure of a show can impact how well children learn from media. For instance, the **capacity model** (see sidebar) argues that children can more readily learn educational content and the story's narrative are tightly woven together (Fisch, 2000).

Context.   Rewatching the same video-based educational content multiple times helps toddlers and preschoolers imitate and learn from what they see on the screen

(Crawley et al, 1999; Krcmar, 2010; Linebarger & Vaala, 2010). Furthermore, consuming media with adults in the room impacts children's learning from educational media. For instance, a mother's mere presence in the room can improve a child's learning, although children learn the most when the adult actively engages them in conversations about what is happening on the screen (Wright et al., 1990). When caregivers co-view educational media with children, it allows them to interpret and explain difficult concepts to children and relate the material to the child's life (e.g., "See the green ball? You have a green ball, too!") (Fender et al., 2010). Co-viewing is also effective when on-screen prompts give parents specific talking points to discuss with their child about a program (Fisch et al., 2008).

Children benefit from co-viewing educational media content with a parent or caregiver who can interpret and explain concepts.

To help facilitate and encourage co-viewing, *Sesame Street* includes content that adults will enjoy and find humorous (Strasburger et al., 2009). It has a long history of parodying popular songs and TV programs. For example, PBS's *Downton Abbey* became *Upside Downton Abbey* to explain the effects of gravity, Netflix's *Stranger Things* was spoofed as *Sharing Things* to highlight the importance of sharing, and HBO's *Game of Thrones* was Muppet-fied as *Game of Chairs* to teach children about playing musical chairs.

Interactive vs. Passive Media

Jordan and Vaala (2020) lament that research testing how children can learn from interactive compared to passive media has lagged behind the ever-changing media environment. The boundaries between what is considered "interactive" and "passive" are continually being blurred, which makes it more difficult to answer the question of whether interactive media are better at teaching children than passive media:

> For example, numerous television programs—typically considered a "passive medium—such as *Dora the Explorer* and *Blue's Clues* are interactive in the sense that they invite children to find clues on the screen and "help" the protagonists by yell-

ing out answers. On the other hand, children's mobile apps—typically considered interactive—can play video content much like viewing a typical, non-interactive television show. (p. 295)

Children's Books: Pixels vs. Paper.   Researchers have investigated how children learn from e-books compared to traditional print books. Interactive features in e-books can vary. For example, some have "hotspots" that move or make noise when children tap them. Sometimes these interactive features are directly connected to the educational content of the book, or they may be distracting (Jordan & Vaala, 2020; see also, Willoughby et al., 2015).

Experimental studies into the effectiveness of interactive e-books have produced mixed results. For instance, some experiments found that children's learning from interactive digital books was similar or worse compared to traditional print books or noninteractive digital versions (Kelley & Kinney, 2017; Strouse & Ganea, 2017b). However, findings from other studies indicate slightly superior learning from interactive e-books, depending on how the books were designed (Bus et al., 2015; Takacs et al., 2015).

Children are more attentive to e-books and could recall more information from them compared to the same book in a print format (Courage et al., 2021). For example, children who read the e-book version were able to correctly identify a previously unknown animal that was labeled in the book more often than those who read the print version (Strouse & Ganea, 2017a). In addition to paying more attention, toddlers exhibited more positive emotions and made themselves more available for reading in the e-book condition. Furthermore, both attention and availability for reading mediated children's learning in the experiment, "suggesting that electronic books supported children's learning by way of increasing their engagement and attention" (p. 11).

In a study by Courage et al. (2021), 2- and 3-year-olds in the e-book group took significantly more time to finish the book than those in the print condition. "This additional time might have been related children's engagement with the e-book features. It might also have provided children with more time to process the story details and enabled better content recognition" (p. 14). The researchers note that results should be interpreted with caution until more research can be conducted into how toddlers learn from digital and paper books.

Other Screen-Based Media: Interactive vs. Non-Interactive.   As more and more children—especially very young children—grow up surrounded by screens, some researchers are exploring whether interactive features can help children overcome the video deficit we discussed earlier in this chapter. For instance, an experiment by Myers et al. (2017) examined whether toddlers (12- to 25-month-olds) could form a relationship with and learn from on-screen adult partners. Some children had socially contingent (i.e., real-time, two-way interaction) FaceTime conversations with their partner, while others watched pre-recorded videos. Both real-time and pre-recorded partners presented the same information to the children. After one week, children in the FaceTime condition both preferred and recognized their partner, but those in the pre-recorded video group did not. Additionally, children who engaged with their partner over FaceTime learned more new patterns, and the oldest children in this group also learned more new words. In short, the findings "build on existing research by showing that interactive video chat can be a medium for learning and social relationships in the second year" (p. 10). Roseberry et al. (2014) note that children, even at a young age, are adept at distinguishing between real contingency and pre-recorded screen-based interactions because "simply posing questions to children and pausing for the answer did not result in language learning if the children were not able to interact contingently with the person on video" (p. 967).

Children under the age of 2 can learn from screen-based media if it is a real-time, two-way interactive video chat.

A growing number of studies have examined the educational effects of interactive versus passive media use on children's ability to transfer knowledge to other contexts. A pair of 2016 studies found that preschoolers were better able to transfer knowledge from a digital game to other settings or problems when they watched a video of an experimenter playing the game, rather than playing the same game themselves (Aladé & Nathanson, 2016; Schroeder & Kirkorian, 2016).

There were similar results in a study of the ability of 24- to 40-month-olds to learn new words from a tablet-based app (Ackermann et al., 2020). Children in the "active" condition could pick which objects on the screen to tap, and then they would hear the name of the object. Meanwhile, children in the passive condition could only watch and hear what the children in the active condition chose. Later, all children were tested on the app to see whether they could correctly tap on the photo of a particular object. Children in the passive condition performed better at matching the word to its photo than did those in the active condition. Interestingly, data on the children's eye movements revealed that both the passive and active groups looked at the correct photo similarly, even though children in the active group were then more likely to tap a different photo. For a further explanation of these findings and possible implications on the design of interactive media for children, see this chapter's Research Spotlight.

RESEARCH SPOTLIGHT

Word Learning from a Tablet App:
Toddlers Perform Better in a Passive Context
Lena Ackermann, Chang Huan Lo, Nivedita Mani, and Julien Mayor (2020)
PLoS ONE, 15(12), Article 30240519

With the proliferation of touchscreen devices, we have seen numerous interactive apps targeting children that claim to be educational. But can these apps help children learn words? Answering that question was the purpose of this study, which used two experiments to examine the effects of active versus passive participation with an app.

Experiment 1

The first experiment included 130 German-speaking children. They were categorized by age: 24-month-olds (n=42), 30-month-olds (n=44), and 40-month-olds (n=44). Children were paired—or "yoked"—and then assigned to either the active or passive conditions. "In the active condition, participants could select four novel objects to be told the label of, while in the passive condition, participants were automatically given the labels for the objects chosen by their yoked active peers" (p. 4).

Learning Phase

Children in the active condition used the experimental app on an iPad Pro. Pictures of eight novel objects and familiar objects were selected for the experiment. The novel objects were given made-up names for the study. The learning phase consisted of four trials with a verbal prompt asking the children to tap one of two randomly combined images. During the first trial, the verbal prompt was "Look, here are two pictures. You can tap on one," while subsequent trials used a prompt that said "Tap on an object, then you'll hear its name." Once a child tapped on a picture, the unselected image was hidden, and the selected image was then labeled five times. The time it took for a child to tap a photo was recorded and used to time the stimulus for their yoked partner in the passive condition.

Participants in the passive condition were not required to tap on the iPad. Instead, they were exposed to their yoked active partners' selections with the same timing observed in the active condition. The verbal prompt was changed for this condition to "Do you see the two pictures? Are they beautiful?" The children then had to wait for as long as it had taken their active peer to choose between the two novel objects displayed. As with the active condition, the unselected image was hidden followed by the selected image being named five times.

Familiarization Phase

After completing the learning phase, all participants took part in the familiarization phase. This phased used six pairs of familiar objects (i.e., an apple, a car, a baby, a ball, a tree, and a shoe). In this phase, all children were shown a pair of photos and instructed to tap on a certain one (e.g., "Tap on the shoe."). This phase allowed children in the passive phase to become familiar with tapping on the tablet and to keep all participants engaged.

Two-Alternative Forced Choice Test Phase

All participants took part in this phase, which included 12 two-alternative forced choice tasks where each of the novel words heard in the learning phase was tested (paired separately with each of the three other novel objects). In each trial, children were shown two of the four novel objects seen/labeled in the learning phase and asked to tap on the one with the heard novel word. Response times were recorded for each task.

(continued)

Four-Alternative Forced Choice Test Phase

This final phase included 8 four-alternative forced choice tasks. Each novel word was tested twice. This time, children were shown all four of the novel objects and were instructed to select a specific one. Response times were recorded for each of the trials.

Results and Discussion

An analysis of the data revealed a reaction time boost for younger children (24-month-olds) in the passive condition compared to those in the active condition. There were no differences in reaction times for the other age groups. Meanwhile, older children (30- and 40-month-olds) in the passive condition responded with increased accuracy over their peers in the active group. This difference was not seen in the 24-month-old group.

Although these results were in line with other research about increased performance for children in passive conditions, Ackermann and colleagues questioned whether these results were related to differences in performance or competence.

> In other words, do children assigned to the active condition merely perform worse than their passive counterparts while nevertheless having learned the words to an equal degree or do children assigned to the active condition also learn worse than their passive counter parts? (p. 12)

Experiment 2

To answer that question, the researchers conducted a second experiment. Experiment 2's methods were identical to Experiment 1, except that this experiment was conducted with Malay-speaking children and included measuring and recording children's eye movements as they completed tasks.

Results and Discussion

During the learning phase, children in the passive condition looked at the target object significantly longer and more robustly than peers in the active condition, which the researchers suggest could indicate more engagement with the content. Children in the passive condition also had greater accuracy during the test phases. However, there were no differences between the passive and active children in terms of gaze-duration (how long a child looked at the target object).

Furthermore, gaze-duration had no significant effect on accuracy scores in the test phase. As Ackermann et al. summarized, "While children in the passive condition looked longer at the target object in the learning phase *and* outperformed their active counterparts in terms of accuracy, the former did not predict the latter" (p. 21).

General Discussion

Together, these two experiments did find a passive boost among participants when tested on novel word-object association tasks. But this study then went further to try and understand the root cause of that boost.

Compared to children in passive conditions, do children in active conditions not learn and subsequently are less likely to correctly identify novel word-object associations, or did they simply not perform correctly during the testing phase (i.e., not tapping on the correct target object despite knowing what the correct object was)?

In experiment 2, children in both conditions looked at the target object at rates above chance. The researchers concluded that the differences in accuracy for active children during the testing phase stems from their performance related to the tapping task, not their competence in word learning. In other words, there were no differences in active and passive children's competence in word learning, but there were differences in their performance in the app. Ackermann et al. concluded that children may have difficulties changing course during the experiment, moving from actively choosing what they want to learn more information about to indicating what they have learned. This was despite the children being told what they needed to do across the different phases of the experiment. (p. 23)

Ultimately, this study provides evidence that interactive educational apps may not adequately measure a child's learning progress. Any type of learning boost observed from using these types of apps is "highly contingent" on both the structure of the tasks children must perform and of the app itself.

Depending on the structure of the learning experience, an active choice might actually decrease children's performance in certain tasks, without having much impact on their learned competence. Thus, the attentional and locomotor constraints specific to touch-screen usage should be kept in mind when talking about learning from interactive touchscreen media. (p. 23)

Summary

Although many parents and critics fear that decades of children's programming have created generations of mindless zombie viewers, research has demonstrated quite the opposite effect. The time you spent watching Big Bird and Elmo on *Sesame Street* or Blue and her owner try to figure out the puzzle of the day on *Blue's Clues* probably did teach you something.

Educational programming fosters language development (particularly vocabulary acquisition) in preschoolers, as well as developing flexible thinking and problem-solving skills. Children's shows improve both reading skills and comprehension. Shows for older children focusing on math and science have a strong track record of improving problem-solving skills and encouraging exploration.

There have been mixed results from programs and DVDs targeted at very young children While infants and toddlers are able to imitate what they see on the TV screen, they often are not able to learn vocabulary words from watching these types of media; however, as they grow older, their ability to learn improves. In general, children under the age of 2 struggle to connect what they see on a screen to the real world. This is known as the video deficit.

Researchers continue to study the factors that can influence a child's ability to learn from media. These factors generally fall into three categories: the child, the content, and the context. Children's learning increases when they have some familiarity with the content. Learning can also be enhanced when children co-view educational media content with a caregiver.

In recent years, scholars have turned their attention toward interactive tablet-based educational media, such as e-books and apps. Results of studies comparing e-books to traditional books have been mixed. Young children are capable of learning from other screen-based content, such as real-time video chats. Some research has found that children who passively consume screen media (watching, rather than physically interacting with a touchscreen) exhibit greater learning than those who engage in interactive use. However, other research indicates that children in both passive and active conditions can learn equally well, but children engaging in more active consumption (e.g., tapping on a touchscreen) may simply not perform as well when asked to demonstrate what they have learned.

No matter whether children's media is made up of pixels or paper or watched on TVs or touchscreens, research shows that children are active consumers of content. And that demand will only continue to grow, giving researchers new avenues to explore for decades to come.

18

Effects of Video Games

If Pac-Man had affected us as kids, we'd all be running around in dark rooms, munching pills and listening to repetitive electronic music.

—Marcus Brigstocke, comedian

I like video games, but they're really violent. I'd like to play a video game where you help the people who were shot in all the other games. It'd be called *Really Busy Hospital*.

—Demetri Martin, comedian

There is no doubt about the popularity of video games. There is also little doubt about the ongoing debate about their effects. Since the release of *Odyssey* and *Pong* in the 1970s, the home video game market has boomed. In 2010, spending on video games, consoles, and other game-related accessories in the United States was $25.1 billion (Entertainment Software Association [ESA], 2011). In 2021, video game spending reached $60.4 billion (NPD Group, 2022). There has also been an increase in esports at colleges and universities, which allows students to compete in games like *League of Legends*, *Overwatch*, and *Fortnite*. Major money can be won playing games. Kyle "Bugha" Giersdorf won $3 million at the Fortnite World Cup in 2019—and he was just 16 years old (Snider, 2019)!

Much like the rise of television, video games have been and will continue to be the focus of many research studies, as well as a source of public debate about the effects that the games have on their players. In this chapter, we begin with a brief look at the modern gamer before exploring three of the main areas in video game research: concerns about negative effects of violent video games; video game addiction and internet gaming disorder; and the positive effects of video games.

A Look at the Modern Gamer

Roughly 227 million people in the United States play video games (ESA, 2021). Although a common stereotype for gamers is that they are teenage boys, statistics and other research into gaming populations paint a very different picture of today's average gamer.

Gender

Gaming is not just for nerdy guys living in their parents' basement, as the stereotype would have us believe. Across all players and ages, females make up nearly half (48%) of gamers (ESA, 2022). Despite females' growing presence in the gaming world, males are still more likely to play games and play them more often (Griffiths et al., 2004; Lenhart, 2015; Terlecki et al., 2011).

Overall, video games play a critical role in both the development and maintenance of teen boys' friendships (Lenhart, 2015). Boys are more likely to meet new friends while gaming compared to girls (57% to 13% respectively). Boys often play games with others on a daily or weekly basis, both in person (42%) and online (55%). Meanwhile, girls are *less* likely to play video games if they have a real-world opportunity to engage in other social activities (Lucas & Sherry, 2004). More women than men reported playing video games to unwind (ESA, 2021, 2022).

Age

Although games were once solely targeted to kids and teens, the gaming industry is now appealing to gamers of all ages. According to the ESA (2022), 71% of U.S. kids play video games, and 65% of U.S. adults are gamers. The average video game player is in their early thirties (ESA, 2019, 2021, 2022). When looking across all ages, 76% of gamers are over 18 years old, with 18- to 34-year-olds making up the largest segment of the gaming population (36%) (ESA, 2022).

Looking at popular game genres by age, the ESA (2022) found that the most preferred genres in the 18–34 range are arcade/other (62%), puzzle and action (55%),

Gaming is popular among all age groups, with the average gamer being in their early thirties. Women make up almost half of all gamers in the United States.

and shooter (54%). Those in the 35–44 group prefer puzzle (69%), arcade/other (64%), and skill/chance (52%) genres. The puzzle game genre continues to be the most preferred across older age groups, rising to 82% for gamers 65 and older.

Whereas older players often enjoy the physical and mental challenges video games present, younger players also cited violence as their favorite aspect of video games (Griffiths et al., 2004). This preference only fuels the cycle of research into video game violence and its effects on youth, which will be discussed later in this chapter.

Personality Factors

Gamers who play daily have lower levels of extraversion and conscientiousness (i.e., the tendency to be careful, efficient, organized, and self-disciplined) and higher levels of exploitation and entitlement (both of which are facets of narcissism) compared to less frequent players (Potard et al., 2020). Extraversion correlated positively with playing sports games but negatively with role-playing and first-person shooter games. Conscientiousness negatively correlated with role-playing, strategy, and action/adventure games. Openness (i.e., the tendency to be broad-minded, imaginative, creative, and curious) positively correlated with role-playing games and negatively with sports games and first-person shooters.

People with high levels of openness and lower levels of agreeableness (i.e., altruism, empathy, nurturance, nonaggression, and trust) prefer to play violent video games (Chory & Goodboy, 2011). Additionally, players who were more open, extroverted, and neurotic (defined as anxious, shy, emotionally unstable, with low self-esteem) but were less agreeable preferred games with stronger violence. Moreover, players with highly aggressive personalities play video games in more violent ways than do nonviolent players (Peng et al., 2008).

Effects of Violent Video Games

As with any issue that may impact our society (especially children), there are opposing sides in the debate about the negative effects resulting from playing violent video games. Although much of the academic debate centers around methodological differences, differing interpretations of data (see Anderson et al., 2010; Bushman et al., 2010; Ferguson & Kilburn, 2010; Ferguson & Konijn, 2015), or disagreements about consensus among scholars (see Bushman et al., 2015b; Anderson et al., 2015; Ivory et al., 2015; Bushman et al., 2015a, in that order), the debate in the public forum is often boiled down to whether violent games will make gamers commit acts of aggression or violence in the real world.

One example of the public firestorm surrounding violent video games was the debate over *School Shooter: North American Tour 2012*, an online first-person shooter game where players earned points by killing innocent students and teachers using the same weapons that real-life gunmen Eric Harris and Dylan Klebold used in their shooting rampage in Columbine High School in 1999 and that Seung-Hui Cho used to shoot and kill 32 people at Virginia Tech in 2007 (Rhen, 2011). In an interview with *The Escapist*, an online magazine devoted to video games, the creator and developer of

School Shooter said the game was not harmful to the players nor disrespectful to the families of the Columbine or Virginia Tech victims (Tito, 2011a). In fact, the developer claimed the game was designed so that players "can just shut off their brains and let their reflexes take over," and went on to praise the game for its "preventative quality," which would "satisfy those with the idea to commit spree killings in their head enough to keep them from doing so" (Tito, 2011a, p. 3). Public outcry against the game, both for its lack of taste and sensitivity and the fear of what impact the game would have on players, caused it to be pulled from its host site within a matter of weeks (Tito, 2011b).

The main fear about violent video games like *School Shooter* and franchises like *Call of Duty*, *Grant Theft Auto*, *Red Dead Redemption* and the like is that they will cause increased aggression in players, which could result in real-world violence. While some argue that the games do have a statistically significant, albeit small, impact on players' aggression (see Anderson et al., 2010; Bushman et al., 2010, Prescott et al., 2018), others argue that there is no effect of violent games on players' aggression (see Ferguson, 2007; Ferguson & Kilburn, 2010). Moreover, recent advances in media effects metatheory encourage researchers to shift the focus from medium-specific effects to identifying audience subsets who could be especially susceptible or vulnerable to experiencing an effect from mass media (e.g., Valkenburg & Peter, 2013).

Theoretical Frameworks for Studying Effects of Video Game Violence

In the vast body of literature on the effects of violent video games, two theoretical frameworks are prevalent: social cognitive theory (Bandura, 2001; also see Chapter 4) and the General Aggression Model (GAM; Anderson & Bushman, 2002, 2018; Bushman & Anderson, 2002; also see Chapters 5 and 11). Social cognitive theory has been used to explain possible effects of playing violent games on players' aggressive thoughts, feelings, and behaviors. Put simply, through playing these games (often repeatedly), players learn how to be aggressive and are rewarded for it in the game, which can motivate them to repeat those behaviors in the future.

Anderson and Bushman's (2002, 2018) **General Aggression Model (GAM)** is one of the most complete theoretical frameworks used to explain how violent video games affect players' levels of aggression. Expanding on social cognitive theory, the GAM adds more mechanisms and routes for aggressive behavior and highlights the role of priming (see Chapter 5 for more on priming). When looking at the short-term effects through the GAM, violent gameplay primes aggression-related mental scripts and schemata, which in turn result in an elevated state of aggression. When these mental pathways are primed, they are more readily available for us to act on. Repeated exposure to video game violence over time helps to hardwire these mental structures, which can ultimately result in creating a more aggressive personality. In their review of video games and the "joystick generation," Barenthin and Van Puymbroeck (2006) concluded that "violent video games provide an environment for aggression, with simultaneous exposure to modeling, reinforcement and rehearsal of behaviors" (p. 25).

Other theories give us alternative frameworks for examining and understanding the relationship between video games and aggression. Slater et al.'s (2003) **downward**

spiral model proposes that adolescents with aggressive personalities may seek out violent media, including video games, which then creates a reinforcing and reciprocal cycle that heightens their aggressive tendencies. Slater (2007) further developed this into the **reinforcing spirals model**. This model "proposes that media use and effects are a dynamic process, in which one of the effects of media exposure is in many cases to reinforce existing patterns of identity, attitude, and behavior—including media selection behavior, which is likely to further reinforce such patterns" (Slater, 2017, p. 17089). Slater's spiral models posit that aggressive players seek out violent games to satisfy their needs, thus grounding his work in the uses and gratifications approach (see Chapter 9) and Zillmann and Bryant's (1985) selective exposure theory. Aggressive children can begin this downward spiral with violent video game content as early as third grade (von Salisch et al., 2011).

A key contribution of Slater's spiral models is the introduction of personal characteristics as moderating factors of the effects of violent media. Advances in media effects metatheory have encouraged redirecting focus away from medium-specific effects toward identifying people who are more susceptible and vulnerable to media effects and what personal characteristics come into play. For instance, the **differential susceptibility to media effects model** (**DSMM**; see Chapter 1) proposes that personal characteristics are key in enhancing or counteracting media effects (Valkenburg & Peter, 2013). Ultimately, the DSMM highlights that mass media exposure—in this case, playing violent video games—will affect each player differently. Rather than looking for some sort of "universal" effect on all players, it is important that researchers examine what individual player characteristics are more likely to result to increased aggressiveness. For example, being the target of peer victimization is linked to young people being more susceptible to aggression-related effects of violent media (Slater et al., 2004).

Findings that Support the Existence of Negative Effects of Violent Games

Many studies have investigated the effects of violent games on players' aggression. Overall, the research has focused on the areas of aggressive thoughts and behaviors, physical arousal, and prosocial activities. Multiple studies conducted by Anderson and his colleagues used meta-analytical research methods (synthesizing the statistical findings of multiple studies into one overall analysis) to show that playing violent video games resulted in higher levels of aggressive thoughts, emotions, and behaviors, as well as decreases in empathy and helping behaviors, when compared to nonplayers (e.g., Anderson, 2004; Anderson et al., 2004, 2010). The American Psychological Association (2015, 2019, 2020) reached the same conclusion, noting that studies using a variety of methods, samples, and measurements have revealed a small but consistent relationship between playing violent video games and increases in aggression. However, the APA cautions that these findings do not provide scientific evidence that violent video games is connected to real-world violence.

Multiple meta-analyses and longitudinal studies have examined how playing violent games is linked to later aggression, and they have arrived at a similar conclusion: higher amounts of violent video gameplay lead to increases in aggression at a later time (Anderson et al., 2008, 2010; APA, 2015, 2019, 2020; Greitemeyer & Mügge,

2014; Greitemeyer & Sagioglou, 2017; Möller & Krahé, 2009; Prescott et al., 2018). This effect was seen in gaming populations from around the world, not just the United States. Prescott et al.'s (2018) meta-analysis found that video game violence's effect on players was moderated by ethnicity. White participants experienced the strongest effect, while Hispanic participants experienced no significant effects. Asian participants fell in between those two groups.

Rewarding violent behaviors during video gameplay can increase hostile emotions and behaviors (Carnagey & Anderson, 2005). Greitemeyer and McLatchie (2011) discovered that one mechanism that can increase aggressive behavior is dehumanization, which is the act of viewing others as less (or less than) human. Gamers also become desensitized to the violence seen on the screen (e.g., Anderson et al., 2010; Carnagey et al., 2007; Engelhardt et al., 2011). In fact, people who have little experience with video games exhibit greater desensitization toward violent acts after playing a violent video game, whereas long-time players displayed little change (Engelhardt et al., 2011). This would seem to indicate that long-time players are already extremely desensitized to violence, and therefore do not react to it as readily.

Whereas Engelhardt et al. (2011) looked at differences between inexperienced and experienced players, Gentile et al. (2016) examined differences between players who habitually play violent games and those who habitually play nonviolent games. Functional MRI scans revealed that gamers who usually play nonviolent games had increases in parts of the brain that are responsible for emotional responses—typically disgust and fear—while playing a violent game. Meanwhile, players who regularly play violent games showed active suppression in those same parts of the brain, which the researchers said "may be an indication of a long-term desensitization effect from prior violent game play" (p. 48).

Playing a violent game in 3D can result in greater feelings of anger due to the more immersive gaming experience (Lull & Bushman, 2016). Violent video games can also increase hostile sexism in male players when their in-game opponent is a sexualized female character (LaCroix et al., 2018). This effect was stronger when players felt more immersed in the game.

How Long Can Effects on Thoughts, Feelings, and Behaviors Last?   Most of us know the thrill of finally beating a challenging level of a video game. We may bask in the glory of our triumph for a few minutes or hours (of course, some of you probably bask in the glory all day and miss a few classes in the process), but if the game was violent, how long do the short-term effects last on our minds and in our bodies? Playing *Mortal Kombat: Deadly Alliance* for 15 minutes resulted in significant increases in physical arousal (i.e., heart rate) and aggressive thoughts and behaviors (Barlett et al., 2009). The hostile thoughts and feelings lasted less than four minutes after the end of the game. However, aggressive behavior and elevated heart rate lasted at least four minutes but returned to normal around the 10-minute mark. Notably, the researchers caution that there is the possibility that aggressive behavior and increased arousal could last longer than 10 minutes. (Learn more about this study in Research Spotlight 1.)

How Long Do the Short-Term Violent Video Game Effects Last?
Christopher Barlett, Omar Branch, Christopher Rodeheffer, and Richard Harris (2009)
Aggressive Behavior, 35, 225–236

In this two-part study, Barlett et al. examined how long our minds, bodies, and behaviors are affected by playing a violent video game.

Research Questions
In order to examine the short-term effects of violent video games, the researchers tested the following three research questions.

1. Will long-term exposure to violent video games increase aggressive behavior?

2. Does violent video gameplay increase aggressive behavior immediately after gameplay has concluded?

3. How long does this heightened aggression last?

Study 1
Although the main objective of this study was to answer the third research question, Barlett et al. had to first prove that their stimulus material fulfilled the requirements of the first two questions.

Method
To accomplish this task, 91 students (69 male, 22 female; mean age: 19.45 years) from a general psychology class were recruited in exchange for class credit. The participants, who came to the lab one at a time, were told they would be taking part in two unrelated studies: one for video games, the other for food preference. The participants were randomly assigned into experimental and control groups. The experimental group played a violent video game (i.e., *Mortal Kombat: Deadly Alliance* on a PlayStation 2), while the control group played a nonviolent game (i.e., *Hard Hitter Tennis* for the PlayStation 2). The groups were subdivided into 4-minute and 9-minute conditions.

To begin, each participant filled out questionnaires about aggression and hostility and completed one-third of the Word Completion Task. This instrument provided participants with word fragments, such as K I __ __. Participants were asked to quickly fill in the blanks to complete the word, which could, for instance, be filled in as K I L L or K I S S. Participants were then given a brief tutorial on how to play the game before the timed gameplay session began. While each participant was playing either the violent or nonviolent game, the experimenter set out materials for the Hot Sauce Paradigm, which is used to assess overt aggressive behavior based on how much hot sauce the participant would force someone who does not like spicy foods to eat. The materials included four bottles of hot sauce, a plastic spoon, four popsicle sticks, and two plastic cups. While the participant continued to play, the experimenter told them they were stepping out for a few minutes to assist another participant who was taking part in a food preference study. (In fact, this "other participant" and the food preference study did not exist.)

When the experimenter returned and gameplay ended, participants' heart rate was measured, and they were given questions to assess their hostility and another third of the Word Completion Task. Participants then answered questions about their preferences for sweet, savory, spicy, hot, bland, and salty foods.

After completing the assessments, participants were given a food preference questionnaire from the "other participant" down the hall. It clearly indicated that the other participant did not like spicy foods. The participants were told that the other person would have to eat all of which-

(continued)

ever hot sauce they selected for them. After tasting each sauce with a popsicle stick to see how spicy each one was, participants poured the sauce of their choice into a cup for the other person to eat. After pouring the desired amount of sauce into the cup, the experimenter took it and left the room under the pretense of going to give it to the "other participant."

For those in the 4-minute condition, the researcher actually stepped into the hallway, set the cup on the floor, and then reentered the room, telling the participant that they had handed the cup to a research assistant to take to the other person. At this point, about four minutes had elapsed since the end of gameplay.

The participants' heart rate was measured, and the researcher gave the participant another set of hostility and word completion questionnaires and the final third of the Word Completion Task for the "second study" they were participating in (i.e., the fictitious food preference study). The participants were told that if the questionnaires seemed similar to the other sets, it was because both studies were examining similar variables.

After completion, the participants were thanked and debriefed.

Participants in the 9-minute condition underwent identical procedures, except that when the experimenter left to take the hot sauce to the other person, they did not reenter the room for five minutes.

Results

The violent games did result in significant increases in physical arousal and aggressive thoughts and feelings compared to those in the nonviolent game condition. Aggressive thoughts and feelings lasted less than four minutes, meaning that by the time they conducted the hot sauce test, aggressive thoughts and feelings had returned to baseline, no matter which delay condition participants were in. Meanwhile, the effects on physical arousal (i.e., heart rate) lasted more than four minutes but less than nine minutes.

Study 2

The first study focused on internal variables (i.e., feelings, thoughts, and heart rate) that influence aggressive behavior. The researchers conducted a second experiment to determine how long the effects on overt aggressive behavior last after gameplay.

Method

Ninety-one participants (48 male, 43 female; mean age: 18.60 years) were recruited for this part of the study. Because the first study demonstrated that the violent video game did lead to increases in aggression, no control group was used in the second study. Participants were randomly assigned to three time-delayed conditions: 0-minute delay, 5-minute delay, and 10-minute delay.

Similar to the first study, participants played the violent video game for 15 minutes. Depending on which condition each participant was assigned to, they completed the Hot Sauce Paradigm zero, five, or ten minutes after their gaming session had ended.

Results

After conducting several statistical analyses, the data revealed that aggressive behavior resulting from the violent video game lasted between five and 10 minutes.

Overall Findings

Combined, these two studies shed new light on the short-term effects of violent video gameplay. Whereas aggressive thoughts and feelings dissipate within four minutes of ending a violent game, the effects on arousal and behavior last slightly longer, between five and 10 minutes. This may seem like a small window for aggressive behavior, but the authors admitted that the effects could last much longer.

Measuring Increases in Aggressive Thoughts, Feelings, and Behaviors.   By this point, you may be wondering how increased aggression is measured in these studies. Do researchers see if a gamer goes out and punches another person? Of course not! (The Institutional Review Board at any university would never approve such a study.) High-quality nonexperimental studies usually use standardized questionnaires as their means of measurement (Anderson et al., 2010; Klimmt & Possler, 2020). Many studies can assess aggressive feelings and thoughts through self-reported data, such as the word completion survey described in Research Spotlight 1. According to Anderson et al. (2010), most high-quality experiments measure a player's aggressive behavior via artificial means, such as blasts of white noise (see Engelhardt et al., 2011) or giving hot sauce to a person who does not like spicy food (see Barlett et al., 2009). Players with higher aggression will select louder volumes and longer durations for the white noise blasts, or they choose to give a person a larger quantity of a spicier hot sauce.

Although these methods may seem silly to us when we read about them, researchers design their studies so that participants are not suspicious of their motives. The noise blasts and hot sauce tests typically provide a reliable means of determining what type of discomfort they are willing to inflict on another human being.

The Argument Against Negative Effects of Violent Video Games

Despite the body of research that shows what Prescott et al. (2018) described as "a statistically significant, reliable effect" (p. 9886), some scholars say this research is flawed. Much of the disagreement is related to methodological issues (Ferguson, 2007; Ferguson & Kilburn, 2010; Freedman, 2002; Olson, 2004), differing interpretations of effect sizes (Hilgard et al., 2017), and alleged publisher bias in academic journals (Ferguson, 2007).

Lee et al. (2009) outlined the general arguments that researchers on this side of the issue cite as major methodological flaws with video game effects studies.

1. Aggression often is not clearly defined, and the terms *aggression* and *violence* are often used interchangeably.

2. Most studies use only one particular game as the stimulus, and it is played for a fixed amount of time.

3. The causal relationship between aggression in real life and playing video games is not straightforward. Variables such as age, gender, and personality come into play.

4. Many studies are conducted with small, nonrandom, nonrepresentative samples.

Regarding the methodological criticisms, the APA (2020) concurs that the lack of precision in using the terms "violence" and "aggression" is problematic, noting "all violence, including lethal violence, is aggression, but not all aggression is violence" (p. 2). The APA attributes part of this issue to differences across disciplines, such as criminology, epidemiology, and psychology. (For more about the difference between aggression and violence, see Chapter 11.)

Additionally, the APA Task Force on Violent Media (2015) acknowledged that the controlled environment of most laboratory experiments does reduce the ecological validity (i.e., the extent to which the results can be generalized to the real world) of their findings. They also noted that research into the effects of violent video games primarily utilizes young adult participants. Far less research is conducted with younger participants, but the task force cited ethical issues of exposing children to possibly harmful stimuli as one reason for a lack of research focusing on younger gamers. Prescott et al. (2018) addressed Ferguson's (2007) claim of alleged publication bias in their meta-analysis. They "observed no evidence that studies with null or negative sizes have been underrepresented in the literature" (p. 9886).

Are Violent Video Games to Blame for Real-World Mass Shootings?

Often after a mass shooting, there is a flurry of debate about the possible role violent video games may have played in causing the shooter to pull the trigger. Although the public and politicians are quick to blame video games, decades of research show there is *no* causal relationship between violent video games and mass shootings (e.g., APA 2015, 2019, 2020; Baldaro et al., 2004; Markey, Markey, & French, 2015; Williams & Skoric, 2005). Ferguson (2007) asked the reasonable question:

> Is it possible that a behavior with such a high base rate (i.e., video game playing) is useful in explaining a behavior with a very low base rate (i.e., school shootings)? Put another way, can an almost universal behavior truly predict a rare behavior? (p. 310)

Empirical evidences tells us that the answer is a firm "no." For example, a study of real-world violence and violent video games concluded that "no evidence was found to suggest that this medium was a major (or minor) contributing cause of violence in the United States" (Markey, Markey, & French, 2015, p. 290). In response to politicians and members of the media incorrectly linking violent video games to real-world violence, the APA (2020) explicitly states that its resolution affirming the relationship between violent video games and aggression

> should not be misinterpreted or misused by attributing violence, such as mass shootings, to violent video game use. Violence is a complex social problem that likely stems from many factors that warrant attention from researchers, policy makers and the public. Attributing violence to violent video gaming is not scientifically sound and draws attention away from other factors. (p. 1)

Furthermore, based on a review of research into school shootings, Klimmt and Possler (2020) concluded,

> Using violent games may be one specific way in which perpetrators try to materialize their fantasies of violence (i.e., a selection effect), but this possibility does not imply a primary causal role of video game violence in motivating perpetrators of mass murder. Public accusations of video games as the main origin of such killings are thus not justified from a scientific point of view. (p. 349)

In fact, as violent video games gained popularity in the United States, youth violence dropped (Ferguson, 2015). It is important to acknowledge that although the correlation was "remarkably strong" (p. 204), it did not indicate a causal relationship.

Notably, gun-based gameplay can influence young adults' attitudes about gun control policies and public safety. College students with more experience playing violent video games (including first-person shooter games) who used realistic gun-like

Playing a video game that has a gun-like controller influences the attitudes of young adults toward public safety and gun control policies.

controllers were less likely to support gun control (Lapierre & Farrar, 2016). Furthermore, participants who were more experienced with gun-like controllers were more likely to believe that greater access to guns would result in greater public safety. The researchers posited that "if guns can help you succeed and keep you safe in the game environment, frequent players may adopt similar attitudes toward real-life firearms in real-world settings" (p. 10).

A Summary of the Effects of Violent Video Games

Klimmt and Possler (2020) reviewed violent video games, reaching three conclusions.

1. The body of research shows playing violent video games "bears a risk of producing higher levels of aggression-related outcomes" (p. 349).

2. However, when looking at the entire gaming population, the average effect size on aggressive thoughts, feelings, and behaviors is small.

3. Personal characteristics of video gamers can "increase the susceptibility to aggression-promoting consequences of violent games substantially" (p. 349).

The Ongoing Debate about Video Game Addiction

It is common to hear parents express concerns about their children being addicted to video games, and mainstream media reports where video games are a part of the story often grab public attention. For example, a South Korean couple was arrested in 2010 after their 3-month-old daughter died of starvation after the couple repeatedly spent up to 12 hours a day in an internet café playing a video game (Cho, 2010). You may ask yourself, "What game could be so interesting that they would neglect their baby girl like that?" According to police, the couple was playing a game called *Prius Online*—where they were raising a "virtual daughter." Other South Koreans' deaths have also been attributed to extreme video game binges. In 2002, a 24-year-old man died after playing video games for 86 hours straight, and a 28-year-old man died a few years later from a heart attack after playing *StarCraft* for 50 hours (M. Kim, 2019). Specialized clinics across South Korea have treated more than 17,000 people for what they call "game overindulgence" (V. Kim, 2019). Video game addiction is referred to by many different names throughout the literature, including problematic or pathological gaming.

The World Health Organization (WHO) included "gaming disorder" in the 11th edition of the International Classification of Diseases (World Health Organization, 2018). The American Psychiatric Association added "internet gaming disorder" to Section III of the *Diagnostic and Statistical Manual of Mental Disorders* (*DSM-5*; APA, 2013a), calling it "a condition warranting more clinical research and experience before it might be considered for inclusion in the main book as a formal disorder" (APA, 2013b, para. 1). Currently, the only behavioral addiction listed in the *DSM-5* is gambling disorder (APA, n.d.). Addictions to alcohol, tobacco, opioids, etc. fall under substance-related disorders. Scans of so-called video game addicts' brains are very similar to scans of people suffering from substance abuse (Han et al., 2010; Weinstein, 2010).

The APA's (2013a) proposed symptoms of internet gaming disorder include:

1. Being preoccupied with gaming
2. Experiencing withdrawal symptoms (e.g., anxiety, sadness, irritability) when gaming is not possible or taken away
3. Experiencing tolerance, which means gamers need to increase the amount of time playing to satisfy their urge to play
4. Being unable to reduce the time spent gaming or having unsuccessful attempts to quit gaming
5. Choosing gaming over other activities or losing interest in previously enjoyed activities because of gaming
6. Continuing to play video games despite problems
7. Lying to family members about how much time is spent gaming
8. Using video games to relieve negative moods (e.g., hopelessness or guilt)
9. Risking or losing a relationship or job because of gaming

Under the APA's criteria, a person could be diagnosed with internet gaming disorder if they experience significant distress or impairment from five or more of listed symptoms in a year. Meanwhile, the WHO's criteria for diagnosing someone with internet gaming disorder is much broader, requiring no clear symptoms other than video games interfering with other activities.

Przybylski et al. (2017) were the first to study internet gaming disorder using APA's criteria. Only 2.4% of gamers had five or more symptoms. However, only 0.3% to 1% also reported feelings of distress, which would make them meet the threshold for a possible internet gaming disorder diagnosis. Although those who met the criteria for a possible diagnosis had lower levels of physical activity and mental health and higher social activity compared to other gamers, none of the differences were statistically significant, which is contrary to widely held notions that internet gaming disorder is related to poorer health (Markey & Ferguson, 2017). Reviewing Przybylski et al.'s findings, Markey and Ferguson (2017) conclude that "video game addiction might be a real thing, but it is not the epidemic that some have made it out to be" (p. 196). (For a look at how pathological video game use can change over time, check out Research Spotlight 2.)

A recent survey of scholars who study the impact of video games on behavior found a lack of consensus about the validity of the *DSM-5*'s criteria for internet gaming disorder and the WHO's diagnosis of gaming disorder (Ferguson & Colwell, 2019). However, the survey did find that a majority (60.8%) agreed that pathological gaming could be a type of mental health problem.

RESEARCH SPOTLIGHT 2

Pathological Video Game Symptoms from Adolescence to Emerging Adulthood:
A 6-Year Longitudinal Study of Trajectories, Predictors, and Outcomes
Sarah M. Coyne, Laura A. Stockdale, Wayne Warburton,
Douglas A. Gentile, Chongming Yang, and Brett. M. Merrill (2020)
Developmental Psychology, 56(7), 1385–1396

Many studies examine the short-term impact of playing video games, but there are fewer longitudinal studies that show effects over time. In this longitudinal study, Coyne et al. examined how pathological symptoms can increase or decrease over time, what predicts pathological use, and what the resulting outcomes are.

Predictions

Rather than formulating research questions or articulating labeled hypotheses, Coyne et al. made the following predictions:

1. A small group of gamers will exhibit high levels of pathological video game use throughout the study.

2. Being male; having high depression, anxiety, and shyness; coming from a single parent home; and low parental knowledge will predict high pathological symptoms.

3. The group with higher levels of pathological symptoms will exhibit worse function over time (such as higher anxiety and depression, aggression, shyness, delinquency, and problematic cell phone use; lower prosocial behavior and empathy; worse financial or vocational situations).

4. A small percentage of pathological gamers will display "turn-around behaviors," where pathological gaming will decrease over time.

Method

Of the 385 adolescent participants, 53% were female. Participants were between 14 and 16 years old, with a mean age of 15.01, at the start of the study. The majority (70%) of participants were European American, 12% were multiethnic, 10% were African American, and 5% were Asian American. The remaining participants were another ethnicity. Most participants (70%) lived in a two-parent (married) home. Almost all (99.2%) were in high school at the beginning of the study. At the end of the study, 74% were in college or vocational training programs, 20% graduated high school but did not pursue further education, 2.3% had graduated college, and 2% had dropped out of high school.

(continued)

Researchers gathered data from the participants in six waves approximately one year apart. (This study started data collection before the APA published its proposed criteria for internet gaming disorder, but the criteria used were adapted from those for pathological gambling, which is often viewed as a similar condition.) Pathological video game use was measured in each wave. Depression, anxiety, aggression, delinquency, empathy, prosocial behavior, and shyness were measured in Waves 1 and 6. Parental knowledge of the participants' behaviors and activities were measured only in Wave 1. Financial stress and problematic cell phone use were measured during Wave 6.

Results

The participants were divided into different classes based on their level of pathological game use and how it changed over the course of six years. The study identified three trajectories for pathological gaming tendencies: increasing, moderate, and nonpathological. 10.1% (n=39) displayed the highest level of pathological gaming symptoms at the start of the study. Over the course of six years, their symptoms progressively increased, with a noticeable jump in the final two waves. This class was labeled as the "increasing symptoms" group. The next class exhibited moderate levels of pathological video game use at the beginning of the study, but their symptoms did not change over time. 17.95% (n=69) of the participants fell into this "moderate symptoms" group. The overwhelming majority of participants, (72%, n=277) showed few symptoms at the beginning of the study, had an increase in Wave 3, and then decreased in each subsequent wave. This group was labeled "nonpathological."

Statistical analyses revealed very few predictors of pathological video game use. Both the increasing and moderate groups were significantly more likely to be male in comparison to the nonpathological group. (This is in line with other research findings that males are more likely to be video game addicts or problematic users [e.g., Mentzoni et al., 2011].) The increasing group's prosocial behavior was also significantly lower than the moderate group. Prosocial behaviors act as a "protective factor" against the development of pathological video game use. No other variables predicted class membership.

Regarding outcomes, the increasing and moderate groups both had higher levels of aggression, shyness, and depression compared to the nonpathological group at the end of the study. The increasing group also had higher anxiety and problematic cell phone use than the nonpathological group. The researchers noted that the increasing and moderate groups were similar, except for the increasing group's higher problematic cell phone use. There were no other differences among the classes when looking at prosocial behavior, empathy, delinquency, financial stress, or vocational situation.

The authors said this study provides further evidence that gaming disorder is not merely the symptom of some other problem, such as depression. They pointed to their findings that showed the increasing and moderate groups had significantly poorer mental health and social and behavior problems in Wave 6 compared to the nonpathological group, despite those variables not being statistically different among the groups in Wave 1. However, more longitudinal research is needed.

They also highlighted the moderate group's higher levels of shyness, aggression, and depression compared to the nonpathological players as a possible cause for concern, noting that having some symptoms—but not the five needed for a diagnosis as recommended in the *DSM-5*—could warrant a classification of preclinical or problematic. (Under the current APA recommendations, someone would either have or not have gaming disorder.)

Finally, the scholars indicated that their findings counter stereotypes of gamers living in their parents' basement because they are not able to financially support themselves or get a job. Pathological video game users appear to be just as financially stable and capable of moving forward in life as nonpathological users, at least in their early 20s.

There are also concerns among scholars that the criteria for diagnosing internet gaming disorder are too broad, which could cause some normal gameplay to be classified as pathological (e.g., Ferguson & Colwell, 2019; Markey & Ferguson, 2017; Przybylski et al., 2017). Ferguson and Colwell (2019) said that whereas using alcohol or heroin to reduce stress could be a sign of addiction, "doing the same with video games is little different from the use of any other hobby" (p. 2). Given the differing views on the issue of internet gaming disorder or video game addiction, much more research and refinement will be needed to reach a consensus.

Positive Effects of Video Games

Of course, not all of the effects of video games are bad, and there is a great deal of research that focuses on the primary intended effect of playing video games: entertainment (Klimmt & Possler, 2020). Video games offer immersive entertainment experiences (e.g., Klimmt, 2003; Vorderer & Bryant, 2006) where players can form authentic emotional attachments to characters (Coulson et al., 2012). Research on the entertaining aspect of video games focuses on three key features: the interactive nature of players' choices influencing the game, the interplay between interactivity and the narrative framework where players can become a character and feel like they are in the game world, and the social interactions of cooperative or competitive games (see Klimmt & Possler, 2020, for a review).

Scholars are also examining other aspects of gameplay that can impact enjoyment, such as **flow**. Flow is a mental state where a person is fully absorbed in an activity that requires complete focus, attention, and involvement (Csikszentmihalyi, 1988). All of us have experienced flow at some point in our lives. Perhaps you were reading a good book or watching television and didn't hear your phone ring or notice another person enter the room. As an interactive medium, video games present a unique opportunity to study flow. Jin (2011) found that greater flow was achieved when there is an optimal balance between a game's level of difficulty and the player's level of skill. You could think of this balance as the "Goldilocks zone" for gaming: not too hard, not too easy, but just challenging enough to keep you motivated to continue playing. When flow is achieved in the gaming experience, it can be highly enjoyable (Sherry, 2004).

Granic et al.'s (2014) review of positive effects of video games noted cognitive, motivational, emotional, and social benefits. Cognitive benefits included improved spatial and problem-solving skills and enhanced creativity. Motivational benefits arise from learning from in-game failures and developing an optimistic, persistent mindset. Improving players' moods and feelings of pride after overcoming significant in-game challenges are examples of emotional benefits. Social benefits include developing prosocial skills through cooperative play. Cooperative play in violent games can boost helpful behaviors both on and offline and playing violent games in groups can reduce hostile feelings.

Educational Games

In addition to being entertaining, video games are useful and effective tools for education—what is often referred to as "game-based learning" (Prensky, 2001). Countless people remember playing some early educational computer games in elementary school—games like *The Oregon Trail* or *Where in the World Is Carmen Sandiego?*—to learn about life (or death by dysentery) on the American frontier or global geography, respectively. Now it is common to see teachers integrating game-based learning through online platforms like Kahoot! to help students study.

According to educational theories, teaching is more effective if students are motivated to learn, receive instantaneous feedback, and can apply their knowledge in a variety of different contexts (see the education chapters in Ritterfeld et al., 2009, for further review). Video games can accomplish all of these things by challenging students to complete a task or level, and the difficulty of a game can be adjusted to match a player's growing knowledge (Fisch, 2009). However, achieving the right balance between fun and education is a key challenge for designing game-based learning (de Freitas, 2018).

Some of you probably think back to your middle school and high school history classes and remember them as extremely boring—just a bunch of dates and names. Video games, such as *Making History*, can allow students to get "hands-on" experience with the past, so to speak. McDivitt (2006) realized that his high school history students were not really interested in learning about European history leading up to World War II. In a semi-experimental study, McDivitt divided his classes into two groups: the control group continued to receive standard lectures, while the experimental group played *Making History*, a game that allows players to take control of a country between 1938 and 1945. Although McDivitt did not analyze his data with standard statistical methods, students who played the game had a better understanding of historical events leading up to WWII when compared with students who just listened to normal lectures. According to Bellotti et al. (2009), educational games can be enjoyed as much as commercial off-the-shelf games. In their experiment, the researchers developed a massively multiplayer online role-playing game (MMORPG) called *SeaGame* to teach proper behaviors about water-related activities (e.g., boating, jet skiing, scuba diving).

A meta-analysis of educational games and interactive simulations revealed that when used as teaching tools, games have advantages over traditional teaching methods (Vogel et al., 2006). The effects of game-based learning can be enhanced by blending games and face-to-face teaching (de Freitas, 2018). Meta-analyses by Clark et al. (2016) and Wouters et al. (2013) also concluded that video games can be powerful teaching tools that can lead to more learning and information retention in comparison to traditional teaching methods. Allowing students to create their own video games is also an effective teaching method because it encourages students to be creative and develop their own solutions to problems they create (Gaskin & Berente, 2011).

Educators are also incorporating virtual reality into the classroom. Dean et al. (2018) taught college students about gender and social scripts using the VR game *Star Trek Bridge Crew.* They had students play the game with an avatar of a gender different from what they identified as in real life. The researchers observed that the students' "embodied experience in VR clearly led to a more meaningful and experiential learning experience" (p. 5).

Although serious games are primarily looked at as 21st-century *teaching* tools, some researchers report that games may also be a good *assessment* tool. Although conventional paper-and-pencil tests may show teachers *what* a student knows, they tell us little about what students can *do* with that knowledge (Rothman, 2011). Making online assessments, such as quizzes and multiple-choice tests, more game-like can ease test anxiety (Pitoyo et al. 2019) and support student learning by encouraging them to repeatedly engage with course material and improving long-term knowledge retention (Petrovic-Dzerdz, 2019).

Exergames and Games for Health-Based Knowledge

One of the common fears about gaming is that it is turning millions of children and adults into inactive, unhealthy couch potatoes. In fact, just one hour of video gameplay resulted in an increase in what is generally known as "mindless eating," which is eating without feeling hungry (Chaput et al., 2011). Instead of trying to figure out how to lure players away from their consoles, TVs, and tablets, game designers have created games to promote exercise and other healthy activities. Using exergames in educational settings, such as PE classes, can help promote a healthier lifestyle choices and serve as a tool for helping combat high obesity rates in children and adolescents (see Vaghetti et al., 2018, for a review). Playing exergames with the Sony PlayStation for 6 months resulted in reductions in body-mass index (BMI) and total fat percentages, although the results were small (Maddison et al., 2011). A more recent meta-analysis found game-based interventions can produce a small but statistically significant reduction in BMI (Ameryoun et al., 2018).

One of the most well-known consoles for exergames was the Nintendo Wii. Utilizing motion-sensing technology, players moved their bodies to play various games like *Wii Tennis* and *Wii Bowling*. The *Wii Fit* game also included exercises for balance, muscle toning, aerobic activity, and yoga (Cummings & Duncan, 2010). Newer gaming systems have continued the exergame trend, such as *Fitness Boxing* for the Nintendo Switch. Although Nintendo no longer manufactures the Wii, many exergame studies still use the platform as part of their experiments.

In research into the Wii's effectiveness as a tool for improving healthy behaviors, players rated exercising with the Wii higher than traditional exercise activities, such as walking and jogging (Graves et al., 2010). The hula and step games produced equivalent energy expenditures to speed walking (Worley et al., 2011). *Dance Revolution*, which can be played on a variety of game consoles, engages gamers in moderate levels of physical activity (see Anderson et al., 2011, for a review). Location-based games that require players to walk to various places, such as *Pokémon GO* and *Harry Potter: Wizards Unite* (the latter shut down in 2022), can result in increases in physical activity (Barkley et al., 2017; Laato et al., 2020). For more on mobile gaming, see Chapter 20.

Another area of research examines the effects of playing video games on older populations. When the Wii first launched, it was common to see stories on the news about seniors playing the Wii in retirement homes or hospitals, and multiple studies found that using the Wii was very beneficial to older players. Due to the Wii's low cost (compared to expensive medical equipment), therapists used it to improve balance in adults over 65 (Bainbridge et al., 2011). (Although Bainbridge et al.'s findings were not statistically significant, participants did demonstrate *clinically* significant improvements in balance.) Wii usage also improved balance and leg strength in

Playing augmented reality games like *Pokémon GO* could result in increases in physical activity.

women 30 to 58 years old (Nitz et al., 2010). Older adults' use of exergames on the Wii and Xbox Kinect can also reduce loneliness, increase social connections, and boost positive attitudes toward others (see Li et al., 2018, for a review). Additionally, exergames can reduce cognitive decline associated with aging and improve cognitive function for older adults with cognitive impairments and neurodegenerative diseases, such as Alzheimer's (see Stanmore et al., 2017, for a review.) Exergame-based therapy can also be effective for Parkinson's Disease rehabilitation (Garcia-Agundez et al., 2019).

Health-related games have been used to help patients learn to cope with diseases, such as cancer (Cole et al., 2006), diabetes (Brown et al., 1997; Lieberman, 2001), and asthma (Homer et al., 2000; Lieberman, 2001). Using video games in these situations allows patients to safely experiment with behavior change in a virtual world. In a game, patients can learn ways to correctly manage their disease (e.g., checking blood pressure, taking insulin), or they can experience the negative outcomes of mismanagement without ever being in real danger (Lee et al., 2009). A recent study found that playing a health-based computer game that highlighted the risks of smoking had a greater impact than a print brochure on participants' attitudes about smoking and their intention to quit, especially when fear appeals were used (Kim et al., 2020; also see Chapter 15 for more on fear appeals in health communication).

Playing video games has positive effects for those with special needs. Children with Down syndrome who played with Wii showed improvement in sensorimotor functions (Wuang et al., 2011). Using the Wii helped people with mental disabilities engage in daily physical activities (Shih, 2011).

Notably, some types of video games have negative health-related effects. Racing games can increase cognitive access to risk-related emotions and a willingness to engage in risky driving behaviors, and those racing games can also impact health behaviors (Fischer, 2009; Fischer et al., 2007, 2008). Participants who played racing games that glorified risky driving behavior were significantly less likely to take part in a health checkup compared to gamers who played risk-neutral games (Kastenmüller et al., 2014).

Although video games may be a convenient form of exercise for many armchair athletes, playing exergames is not without risks. Some players developed what is known as "Wii-itis" from playing too much *Wii Tennis* (Bonis, 2007), Wii knee (i.e., dislocating the knee) during bowling, and even Achilles Wii-itis where the Achilles tendon ruptures during running or stretching games (Sparks et al., 2011).

Games for Social Change

In addition to education and health, games can be used to increase awareness about political, religious, and social issues. An example of a game that fits into this category is *Crisis in the Gulf*, which was created in response to the 2010 BP oil spill in the Gulf of Mexico. *Darfur Is Dying* is perhaps one of the most viral social video games. The game allows players to experience life as one of the 2.5 million refugees in the Sudan's Darfur region, keeping their refugee camp operational while facing attacks by militias (DarfurIsDying.com, 2008). Playing the game resulted in a greater willingness to help those living in Darfur compared to simply reading the same information (Peng et al., 2010). In another study, researchers allowed inner-city children to design their own video games as a way for them to express and explore social issues in their neighborhoods (Ross & Tomlinson, 2010).

The nonprofit organization Games for Change (gamesforchange.org) seeks to create real-world change through video games and other forms of immersive media. As of 2022, the site hosts more than 150 games designed to engage players with contemporary social issues. For example, the game *Tree* addresses climate change by using virtual reality to allow players to experience the life cycle of a tree in the rain forest, which ends in the tree being cut down and burned by industrial loggers.

Although activist games have been around for decades, more work is needed to better establish video games as a tool for activism and true social change (see Anderson-Barkley & Fogleson, 2018, for a review).

Summary

In this chapter, we have examined the average modern gamer, which is not at all like the commonly held stereotype of teen boys playing in their parents' basement. A majority of U.S. adults play video games. The average gamer is in their early thirties, and almost half of gamers are female.

This chapter also looked at the ongoing debate surrounding the effects of violent video games. Do they result in an increase in aggression? Overall, games can produce a negative effect on aggression; however, the effect is small. There has also been a shift away from examining potential universal effects of violent video games to a more individualized approach that seeks to identify why some people may be more susceptible to the effects of violent games.

We also examined internet gaming disorder, which is more commonly known as video game addiction. Although it has not yet been classified as an official disorder by the American Psychiatric Association, research has found that the brain responds to video game addiction in much the same way as a drug addict's brain to drug use.

Meanwhile, the World Health Organization is acknowledging gaming disorder as a diagnosable condition.

All of the findings about video games are not negative. Serious games have been effective educational tools. This is often credited to the adaptive nature of video games that allow for player input and the constant feedback supplied in an engaging mediated environment. In addition to school use, many serious games have proven to be an effective means of health education. The Nintendo Wii paved the way for the development of new exergames that are both fun and engage players in physical activity. Games are also a means by which people can learn about social issues happening around the world, like *Darfur Is Dying*.

Of course, video games change rapidly, therefore research in this field will be ongoing. Much like a in video game, researchers will encounter new challenges and levels of difficulty as they seek to understand the effects games have on players. For video game researchers, the words GAME OVER will probably never be seen.

19

Effects of the Internet and Social Media

> Before social media, we did without so much attention. No computers, no cellphones. We had rotary phones and Polaroid cameras. Our photo albums sat in the attic. No one ever saw our pictures. It's a good thing too, because I looked like a fat goat in our photos.
>
> —Sean Dietrich, 2015

The internet is easily the most pervasive form of mass media that we encounter in our lives. Internet-based terminology has even become a staple of everyday vocabulary. For instance, Google and Venmo are not just a website and an app that we use; they are verbs in everyday conversation (e.g., "I Googled how to change a tire" or "I'll Venmo you for lunch."). Furthermore, even traditional forms of mass communication drive us toward the internet. Radio stations and magazines promote exclusive content on their websites or apps. Many newspapers have shifted to online-only publication. Hollywood studios can bypass theaters and allow audiences to stream new movies from the comfort of home. Television shows often display hashtags on the screen (e.g., #Jeopardy, #TheVoice, #Dateline) to encourage viewers to talk about the program and engage with fellow viewers on social media. On a much more serious note, hashtags, such as #BlackLivesMatter, can be used to build solidarity and broaden the impact of social movements (Mundt et al., 2018).

As technology continues to make the internet faster and more available, we will find new ways to incorporate online activities into our daily lives. We have the ability to access the internet from anywhere at any time via smartphones. (Learn more about the effects of smartphones in Chapter 20). Automobile manufacturers advertise cars as mobile Wi-Fi hotspots. Smart speakers ensure that the vast quantities of information online are never more than a voice command away. Needless to say, the internet is our constant companion—our lifeline to the world, so to speak.

There are more than 4.5 billion internet users worldwide—59% of the global population—and more than 3.8 billion people use social media (Kemp, 2020). In the

United States, 93% of adults were internet users in 2021, up from just 52% in 2000, (Pew Research Center, 2021a) and 72% use social media, up from 5% in 2005 (Pew Research Center, 2021c). Looking specifically at teens, 45% say they are online "almost constantly," while another 44% go online multiple times each day (Anderson & Jaing, 2018). The vast majority of teens are on social media daily (Twenge et al., 2019). Moreover, the majority of Facebook, Snapchat, Instagram, and YouTube users visit the platforms daily (Pew Research Center, 2021c).

In this chapter, we will explore how and why billions of people worldwide use social media, and we will discuss the evolution of computer-mediated communication. We will also look at the concerns about cyberbullying and the ongoing debate about internet addiction. We close the chapter with a look at digital detoxes and how the internet has affected the workplace.

How Much Time Do We Spend Online and What Do We Do There?

To examine the effects of internet use, we must first look at what people do when they go online (Lin, 2009). U.S. adults spend 10 and a half hours a day with media, and internet use makes up just over 3 hours of that total (Nielsen, 2019). The overwhelming majority—2 hours and 31 minutes—takes place on smartphones, while only 31 minutes takes place on computers.

Numerous reports present data about the different ways we spend time online (e.g., Nielsen, 2019; Parrish, 2016; Verto Analytics, 2018), but all repeatedly indicate that social media use is the dominant online activity. Globally, the average internet user spends almost two and a half hours a day on social networks and messaging apps, with roughly seven accounts across various platforms (GlobalWebIndex, 2020). In a recent survey, teens reported spending more than four hours a day on social media (Piper Sandler, 2021). For instance, Snapchat users check the app an average of 30 times a day.

In the United States, more adults use YouTube (81%), Facebook (69%), and Instagram (40%) than other social media platforms (Auxier & Anderson, 2021; see Figure 19.1). Data into teens' social media use and preferences paints a different picture: 35% said Snapchat was their favorite social media platform, followed by TikTok (30%) and Instagram (22%) (Piper Sandler, 2021). Instagram is the most-used social media for teens—with 81% using the app each month.

Streaming video is another area of heavy use on the internet. Video accounts for almost 60% of downstream traffic on the internet, with Netflix—the most popular video site in the world—alone accounting for 15% (Sandvine, 2018). Globally, Netflix users stream almost 165 million hours of video per day, using more than 494 million gigabytes of bandwidth (Meadows, 2019). Netflix is also the top video streaming platform with teens (Piper Sandler, 2021). YouTube, on the other hand, is the dominant video streaming app on mobile devices (Sandvine, 2018), and people watch over a *billion* hours of content on YouTube every day (YouTube, n.d.).

Although many of us often go online for a specific reason, more than 80% of internet users in the United States say they often or sometimes go online without a specific destination in mind (Digital Future Report, 2018).

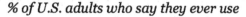

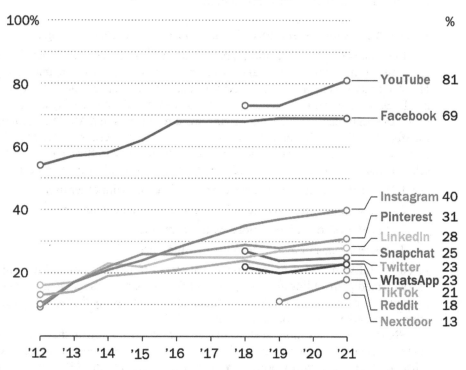

Note: Pre-2018 telephone poll data is not available for YouTube, Snapchat and WhatsApp; pre-2019 telephone poll data is not available for Reddit. Pre-2021 telephone poll data is not available for TikTok. Trend data is not available for Nextdoor.

PEW RESEARCH CENTER (2021)

Figure 19.1   Social media use by U.S. adults.

Effects of Social Media Use

Part of what makes the internet such a unique medium for communication is its technological fluidity (Lin, 2009). We can send and receive information in various ways (e.g., text, pictures, videos, music)—all of which allow us to multitask in an online environment (Lin, 2003). For example, you can binge the latest hit show on Netflix while posting pictures from your roommate's birthday party to Instagram, email your journalism professor about tomorrow's looming deadline, listen to Adele's latest album on Spotify, and watch the latest viral YouTube video all at the same time! Media scholars refer to this type of behavior as **media multitasking** (Roberts et al.,

2005; Zhong et al., 2011). We will begin our look at internet effects by focusing on the most popular internet activity: social media.

Clarifying Social Media and Social Network Site Terminology

In non-academic conversations about platforms like Facebook, Twitter, and Instagram, the terms "social media" and "social network sites" (SNSs) are interchangeable. However, media scholars classify SNSs as a subset of social media (Fox & McEwan, 2020). Because technological advances happen so rapidly, developing a concrete definition of social media can be challenging. As a result, Fox and McEwan (2020) opted for an approach utilizing affordances (i.e., qualities or properties) to better understand social media. In their review, they outlined four universal affordances identified by scholars that differentiate social media from other communication channels:

1. *Interactivity*, both with the system's interface and with other users;
2. *Accessibility* regardless of location, time, and other constraints;
3. *Visibility* of social interactions with others; and
4. *Personalization* of messages to various audiences.

Fox and McEwan also provided a review of other affordances not found on all forms of social media, including *anonymity* or *identifiability* of a user's real name, *editability* of messages, and *network association* that "enables users to visibly link to other users, creating a traceable network of connections" (p. 375).

SNSs are defined more specifically as web-based platforms that allow users to "(1) construct a public or semi-public profile within a bounded system, (2) articulate a list of other users with whom they share a connection, and (3) view and traverse their list of connections and those made by others in the system" (boyd & Ellison, 2007, p. 211).

Examining Social Network Site Effects

Due to Facebook's dominance, both in terms of total internet use and being the top SNS, a great deal of research has been conducted on the platform and the type of people who use it. Although much of the research focuses on reasons why people visit the site and what type of people are likely to share certain types of information, a continually growing body of research examines the effects of using Facebook and other platforms, like Twitter, Instagram, and Snapchat. Research into TikTok is in relatively early stages. Some of the areas of interest in SNS research that we will explore include what factors lead to employing a SNS, the uses and gratifications (U&G) people seek (see Chapter 9 for more about U&G), the effects of profile pictures and the number of friends on SNS users, concerns about privacy, and building and maintaining online social capital.

Social Interaction and Online "Friends." Facebook has 2.93 billion monthly active users and 1.97 billion daily active users (Meta, 2022). According to the Pew Research Center, the most common places for meeting friends online are social media sites; in fact, a majority of 13- to 17-year-olds have made a friend on social media (Lenhart et al., 2015). Many people use Facebook as a tool for keeping up with friends (e.g., Brandtzæg et al., 2010; Coyle & Vaughn, 2008; Joinson, 2008; Lenhart et al., 2010) and relationship maintenance (Ferris & Hollenbaugh, 2018; Park & Lee, 2014). Meta (n.d.), the parent company of Facebook, WhatsApp, and Instagram, says that more than one billion stories are shared daily across their apps and more than 140 billion messages are sent every day. In a study of South Korean college students, social interaction on Instagram significantly influenced intentions to continue using the photo sharing platform (Hwang & Cho, 2018). Most teens who use social media (83%) said they feel more connected to their friend's daily lives, and 70% reported being more aware of their friends' feelings because of social media (Lenhart et al., 2015).

So who, exactly, are our online "friends"? Debatin et al. (2009) highlighted the fact that "the category 'friend' is very broad and ambiguous in the online world; it may include anyone from an intimate to casual acquaintance or a complete stranger of whom only their online identity is known" (p. 87). Several studies (e.g., boyd & Ellison, 2008; Coyle & Vaughn, 2008; Young & Bradford Brown, 2013) have found that SNS users generally do not seek out new people online but rather focus on the relationships with people they already know. However, Facebook has been shown to be an effective means for new friends to become better acquainted (Hsu et al., 2011). There are numerous groups and pages that can connect people with common interests, and hashtags can help people find similar content or profiles.

Personality Factors.   When examining the type of personality factors that affect Facebook use, Amichai-Hamburger and Vinitzky (2010) discovered that those who scored higher on measures of openness were more likely to use Facebook as a communication tool and were more likely to engage with more of Facebook's features. On the other hand, those scoring higher on measures of neuroticism and introversion were more likely to post personal information and photos than those who were less neurotic and more extroverted. Users who are motivated to meet new people online and whose personalities are more agreeable (e.g., they show more trust, kindness, and affection) and less conscientious (e.g., they are less thoughtful and have weaker impulse control) were more dependent on Facebook overall (Ferris & Hollenbaugh, 2018). Those with a lower score on **need for cognition** (NFC)—which is the "propensity to engage in and enjoy cognitively demanding tasks" (B. Zong et al., 2011, p. 1265)—were more likely to use SNSs in general compared to those with a higher NFC score. Moreover, media multitaskers are more likely to use SNSs and stay on the internet for longer periods of time than non-multitaskers. In a recent study, extroversion and social anxiety both significantly correlate to greater SNS use (Cheng et al., 2019).

Narcissism is a personality trait often studied by social media researchers. McCain and Campbell (2018) conducted a meta-analysis of research from around the world, with a combined sample of more than 12,000 participants. They found a positive association between grandiose narcissism—described by the researchers as "the extraverted, grandiose and callous form of narcissism" (p. 309)—and the amount of time spent on social media, frequency of posting, number of friends or followers, and the frequency of posting selfies. In another study, narcissism was associated with posting selfies online, and links between narcissism and posting selfies was stronger for men than for women (Sorokowski et al., 2015). Weiser (2015) noted "that for individuals high in narcissism, posting selfies constitutes a means to not only seek attention and admiration from others . . . but also to convey heightened perceptions of leadership, authority, and dominance" (p. 480). Sheldon and Bryant (2016) examined narcissism and Instagram use. Narcissists wanted to be seen by others in a positive light and used Instagram to appear "cool."

On the other hand, in more recent studies there was no significant relationship between narcissism and social media use (e.g., Barry et al., 2019). Frederick and Zhang (2019) suggest this may be because social media use is so commonplace in today's society that online behaviors previously viewed as self-focused have become normalized to the point that narcissists' behavior no longer stands out when compared to anyone else's.

Effects on Well-Being.   The impact of SNSs on well-being is a popular topic for researchers. Research into this area examines the nature of SNS use, consumed content, and individual traits of users. Much of the research focuses on Facebook, and results are mixed. Some studies demonstrate Facebook use positively impacts well-being (Valenzuela et al., 2009; Yang & Brown, 2016), but others indicate Facebook use has negative impacts on well-being (Blease, 2015; Kalpidou et al., 2011; Satici & Uysal, 2015; Vogel et al., 2014) and life satisfaction (Stieger, 2019). A meta-analysis of 61 studies involving more than 19,000 participants showed that Facebook had a very small negative effect on well-being (Huang, 2017).

In late 2021, Facebook Inc. (now Meta) came under fire after a *Wall Street Journal* article revealed that the company's own research found that Instagram has negative effects on a sizable portion of its users and that the company downplayed those effects in public (Wells et al., 2021). For instance, researchers at Facebook discovered that almost a third of teen girls said when they had negative thoughts about their own bodies, Instagram made them feel even worse. Facebook researchers also determined that among teens who said they had suicidal thoughts, 6% of American and 13% of British users traced those thoughts back to Instagram. The *WSJ* article did report that the internal research concluded that effects of Instagram use were not harmful to the majority of the app's users: "For most teenagers, the effects of 'negative social comparison' are manageable and can be outweighed by the app's utility as a fun way for users to express themselves and connect with friends, the research says" (Wells et al., 2021, para. 47). We will discuss other research findings related to Instagram later in this chapter.

In addition to internal research conducted by social media companies, a great deal of SNS research is conducted on college campuses for two reasons: (1) it is convenient for researchers, many of whom are college professors, and (2) almost all college students use SNSs. Looking specifically at Facebook, earlier research into the platform demonstrated that college freshmen spend more time on the site than upperclassmen (Yang & Brown, 2013) Freshmen students had a stronger emotional connection to Facebook when compared to upperclassmen, and their heavy use of Facebook was connected to lower self-esteem and academic performance (Kalpidou et al., 2011). A larger number of Facebook friends for freshmen was negatively linked to emotional and academic adjustment. First-year students turn to Facebook as a coping strategy to alleviate the stresses of college life. It is also common for college freshmen to use Facebook for keeping up with old high school friends and learning about new people they meet on campus (Ellison et al., 2007, 2011). In other research, college students were more interested in using Facebook to maintain existing social relationships than to search for new connections (Yang & Bradford Brown, 2013). During the first semester of college, freshmen are also more guarded in their self-presentation on Facebook when they initially come on campus; however, they become more relaxed by the end of the first semester (Yang & Bradford Brown, 2016). Conversely, upperclassmen with more Facebook friends displayed more positive relationships for emotional and academic adjustment and stronger attachment to their school (Kalpidou et al., 2011). By the time a student is an upperclassman, they have made more friends on campus and are more engaged in campus activities.

When considering overall internet use, the web can be very beneficial to foreign students as they create new social networks (Lee et al., 2011a). Moreover, students who are more confident in their social skills tend to be more extroverted online, build more online social support, and are more satisfied with their school lives (Liu & LaRose, 2008). Going online can actually *increase* the amount of time spent in face-to-face communication (Carrier et al., 2015). For introverts, Facebook is related to increased face-to-face communication in interpersonal relationships, suggesting that interacting with others on Facebook allows introverts to build rapport and trust in a less threatening social environment, which can then make them more comfortable engaging in face-to-face interactions (Spradlin et al., 2019).

Kim and Lee (2011) discovered that positive self-presentation strategies (i.e., framing yourself with socially desirable qualities—put simply, selectively representing yourself in a positive light) and the number of Facebook friends were positively associated with well-being. Honest self-presentation (i.e., showing your true self, "warts and all") resulted in greater happiness derived from Facebook friends. Generally, a greater amount of authentic self-disclosure on SNSs resulted in higher levels of well-being (Lee et al., 2011b) and self-esteem (Yang & Bradford Brown, 2016). The results of these studies mirror the findings of earlier research (e.g., McKenna et al., 2002) that the foundation of a successful online relationship is honestly revealing one's true self.

Our motivations behind SNS activities can also impact our well-being. When people use Facebook for their own enjoyment and interests, rather than being concerned about other users' opinions, they are more likely to have higher positive affect

Facebook users who share content for their own enjoyment are more likely to have positive emotions and higher self-esteem.

and self-esteem (Manuoğlu & Uysal, 2019). However, "when Facebook activities are motivated by external or internal pressures, they are more likely to be detrimental to one's psychological well-being" (p. 7).

Overall, Seabrook et al.'s (2016) systematic review of 70 studies provides us with a concise summary of the effects of SNSs on well-being: Ultimately, it is the tone and nature of SNS interactions that impacts well-being and self-esteem. Positive and supportive online interactions are associated with positive well-being and life satisfaction; conversely, negative interactions and social comparisons are related to higher levels of depression, anxiety, and loneliness.

Other Effects of SNS Use.   The type of content we see on social media can affect our emotions. An experiment by Kramer et al. (2014) manipulated the amount of positive or negative posts more than 690,000 Facebook users saw in their news feeds. When the number of positive posts in their news feeds were reduced, their own posts contained fewer positive words and more negative words. When the number of negative posts were reduced, the opposite pattern occurred, thus providing evidence that being exposed to others' expressions of emotion on social media can lead us to experience the same emotions, without being aware of the influence. This is known as *emotional contagion*. For Facebook users with high self-esteem, seeing positive posts from close friends can result in feeling happier, but positive posts from distant friends can make them feel worse (Liu et al, 2016). Conversely, negative posts from close Facebook friends can also make high self-esteem users feel worse, while seeing negative posts from distant friends can make them feel better. For more on this study, check out this chapter's Research Spotlight.

RESEARCH SPOTLIGHT

Do Our Facebook Friends Make Us Feel Worse?
A Study of Social Comparison and Emotion
Jiangmeng Liu, Cong Li, Nick Carcioppolo, and Michael North (2016)
Human Communication Research, 42(4), 619–640

The researchers examined the relationship between engaging in social comparison on Facebook and how our emotions can be influenced by content posted by friends on the platform. The researchers based the study on Festinger's (1954) social comparison theory. They examined the impact of self-esteem on how Facebook users compared themselves to positive and negative posts made by both close and distant friends. Their study looked at both upward social comparison (comparison with someone seemingly "superior") and downward social comparison (comparison with someone seemingly "inferior").

Hypotheses

Based on prior research that found upward comparison can have negative effects on a person, while downward comparison can result in positive effects, the researchers developed the following hypothesis.

H1a: When exposed to positive Facebook posts (upward social comparison information), people will exhibit a more negative emotional response than when exposed to negative posts (downward social comparison information).

Meanwhile, prior research into emotional contagion (where people experience the same emotions as others with whom they interact) suggested the following competing hypothesis:

H1b: When exposed to positive Facebook posts, people will exhibit more positive emotion than when exposed to negative posts.

Because of conflicting results in previous research examining the effect of relational closeness on social comparison, the researchers proposed two more competing hypotheses:

H2a: Relational closeness will moderate the influence of Facebook social comparison on individuals' emotions such that when targets are close friends, the social comparison effect will be more salient, generating more negative emotions after exposure to positive posts and more positive emotions after exposure to negative posts, than when targets are distant friends.

H2b: Relational closeness will moderate the influence of Facebook social comparison on individuals' emotions such that when targets are close friends, the reflecting process will function, generating more positive emotions after exposure to positive posts and more negative emotions after exposure to negative posts. When targets are distant friends, the social comparison effect will occur, generating more negative emotions after exposure to positive posts and more positive emotions after exposure to negative posts.

Factoring in the results of other studies on self-esteem and social comparison, the researchers put forth their final hypothesis.

H3: There will be a three-way interaction between relational closeness, self-esteem, and comparison directions. The two-way interaction between relational closeness and comparison directions on emotion will be more prominent for people with high self-esteem than for those with low self-esteem.

Method

The researchers used Craigslist to recruit 163 participants. They ranged in age from 18 to 65, with an average age of just under 33 years old. There were slightly more female participants (53.4%) than male participants (46.6%). Most participants identified themselves as Hispanic (52.8%). Non-Hispanic Caucasians made up 25.8%, while African Americans made up 16.6%. Asians made up 1.2%, and 3.7% identified as Other.

During the laboratory experiment, participants filled out a questionnaire measuring their Facebook usage and self-esteem. Participants were then randomly assigned to one of the two experimental conditions by going onto Facebook and picking either a close or distant friend's profile from their own list of friends. After picking a friend, participants answered a few questions about the friend, including name, age, gender. Researchers also measured how long the friends had known each other, relational closeness, and contact frequency.

The participants were then asked to browse the 10 most recent original posts from the chosen friend's timeline. (These posts had to be text, photos, videos, or other content created by the friend, not content they were tagged in or had shared from other sources.) Next, participants were asked to browse the posts and rate them on a scale of -3 to +3. "No direction or hint was given in the experiment to remind participants to make a social comparison with their friends," the researchers wrote. "Therefore, if the results demonstrated the existence of social comparison, this comparison likely occurred subconsciously" (p. 9).

Researchers then averaged the scores of the 10 posts. The higher the average, the more likely upward comparison occurred; the lower it was, the more likely downward comparison occurred. Participants were given a final questionnaire to assess their emotions. Researchers then thanked the participants and provided a small cash payment for taking part in the study.

Findings

After statistical analyses were performed, H1a, which predicted that exposure to positive posts would result in more negative emotions and vice versa, was not supported. Meanwhile

(continued)

H1b, which predicted that participants could "catch" emotions of their Facebook friend via emotional contagion, was partially supported. The effect of self-esteem on explicit measurements of positive and negative emotion was statistically significant.

Looking at the next two hypotheses, which focused on relational closeness and social comparison, researchers found that participants were happier when their close friends "were superior in posts," and they showed more negative emotions when the friends posted inferior content. Based on these findings, H2a was rejected, but H2b received partial support. The emotional influence of content on Facebook was more salient for high self-esteem people than for those with low self-esteem.

Lastly, participants with high self-esteem mirrored the emotions of their close friends, meaning they "felt better if their friends were doing well, whereas they exhibited negative emotions if their friends were struggling" (p. 14). When high self-esteem participants viewed posts from distant friends, the pattern reversed. Distant friends' positive posts resulted in negative feelings via upward social comparison, and negative posts elicited positive feelings through downward social comparison. Meanwhile, this interaction was not found in participants with low self-esteem. Rather, they were less impacted by posts on Facebook regardless of whether the friend was close or distant. "This result supports the notion that low-self-esteem individuals tend to protect their well-being by avoiding comparison information, whereas high-self-esteem individuals tend to seek self-enhancement even at the risk of negative outcomes" (p. 15). Therefore, H3 was supported.

Yuen et al. (2019) compared the effects of browsing the internet versus using Facebook. Overall, Facebook use was viewed as a less meaningful online activity that negatively impacted mood, compared to general online browsing. Of the various impacts on mood, passive use (i.e., looking at content posted by others but not engaging with it or posting their own content) had the largest negative effect on mood.

SNS users were more dissatisfied with their own bodies after viewing Facebook profiles of attractive users (Haferkamp & Krämer, 2011). This dissatisfaction arose from beliefs that the users could never attain the level of physical beauty seen on attractive users' profiles. Additionally, male participants were more dissatisfied with their own careers after viewing the profiles of successful users. **Social comparison theory** predicts such findings (Festinger, 1954). Seeing people who are attractive, fit, and healthy lowered self-esteem among study participants (Vogel et al., 2014). In a study of middle and high school girls, time spent looking at photos on Facebook—not total time spent on Facebook or the internet—was associated with greater weight dissatisfaction, drive for thinness, self-objectification, and thin ideal internalization (Meier & Gray, 2014). Similarly, frequency of Instagram use correlated with general and physical appearance anxiety, body dissatisfaction, and depressive symptoms in 18- to 35-year-old women (Sherlock & Wagstaff, 2019).

On Instagram, so-called "fitspiration" photos—which are intended to inspire others to adopt healthier lifestyles through exercise and nutrition—can have negative impacts on women's body image. Seeing fitspiration images resulted in increased body dissatisfaction and negative mood for Instagram users (Rounds & Stutts, 2021; Tiggermann & Zaccardo, 2015). Exposure to beauty and fitness images also significantly decreased women's self-rated attractiveness (Sherlock & Wagstaff, 2019). Exposure to fitspiration images could be harmful in the long-term, especially when considering that achieving these ideals is unrealistic for many users.

Another negative effect of SNS use is the fear of privacy invasion. A study of Canadian college students found that while their Facebook, Snapchat, and Instagram accounts tend to be private, their own blogs or websites, LinkedIn, Tumblr, Twitter, and Pinterest profiles tend to be public (Jacobson & Gruzd, 2020). Many college students are uncomfortable with potential employers "cybervetting" job applicants based on what they have posted on social media. However, this does not stop college students from posting questionable content (Miller et al., 2010). In a survey of hiring managers, 70% use SNSs to find out more about job applicants, and nearly 60% say they chose *not* to hire a candidate because of content posted on SNSs (CareerBuilder, 2018). Furthermore, cybervetting does not necessarily stop once you are hired. Almost half of employers check their current employees' social media accounts—one in ten employers check daily—and a third have reprimanded or fired an employee because of content they posted online.

Older Facebook users are afraid that burglars will monitor their social media posts to determine if they are at home (Brandtzæg et al., 2010). These fears are not unwarranted. For instance, police in Hoover, Alabama, arrested two young men who used Facebook to track when people were out of town and then broke into their homes (Ray, 2009).

Evolutions in Computer-Mediated Communication

Although SNSs or texting may serve many of our computer-mediated communication (CMC) needs, many people continue to utilize email for communication. The Radicati Group (2019), a technology market research firm, predicts the total number of consumer and business emails sent per day will top 347 billion by the end of 2023, up from 293 billion in 2019. Over half of the global population used email in 2019, and more than 4.3 billion are predicted to do so by the end of 2023.

A key feature of this type of CMC is that the messages are asynchronous (Lin, 2009). Users are not communicating in real time, allowing them to send and receive messages at their convenience. However, you should not wait too long to reply. Sought after job candidates who take longer to reply to emails were rated more negatively by managers (Kalman & Rafaeli, 2011). Similarly, taking longer to respond to texts from a friend can result in decreased levels of social attraction, wanting to spend time with the other person, and feelings of friendship (Heston & Birnholtz, 2017).

Researchers have been studying CMC for decades. (Check out the sidebar on the "Internet Paradox" for more about an early CMC study.) During that time, computers and other digital technologies have advanced at breakneck speeds. Furthermore, technological advances in communication technologies, such as Zoom and FaceTime, blur the lines between CMC, mediated communication, and human communication. As a result, Carr (2020) argues for "a movement away from emphasizing *computers* in CMC and increasing the focus on the process of *mediation* in human communication" (p. 10). Furthermore, he says that labeling communication as CMC simply because a digital channel was utilized may not be enough to distinguish a study or accurately apply theoretical perspectives.

In his call to redefine the field of CMC research, Carr (2020) outlines several factors that have contributed to the dilution of the original conceptualization of CMC.

The Internet Paradox

The first major study to examine the impact of internet use on communication was conducted by Kraut et al. (1998). They collected data during the mid-1990s, when the internet was still a relatively new form of communication for the public. The researchers determined that participants used the internet largely for communication; however, heavier users were more lonely, depressed, and socially isolated than peers who utilized the internet less. The paradox was that despite high levels of communication with others via the internet, those that communicated the most were lonely and isolated.

The study was criticized for a variety of methodological flaws (see Gross et al., 2002; Shapiro, 1999, for a review). As a result, Kraut et al. (2002) conducted a follow-up study. Users who were more extroverted actually benefited from online socialization more than their less social counterparts in a variety of outcomes, including psychological well-being, trust in people, face-to-face communication, and social involvement.

Of course, with the rise of SNSs, it is easy to maintain contact with friends and family around the world, which mirrors findings from earlier research that internet use can expand social networks (Dimaggio et al., 2001) and help us keep in touch with those we know across great distances (Howard et al., 2001).

The first of these is the fact that what we consider a "computer" has changed from a CPU, keyboard, and monitor into any number of digital devices ranging from tablets to smartphones to smartwatches and more. Additionally, computers are no longer simply communication channels. They can be senders and receivers alike—for instance, consider conversations you may have had with digital assistants like Siri and Alexa.

An additional factor in redefining CMC research is that CMC no longer necessarily means that nonverbal and symbolic cues are reduced in online communication (Carr, 2020). Earlier approaches to CMC viewed our online exchanges as "socially-lean interactions" (p. 12) where many of the communicative cues present in face-to-face (FtF) interactions were filtered out. Over the years, numerous ways of incorporating nonverbal cues into text-based exchanges have been developed, such as emoticons and emoji. Using context-appropriate emoji on Twitter can make tweets more believable and easier to understand compared to ones with no emoji or with emoji that do not match the context of the tweet (Daniel & Camp, 2020). (See Chapter 20 for more about emoji use.) Meanwhile, other advances in digital technologies (e.g., video calls and virtual reality) have enabled the transmission of other nonverbal and symbolic cues, making mediated communication a richer experience.

Emoji allow us to communicate nonverbal information in emails, texts, and social media posts.

Carr (2020) also highlights that "the false diametric separating FtF and CMC has collapsed, and the mere use of computers no longer preordains relational outcomes. FtF communication has long been the gold standard against which CMC is compared, with the assumption CMC functioned to stymie relational development" (pp. 12–13). However, decades of research indicate that relational outcomes from CMC can equal or even surpass those of in-person interactions. Recently, teens who texted and used other forms of CMC (which this study defined as talking on the phone, video chatting, or sending messages via the internet) to communicate with friends reported feeling closer to their friends; similarly, texting more with their parents resulted in feeling closer to them (Manago et al., 2020). Ultimately, with computers as omnipresent tools in our daily lives, Carr (2020) concludes that "the role of mediation will become more critical than the particular device or its transmission properties in understanding human communication" (p. 25).

Online Social Capital

As SNSs allow us to connect with family, friends, acquaintances, and even strangers, the effect that the internet and social media have on social capital has been of particular interest to researchers. Put broadly, **social capital** is defined as the resources accrued from individuals in a network (Coleman, 1988). On an individual level, "social capital allows for a person to draw on resources from other members of the networks to which he or she belongs" (Ellison et al., 2007, p. 1145). Of course, within our own social networks, there are varying levels of closeness to certain individuals. These variations divide social capital into two types: bridging and bonding (Putnam, 2000). *Bridging social capital* refers to people with whom we are acquainted but not especially close. These relationships are generally known as "weak ties." These ties provide us with access to useful information and services but typically do not provide emotional support (Granovetter, 1982). On the other hand, *bonding social capital* is found in close-knit relationships that do provide emotional support (Ellison et al., 2007).

Social capital is of particular salience to college students, who are often removed from old social networks when they head off to college. Ellison et al. (2007) introduced a third type of social capital: *maintained social capital*, which refers to a person's ability to stay connected with old social networks despite not being physically connected anymore. There is a strong relationship between Facebook use and the three types of social capital, with bridging social capital having the strongest relationship of the three.

College-aged Facebook users only perceive social capital benefits when they engage in information-seeking behaviors to learn more about people around them, rather than when using the site to meet new people or to maintain relationships with close friends (Ellison et al., 2011). Personal information on someone's Facebook page serves as a "social lubricant" (p. 887) to facilitate connections. The number of actual friends on Facebook predicted bridging social capital, but not the total number of Facebook friends. Once the number of actual friends passes the 400–500 range, social capital reaches a point of diminishing returns. Engaging in "Facebook Relationship Maintenance Behaviors"—such as liking or commenting on a friend's post or posting a Happy Birthday message on their wall—was correlated with greater perceived bridging social capital (Ellison et al., 2014).

Choi et al. (2011) conducted an international study of SNS use and social capital between American and Korean college students. American students had larger networks of friends (n=392) that consisted of many weak ties. Conversely, Korean students had smaller networks (n=79), but their networks consisted of a balance between strong and weak ties. The American students reported more bridging social capital from their networks, but both American and Korean students reported roughly equal levels of bonding social capital. The researchers concluded that SNS use reflected dominant cultural values of each country. Later research supported the finding that Korean students have smaller numbers of SNS friends than U.S. students but suggested that culture may be best explored at the individual level rather than at the national level (LaRose et al., 2014).

Facebook has the greatest social capital gains for users with low self-esteem (Ellison et al., 2007). People with lower self-esteem are usually shyer, and using online communication enables them to form connections more easily than in person. One study participant noted that Facebook "breaks the ice for certain people . . . people that you don't necessarily know really, really well, and you might not want to call them up because a phone call could be awkward, but it's really easy to send them a two-sentence message" (Steinfield et al., 2008, p. 443).

A recent meta-analysis by Cheng et al. (2019) analyzed studies from around the globe and found that people who have high social anxiety or high emotional loneliness are more likely to use SNSs to compensate for a lack of social resources. However, these people may actually receive few online resources because their online social networks are made mainly of weak ties. Conversely, more extroverted people—who often already have stronger social skills and larger social networks—gain additional social capital through online interactions, thus supporting the "rich-get-richer" hypothesis. This is also known as the *social enhancement hypothesis*.

Cyberbullying

Rates of cyberbullying have continued to rise in recent years, and there have been numerous stories of teens who have taken their own lives as a result of being the victims of cyberbullies. In fact, when cyberbullying is discussed in mainstream media, it often focuses on incidents that result in suicide (Milosevic, 2015). More than a third of middle and high school students in the United States say they have been the victim of cyberbullying in their lifetimes, and approximately 15% say they have cyberbullied someone (Hinduja & Patchin, 2019). Girls are somewhat more likely to have been the victim of cyberbullying (38.5% compared to 34.5% for boys). Girls are more likely to be the victim of someone spreading rumors about them online, whereas boys are more likely to be the victim of online threats of physical violence.

Characteristics of Cyberbullies. Kowalski et al.'s (2014) meta-analysis of 131 cyberbullying studies identified several characteristics of people who engage in cyberbullying behaviors. Overall, research indicates that cyberbullying is highly related to

Girls are somewhat more likely to be cyberbullied; they are more likely to experience being the target of online rumors.

traditional face-to-face bullying and to cybervictimization. This means that perpetrators tend to engage in both face-to-face and online bullying, and they are themselves victims of cyberbullying. They are more likely to believe that cyberbullying behaviors are acceptable, and they have higher levels of moral disengagement.

Furthermore, those who engage in more cyberbullying behaviors also reported more alcohol and drug use as well as lower levels of academic performance. The meta-analysis also identified numerous negative psychological variables linked with engaging in cyberbullying behavior, including higher levels of loneliness, depression, and anxiety and lower levels of life-satisfaction and self-esteem. Many of these variables also apply to cyberbullying victims—perhaps because many cyberbullies are also victims of cyberbullying behaviors.

The Influence of Online Anonymity.   Online anonymity is an important risk factor that can predict cyberbullying behavior. The more anonymous a person feels online, the more likely they are to cyberbully others (Barlett et al., 2016). So why does being anonymous in an online environment result in negative behaviors? Suler (2004) identified anonymity as one of the main factors that leads to the online disinhibition effect, which explains why people behave differently in online environments than they would in the real world. Essentially, actions taken by an individual while online are disassociated from who they are in real life.

> The online self becomes a compartmentalized self. In the case of expressed hostilities or other deviant actions, the person can avert responsibility for those behaviors. . . . In fact, people might even convince themselves that those online behaviors "aren't me at all." (p. 322)

Barlett and Gentile (2012) included anonymity as a key component in their Barlett Gentile Cyberbullying Model (BGCM). The learning-based social-cognitive model explains the psychological processes involved in engaging in cyberbullying behavior. Essentially, the BGCM says that continued cyberbullying behaviors lead to (a) the perception of online anonymity and (b) the belief that a person's physical characteristics (i.e., muscularity, size, and stature) are irrelevant online. Those two factors can result in the development of positive attitudes toward cyberbullying, which can then predict future acts of cyberbullying. This model was later supported by longitudinal data (Barlett & Kowalewski, 2019). Anonymity combined with aggressive social modeling—in this case, seeing aggressive online behavior from others—can also lead to an increase in uncharacteristic online aggression (Zimmerman & Ybarra, 2016). Exposure to media violence, however, is not a direct predictor of cyberbullying behavior (Barlett et al., 2019).

Cyberbullying Interventions.   Parental monitoring of online activities can reduce cyberbullying (Kowalski et al., 2014). Empathy has also been shown to correlate negatively with cyberbullying behavior (Ang & Goh, 2010, Kowalski et al., 2014). Video-based training that focuses on promoting empathy in preteens and teens can reduce cyberbullying behaviors (Schultze-Krumbholz et al., 2016).

A study that examined homosexuality and cyberbullying on Facebook revealed that people were more likely to intervene when they possessed high levels of empathy and extroversion, as well as positive attitudes toward the homosexual community (Fries & Gurung, 2013). People high in empathy were more likely to try and change the subject, whereas those high in extroversion or high in support of the homosexual community were more likely to confront the cyberbully.

Reducing college students' perceptions of online anonymity can also reduce cyberbullying (Barlett et al., 2020). The researchers had students watch three brief videos that detailed how IP addresses can be traced back to a specific computer, how posts made via apps can be traced to specific phones or tablets, and how law enforcement tracked specific posts back to the original senders. They then monitored participants' cyberbullying behavior over a two-month period and observed significant decreases in both anonymity perceptions and toxic online disinhibition.

Internet Addiction

Although video game addiction is an area of concern in the study of internet use (see Chapter 18), a large body of research focuses on addiction-like qualities related to the internet in general. Research into internet addiction is growing; however, it is hampered by a lack of consensus among scholars as to exactly what it means to be an internet addict and by methodological limitations (Zajac et al., 2017). Ryding and Kaye (2018) went so far as to call internet addiction a "conceptual minefield" (p. 225).

Terminology can differ from study to study. In addition to "internet addiction," we see terms like "problematic internet use," "pathological internet use," "internet dependence," "excessive internet use," and "virtual addiction." Despite the wide variety of terms, Poli (2017) estimated that approximately 2% of the global adult population could be considered addicted to the internet.

Early studies (e.g., Brenner, 1997; Griffiths, 2000; Young, 1996) adopted the term "internet addict," which, as Lin (2009) highlighted, implies that the user is dependent on internet usage. Indeed, much of the disagreement about internet addiction is that it is often conceptualized as an addiction to a singular thing, rather than viewing the internet as a gateway to a plethora of possible activities (van Rooij & Prause, 2014). For instance, you can go online to play games, check email, socialize, conduct research for a class project, shop, etc. So perhaps people become addicted to certain online experiences, rather than to the medium itself (Widyanto et al., 2011). Lachmann et al. (2019) described the differences between being addicted to the internet versus addiction to certain online activities:

> Individuals suffering from generalized internet addiction could not have developed their dysfunctional behavior (e.g., shopping, gambling, etc.) without the internet, that is, the problematic internet use itself determines subsequent specific problem behaviors. On the other hand, individuals suffering from specific internet addiction are using the internet only as an instrument to satisfy their needs (e.g., shopping, gambling, and gaming) but are not dependent on the internet per se. The same problematic behavior could exist in the real world outside of cyberspace. (p. 182)

Ryding and Kaye (2018) argue that the term "internet addiction" is too broad to understand the nuances of online addictive behavior, noting that "an individual who spends excessive time online for shopping is qualitatively different from someone who watches or downloads porn excessively. These represent distinct behaviors which are arguably underpinned by different gratifications" (p. 226). (For more on uses and gratifications, see Chapter 9.)

Of course, determining if someone is truly addicted to the internet has led to a debate among scholars. The American Psychological Association (n.d.) defines internet addiction as "a behavioral pattern characterized by excessive or obsessive online and offline computer use that leads to distress and impairment." In the United States, there currently is no approved medical diagnosis for internet addiction. Furthermore, internet addiction is not recognized by the American Psychiatric Association or the World Health Organization or as a disorder. However, the WHO says it is a subject for possible future classification (Borter, 2019).

Other researchers have contended that excessive internet use is not a sign of addiction but rather a form of deficient impulse control (e.g., LaRose & Eastin, 2002; LaRose et al., 2003). Extending this line of thought to social media use, LaRose et al. (2014) commented, "It may be the result of a failure to control specific behaviors at a particular point in time that, as is the case with most so-called technology addictions . . . most individuals are able to recover from on their own" (p. 70). One possible reason that excessive users are unable to self-regulate their online usage is that they are unaware of their behavior, thus making it harder to control (LaRose et al., 2003). After all, how can you control a habit that you do not even realize you have?

Researchers have looked at the reasons why people use the internet for explanations of excessive use. Caplan (2005) observed that people who have lower social skills prefer CMC and therefore use the internet more often, which can lead to negative symptoms linked to problematic internet usage. Using the internet for entertainment was another important risk factor for problematic internet use (Ceyhan, 2011). Kishore et al. (2019) identified using the internet for entertainment as a contributing factor to internet addiction. (Notice the different terminology.) Other research has examined personality factors associated with internet addiction. For instance, Lachmann et al. (2019) identified overlapping personality traits among people who exhibited problematic internet use and problematic smartphone use. Common traits included high neuroticism and low agreeableness and conscientiousness. There was also a "very robust" association between low levels of self-directedness—a personality trait related to a person's willpower and contentment with themselves—and higher problematic use of both the internet and smartphones. In fact, the researchers suggest that lower willpower may be the root of digital addictive tendencies.

In an effort to expand our understanding of internet addiction, some researchers have looked into possible differences between internet addiction, problematic internet use, and nonproblematic internet use. Zhou et al.'s (2018) study of Chinese adolescents identified differences among those three categories, and they suggested that problematic internet use could be viewed as a transitional stage toward internet addiction. In another study of Chinese college students, the association between problematic internet use and mental health issues peaked during sophomore year (Zhou et al., 2020).

Other studies have found connections between internet addiction and several negative outcomes, including higher rates of depression and insomnia (Jain et al., 2020) and decreases in self-confidence, self-esteem, social and academic self-efficacy (Baturay & Toker, 2019). Internet addiction can also trigger loneliness.

Several studies have proposed methods of treating internet addiction, particularly in children and adolescents (see Zajac et al., 2017, for a review). Children who are often bored during free time were more likely to become excessive internet users; however, increased participation in family activities and parental monitoring of internet use could greatly decrease the likelihood of problematic use (Lin et al., 2009). For Chinese adolescents diagnosed with internet addiction, family-based group interventions were far more effective than conventional intervention methods (X. Zhong et al., 2011). However, it is challenging to draw conclusions about proposed treatments from recent research because of various methodological limitations and a lack of studies focusing on any specific treatment (Zajac et al., 2017). Therefore, so-called internet addiction treatments should still be considered experimental.

Scholars are also starting to pay more attention to the areas of social media addiction and problematic social media use. People who prefer Instagram, Snapchat, and Facebook reported more problematic social media use; being female, conscientious, introverted, agreeable, and neurotic were also associated with problematic social media use (Kircaburun et al., 2020). In another study, higher social anxiety and lower happiness levels predicted social media addiction for college students (Baltaci, 2019). And another researcher found that Facebook addiction negatively impacts well-being (Satici, 2019).

Digital Detoxing.   In today's always-on digital society, it is almost impossible to avoid technology. Perceived digital overuse is strongly and negatively associated with well-being (Büchi et al., 2019). Although the demands of connecting with friends online can have positive effects on our mood and well-being (e.g., LaRose et al., 2014), there are times where we just want (and need) to digitally disconnect. Franks et al. (2018) interviewed people who gave up Facebook for a period of time, and they identified four reasons for taking what the researchers called a "Facebook sabbatical": (1) information overload, (2) problematic overuse and antisocial behavior, (3) the "pressure cooker" environment marked by scrutiny and comparison, and (4) so-called Facebook wars and keyboard warriors. Facebook sabbaticals are cyclical, meaning young adults repeatedly engaged in them for temporary escapes from the stress caused by Facebook use.

Taking a break from Facebook resulted in increased life satisfaction and more positive emotions (Tromholt, 2017). Taking a "Facebook vacation" could also help lower stress when the amount of information on the platform becomes overwhelming; however, giving up Facebook also resulted in lower well-being (Vanman et al., 2018). (This could be because the participants who were randomly assigned to give up Facebook may not have been prepared to take a break and may have felt cut off from their friends unexpectedly.) When females took a break from Facebook, they proactively sought out and engaged with their offline social connections, but males did not (Franks et al., 2018). Instagram users also take breaks from the platform as a way to restore balance to their relationships and well-being and to regain control over time spent on the platform (Jorge, 2019).

A key feature of a digital detox is that the disconnection is *temporary*. Users eventually resume using the platforms in a more balanced way (Franks et al., 2018; Jorge, 2019). Fear of missing out (FOMO) and peer pressure are key motivators for males to return to Facebook, whereas females logged back in because of Facebook's "ability to complement and enhance their refreshed offline relationships that were reaffirmed during their sabbatical" (Franks et al., 2018, p. 9). Taking a brief break also helps people better appreciate the benefits of social media.

> Voluntary disconnection from the digital is shown among users as necessary to appreciate and value the utility of Instagram and other social media as central to contemporary social life. Thus, it restores value of the current social media system rather than undermines it. (Jorge, 2019, p. 17)

Interestingly, people's views of compulsive connection to Facebook also change over time, turning the site into a "personal service platform." In a longitudinal study, younger users employed more emotive language to highlight social aspects of using Facebook (Sujon et al., 2018). However, in the span of just five years, those same participants later described Facebook in more practical ways, indicating how it became engrained as a part of their everyday lives. The researchers argued that users have "domesticated" Facebook and employ it "for organizing the *conduct* of their lives, rather than making social contacts. . . . Facebook may be a little boring, but it is also a useful platform for structuring and organizing personal social networks, family connections, and personal archives" (p. 9).

Internet and the Changing Workplace

Companies and organizations are increasingly using the internet to communicate externally with their customers and internally with employees. One well-known method of integrating the internet into the work environment is telework, also known as telecommuting, where technology allows an employee to work from home rather than at the office (Sullivan, 2003). Some scholars argue that those terms could be seen as outdated (Messenger & Gschwind, 2016), but they are still widely used in research studies. Companies allow employees to telework because it can be a cost-saving measure (Harris, 2003; Peters & den Dulk, 2003), and it helps workers remain productive while staying home due to illness (Ahmed et al., 2020).

Video conferencing technologies, such as Skype, Zoom, and Microsoft Teams, are one way that people are able to work remotely, allowing them to participate in work-related activities while physically away from the office. For instance, many universities across the country encouraged professors to hold synchronous online class meetings via Zoom during the COVID-19 pandemic. Meanwhile, Twitter made the drastic move to allow some employees to work from home *forever*. Prior to the COVID-19 pandemic, 40% of U.S. workers had jobs that could be completed via telework, with college graduates, women, Asians, and white workers most likely to be able to telework (Kochhar & Passel, 2020).

Video conferencing facilitates engaging with coworkers when physically distant, but remote work can blur the line between work and home life.

Research into the effects of working from home has resulted in conflicting findings. Teleworking can help employees balance the demands of their job and home life (Britton et al., 2004) and result in higher levels of job satisfaction and performance (Vega et al., 2015). Working from home can help employees spend more time with their family and friends (Grincevičiené, 2020). However, other research indicates that it blurs the line between work and personal life. Working solely from home can lead to employees becoming preoccupied with work, which can interfere with family responsibilities (Eddleston & Mulki, 2017).

A report analyzing global trends in telework concluded that remote employees spend more time working each week than their office-bound counterparts and allow their professional and personal lives to overlap, which leads to increased stress (Eurofound & the International Labour Office, 2019). Compared to working in the workplace, Song and Gao (2020) found that "teleworking, regardless of being conducted on weekdays or weekends/holidays, is always associated with a higher level of stress" (p. 2659).

In addition to stress, teleworkers can also feel lonely and isolated (Mann & Holdsworth, 2003). Although much remote work may be done alone, sometimes workers are required to work in virtual teams. Field studies found that virtual teams can overcome challenges and achieve goals and that they are viable alternatives to in-person teams (Purvanova, 2014). See Allen et al. (2015) for further review of telework research.

The vast body of research on the pros and cons of telework suggests that hybrid work arrangements, such as splitting time between working in the office and working from home throughout the week, "appear to result in a more positive balance between the benefits and drawbacks" of remote work (Eurofound & the International Labour Office, 2019).

Aside from the conflicting effects, telework is successful only if both the company and the employee are committed to the arrangement (Atkin & Lau, 2007). Greer and Payne (2014) outlined a number of strategies to overcome the challenges of working remotely. These strategies include, but are not limited to, using advanced technology similar to what is available at the office, being accessible, creating a space at home that is conducive to working, and communicating with family members about reducing distractions during designated work time.

One other aspect of the internet in the workplace that nearly every employee with online access will face is surfing the web for pleasure. Taking short breaks to surf the web actually improved worker productivity by as much as 9% (Coker, 2011). Younger workers and junior employees are more inclined to use social media at work for both personal and professional reasons, but they have more concerns about privacy intrusion that could occur by adding work colleagues as friends on social media (Walden, 2016). Meanwhile, senior employees are more likely to view social media use in the workplace as a distraction.

Summary

As we have seen, the internet is incorporated into our lives unlike any other type of mass media. In fact, much of our mass media consumption takes place via the internet—from watching a show on Netflix to playing a video game to listening to Spotify and more.

SNSs dominate our time online, providing us with ways to keep in touch with friends and family, build social capital with people we know, and allowing us to draw on the resources of those in our networks. A great deal of research has examined how social media affects our emotions and well-being.

CMC has evolved significantly in recent years, and researchers are continuing to explore the effects that technology has on human communication. Meanwhile, email use is projected to continue growing in future years. Cyberbullying continues to be a problem. Anonymity is a key factor in cyberbullying, but research suggests that empathy and reducing perceptions of anonymity can help reduce those behaviors.

The issue of whether to include internet addiction as a formal mental health disorder is currently being considered by the American Psychiatric Association. Meanwhile, digital detoxing is also a growing area of research as people seek to find more balance in their media-saturated lives.

Lastly, the internet has impacted how, where, and when we work. Research has shown that communication technology that allows employees to work from home helps them maintain a better balance between their job and personal responsibilities, but telecommuting can also blur the lines between work and home life and result in feeling more stress.

In the coming years, we will likely see an increase in longitudinal studies concerning internet use, which will shed more light on the long-term effects of internet usage. Until then, a growing body of research continues to point to some specific effects of internet use (e.g., psychological well-being). With each Facebook status update, photo posted to Instagram, and viral TikTok video, researchers grow closer to understanding more about the effects of the internet and social media on our daily lives.

20

Effects of
Mobile Communication

> I feel about my phone the way horror-movie ventriloquists feel about their dummies: It's smarter than me, better than me, and I will kill anyone who comes between us.
>
> —Colson Whitehead, 2014

Wireless communication technology has become one of the defining media of our time. In fact, mobile technology is the fastest growing communication medium of all time (Castells, 2009; Castells et al., 2007). In the United States, 97% of Americans owned some kind of mobile phone in 2021, with 85% of Americans owning a smartphone (Pew Research Center, 2021b). Nearly all (95%) of U.S. teens either own or have access to a smartphone (Anderson & Jiang, 2018). Smartphone ownership in the United States has more than doubled since the Pew Research Center (2021b) began tracking it in 2011, when only 35% of Americans owned a smartphone. A third of U.S. households have three or more smartphones (Olmstead, 2017), and more homes are using mobile phones than landlines for telephone service (Blumberg & Luke, 2017).

Mobile phones are everywhere, and they have become an integral part of everyday communication and life in general. We use mobile technology to stay in touch with friends and family members on a daily basis. Surveys of U.S. smartphone habits show we are increasingly using them to get directions to or recommendations about a location, listen to music on services like Spotify and Apple Music, take part in video chats, and watch TV and movies on apps like Netflix and Hulu (Anderson, 2016). A majority of smartphone owners use their phones to avoid boredom; follow breaking news; and share pictures, video, and updates about events happening in their community (Pew Research Center, 2015). An overwhelming majority of teens use their phones to simply pass time, connect with people, and learn new things (Schaeffer, 2019). You probably have your phone either in your pocket or in your hand while you read this (or it is at least within arm's reach). For most of you, life without a mobile phone would, no doubt, seem impossible. In fact, nearly half of smartphone owners say they could not live without their phone (Pew Research Center, 2015), and 42% of U.S. teens said they feel anxious when they do not have their phone (Jiang, 2018a).

Smartphones combine many forms of media (e.g., music, movies, internet, video games) into a device that can fit in your pocket. Not only do we have more types of media to engage with than ever before but mobile technology also gives us the ability to take them with us anywhere . . . at least anywhere with good service or Wi-Fi.

Since the 1980s, our culture has morphed into a network-based society in which people interact with those with whom they share interests—not with whom they share physical space (Castells, 2000). Castells et al. (2007) use the term "space of flows" to describe how mobile phones disconnect the concepts of spaces and places from fixed locations. Because communication via mobile technology is not tethered to a fixed location, "the mobile phone allows people to free themselves from the place-based context of their interaction, shifting their frame of reference to the communication itself; that is to a space made of communication flows" (Castells et al., 2007, p. 172). For example, if you were to call your best friend's smartphone right now, they could be riding the bus, sitting in class, or about to walk into a movie. No longer are you calling a designated place, such as your friend's apartment; rather, you are calling an individual who could be in any number of locations. This may seem obvious to you. However, prior to mobile phones, generations of people knew exactly where the person they were calling was going to be if they answered. Now, unless dialing a landline number, you do not necessarily know the location of the person you are calling.

In addition to changing how we think about *where* communication takes place, mobile technology has altered how we think about *when* we communicate. "Timeless time" is what Castells et al. (2007) call mobile communication that upends traditional communication schedules and patterns. For example, work-related communication is no longer confined to the traditional 9-to-5 workday. Your boss may text you late at night to tell you to come in early the next morning, or you may handle a few work emails while you are on vacation. Here is an example of timeless time many of you can probably relate to: It is 11:30 at night, and you have a question about a class assignment due the next day. You email your professor, and (lucky for you) your night-owl professor sends you a response right away via a smartphone. Not all that long ago, this type of late-night conversation between you and a professor would be unfathomable.

In addition to changing where and when communication takes place, mobile technology has fundamentally changed *how* we communicate and *what* we communicate about.

> The relationship between communication technologies and their users changed from that of receiving broadcast messages to actively seeking, producing, and distributing content while using the same media for point-to-point networking. (Campbell & Ling, 2009, p. 593)

Smartphones allow us to do so much more than just make phone calls. We can look up anything we need to know online, upload selfies to Instagram, start a Facebook Live video, respond to a group text, take part in the latest viral TikTok challenge, and the list goes on. For many people, smartphones have become a part of who they are. (Your parents have probably commented at some point that it seems like your phone is glued to your hand.) We do not just pick up the phone when it rings or when we get a text. Instead, we pick it up to connect in some way with the larger world.

Thus, we must expand the media effects paradigm to reflect this change in society. In a relatively short time, mobile communication technology has drastically changed the way we live. In this chapter, we will explore those changes, including how we coordinate our lives with others, how we relate to other people, the role and effects that mobile phones have on youth culture, and the transformation of public spaces into private realms. We will also look at the effects of texting and so-called smartphone addiction. However, we will begin with a brief look at the call that changed it all.

The Birth of the "Brick"

Although wireless communication technology—such as radio—had been in existence for several decades before the world's first public cell phone call on April 3, 1973, the technology was not suitable for everyday personal use. The early wireless technology restricted users to a physical location. Early car phones were so large that the equipment needed to power them had to be stored in the trunk (Greene, 2011).

One day in the late 1960s, Martin Cooper, the general manager of Motorola's division of communication systems, watched an episode of the sci-fi show *Star Trek*. He saw Captain Kirk walking on an alien planet and talking to his crew aboard the *Enterprise* via his small, hand-held communicator. "Suddenly, there was Captain Kirk talking on his communicator—talking!" Cooper recalled in the documentary about the influence of *Star Trek* on the real world (Jones, 2005). Unsatisfied with the limited abilities of wireless technology, the objective for Cooper and his team was to make wireless communication as easy as it looked on *Star Trek*. (Cooper has also credited comic book detective Dick Tracy's two-way wristwatch radio as inspiration for the creation of mobile phones.)

A few years later, Cooper was walking down a busy Manhattan sidewalk on his way to a press conference to unveil Motorola's first cell phone—which was so large and bulky that it was nicknamed the "brick." During his walk, he called his chief competitor at Bell Labs on the brick to tell them that he had beaten them to the punch (Greene, 2011).

Martin Cooper demonstrating an early brick-style cell phone.

Effects on Social Coordination

Mobile communication fundamentally changes how we perceive space and time (Castells et al., 2007; Ling & Campbell, 2008). As a result, it impacts how we coordinate our lives with others, giving us the ability to directly contact someone in real time while we (and/or they) are on the go (Ling, 2017). This is known as "microcoordination" (Ling, 2004; Ling & Yttri, 2002). Campbell and Ling (2020) posited that effects of mobile phone use "are perhaps most obvious in social behavior" (p. 390). Ling and Yttri (1999, 2002) outlined several aspects of social coordination that mobile phones have transformed, including logistics, scheduling, and ongoing refinement of plans. Although the benefits and impacts related to mobile communication and social coordination may seem obvious, Campbell and Ling (2020) note that this area of media research continues to be active and serves to "illuminate how the transition toward smartphones and applications has altered the narrative about mobile technology's effects on social life" (p. 390).

Logistics

Mobile phones give us the power to change plans or give new instructions to someone on the fly. For example, imagine you are preparing to head to class to take your midterm, but just before leaving your dorm room, you get a text from classmate saying that your professor is sick and class is canceled. Instead of walking across campus to discover this for yourself, you and your friend are able to make impromptu plans to go to the library and study together.

Scheduling

Mobile phones give us the ability to soften our schedules when making arrangements with other people. In other words, they give us more flexibility. For example, when you are running late to meet your friends for dinner, you can simply call or text to let them know. This allows them to adjust their schedules so that they will not have to sit around waiting for you.

Ongoing Refinement

Because mobile phones enable us to call anyone at any place at any time, we are able to coordinate with other people on an as-needed basis. Imagine that you go with your friends to the mall. While in the car, the group discusses what the plans for the evening will include: shopping, dinner, and a movie. However, you do not plan where to eat or what movie to see. Once at the mall, some of your friends split off from the group to go to various stores. Everyone is confident that calls on their cell phones will take care of details about where to meet for dinner and to find out what movie the group will see.

Microcoordination 2.0

Originally, mobile microcoordination was thought of in terms of one-to-one communication, such as calling or texting a single person. However, technological advances in the last decade, like group texts and messaging apps (e.g., iMessage, WhatsApp, and Facebook Messenger) have changed the way scholars think about and understand mobile communication (Campbell & Ling, 2020). For instance, with those types of apps, it is possible for groups of people to communicate collectively in a shared digital space, not just on an individual level. Ling and Lai (2016) call this type of group-level coordination "microcoordination 2.0." The researchers observed that mobile group communication can simplify planning, accomplish specific tasks (e.g., planning a wedding or a party), and enable social interaction. Conversely, users can sometimes be overwhelmed by the number of messages in a group chat or forced into awkward situations when added to a group message without their consent.

Coordinating Face-to-Face Interactions

Another aspect of coordination affected by mobile phones is face-to-face (FtF) encounters. Although some researchers have feared that mediated communication can be detrimental to FtF sociability (see Kraut et al., 1998), studies have shown that mobile communication can actually result in more real-life encounters with people we know (e.g., Hashimoto et al., 2000; Ishii, 2006). A recent study found that teens who texted their friends more often also spent more face-to-face time with friends (Manago et al., 2020). For example, texting with your friend about working out may result in the two of you meeting at the gym to exercise together.

Mobile communication, such as texting, can lead to more face-to-face time with people we know in the real world.

Effects on Relational Communication

By nature, the mobile phone is a very personal piece of technology. "Mobile phones have become so intimately a part of us that they have come to represent an extension of our physical selves—an umbilical cord, anchoring the information society's digital infrastructure to our very bodies" (Harkin, 2003, p. 16). Many of us customize our phones with colored cases, download custom ringtones, and use personal photographs as lock and home screens. Often phones are viewed as a type of fashion accessory (Fortunati, 2005a; Ling, 2004).

Maintaining Perpetual Contact

Mobile phones have impacted relational communication through "perpetual contact" (Katz & Aakhus, 2002) and "connected presence" (Licoppe, 2004). Even when we are not communicating with another person, just knowing that communication is *possible* changes how we relate to each other and to technology (Campbell, 2008). Mobile communication allows—and in many ways encourages—us to be available to others anytime anywhere (Ling, 2017; Schrock, 2015; Vorderer et al., 2016). In fact, an overwhelming majority of Americans say they rarely or never turn their phone off (Rainie & Zickuhr, 2015). Phone calls and texts can come at any time throughout the day or night, and "the continuous nature of this flow of irregular interaction helps to maintain the feeling of a permanent connection, an impression that the link can be activated at any time" (Licoppe, 2004, p. 141). Riordan (2017) expanded on that thought, saying,

> We are never more than a text message away, whether at work, running errands, at home, or even in bed. This constant connection via communication means that at any given moment we may be called on to fulfill the role of employee, parent, spouse, friend, daughter or son, or more. (p. 15)

Ultimately, this heightened sense of connection results in the strengthening of our social bonds (Campbell & Ling, 2009).

Texting and Relational Communication

Text messages are a large part of communication via mobile phones. Lenhart et al.'s (2015) analysis of how teens use communication technology in their friendships found that 80% of teens say they share their phone number when meeting a new friend with the expectation that they will maintain contact via text, and 54% said their phone number for texting is the first piece of contact information they give to a new friend, compared to only 9% for voice calls. Although many of you, no doubt, do not give a second thought about sending text messages, scholars suggest that "in actuality they are symbolic gestures of companionship, even intimacy" (Campbell & Ling, 2009, p. 596). In a sense, they are similar to passing notes (Ling, 2004), and can be regarded as "digital gifts" (Johnsen, 2003) that play a critical role in connecting us to others. Ling and Yttri (2002) explained how this idea of connectedness works.

> The receiver is in the thoughts of the sender and when they meet they will be able to base a certain portion of their further interaction on the exchange of messages. The messages serve to tie the group together through the development of a common history or narrative. (pp. 158–159)

Put another way, text messages can function as building blocks for future FtF interactions by laying a common groundwork for all those involved. This shared history can help us feel more connected.

Emerging from the "Telecocoon"

Some scholars fear that too much connectedness among members of a tight-knit group could actually prove harmful to forming new relations outside of close networks. Some research has shown that heavy reliance on mobile phones has a so-called "tele-cocooning" effect, in which we are insulated inside our close-knit social group (Habu-chi, 2005; Ito et al., 2008). One possible result of social cocooning is that those who are cocooned could feel less connected to the "outside" world and are kept from hearing alternative ideas and voices (Campbell & Ling, 2008; Ling, 2008). For adolescents, texting is also associated with being more cautious and less socially tolerant when dealing with others (Kobayashi & Boase, 2014). Additionally, 43% of 13- to 17-year-olds (Schaeffer, 2019) and 47% of 18- to 29-year-olds (Pew Research Center, 2015) admitted to using their smartphone to avoid interacting with people around them.

Despite concerns that mobile technology and telecocooning lead to increased social isolation, mobile phones can have the opposite effect. In fact, our phones can both strengthen close relationships and connect us to people outside of our inner social circle (Wilken, 2011). Campbell and Ling (2020) stated that "rather than reaching in to core ties at the expense of reaching out beyond them, the effects of smart-phone use can be characterized as reaching in *and* reaching out, with the technology serving as an added layer of social connectivity" (p. 393).

Rainie and Wellman (2012) compared smartphones to Swiss Army knives, high-lighting how using apps for various purposes (e.g., social media, gaming, navigation, etc.) can broaden a person's social connections. Hampton et al. (2011) linked owning a mobile phone, instant messaging, and sharing photos online to having a larger group of core confidants. Mobile technology may also help us learn more about our close friends and family because "the use of new media makes some personal characteris-tics more observable than in the past. New technologies may not increase diversity as much as they increase awareness of diversity that was always there" (Hampton et al., 2011, p. 150). For example, sharing photos online increased the likelihood of having a core connection from a different political party. How did participants in the study know the political affiliations of others? They could have learned the information from online posts by friends or family. Further examining political discourse, Camp-bell and Kwak (2011b) found that, although political discussions via mobile technol-ogy were slightly lower in small tight-knit groups of like-minded individuals, mobile-based discussions facilitated more open political discussions in larger groups of like-minded people.

Kobayashi et al. (2015) called for further thought about the telecocooning hypoth-esis "because the customizability of smartphones allows them to facilitate increased interaction with weak tie relationships" (p. 331). Their experiment revealed that on-screen reminders on a person's phone can influence them to reach out to people they had not talked to in at least two months. The reminders were especially effective at helping people reconnect with former classmates.

"Technoference" in Romantic Relationships

We have discussed how mobile communication technology impacts our connec-tions to acquaintances, friends, and others we are close to, but what about the people we love the most? Research shows that mobile technology and our connection to it can impact our romantic relationships. McDaniel and Coyne (2016) examined how computers, mobile phones, and television create "technoference," which they defined as "everyday intrusions or interruptions in couple interactions or time spent together that occur due to technology" (p. 85). Technoference is relatively common and can pave the way for conflict between romantic partners. "When individuals place their technology above their partner, even if only for a brief moment, they can sow conflict in their romantic relationship, which may lead to negative outcomes" (p. 94), such as greater depressive symptoms and lower life satisfaction.

Technoference has been linked to negative relational outcomes.

In another study looking specifically at smartphones and romantic relationships, smartphone use alone did not impact either relationship satisfaction or relationship uncertainty, "rather it is the increased psychological attachment to the devices that is linked to negative relational outcomes" (Lapierre & Lewis, 2018, p. 395). For instance, if one partner becomes increasingly dependent on their smartphone, the other partner feels worse about the health of their romantic relationship.

McDaniel and Coyne (2016) suggest that couples talk openly and honestly about technology-related conflict in their relationship and find ways to lessen potential conflict. This could include silencing or turning off devices while interacting with each other, or it could mean technology use is allowed, as long as it is not extensive. These strategies can differ from couple to couple, "but it will require an open and continuous dialogue between partners" (p. 94).

Effects on Youth Culture

The widespread adoption of mobile communication has reshaped many traditional issues of how teens transition into adulthood (Campbell & Ling, 2009). In years past, many teens were brought up to follow in the same footsteps as their parents.

Today, however, cultural change occurs so quickly that children's experiences are drastically different from those of their parents or even older siblings.

Connecting with Friends

Adolescents must learn how to function in society. Interactions with peers play a large role in learning to navigate in the world, and mobile phones are a perfect tool for teen interaction. The average high school senior in the United States spends approximately two hours a day texting (Twenge et al., 2019). Text messaging is the most-used method of daily communication among friends (Lenhart et al., 2015). Teen girls are more likely to text, call, and use social media to get in touch with friends, whereas teen boys are more likely to connect with their closest friends through video games (Lenhart et al., 2015).

Constant contact with friends via mobile phones strengthens feelings of in-group belonging (e.g., Ling, 2004, 2008; Ling & Yttri, 2002). Many teens said that the desire to "always be available" was the main reason they got a cell phone (Nielsen, 2010). In one survey, 57% of teens said they often or sometimes felt as if they had to respond to text messages immediately (Jiang, 2018a).

Sexting: Risky Behavior or the New Normal?

Sexting, which is defined as "the sharing of sexually-explicit images, videos, or messages through electronic means" (Madigan et al., 2018), is another major area of concern regarding the effects of smartphones. According to Doring (2014), there are two primary views of sexting. The most common is that sexting is an inherently risky behavior that needs to be addressed through intervention and prevention. The second is that sexting is viewed as both a normal and healthy means of sexual expression in relationships. Regarding the first view, a meta-analysis of sexting studies found sexting behavior was only weakly to moderately related to sexual activity, having unprotected sex, and a person's number of sexual partners (Kosenko et al., 2017). "All we know is that sexting and sexual behavior co-occur. Sexting might act as a gateway to other sexual activity, but it is just as likely that sexting is simply part of an already sexually active person's sexual repertoire" (p. 153).

In another meta-analysis conducted by Madigan et al. (2018), consensual sexting is becoming more commonplace among teens, with one in seven teens having sent a sext and one in four having received sexts. "Efforts and resources to criminalize sexts should be redirected to educational programs on digital citizenship and healthy relationships" (p. 333). Children get their first smartphones not long after turning 10 years old, which prompted the researchers to call for parents, pediatricians, and middle school educators to have conversations with tweens about sexting and navigating the digital world. In the meta-analysis, one in eight youths had engaged in forwarding a sext or having a sext forwarded without their consent. Few studies have addressed this type of sexting behavior, and more research needs to be done to better understand possible effects.

Mobile Phone Use in the Classroom

Some negative effects of cell phone use are related to academic performance. Among high school students, heavy usage was linked to higher failure rates in class, including repeating a grade (Sánchez-Martínez & Otero, 2009). In a study of 8th and 11th grade students, compulsive texting was negatively related to female students' grades, school bonding, and scholastic competence, while male students showed no significant effects (Lister-Landman et al., 2017).

At the collegiate level, students using their phones in class are less likely to be able to identify lecture material (End et al., 2010). Texting during class results in lower test scores (Ellis et al., 2010). Students with higher rates of texting in class had lower overall GPAs (Harman & Sato, 2011). Schneider's (2018) review of relevant literature on the subject concluded that using a phone during class was associated with worse performance on class-specific tasks, such as quiz grades and note taking, and overall lower academic performance. Furthermore, heavy smartphone use in class can prohibit students from making firm real-world connections with classmates, which inhibits the creation of a supportive and cooperative learning environment (Soomro et al., 2019). You have been warned. . . .

Effects of Texting

Texting has become an important form of mobile communication. Despite messages often being short (Ling, 2006), they can cover a wide range of topics, ranging from social coordination to emotional expression (Ling, 2005). However, unlike face-to-face communication or a voice call, texting removes traditional nonverbal cues, such as facial expression and tone of voice, from communicative acts. Instead, we see capitalization, punctuation, emoticons, and emoji serving as nonverbal cues.

Communicating Affect and Tone via Emoticons and Emoji

Computer-mediated communication and mobile-mediated communication have developed their own language, so to speak. Many people created their own shorthand for communicating with their friends. Texts like "where u @?," "call me l8r," and "i luv u <3" can become a "badge of membership" signifying one's belonging in certain social networks (Campbell & Ling, 2009). Moreover, shorthand codes like LOL, ROFLMFAO, and TTYL are often found in various forms of online communication. Whereas this style of communication may come naturally to younger generations, parents and grandparents often struggle to decipher the meanings behind this "alphabet soup." (Many of you have probably heard stories about someone's older relative thinking LOL meant "lots of love" rather than "laughing out loud," which can lead to some unintentionally funny and/or awkward text exchanges.)

In addition to those shorthand codes, emoticons, such as :) and :(, help convey emotion in email and instant messages. They can also help to clarify a sender's intent. Some emoticons, such as :p (tongue) and ;) (wink) indicate sarcasm (Thompson & Filik, 2016). Emoji are viewed as an advanced version of emoticons (Aull, 2019) that have largely replaced them (Thomson et al., 2018). In fact, typing :p in Word automatically produces 😝; typing ;) produces ☺. Emoji are more effective than emoticons in terms of expressiveness and content richness (Rodriques et al., 2017). Today, people (especially females) use emoji more frequently than emoticons and report more positive attitudes and deeper levels of identification with emoji (Prada et al., 2018).

Since their initial release in 1999, emoji have been adopted widely, particularly on mobile devices. We employ them in texts, emails, Instagram stories, etc. From faces to animals to food and more, "emojis exist at an intersection of effective communication, play, and personal expression" (Riordan, 2017). Emoji use is a hot topic for researchers, especially in the areas of computer sciences and communication, but scholars in the fields of marketing, medicine, education, psychology, linguistics, and behavioral science are also actively studying emoji (Bai et al., 2019). Emoji have become so ingrained in our daily digital lives that the Oxford Dictionary named the "face with tears of joy" emoji (😂 also known as the "crying while laughing" emoji) as its "Word of the Year" in 2015 (Steinmetz, 2015). Some college courses incorporate in-class exercises to help college students better understand emoji use in interpersonal communication (e.g., Yang, 2020).

Much like emoticons, emoji can help communicate tone and reduce ambiguity (Kaye et al., 2016). However, some emoji can make a sender's intent more ambiguous. For instance, 🙏 the "folded hands" emoji can symbolize prayer, but some interpret it as clapping or a high five (Bai et al., 2019). Despite some possible misinterpretations, emoji use can preserve and enhance social relationships (Riordan, 2017). Non-face emoji can also communicate emotions, specifically joy (Riordan, 2017). Skovholt et al. (2014) and Riordan (2017) found emoji can increase positive emotions for message receivers, but emoji cannot change the overall valence of the message. In other words, emoji can soften the negative tone of a message, but they do not change a negative message into a positive one. Moreover, using multiple emoji in a message has little impact on a receiver's interpretation of the message (Riordan, 2017; Riordan & Trichtinger, 2016). However, the gender of the sender can influence how receivers interpret emoji in text messages (Butterworth et al., 2019). See the Research Spotlight in this chapter for more on this study.

RESEARCH SPOTLIGHT

Sender Gender Influences Emoji Interpretation in Text Messages
Sarah E. Butterworth, Traci A Giuliano, Justin White, Lizette Cantu, and Kyle C. Fraser (2019)
Frontiers in Psychology, 10, Article 784

Emoji are commonly used in text-based communication, and Butterworth et al. wanted to understand if the gender of the sender could influence how a recipient interpreted the emoji in text messages.

They reviewed research that identified differences in emoji use between men and women and stereotypes regarding gendered communication, Butterworth et al. formulated two hypotheses:

H1: A text message containing affectionate emojis would be perceived as more appropriate and likable when it came from a female sender than a male sender, and

H2: A text message containing an emoji that was less overtly affectionate but still friendly would be considered equally appropriate and likeable whether it came from a female sender or a male sender. (p. 2)

(continued)

Method

Eighty Southwestern University (Texas) undergraduates (39 female, 40 male, 1 unreported; mean age: 20.14 years) agreed to participate, completing a brief survey on "workplace correspondence." The participants viewed a screen shot of a hypothetical text message from a person thanking their coworker for a job-related favor: "Hey Katie, I'm sorry I couldn't come in yesterday. I'm feeling a lot better today though. Thanks for covering my shift." The text was always addressed to a female coworker but was sent from either a fictional female ("Rebecca") or fictional male ("Steven"). The text included either a combination of affectionate emoji (i.e., a kissing-face emoji and a red heart emoji) or a friendly emoji (i.e., a smiley face).

After seeing one of the hypothetical messages, participants provided feedback using 7-point Likert scales about the appropriateness of the message, rating prompts (e.g., "The text shows a proper tone between employees," "[Rebecca/Steven] acted professionally in this case," "Katie probably felt uncomfortable receiving this text," etc.) from 1 (Strongly Disagree) to 7 (Strongly Agree). Participants also rated the likability of the sender by rating prompts (e.g., "I would like to work with someone like [Rebecca/Steven]," "I feel as though I would get along well with [Rebecca/Steven]," etc.).

Results

The results of a pair of 2 (Sender's Gender) x 2 (Emoji Type) between-subject analyses of variance (ANOVAs) revealed that texts containing affectionate emoji were generally viewed less appropriate than texts with a friendly emoji. The text containing affectionate emoji was perceived as less appropriate when sent by a man than when it was sent by a woman. Additionally, senders of texts with affectionate emoji were viewed as less likeable than senders of friendly emoji.

Texts with the friendly smiley face emoji were viewed as appropriate for both genders. Unexpectedly, a man who sent a text with a friendly emoji was perceived as more likeable than a woman who sent the same text.

These findings are consistent with previous research into gender stereotypes and communication, affirming that

> people generally perceive affectionately emotive women as more appropriate than affectionately emotive men. Because men are not expected to show as much emotion in their communication, however, when they do show emotion they may potentially receive more of a positive reaction than women do . . . [and they] are perhaps more celebrated for acting in a way that is inherently more expected in female communication. (pp. 3–4)

In the previous section, it was noted that sexting was becoming more commonplace in teens' romantic relationships. Studies have also examined adult usage of emoji in their romantic relationships. Adults who are more extroverted and have had more casual sexual partners are more likely to use emoji (e.g., the tongue, eggplant, smirking face, and winking face) in sexually suggestive ways (Thomson et al., 2018). Emoji use with a potential romantic partner was associated with an increased likelihood of a second date or meet-up, more frequent sexual activity, and a higher number of sexual partners in the previous year (Gesselman et al., 2019). Using emoji can satisfy needs for intimate communication and interpersonal closeness, making emoji "an important aspect of social behavior in today's digital world that can be used strategically as affective signals, particularly in the domain of human courtship" (p. 12).

Texting While Driving

In their review of mobile phone and driving performance studies, Chen and Yan (2013) found that studies repeatedly indicated that hands-free phone use was considered as dangerous as handheld use and that using a phone while driving was linked to longer reaction times and poorer vehicle control. On average, texting while driving led to five times more crashes than when drivers did not text (Bendak, 2015). Texting while driving resulted in drivers taking their eyes of the road 25% to almost 32% of the time compared to less than 2% of the time for non-texting drivers. Bendak concluded that "any form of texting significantly increases the risk of crashing and, therefore, should be discouraged by developing new and innovative ways to involve the public and improve awareness" (p. 392).

As of 2021, 48 states ban texting for all drivers (Governors Highway Safety Association, 2021). Despite these bans, thousands of crashes are attributed to texting and driving. So why do people continue to engage in this dangerous behavior? One study suggested people with lower levels of self-control and those who have a higher propensity toward risk may be more motivated to text while driving (Gupta et al., 2016). Another proposed that college students who think they are capable of multitasking, overestimate their driving skills, and believe they are in control are more likely to use their phone while driving (Schlehofer et al., 2010). Students who used their phones more while driving in a driving simulator also had worse real-world driving records. Adults text behind the wheel because they believe they can still drive safely while texting (Kareklas & Muehling, 2014). Priming people with public service announcements (PSAs) that include verbal and/or visual cues about death or dying can make them view texting and driving more negatively and reduce intentions of texting while driving in the future. (For more on priming, refer to Chapter 5.)

Texting while driving results in drivers taking their eyes off the road.

Private Use in Public Space

The rapid adoption of mobile phones has transformed our social landscape into a place where individuals are privately using public spaces. Because societal rules for public behavior and phone conversations often conflict with each other (Love & Kewley, 2005; Palen et al., 2001), the lines between public and private spaces are often blurred (Campbell & Ling, 2009).

We have seen that using mobile phones makes it easier for us to communicate with friends and family. Campbell and Ling (2009) pointed out that it often does so at the expense of people who must listen to our ringtones, text message alerts, and half-conversations when they occur in public spaces. More than half of Americans say they frequently or occasionally overhear people on the phone discussing intimate details about their lives in public (Rainie & Zickuhr, 2015). A few studies demonstrated that some people find it entertaining to overhear someone's cell phone conversation (Fortunati, 2005b; Paragas, 2003); however, most people do not like having to hear a person talking on their phone (Monk et al., 2004). In fact, listening to one side of a mobile phone conversation, called a "halfalogue," is more distracting than if the person could hear both sides of the conversation (Emberson et al., 2010). A majority of Americans, especially younger generations, believe it is generally acceptable to talk on a phone while on public transportation, waiting in line, or when walking down the street (Rainie & Zickuhr, 2015).

More than half of Americans say they often or sometimes overhear someone on the phone talking about very personal matters in public.

Earlier in this chapter, we discussed the idea of mobile phones creating social cocooning. In a public space, we may experience cocooning due to the nature of mobile phone use.

> While generally we must be open to both intimates and strangers when we interact in daily life, the mobile phone tips the balance in the favor of the intimate sphere of friends and family. In a situation where there otherwise might have been the oppor-

tunity for talking with a stranger (e.g., waiting for a bus or standing in the checkout line), we can instead gossip, flirt, or joke with friends, intimates, or family members. (Ling, 2008, pp. 159–160)

In the situations that Ling described, we are exhibiting what Gergen (2002) called *absent presence*—our bodies are physically present, but our minds are elsewhere engaged in conversation via mobile technology. A study by the Pew Research Center examined mobile phone use in public spaces and found that 70% of people frequently or occasionally used their phone in public to plan get-togethers with others, and 67% frequently or occasionally used their phone in public to catch up with friends and family (Rainie & Zickuhr, 2015). These findings lend credence to the assertion that our phone use in a public space focuses our attention on our inner social circle. Almost a quarter of mobile phone users reported at least occasionally using their phone to avoid others in public.

Campbell and Kwak (2011a) investigated how people using mobile technology engaged with others in public. Interestingly, when people used mobile technology for informational purposes (i.e., coordination and to check up on the news), they were significantly more likely to engage in a conversation with a stranger. Conversely, when people used mobile technology for relational purposes (i.e., more intimate conversations with friends and family), they were less likely to talk to strangers. Campbell and Kwak suggested that the link between informational use of mobile technology and the increase in talking to strangers is that information use gives people something to talk about (e.g., current events, sports, weather).

Mobile Gaming in Public Spaces

Katz and Acord (2008) noted the increasing popularity of mobile gaming, which Campbell and Kwak (2011a) said can have significant implications on patterns of mobile technology use and talking to strangers in public. In fact, improvements in wireless technology (e.g., faster speeds, greater bandwidth) have improved mobile phones' data transfer capabilities, allowing millions of people to play mobile games (Soh & Tan, 2008). Casual games like *Words with Friends*, *Angry Birds*, and *Candy Crush* are very popular. Since the release of the original *Angry Birds* in 2009, the franchise has racked up more than four billion global downloads (Rovio, 2019). Rovio, the company that created *Angry Birds*, reported in 2010 that global users collectively played for 200 million minutes each day. Phrasing the statistic differently, people around the world catapulted colorful birds at green pigs for 16 years' worth of time every hour (Wortham, 2010). In addition to being popular, mobile games can also be incredibly profitable. For instance, the original *Angry Birds* cost about $100,000 to develop. Its sequel, *Angry Birds 2*, earned almost $132 million in 2018 (Rovio, 2019). Mobile gaming earned $49 billion in revenue in 2019 and is projected to hit more than $56 billion in 2024 (Green, 2019).

Because many of the levels on *Angry Birds* take less than a minute to complete, the game is ideal for playing in spare moments (Richmond, 2010)—as are many other app-based mobile games. These moments often tend to be in public. In addition to people simply playing games in public spaces, we also see location-based mobile gameplay expanding into public spaces through advances in augmented reality. Interactive mobile gaming changes the way we perceive physical spaces, blurring the line between private and public spaces (de Souza e Silva & Sutko, 2008).

> The use of location-awareness in mobile devices and the superimposition of the game narrative on the physical space transforms the intrinsic connection between mobile users and physical spaces. For the connected user, the surrounding space is no longer something to be disconnected from, but something to be linked to. (p. 459)

Recently, *Pokémon Go* gained worldwide popularity as players explored their communities to find and collect various characters (Licoppe, 2017). *Pokémon Go* players felt happier and more successful after playing; the game also motivated players to spend more time outdoors and walking (Williams & Slak-Valek, 2019). The game can boost tourism by increasing visitation to local attractions, with some visiting new cities and countries to collect characters. For instance, one player took a 12-day trip across the globe—with stops in Paris, Sydney, Hong Kong, and Tokyo—to catch all of the characters (Weinburger, 2016).

Effects on Workplace Communication

In addition to personal use, mobile technology is also affecting the way people work, presenting both benefits and challenges (e.g., Andriessen & Vartiainen, 2006; Julsrud, 2005; Julsrud & Bakke, 2008). Although many of you may be familiar with the concept of telework or working from home via the internet (see Chapter 19), mobile phones have given rise to mobile work (Campbell & Ling, 2009). Similar to teleworkers, mobile workers primarily work away from an office; however, mobile workers tend to be on the go, whether it is working from various sites within a given location or constantly moving from one place to the next in a more nomadic fashion (Lilischkis, 2003). The benefits of mobile work include increased adaptability, flexibility, and access to resources (Campbell & Ling, 2009). In fact, a majority of smartphone owners say their phone represents "freedom" (Pew Research Center, 2015).

No doubt, mobile work sounds appealing if you dread being stuck in an office or cubicle all day, but it is not without potential pitfalls. Mobile communication lowers the boundaries between work and home, allowing work matters to spill into family time (recall Castells et al.'s [2007] concept of timeless time discussed earlier in this chapter). Mobile work can cause increased stress for both men and women (Barley et al., 2011). The spillover can go both ways. Women particularly felt the stressful effects of mobile communication due to the fact that family issues often seep into their workplace (Chesley, 2005). However taking multiple "microbreaks" during the workday to text friends or family members—or even taking a minute or two to play a mobile game—can help alleviate work-related stress (Kim & Park, 2017). Employees spend about 22 minutes a day on their smartphones for non-work-related activities.

When it comes to communicating with coworkers via mobile technology, employees must be careful when juggling multiple conversations simultaneously. Texting, instant messaging, and emailing on mobile devices make is easier to juggle multiple work conversations at the same time (Cameron & Webster, 2011). However, if a worker is not forthcoming about multiple concurrent conversations—such as emailing from a smartphone while on a conference call—colleagues could perceive incivility and the simultaneous activity could create mistrust.

Email can be a source of work-related stress and anxiety. Mobile technology enabled employees to spend more time emailing, which caused greater feelings of being overloaded, but workers' perceptions of being able to cope with the overload increased as they processed more email (Barley et al., 2011). Ultimately, mobile technologies in the work environment have created what some call the "autonomy paradox"—mobile devices give workers more autonomy through flexibility and control over work-related communication but also raise expectations that employees should always be available and respond to email, which makes disconnecting from work more challenging, thus reducing one's autonomy (Mazmanian et al., 2013). Recent studies examined workplace "telepressure" (i.e., the urge to answer work-related messages quickly). Not only did it lead people to use their smartphones while at work (Van Laethem et al., 2018) but also during their off hours (Cambier et al., 2019). Moreover, work-related smartphone use limited employees' abilities to disconnect from their jobs during non-work hours.

Checking email less frequently resulted in people feeling less stressed, which, in turn, resulted in a higher sense of well-being (Kishlev & Dunn, 2014). Concerns about the pressure to be constantly checking one's inbox have led to legislation to help employees disconnect from digital demands outside of work. Portugal passed a law in 2021 making it illegal for employers to call, text, or email employees outside of their normal work hours (Horowitz, 2021). Similarly, France enacted a law in 2017 requiring companies with more than 50 employees to implement policies to prevent work emails from intruding into an employee's off hours (Rubin, 2017). These policies included avoiding the "reply all" option on emails or blocking off chunks of time (e.g., 9 p.m. to 7 a.m.) where workers are not expected to reply to work emails. France's law came after German automaker Daimler enacted an optional policy to replace the traditional out-of-office reply while an employee is on vacation. Instead of returning to work to face an inbox full of new emails, Daimler allowed employees to turn on the "Mail on Holiday" feature, which deleted any incoming email and sent a reply with contact information for another employee for any urgent matters (Gibson, 2014).

Smartphone Addiction and Nomophobia

As this chapter has detailed, there are numerous concerns about the effects of mobile phone use, especially smartphones. Much of what has been covered in this chapter focuses on effects of mobile phones on social behavior, but there are also psychological effects to consider. The primary psychological effect that has captured both media and academic attention is so-called smartphone addiction. In fact, Shambare et al. (2012) asserted that mobile phone addiction is "possibly the biggest non-drug addiction of the 21st century" (p. 573).

Although numerous studies have examined smartphone addiction—far more than can be covered here—Campbell and Ling (2020) point out that questions remain about whether smartphone addiction is even real. Smartphone addiction is not included in the *Diagnostic and Statistical Manual for Mental Health Disorders*, nor is it recognized in the psychological community (APA, 2013). Although compulsive smartphone use can lead to many problems, it does not mean that a compulsive smartphone user is necessarily addicted (Campbell & Ling, 2020). Panova and Carbonell (2018) compared research on smartphone addiction to criteria for behavioral addiction and reached this conclusion:

> Although the majority of research in the field declares that smartphones are addictive or takes the existence of smartphone addiction as granted, we did not find sufficient support from the addiction perspective to confirm the existence of smartphone addiction at this time. The behaviors observed in the research could be better labeled as problematic or maladaptive smartphone use and their consequences do not meet the severity levels of those caused by addiction. (p. 252)

Campbell and Ling (2020) suggest problematic phone use could be looked at as a habit, rather than an addiction. LaRose (2010) noted that perhaps more than half of all media usage behaviors are habitual. Considering our phones' ever-present role in our daily lives, it is certainly possible that much of our use is simply out of habit.

Another growing area of mobile phone dependency research examines the effects of *not* having our phone with us. Researchers call the fear of not having our phone with us **nomophobia**. A recent review of nomophobia research indicates that the condition negatively affects academic performance, physical and mental health, personality, self-esteem, stress, and anxiety (Rodriguez-Garcia et al., 2020). Separating college students from their iPhones negatively impacted their attention while trying to complete cognitive tasks (i.e., word search puzzles) and increased participants' blood pressure and self-reported levels of anxiety and unpleasantness, especially when they could hear their phones ringing (Clayton et al., 2015). As mentioned earlier in this chapter, more than 40% of U.S. teens said not having their phone made them feel anxious (Jiang, 2018a). Rodriguez-Garcia et al. (2020) conclude that nomophobia is a public health problem and call for research on the issue to continue.

Summary

It is easy for us to overlook many of the effects of mobile communication in our daily lives because we often do not give our phone a second thought—unless we forget it, lose it, or the battery dies! In those situations, we are painfully aware of how dependent we have become on it.

Mobile phones give us much greater control and flexibility when it comes to social coordination. We can tackle logistical issues, shuffle our schedule, or firm up plans with a single phone call or text. Mobile phones are a very personal technology. Not only do they facilitate mediated communication with friends and family but they also aid in coordinating FtF meetings. Some research has revealed that mobile phone use can insulate us from contact with those outside of our close-knit groups, but it can also connect us with those beyond our inner social circle.

Youth culture has been transformed by the widespread adoption of mobile technology. Teens stay in constant contact with friends, primarily through texting. Sexting is still a major area of concern, but research suggests it now may be a common part of courtship for teens and adults alike. College students are not immune to the negative consequences of mobile phone use. Generally, phones in the classroom lead to poor performance and low grades.

Mobile phones blur the line between public and private space. When phone calls, which previously were considered private, occur in public, there are many unintended consequences on the people in proximity to the caller. However, some types of mobile phone use help callers strike up conversations with strangers encountered in public spaces. In a similar effect, mobile gaming has turned public spaces into communal gameboards.

Mobile technology has also had a large impact on the workplace. Employees should be mindful of the possible effects of simultaneous multiple conversations with colleagues, which include feelings of distrust. Additionally, work-related smartphone use can make it more difficult for employees to disconnect from their jobs during non-work hours.

With the prevalence of mobile phones in today's society, concerns abound about smartphone addiction, but some scholars say problematic mobile phone use does not rise to the level of an actual addiction. Rather, it should be viewed as a habit. Meanwhile, researchers continue to study the effects of not having our phones with us.

Overall, mobile communication has fundamentally changed the way we think about people, space, and time. The impact on society has been—and will continue to be—substantial.

References

Abel, G. G., Barlow, D. H., Blanchard, E. B., & Guild, D. (1977). The components of rapists' sexual arousal. *Archives of General Psychiatry, 34*(8), 895–903. https://doi.org/10.1001/archpsyc.1977.01770200033002

Abel, S. (1995). The rabbit in drag: Camp and gender construction in the American animated cartoon. *Journal of Popular Culture, 29*(3),183–202. https://doi.org/10.1111/j.0022-3840.1995.00183.x

Abma, J. C., & Martinez, G. M. (2017). Sexual activity and contraceptive use among teenagers in the United States, 2011-2015. *National Health Statistics Report*, (104), 1–23. https://www.cdc.gov/nchs/data/nhsr/nhsr104.pdf

Abraham, L., & Appiah, O. (2006). Framing news stories: The role of visual imagery in priming racial stereotypes. *The Howard Journal of Communications, 17*(3), 183–203. https://doi.org/10.1080/10646170600829584

Abrams, J., & Giles, H. (2007). Ethnic identity gratifications selection and avoidance by African Americans: A group vitality and social identity perspective. *Media Psychology, 9*(1), 115–134. https://doi.org/10.1080/15213260709336805

Abramson, P. R., Perry, L., Seeley, T., Seeley, D., & Rothblatt, A. (1981). Thermographic measurement of sexual arousal: A discriminant validity analysis. *Archives of Sexual Behavior, 10*(2), 175–176. https://doi.org/10.1007/BF01542177

Ackermann, L., Lo, C. H., Mani, N., & Mayor, J. (2020). Word learning from a tablet app: Toddlers perform better in a passive context. *PLOS ONE, 15*(12), Article e0240519. https://doi.org/10.1371/journal.pone.0240519

Adams, C. & Harder, B. M. (2019). Lifestyles are risky, too: The social construction of risk and empowerment in prescription drug direct-to-consumer advertisements. *Health, Risk & Society, 21*(1-2), 17–34. https://doi.org/10.1080/13698575.2019.1601684

Adobe. (2019, June 4). *Despite 25 years of ad growth, diversity remains a challenge.* https://blog.adobe.com/en/publish/2019/06/04/despite-25-years-of-advertising-growth-diversity-remains-a-challenge.html#gs.6q686c

Ahmed, F., Kim, S., Nowalk, M., King, J. P., Van-Wormer, J. J., Gaglani, M....Uzicanin, A. (2020). Paid leave and access to telework as work attendance determinants during acute respiratory illness, United States, 2017–2018. *Emerging Infectious Diseases, 26*(1), 26-33. https://doi.org/10.3201/eid2601.190743

Aitken, P. P., Leathar, D. S., & O'Hagan, F. J. (1985). Children's perceptions of advertisements for cigarettes. *Social Science Medicine, 2*, 785–797. https://doi.org/10.1016/0277-9536(85)90127-3

Aitken, P. P., Leathar, D. S., & Squair, S. I. (1986). Children's awareness of cigarette brand sponsorship of sports and games in the UK. *Health Education Research, 1*(3), 203–211. https://doi.org/10.1093/her/1.3.203

Ajzen, I. (1988). *Attitudes, personality, and behavior.* Dorsey.

Ajzen, I. (1991). The theory of planned behavior. *Organizational Behavior and Human Decision Processes, 50*(2), 179–211. https://doi.org/10.1016/0749-5978(91)90020-T

Akerman, A., Bryant, J. A., & Diaz-Wionczek, M. (2011). Educational preschool programming in the US: An ecological and evolutionary story. *Journal of Children and Media, 5*(2), 204–220. https://doi.org/10.1080/17482798.2011.558284

Al Abbas, A. A. K. (2018). *The effect of parental interventions on food buying behaviour of children subjected to social media food advertising* [Doctoral dissertation, Brunel University]. http://bura.brunel.ac.uk/handle/2438/18415

Aladé, F., & Nathanson, A. I. (2016). What preschoolers bring to the show: The relation between viewer characteristics and children's learning from educational television. *Media Psychology*,

19(3), 406–430. https://doi.org/10.1080/15213269.2015.1054945

Alba, J. W., & Marmorstein, H. (1987). The effects of frequency knowledge on consumer decision making. *Journal of Consumer Research, 14*(1), 14–25. https://doi.org/10.1086/209089

Albada, K. F. (2014). Media content: Televised entertainment. In T. L. Thompson (Ed.), *Encyclopedia of health communication* (Vol. 2, pp. 815–819). Sage.

Alexopoulos, C., & Taylor, L. D. (2020). Risky business: Sexual risk and responsibility messages in teen sex romps. *Sexuality & Culture, 34*, 2161–2182. https://doi.org/10.1007/s12119-020-09742-4

Alhabash, S., & Ma, M. (2017). A tale of four platforms: Motivations and uses of Facebook, Twitter, Instagram, and Snapchat among college students? *Social Media + Society, 3*(1). https://doi.org/10.1177/2056305117691544

Ali, F. R. M., Marynak, K. L., Kim, Y., Binns, S., Emery, S. L., Gomez, Y., & King, B. A. (2020). E-cigarette advertising expenditures in the United States, 2014–2018. *Tobacco Control, 29*(e1), e124–e126. https://doi.org/10.1136/tobaccocontrol-2019-055424

Alkazemi, M. F., & Wanta, W. (2018). The effect of oil prices on the media agenda: A model of agenda building. *Newspaper Research Journal, 39*(2), 232–244. https://doi.org/10.1177/0739532918775655

Allen, J. J., Ash, S. M., & Anderson, C. A. (2022). Who finds media violence funny? Testing the effects of media violence exposure and dark personality traits. *Psychology of Popular Media, 11*(1), 35–46. https://doi.org/10.1037/ppm0000296

Allen, M., D'Alessio, D., & Emmers-Sommer, T. M. (1999). Reactions of criminal sexual offenders to pornography: A meta-analytic summary. In M. Roloff (Ed.), *Communication yearbook 22* (pp. 139–169). Sage.

Allen, M., D'Alessio, D., Emmers, T. M., & Gebhardt, L. (1996). The role of educational briefings in mitigating effects of experimental exposure to violent sexually explicit material: A meta-analysis. *Journal of Sex Research, 33*(2), 135–141. https://doi.org/10.1080/00224499609551825

Allen, M., Emmers-Sommer, T. M., D'Alessio, D., Timmerman, L., Hanzal, A., & Korus, J. (2007). The connection between the physiological and psychological reactions to sexually explicit materials: A literature summary using meta-analysis. *Communication Monographs, 74*(4), 541–560. https://doi.org/10.1080/03637750701578648

Allen, T. D., Golden, T. D., & Shockley, K. M. (2015). How effective is telecommuting? Assessing the status of our scientific findings. *Psychological Science in the Public Interest, 16*(2), 40–68. https://doi.org/10.1177/1529100615593273

Althaus, S. L., & Kim, Y. M. (2006). Priming effects in complex information environments: Reassessing the impact of news discourse on presidential approval. *Journal of Politics, 68*, 960–976. https://doi.org/10.1111/j.1468-2508.2006.00483.x

Althaus, S. L., & Tewksbury, D. (2002). Agenda setting and the "new" news: Patterns of issue importance among readers of the paper and online versions of *The New York Times*. *Communication Research, 29*, 180–207. https://doi.org/10.1177/0093650202029002004

Amazeen, M. A., & Bucy, E. P. (2019). Conferring resistance to digital information: The inoculating influence of procedural news knowledge. *Journal of Broadcasting & Electronic Media, 63*(3), 415–432. https://doi.org/10.1080/08838151.2019.1653101

American Academy of Pediatrics. (1999). Media education. *Pediatrics, 104*, 341–343. https://doi.org/10.1542/peds.104.2.341

American Academy of Pediatrics. (2001). Children, Adolescents, and Television. *Pediatrics, 107*, 423–426. https://doi.org/10.1542/peds.107.2.423

American Academy of Pediatrics, American Academy of Child and Adolescent Psychiatry, American Psychological Association, American Medical Association, American Academy of Family Physicians, & American Psychiatric Association. (2000). *Joint statement on the impact of entertainment violence on children.* http://www.craiganderson.org/wp-content/uploads/caa/VGVpolicyDocs/00AAP%20-%20Joint%20Statement.pdf

American Medical Association. (2007a). *Emotional and behavioral effects, including addictive potential, of video games* (CSAPH Report 12-A-07). Retrieved from http://www.ama-assn.org/ama1/pub/upload/mm/467/csaph12a07.doc

American Psychiatric Association. (n.d.) *Internet gaming*. https://www.psychiatry.org/patients-families/internet-gaming

American Psychiatric Association. (2013a). *Diagnostic and statistical manual of mental disorders* (5th ed.) https://doi.org/10.1176/appi.books.9780890425596

American Psychiatric Association. (2013b). *Internet gaming disorder.* https://www.psychiatry.org/File%20Library/Psychiatrists/Practice/DSM/APA_DSM-5-Internet-Gaming-Disorder.pdf

American Psychological Association. (n.d.). *Internet addiction.* https://dictionary.apa.org/internet-addiction

American Psychological Association Task Force on Media Violence. (2015). *Technical report on the review of violent video game literature.* https://www.apa.org/pi/families/review-video-games.pdf

American Psychological Association. (2019). *APA task force report on violent video games.* https://www.apa.org/science/leadership/bsa/report-violent-video-games.pdf

American Psychological Association. (2020). *APA resolution on violent video games: February 2020 revision* to the 2015 resolution. https://www.apa.org/about/policy/resolution-violent-video-games.pdf

Ameryoun, A., Sanaeinasab, H., Saffari, M., & Koenig, H. G. (2018). Impact of game-based health promotion programs on body mass index in overweight/obese children and adolescents: A systematic review and meta-analysis of randomized controlled trials. *Childhood Obesity, 14*(2), 67–80. https://doi.org/10.1089/chi.2017.0250

Amichai-Hamburger, Y., & Vinitzky, G. (2010). Social network use and personality. *Computers in Human Behavior, 26*, 1289–1295. https://doi.org/10.1016/j.chb.2010.03.018

Ancu, M., & Cozma, R. (2009). MySpace politics: Uses and gratifications of befriending candidates. *Journal of Broadcasting & Electronic Media, 53*(4), 567–583. https://doi.org/10.1080/08838150903333064

Anderson, C. A. (2004). An update on the effects of playing violent video games. *Journal of Adolescence, 27*, 113–122. https://doi.org/10.1016/j.adolescence.2003.10.009

Anderson, C. A., Andrighetto, L., Bartholow, B. D., Bègue, L., Boxer, P., Brockmyer, J. F., Burgess, M. C. R., Calvete, E., Cantor, J., Coyne, S. M., Dill-Shackleford, K., Donnerstein, E., Gabbiadini, A., Gibson, B., Hasan, Y., Lueke, A. K., Orue, I., Riva, P., Strasburger, V. C., . . . Warburton, W. (2015). Consensus on media violence effects: Comment on Bushman, Gollwitzer, and Cruz (2015). *Psychology of Popular Media Culture, 4*(3), 215–221. https://doi.org/10.1037/ppm0000063

Anderson, C. A., Berkowitz, L., Donnerstein, E., Huesmann, L. R., Johnson, J. D., Linz, D., Malamuth, N. M., & Wartella, E. (2003). The influence of media violence on youth. *Psychological Science in the Public Interest, 4*(3), 81–110. https://doi.org/10.1111/j.1529-1006.2003.pspi_1433.x

Anderson, C. A., & Bushman, B. J. (2001). Effects of violent video games on aggressive behavior, aggressive cognition, aggressive affect, physiological arousal, and prosocial behavior: A meta-analytic review of the scientific literature. *Psychological Science, 12*, 353–359. https://doi.org/10.1111/1467-9280.00366

Anderson, C. A., & Bushman, B. J. (2002). Human aggression. *Annual Review of Psychology, 53*, 27–51. https://doi.org/10.1146/annurev.psych.53.100901.135231

Anderson, C. A., & Bushman, B. J. (2018). Media violence and the general aggression model. *Journal of Social Issues, 74*(2), 386–413. https://doi.org/10.1111/josi.12275

Anderson, C. A., & Carnagey, N. L. (2009). Causal effects of violent sports video games on aggression: Is it competitiveness or violent content? *Journal of Experimental Social Psychology, 45*(4), 731–739. https://doi.org/10.1016/j.jesp.2009.04.019

Anderson, C. A., & Carnagey, N. L. (2014). *The role of theory in the study of media violence: The general aggression model*. In D. A. Gentile (Ed.), *Media violence and children: A complete guide for parents and professionals* (2nd ed., pp. 103–133). Praeger/ABC-CLIO.

Anderson, C. A., Carnagey, N. L., Flanagan, M., Benjamin, A. J., Eubanks, J., & Valentine, J. C. (2004). Violent video games: Specific effects of violent content on aggressive thoughts and behavior. In M. Zanna (Ed.), *Advances in experimental social psychology* (Vol. 36, pp. 199–249). Elsevier.

Anderson, C. A., & Dill, K. E. (2000). Video games and aggressive thoughts, feelings, and behavior in the laboratory and in life. *Journal of Personality and Social Psychology, 78*, 772–790. https://doi.org/10.1037/0022-3514.78.4.772

Anderson, C. A., Gentile, D. A., & Dill, K. E. (2011). Prosocial, antisocial, and other effects of recreational video games. In D. G. Singer & J. L. Singer (Eds.), *Handbook of children and the media* (2nd ed., pp. 249–272). Sage.

Anderson, C. A., & Murphy, C. R. (2003). Violent video games and aggressive behavior in young women. *Aggressive Behavior, 29*(5), 423–429. https://doi.org/10.1002/ab.10042

Anderson, C. A., Sakamoto, A., Gentile, D. A., Ihori, N., Shibuya, A., Yukawa, S., Naito, M., & Kobayashi, K. (2008). Longitudinal effects of violent video games on aggression in Japan and the United States. *Pediatrics, 122*(5), e1067–e1072. https://doi.org/10.1542/peds.2008-1425

Anderson, C. A., Shibuya, A., Ihori, N., Swing, E. L., Bushman, B. J., Sakamoto, A., Rothstein, H. R., & Saleem, M. (2010). Violent video game effects on aggression, empathy, and prosocial behavior in eastern and western countries: A meta-analytic review. *Psychological Bulletin, 136*(2), 151–173. https://doi.org/10.1037/a0018251

Anderson, D. R., Bryant, J., Wilder, A., Santomero, A., Williams, M., & Crawley, A. M. (2000). Researching *Blue's Clues*: Viewing behavior and impact. *Media Psychology, 2*(2), 179–194. https://doi.org/10.1207/S1532785XMEP0202_4

Anderson, D. R., Huston, A. C., Wright, J. C., & Collins, P. A. (1998). *Sesame Street* and educational television for children. In R. G. Noll & M. E. Price (Eds.), *A communications cornucopia: Markle Foundation essays on information policy* (pp. 279–296). Brookings Institution Press.

Anderson, D. R., Lorch, E. P., Field, D. E., & Sanders, J. (1981). The effects of TV program comprehensibility on preschool children's visual attention to television. *Child Development, 52*(1), 151–157. https://doi.org/10.2307/1129224

Anderson, I. K. (2011). The uses and gratifications of online care pages: A study of CaringBridge.

Health Communication, 26, 546–559. https://doi.org/10.1080/10410236.2011.558335

Anderson, J. (1983). *The architecture of cognition.* Oxford University Press.

Anderson, J., & Bower, G. (1973). *Human associative memory.* Winston.

Anderson, J. A., & Meyer, T. P. (1975). Functionalism and the mass media. *Journal of Broadcasting, 19,* 11–22. https://doi.org/10.1080/08838157509363766

Anderson, M., & Jiang, J. (2018). *Teens, social media & technology 2018.* Pew Research Center. https://www.pewresearch.org/internet/wp-content/uploads/sites/9/2018/05/PI_2018.05.31_TeensTech_FINAL.pdf

Anderson, R. B. (1995). Cognitive appraisal of performance capability in the prevention of drunken driving: A test of self-efficacy theory. *Journal of Public Relations Research, 7*(3), 205–229. https://doi.org/10.1207/s1532754xjprr0703_03

Anderson, R. B. (2000). Vicarious and persuasive influences on efficacy expectations and intentions to perform breast self-examination. *Public Relations Review, 26*(1), 97–114. https://doi.org/10.1016/S0363-8111(00)00033-3

Anderson, R. B., & McMillion, P. Y. (1995). Effects of similar and diversified modeling on African American women's efficacy expectations to perform breast self-examination. *Health Communication, 7*(4), 327–343. https://doi.org/10.1207/s15327027hc0704_3

Anderson-Barkley, T., & Foglesong, K. (2018). Activism in video games: A new voice for social change. In K. L. Gray & D. J. Leonard (Eds.), *Woke gaming: Digital challenges to oppression and social injustice* (pp. 252–269). University of Washington Press.

Andriessen, J. H., & Vartiainen, M. (2006). *Mobile virtual work: A new paradigm?* Springer.

Andsager, J. L. (2000). How interest groups attempt to shape public opinion with competing news frames. *Journalism & Mass Communication Quarterly, 77*(3), 577–592. https://doi.org/10.1177/107769900007700308

Andsager, J., & Roe, K. (2003). "What's your definition of dirty, baby?": Sex in music video. *Sexuality & Culture: An Interdisciplinary Quarterly, 7*(3), 79–97. https://doi.org/10.1007/s12119-003-1004-8

Ang, R. P., & Goh, D. H. (2010). Cyberbullying among adolescents: The role of affective and cognitive empathy, and gender. *Child Psychiatry and Human Development, 41*(4), 387–397. https://doi.org/10.1007/s10578-010-0176-3

Angelini, J. R., Billings, A. C., MacArthur, P. J., Bissell, K., Smith, L. R. (2014). Competing separately, medaling equally: Racial depictions of athletes in NBC's primetime broadcast of the 2012 London Olympic games. *Howard Journal of Communication, 25*(2), 115–133. https://doi.org/10.1080/10646175.2014.888380

Angell, J. R. (1941). Radio and national morale. *The American Journal of Sociology, 47*(3), 352–359. https://doi.org/10.1086/218915

Antunes, F. (2017). Rethinking PG-13: Ratings and the boundaries of childhood horror. *Journal of Film and Video, 69*(1), 27–43. https://doi.org/10.5406/jfilmvideo.69.1.0027

Anyiwo, N., Ward, L. M., Day Fletcher, K., & Rowley, S. (2018). Black adolescents' television usage and endorsement of mainstream gender roles and the strong Black woman schema. *Journal of Black Psychology, 44*(4), 371–397. https://doi.org/10.1177/0095798418771818

Applegate, E. (1998). *Personalities and products: A historical perspective on advertising in America.* Greenwood.

Applequist, J., & Ball, J. G. (2018). An updated analysis of direct-to-consumer television advertisements for prescription drugs. *Annals of Family Medicine, 16*(3), 211–216. https://doi.org/10.1370/afm.2220

Arceneaux, K., & Johnson, M. (2013). *Changing minds or changing channels? Partisan news in an age of choice.* University of Chicago Press.

Arendt, F. (2017). Impulsive facial-threat perceptions after exposure to stereotypic crime news. *Communication Research, 44*(6), 793–816. https://doi.org/10.1177/0093650214565919

Armstrong, G., Neuendorf, K., & Brentar, J. (1992). TV entertainment, news, and racial perceptions of college students. *Journal of Communication, 42*(3), 153–176. https://doi.org/10.1111/j.1460-2466.1992.tb00804.x

Ashby, S. L., Arcari, C. M., & Edmonson, M. B. (2006). Television viewing and risk of sexual initiation by young adolescents. *Archives of Pediatrics & Adolescent Medicine, 160*(4), 375–380. https://doi.org/10.1001/archpedi.160.4.375

Atkin, C. (1983). Effects of realistic TV violence vs. fictional violence on aggression. *Journalism Quarterly, 60*(4), 615–621. https://doi.org/10.1177/107769908306000405

Atkin, C. K. (1990). Effects of televised alcohol messages on teenage drinking patterns. *Journal of Adolescent Health Care, 11*(1), 10–24. https://doi.org/10.1016/0197-0070(90)90125-L

Atkin, C. K., & Freimuth, V. (2013). Guidelines for formative research in campaign design. In R. E. Rice & C. K. Atkin (Eds.), *Public communication campaigns* (4th ed., pp. 53–68). Sage.

Atkin, C., Hocking, J., & Block, M. (1984). Teenage drinking: Does advertising make a difference? *Journal of Communication, 34*(2), 157–167. https://doi.org/10.1111/j.1460-2466.1984.tb02167.x

Atkin, D. J., & Lau, T. Y. (2007). Information technology and organizational telework. In C. A. Lin & D. J. Atkin (Eds.), *Communication technology and social change: Theory and implications* (pp. 79–100). Lawrence Erlbaum Associates.

Atwell Seate, A., Cohen, E. L., Fujioka, Y., & Hoffner, C. (2012). Exploring gun ownership as a social identity to understanding the perceived media influence of the Virginia Tech news coverage on attitudes toward gun control policy. *Communication Research Reports, 29*(2), 130–139. https://doi.org/10.1080/08824096.2012.667773

Atwell Seate, A., Ma, R., Chien, H.-Y., & Mastro, D. (2018). Cultivating intergroup emotions: An intergroup threat theory approach. *Mass Communication and Society, 21*(2), 178–197. https://doi.org/10.1080/15205436.2017.1381262

Atwell Seate, A., & Mastro, D. (2017). Exposure to immigration in the news: The impact of group-level emotions on intergroup behavior. *Communication Research, 44*(6), 817–840. https://doi.org/10.1177/0093650215570654

Aubrey, J. S. (2004). Sex and punishment: An examination of sexual consequences and the sexual double standard in teen programming. *Sex Roles, 50*, 505–514. https://doi.org/10.1023/B:SERS.0000023070.87195.07

Aubrey, J. S., & Frisby, C. M. (2011). Sexual objectification in music videos: A content analysis comparing gender and genre. *Mass Communication & Society, 14*(4), 475–501. https://doi.org/10.1080/15205436.2010.513468

Aubrey, J. S., & Smith, S. E. (2016). The impact of exposure to sexually oriented media on the endorsement of hookup culture. *Mass Communication and Society, 19*, 74–101. https://doi.org/10.1080/15205436.2015.1070875

Aubrey, J. S., & Yan, K. (2020). Gender-based media stereotypes and their effects on audiences: The more gender changes, the more media representation stays the same. In A. C. Billings & S. Parrott (Eds.), *Media stereotypes: From ageism to xenophobia* (pp. 73–91). Peter Lang.

Aubrey, J. S., Yan, K., Terán, L., & Roberts, L. (2020). The heterosexual script on tween, teen, and young-adult television programs: A content analytic update and extension. *Journal of Sex Research, 57*(9), 1134–1145. https://doi.org/10.1080/00224499.2019.1699895

Aull, B. (2019). A study of phatic emoji use in WhatsApp communication. *Internet Pragmatics, 2*(2), 206–232. https://doi.org/10.1075/ip.00029.aul

Austin, E. W., Chen, M.-J., & Grube, J. W. (2006). How does alcohol advertising influence underage drinking? The role of desirability, identification and skepticism. *Journal of Adolescent Health, 38*(4), 376–384. https://doi.org/10.1016/j.jadohealth.2005.08.017

Austin, E. W., & Knaus, C. (2000). Predicting the potential for risky behavior among those "too young" to drink, as the result of appealing advertising. *Journal of Health Communication, 5*(1), 13–27. https://doi.org/10.1080/108107300126722

Axsom, D., Yates, S., & Chaiken, S. (1987). Audience response as a heuristic cue in persuasion. *Journal of Personality and Social Psychology, 53*(1), 30–40. https://doi.org/10.1037/0022-3514.53.1.30

Baams, L., Overbeek, G., Dubas, J. S., Doornwaard, S. M., Rommes, E., & van Aken, M. A. (2015). Perceived realism moderates the relation between sexualized media consumption and permissive sexual attitudes in Dutch adolescents. *Archives of Sexual Behavior, 44*(3), 743–754. https://doi.org/10.1007/s10508-014-0443-7

Babrow, A. S. (1988). Theory and method in research on audience motives. *Journal of Broadcasting & Electronic Media, 32*(4), 471–487. https://doi.org/10.1080/08838158809386717

Baden, C., & Lecheler, S. (2012). Fleeting, fading, or far-reaching? A knowledge-based model of the persistence of framing effects. *Communication Theory, 22*(4), 359–382. https://doi.org/10.1111/j.1468-2885.2012.01413.x

Bai. Q., Dan, Q., Mu, Z., & Yang, M. (2019). A systematic review of emoji: Current research and future perspectives. *Frontiers in Psychology, 10*, 1–16. https://doi.org/10.3389/fpsyg.2019.02221

Bailey, A. A. (2006). A year in the life of the African-American male in advertising: A content analysis. *Journal of Advertising, 35*(1), 83–104. https://doi.org/10.2753/JOA0091-3367350106

Bainbridge, E., Bevans, S., Keeley, B., & Oriel, K. (2011). The effects of Nintendo Wii Fit on community-dwelling older adults with perceived balance deficits: A pilot study. *Physical & Occupational Therapy in Geriatrics, 29*(2), 126–135. https://doi.org/10.3109/02703181.2011.569053

Baker, C. N. (2005). Images of women's sexuality in advertisements: A content analysis of Black- and White-oriented women's and men's magazines. *Sex Roles: A Journal of Research, 52*(1-2), 13–27. https://doi.org/10.1007/s11199-005-1190-y

Baldaro, B., Tuozzi, G., Codispoti, M., Montebarocci, O., Barbagli, F., Trombini, E., & Rossi, N. (2004). Aggressive and non-violent videogames: Short-term psychological and cardiovascular effects on habitual players. *Stress and Health: Journal of the International Society for the Investigation of Stress, 20*(4), 203–208. https://doi.org/10.1002/smi.1015

Ball, S., & Bogatz, G. A. (1970). *The first year of Sesame Street: An evaluation.* Educational Testing Service.

Ball, S., & Bogatz, G. A. (1973). *Reading with television: An evaluation of The Electric Company.* Educational Testing Service.

Ball, S., Bogatz, G. A., Karazow, K. M., & Rubin, D. B. (1974). *Reading with television: A follow-up evaluation of The Electric Company.* Educational Testing Service.

Ball-Rokeach, S. J., & DeFleur, M. L. (1976). A dependency model of mass-media effects. *Communication Research, 3*(1), 3–21. https://doi.org/10.1177/009365027600300101

Ball-Rokeach, S. J., Rokeach, M., & Grube, J. W. (1984a, November). The great American values test. *Psychology Today, 34*, 41.

Ball-Rokeach, S. J., Rokeach, M., & Grube, J. W. (1984b). *The great American values test: Influencing behavior and belief through television.* Free Press.

Baltaci, Ö. (2019). The predictive relationships between the social media addiction and social anxiety, loneliness, and happiness. *International Journal of Progressive Education, 15*(4), 73–82. https://doi.org/10.29329/ijpe.2019.203.6

Bancroft, J., & Mathews, A. (1971). Autonomic correlates of penile erection. *Journal of Psychosomatic Research, 15,* 159–167. https://doi.org/10.1016/0022-3999(71)90003-1

Bandura, A. (1965a). Influence of models' reinforcement contingencies on the acquisition of imitative responses. *Journal of Personality and Social Psychology, 1*(6), 589–595. https://doi.org/10.1037/h0022070

Bandura, A. (1965b). Vicarious processes: A case of no-trial learning. In L. Berkowitz (Ed.), *Advances in experimental social psychology* (Vol. 2, pp. 1–55). Academic.

Bandura, A. (1973). *Aggression: A social learning analysis.* Prentice-Hall.

Bandura, A. (1977). *Social learning theory.* Prentice-Hall.

Bandura, A. (1978). A social learning theory of aggression. *Journal of Communication, 28*(3), 12–29. https://doi.org/10.1111/j.1460-2466.1978.tb01621.x

Bandura, A. (1979). Psychological mechanisms of aggression. In M. von Cranach, K. Foppa, W. Lepenies, & D. Ploog (Eds.), *Human ethology: Claims and limits of a new discipline* (pp. 316–356). Cambridge University Press.

Bandura, A. (1982). Self-efficacy mechanism in human agency. *American Psychologist, 37*(2), 122–147. https://doi.org/10.1037/0003-066X.37.2.122

Bandura, A. (1986). *Social foundations of thought and action: A social cognitive theory.* Prentice-Hall.

Bandura, A. (1989). Self-regulation of motivation and action through internal standards and goal systems. In L. A. Pervin (Ed.), *Goal concepts in personality and social psychology* (pp. 19–85). Lawrence Erlbaum Associates.

Bandura, A. (1991). Social cognitive theory of moral thought and action. In W. M. Kurtines & J. L. Gerwitz (Eds.), *Handbook of moral behavior and development* (Vol. 1, pp. 45–103). Lawrence Erlbaum Associates.

Bandura, A. (1992). Self-efficacy mechanism in psychobiological functioning. In R. Schwarzer (Ed.), *Self-efficacy: Thought control of action* (pp. 355–394). Hemisphere.

Bandura, A. (1994). Social cognitive theory of mass communication. In J. Bryant & D. Zillmann (Eds.), *Media effects: Advances in theory and research* (pp. 61–90). Lawrence Erlbaum Associates.

Bandura, A. (2002). Social cognitive theory of mass communication. In J. Bryant & D. Zillmann (Eds.), *Media effects: Advances in theory and research* (2nd ed., pp. 121–153). Lawrence Erlbaum Associates.

Bandura, A. (2004). Health promotion by social cognitive means. *Health Education & Behavior, 31*(2), 143–164. https://doi.org/10.1177/1090198104263660

Bandura, A. (2006). On integrating social cognitive and social diffusion theories. In A. Singhal & J. Dearing (Eds.), *Communication of innovations: A journey with Ev Rogers* (pp. 111–135). Sage.

Bandura, A. (2009). Social cognitive theory of mass communication. In J. Bryant & M. B. Oliver (Eds.), *Media effects: Advances in theory and research* (3rd ed., pp. 94–124). Routledge.

Bandura, A., Ross, D., & Ross, S. A. (1963a). Imitation of film-mediated aggressive models. *The Journal of Abnormal and Social Psychology, 66*(1), 3–11. https://doi.org/10.1037/h0048687

Bandura, A., Ross, D., & Ross, S. A. (1963b). Vicarious reinforcement and imitative learning. *The Journal of Abnormal and Social Psychology, 67*(6), 601–607. https://doi.org/10.1037/h0045550

Bandura, A., Underwood, B., & Fromson, M. E. (1975). Disinhibition of aggression through diffusion of responsibility and dehumanization of victims. *Journal of Research in Personality, 9*(4), 253–269. https://doi.org/10.1016/0092-6566(75)90001-X

Bandura, A., & Walters, R. H. (1963). *Social learning and personality development.* Holt, Rinehart and Winston.

Bane, K. C. (2019). Tweeting the agenda: How print and alternative web-only news organizations use Twitter as a source. *Journalism Practice, 13*(2), 191–205. https://doi.org/10.1080/17512786.2017.1413587

Banning, S. A. (2007). Factors affecting the marketing of a public safety message: The third-person effect and uses of gratifications theory in public reaction to a crime reduction program. *Atlantic Journal of Communication, 15*(1), 1–18. https://doi.org/10.1080/15456870701212716

Barbaree, H. E., Marshall, W. L., & Lanthier, R. D. (1979). Deviant sexual arousal in rapists. *Behavior Research and Therapy, 17*(3), 215–222. https://doi.org/10.1016/0005-7967(79)90036-6

Barenthin, J., & Van Puymbroeck, M. (2006, August). Research update: The joystick generation. *Parks & Recreation, 48*(8), 24–29.

Bargh, J. A., Bond, R. N., Lombardi, W. J., & Tota, M. E. (1986). The additive nature of chronic and temporary sources of construct accessibility. *Journal of Personality and Social Psychology, 50*(5), 869–878. https://doi.org/10.1037/0022-3514.50.5.869

Bargh, J., & Chartrand, T. (2000). The mind in the middle: A practical guide to priming and automaticity research. In H. Reis & C. Judd (Eds.), *Handbook of research methods in social and personality psychology* (pp. 253–285). Cambridge University Press.

Barker, A. B., Britton, J., Thomson, E., Hunter, A., Opazo Breton, M., & Murray, R. L. (2020). A content analysis of tobacco and alcohol audiovisual content in a sample of UK reality TV programmes. *Journal of Public Health, 42*(3), 561–569. https://doi.org/10.1093/pubmed/fdz043

Barkley, J. E., Lepp, A., & Glickman, E. L. (2017). "Pokémon Go!" may promote walking, discourage sedentary behavior in college students. *Games for Health Journal, 6*(3), 165–170. https://doi.org/10.1089/g4h.2017.0009

Barlett, C., Branch, O., Rodeheffer, C., & Harris, R. (2009). How long do the short-term violent video game effects last? *Aggressive Behavior, 35,* 225–236. https://doi.org/10.1002/ab.20301

Barlett, C. P., & Gentile, D. A. (2012). Attacking others online: The formation of cyberbullying in late adolescence. *Psychology of Popular Media Culture, 1*(2), 123–135. https://doi.org/10.1037/a0028113

Barlett, C. P., Gentile, D. A., & Chew, C. (2016). Predicting cyberbullying from anonymity. *Psychology of Popular Media Culture, 5*(2), 171–180. https://doi.org/10.1037/ppm0000055

Barlett, C. P., Heath, J. B., Madison, C. S., DeWitt, C. C., & Kirkpatrick, S. M. (2020). You're not anonymous online: The development and validation of a new cyberbullying intervention curriculum. *Psychology of Popular Media, 9*(2), 135–144. https://doi.org/10.1037/ppm0000226

Barlett, C. P., & Kowalewski, D. A. (2019). Learning to cyberbully: An extension of the Barlett Gentile cyberbullying model. *Psychology of Popular Media Culture, 8*(4), 437–443. https://doi.org/10.1037/ppm0000183

Barlett, C. P., Kowalewski, D. A., Kramer, S. S., & Helmstetter, K. M. (2019). Testing the relationship between media violence exposure and cyberbullying perpetration. *Psychology of Popular Media Culture, 8*(3), 280–286. https://doi.org/10.1037/ppm0000179

Barley, S. R., Meyerson, D. E., & Grodal, S. (2011). E-mail as a source and symbol of stress. *Organization Science, 22*(4), 887–906. https://doi.org/10.1287/orsc.1100.0573

Barnes, S. J., & Böhringer, M. (2011). Modeling use continuance behavior in microblogging services: The case of Twitter. *Journal of Computer Information Systems, 51*(4), 1–10. https://doi.org/10.1080/08874417.2011.11645496

Barnidge, M. (2018). Social affect and political disagreement on social media. *Social Media + Society, 4*(3). https://doi.org/10.1177/2056305118797721

Barnidge, M., Gil de Zúñiga, H., & Diehl, T. (2017). Second screening and political persuasion on social media. *Journal of Broadcasting & Electronic Media, 61*(2), 309–331. https://doi.org/10.1080/08838151.2017.1309416

Baron, L., & Straus, M. A. (1987). Four theories of rape: A macrosociological analysis. *Social Problems, 34,* 467–490.

Baron, R. A., & Bell, P. A. (1973). Effects of heightened sexual arousal on physical aggression. *Proceedings of the 81st Annual Convention of the American Psychological Association, 8,* 171–172.

Barr, R. (2013). Memory constraints on infant learning from picture books, television, and touchscreens. *Child Development Perspectives, 7*(4), 205–210. https://doi.org/10.1111/cdep.12041

Barr, R., & Hayne, H. (1999). Developmental changes in imitation from television during infancy. *Child Development, 70*(5), 1067–1081. https://doi.org/10.1111/1467-8624.00079

Barry, A. E., Padon, A. A., Whiteman, S. D., Hicks, K. K., Carreon, A. K., Crowell, J. R., Willingham, K. L., & Merianos, A. L. (2018). Alcohol advertising on social media: Examining the content of popular alcohol brands on Instagram. *Substance Use & Misuse, 53*(14), 2413–2420. https://doi.org/10.1080/10826084.2018.1482345

Barry, C. T., Reiter, S. R., Anderson, A. C., Schoessler, M. L., & Sidoti, C. L. (2019). "Let me take another selfie": Further examination of the relation between narcissism, self-perception, and Instagram posts. *Psychology of Popular Media Culture, 8*(1), 22–33. https://doi.org/10.1037/ppm0000155

Barthel, M., Mitchell, A., & Holcomb, J. (2016, December 15). *Many Americans believe fake news is sowing confusion.* Pew Research Center. https://www.journalism.org/2016/12/15/many-americans-believe-fake-news-is-sowing-confusion/

Bartholow, B. D. (2018). The aggressive brain: Insights from neuroscience. *Current Opinion in Psychology, 19,* 60–64. https://doi.org/10.1016/j.copsyc.2017.04.002

Bartholow, B. D., & Anderson, C. A. (2002). Effects of violent video games on aggressive behavior: Potential sex differences. *Journal of Experimental Social Psychology, 38*(3), 283–290. https://doi.org/10.1006/jesp.2001.1502

Bartholow, B. D., Bushman, B. J., & Sestir, M. A. (2006). Chronic violent video game exposure and desensitization to violence: Behavioral and event-related brain potential data. *Journal of Experimental Social Psychology, 42*(4), 532–539. https://doi.org/10.1016/j.jesp.2005.08.006

Barton, K. M. (2009). Reality television programming and diverging gratifications: The influence of content on gratifications obtained. *Journal of Broadcasting & Electronic Media, 53*(3), 460–476. https://doi.org/10.1080/08838150903102659

Bartsch, R. A., Burnett, T., Diller, T. R., & Rankin-Williams, E. (2000). Gender representation in television commercials: Updating an update. *Sex Roles: A Journal of Research, 43*(9-10), 735–743. https://doi.org/10.1023/A:1007112826569

Bashirian, S., Jenabi, E., Khazaei, S., Barati, M., Karimi-Shahanjarini, A., Zareian, S., Rezapur-Shahkolai, F., & Moeini, B. (2020). Factors associated with preventive behaviours of COVID-19 among hospital staff in Iran in 2020: An application of the Protection Motivation Theory. *The Journal of Hospital Infection, 105*(3), 430–433. https://doi.org/10.1016/j.jhin.2020.04.035

Basil, M., & Witte, K. (2014). Fear appeals and extended parallel process model. In T. L. Thompson (Ed.), *Encyclopedia of health communication* (Vol. 1, pp. 498–500). Sage.

Bass, S. B., Ruzek, S. B., Gordon, T. F., Fleisher, L., McKeown, N., & Moore, D. (2006). Relationship of internet health information use with patient behavior and self-efficacy: Experiences of newly diagnosed cancer patients who contact the national Cancer Institute's Cancer Information Service. *Journal of Health Communication, 11*(2), 219–236. https://doi.org/10.1080/10810730500526794

Baturay, M. H., & Toker, S. (2019). Internet addiction among college students: Some causes and effects. *Education and Information Technologies, 24,* 2863–2885. https://doi.org/10.1007/s10639-019-09894-3

Baxter, R. L., Deriemer, C., Landini, A., Leslie, L., & Singletary, M. W. (1985). A content analysis of music videos. *Journal of Broadcasting & Electronic Media, 29*(3), 333–340. https://doi.org/10.1080/08838158509386589

Bazzini, D. G., McIntosh, W. D., Smith, S. M., Cook, S., & Harris, C. (1997). The aging women in popular film: Underrepresented, unattractive, unfriendly, and unintelligent. *Sex Roles: A Journal of Research, 36*(7-8), 531–543. https://doi.org/10.1007/BF02766689

Becker, A. E. (2004). Television, disordered eating, and young women in Fiji: Negotiating body image and identity during rapid social change. *Culture, Medicine & Psychiatry, 28*(4), 533–559. https://doi.org/10.1007/s11013-004-1067-5

Becker, A. E., Burwell, R. A., Navara, K., & Gilman, S. E. (2003). Binge eating and binge eating disorder in a small-scale, indigenous society: The view from Fiji. *International Journal of Eating Disorders, 34*(4), 423–431. https://doi.org/10.1002/eat.10225

Becker, L. B., & Kosicki, G. M. (1991). Einege historische und aktuelle Anmerkungenzura merikanischenWirkungforschung und der Versucheiner transaktionalen analyse [Some historical notes and contemporary comments on American message-producer/message-receiver transaction]. In W. Fruh (Ed.), *Medienwirkungen: Das dynamisch-transaktionale Modell: Theorie und emirischeforschung* (pp. 193–213). Westdeutscher Verlag.

Becker, L., & McCombs, M. E. (1978). The role of the press in determining voter reaction to presidential primaries. *Human Communication Research, 4,* 301–307. https://doi.org/10.1111/j.1468-2958.1978.tb00716.x

Becker, L. B., McCombs, M. E., & McLeod, J. M. (1975). The development of political cognitions. In S. H. Chaffee (Ed.), *Political communication* (pp. 21–64). Sage.

Behm-Morawitz, E., Aubrey, J. S., Pennell, H., & Kim, K. B. (2019). Examining the effects of MTV's *16 and Pregnant* on adolescent girls' sexual health: The implications of character affinity, pregnancy risk factors, and health literacy on message effectiveness. *Health Communication, 34*(2), 180–190. https://doi.org/10.1080/10410236.2017.1399506

Behm-Morawitz, E., & Mastro, D. E. (2008). Mean girls? The influence of gender portrayals in teen movies on emerging adults' gender-based attitudes and beliefs. *Journalism & Mass Communication Quarterly, 85*(1), 131–146. https://doi.org/10.1177/107769900808500109

Bell, E. (1995). Somatexts at the Disney shop: Constructing the pentimentos of women's animated bodies. In E. Bell, L. Haas, & L. Sells (Eds.), *From mouse to mermaid: The politics of film, gender, and culture* (pp. 107–124). Indiana University Press.

Bellotti, F., Berta, R., De Gloria, A., & Primavera, L. (2009). Enhancing the educational value of video games. *Computers in Entertainment, 7*(2), Article 23. https://doi.org/10.1145/1541895.1541903

Bendak, S. (2015). Objective assessment of the effects of texting while driving: A simulator study. *International Journal of Injury Control and Safety Promotion, 22*(4), 387–392. http://dx.doi.ord/10.1080/17457300.2014.942325

Benelli, E. (2003). The role of the media in steering public opinion on health care issues. *Health Policy, 63*(2), 179–186. https://doi.org/10.1016/s0168-8510(02)00064-7

Benford, R. D. (2013). Master frame. In D. A. Snow, D. della Porta, B. Klandermans, & D. McAdam (Eds.), *The Wiley-Blackwell encyclopedia of social and political movements.* https://doi.org/10.1002/9780470674871.wbespm126

Bennett, W. L., & Iyengar, S. (2008). A new era of minimal effects? The changing foundations of political communication. *Journal of Communication, 58*(4), 707–731. https://doi.org/10.1111/j.1460-2466.2008.00410.x

Bennett, W. L., Lawrence, R. G., & Livingston, S. (2006). None dare call it torture: Indexing and the limits of press independence in the Abu Ghraib scandal. *Journal of Communication, 56* (3), 467–485. https://doi.org/10.1111/j.1460-2466.2006.00296.x

Bennett, W. L., Lawrence, R. G., & Livingston, S. (2007). *When the press fails: Political power and the news media from Iraq to Katrina.* University of Chicago Press.

Bennett, W. L., & Livingston, S. (2018). The disinformation order: Disruptive communication and the decline of democratic institutions. *European Journal of Communication, 33*(2), 122–139. https://doi.org/10.1177/0267323118760317

Bennett, W. L., & Manheim, J. B. (2006). The one-step flow of communication. *The ANNALS of the American Academy of Political and Social Science, 608*(1), 213–232. https://doi.org/10.1177/0002716206292266

Bent, S. (1969). *Newspaper crusaders: A neglected story.* Books for Libraries Press.

Bentivegna, S., & Boccia Artieri, G. (2020). Rethinking public agenda in a time of high-choice media environment. *Media and Communication, 8*(4), 6–15. http://doi.org/10.17645/mac.v8i4.3166

Berelson, B. (1948). Communications and public opinion. In W. Schramm (Ed.), *Communications in modern society* (pp. 168–185). University of Illinois Press.

Berelson, B. (1949). What "missing the newspaper" means. In P. F. Lazarsfeld & F. N. Stanton (Eds.), *Communications research 1948–1949* (pp. 111–129). Harper.

Berelson, B., & Janowitz, M. (Eds.). (1950). *Reader in public opinion and communication.* Free Press.

Berelson, B. R., Lazarsfeld, P. F., & McPhee, W. N. (1954). *Voting: A study of opinion formation in a presidential campaign.* University of Chicago Press.

Berkey, C. S., Rockett, H. R., Field, A. E., Gillman, M. W., Frazier, A. L., Camargo, C. A., Jr., & Colditz, G. A. (2000). Activity, dietary intake, and weight changes in a longitudinal study on preadolescent and adolescent boys and girls. *Pediatrics, 105*(4), 446–452. https://doi.org/10.1542/peds.105.4.e56

Berkowitz, L. (1962). Violence in the mass media. In L. Berkowitz (Ed.), *Aggression: A social psychological analysis* (pp. 229–255). McGraw-Hill.

Berkowitz, L. (1965). Some aspects of observed aggression. *Journal of Personality and Social Psychology, 2*(3), 359–369. https://doi.org/10.1037/h0022221

Berkowitz, L. (1974). Some determinants of impulsive aggression: The role of mediated associations with reinforcements for aggression. *Psychological Review, 81*(2), 165–176. https://doi.org/10.1037/h0036094

Berkowitz, L. (1984). Some effects of thoughts on anti- and prosocial influences of media events: A cognitive-neoassociation analysis. *Psychological Bulletin, 95*(3), 410–427. https://doi.org/10.1037/0033-2909.95.3.410

Berkowitz, L. (1990). On the formation and regulation of anger and aggression: A cognitive-neoassociationistic analysis. *American Psychologist, 45*(4), 494–503. https://doi.org/10.1037/0003-066X.45.4.494

Berkowitz, L. (1994). Is something missing? Some observations prompted by the cognitive-neoassociationist view of anger and emotional aggression. In L. R. Huesmann (Ed.), *Aggressive behavior: Current perspectives* (pp. 35–57). Plenum Press.

Berkowitz, L. (1997). Some thoughts extending Bargh's argument. In R. S. Wyer (Ed.), *The automaticity of everyday life: Advances in social cognition* (Vol. 10, pp. 83–92). Lawrence Erlbaum Associates.

Berkowitz, L., & Alioto, J. T. (1973). The meaning of an observed event as a determinant of its aggressive consequences. *Journal of Personality and Social Psychology, 28*(2), 206–217. https://doi.org/10.1037/h0035730

Berkowitz, L., Corwin, R., & Heironimous, M. (1963). Film violence and subsequent aggressive tendencies. *Public Opinion Quarterly, 27*(2), 217–229. https://doi.org/10.1086/267162

Berkowitz, L., & Geen, R. G. (1966). Film violence and the cue properties of available targets. *Journal of Personality and Social Psychology, 3*(5), 525–530. https://doi.org/10.1037/h0023201

Berkowitz, L., & Heimer, K. (1989). On the construction of the anger experience: Aversive events and negative priming in the formation of feelings. In L. Berkowitz (Ed.), *Advances in experimental social psychology* (Vol. 22, pp. 1–37). Academic.

Berkowitz, L., & Rawlings, E. (1963). Effects of film violence on inhibitions against subsequent aggression. *The Journal of Abnormal and Social Psychology, 66*(5), 405–412. https://doi.org/10.1037/h0046639

Berlyne, D. E. (1967). Arousal and reinforcement. In D. Levine (Ed.), *Nebraska Symposium on Motivation* (Vol. 15, pp. 1–110). University of Nebraska Press.

Berlyne, D. E. (1971). *Aesthetics and psychobiology.* Prentice-Hall.

Bernard, P., Legrand, S., & Klein, O. (2018). From bodies to blame: Exposure to sexually objectifying media increases tolerance toward sexual harassment. *Psychology of Popular Media Culture, 7*(2), 99–112. https://doi.org/10.1037/ppm0000114

Bever, L. (2018, January 17). Teens are daring each other to eat Tide pods. We don't need to tell you that's a bad idea. *The Washington Post.* https://www.washingtonpost.com/news/to-your-health/wp/2018/01/13/teens-are-daring-each-other-to-eat-tide-pods-we-dont-need-to-tell-you-thats-a-bad-idea/

Bhattacharya, S., Bashar, M., Srivastava, A., & Singh, A. (2019). NOMOPHOBIA: NO Mobile Phone PhoBIA. *Journal of Family Medicine & Primary Care, 8*(4), 1297–1300. 10.4103/jfmpc.jfmpc_71_19

Biener, L., & Siegel, M. (2000). Tobacco marketing and adolescent smoking: More support for a causal inference. *American Journal of Public Health, 90*(3), 407–411. https://doi.org/10.2105/AJPH.90.3.407

Bilandzic, H., & Busselle. R. W. (2008). Transportation and transportability in the cultivation of genre-consistent attitudes and estimates. *Journal of Communication, 58*(3), 508–529. https://doi.org/10.1111/j.1460-2466.2008.00397.x

Bilandzic, H., & Rössler, P. (2004). Life according to television. Implications of genre-specific cultivation effects: The gratification/cultivation model. *Communications: The European Journal of Communication Research, 29*(3), 295–326. https://doi.org/10.1515/comm.2004.020

Billings, A. C., & Parrott, S. (2020a). Introduction: The practice of studying media stereotypes. In A. C. Billings & S. Parrott (Eds.), *Media stereotypes: From ageism to xenophobia* (pp. 1–13). Peter Lang.

Billings, A. C., & Parrott, S. (Eds.). (2020b). *Media stereotypes: From ageism to xenophobia.* Peter Lang. https://doi.org/10.3726/b15280

Birch, H. B., & Bortner, M. (1966). Stimulus competition and category usage in normal children. *The Journal of Genetic Psychology: Research and Theory on Human Development, 109*(2), 195–204. https://doi.org/10.1080/00221325.1966.10533696

Birnbaum, D. W., & Croll, W. L. (1984). The etiology of children's stereotypes about sex differences in emotionality. *Sex Roles: A Journal of Research, 10*(9-10), 677–691. https://doi.org/10.1007/BF00287379

Blackstone, G. E., Cowart, H. S., & Saunders, L. M. (2017). TweetStorm in #ferguson: How news organizations framed dominant authority, anti-authority, and political figures in a restive community. *Journal of Broadcasting & Electronic Media, 61*(3), 597–614. https://doi.org/10.1080/08838151.2017.1344670

Blaha, M. J. (n.d.). 5 vaping facts you need to know. *Johns Hopkins Medicine.* https://www.hopkinsmedicine.org/health/wellness-and-prevention/5-truths-you-need-to-know-about-vaping

Bleakley, A., Ellithorpe, M. E., Hennessy, M., Jamieson, P. E., Khurana, A., & Weitz, I. (2017). Risky movies, risky behaviors, and ethnic identity among Black adolescents. *Social Science & Medicine, 195*, 131–137. https://doi.org/10.1016/j.socscimed.2017.10.024

Bleakley, A., Ellithorpe, M. E., Hennessy, M., Khurana, A., Jamieson, P., & Weitz, I. (2017). Alcohol, sex, and screens: Modeling media influence on adolescent alcohol and sex co-occurrence. *Journal of Sex Research, 54*(8), 1026–1037. https://doi.org/10.1080/00224499.2017.1279585

Bleakley, A., Hennessy, M., & Fishbein, M. (2011). A model of adolescents' seeking of sexual content in their media choices. *Journal of Sex Research, 48*(4), 309–315. https://doi.org/10.1080/00224499.2010.497985

Bleakley, A., Hennessy, M., Fishbein, M., & Jordan, A. (2008). It works both ways: The relationship between exposure to sexual content in the media and adolescent sexual behavior. *Media Psychology, 11*, 443–461. https://doi.org/10.1080/15213260802491986

Bleakley, A., Jamieson, P. E., & Romer, D. (2012). Trends of sexual and violent content by gender in top-grossing U.S. films, 1950–2006. *Journal of Adolescent Health, 51*(1), 73–79. https://doi.org/10.1016/j.jadohealth.2012.02.006

Blease, C. R. (2015). Too many "friends," too few "likes"? Evolutionary psychology and "Facebook depression." *Review of General Psychology, 19*(1), 1–13. https://doi.org/10.1037/gpr0000030

Block, C. (1972). White backlash to Negro ads: Fact or fantasy? *Journalism Quarterly, 49*(2), 258–262. https://doi.org/10.1177/107769907204900205

Bloom, P. N., Hogan, J. E., & Blazing, J. (1997). Sports promotion and teen smoking and drinking: An exploratory study. *American Journal of Health Behavior, 2*, 100–109.

Blumer, H. G. (1933). *Movies and conduct.* Macmillan.

Blumer, H. G. (1951). The mass, the public, and public opinion. In A. M. Lee (Ed.), *New outlines of the principles of sociology* (2nd rev. ed.). Barnes & Noble.

Blumer, H. G., & Hauser, P. M. (1933). *Movies, delinquency and crime.* Macmillan.

Blumler, J. G. (1979). The role of theory in uses and gratifications studies. *Communication Research, 6,* 9–36. https://doi.org/10.1177/009365027900600102

Blumler, J. G., & McLeod, J. M. (1974). Communication and voter turnout in Britain. In T. Legatt (Eds.), *Sociological theory and social research* (pp. 265–312). Sage.

Bodenhausen, G., Schwarz, N., Bless, H., & Wanke, M. (1995). Effects of atypical exemplars on racial beliefs: Enlightened racism or generalized appraisals? *Journal of Experimental Social Psychology, 31*(1), 48–63. https://doi.org/10.1006/jesp.1995.1003

Bogatz, G. A., & Ball, S. (1971). *The second year of Sesame Street: A continuing evaluation.* Educational Testing Service.

Bolls., P. D., Weber, R., Lang, A., & Potter, R. F. (2020). Media psychophysiology and neuroscience: Bringing brain science into media processes and effects research. In M. B. Oliver, A. A. Raney, & J. Bryant (Eds.), *Media effects: Advances in theory and research* (4th ed., pp. 195–210). Routledge.

Bolsen, T. (2011). The construction of news: Energy crises, advocacy messages, and frames toward conservation. *International Journal of Press/Politics, 16*(2), 143–162. https://doi.org/10.1177/1940161210392782

Bond, B. J. (2015). Portrayals of sex and sexuality in gay- and lesbian-oriented media: A quantitative content analysis. *Sexuality & Culture: An Interdisciplinary Quarterly, 19*(1), 37–56. https://doi.org/10.1007/s12119-014-9241-6

Bond, B., & Harrison, K. (2008). *Media-induced fright during a national tragedy: The case of the Virginia Tech massacre.* National Communication Association conference paper.

Bond, R. M., Fariss, C. J., Jones, J. J., Kramer, A. D., Marlow, C., Settle, J. E., & Fowler, J. H. (2012). A 61-million-person experiment in social influence and political mobilization. *Nature, 489*(7415), 295–298.https://doi.org/10.1038/nature11421

Bonis, J. (2007). Acute Wiiitis. *The New England Journal of Medicine, 356,* 2431–2432. https://doi.org/10.1056/NEJMc070670

Booker, M. K. (2010). *Disney, Pixar, and the hidden messages of children's films.* Santa Praeger.

Borah, P. (2014). Does it matter where you read the news story? Interaction of incivility and news frames in the political blogosphere. *Communication Research, 41,* 809–827. https://doi.org/10.1177/0093650212449353

Borah, P. (2018). Addressing theoretical and methodological challenges of doing news framing analysis in the contemporary media landscape. In P. D'Angelo (Ed.), *Doing news framing analysis II: Empirical and theoretical perspectives* (2nd ed., pp. 163–188). Routledge.

Born, M. (1949). *Natural philosophy of cause and chance.* Clarendon Press.

Borter. G. (2019, January 27). *The digital drug: Internet addiction spawns U.S. treatment programs.* Reuters. https://www.reuters.com/article/us-usa-internet-addiction-feature/the-digital-drug-internet-addiction-spawns-u-s-treatment-programs-idUSKCN1PL0AG

Bőthe, B., Tóth-Király, I., Bella, N., Potenza, M. N., Demetrovics, Z., & Orosz, G. (2021). Why do people watch pornography? The motivational basis of pornography use. *Psychology of Addictive Behaviors, 35*(2), 172–186. https://doi.org/10.1037/adb0000603

Botta, R. (2000). The mirror of television: A comparison of Black and White adolescents' body image. *Journal of Communication, 50*(3), 144–159. https://doi.org/10.1111/j.1460-2466.2000.tb02857.x

Boursier, V., Gioia, F., Griffiths, M. D. (2020). Objectified body consciousness, body image control in photos, and problematic social networking: The role of appearance control beliefs. *Frontiers in Psychology, 11,* Article 147. https://doi.org/10.3389/fpsyg.2020.00147

Bowen, L., & Schmid, J. (1997). Minority presence and portrayal in mainstream magazine advertising: An update. *Journalism & Mass Communication Quarterly, 74*(1), 134–146. https://doi.org/10.1177/107769909707400111

boyd, d. m., & Ellison, N. B. (2007). Social network sites: Definition, history, and scholarship. *Journal of Computer-Mediated Communication, 13,* 210–230. https://doi.org/10.1111/j.1083-6101.2007.00393.x

Boydstun, A., Vliegenthart, R., & Baker, M. (2017). The conditional nature of presidential agenda influence on TV news: The case of education. *International Journal Of Communication, 11*(22). https://ijoc.org/index.php/ijoc/article/view/5997

Boyland, E. J., & Whalen, R. (2015). Food advertising to children and its effects on diet: Review of recent prevalence and impact data. *Pediatric Diabetes, 16*(5), 331–337. https://doi.org/10.1111/pedi.12278

Boyle, M. P., Schmierbach, M., Armstrong, C. L., Cho, J., McCluskey, M., McLeod, D. M., & Shah, D. V. (2006). Expressive responses to news stories about extremist groups: A framing experiment. *Journal of Communication, 56*(2), 271–288. https://doi.org/10.1111/j.1460-2466.2006.00019.x

Boyle, T. P. (2001). Intermedia agenda setting in the 1996 presidential election. *Journalism & Mass Communication Quarterly, 78,* 26–44. https://doi.org/10.1177/107769900107800103

Bradley, S. D. (2007). Neural network simulations support heuristic processing model of cultivation effects. *Media Psychology, 10,* 449–469. https://doi.org/10.1080/15213260701533078

Bradtzæg, P. B., Lüders, M., & Skjetne, J. H. (2010). Too many Facebook "friends"? Content sharing and sociability versus the need for privacy in social network sites. *International Journal of Human-Computer Interaction, 26,* 1006–1030. https://doi.org/10.1080/10447318.2010.516719

BrainyQuote.com. (2011). Cell phone quotes. Retrieved from http://www.brainyquote.com/quotes/keywords/cell_phone.html

Braithwaite, I., Stewart, A. W., Hancox, R. J., Beasley, R., Murphy, R., Mitchell, E. A., & ISAAC Phase Three Study Group. (2013). The worldwide association between television viewing and obesity in children and adolescents: Cross sectional study. *PloS One, 8*(9), Article e74263. https://doi.org/10.1371/journal.pone.0074263

Branje, C., Nespoil, G., Russo, F., & Fels, D. I. (2014). The effect of vibrotactile stimulation on the emotional response to horror films. *Computers in Entertainment, 11*(1), Article 5. https://doi.org/10.1145/2543698.2543703

Brenner, V. (1997). Psychology of computer use: XLVII. Parameters of internet use, abuse and addiction: The first 90 days of the Internet Usage Survey. *Psychological Reports, 80*(3, Pt 1), 879–882. https://doi.org/10.2466/pr0.1997.80.3.879

Brewer, P. R. (2002). Framing, value words, and citizens' explanations of their issue opinions. *Political Communication, 19,* 303–316. https://doi.org/10.1080/01957470290055510

Brewer, P. R., & Ley, B. L. (2010). Media use and public perceptions of DNA evidence. *Science Communication, 32*(1), 93–117. https://doi.org/10.1177/1075547009340343

Brickner, M. A., Harkins, S. G., & Ostrom, T. M. (1986). Effects of personal involvement: Thought-provoking implications for social loafing. *Journal of Personality and Social Psychology,* *51*(4), 763–769. https://doi.org/10.1037/0022-3514.51.4.763

Bridges, A. J., Wosnitzer, R., Scharrer, E., Sun, C., & Liberman, R. (2010). Aggression and sexual behavior in best-selling pornography videos: A content analysis update. *Violence Against Women,* *16*(10), 1065–1085. https://doi.org/10.1177/1077801210382866

Briñol, P., & Petty, R. E. (2004). Self-validation processes: The role of thought confidence in persuasion. In G. Haddock & G. Maio (Eds.), *Contemporary perspectives in the psychology of attitudes* (pp. 205–226). Psychology Press.

Briñol, P., & Petty, R. E. (2009). *Persuasion: Insights from the self-validation hypothesis.* In M. P. Zanna (Ed.), *Advances in experimental social psychology. Advances in experimental social psychology, Vol. 41* (pp. 69–118). Elsevier Academic Press. https://doi.org/10.1016/S0065-2601(08)00402-4

Briñol, P., Petty, R. E., & Barden, J. (2007). Happiness versus sadness as a determinant of thought confidence in persuasion: A self-validation analysis. *Journal of Personality and Social Psychology, 93*(5), 711–727. https://doi.org/10.1037/0022-3514.93.5.711

Briñol, P., Petty, R. E., & McCaslin, M. J. (2008). Automatic and deliberative attitude change from thoughtful and non-thoughtful processes. In R. E. Petty, R. H. Fazio, & P. Briñol (Eds.), *Attitudes: Insights from the new implicit measures* (pp. 285–326). Psychology Press.

Britton, J., Halfpenny, P., Devine, F., & Mellor, R. (2004). The future of regional cities in the information age: The impact of information technology on Manchester's financial and business service sector. *Sociology, 38,* 795–814. https://doi.org/10.1177/0038038504045865

Brock, T. C., & Buss, A. H. (1962). Dissonance, aggression, and evaluation of pain. *The Journal of Abnormal and Social Psychology, 65*(3), 197–202. https://doi.org/10.1037/h0048948

Brock, T. C., & Buss, A. H. (1964). Effects of justification for aggression and communication with the victim on postaggression dissonance. *Journal of Abnormal and Social Psychology, 68,* 404–412. https://doi.org/10.1037/h0042571

Brodie, M., Hamel, E. C., Altman, D. E., Blendon, R. J., & Benson, J. M. (2003). Health news and the American public, 1996–2002. *Journal of Health Politics, Policy and Law, 28*(5), 927–950. https://doi.org/10.1215/03616878-28-5-927

Brookey, R. A., & Westerfelhaus, R. (2005). The digital auteur: Branding identity on the *Monsters, Inc.* DVD. *Western Journal of Communication, 69*(2), 109–128. https://doi.org/10.1080/10570310500076734

Brooks, M. E., Bichard, S., & Craig, C. (2016). What's the score? A content analysis of mature adults in

Super Bowl commercials. *Howard Journal of Communication, 27*(4), 347–366. https://doi.org/10.1080/10646175.2016.1206046

Brown, J. D., Campbell, K., & Fischer, L. (1986). American adolescents and music videos: Why do they watch? *Gazette, 37*(1–2), 19–32. https://doi.org/10.1177/001654928603700104

Brown, J. D., L'Engle, K. L., Pardun, C. J., Guo, G., Kenneavy, K., & Jackson, C. (2006). Sexy media matter: Exposure to sexual content in music, movies, television, and magazines predicts Black and white adolescents' sexual behavior. *Pediatrics, 117*(4), 1018–1027. https://doi.org/10.1542/peds.2005-1406

Brown, J. D., & Walsh-Childers, K. (1994). Effects of media on personal and public health. In J. Bryant & D. Zillmann (Eds.), *Media effects: Advances in theory and research.* Lawrence Erlbaum Associates.

Brown, S. J., Lieberman, D. A., Gemeny, B. A., Fan, Y. C., Wilson, D. M., & Pasta, D. J. (1997). Educational computer game for juvenile diabetes: Results of a controlled trial. *Medical Informatics, 22*(1), 77–89. https://doi.org/10.3109/14639239709089835

Brownfield, E. D., Bernhardt, J. M., Phan, J. L., Williams, M. V., & Parker, R. M. (2004). Direct-to-consumer drug advertisements on network television: An exploration of quantity, frequency, and placement. *Journal of Health Communication, 9*(6), 491–497. https://doi.org/10.1080/10810730490523115

Brugman, B. C., Burgers, C., & Steen, G. J. (2017). Recategorizing political frames: A systematic review of metaphorical framing in experiments on political communication. *Annals of the International Communication Association, 41*(2), 181–197. https://doi.org/10.1080/23808985.2017.1312481

BrummertLennings, H. I., & Warburton, W. A. (2011). The effect of auditory versus visual violent media exposure on aggressive behavior: The role of song lyrics, video clips and musical tone. *Journal of Experimental Social Psychology, 47*(4), 794–799. https://doi.org/10.1016/j.jesp.2011.02.006

Bruntz, G. G. (1938). *Allied propaganda and the collapse of the German empire in 1918.* Stanford University Press.

Bruselle, R., & Crandall, H. (2002). Television viewing and perceptions about race differences in socioeconomic success. *Journal of Broadcasting & Electronic Media, 46,* 256–282. https://doi.org/10.1207/s15506878jobem4602_6

Bryant, J. (1986). The road most traveled: Yet another cultivation critique. *Journal of Broadcasting & Electronic Media, 30,* 231–244. https://doi.org/10.1080/08838158609386621

Bryant, J. A., & Bryant, J. (2003). Effects of entertainment televisual media on children. In E. L. Palmer & B. M. Young (Eds.), *The faces of televi-*

sual media: Teaching, violence, selling to children (2nd ed., pp. 195–217). Lawrence Erlbaum Associates.

Bryant, J., McCollum, J., Ralston, L., Raney, A., McGavin, L., Miron, D., Maxwell, M., Venugopalan, G., Thompson, S., Dewitt, D., Lewis, K., Mundorf, N., & Smith, S. (1997). Report 8: Effects of two years' viewing of *Allegra's Window* and *Gullah Gullah Island*. Report to Nick, Jr. University of Alabama, Institute for Communication Research.

Bryant, J., Mulliken, L., Maxwell, M., Mundorf, N., Mundorf, J., Wilson, B., Smith, S., McCollum, J., & Owens, J. W. (1999). Effects of two years' viewing of *Blue's Clues*. University of Alabama, Institute for Communication Research.

Bryant, J., & Rockwell, S. C. (1994). Effects of massive exposure to sexually oriented prime-time television programming on adolescents' moral judgment. In D. Zillmann, J. Bryant, & A. Huston (Eds.), *Media, children, and the family: Social scientific, psychodynamic, and clinical perspectives*. Lawrence Erlbaum Associates.

Bryant, J., & Zillmann, D. (1984). Using television to alleviate boredom and stress: Selective exposure as a function of induced excitational states. *Journal of Broadcasting, 28*, 1–20. https://doi.org/10.1080/08838158409386511

Brydon, S. G. (2009). Men at the heart of mothering: Finding mother in *Finding Nemo*. *Journal of Gender Studies, 18*, 131–146. https://doi.org/10.1080/09589230902812448

Büchi, M., Festic, N., & Latzer, M. (2019). Digital overuse and subjective well-being in a digitized society. *Social Media + Society, 5*(4). https://doi.org/10.1177/2056305119886031

Buerkel-Rothfuss, N. L., & Mayes, S. (1981). Soap opera viewing: The cultivation effect. *Journal of Communication, 31*(3), 108–115. https://doi.org/10.1111/j.1460-2466.1981.tb00433.x

Bulkow, K., Urban, J., & Schweiger, W. (2013). The duality of agenda-setting: The role of information processing. *International Journal of Public Opinion Research, 25*(1), 43–63. https://doi.org/10.1093/ijpor/eds003

Burgers, C., Konijn, E. A., & Steen, G. J. (2016). Figurative framing: Shaping public discourse through metaphor, hyperbole, and irony. *Communication Theory, 26*(4), 410–430. https://doi.org/10.1111/comt.12096

Burgess, M. C. R., Dill, K. E., Stermer, S. P., Burgess, S. R., & Brown, B. P. (2011). Playing with prejudice: The prevalence and consequences of racial stereotypes in video games. *Media Psychology, 14*(3), 289–311. https://doi.org/10.1080/15213269.2011.596467

Burgoon, M., & Klingle, R. S. (1998). Gender differences in being influential and/or influenced: A challenge to prior explanations. In D. J. Canary & K. Dindia (Eds.), *Sex differences and similarities in communication: Critical essays and empirical investigations of sex and gender in interaction* (pp. 257–285). Lawrence Erlbaum Associates.

Burnkrant, R., & Unnava, R. (1989). Self-referencing: A strategy for increasing processing of message content. *Personality and Social Psychology Bulletin, 15*(4), 628–638. https://doi.org/10.1177/0146167289154015

Bus, A. G., Takacs, Z. K., & Kegel, C. A. T. (2015). Affordances and limitations of electronic storybooks for young children's emergent literacy. *Developmental Review, 35*, 79–97. https://doi.org/10.1016/j.dr.2014.12.004

Busby, D. M., Chiu, H.-Y., Olsen, J. A., & Willoughby, B. J. (2017). Evaluating the dimensionality of pornography. *Archives of Sexual Behavior, 46*, 1723–1731. https://doi.org/10.1007/s10508-017-0983-8

Bush, R., Resnick, A., & Stern, B. (1980). A content analysis of the portrayal of black models in magazine advertising. In R. Bagozzi et al. (Eds.), *Marketing in the 80's: Changes and challenges* (pp. 484–487). American Marketing Association.

Bushman, B. J. (2016). Violent media and hostile appraisals: A meta-analytic review. *Aggressive Behavior, 42*(6), 605–613. https://doi.org/10.1002/ab.21655

Bushman, B. J., & Anderson, C. A. (2002). Violent video games and hostile expectations: A test of the general aggression model. *Personality & Social Psychology Bulletin, 28*, 1679–1686. https://doi.org/10.1177/014616702237649

Bushman, B. J., & Anderson, C. A. (2009). Comfortably numb: Desensitizing effects of violent media on helping others. *Psychological Science, 20*(3), 273–277. https://doi.org/10.1111/j.1467-9280.2009.02287.x

Bushman, B. J., Gollwitzer, M., & Cruz, C. (2015a). Agreement across stakeholders is consensus: Response to Ivory et al. (2015). *Psychology of Popular Media Culture, 4*(3), 230–235. https://doi.org/10.1037/ppm0000061

Bushman, B. J., Gollwitzer, M., & Cruz, C. (2015b). There is broad consensus: Media researchers agree that violent media increase aggression in children, and pediatricians and parents concur. *Psychology of Popular Media Culture, 4*(3), 200–214. https://doi.org/10.1037/ppm0000046

Bushman, B. J., Rothstein, H. R., & Anderson, C. A. (2010). Much ado about something: Violent video game effects and a school of red herring: Reply to Ferguson and Kilburn (2010). *Psychological Bulletin, 136*(2), 182–187. https://doi.org/10.1037/a0018718

Busselle, R. (2003). Television exposure, parents' precautionary warnings and young adults' perceptions of crime. *Communication Research, 30*(5), 530–556. https://doi.org/10.1177/0093650203256360

Busselle, R. (2017). Schema theory and mental models. In P. Rössler (Ed.), *International encyclopedia of media effects* (Vol. 4, pp. 1753–1760). Wiley-Blackwell. https://doi.org/10.1002/9781118783764.wbieme0079

Busselle, R., & Van den Bulck, J. (2020). Cultivation theory, media, stories, processes, and reality. In M. B. Oliver, A. A. Raney, & J. Bryant (Eds.), *Media effects: Advances in theory and research* (4th ed., pp. 69–82). Routledge.

Butterworth, S. E., Giuliano, T. A., White, J., Cantu, L., & Fraser, K. C. (2019). Sender gender influences emoji interpretation in text messages. *Frontiers in Psychology, 10*, Article 784. https://doi.org/10.3389/fpsyg.2019.00784

Buzzuto, J. C. (1975). Cinematic neurosis following "The Exorcist": Report of four cases. *Journal of Nervous and Mental Disease, 161*(1), 43–48. https://doi.org/10.1097/00005053-197507000-00005

Cacciatore, M.A., Scheufele, D. A., & Iyengar, S. (2016). The end of framing as we know it . . . and the future of media effects. *Mass Communication and Society, 19*(7), 7–23. https://doi.org/10.1080/15205436.2015.1068811

Calvert, S. L. (1995). *Impact of televised songs on children's and young adults' memory of verbally-presented content.* Unpublished manuscript, Department of Psychology, Georgetown University, Washington, DC.

Calvert, S. L., & Pfordresher, P. Q. (1994, August). *Impact of a televised song on students' memory of information.* Poster presented at the annual meeting of the American Psychological Association, Los Angeles, CA.

Calvert, S. L., Rigaud, E., & Mazella, J. (1991). *Presentational features for students' recall of televised educational content.* Poster presented at the biennial meeting of the Society for Research in Child Development, Seattle, WA.

Calvert, S. L., & Tart, M. (1993). Song versus verbal forms for very-long-term, long-term, and short-term verbatim recall. *Journal of Applied Developmental Psychology, 14,* 245–260. https://doi.org/10.1016/0193-3973(93)90035-T

Camaj, L., & Northup, T. (2019). Dual-screening the candidate image during presidential debates: The moderating role of Twitter and need to evaluate for the effects on candidate perceptions. *Journals of Broadcasting & Electronic Media, 63*(1), 20–38. https://doi.org/10.1080/08838151.2019.1574117

Camaj, L. (2014). Need for orientation, selective exposure, and attribute agenda-setting effects. *Mass Communication and Society, 17,* 689–713. https://doi.org/10.1080/15205436.2013.835424

Cambier, R., Derks, D., & Vlerick, P. (2019). Detachment from work: A diary study on telepressure, smartphone use and empathy. *Psychologica Belgica, 59*(1), 227–245. https://doi.org/10533/pb.477

Cambre, M. A., & Fernie, D. (1985). *Formative evaluation of Season IV, 3-2-1 Contact: Assessing the appeal of four weeks of educational television programs and their influence on children's science comprehension and science interest.* Children's Television Workshop.

Campbell, R., Martin, C. R., & Fabos, B. (2019). *Media & culture: An introduction to mass communication.* (12th ed.). Bedford/St. Martin's.

Campbell, S. W. (2008). Mobile technology and the body: Apparatgeist, fashion, and function. In J. Katz (Ed.), *Handbook of mobile communication studies* (pp. 153–164). MIT Press.

Campbell, S. W., & Kwak, N. (2011a). Mobile communication and civil society: Linking patterns and places of use to engagement with others in public. *Human Communication Research, 37*(2), 207–222. https://doi.org/10.1111/j.1468-2958.2010.01399.x

Campbell, S. W., & Kwak, N. (2011b). Mobile communication and strong network ties: Shrinking or expanding spheres of public discourse? *New Media & Society, 14*(2), 262–280. https://doi.org/10.1177/1461444811411676

Campbell, S. W., & Ling, R. (2008). Conclusion: Mobile communication in space and time—Furthering the theoretical dialogue. In R. Ling & S. Campbell (Eds.), *The mobile communication research series: Reconstruction of space and time through mobile communication practices* (pp. 251–260). Transaction.

Campbell, S. W., & Ling, R. (2009). Effects of mobile communication. In J. Bryant & M. B. Oliver (Eds.), *Media effects: Advances in theory and research* (3rd ed., pp. 592–606). Routledge.

Campbell, S. W., & Ling, R. (2020). Effects of mobile communication: Revolutions in an evolving field. In M. B. Oliver, A. A. Raney, & J. Bryant (Eds.), *Media effects: Advances in theory and research* (4th ed., pp. 389–403). Routledge.

Cantor, J. (1994). Fright reactions to mass media. In J. Bryant & D. Zillmann (Eds.), *Media effects: Advances in theory and research* (pp. 213–245). Lawrence Erlbaum Associates.

Cantor, J. (1998). *"Mommy, I'm scared": How TV and movies frighten children and what we can do to protect them.* Harcourt Brace.

Cantor, J. (1999). Comments on the coincidence: Comparing the findings on retrospective reports of fear. *Media Psychology, 1,* 141–143. https://doi.org/10.1207/s1532785xmep0102_3

Cantor, J. (2004). "I'll never have a clown in my house"—Why movie horror lives on. *Poetics Today, 25*(2), 283–304. https://doi.org/10.1215/03335372-25-2-283

Cantor, J. (2009). Fright reactions to mass media. In J. Bryant & M. B. Oliver (Eds.), *Media effects: Advances in theory and research* (3rd ed.). Routledge.

Cantor, J. (2017). Fright responses to media. In P. Rössler (Ed.), *International encyclopedia of media effects* (Vol. 2, pp. 652–664). Wiley-Blackwell. https://doi.org/10.1002/9781118783764.wbieme0165

Cantor, J., Byrne, S., Moyer-Gusé, E., & Riddle, K. (2010). Descriptions of media-induced fright reactions in a sample of US elementary school children. *Journal of Children and Media, 4*(1), 1–17. https://doi.org/10.1080/17482790903407242

Cantor, J., & Harrison, K. (2022). Parents reports of children's fright reactions to news of the COVID-19 pandemic: Results from a national U.S. sample. *Media Psychology.* Advance online publication. https://doi.org/10.1080/15213269.2021.2009878

Cantor, J., & Hoffner, C. (1987, April). *Children's fear reactions to a televised film as a function of perceived immediacy of depicted threat.* Paper presented at the Convention of the Society for Research in Child Development, Baltimore.

Cantor, J., & Hoffner, C. (1990). Children's fear reactions to a televised film as a function of perceived immediacy of depicted threat. *Journal of Broadcasting & Electronic Media, 34*(4), 421–442. https://doi.org/10.1080/08838159009386753

Cantor, J., Mares, M. L., & Oliver, M. B. (1993). Parents' and children's emotional reactions to televised coverage of the Gulf War. In B. Greenberg & W. Gantz (Eds.), *Desert Storm and the mass media* (pp. 325–340). Hampton Press.

Cantor, J., & Nathanson, A. (1996). Children's fright reactions to television news. *Journal of Communication, 46*(4), 139–152. https://doi.org/10.1111/j.1460-2466.1996.tb01510.x

Cantor, J., & Omdahl, B. (1991). Effects of fictional media depictions of realistic threats on children's emotional responses, expectations, worries, and liking for related activities. *Communication Monographs, 58*(4), 384–401. https://doi.org/10.1080/03637759109376237

Cantor, J., & Omdahl, B. (1999). Children's acceptance of safety guidelines after exposure to televised dramas depicting accidents. *Western Journal of Communication, 63*(1), 57–71. https://doi.org/10.1080/10570319909374628

Cantor, J., & Reilly, S. (1982). Adolescents' fright reactions to television and films. *Journal of Communication, 32*(1), 87–99. https://doi.org/10.1111/j.1460-2466.1982.tb00480.x

Cantor, J., & Sparks, G. G. (1984). Children's fear responses to mass media: Testing some Piagetian predictions. *Journal of Communication, 34*(2), 90–103. https://doi.org/10.1111/j.1460-2466.1984.tb02162.x

Cantor, J., Sparks, G. G., & Hoffner, C. (1988). Calming children's television fears: Mr. Rogers vs. The Incredible Hulk. *Journal of Broadcasting & Electronic Media, 32*(3), 271–288. https://doi.org/10.1080/08838158809386702

Cantor, J., & Wilson, B. J. (1984). Modifying fear responses to mass media in preschool and elementary school children. *Journal of Broadcasting, 28,* 431–443. https://doi.org/10.1080/08838158409386552

Cantor, J., Wilson, B. J., & Hoffner, C. (1986). Emotional responses to a televised nuclear holocaust film. *Communication Research, 13*(2), 257–277. https://doi.org/10.1177/009365086013002006

Cantor, J., Ziemke, D., & Sparks, G. G. (1984). Effect of forewarning on emotional responses to a horror film. *Journal of Broadcasting, 28*(1), 21–31. https://doi.org/10.1080/08838158409386512

Cantor, J., Zillmann, D., & Bryant, J. (1975). Enhancement of experienced sexual arousal in response to erotic stimuli through misattribution of unrelated residual excitation. *Journal of Personality and Social Psychology, 32*(1), 69–75. https://doi.org/10.1037/h0076784

Cantril, H. (1940). *The invasion from Mars: A study in the psychology of panic.* Princeton University Press.

Caplan, S. E. (2005). A social skill account of problematic internet use. *Journal of Communication, 55*(4), 721–736. https://doi.org/10.1111/j.1460-2466.2005.tb03019.x

Cappella, J. N., & Jamieson, K. H. (1994). Broadcast adwatch effects: A field experiment. *Communication Research, 21,* 342–365. https://doi.org/10.1177/009365094021003006

Cappella, J. N., & Jamieson, K. H. (1997). *Spiral of cynicism: The press and the public good.* Oxford University Press.

CareerBuilder. (2018, August 9). *More than half of employers have found content on social media that has caused them NOT to hire a candidate, according to a recent CareerBuilder survey.* http://press.careerbuilder.com/2018-08-09-More-Than-Half-of-Employers-Have-Found-Content-on-Social-Media-That-Caused-Them-NOT-to-Hire-a-Candidate-According-to-Recent-CareerBuilder-Survey

Carey, J. W. (1996). The Chicago School and mass communication research. In E. E. Dennis & E. Wartella (Eds.), *American communication research: The remembered history* (pp. 21–38). Lawrence Erlbaum Associates.

Carey, J. W., & Kreiling, A. L. (1974). Popular culture and uses and gratifications: Notes toward an accommodation. In J. G. Blumler & E. Katz (Eds.), *The uses of mass communications: Current perspectives on gratifications research* (pp. 225–248). Sage.

Carnagey, N. L., & Anderson, C. A. (2005). The effects of reward and punishment in violent video games on aggressive affect, cognition, and behavior. *Psychological Science, 16*(11), 882–889. https://doi.org/10.1111/j.1467-9280.2005.01632.x

Carnagey, N. L., Anderson, C. A., & Bushman, B. J. (2007). The effect of video game violence on physiological desensitization to real-life violence. *Journal of Experimental Social Psychology, 43*(3), 489–496. https://doi.org/10.1016/j.jesp.2006.05.003

Carr, C. T. (2020). CMC is dead, long live CMC! Situating computer-mediated communication scholarship beyond the digital age. *Journal of Computer-Mediated Communication, 25*(1), 9–22. https://doi.org/10.1093/jcmc/zmz018

Carrier, L. M., Spradlin, A., Bunce, J. P., & Rosen, L. D. (2015). Virtual empathy: Positive and negative impacts of going online upon empathy in young adults. *Computers in Human Behavior, 52*, 39–48. https://doi.org/10.1016/j.chb.2015.05.026

Cassino, D., & Erisen, C. (2010). Priming Bush and Iraq in 2008: A survey experiment. *American Politics Research, 38*(2), 372–394. https://doi.org/10.1177/1532673X09346799

Castells, M. (2000). *The rise of the network society* (2nd ed.). Blackwell.

Castells, M. (2009). *Communication power.* Oxford University Press.

Castells, M., Fernandez-Ardevol, M., Qiu, J., & Sey, A. (2007). *Mobile communication and society: A global perspective.* MIT Press.

Centers for Disease Control and Prevention. (2016). E-cigarette ads and youth. *VitalSigns.* https://www.cdc.gov/vitalsigns/pdf/2016-01-vital-signs.pdf

Ceyhan, A. A. (2011). University students' problematic internet use and communication skills according to the internet use purposes. *Educational Sciences: Theory & Practice, 11*, 69–77.

Chadee, D., Smith, S., & Ferguson, C. J. (2019). Murder she watched: Does watching news or fictional media cultivate fear of crime? *Psychology of Popular Media Culture, 8*(2), 125–133. https://doi.org/10.1037/ppm0000158

Chaffee, S. H. (1977). Mass media effects. In D. Lerner & L. Nelson (Eds.), *Communication research* (pp. 210–241). University of Hawaii Press.

Chaffee, S. H. (1982). Mass media and interpersonal channels: Competitive, convergent or complementary? In G. Gumpert & R. Cathcart (Eds.), *Inter/media: Interpersonal communication in a media world* (pp. 57–77). Oxford University Press.

Chaffee, S. H., & Hochheimer, J. L. (1985). The beginnings of political communication research in the United States: Origins of the "limited effects" model. In E. M. Rogers & F. Balle (Eds.), *The media revolution in America and Western Europe* (pp. 60–95). Ablex.

Chaiken, S. (1980). Heuristic versus systematic information processing and the use of source versus message cues in persuasion. *Journal of Personality and Social Psychology, 39*(5), 752–766. https://doi.org/10.1037/0022-3514.39.5.752

Chaiken, S. (1987). The heuristic model of persuasion. In M. P. Zanna, J. Olson, & C. P. Herman (Eds.), *Social influence: The Ontario symposium, 5* (pp. 3–39). Lawrence Erlbaum Associates.

Chaiken, S., Wood, W., & Eagly, A. H. (1996). Principles of persuasion. In E. T. Higgins & A. W. Kruglanski (Eds.), *Social psychology: Handbook of basic principles* (pp. 702–742). Guilford Press.

Chang, C. (2015). Motivated processing: How people perceive news covering novel or contradictory health research findings. *Science Communication, 37*(5), 602–634. https://doi.org/10.1177/1075547015597914

Chaput, J.-P., Visby, T., Nyby, S., Klingenberg, L., Gregersen, N. T., Tremblay, A., Astrup, A., & Sjödin, A. (2011). Video game playing increases food intake in adolescents: A randomized cross-over study. *The American Journal of Clinical Nutrition, 93*(6), 1196–1203. https://doi.org/10.3945/ajcn.110.008680

Charters, W. W. (193350). *Motion pictures and youth: A summary.* Macmillan.. In B. Berelson & M. Janowitz (Eds.), *Reader in public opinion and communication* (pp. 397–406). Free Press.

Chen, G. M., Riedl, M. J., Shermak, J. L., Brown, J., & Tenenboim, O. (2019). Breakdown of democratic norms? Understanding the 2016 US presidential election through online comments. *Social Media + Society, 5*(2). https://doi.org/10.1177/2056305119843637

Chen, Q., & Yan, Z. (2013). New evidence of impacts of cell phone use on driving performance: A review. *International Journal of Cyber Behavior, Psychology and Learning, 3*(3), 46–51. https://doi.org/10.4018/ijcbpl.2013070104

Chen, S., & Chaiken, S. (1999). The heuristic-systematic model in its broader context. In S. Chaiken & Y. Trope (Eds.), *Dual-process theories in social psychology* (pp. 73–96). The Guilford Press.

Chen, Y.-Y., Li, C.-M., Liang, J.-C., & Tsai, C.-C. (2018). Health information obtained from the internet and changes in medical decision making: Questionnaire development and cross-sectional survey. *Journal of Medical Internet Research, 20*(2), Article e47. https://doi.org/10.2196/jmir.9370

Cheng, C., Wang, H.-Y., Sigerson, L., & Chau, C.-L. (2019). Do the socially rich get richer? A nuanced perspective on social network site use and online social capital accrual. *Psychological Bulletin, 145*(7), 734–764. http://doi.org/10.1037/bul0000198

Chernov, G., & McCombs, M. (2019). Philosophical orientations and theoretical frameworks in media effects: Agenda setting, priming and their comparison with framing. *The Agenda Setting Journal, 3*(1), 63–81. https://doi.org/10.1075/asj.18016.che

Chesley, N. (2005). Blurring boundaries? Linking technology use, spillover, individual distress, and family satisfaction. *Journal of Marriage and Family, 67,* 1237–1248. https://doi.org/10.1111/j.1741-3737.2005.00213.x

Chia, S. C. (2006). How peers mediate media influence on adolescents' sexual attitudes and sexual behavior. *Journal of Communication, 56*(3), 585–606. https://doi.org/10.1111/j.1460-2466.2006.00302.x

Cho, H., Wilson, K., & Choi, J. (2011). Perceived realism of television medical dramas and perceptions about physicians. *Journal of Media Psychology: Theories, Methods, and Applications, 23*(3), 141–148. https://doi.org/10.1027/1864-1105/a000047

Cho, J. (2010). *Game addicts arrested for starving baby to death.* ABC News. http://abcnews.go.com/international/thelaw/baby-death-alleged-result-parents-online-games-addiction/story?id=10007040

Choi, S. M., Kim, Y., Sung, Y., & Sohn, D. (2011). Bridging or bonding? A cross-cultural study of social relationships in social networking sites. *Information, Communication & Society, 14,* 107–129. https://doi.org/10.1080/13691181003792624

Chong, Y. M. G., Teng, K. Z. S., Siew, S. C. A., & Skoric, M. M. (2012). Cultivation effects of video games: A longer-term experimental test of first- and second-order effects. *Journal of Social and Clinical Psychology, 31*(9), 952–971. https://doi.org/10.1521/jscp.2012.31.9.952

Chory, R. M., & Goodboy, A. K. (2011). Is basic personality related to violent and non-violent video game play and preferences? *Cyberpsychology, Behavior, and Social Networking, 14,* 191–198. https://doi.org/10.1089/cyber.2010.0076

Christensen, P., & Wood, W. (2007). Effects of media violence on viewers' aggression in unconstrained social interaction. In R. W. Preiss, B. M. Gayle, N. Burrell, M. Allen, & J. Bryant (Eds.), *Mass media effects research: Advances through meta-analysis* (pp. 145–168). Lawrence Erlbaum Associates.

Christenson, P. G. (1992). The effects of parental advisory labels on adolescent music preferences. *Journal of Communication, 42*(1), 106–113. https://doi.org/10.1111/j.1460-2466.1992.tb00772.x

Christenson, P. G., Henriksen, L., & Roberts, D. F. (2000). *Substance use in popular prime time television.* Office of National Drug Control Policy.

Chrousos, G. P., & Mentis, A. A. (2020). Medical misinformation in mass and social media: An urgent call for action, especially during epidemics. *European Journal of Clinical Investigation, 50*(5), Article e13227. https://doi.org/10.1111/eci.13227

Chung, J. E. (2014). Medical dramas and viewer perception of health: Testing cultivation effects. *Human Communication Research, 40*(3), 333–349. https://doi.org/10.1111/hcre.12026

Clancy-Hepburn, K., Hickey, A. A., & Neville, G. (1974). Children's behavior responses to TV food advertisements. *Journal of Nutrition Education, 7,* 93–96. https://doi.org/10.1016/S0022-3182(74)80118-4

Clarens, C. (1967). *An illustrated history of the horror film.* Putnam.

Clark, D., Nagler, R. H., & Niederdeppe, J. (2019). Confusion and nutritional backlash from news media exposure to contradictory information about carbohydrates and dietary fats. *Public Health Nutrition, 22*(18), 3336–3348. https://doi.org/10.1017/S1368980019002866

Clark, D. B., Tanner-Smith, E. E., & Killingsworth, S. S. (2016). Digital games, design, and learning: A systematic review and meta-analysis. *Review of Educational Research, 86*(1), 79–122. https://doi.org/10.3102/0034654315582065

Clarke, M. M. (2005, June). A scholastic achievement: Building an entertainment division? Forte aced the test. *Broadcasting & Cable, 135*(25), 30.

Clarke, P., & Kline, F. G. (1974). Media effects reconsidered: Some new strategies for communication research. *Communication Research, 1*(2), 224–240. https://doi.org/10.1177/009365027400100205

Clasen, M., Kjeldgaard-Christiansen, J., & Johnson, J. A. (2020). Horror, personality, and threat simulation: A survey on the psychology of scary media. *Evolutionary Behavioral Sciences, 14*(3), 213–230. https://doi.org/10.1037/ebs0000152

Clayton, K., Crabtree, C. & Horiuchi, Y. (2022). Do identity frames impact support for multiracial candidates? The case of Kamala Harris. *Journal of Experimental Political Science,* 1-12. https://doi.org/10.1017/XPS.2021.33

Clayton, R. B., Leshner, G., & Almond, A. (2015). The extended iself: The impact of iphone separation on cognition, emotion, and physiology. *Journal of Computer-Mediated Communication, 20*(2), 119–135. https://doi.org/10.1111/jcc4.12109

Cline, V. B. (1994). Pornography effects: Empirical and clinical evidence. In D. Zillmann, J. Bryant, & A. Huston (Eds.), *Media, children, and the family: Social scientific, psychodynamic, and clinical perspectives.* Lawrence Erlbaum Associates.

Cline, V. B., Croft, R. G., & Courrier, S. (1973). Desensitization of children to television violence. *Journal of Personality and Social Psychology, 27*(3), 360–365. https://doi.org/10.1037/h0034945

Coenen, L., & Van den Bulck, J. (2016). Cultivating the opinionated: The need to evaluate moderates the relationship between crime drama viewing and scary world evaluations. *Human Communication Research, 42*(3), 421–440. https://doi.org/10.1111/hcre.12080

Cohen, B. C. (1963). *The press and foreign policy.* Princeton University Press.

Cohen, R. A., & Adams, P. F. (2011). Use of the internet for health information: United States, 2009.

Centers for Disease Control and Prevention. https://www.cdc.gov/nchs/products/data-briefs/db66.htm

Coker, B. L. S. (2011). Freedom to surf: The positive effects of workplace internet leisure browsing. *New Technology, Work and Employment, 26,* 238–247. https://doi.org/10.1111/j.1468-005X.2011.00272.x

Cole, S. W., Kato, P. M., Marin-Bowling, V. M., Dahl, G. V., & Pollock, B. H. (2006). Clinical trial of *Re-Mission:* A computer game for young people with cancer. *Cyberpsychology & Behavior, 9,* 665–666. https://doi.org/10.1089/cpb.2006.9.653

Coleman, J. S. (1988). Social capital in the creation of human capital. *American Journal of Sociology, 94*(Supplement), S95–S120. http://www.jstor.org/stable/2780243

Coleman, R., Thorson, E., & Wilkins, L. (2011). Testing the effect of framing and sourcing in health news stories. *Journal of Health Communication, 16*(9), 941–954. https://doi.org/10.1080/10810730.2011.561918

Colfax, J. D., & Steinberg, S. F. (1972). The perpetuation of racial stereotypes: Blacks in mass circulation magazine advertisements. *Public Opinion Quarterly, 36*(1), 8–18. https://doi.org/10.1086/267971

Collins, A., & Loftus, E. (1975). A spreading-activation theory of semantic processing. *Psychological Review, 82*(6), 407–428. https://doi.org/10.1037/0033-295X.82.6.407

Collins, L., Glasser, A. M., Abudayyeh, H., Pearson, J. L., & Villanti, A. C. (2019). E-cigarette marketing and communication: How e-cigarette companies market e-cigarettes and the public engages with e-cigarette information. *Nicotine & Tobacco Research, 21*(1), 14–24. https://doi.org/10.1093/ntr/ntx284

Collins, R. L., Ellickson, P. L., McCaffrey, D., & Hambarsoomians, K. (2007). Early adolescent exposure to alcohol advertising and its relationship to underage drinking. *Journal of Adolescent Health, 40*(6), 527–534. https://doi.org/10.1016/j.jadohealth.2007.01.002

Collins, R. L., Elliot, M. N., Berry, S. H., Kanouse, D. E., Kunkel, D. K., Hunter, S. B., & Miu, A. (2004). Watching sex on TV predicts adolescent initiation of sexual behavior. *Pediatrics, 114,* e280–e289. https://doi.org/10.1542/peds.2003-1065-L

Collins, R. L., Strasburger, V. C., Brown, J. D., Donnerstein, E., Lenhart, A., & Wardd, L. M. (2017). Sexual media and childhood well-being and health. *Pediatrics, 140*(Supplement 2), S162–S166. https://doi.org/10.1542/peds.2016-1758X

Collins, W. A. (1973). Effect of temporal separation between motivation, aggression, and consequences: A developmental study. *Developmental Psychology, 8*(2), 215–221. https://doi.org/10.1037/h0034143

Collins, W. A., Wellman, H. M., Keniston, A. H., & Westby, S. D. (1978). Age-related aspects of comprehension and inference from a televised dramatic narrative. *Child Development, 49*(2), 389–399. https://doi.org/10.2307/1128703

Coltrane, S., & Messineo, M. (2000). The perpetuation of subtle prejudice: Race and gender imagery in 1990s television advertising. *Sex Roles: A Journal of Research, 42*(5-6), 363–389. https://doi.org/10.1023/A:1007046204478

Committee on Food Marketing and the Diets of Children and Youth. (2006). *Food marketing to children and youth: Threat or opportunity?* National Academy Press.

Comstock, G. (1980). New emphasis in research on the effects of television and film violence. In E. Palmer & A. Dorr (Eds.), *Children and the faces of television* (pp. 129–148). Academic.

Comstock, G., Chaffee, S., Katzman, N., McCombs, M., & Roberts, D. (1978). *Television and human behavior.* Columbia University Press.

Conway, B. A., Kenski, K., & Wang, D. (2015). The rise of Twitter in the political campaign: Searching for intermedia agenda-setting effects in the presidential primary. *Journal of Computer-Mediated Communication, 20*(4), 363–380. https://doi.org/10.1111/jcc4.12124

Conway, L. G. III, Repke, M. A., & Houck, S. C. (2017). Donald Trump as a cultural revolt against perceived communication restriction: Priming political correctness norms causes more Trump support. *Journal of Social and Political Psychology, 5*(1), 244–259. https://doi.org/10.5964/jspp.v5i1.732

Conway-Silva, B. A., Filer, C. R., Kenski, K., & Tsetsi, E. (2018). Reassessing Twitter's agenda-building power: An analysis of intermedia agenda-setting effects during the 2016 presidential primary season. *Social Science Computer Review, 36*(4), 469–483. https://doi.org/10.1177/0894439317715430

Coon, K. A., Goldberg, J., Rogers, B. L., & Tucker, K. (2001). Relationships between use of television during meals and children's food consumption patterns. *Pediatrics, 107*(1), e7. https://doi.org/10.1542/peds.107.1.e7

Cooper, J., & Mackie, D. (1986). Video games and aggression in children. *Journal of Applied Social Psychology, 16*(8), 726–744. https://doi.org/10.1111/j.1559-1816.1986.tb01755.x

Cooper, R., & Tang, T. (2009). Predicting audience exposure to television in today's media environment: An empirical integration of active-audience and structural theories. *Journal of Broadcasting & Electronic Media, 53*(3), 400–418. https://doi.org/10.1080/08838150903102204

Coppock, A., Hill, S. J., & Vavreck, L. (2020). The small effects of political advertising are small regardless of context, message, sender, or receiver: Evidence from 59 real-time randomized experiments. *Science Advances, 6*(36), Article eabc4046. https://doi.org/10.1126/sciadv.abc4046

Cornelius, M. E., Wang, T. W., Jamal, A., Loretan, C. G., & Neff, L. J., (2020). Tobacco product use among adults—United States, 2019. *Morbidity and Mortality Weekly Report, 69*(46), 1736–1742. http://doi.org/10.15585/mmwr.mm6946a4

Cotliar, S. (2009, February 20). Clintons bid farewell to Socks the cat. *People.* http://www.people.com/people/article/0,20260477,00.html

Courage, M. L., Frizzell, L. M., Walsh, C. S., & Smith, M. (2021). Toddlers using tablets: They engage, play, and learn. *Frontiers in Psychology, 12,* Article 564479. https://doi.org/10.3389/fpsyg.2021.564479

Courage, M. L., & Howe, M. L. (2010). To watch or not to watch: Infants and toddlers in a brave new electronic world. *Developmental Review, 30*(2), 101–115. https://doi.org/10.1016/j.dr.2010.03.002

Court, J. H. (1984). Sex and violence: A ripple effect. In N. M. Malamuth & E. Donnerstein (Eds.), *Pornography and sexual aggression* (pp. 143–172). Academic Press.

Covert, J. J., & Dixon, T. L. (2008). A changing view: Representation and effects of the portrayal of women of color in mainstream women's magazines. *Communication Research, 35*(2), 232–256. https://doi.org/10.1177/0093650207313166

Cowan, G., & Campbell, R. R. (1994). Racism and sexism in interracial pornography: A content analysis. *Psychology of Women Quarterly, 18*(3), 323–338. https://doi.org/10.1111/j.1471-6402.1994.tb00459.x

Cowan, G., Lee, C., Levy, D., & Snyder, D. (1988). Dominance and inequality in x-rated videocassettes. *Psychology of Women Quarterly, 12*(3), 299–311. https://doi.org/10.1111/j.1471-6402.1988.tb00945.x

Cowan, G., & O'Brien, M. (1990). Gender and survival vs. death in slasher films: A content analysis. *Sex Roles: A Journal of Research, 23*(3–4), 187–196. https://doi.org/10.1007/BF00289865

Cowart, H. (2020). What to think about: The applicability of agenda-setting in a social media context. *The Agenda Setting Journal, 4*(2), 195–218. https://doi.org/10.1075/asj.19001.cow

Cowley, M., & Smith, B. (1939). *Books that changed our minds.* Doubleday, Doran & Company.

Coyle, C. L., & Vaughn, H. (2008). Social networking: Communication revolution or evolution? *Bell Labs Technical Journal, 13*(2), 13–18. https://doi.org/10.1002/bltj.20298

Coyne, S. M., Stockdale, L. A., Warburton, W., Gentile, D. A., Yang, C., & Merrill, B. M. (2020). Pathological video game symptoms from adolescence to emerging adulthood: A 6-year longitudinal study of trajectories, predictors, and outcomes. *Developmental Psychology, 56*(7), 1385–1396. https://doi.org/10.1037/dev0000939

Craig, R. S. (1992). The effect of television day part on gender portrayals in television commercials: A content analysis. *Sex Roles: A Journal of Research, 26*(5-6), 197–211. https://doi.org/10.1007/BF00289707

Cranwell, J., Opazo-Breton, M., & Britton, J. (2016). Adult and adolescent exposure to tobacco and alcohol content in contemporary YouTube music videos in Great Britain: A population estimate. *Journal of Epidemiology & Community Health, 70*(5), 488–492. https://doi.org/10.1136/jech-2015-206402

Cranwell, J., Whittamore, K., Britton, J., & Leonardi-Bee, J. (2016). Alcohol and tobacco content in UK video games and their association with alcohol and tobacco use among young people. *Cyberpsychology, Behavior and Social Networking, 19*(7), 426–434. https://doi.org/10.1089/cyber.2016.0093

Crawley, A. M., Anderson, D. R., Wilder, A., Williams, M., & Santomero, A. (1999). Effects of repeated exposures to a single episode of the television program *Blue's Clues* on the viewing behaviors and comprehension of preschool children. *Journal of Educational Psychology, 91*(4), 630–637. https://doi.org/10.1037/0022-0663.91.4.630

Csikszentmihalyi, M. (1988). The flow experience and its significance for human psychology. In M. Csikszentmihalyi & I. S. Csikszentmihalyi (Eds.), *Optimal experience: Psychological studies of flow in consciousness* (pp. 15–35). Cambridge University Press.

Cummings, J., & Duncan, E. (2010). Changes in affect and future exercise intentions as a result of exposure to a regular exercise programme using Wii Fit. *Sport & Exercise Psychology Review, 6*(2), 31–41.

Curnalia, R. M. L., & Mermer, D. L. (2014). The "ice queen" melted and it won her the primary: Evidence of gender stereotypes and the double bind in news frames of Hillary Clinton's "emotional moment." *Qualitative Research Reports in Communication, 15*(1), 26–32. https://doi.org/10.1080/17459435.2014.955589

Curry, T. J., Jarosch, J., & Pacholok, S. (2005). Are direct to consumer advertisements of prescription drugs educational? Comparing 1992 to 2002. *Journal of Drug Education, 35*(3), 217–232. https://doi.org/10.2190/1VAK-BCNG-EHCC-BVLD

Custers, K., & Van den Bulck, J. (2012). Fear effects by the media. *European Journal of Pediatrics, 171*(4), 613–616. https://doi.org/10.1007/s00431-011-1632-1

Cyberchase. (n.d.). *About* [Facebook page]. Retrieved September 5, 2022, from https://www.facebook.com/cyberchase/about/?ref=page_internal

Czyzewska, M., & Ginsburg, H. J. (2007). Explicit and implicit effects of anti-marijuana and anti-tobacco TV advertisements. *Addictive Behaviors, 32*, 114–127. https://doi.org/10.1016/j.addbeh.2006.03.025

D'Abreu, L. C. F., & Krahé, B. (2014). Predicting sexual aggression in male college students in Brazil. *Psychology of Men & Masculinity, 15*(2), 152–162. https://doi.org/10.1037/a0032789

Dalisay, F., & Tan, A. (2009). Assimilation and contrast effects in the priming of Asian American and African American stereotypes through TV exposure. *Journalism & Mass Communication Quarterly, 86*(1), 7–22. https://doi.org/10.1177/107769900908600102

Daniel, T. A., & Camp, A. L. (2020). Emojis affect processing fluency on social media. *Psychology of Popular Media, 9*(2), 208–213. https://doi.org/10.1037/ppm0000219

Daniels, E. A., & Zurbriggen, E. L. (2016). The price of sexy: Viewers' perceptions of a sexualized versus nonsexualized Facebook profile photograph. *Psychology of Popular Media Culture, 5*(1), 2–14. https://doi.org/10.1037/ppm0000048

Danowski, J. A., Gluesing, J., & Riopelle, K. (2011). The revolution of diffusion theory caused by new media. In A. Vishwanath & G. A. Barnett (Eds.), *The diffusion of innovation: A communication sciences perspective* (pp. 123–144). Peter Lang.

DarfurIsDying.com (2008). About the game. http://www.darfurisdying.com/aboutgame.html

Darlington, L., & Talbot, E. B. (1898). Minor studies from the psychological laboratory of Cornell University: Distraction by musical sounds; the effect of pitch upon attention. *The American Journal of Psychology, 99*, 332–345. https://doi.org/10.2307/1411298

Davidson, E. S., Yasuna, A., & Tower, A. (1979). The effects of television cartoons on sex-role stereotyping in young girls. *Child Development, 50,* 597–600.

Davies, D. R. (1998). The contemporary newspaper, 1945–present. In W. D. Sloan (Ed.), *The age of mass communication* (pp. 453–469). Vision Press.

Davies, P. G., Spencer, S. J., Quinn, D. M., & Gerhardstein, R. (2002). Consuming images: How television commercials that elicit stereotype threat can restrain women academically and professionally. *Personality and Social Psychology Bulletin, 28*(12), 1615–1628. https://doi.org/10.1177/014616702237644

Davis, K. C., Norris, J., George, W. H., Martell, J., & Heiman, J. R. (2006). Men's likelihood of sexual aggression: The influence of alcohol, sexual arousal, and violent pornography. *Aggressive Behavior, 32*(6), 581–589. https://doi.org/10.1002/ab.20157

Davis, R. M., & Kendrick, J. S. (1989). The Surgeon General's warning in outdoor cigarette advertising: Are they readable? *Journal of the American Medical Association, 261*(1), 90–94. https://doi.org/10.1001/jama.1989.03420010100041

Davison, W. P. (1983). The third-person effect in communication. *Public Opinion Quarterly, 47*(1), 1–15. https://doi.org/10.1086/268763

Dean, S., Eschenfelder, C., Woodard, J., & Enlow. V. (2018). Teaching on the holodeck: Gender and social scripts among the crew of the virtual Star Trek Enterprise. *Journal of Media Education, 9*(4), 5–12. https://en.calameo.com/read/0000917890ff24424c30e

Dearing, J. W., & Rogers, E. M. (1996). *Agenda-setting.* Sage. https://doi.org/10.4135/9781452243283

Debatin, B., Lovejoy, J. P., Horn, A.-K., & Hughes, B. N. (2009). Facebook and online privacy: Attitudes, behaviors, and unintended consequences. *Journal of Computer-Mediated Communication, 15*(1), 83–108. https://doi.org/10.1111/j.1083-6101.2009.01494.x

De Cock, R. (2012). Mediating Flemish children's reactions of fear and sadness to television news and its limitations. *Journal of Children and Media, 6*(2), 485–501. https://doi.org/10.1080/17482798.2012.740414

de Freitas, S. (2018). Are games effective learning tools? A review of educational games. *Journal of Educational Technology & Society, 21*(2), 74–84.

Dennis, E. E., & Wartella, E. (Eds.) (1996). *American communication research: The remembered history.* Lawrence Erlbaum Associates.

Dennison, B. A., Erb, T. A., & Jenkins, P. l. (2002). Television viewing and television in bedroom associated with overweight risk among low-income preschool children. *Pediatrics, 109*(6), 1028–1035. https://doi.org/10.1542/peds.109.6.1028

Department of Health and Social Security and the Welsh Office. (1987). *AIDS: Monitoring response to the public education campaign, Feb. 1986–Feb. 1987.* H. M. Stationery Office.

Derry, C. (1987). More dark dreams: Some notes on the recent horror film. In G. A. Waller (Ed.), *American horrors: Essays on the modern American horror film* (pp. 162–174). University of Illinois Press.

De Souza e Silva, A., & Sutko, D. M. (2008) Playing life and living play: How hybrid reality games reframe space, play, and the ordinary. *Critical Studies in Mass Communication, 25*(5), 447–465. https://doi.org/10.1080/15295030802468081

DeSteno, D., Petty, R. E., Rucker, D. D., Wegener, D. T., & Braverman, J. (2004). Discrete emotions and persuasion: The role of emotion-induced expectancies. *Journal of Personality and Social Psychology, 86*(1), 43–56. https://doi.org/10.1037/0022-3514.86.1.43

DeSteno, D., Petty, R. E., Wegener, D. T., & Rucker, D. D. (2000). Beyond valence in the perception of likelihood: The role of emotion specificity.

Journal of Personality and Social Psychology, 78(3), 397–416. https://doi.org/10.1037/0022-3514.78.3.397

Deutsch, K. (1966). *The nerves of government*. Free Press.

DeWall, C. N., & Anderson, C. A. (2011). *The general aggression model*. In P. R. Shaver & M. Mikulincer (Eds.), *Herzilya series on personality and social psychology. Human aggression and violence: Causes, manifestations, and consequences* (pp. 15–33). American Psychological Association. https://doi.org/10.1037/12346-001

DeWall, C. N., Anderson, C. A., & Bushman, B. J. (2011). The general aggression model: Theoretical extensions to violence. *Psychology of Violence, 1*(3), 245–258. https://doi.org/10.1037/a0023842

Dibble, J. L., Hartmann, T., & Rosaen, S. F. (2016). Parasocial interaction and parasocial relationship: Conceptual clarification and a critical assessment of measures. *Human Communication Research, 42*(1), 21–44. https://doi.org/10.1111/hcre.12063

Dicken-Garcia, H. (1998). The popular press, 1833–1865. In W. D. Sloan (Ed.), *The age of mass communication* (pp. 147–170). Vision Press.

Dietrich, S. (2015). *Sean of the south: Volume II*. Published by the author.

Dietz, W. H. (1990). You are what you eat: What you eat is what you are. *Journal of Adolescent Health Care, 11*(1), 76–81. https://doi.org/10.1016/0197-0070(90)90133-M

Dietz, W. H., & Gortmaker, S. L. (1985). Do we fatten our children at the TV set? Television viewing and obesity in children and adolescents. *Pediatrics, 75*(5), 807–812. https://doi.org/10.1542/peds.75.5.807

DiFranza, J. R., Richards, J. W., Paulman, P. M., Wolf-Gillespie, N., Fletcher, C., Jaffe, R. D., & Murray, D. (1991). RJR Nabisco's cartoon camel promotes Camel cigarettes to children. *Journal of the American Medical Association, 266*(22), 3149–3153. https://doi.org/10.1001/jama.1991.03470220065028

Digital Future Report. (2018). *The 2018 digital future report: Surveying the digital future year sixteen*. Center for the Digital Future at USC Annenberg. https://www.digitalcenter.org/wp-content/uploads/2018/12/2018-Digital-Future-Report.pdf

Dill, K. E., & Dill, J. G. (1998). Video game violence: A review of the empirical literature. *Aggression and Violent Behavior, 3,* 407–428. https://doi.org/10.1016/S1359-1789(97)00001-3

Dillard, J. P. (2020). Currents in the study of persuasion. In M. B. Oliver, A. A. Raney, & J. Bryant (Eds.), *Media effects: Advances in theory and research* (4th ed., pp. 115–129). Routledge.

Dillman Carpentier, F. R., Northup, C. T., & Parrott, M. S. (2014). Revisiting media priming effects of sexual depictions: Replication, extension, and consideration of sexual depiction strength. *Media Psychology, 17*(1), 34–54. https://doi.org/10.1080/15213269.2013.870045

Dillman Carpentier, F. R., Parrott, M. S., & Northup, C. T. (2014). When first comes love (or lust): How romantic and sexual cues bias first impressions in online social networking. *The Journal of Social Psychology, 154,* 423–440. https://doi.org/10.1080/00224545.2014.933158

Dillman Carpentier, F. R., Stevens, E. M., Wu, L., & Seely, N. (2017). Sex, love, and risk-n-responsibility: A content analysis of entertainment television. *Mass Communication and Society, 20*(5), 686–709. https://doi.org/10.1080/15205436.2017.1298807

Dimaggio, P., Hargittai, E., Neuman, W. R., & Robinson, J. P. (2001). Social implications of the internet. *Annual Review of Sociology, 27,* 307–336. https://doi.org/10.1146/annurev.soc.27.1.307

Dimitrova, D. V., & Connolly-Ahern, C. (2007). A tale of two wars: Framing analysis of online news sites in Coalition countries and the Arab world during the Iraq War. *The Howard Journal of Communication, 18,* 153–168. https://doi.org/10.1080/10646170701309973

Dixon, T. L. (2006). Psychological reactions to crime news portrayals of Black criminals: Understanding the moderating roles of prior news viewing and stereotype endorsement. *Communication Monographs, 73,* 162–187. https://doi.org/10.1080/03637750600690643

Dixon, T. L. (2007). Black criminals and white officers: The effects of racially misrepresenting law breakers and law defenders on television news. *Media Psychology, 10,* 270–291. https://doi.org/10.1080/15213260701375660

Dixon, T. L. (2017). Good guys are still always in white? Positive change and continued misrepresentation of race and crime on local television news. *Communication Research, 44*(6), 775–792. https://doi.org/10.1177/0093650215579223

Dixon, T. L. (2020). Media stereotypes: Content, effects, and theory. In M. B. Oliver, A. A. Raney, & J. Bryant (Eds.), *Media effects: Advances in theory and research* (4th ed., pp. 243–257). Routledge.

Dixon, T., & Azocar, C. (2007). Priming crime and activating Blackness: Understanding the psychological impact of the overrepresentation of Blacks as lawbreakers on television news. *Journal of Communication, 57*(2), 229–253. https://doi.org/10.1111/j.1460-2466.2007.00341.x

Dixon, T., Azocar, C., & Casas, M. (2003). The portrayal of race and crime on television network news. *Journal of Broadcasting & Electronic Media, 47*(4), 498–523. https://doi.org/10.1207/s15506878jobem4704_2

Dixon, T., & Linz, D. (2000a). Overrepresentation and underrepresentation of African Americans and

Latinos as lawbreakers on television news. *Journal of Communication, 50*(2), 131–154. https://doi.org/10.1111/j.1460-2466.2000.tb02845.x

Dixon, T., & Linz, D. (2000b). Race and the misrepresentation of victimization on local television news. *Communication Research, 27*(5), 547–573. https://doi.org/10.1177/009365000027005001

Dixon, T., & Maddox, K. (2005). Skin tone, crime news, and social reality judgments: Priming the stereotype of the dark and dangerous black criminal. *Journal of Applied Social Psychology, 35*(8), 1555–1570. https://doi.org/10.1111/j.1559-1816.2005.tb02184.x

Djerf-Pierre, M., & Shehata, A. (2017). Still an agenda setter: Traditional news media and public opinion during the transition from low to high choice media environments. *Journal of Communication, 67*(5), 733–757. https://doi.org/10.1111/jcom.12327

Domke, D., McCoy, K., & Torres, M. (1999). News media, racial perceptions, and political cognition. *Communication Research, 26*(5), 570–607. https://doi.org/10.1177/009365099026005003

Donnerstein, E. (1980). Aggressive erotica and violence against women. *Journal of Personality and Social Psychology, 39*(2), 269–277. https://doi.org/10.1037/0022-3514.39.2.269

Doob, A. N., & MacDonald, G. E. (1979). Television viewing and fear of victimization: Is the relationship causal? *Journal of Personality and Social Psychology, 37*(2), 170–179. https://doi.org/10.1037/0022-3514.37.2.170

Door, A. (1980). When I was a child I thought as a child. In S. B. Withey & R. P. Abeles (Eds.), *Television and social behavior: Beyond violence and children* (pp. 191–230). Lawrence Erlbaum Associates.

Dorfman, L., & Wallack, L. (2007). Moving nutrition upstream: The case for reframing obesity. *Journal of Nutrition Education and Behavior, 39*(2), S45–S50. https://doi.org/10.1016/j.jneb.2006.08.018

Douglas, D. (1966). *Horror!* Macmillan.

Downs, E., & Oliver, M. B. (2016). How can Wii learn from video games? Examining relationships between technological affordances & socio-cognitive determinates on affective and behavioral outcomes. *International Journal of Gaming and Computer-Mediated Simulations, 8*(1), 28–43. https://doi.org/10.4018/IJGCMS.2016010103

Drabman, R. S., & Thomas, M. H. (1974). Does media violence increase children's toleration of real-life aggression? *Developmental Psychology, 10*(3), 418–421. https://doi.org/10.1037/h0036439

Duke, J. C., MacMonegle, A. J., Nonnemaker, J. M., Farrelly, M. C., Delahanty, J. C., Zhao, X., Smith, A. A., Rao, P., & Allen, J. A. (2019). Impact of The Real Cost media campaign on youth smoking initiation. *American Journal of Preventive Medicine, 57*(5), 645–651. https://doi.org/10.1016/j.amepre.2019.06.011

Dukes, K. N., & Gaither, S. E. (2017). Black racial stereotypes and victim blaming: Implications for media coverage and criminal proceedings in cases of police violence against racial and ethnic minorities. *Journal of Social Issues, 73*(4), 789–807. https://doi.org/10.1111/josi.12248

Duncker, K. (1938). Experimental modification of children's food preferences through social suggestion. *The Journal of Abnormal and Social Psychology, 33*(4), 489–507. https://doi.org/10.1037/h0056660

DvirGvirsman, S. (2014). It's not that we don't know, it's that we don't care: Explaining why selective exposure polarizes attitudes. *Mass Communication and Society, 17*(1), 74–97. https://doi.org/10.1080/15205436.2013.816738

Dysinger, W. S., & Ruckmick, C. A. (1933). *The emotional responses of children to the motion picture situation.* Macmillan.

Early Childhood Learning & Knowledge Center. (2020, July 17). *Head Start approach to school readiness—Overview.* https://eclkc.ohs.acf.hhs.gov/school-readiness/article/head-start-approach-school-readiness-overview

Eastman, H., & Liss, M. (1980). Ethnicity and children's preferences. *Journalism Quarterly, 57*(2), 277–280. https://doi.org/10.1177/107769908005700211

Eccles, A., Marshall, W. L., & Barbaree, H. E. (1988). The vulnerability of erectile measures to repeated assessments. *Behavior Research and Therapy, 26*(2), 179–183. https://doi.org/10.1016/0005-7967(88)90117-9

Eddleston, K. A., & Mulki, J. (2017). Toward understanding remote workers' management of work-family boundaries: The complexity of workplace embeddedness. *Group & Organization Management, 42*(3), 346–387. https://doi.org/10.1177/1059601115619548

Edelman, M. (1993). Contestable categories and public opinion. *Political Communication, 10*(3), 231–242. https://doi.org/10.1080/10584609.1993.9962981

Edy, J. A., & Meirick, P. C. (2007). Wanted, dead or alive: Media frames, frame adoption, and support for the war in Afghanistan. *Journal of Communication, 57*(1), 119–141. https://doi.org/10.1111/j.1460-2466.2006.00332.x

Eisenberg, A. L. (1936). *Children and radio programs.* Columbia University Press.

Eisenstein, E. L. (1979). *The printing press as an agent of change: Communications and cultural transformations in early modern Europe.* Cambridge University Press.

Eisenstein, E. L. (1983). *The printing revolution in early modern Europe.* Cambridge University Press.

Eleuteri, S., Saladino, V., & Verrastro, V. (2017). Identity, relationships, sexuality, and risky behaviors of adolescents in the context of social media. *Sexual and Relationship Therapy, 32*(3–4), 354–365. https://doi.org/10.1080/14681994.2017.1397953

Ellickson, P. L., Collins, R. L., Hambarsoomians, K., & McCaffrey, D. F. (2005). Does alcohol advertising promote adolescent drinking? Results from a longitudinal assessment. *Addiction (Abingdon, England), 100*(2), 235–246. https://doi.org/10.1111/j.1360-0443.2005.00974.x

Elliott, P. (1974). Uses and gratifications research: A critique and a sociological alternative. In J. G. Blumler & E. Katz (Eds.), *The uses of mass communications: Current perspectives on gratifications research* (pp. 249–268). Sage.

Ellis, Y., Daniels, B., & Jauregui, A. (2010). The effect of multitasking on the grade performance of business students. *Research in Higher Education Journal, 8,* 1–10.

Ellison, N. B., Steinfield, C., & Lampe, C. (2007). The benefits of Facebook "friends": Social capital and college students' use of online social network sites. *Journal of Computer-Mediated Communication, 12*(4), 1142–1168. https://doi.org/10.1111/j.1083-6101.2007.00367.x

Ellison, N. B., Steinfield, C., & Lampe, C. (2011). Connection strategies: Social capital implications of Facebook-enabled communication practices. *New Media & Society, 13*(6), 873–892. https://doi.org/10.1177/1461444810385389

Ellison, N. B., Vitak, J., Gray, R., & Lampe, C. (2014). Cultivating social resources on social network sites: Facebook relationship maintenance behaviors and their role in social capital processes. *Journal of Computer-Mediated Communication, 19*(4), 855–870. https://doi.org/10.1111/jcc4.12078

Ellithorpe, M. E., Bleakley, A., Hennessy, M., Weitz, I., Jamieson, P., & Khurana, A. (2017). Differences in the portrayal of health risk behaviors by Black and white characters in popular films. *Journal of Health Communication, 22*(6), 451–458. https://doi.org/10.1080/10810730.2017.1290165

Elsey, J. W. B., van Andel, K., Kater, R. B., Reints, I. M., & Spiering, M. (2019). The impact of virtual reality versus 2D pornography on sexual arousal and presence. *Computers in Human Behavior, 97,* 35–43. https://doi.org/10.1016/j.chb.2019.02.031

Elwood, W. N., & Ataabadi, A. N. (1996). Tuned in and turned off: Out-of-treatment injection drug and crack users' response to media intervention campaigns. *Communication Reports, 9*(1), 49–59. https://doi.org/10.1080/08934219609367634

Emberson, L. L., Lupyan, G., Goldstein, M. H., & Spivey, M. J. (2010). Overheard cell-phone conversations: When less speech is more distracting. *Psychological Science, 21,* 1383–1388. https://doi.org/10.1177/0956797610382126

End, C. M., Worthman, S., & Mathews, M. B. (2010). Costly cell phones: The impact of cell phone rings on academic performance. *Teaching of Psychology, 37*(1), 55–57. https://doi.org/10.1080/00986280903425912

Engelhardt, C. R., Bartholow, B. D., Kerr, G. T., & Bushman, B. J. (2011). This is our brain on violent video games: Neural desensitization to violence predicts increased aggression following violent video game exposure. *Journal of Experimental Psychology, 47,* 1033–1036. https://doi.org/10.10/j.jesp.2011.03.027

Entertainment Software Association (ESA). (2011). *2011 essential facts about the computer and video game industry.* https://etcjournal.files.wordpress.com/2011/11/esa_ef_2011.pdf

Entertainment Software Association. (2019). *2019 essential facts about the computer and video game industry.* https://www.theesa.com/wp-content/uploads/2019/05/ESA_Essential_facts_2019_final.pdf

Entertainment Software Association. (2021). *2021 essential facts about the video game industry.* https://www.theesa.com/resource/2021-essential-facts-about-the-video-game-industry/

Entertainment Software Association. (2022). *2022 essential facts about the video game industry.* https://www.theesa.com/resource/2022-essential-facts-about-the-video-game-industry/

Entman, R. M. (1993). Framing: Toward clarification of a fractured paradigm. *Journal of Communication, 43,* 51–58. https://doi.org/10.1111/j.1460-2466.1993.tb01304.x

Entman, R. M. (2010). Media framing biases and political power: Explaining slant in news of Campaign 2008. *Journalism, 11*(4), 389–408. https://doi.org/10.1177/1464884910367587

Erbland, K. (2019, July 9). *Before Netflix, Hollywood studios banned most on-screen smoking years ago.* IndieWire. https://www.indiewire.com/2019/07/hollywood-studios-banned-on-screen-smoking-1202156534/

Eron, L. D., Huesmann, L. R., Lefkowitz, M. M., & Walder, L. O. (1972). Does television violence cause aggression? *American Psychologist, 27*(4), 253–263. https://doi.org/10.1037/h0033721

Eschholz, S., Bufkin, J., & Long, J. (2002). Symbolic reality bites: Women and racial/ethnic minorities in modern film. *Sociological Spectrum, 22*(3), 299–334. https://doi.org/10.1080/02732170290062658

Esser, F. (2008). History of med effects. In W. Donsbach (Ed.), *The international encyclopedia of communication* (pp. 2891-2896). Blackwell.

Eurofound & the International LabourOffice. (2019). *Working anytime, anywhere: The effects on the world of work.* https://www.eurofound.europa.eu/publications/report/2017/working-anytime-anywhere-the-effects-on-the-world-of-work

Evans, H. K., Cordova, V., & Sipole, S. (2014). Twitter style: An analysis of how house candidates used Twitter in their 2012 campaigns. *PS: Political Science and Politics, 47*, 454–461. https://doi.org/10.1017/S1049096514000389

Evans, W. (1984). Monster movies: A sexual theory. In B. K. Grant (Ed.), *Planks of reason: Essays on the horror film* (pp. 53–64). Scarecrow Press.

Eveland, W. P. (2004). The effect of political discussion in producing informed citizens: The roles of information, motivation, and elaboration. *Political Communication, 21*(2), 177–193. https://doi.org/10.1080/10584600490443877

Eveland, W. P., Hayes, A. F., Shah, D. V., & Kwak, N. (2005). Understanding the relationship between communication and political knowledge: A model comparison approach using panel data. *Political Communication, 22*(4), 423–446. https://doi.org/10.1080/10584600500311345

Ewoldsen, D. R., & Rhodes, N. (2020). Media priming and accessibility. In M. B. Oliver, A. A. Raney, & J. Bryant (Eds.), *Media effects: Advances in theory and research* (4th ed., pp. 83–99). Routledge.

Ey, L.-A. (2016). Sexualized music media and children's gender role and self-identity development: A four-phase study. *Sex Education, 16*(6), 634–648. https://doi.org/10.1080/14681811.2016.1162148

Eysenbach, G., & Köhler, C. (2002). How do consumers search for and appraise health information on the World Wide Web? Qualitative study using focus groups, usability tests, and in-depth interviews. *British Medical Journal, 324*, 573–577. https://doi.org/10.1136/bmj.324.7337.573

Eysenbach, G., Powell, J., Kuss, O., & Sa, E. R. (2002). Empirical studies assessing the quality of health information for consumers on the World Wide Web: A systematic review. *Journal of the American Medical Association, 287*(20), 2691–2700. https://doi.org/10.1001/jama.287.20.2691

Ezati Rad, R., Mohseni, S., KamalzadehTakhti, H., Azad, M. H., Shahabi, N., Aghamolaei, T., & Norozian, F. (2021). Application of the protection motivation theory for predicting COVID-19 preventive behaviors in Hormozgan, Iran: A cross-sectional study. *BMC Public Health, 21*, Article 466. https://doi.org/10.1186/s12889-021-10500-w

Fabes, R. A., & Martin, C. L. (1991). Gender and age stereotypes of emotionality. *Personality and Social Psychology Bulletin, 17*(5), 532–540. https://doi.org/10.1177/0146167291175008

Facebook. (2021). *Facebook reports third quarter 2021 results*. https://s21.q4cdn.com/399680738/files/doc_news/Facebook-Reports-Third-Quarter-2021-Results-2021.pdf

Falkowski, J., & Steptoe, A. (1983). Biofeedback-assisted relaxation in the control of reactions to a challenging task and anxiety-provoking film. *Behaviour Research and Therapy, 21*(2), 161–167. https://doi.org/10.1016/0005-7967(83)90162-6

Fals-Stewart, W. (2003). The occurrence of partner physical aggression on days of alcohol consumption: A longitudinal diary study. *Journal of Consulting and Clinical Psychology, 71*(1), 41–52. https://doi.org/10.1037/0022-006X.71.1.41

Fardouly, J., Diedrichs, P. C., Vartanian, L. R., & Halliwell, E. (2015). The mediating role of appearance comparisons in the relationship between media usage and self-objectification in young women. *Psychology of Women Quarterly, 39*(4), 447–457. https://doi.org/10.1177/0361684315581841

Farrar, K., & Krcmar, M. (2006). Measuring state and trait aggression: A short, cautionary tale. *Media Psychology, 8*(2), 127–138. https://doi.org/10.1207/s1532785xmep0802_4

Fazio, R. H. (1990). Multiple processes by which attitudes guide behavior: The MODE model as an integrative framework. *Advances in Experimental Social Psychology, 23*, 75–102. https://doi.org/10.1016/S0065-2601(08)60318-4

Fazio, R. H., Jackson, J. R., Dunton, B. C., & Williams, C. J. (1995). Variability in automatic activation as an unobtrusive measure of racial attitudes: A bona fide pipeline? *Journal of Personality and Social Psychology, 69*(6), 1013–1027. https://doi.org/10.1037/0022-3514.69.6.1013

Fazio, R. H., & Olson, M. A. (2003). Implicit measures in social cognition research: Their meaning and use. *Annual Review of Psychology, 54*, 297–327. https://doi.org/10.1146/annurev.psych.54.101601.145225

Fazio, R. H., & Williams, C. J. (1986). Attitude accessibility as a moderator of the attitude–perception and attitude–behavior relations: An investigation of the 1984 presidential election. *Journal of Personality and Social Psychology, 51*(3), 505–514. https://doi.org/10.1037/0022-3514.51.3.505

Febvre, L., & Martin, H-J. (1984). The *coming of the book: The impact of printing 1450–1800* (D. Gerard, trans.). Verso Editions.

Federal Trade Commission. (2021a). *Federal Trade Commission cigarette report for 2019*. https://www.ftc.gov/system/files/documents/reports/federal-trade-commission-cigarette-report-2019-smokeless-tobacco-report-2019/cigarette_report_for_2019.pdf

Federal Trade Commission. (2021b). *Federal Trade Commission smokeless tobacco report for 2019*. https://www.ftc.gov/system/files/documents/reports/federal-trade-commission-cigarette-report-2019-smokeless-tobacco-report-2019/2019_smokeless_tobacco_report.pdf

Federman, J. (Ed.). (1998). *National television violence study: Vol. 3, Executive summary*. Center for communication and social policy, University of California.

Feezell, J. T. (2018). Agenda setting through social media: The importance of incidental news exposure and social filtering in the digital era. *Political*

Research Quarterly, 71(2), 482–494. https://doi.org/10.1177/1065912917744895

Feldman, L. (2013). Learning about politics from *The Daily Show*: The role of viewer orientation and processing motivations. *Mass Communication & Society, 16*(4), 586–607. https://doi.org/10.1080/15205436.2012.735742

Feldman, L., Maibach, E. W., Roser-Renouf, C., & Leiserowitz, A. (2012). Climate on cable: The nature and impact of global warming coverage on Fox News, CNN, and MSNBC. *The International Journal of Press/Politics, 17*(1), 3–31. https://doi.org/10.1177/1940161211425410

Fender, J. G., Richert, R. A., Robb, M. B., & Wartella, E. (2010). Parent teaching focus and toddlers' learning from an infant DVD. *Infant and Child Development, 19*(6), 613–627. https://doi.org/10.1002/icd.713

Fenton, F. (1910). The influence of newspaper presentations upon the growth of crime and other antisocial activity. *The American Journal of Sociology, 16*(3), 342–371.

Fenton, F. (1911). The influence of newspaper presentations upon the growth of crime and other antisocial activity (cont.). *The American Journal of Sociology, 16*(4), 538–564.

Ferguson, C. J. (2007). The good, the bad and the ugly: A meta-analytic review of positive and negative effects of violent video games. *Psychiatric Quarterly, 78,* 309–316. https://doi.org/10.1007/s11126-007-9056-9

Ferguson, C. J. (2015). Does movie or video game violence predict societal violence? It depends on what you look at and when. *Journal of Communication, 65*(1), 193–212. https://doi.org/10.1111/jcom.12142

Ferguson, C. J., & Colwell, J. (2019). Lack of consensus among scholars on the issue of video game "addiction". *Psychology of Popular Media Culture.* Advance online publication. https://doi.org/10.1037/ppm0000243

Ferguson, C. J., Contreras, S., & Kilburn, M. (2014). Advertising and fictional media effects on healthy eating choices in early and later childhood. *Psychology of Popular Media Culture, 3*(3), 164–173. https://doi.org/10.1037/ppm0000016

Ferguson, C. J., & Hartley, R. D. (2022). Pornography and sexual aggression: Can meta-analysis find a link?. *Trauma, Violence, & Abuse, 23*(1), 278–287. https://doi.org/10.1177/1524838020942754

Ferguson, C. J., & Kilburn, J. (2009). The public health risks of media violence: A meta-analytic review. *The Journal of Pediatrics, 154*(5), 759–763. https://doi.org/10.1016/j.jpeds.2008.11.033

Ferguson, C. J., & Kilburn, J. (2010). Much ado about nothing: The misestimation and overinterpretation of violent video game effects in Eastern and Western nations: Comment on Anderson et al.

(2010). *Psychological Bulletin, 136,* 174–178. https://doi.org/10.1037/a0018566

Ferguson, C. J., & Konijn, E. A. (2015). She said/he said: A peaceful debate on video game violence. *Psychology of Popular Media Culture, 4*(4), 397–411. https://doi.org/10.1037/ppm0000064

Ferguson, C. J., Nielsen, R., & Markey, P. M. (2017). Does sexy media promote teen sex? A meta-analytic and methodological review. *The Psychiatric Quarterly, 88*(2), 349–358. https://doi.org/10.1007/s11126-016-9442-2

Ferris, A. L., & Hollenbaugh, E. E. (2018). A uses and gratification approach to exploring antecedents to Facebook dependency. *Journal of Broadcasting & Electronic Media, 62*(1), 51–70. https://doi.org/10.1080/08838151.2017.1375501

Ferris, A. L., Smith, S. W., Greenberg, B. S., & Smith, S. L. (2007). The content of reality dating shows and viewer perceptions of dating. *Journal of Communication, 57*(3), 490–510. https://doi.org/10.1111/j.1460-2466.2007.00354.x

Feshbach, N. D. (1982). Sex differences in empathy and social behavior in children. In N. Eisenberg (Ed.), *The development of prosocial behavior* (pp. 315–338). Academic Press.

Feshbach, S. (1955). The drive-reducing function of fantasy behavior. *The Journal of Abnormal and Social Psychology, 50*(1), 3–11. https://doi.org/10.1037/h0042214

Feshbach, S. (1961). The stimulating versus cathartic effects of vicarious aggressive activity. *Journal of Abnormal and Social Psychology, 63,* 381–385. https://doi.org/10.1037/h0048863

Feshbach, S., & Singer, R. D. (1971). *Television and aggression: An experimental field study.* Jossey-Bass.

Festinger, L. (1954). A theory of social comparison processes. *Human Relations, 7,* 117–140. https://doi.org/10.1177/001872675400700202

Festinger, L. (1957). *A theory of cognitive dissonance.* Row, Peterson.

Festinger, L., Schachter, S., & Bach, K. (Eds.). (1950). *Social pressures in informal groups: A study of human factors in housing.* Stanford University Press.

Fikkers, K. M., & Piotrowski, J. T. (2019). Content and person effects in media research: Studying differences in cognitive, emotional, and arousal responses to media content. *Media Psychology.* Advance online publication. https://doi.org/10.1080/15213269.2019.1608257

Fikkers, K. M., Piotrowski, J. T., Lugtig, P., & Valkenburg, P. M. (2016). The role of perceived peer norms in the relationship between media violence exposure and adolescents' aggression. *Media Psychology, 19*(1), 4–26. https://doi.org/10.1080/15213269.2015.1037960

Fikkers, K. M., Piotrowski, J. T., & Valkenburg, P. M. (2016). Beyond the lab: Investigating early adolescents' cognitive, emotional, and arousal responses to violent games. *Computers in Human Behavior, 60*, 542–549. https://doi.org/10.1016/j.chb.2016.02.055

Fikkers, K. M., Piotrowski, J. T., Weeda, W. D., Vossen, H. G. M., & Valkenburg, P. M. (2013). Double dose: High family conflict enhances the effect of media violence exposure on adolescents' aggression. *Societies, 3*(3), 280–292. https://doi.org/10.3390/soc3030280

Finklea, B. W. (2011a, August 10–13). *Pixar's "new man": A textual and thematic analysis of masculinity in the* Toy Story *trilogy* [Poster presentation]. Association for Education of Journalism and Mass Communication 95th Annual Meeting, St. Louis, MO, United States.

Finklea, B. W. (2011b, April 10–13). Rooting for the serial killer: Disposition theory, justice, and morality in Showtime's *Dexter* [Paper presentation]. Broadcast Education Association 56th Annual Meeting, Las Vegas, NV, United States.

Finklea, B. W. (2014). *Examining masculinities in Pixar films: What it means to be a boy, whether human, fish, car, or toy* [Doctoral dissertation, University of Alabama]. University of Alabama Institutional Repository. https://ir.ua.edu/bitstream/handle/123456789/1977/file_1.pdf?sequence=1&isAllowed=y

Finklea, B. W. (2017a) Media effects: Comprehensive theories. In P. Rössler (Ed.), *International Encyclopedia of Media Effects* (Vol. 3, pp. 930–942). Wiley-Blackwell. https://doi.org/10.1002/9781118783764.wbieme0029

Finklea, B. W. (2017b). Nurturing new men and polishing imperfect fathers via hetero- and homosocial relationships in Pixar films. In R. A. Lind (Ed.) *Race and gender in electronic media: Content, context, culture* (pp. 89–104). New York, NY: Routledge.

Finklea, B. W., & Hardig, S. B. (2016). Seen but not heard: Exploring muted group theory in Pixar's *The Incredibles, WALL-E*, and *Brave*. In K. G. Roberts (Ed.) *Communication theory and millennial popular culture: Essays and applications* (pp 119–127). Peter Lang.

Finn, S. (1992). Television addiction? An evaluation of four competing media-use models. *Journalism Quarterly, 69*, 422–435. https://doi.org/10.1177/107769909206900216

Finnerty-Myers, K. (2011). Understanding the dynamics behind the relationship between exposure to negative consequences of risky sex on entertainment television and emerging adults' safe-sex attitudes and intentions. *Mass Communication & Society, 14*(6), 743–764. https://doi.org/10.1080/15205436.2010.540057

Fisch, S. M. (2000). A capacity model of children's comprehension of educational content on televi-

sion. *Media Psychology, 2*(1), 63–91. https://doi.org/10.1207/S1532785XMEP0201_4

Fisch, S. M. (2002). Vast wasteland or vast opportunity?: Effects of educational television on children's academic knowledge, skills, and attitudes. In J. Bryant & D. Zillmann (Eds.), *Media effects: Advances in theory and research* (2nd ed.). Lawrence Erlbaum Associates.

Fisch, S. M. (2003). *The impact of Cyberchase on children's mathematical problem solving: Cyberchase season 2 summative study.* MediaKidz Research & Consulting. https://www.informalscience.org/sites/default/files/report_257.PDF

Fisch, S. M. (2005, April). *Transfer of learning from educational television: Near and far transfer from Cyberspace.* Poster session presented at the biennial meeting of the Society for Research in Child Development, Atlanta, GA.

Fisch, S. M. (2009). Educational television and interactive media for children: Effects on academic knowledge, skills, and attitudes. In J. Bryant & M. B. Oliver (Eds.), *Media effects: Advances in theory and research* (3rd ed., pp. 402–435). Routledge.

Fisch, S. M., Akerman, A., Morgenlander, M., McCann Brown, S. K., Fisch, S. R. D., Schwartz, B. B., & Tobin, P. (2008). Coviewing preschool television in the US: Eliciting parent-child interaction via onscreen prompts. *Journal of Children and Media, 2*, 163–173. https://doi.org/10.1080/17482790802078680

Fisch, S. M., & Truglio, R. T. (Eds.). (2001). *"G" is for "growing": Thirty years of research on children and Sesame Street.* Lawrence Erlbaum Associates.

Fischer, P. M., Richards, J. W., Berman, E. J., & Krugman, D. M. (1989). Recall and eye tracking study of adolescents viewing tobacco advertisements. *Journal of the American Medical Association, 261*(1), 84–89. https://doi.org/10.1001/jama.1989.03420010094040

Fischer, P. M., Schwartz, M. P., Richards, J. W., Jr., Goldstein, A. O., & Rojas, T. H. (1991). Brand logo recognition by children aged 3 to 6 years. Mickey Mouse and Old Joe the Camel. *JAMA, 266*(22), 3145–3148. https://doi.org/10.1001/jama.1991.03470220061027

Fishbein, M., & Ajzen, I. (1975). *Belief, attitude, intention and behavior: An introduction to theory and research.* Addison-Wesley.

Fishbein, M., & Ajzen, I. (1976). Misconceptions about the Fishbein model: Reflections on a study by Songer-Nocks. *Journal of Experimental Social Psychology, 12*(6), 579–584. https://doi.org/10.1016/0022-1031(76)90036-6

Fishbein, M., & Ajzen, I. (2010). *Predicting and changing behavior: The reasoned action approach.* Psychology Press.

Fisher, D. A., Hill, D. L., Grube, J. W., Bersamin, M. M., Walker, S., & Gruber, E. L. (2009). Televised sexual content and parental mediation: Influences on adolescent sexuality. *Media Psychology, 12,* 121–147. https://doi.org/10.1080/15213260902849901

Fisher, W. A., Kohut, T., Di Gioacchino, L. A., & Fedoroff, P. (2013). Pornography, sex crime, and paraphilia. *Current Psychiatry Reports, 15,* Article 362. https://doi.org/10.1007/s11920-013-0362-7

Fiske, S. T., & Taylor, S. E. (1991). *Social cognition* (2nd ed.). McGraw-Hill.

Flagg, B. N. (2012). *Summative evaluation of SciGirls season two television series & website.* https://www.informalscience.org/sites/default/files/SG2_SummativeEval_2012.pdf

Flavell, J. (1963). *The developmental psychology of Jean Piaget.* Van Nostrand.

Flerx, V. C., Fidler, D. S., & Rogers, R. W. (1976). Sex role stereotypes: Developmental aspects and early intervention. *Child Development, 47*(4), 998–1007. https://doi.org/10.2307/1128436

Floyd, D. L., Prentice-Dunn, S., & Rogers, R. W. (2000). A meta-analysis of research on protection motivation theory. *Journal of Applied Social Psychology, 30,* 407–429. https://doi.org/10.1111/j.1559-1816.2000.tb02323.x

Forsyth, S. R., & Malone, R. E. (2016). Tobacco imagery in video games: Ratings and gamer recall. *Tobacco Control, 25*(5), 587–590. https://doi.org/10.1136/tobaccocontrol-2015-052286

Forsyth, S. R., & McDaniel, P. A. (2021). Tobacco imagery in the 20 best-selling video games of 2018. *Nicotine & Tobacco Research, 23*(8), 1341–1348. https://doi.org/10.1093/ntr/ntaa233

Fortunati, L. (2005a). Mobile phones and fashion in post-modernity. *Telektronikk, 3*(4), 35–48.

Fortunati, L. (2005b). Mobile telephone and the presentation of self. In R. Ling & P. Pedersen (Eds.), *Mobile communications: Re-negotiation of the social sphere* (pp. 203–218). Springer.

Foster, E., & Gamble, E. A. (1906). The effect of music on thoracic breathing. *The American Journal of Psychology, 17,* 406–414.

Foundation for Advancing Alcohol Responsibility. (2016). *Back to school survey 2016.* https://www.responsibility.org/back-school-survey-2016/

Fowler, K., & Thomas, V. (2015). A content analysis of male roles in television advertising: Do traditional roles still hold? *Journal of Marketing Communications, 21*(5), 356–371. https://doi.org/10.1080/13527266.2013.775178

Fox, J., & Bailenson, J. N. (2009). Virtual self-modeling: The effects of vicarious reinforcement and identification on exercise behaviors. *Media Psychology, 12,* 1–25. https://doi.org/10.1080/15213260802669474

Fox, J., & McEwan, B. (2020). Social media. In M. B. Oliver, A. A. Raney, & J. Bryant (Eds.), *Media effects: Advances in theory and research* (4th ed., pp. 373-388). Routledge.

Fox, J., & Potocki, B. (2016). Lifetime video game consumption, interpersonal aggression, hostile sexism, and rape myth acceptance: A cultivation perspective. *Journal of Interpersonal Violence, 31*(10), 1912–1931. https://doi.org/10.1177/0886260515570747

Fox, S. (2006). *Online health search 2006.* Pew Internet and American Life Project. Retrieved from http://www.pewinternet.org/pdfs/PIP_Online_health_ 2006.pdf

Fox, S. (2014, January 15). *The social life of health information.* Pew Research Center. https://www.pewresearch.org/fact-tank/2014/01/15/the-social-life-of-health-information/

Fox, S., & Duggan, M. (2013). *Health online 2013.* Pew Research Center. https://www.pewresearch.org/internet/2013/01/15/health-online-2013/

Franks, J., Chenhall, R., & Keogh, L. (2018). The Facebook sabbatical as a cycle: Describing the gendered experience of young adults as they navigate disconnection and reconnection. *Social Media + Society, 4*(3). https://doi.org/10.1177/2056305118801995

Franz, M. M., Freedman, P., Goldstein, K., & Ridout, T. N. (2008). Understanding the effect of political advertising on voter turnout: A response to Krasno and Green. *The Journal of Politics, 70*(1), 262–268. https://doi.org/10.1017/S0022381607080188

Frederick, C., & Zhang, T. (2019). Narcissism and social media usage: Is there no longer a relationship? *Journal of Articles in Support of the Null Hypothesis, 16*(1), 23–32. Retrieved from https://commons.erau.edu/publication/1322

Freedman, J. (2002). *Media violence and its effects on aggression: Assessing the scientific evidence.* University of Toronto Press.

Freimuth, V. S., Hammond, S. L., & Stein, J. A. (1988). Health advertising: Prevention for profit. *American Journal of Public Health, 78*(5), 557–561. https://doi.org/10.2105/AJPH.78.5.557

Freis, S. D., & Gurung, R. A. R. (2013). A Facebook analysis of helping behavior in online bullying. *Psychology of Popular Media Culture, 2*(1), 11–19. https://doi.org/10.1037/a0030239

French, I. M., & Hamilton, L. D. (2018). Male-centric and female-centric pornography consumption: Relationship with sex life and attitudes in young adults. *Journal of Sex & Marital Therapy, 44*(1), 73–86. https://doi.org/10.1080/0092623X.2017.1321596

Frew, C. (2021, January 20). *18 years later,* Final Destination 2 *has still ruined log trucks for everyone.* Unilad. https://www.unilad.co.uk/featured/18-years-later-final-destination-2-has-still-ruined-log-trucks-for-everyone/

Fridkin, K., Kenney, P. J., & Wintersieck, A. (2015). Liar, liar, pants on fire: How fact-checking influences citizens' reactions to negative advertising.

Political Communication, 32(1), 127–151. https://doi.org/10.1080/10584609.2014.914613

Fridkin, K., Wintersieck, A., Courey, J., & Thompson, J. (2017). Race and police brutality: The importance of media framing. *International Journal of Communication, 11*, 3394–3414. https://ijoc.org/index.php/ijoc/article/viewFile/6950/2117

Frisby, C. M., & Aubrey, J. S. (2012). Race and genre in the use of sexual objectification in female artists' music videos. *Howard Journal of Communications, 23*(1), 66–87. https://doi.org/10.1080/10646175.2012.641880

Frissen, T., De Coninck, D., Matthys, K., & d'Haenens, L. (2020). Longitudinal evidence of how media audiences differ in public health perceptions and behaviors during a global pandemic. *Frontiers in Public Health, 8*, Article 583408. https://doi.org/10.3389/fpubh.2020.583408

Fritz, N., Malic, V., Paul, B., & Zhou, Y. (2020). A descriptive analysis of the types, targets, and relative frequency of aggression in mainstream pornography. *Archives of Sexual Behavior, 49*, 3041–3053. https://doi.org/10.1007/s10508-020-01773-0

Fritz, N., Malic, V., Paul, B., & Zhou, Y. (2021). Worse than objects: The depiction of Black women and men and their sexual relationship in pornography. *Gender Issues, 38*, 100–120. https://doi.org/10.1007/s12147-020-09255-2

Frosch, D. L., Krueger, P. M., Hornik, R. C., Cronholm, P. F., & Barg, F. K. (2007). Creating demand for prescription drugs: A content analysis of television direct-to-consumer advertising. *Annals of Family Medicine, 5*, 6–13. https://doi.org/10.1370/afm.611

Frutos, A. M., & Merrill, R. M. (2017). Explicit sexual movie viewing in the United States according to selected marriage and lifestyle, work and financial, religion and political factors. *Sexuality & Culture, 21*, 1062–1082. https://doi.org/10.1007/s12119-017-9438-6

Fryberg, S. (2003). Really? You don't look like an American Indian: Social representations and social group identities. *Dissertation Abstracts International* (Vol. 64).

Fujioka, Y. (2005). Black media images as a perceived threat to African American ethnic identity: Coping responses, perceived public perception, and attitudes towards affirmative action. *Journal of Broadcasting & Electronic Media, 49*(4), 450–467. https://doi.org/10.1207/s15506878jobem4904_6

Funk, J. B., Baldacci, H. B., Pasold, T., & Baumgardner, J. (2004). Violence exposure in real-life, video games, television, movies, and the internet: Is there desensitization? *Journal of Adolescence, 27*, 23–39. https://doi.org/10.1016/j.adolescence.2003.10.005

Funkhouser, G. R. (1973). The issues of the sixties: An exploratory study in the dynamics of public opinion. *Public Opinion Quarterly, 37*(1), 62–75. https://doi.org/10.1086/268060

Furnham, A., & Lay, A. (2019). The universality of the portrayal of gender in television advertisements: A review of the studies this century. *Psychology of Popular Media Culture, 8*(2), 109–124. https://doi.org/10.1037/ppm0000161

Gabrielli, J., Corcoran, E., Genis, S., McClure, A. C., & Tanski, S. E. (2021). Exposure to television alcohol brand appearances as predictor of adolescent brand affiliation and drinking behaviors. *Journal of Youth and Adolescence.* Advance online publication. https://doi.org/10.1007/s10964-021-01397-0

Galdi, S., Maass, A., & Cadinu, M. (2014). Objectifying media: Their effect on gender role norms and sexual harassment of women. *Psychology of Women Quarterly, 38*(3), 398–413. https://doi.org/10.1177/0361684313515185

Gamson, W. A., & Modigliani, A. (1987). The changing culture of affirmative action. In R. G. Braungart & M. M. Braungart (Eds.), *Research in Political Sociology* (Vol. 3, pp.137–177). JAI Press.

Ganahl, D. J., Prinsen, T. J., & Netzley, S. B. (2003). A content analysis of prime time commercials: A contextual framework of gender representation. *Sex Roles: A Journal of Research, 49*(9-10), 545–551. https://doi.org/10.1023/A:1025893025658

Garcia-Agundez, A., Folkerts, A.-K., Konrad, R., Caserman, P., Tregel, T., Goosses, M., Göbel, S., & Kalbe, E. (2019). Recent advances in rehabilitation for Parkinson's Disease with exergames: A systematic review. *Journal of NeuroEngineering and Rehabilitation, 16*, Article 17. https://doi.org/10.1186/s12984-019-0492-1

Garrett, R. K., DvirGvirsman, S., Johnson, B. K., Tsfati, Y., Neo, R., & Dal, R. (2014). Implications of pro-and counterattitudinal information exposure for affective polarization. *Human Communication Research, 40*(3), 309–332. https://doi.org/10.1111/hcre.12028

Gaskin, J., & Berente, N. (2011). Video game design in the MBA curriculum: An experiential learning approach for teaching design thinking. *Communications of the Association for Information Systems, 29*, 103–122. https://doi.org/10.17705/1CAIS.02906

Gawronski, B., & Bodenhausen, G. V. (2006). Associative and propositional processes in evaluation: An integrative review of implicit and explicit attitude change. *Psychological Bulletin, 132*(5), 692–731. https://doi.org/10.1037/0033-2909.132.5.692

Gearhart, S., & Zhang, W. (2014). Gay bullying and online opinion expression: Testing spiral of silence in the social media environment. *Social Science Computer Review, 32*(1), 18–36. https://doi.org/10.1177/0894439313504261

Geen, R. G. (1975). The meaning of observed violence: Real vs. fictional violence and consequent effects on aggression and emotional arousal. *Journal of Research in Personality, 9*(4), 270–281. https://doi.org/10.1016/0092-6566(75)90002-1

Geen, R. G., & Rakosky, J. J. (1973). Interpretations of observed aggression and their effect on GSR. *Journal of Experimental Research in Personality, 6*(4), 289–292.

Geena Davis Institute on Gender in Media. (2019). *Rewrite her story: The state of the world's girls 2019.* https://seejane.org/wp-content/uploads/2019-rewrite-her-story-plan-international-report.pdf

Geis, F. L., Brown, V., Jennings-Walstedt, J., & Porter, N. (1984). TV commercials as achievement scripts for women. *Sex Roles: A Journal of Research, 10*(7-8), 513–525. https://doi.org/10.1007/BF00287260

Gentile, D. A., Coyne, S., & Walsh, D. A. (2011). Media violence, physical aggression, and relational aggression in school age children: A short-term longitudinal study. *Aggressive Behavior, 37*(2), 193–206. https://doi.org/10.1002/ab.20380

Gentile, D. A., Swing, E. L., Anderson, C. A., Rinker, D., & Thomas, K. M. (2016). Differential neural recruitment during violent video game play in violent- and nonviolent-game players. *Psychology of Popular Media Culture, 5*(1), 39–51. https://doi.org/10.1037/ppm0000009

Gerbner, G. (1970). Cultural indicators: The case of violence in television drama. *Annals of the American Academy of Political and Social Science, 388,* 69–81. https://doi.org/10.1177/000271627038800108

Gerbner, G. (1972). Violence in television drama: Trends and symbolic functions. In G. A. Comstock & E. Rubinstein (Eds.), *Television and social behavior: Vol. 1. Media content and control* (pp. 28–187). U.S. Government Printing Office. https://web.asc.upenn.edu/gerbner/Asset.aspx?assetID=2584

Gerbner, G. (1997). Gender and age in primetime television. In S. Kirschner & D. A. Kirschner (Eds.), *Perspectives on psychology and the media* (pp. 69–94). American Psychological Society.

Gerbner, G., & Gross, L. (1976). Living with television: The violence profile. *Journal of Communication, 26*(2), 172–194. https://doi.org/10.1111/j.1460-2466.1976.tb01397.x

Gerbner, G., Gross, L., Eleey, M. F., Jackson-Beeck, M., Jeffries-Fox, S., & Signorielli, N. (1977). Television violence profile no. 8: The highlights. *Journal of Communication, 27*(2),171–180. https://doi.org/10.1111/j.1460-2466.1977.tb01845.x

Gerbner, G., Gross, L., Jackson-Beeck, M., Jeffries-Fox, S., & Signorielli, N. (1978). Cultural indicators: Violence profile no. 9. *Journal of Communication, 28*(3), 176–207. https://doi.org/10.1111/j.1460-2466.1978.tb01646.x

Gerbner, G., Gross, L., Morgan, M., & Signorielli, N. (1980). The "mainstreaming" of America: Violence profile no. 11. *Journal of Communication, 30*(3), 10–29. https://doi.org/10.1111/j.1460-2466.1980.tb01987.x

Gerbner, G., Gross, L., Morgan, M., & Signorielli, N. (1994). Growing up with television: The cultivation perspective. In J. Bryant & D. Zillmann (Eds.), *Media effects: Advances in theory and research* (pp. 17–41). Lawrence Erlbaum Associates.

Gerbner, G., Gross, L., Morgan, M., Signorielli, N., & Shanahan, J. (2002). Growing up with television: Cultivation processes. In J. Bryant & D. Zillmann (Eds.), *Media effects: Advances in theory and research* (2nd ed.). Lawrence Erlbaum Associates.

Gerbner, G., & Signorielli, N. (1979). *Women and minorities in television drama 1969–1978.* Annenberg School of Communication, University of Pennsylvania.

Gergen, K. J. (2002). The challenge of absent presence. In J. Katz & M. Aakhus (Eds.), *Perpetual contact: Mobile communication, private talk, public performance* (pp. 227–241). Cambridge University Press.

Gesselman, A. N., Ta, V. P., & Garcia, J. R. (2019). Worth a thousand interpersonal words: Emoji as affective signals for relationship-oriented digital communication. *PLOS ONE, 14*(8), Article e0221297. https://doi.org/10.1371/journal.pone.0221297

GfK Roper Youth Report. (2016). *Influences on youth decisions about drinking.* http://i2.cdn.turner.com/cnn/2016/images/09/07/influencesonyouthsdecisionsaboutdrinking-2016-03-11.pdf

Ghanem, S. (1997). Filling in the tapestry: The second level of agenda setting. In M. E. McCombs, D. L. Shaw, & D. Weaver (Eds.), *Communication and democracy: Exploring the intellectual frontiers in agenda-setting theory* (pp. 3–14). Lawrence Erlbaum Associates.

Gibson, M. (2014, August 15). Here's a radical way to end vacation email overload. *Time.* https://time.com/3116424/daimler-vacation-email-out-of-office/

Gilbody, S., Wilson, P., & Watt, I. (2005). Benefits and harms of direct to consumer advertising: A systematic review. *Quality & Safety in Health Care, 14*(4), 246–250. https://doi.org/10.1136/qshc.2004.012781

Gilens, M. (1999). *Why Americans hate welfare: Race, media and the politics of antipoverty policy.* University of Chicago Press.

Gillam, K., & Wooden, S. R. (2008). Post-princess models of gender: The new man in Disney/Pixar. *Journal of Popular Film and Television, 36,* 2–8. https://doi.org/10.3200/JPFT.36.1.2-8

Gilliam, F., & Iyengar, S. (2000). Prime suspects: The influence of local television news on the viewing public. *American Journal of Political Science, 44*(3), 560–573. https://doi.org/10.2307/2669264

Gilliam, F. D., Iyengar, S., Simon, A., & Wright, O. (1996). Crime in black and white: The violent, scary world of local news. *Harvard International Journal of Press/Politics, 1*(3), 6–23. https://doi.org/10.1177/1081180X96001003003

Girodo, M., & Pellegrini, W. (1976). Exercise-produced arousal, film-induced arousal and attribution of internal state. *Perceptual and Motor Skills, 42*(3, Pt 1), 931–935. https://doi.org/10.2466/pms.1976.42.3.931

Gitlin, T. (1978). Media sociology: The dominant paradigm. *Theory and Society, 6,* 205–253.

Givens, S. B., & Monahan, J. L. (2005). Priming mammies, jezebels, and other controlling images: An examination of the influence of mediated stereotypes on perceptions of an African American woman. *Media Psychology, 7,* 87–106. https://doi.org/10.1207/S1532785XMEP0701_5

Glantz, S., Kacirk, K. W., & McCulloch, C. (2004). Back to the future: Smoking in movies in 2002 compared with 1950 levels. *American Journal of Public Health, 94*(2), 261–263. https://doi.org/10.2105/ajph.94.2.261

GlobalWebIndex. (2020). *Social: GlobalWebIndex's flagship report on the latest trends in social media.*https://www.globalwebindex.com/hubfs/Downloads/2019%20Q2-Q3%20Social%20Report.pdf?utm_campaign=Social%20media%20report%202020&utm_source=hs_automation&utm_medium=email&utm_content=82864869&_hsenc=p2ANqtz-8A2ENwBrZmPdt-coC6VVY2UQ0jHQf2Rz64Cfy5GgPNjrZ5jJUgL9n5RDVMXLOB2VJgFBO_c4dBhKsgYk3_W3gTvYaZtQ&_hsmi=82864869

Goffman, E. (1974). *Frame analysis: An essay on the organization of experience.* Harvard University Press.

Goidel, R., Freeman, C., & Procopio, S. (2006). The impact of television on perceptions of juvenile crime. *Journal of Broadcasting & Electronic Media, 50*(1), 119–139. https://doi.org/10.1207/s15506878jobem5001_7

Golbeck, J., Grimes, J. M., Rogers, A. (2010). Twitter use by the U.S. Congress. *Journal of the American Society for Information Science and Technology, 61,* 1612–1621. https://doi.org/10.1002/asi.21344

Goldberg, M. E., Gorn, G. J., & Gibson, W. (1978). TV messages for snack and breakfast foods: Do they influence children's preferences? *Journal of Consumer Research, 5*(2), 73–81. https://doi.org/10.1086/208717

Goldstein, A. O., Fischer, P. M., Richards, J. W., & Creten, D. (1987). Relationship between high school student smoking and recognition of cigarette advertisements. *Journal of Pediatrics, 110*(3), 488–491. https://doi.org/10.1016/S0022-3476(87)80523-1

Goldstein, A. O., Sobel, R. A., & Newman, G. R. (1999). Tobacco and alcohol use in G-rated children's animated films. *Journal of the American Medical Association, 281*(12), 1131–1136. https://doi.org/10.1001/jama.281.12.1131

Gollust, S. E., Lantz, P. M., & Ubel, P. A. (2009). The polarizing effect of news media messages about the social determinants of health. *American Journal of Public Health, 99*(12), 2160–2167. https://doi.org/10.2105/AJPH.2009.161414

Goranson, R. (1969). *Observed violence and aggressive behavior: The effects of negative outcomes to the observed violence* (Unpublished doctoral dissertation). University of Wisconsin-Madison.

Gordon, B. R., Lovett, M. J., Luo, B., & Reeder, J. C., III. (2022). Disentangling the effects of ad tone on voter turnout and candidate choice in presidential elections. *Management Science.* Advance online publication. https://doi.org/10.1287/mnsc.2022.4347

Gorham, B. (2006). News media's relationship with stereotyping: The linguistic intergroup bias in response to crime news. *Journal of Communication, 56*(2), 289–308. https://doi.org/10.1111/j.1460-2466.2006.00020.x

Gottfried, J., Barthel, M., & Shearer, E. (2016, February 4). *The 2016 presidential campaign—A news event that's hard to miss.* Pew Research Center. https://www.journalism.org/2016/02/04/the-2016-presidential-campaign-a-news-event-thats-hard-to-miss/

Gottfried, J. A., Vaala, S. E., Bleakley, A., Hennessy, M., & Jordan, A. (2013). Does the effect of exposure to TV sex on adolescent sexual behavior vary by genre?. *Communication Research, 40*(1), 73–95. https://doi.org/10.1177/0093650211415399

Governors Highway Safety Association. (2021, December). Distracted driving. https://www.ghsa.org/state-laws/issues/distracted%20driving

Grabe, M. E., & Drew, D. G. (2007). Crime cultivation: Comparisons across media genres and channels. *Journal of Broadcasting & Electronic Media, 51*(1), 147–171. https://doi.org/10.1080/08838150701308143

Grabe, M. E., Kamhawi, R., & Yegiyan, N. (2009). Informing citizens: How people with different levels of education process television, newspaper, and web news. *Journal of Broadcasting & Electronic Media, 53*(1), 90–111. https://doi.org/10.1080/08838150802643860

Granberg, D., & Brown, T. A. (1989). On affect and cognition in politics. *Social Psychology Quarterly, 52*(3), 171–182. https://doi.org/10.2307/2786712

Granic, I., Lobel, A., & Engels, R. C. M. E. (2014). The benefits of playing video games. *American Psychologist, 69*(1), 66–78. https://doi.org/10.1037/a0034857

Granovetter, M. S. (1982). The strength of weak ties: A network theory revisited. In P. V. Mardsen & N. Lin (Eds.), *Social structure and network analysis* (pp. 105–130). Sage.

Grant, B. F. (2000). Estimates of US children exposed to alcohol abuse and dependence in the family. *American Journal of Public Health, 90,* 112–115. https://doi.org/10.2105/ajph.90.1.112

Graves, L. E. F., Ridgers, N. D., Williams, K., Stratton, G., Atkinson, G., & Cable, N. T. (2010). The physiological cost of enjoyment of Wii Fit in adolescents, young adults, and older adults. *Journal of Physical Activity and Health, 7*(3), 393–401. https://doi.org/10.1123/jpah.7.3.393

Graybill, D., Kirsch, J., & Esselman, E. (1985). Effects of playing violent versus nonviolent video games on the aggressive ideation of aggressive and nonaggressive children. *Child Study Journal, 15,* 199–205.

Green, A. (2019). *Mobile gaming generated 60% of the global video games revenue in 2019.* Golden Casino News. https://goldencasinonews.com/blog/2019/12/30/mobile-gaming-generated-60-of-the-global-video-games-revenue-in-2019/

Greenberg, B. S. (1974). Gratifications of television viewing and their correlates for British children. In J. G. Blumler & E. Katz (Eds.), *The uses of mass communications: Current perspectives on gratifications research* (pp. 71–92). Sage.

Greenberg, B. S. (1994). Content trends in media sex. In D. Zillmann, J. Bryant, & A. C. Huston (Eds.), *Media, children, and the family: Social scientific, psychodynamic, and clinical perspectives.* Lawrence Erlbaum Associates.

Greenberg, B. S., Brown, J. D., & Buerkel-Rothfuss, N. L. (1993). *Media, sex, and the adolescent.* Hampton Press.

Greenberg, B. S., & Hofschire, L. (2000). Sex on entertainment television. In D. Zillmann & P. Vorderer (Eds.), *Media entertainment: The psychology of its appeal* (pp. 93–111). Lawrence Erlbaum Associates.

Greenberg, B. S., & Linsangan, R. (1993). Gender differences in adolescents' media use, exposure to sexual content, parental mediation and self-perceptions. In B. S. Greenberg, J. Brown, & N. Buerkel-Rothfuss (Eds.), *Media, sex and the adolescent* (pp. 134–144). Hampton Press.

Greenberg, B. S., Mastro, D., & Brand, J. E. (2002). Minorities and the mass media: Television into the 21st century. In J. Bryant & D. Zillmann (Eds.), *Media effects: Advances in theory and research* (2nd ed., pp. 333–351). Lawrence Erlbaum Associates.

Greenberg, B. S., Stanley, C., Siemicki, M., Heeter, C., Soderman, A., & Linsangan, R. (1993). Sex content on soaps and primetime television series most viewed by adolescents. In B. S. Greenberg, J. D. Brown, & N. L. Buerkel-Rothfuss (Eds.), *Media, sex and the adolescent.* Hampton Press.

Greenberg, L., D'Andrea, G., & Lorence, D. (2004). Setting the public agenda for online health search: A white paper and action agenda. *Journal of Medical Internet Research, 6*(2), Article e18. https://doi.org/10.2196/jmir.6.2.e18

Greene, B. (2011). *38 years ago he made the first cell phone call.* CNN. http://www.cnn.com/2011/OPINION/04/01/greene.first.cellphone.call/index.html

Greene, K., & Krcmar, M. (2005). Predicting exposure to and liking of media violence: A uses and gratifications approach. *Communication Studies, 56,* 71–93. https://doi.org/10.1080/0008957042000332250

Greenwald, A. G. (1968). Cognitive learning, cognitive response to persuasion, and attitude change. In A. Greenwald, T. Brock, & T. Ostrom (Eds.), *Psychological foundations of attitudes* (pp. 147–170). Academic Press.

Greenwald, A. G., McGhee, D. E., & Schwartz, J. L. K. (1998). Measuring individual differences in implicit cognition: The implicit association test. *Journal of Personality and Social Psychology, 74*(6), 1464–1480. https://doi.org/10.1037/0022-3514.74.6.1464

Greer, T. W., & Payne, S. C. (2014). Overcoming telework challenges: Outcomes of successful telework strategies. *The Psychologist-Manager Journal, 17*(2), 87–111. https://doi.org/10.1037/mgr0000014

Greitemeyer, T., & McLatchie, N. (2011). Denying humanness to others: A newly discovered mechanism by which violent video games increase aggressive behavior. *Psychological Science, 22,* 659–665. https://doi.org/10.1177/0956797611403320

Greitemeyer, T., & Mügge, D. O. (2014). Video games do affect social outcomes: A meta-analytic review of the effects of violent and prosocial video game play. *Personality and Social Psychology Bulletin, 40*(5), 578–589. https://doi.org/10.1177/0146167213520459

Greitemeyer, T., & Sagioglou, C. (2017). The longitudinal relationship between everyday sadism and the amount of violent video game play. *Personality and Individual Differences, 104,* 238–242. https://doi.org/10.1016/j.paid.2016.08.021

Grieco, E. (2020, April 1). *American's main sources for political news vary by party and age.* Pew Research Center. https://www.pewresearch.org/fact-tank/2020/04/01/americans-main-sources-for-political-news-vary-by-party-and-age/

Griffiths, M. (2000). Does internet and computer "addiction" exist? Some case study evidence. *CyberPsychology & Behavior, 3*(2), 211–218. https://doi.org/10.1089/109493100316067

Griffiths, M. D., Davies, M. N. O., & Chappell, D. (2004). Online computer gaming: A comparison of adolescent and adult gamers. *Journal of Adolescence, 27,* 87–96. https://doi.org/10.1016/j.adolescence.2003.10.007

Grimes, T., & Bergen, L. (2008). The epistemological argument against a causal relationship between media violence and sociopathic behavior among psychologically well viewers. *American Behavioral Scientist, 51*(8), 1137–1154. https://doi.org/10.1177/0002764207312008

Grimsted, D. (1998). *American mobbing, 1828–1861: Toward civil war.* Oxford University Press.

Grincevičienė, N. (2020). The effect of the intensity of telework on employees' work-life balance. *Buhalterinės Apskaitos Teorija Ir Praktika, 21*(1). https://doi.org/10.15388/batp.2020.16

Grindal, T., Silander, M., Maxon, T., Hupert, N., Vahey, P., & Pasnik, S. (2019). *Early science and engineering: The impact of* The Cat in the Hat Knows a Lot About That! *on learning.* Education Development Center, Inc., and SRI International. https://files.eric.ed.gov/fulltext/ED603162.pdf

Gross, E. F., Juvonen, J., & Gable, S. L. (2002). Internet use and well-being in adolescence. *Journal of Social Issues, 58*(1), 75–90. https://doi.org/10.1111/1540-4560.00249

Grossman, M., & Wood, W. (1993). Sex differences in intensity of emotional experience: A social role interpretation. *Journal of Personality and Social Psychology, 65*(5), 1010–1022. https://doi.org/10.1037/0022-3514.65.5.1010

Grubbs, J. B., Wright, P. J., Braden, A. L., Wilt, J. A., & Kraus, S. W. (2019). Internet pornography use and sexual motivation: A systematic review and integration. *Annals of the International Communication Association, 43*(2), 117–155. https://doi.org/10.1080/23808985.2019.1584045

Grube, J. W. (2004). Alcohol in the media: Drinking portrayals, alcohol advertising, and alcohol consumption among youth. In R. J. Bonnie & M. E. O'Connell (Eds.), *Reducing underage drinking: A collective responsibility* (pp. 597–622). The National Academy of Sciences.

Guenther-Grey, C. A., Schnell, D., Fishbein, M., & AIDS Community Demonstration Projects. (1995). Sources of HIV/AIDS information among female sex traders. *Health Education Research, 10*(3), 385–390. https://doi.org/10.1093/her/10.3.385

Guernsey, L. (2007). *Into the minds of babes: How screen time affects children from birth to age five.* Basic Books.

Gunter, B. (1987). *Television and the fear of crime.* John Libbey.

Gunter, B. (1994). The question of media violence. In J. Bryant & D. Zillmann (Eds.), *Media effects: Advances in theory and research* (pp. 163–211). Lawrence Erlbaum Associates.

Gunter, B. (2002). *Media sex: What are the issues?* Lawrence Erlbaum Associates.

Gunter, B., & Furnham, A. (1984). Perceptions of television violence: Effects of programme genre and type of violence on viewers' judgements of violent portrayals. *British Journal of Social Psychology, 23*(2), 155–164. https://doi.org/10.1111/j.2044-8309.1984.tb00624.x

Guo, L. (2012). The application of social network analysis in agenda setting research: A method-ological exploration. *Journal of Broadcasting & Electronic Media, 56*(4), 616–631. https://doi.org/10.1080/08838151.2012.732148

Guo, L. (2013). Toward the third level of agenda setting theory: A network agenda setting model. In T. J. Johnson (Ed.), *Agenda setting in a 2.0 world: New agendas in communication* (pp. 112–133). Routledge.

Guo, L. (2017). Agenda-setting: Individual-level effects versus aggregate-level effects. In P. Rössler (Ed.), *International encyclopedia of media effects* (Vol. 1, pp. 25–37). Wiley-Blackwell. https://doi.org/10.1002/9781118783764.wbieme0031

Guo, L., & McCombs, M. (2011, May 26–30). *Network agenda setting: A third level of media effects.* [Paper presentation]. International Communication Association 61st Annual Conference, Boston, MA, United States.

Guo, L., & Vargo, C. (2015). The power of message networks: A big-data analysis of the network agenda setting model and issue ownership. *Mass Communication and Society, 18*, 557–576. https://doi.org/10.1080/15205436.2015.1045300

Guo, L., Vu, H. T., & McCombs, M. (2012). An expanded perspective on agenda-setting effects: Exploring the third level of agenda setting. *Revista de Communicación, 11*, 51–68. https://revistadecomunicacion.com/pdf/2012/Art051-068.pdf

Gupta, P. B., Burns, D. J., & Boyd, H. (2016). Texting while driving: An empirical investigation of students' attitudes and behaviors. *Information Systems Management, 33*(1), 88–101. https://doi.org/10.1080/10580530.2016.1117884

Gurevitch, M., & Blumler, J. G. (1990). Political communication systems and democratic values. In J. Lichtenberg (Ed.), *Democracy and the mass media* (pp. 269–289). Cambridge University Press.

Gwinn, A. M., Lambert, N. M., Fincham, F. D., & Maner, J. K. (2013). Pornography, relationship alternatives, and intimate extradyadic behavior. *Social Psychological and Personality Science, 4*(6), 699–704. https://doi.org/10.1177/1948550613480821

Gypson, K. (2019, January 10). *Freshmen US lawmakers setting new rules for social media.* VOA. https://www.voanews.com/usa/us-politics/freshman-us-lawmakers-setting-new-rules-social-media

Ha, L. (2020). Advertising effects and advertising effectiveness. In M. B. Oliver, A. A. Raney, & J. Bryant (Eds.), *Media effects: Advances in theory and research* (4th ed., pp. 275–289). Routledge.

Habuchi, I. (2005). Accelerating reflexivity. In M. Ito, D. Okabe, & M. Matsuda (Eds.), *Personal portable, pedestrian: Mobile phones in Japanese life* (pp. 165–182). MIT Press.

Haferkamp, N., & Krämer, N. C. (2011). Social comparison 2.0: Examining the effects of online profiles on social-networking sites. *Cyberpsychology,*

Behavior, and Social Networking, 14, 209–314. https://doi.org/10.1089/cyber.2010.0120

Hakluyt, R. (1850). *Divers voyages touching the discovery of America and the islands adjacent.* The Hakluyt Society. https://www.loc.gov/item/04000242/ (Original work published 1582)

Hald, G. M., & Malamuth, N. N. (2015). Experimental effects of exposure to pornography: The moderating effect of personality and mediating effect of sexual arousal. *Archives of Sexual Behavior, 44*(1), 99–109. https://doi.org/10.1007/s10508-014-0291-5

Hale, J. L., & Dillard, J. P. (1995). Fear appeals in health promotion campaigns: Too much, too little, or just right? In E. Maibach & R. L. Parrott (Eds.), *Designing health messages: Approaches from communication theory and public health practice* (pp. 65–80). Sage.

Hall, C. C. (Ed.), & Jameson, J. F. (1910). A relation of Maryland: together with a map of the countrey, the conditions of plantation, His Majesties charter to the Lord Baltemore. In C. C. Hall (Ed.), *Original narratives of early American history: Narratives of early Maryland 1633–1684* (pp. 65–112). American Historical Society. (Original work published 1635)

Hall, E. R., Fisch, S. M., Esty, E. T., Debold, E., Miller, B. A., Bennett, D. T., & Sloan, S. V. (1990). *Children's problem-solving behavior and their attitudes toward mathematics: A study of the effects of Square One TV* (Vols. 1–5). Children's Television Workshop.

Hamari, J., Malik, A., Koski, J., & Johri, A. (2019). Uses and gratifications of Pokémon Go: Why do people play mobile location-based augmented reality games? *International Journal of Human-Computer Interaction, 35*(9), 804–819. https://doi.org/10.1080/10447318.2018.1497115

Hampton, K., Rainie, L., Lu, W., Dwyer, M., Shin, I., & Purcell, K. (2014, August 26). *Social media and the "spiral of silence."* Pew Research Center. https://www.pewresearch.org/internet/2014/08/26/social-media-and-the-spiral-of-silence/

Hampton, K. N., Sessions, L. F., & Her, E. J. (2011). Core networks, social isolation, and new media: How internet and mobile phone use is related to network size and diversity. *Information, Communication & Society, 14*(1), 130–155. https://doi.org/10.1080/1369118X.2010.513417

Han, D. H., Kim, Y. S., Lee, Y. S., Min, K. J., & Renshaw, P. F. (2010). Changes in cue-induced, prefrontal cortex activity with video-game play. *Cyberpsychology, Behavior, and Social Networking, 13*, 655–661. https://doi.org/10.1089/cyber.2009.0327

Han, J., & Yzer, M. (2020). Media-induced misperception further divides public opinion: A test of self-categorization theory of attitude polariza-tion. *Journal of Media Psychology: Theories, Methods, and Applications, 32*(2), 70–81. https://doi.org/10.1027/1864-1105/a000259

Hancock, D., & McMurty, L. (2017). "Cycles upon cycles, stories upon stories": Contemporary audio media and podcast horror's new frights. *Palgrave Communications, 3*, Article 17075. https://doi.org/10.1057/palcomms.2017.75

Hanewinkel, R., Sargent, J. D., Hunt, K., Sweeting, H., Engels, R. C. M. E., Scholte, R. H. J., Mathis, F., Florek, E., & Morgenstern, M. (2014). Portrayal of alcohol consumption in movies and drinking initiation in low-risk adolescents. *Pediatrics, 133*(6), 973–982. https://doi.org/10.1542/peds.2013-3880

Hare, R. D., & Blevings, G. (1975). Defensive responses to phobic stimuli. *Biological Psychology, 3*(1), 1–13. https://doi.org/10.1016/0301-0511(75)90002-2

Haridakis, P., & Humphries, Z. (2019). Uses and gratifications. In D. W. Stacks, M. B. Salwen, & K. C. Eichhorn (Eds.), *An integrated approach to communication theory and research* (3rd ed., pp. 139–152). Routledge.

Haridakis, P. M., & Rubin, A. M. (2005). Third-person effects in the aftermath of terrorism. *Mass Communication & Society, 8*(1), 39–59. https://doi.org/10.1207/s15327825mcs0801_4

Hariot, T. (1972). *A briefe and true report of the new found land of Virginia, by Thomas Hariot. The complete 1590 Theodor de Bry edition.* Dover. (Original work published 1590)

Harkin, J. (2003). *Mobilisation: The growing public interest in mobile technology.* Demos.

Harman, B. A., & Sato, T. (2011). Cell phone use and grade point average among undergraduate university students. *College Student Journal, 45*, 544–549.

Harmon, M., & Muenchen, R. (2009). Semantic framing in the build-up to the Iraq War: Fox v. CNN and other U.S. broadcast news programs. *ETC: A Review of General Semantics, 66*(1), 12–26. http://www.jstor.org/stable/42578893

Harris, L. (2003). Home-based teleworking and the employment relationship: Managerial challenges and dilemmas. *Personnel Review, 32*, 422–439. https://doi.org/10.1108/00483480310477515

Harris, R. J. (1994). The impact of sexually explicit media. In J. Bryant & D. Zillmann (Eds.), *Media effects: Advances in theory and research* (pp. 247–272). Lawrence Erlbaum Associates.

Harris, R. J., & Barlett, C. P. (2009). Effects of sex in the media. In J. Bryant & M. B. Oliver (Eds.), *Media effects: Advances in theory and research* (3rd ed., pp. 304–324). Routledge.

Harris, R. J., & Scott, C. L. (2002). Effects of sex in the media. In J. Bryant & D. Zillmann (Eds.), *Media effects: Advances in theory and research* (2nd ed., pp. 307–332). Lawrence Erlbaum Associates.

Harrison, K., & Cantor, J. (1999). Tales from the screen: Enduring fright reactions to scary media. *Media Psychology, 1*(2), 97–116. https://doi.org/10.1207/s1532785xmep0102_1

Harrison, R. L., Thomas, K. D., & Cross, S. N. N. (2017). Restricted visions of multiracial identity in advertising. *Journal of Advertising, 46*(4), 503–520. https://doi.org/10.1080/00913367.2017.1360227

Harvard Medical School. (n.d.). *Alcohol abuse.* https://www.health.harvard.edu/addiction/alcohol-abuse

Harvard Medical School. (2017, February 14). *Do not get sold on drug advertising.* https://www.health.harvard.edu/drugs-and-medications/do-not-get-sold-on-drug-advertising

Harwood, J. (1997). Viewing age: Lifespan identity and television viewing choices. *Journal of Broadcasting & Electronic Media, 41*(2), 203–213. https://doi.org/10.1080/08838159709364401

Hashimoto, Y., Ishii, K., Nakamura, I., Korenaga, R., Tsuji, D., & Mori, Y. (2000). Keitai denwa wo chuushin to surutsusin media riyonikansurucho-sakenkyu [A study on mobile phone and other communication media usage]. *Tokyo Daigaku Shyakai Joho KenkyusyoChosaKenkyu, Kiyo, 14,* 180–192.

Hatch, S., G., Esplin, C. R., Aaron, S. C., Dowdle, K. K., Fincham, F. D., Hatch, H. D., & Braithwaite, S. R., (2020). Does pornography consumption lead to intimate partner violence perpetration? Little evidence for temporal precedence. *The Canadian Journal of Human Sexuality, 29*(3), 289–296. https://doi.org/10.3138/cjhs.2019-0065

Hatchett, A., Hallam, J. S., & Ford, M. A. (2013). Evaluation of a social cognitive theory-based email intervention designed to influence the physical activity of survivors of breast cancer. *Psycho-oncology, 22*(4), 829–836. https://doi.org/10.1002/pon.3082

Hawkins, R. P., & Pingree, S. (1981). Using television to construct social reality. *Journal of Broadcasting, 25*(4), 347–364. https://doi.org/10.1080/08838158109386459

Hawkins, R. P., & Pingree, S. (1982). Television's influence on social reality. In D. Pearl, L. Bouthilet, & J. Lazar (Eds.), *Television and behavior: Ten years of scientific progress and implications for the eighties* (DHHS Publication No. ADM 82–1196, Vol. 2, pp. 224–247). U.S. Government Printing Office. https://files.eric.ed.gov/fulltext/ED228979.pdf

Hawkins, R. P., & Pingree, S. (1990). Divergent psychological processes in constructing social reality from mass media content. In N. Signorielli & M. Morgan (Eds.), *Cultivation analysis: New directions in media effects research* (pp. 35–50). Sage.

Hayat, T., & Samuel-Azran, T. (2017). Dual-screening the candidate image during presidential debates: The moderating role of Twitter and need to evaluate for the effects on candidate perceptions. *Jour-nal of Broadcasting & Electronic Media, 63*(1), 20–38. https://doi.org/10.1080/08838151.2019.1574117

Healy, J. M. (1990). *Endangered minds: Why our children don't think.* Simon & Schuster.

Hearold, S. (1986). A synthesis of 1043 effects of television on social behavior. In G. Comstock (Ed.), *Public communication and behavior* (Vol. 1, pp. 65–133). Academic Press.

Heath, R. L., & Bryant, J. (2000). *Human communication theory and research: Concepts, contexts, and challenges.* Lawrence Erlbaum Associates.

Hedding, K. J., & Ripka, K. (2018). What's political Twitter talking about? Setting the media agenda for the 2016 presidential debates among influential left, center, and right political media. *The Agenda Setting Journal, 2*(2), 168–190. https://doi.org/10.1075/asj.18018.hed

Heesacker, M., Petty, R. E., & Cacioppo, J. T. (1983). Field dependence and attitude change: Source credibility can alter persuasion by affecting message-relevant thinking. *Journal of Personality, 51,* 653–666. https://doi.org/10.1111/j.1467-6494.1983.tb00872.x

Heider, F. (1959). *The psychology of interpersonal relations* (2nd ed.). Wiley.

Heider, F., & Simmel, M. (1944). An experimental study of apparent behavior. *American Journal of Psychology, 57,* 243–259. https://doi.org/10.2307/1416950

Hellsten, I. (2003). Focus on metaphors: The case of "Frankenfood" on the web. *Journal of Computer-Mediated Communication, 8*(4), Article JCMC841. https://doi.org/10.1111/j.1083-6101.2003.tb00218.x

Helm, A. F., & Spencer, R. (2019). Television use and its effects on sleep in early childhood. *Sleep Health, 5*(3), 241–247. https://doi.org/10.1016/j.sleh.2019.02.009

Henriksen, L., & Flora, J. A. (2001). *Effects of adolescents' exposure to retail tobacco advertising* [Paper presentation]. 51st Annual International Communication Association Conference, Washington, DC, United States.

Herbenick, D., Fu, T.-C., Wright, P., Paul, B., Gradus, R., Bauer, J., & Jones, R. (2020). Diverse sexual behaviors and pornography use: Findings from a nationally representative probability survey of Americans aged 18 to 60 years. *The Journal of Sexual Medicine, 17*(4), 623–633. https://doi.org/10.1016/j.jsxm.2020.01.013

Herbozo, S., Tantleff-Dunn, S., Gokee-Larose, J., & Thompson, J. K. (2004). Beauty and thinness messages in children's media: A content analysis. *Eating Disorders, 12*(1), 21–34. https://doi.org/10.1080/10640260490267742

Herzog, H. (1940). Professor quiz: A gratification study. In P. F. Lazarsfeld (Ed.), *Radio and the printed page* (pp. 64–93). Duell, Sloan, & Pearce.

Herzog, H. (1944). What do we really know about daytime serial listeners? In P. F. Lazarsfeld & F. N. Stanton (Eds.), *Radio research 1942–1943* (pp. 3–33). Duell, Sloan, & Pearce.

Hess, R. D., & Goldman, H. (1962). Parents' views of the effects of television on their children. *Child Development, 33,* 411–426. https://doi.org/10.2307/1126454

Heston, M., & Birnholtz, J. (2017, May 25-29). *Worth the wait? The effect of responsiveness on interpersonal attraction among known acquaintances* [Paper presentation]. 67th Annual International Communication Association Conference, San Diego, CA, United States.

Hestroni, A. (2007). Three decades of sexual content on prime-time network programming: A longitudinal meta-analytic review. *Journal of Communication, 57,* 318–348. https://doi.org/10.1111/j.1460-2466.2007.00345.x

Hestroni, A. (2008). Geo-cultural proximity, genre exposure, and cultivation. *Communications, 33,* 69–90. https://doi.org/10.1515/COMMUN.2008.004

Hestroni, A., Elphariach, H., Kapuza, R., & Tsfoni, B. (2007). Geographical proximity, cultural imperialism, and the cultivation effect. *Communication Monographs, 74*(2), 181–199. https://doi.org/10.1080/03637750701390077

Higgins, E. T., Bargh, J. A., & Lombardi, W. J. (1985). Nature of priming effects on categorization. *Journal of Experimental Psychology: Learning, Memory, and Cognition, 11*(1), 59–69. https://doi.org/10.1037/0278-7393.11.1.59

Hilgard, J., Engelhardt, C. R., Bartholow, B. D., & Rouder, J. N. (2017). How much evidence is p > .05? Stimulus pre-testing and null primary outcomes in violent video games research. *Psychology of Popular Media Culture, 6*(4), 361–380. https://doi.org/10.1037/ppm0000102

Hill, C., Davis, H., Holman, R., & Nelson, G. (1984). *Video violence and children.* H. M. Stationery Office.

Himmelweit, H. T., Oppenheim, A. N., & Vince, P. (1958). *Television and the child.* Oxford University Press.

Hinduja, S. & Patchin, J. W. (2019). *2019 cyberbullying data.* Cyberbullying Research Center. https://cyberbullying.org/2019-cyberbullying-data

Hirsh, P. (1980). The "scary" world of the non-viewer and other anomalies: A reanalysis of Gerbner et al.'s findings on cultivation analysis Part 1. *Communication Research, 7*(4), 403–456. https://doi.org/10.1177/009365028000700401

Hoekstra, S. J., Harris, R. J., & Helmick, A. L. (1999). Autobiographical memories about the experience of seeing frightening movies in childhood. *Media Psychology, 1*(2), 117–140. https://doi.org/10.1207/s1532785xmep0102_2

Hoewe, J. (2020). Toward a theory of media priming. *Annals of the International Communication Association,* 44(2), 312–321. https://www.tandfonline.com/doi/abs/10.1080/23808985.2020.1815232

Hoewe, J., & Sherrill, L. A. (2019). The influence of female lead characters in political TV shows: Links to political engagement. *Journal of Broadcasting & Electronic Media, 63*(1), 59–76. https://doi.org/10.1080/08838151.2019.1570782

Hoewe, J., Wiemer, E. C., Adekunle, T., Barton, R., Jett, J., & Pijanowski, A. (2020). Linking political TV shows with female lead characters to political engagement: The roles of parasocial processes and gender identity. *Journal of Broadcasting & Electronic Media, 64*(5), 672–692. https://doi.org/10.1080/08838151.2020.1849703

Hoff, E. E. (1998). The press and a new America, 1865–1900. In W. D. Sloan (Ed.), *The age of mass communication* (pp. 233–250). Vision Press.

Hoffner, C. (1995). Adolescents' coping with frightening mass media. *Communication Research, 22*(3), 325–346. https://doi.org/10.1177/009365095022003003

Hoffner, C. (2009). Affective responses and exposure to frightening films: The role of empathy and different types of content. *Communication Research Reports, 26*(4), 285–296. https://doi.org/10.1080/08824090903293700

Hoffner, C., & Cantor, J. (1985). Developmental differences in responses to a television character's appearance and behavior. *Developmental Psychology, 21*(6), 1065–1074. https://doi.org/10.1037/0012-1649.21.6.1065

Hoffner, C., & Cantor, J. (1990). Forewarning of a threat and prior knowledge of outcome: Effects on children's emotional responses to a film sequence. *Human Communication Research, 16*(3), 323–354. https://doi.org/10.1111/j.1468-2958.1990.tb00214.x

Hoffner, C., & Levine, K. J. (2005). Enjoyment of mediated fright and violence: A meta-analysis. *Media Psychology, 7*(2), 207–237. https://doi.org/10.1207/S1532785XMEP0702_5

Holbert, L., Shah, D., & Kwak, N. (2004). Fear, authority, and justice: Crime-related TV viewing and endorsements of capital punishment and gun ownership. *Journalism & Mass Communication Quarterly, 81*(2), 343–363. https://doi.org/10.1177/107769900408100208

Holbert, R. L. (2005). A typology for the study of entertainment television and politics. *American Behavioral Scientist, 49*(3), 436–453. https://doi.org/10.1177/0002764205279419

Holbert, R. L., Garrett, R. K., & Gleason, L. S. (2010). A new era of minimal effects? A response to Bennett and Iyengar. *Journal of Communication, 60*(1), 15–34. https://doi.org/10.1111/j.1460-2466.2009.01470.x

Holbert, R. L., & Hansen, G. J. (2006). *Fahrenheit 9-11,* need for closure and the priming of affective ambivalence: An assessment of intra-affective structures by party identification. *Human Communication Research, 32*(2), 109–129. https://doi.org/10.1111/j.1468-2958.2006.00005.x

Holbrook, R. A., & Hill, T. G. (2005). Agenda-setting and priming in prime time television: Crime dramas as political cues. *Political Communication, 22*(3), 277–295. https://doi.org/10.1080/10584600591006519

Holton, A., Lee, N., & Coleman, R. (2014). Commenting on health: A framing analysis of user comments in response to health articles online. *Journal of Health Communication, 19*(7), 825–837. https://doi.org/10.1080/10810730.2013.837554

Homer, C., Susskind, O., Alpert, H. R., Owusu, C., Schneider, L., Rappaport, L. A., & Rubin, D. H. (2000). An evaluation of an innovative multimedia educational software program for asthma management: Report of a randomized, controlled trial. *Pediatrics, 106*(1 Pt 2), 210–215.

Horowitz, J. (2021, November 11). *In Portugal, it's now illegal for your boss to call outside work hours.* CNN. https://www.cnn.com/2021/11/11/success/portugal-employer-contact-law/index.html?fbclid=IwAR16Ax8nOb2pcQoKZCBT0RHLlqt7gM-Wdel_OT87A0PHqpcAdqRMjunAGX8

Horton, D., & Wohl, R. R. (1956). Mass communication and para-social interaction. *Psychiatry, 19*(3), 215–229. https://doi.org/10.1080/00332747.1956.11023049

Hovland, C. I. (1954). Effects of the mass media on communication. In G. Lindzey (Ed.), *Handbook of social psychology* (Vol. 2, pp. 1062–1103). Addison-Wesley.

Hovland, C. I., Lumsdaine, A., & Sheffield, F. (1949). *Experiments on mass communication.* Princeton University Press.

Howard, D. J. (1990). Rhetorical question effects on message processing and persuasion: The role of information availability and the elicitation of judgment. *Journal of Experimental Social Psychology, 26*(3), 217–239. https://doi.org/10.1016/0022-1031(90)90036-L

Howard, P. E. N., Raine, L., & Jones, S. (2001). Days and nights on the internet. *American Behavioral Scientist, 45*(3), 383–404. https://doi.org/10.1177/0002764201045003003

Hsu, C.-W., Wan, C.-C., & Tai, Y.-T. (2011). The closer the relationship, the more interaction on Facebook? Investigating the case of Taiwan users. *Cyberpsychology, Behavior, and Social Networking, 14*, 473–476. https://doi.org/10.1089/cyber.2010.0267

Huang, C. (2017). Time spent on social network sites and psychological well-being: A meta-analysis. *Cyberpsychology, Behavior, and Social Networking, 20*(6), 346–354. https://doi.org/10.1089/cyber.2016.0758

Huckfeldt, R., & Sprague, J. (1995). *Citizens, politics, and social communication.* Cambridge University Press.

Huesmann, L. R. (1982). Violence and aggression. In National Institute of Mental Health, *Television and behavior: Ten years of scientific progress* (Vol. 1, pp. 36–44). U.S. Government Printing Office. https://files.eric.ed.gov/fulltext/ED222186.pdf

Huesmann, L. R., Dubow, E. F., & Yang, G. (2013). Why is it so hard to believe that media violence causes aggression? In K. E. Dill (Ed.), *The Oxford handbook of media psychology* (pp. 159–171). Oxford University Press. https://doi.org/10.13140/2.1.4496.7368

Huesmann, L. R., & Eron, L. D. (Eds.). (1986). *Television and the aggressive child: A cross-national comparison.* Lawrence Erlbaum Associates.

Huesmann, L. R., Moise-Titus, J., Podolski, C. L., & Eron, L. D. (2003). Longitudinal relations between children's exposure to TV violence and their aggressive and violent behavior in young adulthood: 1977–1992. *Developmental Psychology, 39*(2), 201–221. https://doi.org/10.1037//0012-1649.39.2.201

Hughes, M. (1980). The fruits of cultivation analysis: A reexamination of some effects of television watching. *Public Opinion Quarterly, 44*(3), 287–302. https://doi.org/10.1086/268597

Hughes, M. (2019, May 17). *What is the Murph challenge and why is everyone doing it on Memorial Day?* CNN. https://www.cnn.com/2019/05/27/us/memorial-day-murph-challenge-trnd/index.html

Hume, R. (1977, October). Selling the Swedish nightingale: Jenny Lind and P. T. Barnum. *American Heritage, 28*(6), 90–107. https://www.americanheritage.com/selling-swedish-nightingale

Hummer, T. A., Kronenberger, W. G., Wang, Y., & Mathews, V. P. (2019). Decreased prefrontal activity during a cognitive inhibition task following violent video game play: A multi-week randomized trial. *Psychology of Popular Media Culture, 8*(1), 63–75. https://doi.org/10.1037/ppm0000141

Hunt, D., & Ramón, A.-C. (2020a). *Hollywood diversity report 2020: A tale of two Hollywoods Part 1: Film.* UCLA College Social Sciences. https://socialsciences.ucla.edu/wp-content/uploads/2020/02/UCLA-Hollywood-Diversity-Report-2020-Film-2-6-2020.pdf

Hunt, D., & Ramón, A.-C. (2020b). *Hollywood diversity report 2020: A tale of two Hollywoods Part 2: Television.* UCLA College Social Sciences. https://socialsciences.ucla.edu/wp-content/uploads/2020/10/UCLA-Hollywood-Diversity-Report-2020-Television-10-22-2020.pdf

Huntzicker, W. E. (1998). The pioneer press, 1800–1900. In W. D. Sloan (Ed.), *The age of mass communication* (pp. 187–211). Vision Press.

Hurley, R. J., Jensen, J., Weaver, A., & Dixon, T. (2015). Viewer ethnicity matters: Black crime in

TV news and its impact on decisions regarding public policy. *Journal of Social Issues, 71*(1), 155-170. https://doi.org/10.1111/josi.12102

Huston, A. C., Anderson, D. R., Wright, J. C., Linebarger, D. L., & Schmitt, K. L. (2001). *Sesame Street* viewers as adolescents: The recontact study. In S. M. Fisch & R. T. Truglio (Eds.), *"G" is for "growing": Thirty years of research on children and* Sesame Street (pp. 131–144). Lawrence Erlbaum Associates.

Huston, A. C., Wartella, E., & Donnerstein, E. (1998). *Measuring the effects of sexual content in the media: A report to the Kaiser Family Foundation.* The Henry J. Kaiser Family Foundation.

Hwang, H. S., & Cho, J. (2018). Why Instagram? Intention to continue using Instagram among Korean college students. *Social Behavior and Personality, 46*(8), 1305–1316. https://doi.org/10.2224/sbp.6961

Hyde, J. (1994). The media and the diffusion of innovation: The phonograph and radio broadcasting. In J. D. Startt & W. D. Sloan (Eds.), *The significance of the media in American history.* Vision Press.

Hyman, H., & Sheatsley, P. (1947). Some reasons why information campaigns fail. *Public Opinion Quarterly, 11,* 412–423. https://doi.org/10.1086/265867

Ireland, J. L., Birch, P., & Ireland, C. A. (2018). *The Routledge international handbook of human aggression: Current issues and perspectives.* Routledge.

Irwin, A. R., & Gross, A. M. (1995). Cognitive tempo, violent video games, and aggressive behavior in young boys. *Journal of Family Violence, 10*(3), 337–350. https://doi.org/10.1007/BF02110997

Ishii, K. (2006). Implications of mobility: The uses of personal communication media in everyday life. *Journal of Communication, 56*(2), 346–365. https://doi.org/10.1111/j.1460-2466.2006.00023.x

Ito, M., Okabe, D., & Anderson, K. (2008). Portable objects in three global cities: The personalization of urban places. In R. Ling & S. Campbell (Eds.), *The mobile communication research series: Reconstruction of space and time through mobile communication practices* (pp. 67–88). Transaction.

Ivory, J. D., Markey, P. M., Elson, M., Colwell, J., Ferguson, C. J., Griffiths, M. D., Savage, J., & Williams, K. D. (2015). Manufacturing consensus in a diverse field of scholarly opinions: A comment on Bushman, Gollwitzer, and Cruz (2015). *Psychology of Popular Media Culture, 4*(3), 222–229. https://doi.org/10.1037/ppm0000056

Ivry, B. (1998, September 25). In movies, a question of race. *Buffalo News,* p. 3G.

Iyengar, S. (1989). How citizens think about national issues. *American Journal of Political Science, 33*(4), 878–897. https://doi.org/10.2307/2111113

Iyengar, S. (1991). *Is anyone responsible? How television frames political issues.* University of Chicago Press.

Iyengar, S., & Kinder, D. R. (1985). Psychological accounts of agenda setting. In S. Kraus & R. Perloff (Eds.), *Mass media and political thought* (pp. 85–114). Sage.

Iyengar, S., & Kinder, D. R. (1987). *News that matters: Television and American opinion.* University of Chicago Press.

Iyengar, S., Peters, M. D., & Kinder, D. R. (1982). Experimental demonstrations of the "not-so-minimal" consequences of television news programs. *American Political Science Review, 76,* 848–858. https://doi.org/10.2307/1962976

Iyengar, S., & Simon, A. F. (2000). New perspectives and evidence on political communication and campaign effects. *Annual Review of Psychology, 51,* 149–169. https://doi.org/10.1146/annurev.psych.51.1.149

Izard, C. E. (1977). *Human emotions.* Plenum Press.

Jackson, L. A., & Ervin, K. S. (1991). The frequency and portrayal of black families in fashion advertisements. *Journal of Black Psychology, 18*(1), 67–70.

Jacobson, J., & Gruzd, A. (2020). Cybervetting job applicants on social media: the new normal? *Ethics and Information Technology, 22,* 175–195. https://doi.org/10.1007/s10676-020-09526-2

Jahng, M. R. (2019). Watching the rich and famous: The cultivation effect of reality television shows and the mediating role of parasocial experiences. *Media Practice and Education, 20*(4), 319–333. https://doi.org/10.1080/25741136.2018.1556544

Jain, A., Sharma, R., Gaur, K. L., Yadav, N., Sharma, P., Sharma, N., Khan, N., Kumawat, P., Jain, G., Maanjua, M., Sinha, K. M., & Yadav, K. S. (2020). Study of internet addiction and its association with depression and insomnia in university students. *Journal of Family Medicine and Primary Care, 9*(3), 1700–1706. https://doi.org/10.4103/jfmpc.jfmpc_1178_19

James, P. T., Leach, R., Kalamara, E., & Shayeghi, M. (2001). The worldwide obesity epidemic. *Obesity Research, 9*(S4), 228S–233S. https://doi.org/10.1038/oby.2001.123

James, T., Jr. (1982, May). World went mad when mighty Jumbo came to America. *Smithsonian, 13,* 134–152.

Jamieson, K. H., & Cappella, J. N. (2008). *Echo chamber: Rush Limbaugh and the conservative media establishment.* Oxford University Press.

Jenks, J. W. (1895). The guidance of public opinion. *The American Journal of Sociology, 1*(2), 158–169. http://www.jstor.org/stable/2761502

Jennings, N. A., Hooker, S. D., & Linebarger, D. L. (2009). Educational television as mediate literacy environments for preschoolers. *Learning, Media and Technology, 34*(3), 229–242. https://doi.org/10.1080/17439880903141513

Jensen, J. D., King, A. J., Carcioppolo, N., & Davis, L. (2012). Why are tailored messages more effective? A multiple mediation analysis of a breast cancer screening intervention. *Journal of Communication, 62*(5), 851–868. https://doi.org/10.1111/j.1460-2466.2012.01668.x

Jerit, J., Barabas, J., & Bolsen, T. (2006). Citizens, knowledge, and the information environment. *American Journal of Political Science, 50*(2), 266–282. https://www.jstor.org/stable/3694272

Jernigan, D., Noel, J., Landon, J., Thornton, N., & Lobstein, T. (2017). Alcohol marketing and youth alcohol consumption: A systematic review of longitudinal studies published since 2008. *Addiction (Abingdon, England), 112*(S1), 7–20. https://doi.org/10.1111/add.13591

Jin, B. & Jeong, S. (2010). The impact of Korean television drama viewership on the social perceptions of single life and having fewer children in married life. *Asian Journal of Communication, 20*(1), 17–32. https://doi.org/10.1080/01292980903440806

Jin, S.-A A. (2011). "I feel present. Therefore, I experience flow:" A structural equation modeling approach to flow and presence in video games. *Journal of Broadcasting & Electronic Media, 55*(1), 114–136. https://doi.org/10.1080/08838151.2011.546248

Jo, E., & Berkowitz, L. (1994). A priming effect analysis of media influences: An update. In J. Bryant & D. Zillmann (Eds.), *Media effects: Advances in theory and research* (pp. 43–60). Lawrence Erlbaum Associates.

Johns, M. M., Lowry, R., Haderxhanaj, L. T., Rasberry, C. N., Robin, L., Scales, L., Stone, D., & Suarez, N. (2020). Trends in violence victimization and suicide risk by sexual identity among high school students—Youth Risk Behavior Survey, United States, 2015–2019. *Morbidity and Mortality Weekly Report, 69*(1), 19–27. https://www.cdc.gov/healthyyouth/data/yrbs/pdf/2019/su6901-H.pdf

Johnsen, T. E. (2003). The social context of the mobile phone use of Norwegian teens. In J. Katz (Ed.), *Machines that become us: The social context of communication technology* (pp. 161–170). Transaction.

Johnson, B. K., Udvardi, A., Eden, A., & Rosenbaum, J. E. (2020). Spoilers go bump in the night: Impacts of minor and major reveals on horror film enjoyment. *Journal of Media Psychology: Theories, Methods, and Applications, 32*(1), 14–25. https://doi.org/10.1027/1864-1105/a000252

Johnson, B. R. (1980). General occurrence of stressful reactions to commercial motion pictures and elements in films subjectively identified as stressors. *Psychological Reports, 47*(3, Pt 1), 775–786. https://doi.org/10.2466/pr0.1980.47.3.775

Johnson, J. D., Adams, M. S., Hall, W., & Ashburn, L. (1997). Race, media, and violence: Differential racial effects of exposure to violent news stories. *Basic and Applied Social Psychology, 19*(1), 81–90. https://doi.org/10.1207/s15324834basp1901_6

Johnson, R. (1609). *Nova Britannia: Offering most excellent fruites by planting in Virginia: Exciting all such as be well affected to further the same.* London: Printed for Samuel Macham.

Johnson-Laird, P. N. (1983). *Mental models.* Harvard University Press.

Johnson-Laird, P. N. (1989). Mental models. In M. I. Posner (Ed.), *Foundations of cognitive science* (pp. 469–499). MIT Press.

Johnston, J. (1980). *An exploratory study of the effects of viewing the first season of* 3-2-1 Contact. Children's Television Workshop.

Johnston, J., & Ettema, J. S. (1982). *Positive images: Breaking stereotypes with children's television.* Sage.

Johnston, J., & Luker, R. (1983). *The "Eriksson Study": An exploratory study of viewing two weeks of the second season of* 3-2-1 Contact. Children's Television Workshop.

Joinson, A. N. (2008). "Looking at," "looking up," or "keeping up with" people? Motives and uses for Facebook. *CHI 2008 Proceedings* (pp. 1027–1036). ACM. https://doi.org/10.1145/1357054.1357213

Jones, J. (2005). *How William Shatner changed the world* [Film]. Handel Productions.

Jordan, A. B., & Vaala, S. E. (2020). Educational media for children. In M. B. Oliver, A. A. Raney, & J. Bryant (Eds.), *Media effects: Advances in theory and research* (4th ed., pp. 290–307). Routledge.

Jorge, A. (2019). Social media, interrupted: Users recounting temporary disconnection on Instagram. *Social Media + Society, 5*(4). https://doi.org/10.1177/2056305119881691

Josephson, W. L. (1987). Television violence and children's aggression: Testing the priming, social script, and disinhibition predictions. *Journal of Personality and Social Psychology, 53*(5), 882–890. https://doi.org/10.1037/0022-3514.53.5.882

Jozkowski, K. N., Marcantonio, T. L., Rhoads, K. E., Canan, S., Hunt, M. E., & Willis, M. (2019). A content analysis of sexual consent and refusal communication in mainstream films. *The Journal of Sex Research, 56*(6), 754–765. https://doi.org/10.1080/00224499.2019.1595503

Juergen, M. (2010). A brief history of play. *Entrepreneur, 38*(11), 30–36.

Julsrud, T. E. (2005). Behavioral changes at the mobile workplace: A symbolic interactionist approach. In R. Ling & P. Pedersen (Eds.), *Mobile communications: Re-negotiation of the social sphere* (pp. 93–112). Springer-Verlag.

Julsrud, T. E., & Bakke, J. W. (2008). Trust, friendship and expertise: The use of e-mail, mobile dialogues, and SMS to develop and sustain social relations in a distributed work group. In R. Ling & S. W. Campbell (Eds.), *The mobile communication research series: Reconstruction of space and time through mobile communication practices* (pp. 159–190). Transaction.

Jurkowitz, M., Mitchell, A., Shearer, E., & Walker, M. (2020, January 24). *U.S. media polarization and the 2020 election: A nation divided*. Pew Research Center. https://www.journalism.org/wp-content/uploads/sites/8/2020/01/PJ_2020.01.24_Media-Polarization_FINAL.pdf

Kahneman, D. (2003). Maps of bounded rationality: A perspective on intuitive judgment and choice. In T. Frangsmyr (Ed.), *Les Prix Nobel: The Nobel Prizes 2002* (pp. 449–489). Nobel Foundation.

Kahneman, D., & Tversky, A. (1979). Prospect theory—Analysis of decision under risk. *Econometrica, 47*(2), 263–291. https://doi.org/10.2307/1914185

Kahneman, D., & Tversky, A. (1984). Choices, values, and frames. *American Psychologist, 39*(4), 341–350. https://doi.org/10.1037/0003-066X.39.4.341

Kaid, L. L. (1996). Political communication. In M. B. Salwen & D. W. Stacks (Eds.), *An integrated approach to communication theory and research* (pp. 443–457). Lawrence Erlbaum Associates.

Kaid, L. L., Gobetz, R., Garner, J., Leland, C. M., & Scott, D. (1993). Television news and presidential campaigns: The legitimization of televised political advertising. *Social Science Quarterly, 74*(2), 274–285. http://www.jstor.org/stable/42863627

Kalman, Y. M., & Rafaeli, S. (2011). Online pauses and silence: Chronemic expectancy violations in written computer-mediated communication. *Communication Research, 38*(1), 54–69. https://doi.org/10.1177/0093650210378229

Kalpidou, M., Costin, D., & Morris, J. (2011). The relationship between Facebook and the well-being of undergraduate college students. *Cyberpsychology, Behavior, and Social Networking, 14*(4), 183–189. https://doi.org/10.1089/cyber.2010.0061

Kalyanaraman, S., & Bailensen, J. (2020). Virtual reality in media effects. In M. B. Oliver, A. A. Raney, & J. Bryant (Eds.), *Media effects: Advances in theory and research* (4th ed., pp. 404–418). Routledge.

Kang, J. G., & Morgan, M. (1988). Culture clash: US television programs in Korea. *Journalism Quarterly, 65*(2), 431–438. https://doi.org/10.1177/107769908806500225

Kareklas, I., & Meuhling, D. D. (2014). Addressing the texting and driving epidemic: Mortality salience priming effects on attitudes and behavioral intentions. *The Journal of Consumer Affairs, 48*(2), 223–250. https://doi.org/10.1111/joca.12039

Karsay, K., Matthes, J., Buchsteiner, L., & Grosser, V. (2019). Increasingly sexy? Sexuality and sexual objectification in popular music videos, 1995–2016. *Psychology of Popular Media Culture, 8*(4), 346–357. https://doi.org/10.1037/ppm0000221

Kassarjian, H. (1969). The Negro and American advertising: 1946–1965. *Journal of Marketing Research, 6*(1), 29–39. https://doi.org/10.1177/002224376900600102

Kastenmüller, A., Fischer, P., & Fischer, J. (2014). Video racing games increase actual health-related risk-taking behavior. *Psychology of Popular Media Culture, 3*(4), 190–194. https://doi.org/10.1037/a0030559

Katz, D., & Lazarsfeld, P. F. (1955). *Personal influence.* The Free Press.

Katz, E. (1980). On conceptualizing media effects. In T. McCormack (Ed.), *Studies in communication* (Vol. 1, pp. 119–141). JAI Press.

Katz, E. (1988). On conceptualizing media effects. In S. Oskamp (Ed.), *Television as a social issue* (pp. 361–374). Sage.

Katz, E., Gurevitch, M., & Haas, H. (1973). On the use of the mass media for important things. *American Sociological Review, 38*(2), 164–181. https://doi.org/10.2307/2094393

Katz, J. E., & Aakhus, M. A. (Eds.). (2002). *Perpetual contact: Mobile communication, private talk, public performance.* Cambridge University Press.

Katz, J. E., & Acord, S. K. (2008). Mobile games and entertainment. In J. Katz (Ed.), *Handbook of mobile communication studies* (pp. 403–418). MIT Press.

Kaye, L. K., Wall, H. J., & Malone, S. A. (2016). "Turn that frown upside-down": A contextual account of emoticon usage on different virtual platforms. *Computers in Human Behavior, 60*, 463–467. https://doi.org/10.1016/j.chb.2016.02.088

Kean, L. G. (2014). Mediated health campaigns. In T. L. Thompson (Ed.), *Encyclopedia of health communication* (Vol. 2, pp. 833–836). Sage.

Kearney, M. S., & Levine, P. B. (2015). Media influences on social outcomes: The impact of MTV's *16 and Pregnant* on teen childbearing. *American Economic Review, 105*(12), 3597–3632. https://doi.org/10.1257/aer.20140012

Kearney, M. S., & Levine, P. B. (2019). Early childhood education by television: Lessons from *Sesame Street. American Economic Journal: Applied Economics, 11*(1), 318–350. https://doi.org/10.1257/app.20170300

Keller-Hamilton, B., Muff, J., Blue, T., Slater, M. D., Robers, M. E., & Ferketich, A. K. (2018). Tobacco and alcohol on television: A content analysis of male adolescents' favorite shows. *Preventing Chronic Disease, 15*, Article 180062. https://doi.org/10.5888/pcd15.180062

Kelley, E. S., & Kinney, K. (2017). Word learning and story comprehension from digital storybooks: Does interaction make a difference? *Journal of Educational Computing Research, 55*(3), 410–428. https://doi.org/10.1177/0735633116669811

Kelly, H. (1981). Reasoning about realities: Children's evaluations of television and books. In H. Kelly & H. Gardner (Eds.), *Viewing children through television* (pp. 59–71). Jossey-Bass.

Kemp, S. (2020, January 30). *Digital 2020: Global digital overview.* Datareportal. https://datareportal.com/reports/digital-2020-global-digital-overview

Kim, J. L., Collins, R. L., Kanouse, D. E., Elliott, M. N., Berry, S. H., Hunter, S. B., Miu, A., & Kunkel, D. (2006). Sexual readiness, household policies, and other predictors of adolescents' exposure to sexual content in mainstream entertainment television. *Media Psychology, 8*(4), 449–471. https://doi.org/10.1207/s1532785xmep0804_6

Kim, J. W. (2018). Rumor has it: The effects of virality metrics on rumor believability and transmission on Twitter. *New Media & Society, 20*(12), 4807–4825. https://doi.org/10.1177/1461444818784945

Kim, J., & Lee, J.-E. R. (2011). The Facebook paths to happiness: Effects of the number of Facebook friends and self-presentation on subjective well-being. *Cyberpsychology, Behavior, and Social Networking, 14*, 359–365. https://doi.org/10.1089/cyber.2010.0374

Kim, J., Song, H., Merrill, K., Jr, Jung, Y., & Kwon, R. J. (2020). Using serious games for antismoking health campaigns: Experimental study. *JMIR Serious Games, 8*(4), Article e18528. https://doi.org/10.2196/18528

Kim, J., & Wanta, W. (2018). News framing of the U.S. immigration debate during election years: Focus on generic frames. *The Communication Review, 21*(2), 89–115. https://doi.org/10.1080/10714421.2018.1479616

Kim, K., & McCombs, M. (2007). News story descriptions and the public's opinions of political candidates. *Journalism & Mass Communication Quarterly, 84*(2), 299–314. https://doi.org/10.1177/107769900708400207

Kim, M. S. (2019, December 23). Video games are dividing South Korea. *MIT Technology Review.* https://www.technologyreview.com/2019/12/23/238190/video-games-national-crisis-addiction-south-korea/

Kim, M., Popova, L., Halpern-Felsher, B., & Ling, P. M. (2019). Effects of e-cigarette advertisements on adolescents' perceptions of cigarettes. *Health Communication, 34*(3), 290–297. https://doi.org/10.1080/10410236.2017.1407230

Kim, S.-H., Han, M., & Scheufele, D. A. (2010). Think about him this way: Priming, news media, and South Koreans' evaluation of the president. *International Journal of Public Opinion Research, 22*(3), 299–319. https://doi.org/10.1093/ijpor/edp057

Kim, S., & Park, Y. (2017, August 4-8). *A daily investigation of smartphone use and affective well-being at work* [Paper presentation]. Academy of Management Annual Meeting, Atlanta, GA, United States.

Kim, V. (2019, October 17). He played for 72 hours straight: South Korea wrestles with video game addiction. *LA Times.* https://www.latimes.com/world-nation/story/2019-10-17/south-korea-video-game-addiction-mental-health

King, P. (1997). The press, candidate images and voter perceptions. In M. E. McCombs, D. L. Shaw, & D. Weaver (Eds.), *Communication and democracy: Exploring the intellectual frontiers in agenda setting* (pp. 29–40). Lawrence Erlbaum Associates.

King, S. (1981). *Danse macabre.* New York: Everest.

Kircaburun, K., Alhabash, S., Tosuntaş, Ş. B., & Griffith, M. D. (2020). Uses and gratifications of problematic social media use among university students: A simultaneous examination of the big five of personality traits, social media platforms, and social media use motives. *International Journal of Mental Health Addiction, 18*, 525–547. https://doi.org/10.1007/s11469-018-9940-6

Kirkorian, H., Etta, R., Yoo, S. H., Jin, M., & Skora, E. (2017). *Video deficit.* Oxford Bibliographies. https://www.oxfordbibliographies.com/view/document/obo-9780199756841/obo-9780199756841-0187.xml

Kishore, A., Pan, T., & Nasker, N. N. (2019). Internet addiction and its associated factors: Study among the students of a public health school of Kolkata. *International Journal of Health & Allied Sciences, 8*(3), 159-163. https://10.4103/ijhas.IJHAS_43_18

Klaassen, M. J., & Peter, J. (2015). Gender (in)equality in internet pornography: A content analysis of popular pornographic internet videos. *Journal of Sex Research, 52*(7), 721–735. https://doi.org/10.1080/00224499.2014.976781

Klapper, J. T. (1949). *The effects of mass media: A report to the director of the public library inquiry.* Columbia University Bureau of Applied Social Research.

Klapper, J. T. (1960). *The effects of mass communication.* Free Press.

Klapper, J. T. (1963). Mass communication research: An old road resurveyed. *Public Opinion Quarterly, 27*(4), 515–527. https://www.jstor.org/stable/2747097

Kleemans, M., Daalmans, S., Carbaat, I., & Anschütz, D. (2018). Picture perfect: The direct effect of manipulated Instagram photos on body image in adolescent girls. *Media Psychology, 21*(1), 93–110. https://doi.org/10.1080/15213269.2016.1257392

Klimmt, C. (2003). Dimensions and determinates of the enjoyment of playing digital games: A three-level model. In M. Copier & J. Raessens (Eds.), *Level up: Digital games research conference* (pp. 246–257). Utrech University.

Klimmt, C., & Possler, D. (2020). Video games. In M. B. Oliver, A. A. Raney, & J. Bryant (Eds.), *Media effects: Advances in theory and research* (4th ed., pp. 342–356). Routledge.

Kline, L. W. (1907). The psychology of humor. *The American Journal of Psychology, 18*(4), 421–441. https://doi.org/10.2307/1412574

Knutzen, K. E., Moran, M. B., & Soneji, S. (2018). Combustible and electronic tobacco and marijuana products in hip-hop music videos, 2013–2017. *JAMA Internal Medicine, 178*(12), 1608–1615. https://doi.org/10.1001/jamainternmed.2018.4488

Ko, H., Cho, C.-H., & Roberts, M. S. (2005). Internet uses and gratifications: A structural equation model of interactive advertising. *Journal of Advertising, 34*(2), 57–70. https://doi.org/10.1080/00913367.2005.10639191

Kobayashi, T., Boase, J., Suzuki, T., & Suzuki, T. (2015). Emerging from the cocoon? Revisiting the tele-cocooning hypothesis in the smartphone era. *Journal of Computer-Mediated Communication, 20*(3), 330–345. https://doi.org/10.1111/jcc4.12116

Kochhar, R. & Passel, J. S. (2020, May 6). *Telework may save U.S. jobs in COVID-19 downturn, especially among college graduates.* Pew Research Center. https://www.pewresearch.org/fact-tank/2020/05/06/telework-may-save-u-s-jobs-in-covid-19-downturn-especially-among-college-graduates/

Kogen, L., & Dilliplane, S. (2019). How media portrayals of suffering influence willingness to help: The role of solvability frames. *Journal of Media Psychology: Theories, Methods, and Applications, 31*(2), 92–102. https://doi.org/10.1027/1864-1105/a000232

Kohut, T., Balzarini, R. N., Fisher, W. A., Grubbs, J. B., Campbell, L., & Prause, N. (2020). Surveying pornography use: A shaky science resting on poor measurement foundations. *Journal of Sex Research, 57*(6), 722–742. https://doi.org/10.1080/00224499.2019.1695244

Kohut, T., Fisher, W. A., & Campbell, L. (2017). Perceived effects of pornography on the couple relationship: Initial findings of open-ended, participant-informed, "bottom-up" research. *Archives of Sexual Behavior, 46*, 585–602. https://doi.org/10.1007/s10508-016-0783-6

Kohut, T., Landripet, I., & Štulhofer, A. (2021). Testing the confluence model of the association between pornography use and male sexual aggression: A longitudinal assessment in two independent adolescent samples from Croatia. *Archives of Sexual Behavior, 50*, 647–665. https://doi.org/10.1007/s10508-020-01824-6

Koriat, A., Melkman, R., Averill, J. R., & Lazarus, R. S. (1972). The self-control of emotional reactions to a stressful film. *Journal of Personality, 40*(4), 601–619. https://doi.org/10.1111/j.1467-6494.1972.tb00083.x

Kosenko, K., Luurs, G., & Binder, A. R. (2017). Sexting and sexual behavior, 2011-2015: A critical review and meta-analysis of a growing literature. *Journal of Computer-Mediated Communication, 22*(3), 141–160. https://doi.org/10.1111/jcc4.12187

Kosicki, G. M. (1993). Problems and opportunities in agenda-setting research. *Journal of Communication, 43*(2), 100–127. https://doi.org/10.1111/j.1460-2466.1993.tb01265.x

Kowalski, R. M., Giumetti, G. W., Schroeder, A. N., & Lattanner, M. R. (2014). Bullying in the digital age: A critical review and meta-analysis of cyberbullying research among youth. *Psychological Bulletin, 140*(4), 1073–1137. https://doi.org/10.1037/a0035618

Krafka, C. L. (1985). *Sexually explicit, sexually violent, and violent media: Effects of multiple naturalistic exposures and debriefing on female viewers* [Unpublished doctoral dissertation]. University of Wisconsin-Madison.

Krahé, B., & Busching, R. (2015). Breaking the vicious cycle of media violence use and aggression: A test of intervention effects over 30 months. *Psychology of Violence, 5*(2), 217–226. https://doi.org/10.1037/a0036627

Krahé, B. & Möller, I. (2010). Longitudinal effects of media violence on aggression and empathy among German adolescents. *Journal of Applied Developmental Psychology, 31*(5), 401–409. https://doi.org/10.1016/j.appdev.2010.07.003

Krahé, B., Möller, I., Huesmann, L. R., Kirwil, L., Felber, J., & Berger, A. (2011). Desensitization to media violence: Links with habitual media violence exposure, aggressive cognitions, and aggressive behavior. *Journal of Personality and Social Psychology, 100*(4), 630–646. https://doi.org/10.1037/a0021711

Krahé, B., Tomaszewska, P., & Schuster, I. (2022). Links of perceived pornography realism with sexual aggression via sexual scripts, sexual behavior, and acceptance of sexual coercion: A study of German university students. *International Journal of Environmental Research and Public Health, 19*(1), Article 63. https://doi.org/10.3390/ijerph19010063

Kramer, A. D. I., Guillory, J. E., & Hancock, J. T. (2014). Experimental evidence of massive-scale emotional contagion through social networks. *Proceedings of the National Academy of Sciences, 111*(24), 8788–8790. https://doi.org/10.1073/pnas.1320040111

Kraut, R., Kiesler, S., Boneva, B., Cummings, J., Helgeson, V., & Crawford, A. (2002). Internet paradox revisited. *Journal of Social Issues, 58*(1), 49–74. https://doi.org/10.1111/1540-4560.00248

Kraut, R. E., Patterson, M., Lundmark, V., Kiesler, S., Mukhopadhyay, T., & Scherlis, W. (1998). Internet paradox: A social technology that reduces social involvement and psychological well-being? *American Psychologist, 53*(9), 1017–1031. https://doi.org/10.1037/0003-066X.53.9.1017

Krcmar, M. (2010). Assessing the research on media, cognitive development, and infants: Can infants really learn from television and videos? *Journal of Children and Media, 4*(2), 120–134. https://doi.org/10.1080/17482791003629586

Krcmar, M. (2011). Can past experience with television help US infants learn from it? *Journal of Children and Media, 5*(3), 235–247. https://doi.org/10.1080/17482798.2011.584373

Krcmar, M. (2017). Uses and gratifications: Basic concepts. In P. Rössler (Ed.), *International encyclopedia of media effects* (Vol. 4, pp. 1997–2009). Wiley-Blackwell. https://doi.org/10.1002/9781118783764.wbieme0045

Krcmar, M. (2020). Social cognitive theory. In M. B. Oliver, A. A. Raney, & J. Bryant (Eds.), *Media effects: Advances in theory and research* (4th ed., pp. 100–114). Routledge.

Krcmar, M., Farrar, K., & McGloin, R. (2011). The effects of video game realism on attention, retention and aggressive outcomes. *Computers in Human Behavior, 27*(1), 432–439. https://doi.org/10.1016/j.chb.2010.09.005

Krcmar, M., Grela, B., & Lin, K. (2007). Can toddlers learn vocabulary from television? An experimental approach. *Media Psychology, 10*(1), 41–63. https://doi.org/10.108/15213260701300931

Krcmar, M., & Valkenburg, P. M. (1999). A scale to assess children's moral interpretations of justified and unjustified violence and its relationship to television viewing. *Communication Research, 26*(5), 608–634. https://doi.org/10.1177/009365099026005004

Kreslake, J. M., Elkins, A., Thomas, C. N., Gates, S., & Lehman, T. (2019). Use of mass communication by public health programs in nonmetropolitan regions. *Preventing Chronic Disease, 16*, Article E96. https://doi.org/10.5888/pcd16.190014

Kreuter, M. W., Strecher, V. J., & Glassman, B. (1999). One size does not fit all: The case for tailoring print materials. *Annals of Behavioral Medicine, 21*(4), 276–283. https://doi.org/10.1007/BF02895958

Krongard, S., & Tsay-Vogel, M. (2020). Online original TV series: Examining portrayals of violence in popular binge-watched programs and social reality perceptions. *Psychology of Popular Media, 9*(2), 155–164. https://doi.org/10.1037/ppm0000224

Krosnick, J. A. (1988). The role of attitude importance in social evaluation: A study of policy preference, presidential candidate evaluations, and voting behavior. *Journal of Personality and Social Psychology, 55*(2), 196–210. https://doi.org/10.1037/0022-3514.55.2.196

Krosnick, J. A., & Kinder, D. R. (1990). Altering the foundations of support for the president though priming. *American Political Science Review, 84*(2), 497–512. https://doi.org/10.2307/1963531

Ku, G., Kaid, L. L., & Pfau, M. (2003). The impact of web site campaigning on traditional news media and public information processing. *Journalism & Mass Communication Quarterly, 80*(3), 528–547. https://doi.org/10.1177/107769900308000304

Kunkel, D., Biely, E., Eyal, K., Cope-Farrar, K. M., Donnerstein, E., & Fandrich, R. (2003). *Sex on TV 3: Content and context.* Henry J. Kaiser Family Foundation.

Kunkel, D., Cope, K. M., Farinola, W. J. M., Biely, E., Rollin, E., & Donnerstein, E. (1999). *Sex on TV: A biennial report to the Kaiser Family Foundation.* Kaiser Family Foundation.

Kunkel, D., Eyal, K., Donnerstein, E., Farrar, K. M., Biely, E., & Rideout, V. (2007). Sexual socialization messages on entertainment television: Comparing content trends 1997–2002. *Media Psychology, 9*(3), 595–622. https://doi.org/10.1080/15213260701283210

Kuo, H. C., Lee, C.-C., & Chiou, W.-B. (2016). The power of the virtual ideal self in weight control: Weight-reduced avatars can enhance the tendency to delay gratification and regulate dietary practices. *Cyberpsychology, Behavior, and Social Networking, 19*, 80–85. https://doi.org/10.1089/cyber.2015.0203

Kushin, M. J., Yamamoto, M., & Dalisay, F. (2019). Societal majority, Facebook, and the spiral of silence in the 2016 US presidential election. *Social Media + Society, 5*(2). https://doi.org/10.1177/2056305119855139

Kushlev, K., & Dunn, E. W. (2015) Checking email less frequently reduces stress. *Computers in Human Behavior, 43*, 220–228. https://doi.org/10.1016/j.chb.2014.11.005

Kwak, N., Williams, A. E., Wang, X. R., & Lee, H. (2005). Talking politics and engaging in politics: An examination of the interactive relationships between structural features of political talk and discussion engagement. *Communication Research, 32*(1), 87–111. https://doi.org/10.1177/0093650204271400

Laato, S., Hyrynsalmi, S., Rauti, S., Islam, A. N., & Laine, T. H. (2020). Location-based games as Exergames: From Pokémon to the wizarding world. *International Journal of Serious Games, 7*(1), 79–95. https://doi.org/10.17083/ijsg.v7i1.337

Lachmann, B., Duke, É., Sariyska, R., & Montag, C. (2019). Who's addicted to the smartphone and/or the internet? *Psychology of Popular Media Culture, 8*(3), 182–189. https://doi.org/10.1037/ppm0000172

Ladd, J. M. (2012). *Why Americans hate the media and how it matters.* Princeton University Press.

Lampman, C., Rolfe-Maloney, B., David, E. J., Yan, M., McDermott, N., Winters, S., Davis, J., & Lathrop, R. (2002). Messages about sex in the workplace: A content analysis of primetime television. *Sexuality & Culture: An Interdisciplinary Quarterly, 6*(4), 3–21.

Landman, J., & Manis, M. (1983). Social cognition: Some historical and theoretical perspectives. In L. Berkowitz (Ed.), *Advances in experimental social psychology* (Vol. 16, pp. 49–123). Academic.

Lang, K., & Lang, G. E. (1959). The mass media and voting. In E. Burdick & A. J. Brodbeck (Eds.), *American voting behavior* (pp. 217–235). Free Press.

Lapierre, M. A., & Farrar, K. M. (2018). Learning to love guns? Gun-based gameplay's links to gun attitudes. *Psychology of Popular Media Culture, 7*(3), 216–230. https://doi.org/10.1037/ppm0000132

Lapierre, M. A., & Lewis, M. N. (2018). Should it stay or should it go? Smartphones and relational health. *Psychology of Popular Media Culture, 7*(3), 384–398. https://doi.org/10.1037/ppm0000119

Lapierre, M. A., & Vaala, S. E. (2015). Predictors of baby video/DVD ownership: Findings from a national sample of American parents with young children. *Journal of Children and Media, 9*(2), 212–230. https://doi.org/10.1080/17482798.2015.1024001

Lapinski, M. K., & Witte, K. (1998). Health communication campaigns. In L. D. Jackson & B. K. Duffy (Eds.), *Health communication research: A guide to developments and directions* (pp. 139–161). Greenwood.

LaRose, R. (2010). The problem of media habits. *Communication Theory, 20*(2), 194–222. https://doi.org/10.1111/j.1468-2885.2010.01360.x

LaRose, R., Connolly, R., Lee, H., Kang, L., & Hales, K. D. (2014). Connection overload? A cross cultural study on the consequences of social media connection. *Information Systems Management, 31*(1), 59–73. https://doi.org/10.1080/10580530.2014.854097

LaRose, R., & Eastin, M. S. (2002). Is online buying out of control? Electronic commerce and consumer self-regulation. *Journal of Broadcasting & Electronic Media, 46*(4), 549–564. https://doi.org/10.1207/s15506878jobem4604_4

LaRose, R., Lin, C. A., & Eastin, M. S. (2003). Unregulated internet usage: Addiction, habit, or deficient self-regulation? *Media Psychology, 5*(3), 225–253. https://doi.org/10.1207/S1532785XMEP0503_01

Lassen, D. S., & Brown, L. R. (2017). Twitter: The electoral connection? *Social Science Computer Review, 29*(4), 419-436. https://doi.org/10.1177/0894439310382749

Lasswell, H. D. (1927). *Propaganda technique in the World War.* Knopf.

Lasswell, H. D. (1948). The structure and function of communication in society. In L. Bryson (Ed.), *The communication of ideas* (pp. 37–51). Harper.

Lauzen, M. M., & Dozier, D. M. (2002). You look mahvelous: An examination of gender and appearance comments in the 1999–2000 prime-time season. *Sex Roles, 46*, 429–437. https://doi.org/10.1023/A:1020417731462

LaValley, S. A., Kiviniemi, M. T., & Gage-Bouchard, E. A. (2017). Where people look for online health information. *Health Information and Libraries Journal, 34*(2), 146–155. https://doi.org/10.1111/hir.12143

Lazarsfeld, P. F. (1940). *Radio and the printed page.* New York: Duell, Sloan, & Pearce.

Lazarsfeld, P. F. (1949). Forward. In J. T. Klapper, *The effects of mass media: A report to the director of the public library inquiry* (pp. 1–9). New York: Columbia University Bureau of Applied Social Research.

Lazarsfeld, P. F. (1962). Introduction. In S. A. Stouffer, *Social research to test ideas: Selected writings of Samuel A. Stouffer* (pp. xv–xxxi). Free Press.

Lazarsfeld, P. F., Berelson, B. R., & Gaudet, H. (1944). *The people's choice.* Columbia University Press.

Lazarsfeld, P. F., Berelson, B. R., & Gaudet, H. (1948). *The people's choice* (2nd ed.). Columbia University Press.

Lazarus, R. S., Speisman, J. C., Mordkoff, A. M., & Davidson, L. A. (1962). A laboratory study of psychological stress produced by a motion picture film. *Psychological Monographs: General and Applied, 76*(34), 1–35. https://doi.org/10.1037/h0093861

Lazer, D., Vaum, M., Benkler, Y., Berinsky, A., Greenhill, K., Menczer, F., Metzger, M., Nyhan, B., Pennycook, G., Rothschild, D., Schudson, M., Sloman, S., Sunstein, C., Thorson, E., Watts, D., & Zittrain, J. (2018). The science of fake news: Addressing fake news requires a multidisciplinary effort. *Science, 359*(6380), 1094–1096. https://doi.org/10.1126/science.aao2998

Lecheler, S., Keer, M., Schuck, A. R. T., & Hänggli, R. (2015). The effects of repetitive news framing on political opinions over time. *Communication Monographs, 82*(3), 339–358. https://doi.org/10.1080/03637751.2014.994646

Lee, A., & Lee, E. B. (1939). *The fine art of propaganda: A study of Father Coughlin's speeches.* Harcourt, Brace and Company.

Lee, B., Liu, J., Choung, H., & McLeod, D. (2020). Beyond the notion of accessibility bias: Message content as the common source of agenda-setting and priming effects. *Mass Communication & Society, 23*(4), 554–577. https://doi.org/10.1080/15205436.2019.1708403

Lee, B., & McLeod, D. M. (2020). Reconceptualizing cognitive media effects theory and research under the judged usability model. *Review of Communication Research, 8*, 17–50. https://www.rcommunicationr.org/index.php/rcr/article/view/65

Lee, C., & Niederdeppe, J. (2011). Genre-specific cultivation effects: Lagged associations between overall TV viewing, local TV news viewing, and fatalistic beliefs about cancer prevention. *Communication Research, 38*(6), 731–753. https://doi.org/10.1177/0093650210384990

Lee, E.-J. (2012). That's not the way it is: How user-generated comments on the news affect perceived media bias. *Journal of Computer-Mediated Communication, 18*(1), 32–45. https://doi.org/10.1111/j.1083-6101.2012.01597.x

Lee, E.J., & Tandoc, E. C., Jr. (2017). When news meets the audience: How audience feedback online affects news production and consumption. *Human Communication Research, 43*(4), 436–449. https://doi.org/10.1111/hcre.12123

Lee, G., Lee, J., & Kwon, S. (2011). Use of social-networking sites and subjective well-being: A study in South Korea. *Cyberpsychology, Behavior, and Social Networking, 14*(3), 151–155. https://doi.org/10.1089/cyber.2009.0382

Lee, J., & Xu, W. (2018). The more attacks, the more retweets: Trump's and Clinton's agenda setting on Twitter. *Public Relations Review, 44*(2), 201–213. https://doi.org/10.1016/j.pubrev.2017.10.002

Lee, K. M., Peng, W., & Park, N. (2009). Effects of computer/video games and beyond. In J. Bryant & M. B. Oliver (Eds.), *Media effects: Advances in theory and research* (3rd ed., pp. 551–566). Routledge.

Lee, M. J., Bichard, S. L., Irey, M. S., Walt, H. M., & Carlson, A. J. (2009). Television viewing and ethnic stereotypes: Do college students form stereotypical perceptions of ethnic groups as a result of heavy television consumption? *Howard Journal of Communications, 20*(1), 95–110. https://doi.org/10.1080/10646170802665281

Lee, N. Y. (2021). How agenda setting works: A dual path model and motivated reasoning. *Journalism, 22*(9), 2279–2296. https://doi.org/10.1177/1464884919851882

Lee, P. S. N., Leung, L., Lo, V., Xiong, C., & Wu, T. (2011). Internet communication versus face-to-face interaction in quality of life. *Social Indicators Research, 100,* 375–389. https://doi.org/10.1007/s11205-010-9618-3

Lee, S. Y., & Riffe, D. (2017). Who sets the corporate social responsibility agenda in the news media? Unveiling the agenda-building process of corporations and a monitoring group. *Public Relations Review, 43*(2), 293–305. https://doi.org/10.1016/j.pubrev.2017.02.007

Lehr, D. (2016, October 5). When "Birth of a Nation" sparked a riot in Boston. *Boston Globe.* https://www.bostonglobe.com/ideas/2016/10/05/when-birth-nation-sparked-riot-boston/bN9S0ltko6QyRIQiJcr9KJ/story.html

Leippe, M. R., & Elkin, R. A. (1987). When motives clash: Issue involvement and response involvement as determinants of persuasion. *Journal of Personality and Social Psychology, 52*(2), 269–278. https://doi.org/10.1037/0022-3514.52.2.269

Leitner, R. K. (1991). *Comparing the effects on reading comprehension of educational video, direct experience, and print* [Unpublished doctoral thesis]. University of San Francisco, California.

Lenhard, A., Smith, A., Anderson, M., Duggan, M., & Perrin, A. (2015, August). *Teens, technology & friendships.* Pew Research Center. https://www.pewresearch.org/internet/wp-content/uploads/sites/9/2015/08/Teens-and-Friendships-FINAL2.pdf

Lenhart, A., Purcell, K., Smith, A., & Zickuhr, K. (2010). *Social media and young adults: Social media and mobile internet use among teens and adults.* Pew Internet & American Life Project. https://www.pewresearch.org/internet/2010/02/03/social-media-and-young-adults/

Lerner, D., & Nelson, L. M. (1977). *Communication research: A half-century appraisal.* The University Press of Hawaii.

Levendusky, M. S. (2013). Why do partisan media polarize viewers? *American Journal of Political Science, 57*(3), 611–623. https://doi.org/10.1111/ajps.12008

Levin, G. (2017, June 27). Who's watching what: TV shows ranked by racial and ethnic groups. *USA Today.* https://www.usatoday.com/story/life/tv/2017/06/27/whos-watching-what-tv-shows-ranked-racial-and-ethnic-groups/103199848/

Lev-On, A. (2017). Uses and gratifications: Evidence for various media. In P. Rössler (Ed.), *International encyclopedia of media effects* (Vol. 4, pp. 2009–2017). Wiley-Blackwell. https://doi.org/10.1002/9781118783764.wbieme0046

Levy, A., & Stokes, R. (1987). Effects of a health promotion advertising campaign on sales of ready to eat cereals. *Public Health Reports, 102*(4), 398–403.

Levy, M. R., & Windahl, S. (1984). Audience activity and gratifications: A conceptual clarification and exploration. *Communication Research, 11,* 51–78. https://doi.org/10.1177/009365084011001003

Lewin, K. (1951). *Field theory in social science.* Harper.

Li, J., Erdt, M., Chen, L., Cao, Y., Lee, S.-Q., & Theng, Y.-L. (2018). The social effects of exergames on older adults: Systematic review and metric analysis. *Journal of Medical Internet Research, 20*(6), e10486. https://doi.org/10.2196/10486

Licoppe, C. (2004). "Connected" presence: The emergence of a new repertoire for managing social relationships in a changing communication technoscape. *Environment and Planning D: Society and Space, 22*(1), 135–156. https://doi.org/10.1068/d323t

Licoppe, C. (2017). From Mogi to Pokémon Go: Continuities and change in location aware collection games. *Mobile Media and Communication, 5*(1), 24–59. https://doi.org/10.1177/2050157916677862

Lieberman, D. A. (2001). Management of chronic pediatric diseases with interactive health games: Theory and research findings. *Journal of Ambulatory Care Management, 24,* 26–38. https://doi.org/10.1097/00004479-200101000-00004

Liebers, N., & Schramm, H. (2019). Parasocial interactions and relationships with media characters—

An inventory of 60 years of research. *Communication Research Trends, 38*(2), 1–31. https://www.researchgate.net/publication/333748971

Liebert, R. M., Sprafkin, J. N., & Davidson, E. S. (1982). *The early window: Effects of television on children and youth.* Pergamon.

Liggett, T. C. (2005). *Reading Rainbow* and the joy of reading. In J. Flood, S. B. Heath, & D. Lapp (Eds.), *Handbook of research on teaching literacy through the communicative and visual arts* (pp. 834–836). Lawrence Erlbaum Associates.

Lilischkis, S. (2003). *More yo-yos, pendulums and nomads: Trends of mobile and multi-location work in the information society* (Issue report no. 36). Socioeconomic Trends Assessment for the Digital Revolution. https://visionarymarketing.com/wp-content/uploads/2015/05/rapportstar2003-141119060039-conversion-gate01.pdf

Lin, C. A. (2003). An interactive communication technology adoption model. *Communication Theory, 13*(4), 345–365. https://doi.org/10.1111/j.1468-2885.2003.tb00296.x

Lin, C. A. (2009). Effects of the internet. In J. Bryant & M. B. Oliver (Eds.), *Media effects: Advances in theory and research* (3rd ed., pp. 567–591). Routledge.

Lin, C. A., & Xu, Z. (2017). Watching TV series with horror content: Audience attributes, motivations, involvement, and enjoyment. *Journal of Broadcasting & Electronic Media, 61*(4), 638–657. https://doi.org/10.1080/08838151.2017.1375503

Lin, C.-H., Lin, S.-L., & Wu, C.-P. (2009). The effects of parental monitoring and leisure boredom on adolescents' internet addiction. *Adolescence, 44,* 993–1004.

Lin, J.-H. T. (2017). Fear in virtual reality (VR): Fear elements, coping reactions, immediate and next-day fright responses toward a survival horror zombie virtual reality game. *Computers in Human Behavior, 72,* 350–361. https://doi.org/10.1016/j.chb.2017.02.057

Lin, J.-H. T., Wu, D.-Y., & Tao, C.-C. (2017). So scary, yet so fun: The role of self-efficacy in enjoyment of a virtual reality horror game. *New Media & Society, 20*(9), 3223–3242. https://doi.org/10.1177/1461444817744850

Lin, W.-H., Liu, C.-H., & Yi, C.-C. (2020) Exposure to sexually explicit media in early adolescence is related to risky sexual behavior in emerging adulthood. *PloS ONE, 15*(4), Article e0230242. https://doi.org/10.1371/journal.pone.0230242

Linebarger, D. L. (2000). *Summative evaluation of Between the Lions: A final report to WGBH Educational Foundation.* University of Kansas, Juniper Gardens Children's Project. https://citeseerx.ist.psu.edu/viewdoc/download?doi=10.1.1.587.6838&rep=rep1&type=pdf

Linebarger, D. L. (2001). *Summative evaluation of Dora the Explorer, Part 1: Learning outcomes.* Media & Technology Projects, ABCD Ventures.

Linebarger, D. L. (2006). *The* Between the Lions *American Indian literacy initiative research component: A report prepared for the United States Department of Education.* Annenberg School for Communication, University of Pennsylvania. https://www.earlycareresearch.org/sites/default/files/pdf/rc16566.pdf

Linebarger, D. L. (2015). *Super Why!* to the rescue: Can preschoolers learn early literacy skills from educational television? *International Journal for Cross-Disciplinary Subjects in Education, 6*(1), 2060–2069. https://doi.org/10.20533/ijcdse.2042.6364.2015.0286

Linebarger, D. L., & Piotrowski, J. T. (2010). Structures and strategies in children's educational television: The roles of program type and learning strategies in children's learning. *Child Development, 81*(5), 1582–1597. https://doi.org/10.1111/j.1467-8624.2010.01493.x

Linebarger, D. L., & Vaala, S. E. (2010). Screen media and language development in infants and toddlers: An ecological perspective. *Developmental Review, 30*(2), 176–202. https://doi.org/10.1016/j.dr.2010.03.006

Linebarger, D. L., & Walker, D. (2005). Infants' and toddlers' television viewing and language outcomes. *The American Behavioral Scientist, 48*(5), 624–645. https://doi.org/10.1177/0002764204271505

Ling, R. (2004). *The mobile connection: The cell phone's impact on society.* Morgan Kaufman.

Ling, R. (2005). The sociolinguistics of SMS: An analysis of SMS use by a random sample of Norwegians. In R. Ling & P. Pedersen (Eds.), *Mobile communications: Re-negotiation of the social sphere* (pp. 335–350). London: Springer-Verlag.

Ling, R. (2006, December). *The length of text messages and the use of predictive texting* [Paper presention]. Association of Internet Researchers Conference, Brisbane, Australia.

Ling, R. (2008). *New tech, new ties: How mobile communication is reshaping social cohesion.* MIT Press.

Ling, R., & Campbell, S. W. (2008). *The mobile communication research series: Reconstruction of space and time through mobile communication practices.* Transaction Publishers.

Ling, R., & Lai, C.-H. (2016). Microcoordination 2.0: Social coordination in the age of smartphones and messaging apps. *Journal of Communication, 66*(5), 834–856. https://doi.org/10.1111/jcom.12251

Ling, R., & Yttri, B. (2002). "Nobody sits at home and waits for the telephone to ring": Hyper-coordination via mobile phones in Norway. In J. Katz & M. Aakhus (Eds.), *Perpetual contact: Mobile communication, private talk, public performance* (pp. 139–169). Cambridge University Press.

Linz, D., Donnerstein, E., & Penrod, S. (1984). The effects of multiple exposures to filmed violence against women. *Journal of Communication, 34*(3), 130–147. https://doi.org/10.1111/j.1460-2466.1984.tb02180.x

Linz, D. G., Donnerstein, E., & Penrod, S. (1988). Effects of long-term exposure to violent and sexually degrading depictions of women. *Journal of Personality and Social Psychology, 55*(5), 758–768. https://doi.org/10.1037//0022-3514.55.5.758

Linz, D., & Malamuth, N. (1993). *Pornography.* Sage.

Lippe-McGraw, J. (2021). Your *Sports Illustrated* swimsuit 2021 cover models are Megan Thee Stallion, Naomi Osaka and Leyna Bloom. *Sports Illustrated.* https://swimsuit.si.com/swimlife/meet-your-cover-models-2021-mts-naomi-leyna

Lippman, J. R., Ward, L. M., & Seabrook, R. C. (2014). Isn't it romantic? Differential associations between romantic screen media genres and romantic beliefs. *Psychology of Popular Media Culture, 3*(3), 128–140. https://doi.org/10.1037/ppm0000034

Lippmann, W. (1922). *Public opinion.* Harcourt Brace.

Lister-Landman, K. M., Domoff, S. E., & Dubow, E. F. (2015). The role of compulsive texting in adolescents' academic functioning. *Psychology of Popular Media Culture, 6*(4), 311–325. https://doi.org/10.1037/ppm0000100

Liu, C., & Liu, Y. (2020). Media exposure and anxiety during COVID-19: The mediation effect of media vicarious traumatization. *International Journal of Environmental Research and Public Health, 17*(13), Article 4720. https://doi.org/10.3390/ijerph17134720

Liu, J., Li, C., Carcioppolo, N., & North, M. (2016). Do our Facebook friends make us feel worse? A study of social comparison and emotion. *Human Communication Research, 42*(4), 619–640. https://doi.org/10.1111/hcre.12090

Liu, X., & LaRose, R. (2008). Does using the internet make people more satisfied with their lives? The effects of the internet on college students' school life satisfaction. *Cyberpsychology & Behavior, 11*(3), 310–320. https://doi.org/10.1089/cpb.2007.0040

Long, N. E. (1958). The local community as an ecology of games. *American Journal of Sociology, 64*(3), 251–261. https://doi.org/10.1086/222468

Lotz, A. D. (2014). *The television will be revolutionized* (2nd ed.). NYU.

Love, S., & Kewley, J. (2005). Does personality affect people's attitudes towards mobile phone use in public places? In R. Ling & P. Pedersen (Eds.), *Mobile communications: Re-negotiation of the social sphere* (pp. 273–284). Springer-Verlag.

Lowery, S. A., & DeFleur, M. L. (1995). *Milestones in mass communication research: Media effects.* Longman.

Lowry, D. T., & Towles, D. E. (1989). Soap opera portrayals of sex, contraception, and sexually transmitted diseases. *Journal of Communication, 39*(2), 76–83. https://doi.org/10.1111/j.1460-2466.1989.tb01030.x

Lucas, K., & Sherry, J. L. (2004). Sex differences in video game play: A communication-based approach. *Communication Research, 31*(5), 499–523. https://doi.org/10.1177/0093650204267930

Luke, C. (1985). Television discourse processing: A schema theoretic approach. *Communication Education, 34*(2), 91–105. https://doi.org/10.1080/03634528509378591

Lull, R. B., & Bushman, B. J. (2016). Immersed in violence: Presence mediates the effect of 3D violent video gameplay on angry feelings. *Psychology of Popular Media Culture, 5*(2), 133–144. https://doi.org/10.1037/ppm0000062

Lundy, L. K., Ruth, A. M., & Park, T. D. (2008). Simply irresistible: Reality TV consumption patterns. *Communication Quarterly, 56*(2), 208–225. https://doi.org/10.1080/01463370802026828

Luttig, M. D., & Callaghan, T. H. (2016). Is President Obama's race chronically accessible? Racial priming in the 2012 presidential election. *Political Communication, 33*(4), 628–650. https://doi.org/10.1080/10584609.2016.1166168

Lyle, J., & Hoffman, H. R. (1972). Children's use of television and other media. In E. A. Rubinstein, G. A. Comstock, & J. P. Murray (Eds.), *Television and social behavior* (Vol. 4, pp. 129–256). U.S. Government Printing Office. https://www.ojp.gov/pdffiles1/Digitization/148978NCJRS.pdf

Lynch, T., & Martins, N. (2015). Nothing to fear? An analysis of college students' fear experiences with video games. *Journal of Broadcasting & Electronic Media, 59*(2), 298–317. https://doi.org/10.1080/08838151.2015.1029128

Macafee, T., McLaughlin, B., & Rodriguez, N. S. (2019). Winning on social media: Candidate social-mediated communication and voting during the 2016 US presidential election. *Social Media + Society, 5*(1). https://doi.org/10.1177/2056305119826130

Maccoby, N., & Farquhar, J. W. (1975). Communication for health: Unselling heart disease. *Journal of Communication, 25*(3), 114–126. https://doi.org/10.1111/j.1460-2466.1975.tb00613.x

MacKuen, M. (1981). Social communication and the mass policy agenda. In M. MacKuen & S. Coombs (Eds.), *More than news: Media power in public affairs* (pp. 19–144). Sage.

MacMonegle, A. J., Nonnemaker, J., Duke, J. C., Farrelly, M. C., Zhao, X., Delahanty, J. C., Smith, A. A., Rao, P., & Allen, J. A. (2018). Cost-effectiveness analysis of The Real Cost campaign's effect on smoking prevention. *American Journal of Preventive Medicine, 55*(3), 319–325. https://doi.org/10.1016/j.amepre.2018.05.006

Maddison, R., Foley, L., Mhurchu, C. N., Jiang, Y., Jull, A., Prapavessis, H., . . . & Rodgers, A. (2011). Effects of active video games on body composition: A randomized controlled trial. *The*

American Journal of Clinical Nutrition, 94(1), 156–163. https://doi.org/10.3945/ajcn.110.009142

Madigan, S., Ly, A., Rash, C. L., Ouytsel, J. V., & Temple, J. R. (2018). Prevalence of multiple forms of sexting behavior among youth: A systematic review and meta-analysis. *JAMA Pediatrics, 172*(4), 327–335. https://doi.org/10.1001/jamapediatrics.2017.5314

Madison, T. P., & Porter, L. V. (2015). The people we meet: Discriminating functions of parasocial interactions. *Imagination, Cognition and Personality, 35*(1), 47–71. https://doi.org/10.1177/0276236615574490

Maio, G., Haddock, G., Watt, S. E., & Hewstone, M. (2008). Implicit measures in applied contexts: An illustrative examination of anti-racism advertising. In R. E. Petty, R. H. Fazio, & P. Briñol (Eds.), *Attitudes: Insights from the new implicit measures* (pp. 327–357). Psychology Press.

Malamuth, N. M. (1981). Rape fantasies as a function of exposure to violent sexual stimuli. *Archives of Sexual Behavior, 10*(1), 33–47. https://doi.org/10.1007/BF01542673

Malamuth, N. M. (1993). Pornography's impact on male adolescents. *Adolescent Medicine: State of the Art Reviews, 4*(3), 563–576.

Malamuth, N. M. (1996). Sexually explicit media, gender differences, and evolutionary theory. *Journal of Communication, 46*(3), 8–31.

Malamuth, N. M., & Check, J. V. P. (1980). Penile tumescence and perceptual responses to rape as a function of victim's perceived reactions. *Journal of Applied Social Psychology, 10*(6), 528–547. https://doi.org/10.1111/j.1559-1816.1980.tb00730.x

Malamuth, N. M., & Check, J. V. P. (1983). Sexual arousal to rape depictions: Individual differences. *Journal of Abnormal Psychology, 92*(1), 55–67. https://doi.org/10.1037/0021-843X.92.1.55

Malamuth, N. M., & Donnerstein, E. (Eds.). (1984). *Pornography and sexual aggression.* Academic.

Malamuth, N. M., Heim, M., & Feshbach, S. (1980). Sexual responsiveness of college students to rape depictions: Inhibitory and disinhibitory effects. *Journal of Personality and Social Psychology, 38*(3), 399–408. https://doi.org/10.1037/0022-3514.38.3.399

Malamuth, N. M., & Impett, E. A. (2001). Research on sex in the media: What do we know about effects on children and adolescents? In D. Singer & J. Singer (Eds.), *Handbook of children and the media* (pp. 269–278). Sage.

Manago, A. M., Brown, G., Lawley, K. A., & Anderson, G. (2020). Adolescents' daily face-to-face and computer-mediated communication: Associations with autonomy and closeness to parents and friends. *Developmental Psychology, 56*(1), 153–164. https://doi.org/10.1037/dev0000851

Manago, A. M., Ward, L. M., Lemm, K. M., Reed, L., & Seabrook, R. (2015). Facebook involvement, objectified body consciousness, body shame, and sexual assertiveness in college women and men. *Sex Roles: A Journal of Research, 72*(1-2), 1–14. https://doi.org/10.1007/s11199-014-0441-1

Manis, F. R., Keating, D. P., & Morison, F. J. (1980). Developmental differences in the allocation of processing capacity. *Journal of Experimental Child Psychology, 29*(1), 156–169. https://doi.org/10.1016/0022-0965(80)90098-3

Mann, S., & Holdsworth, L. (2003). The psychological impact of teleworking: Stress, emotions and health. *New Technology, Work and Employment, 18*(3), 196–211. https://doi.org/10.1111/1468-005X.00121

Mansbridge, J. (2003). Rethinking representation. *The American Political Science Review, 97*(4), 515–528. http://www.jstor.org/stable/3593021

Manuoğlu, E., & Uysal, A. (2019). Motivation for different Facebook activities and well-being: A daily experience sampling study. *Psychology of Popular Media Culture, 9*(4), 456–464. https://doi.org/10.1037/ppm0000262

Mares, M.-L., & Acosta, E. E. (2008). Be kind to three-legged dogs: Children's literal interpretations of TV's moral lessons. *Media Psychology, 11*(3), 377–399. https://doi.org/10.1080/15213260802204355

Mares, M.-L., Bartsch, A., & Bonus, J. A. (2016). When meaning matters more: Media preferences across the adult life span. *Psychology and Aging, 31*(5), 513–531. https://doi.org/10.1037/pag0000098

Mares, M.-L., & Pan, Z. (2013). Effects of *Sesame Street*: A meta-analysis of children's learning in 15 countries. *Journal of Applied Developmental Psychology, 34*(3), 140–151. https://doi.org/10.1016/j.appdev.2013.01.001

Markey, P. M., & Ferguson, C. J. (2017). Internet gaming addiction: Disorder or moral panic?. *The American Journal of Psychiatry, 174*(3), 195–196. https://doi.org/10.1176/appi.ajp.2016.16121341

Markey, P. M., French, J. E., & Markey, C. N. (2015). Violent movies and severe acts of violence: Sensationalism versus science. *Human Communication Research, 41*(2), 155–173. https://doi.org/10.1111/hcre.12046

Markey, P. M., Markey, C. N., & French, J. E. (2015). Violent video games and real-world violence: Rhetoric versus data. *Psychology of Popular Media Culture, 4*(4), 277–295. https://doi.org/10.1037/ppm0000030

Marquis, L. (2016). Priming. In G. Mazzoleni (Ed.), *The international encyclopedia of political communication* (pp. 1236–1245). Wiley. https://doi.org/10.1002/9781118541555.wbiepc069

Martin, G. N. (2019). (Why) do you like scary movies? A review of the empirical research on psychological responses to horror films. *Frontiers in Psychology, 10*, Article 2298. https://doi.org/10.3389/fpsyg.2019.02298

Martinez, G. M., & Abma, J. C. (2020). Sexual activity and contraceptive use among teenagers aged 15–19 in the United States, 2015–2017. *NCHS Data Brief, 366*. https://www.cdc.gov/nchs/data/databriefs/db366-h.pdf

Martino, S. C., Collins, R. L., Kanouse, D. E., Elliott, M., & Berry, S. H. (2005). Social cognitive processes mediating the relationship between exposure to television's sexual content and adolescents' sexual behavior. *Journal of Personality and Social Psychology, 89*(6), 914–924. https://doi.org/10.1037/0022-3514.89.6.914

Martino, S. C., Setodji, C. M., Dunbar, M. S., & Shadel, W. G. (2019). Increased attention to the tobacco power wall predicts increased smoking risk among adolescents. *Addictive Behaviors, 88*, 1–5. https://doi.org/10.1016/j.addbeh.2018.07.024

Martins, N., & Jensen, R. E. (2014). The relationship between "Teen Mom" reality programming and teenagers' beliefs about teen parenthood. *Mass Communication and Society, 17*(6), 830–852. https://doi.org/10.1080/15205436.2013.851701

Marvin, C. (1988). *When old technologies were new: Thinking about electric communication in the late nineteenth century.* Oxford University Press.

Mastro, D. (2003). A social identity approach to understanding the impact of television messages. *Communication Monographs, 70*(2), 98–113. https://doi.org/10.1080/0363775032000133764

Mastro, D. (2009). Effects of racial and ethnic stereotyping. In J. Bryant & M. B. Oliver (Eds.), *Media effects: Advances in theory and research* (3rd ed., pp. 325–341). Routledge.

Mastro, D., & Behm-Morawitz, E. (2005). Latino representation on primetime television. *Journalism & Mass Communication Quarterly, 82*(1), 110–130. https://doi.org/10.1177/107769900508200108

Mastro, D., Behm-Morawitz, E., & Ortiz, M. (2007). The cultivation of social perceptions of Latinos: A mental models approach. *Media Psychology, 9*(2), 347–365. https://doi.org/10.1080/15213260701286106

Mastro, D., & Do, K. N. (2020). Stereotypes of Latina/o populations. In A. C. Billings & S. Parrott (Eds.), *Media stereotypes: From ageism to xenophobia* (pp. 113–131). Peter Lang.

Mastro, D., & Figueroa-Caballero, A. (2018). Measuring extremes: A quantitative content analysis of prime time TV depictions of body type. *Journal of Broadcasting & Electronic Media, 62*(2), 320–336. https://doi.org/10.1080/08838151.2018.1451853

Mastro, D., & Greenberg, B. S. (2000). The portrayal of racial minorities on primetime television. *Journal of Broadcasting & Electronic Media, 44*(4), 690–703. https://doi.org/10.1207/s15506878jobem4404_10

Mastro, D., & Kopacz, M. (2006). Media representations of race, prototypicality, and policy reasoning: An application of self-categorization theory. *Journal of Broadcasting & Electronic Media, 50*(2), 305–322. https://doi.org/10.1207/s15506878jobem5002_8

Mastro, D., & Stern, S. (2003). Representations of race in television commercials: A content analysis of primetime advertising. *Journal of Broadcasting & Electronic Media, 47*(4), 638–647. https://doi.org/10.1207/s15506878jobem4704_9

Mathai, J. (1983). An acute anxiety state in an adolescent precipitated by viewing a horror movie. *Journal of Adolescence, 6*(2), 197–200. https://doi.org/10.1016/S0140-1971(83)80027-X

Matheson, D. M., Killen, J. D., Wang, Y., Varady, A., & Robinson, T. N. (2004). Children's food consumption during television viewing. *American Journal of Clinical Nutrition, 79*(6), 1088–1094. https://doi.org/10.1093/ajcn/79.6.1088

Mayrhofer, M., & Matthes, J. (2018). Drinking at work: The portrayal of alcohol in workplace-related TV dramas. *Mass Communication & Society, 21*(1), 94–114. https://doi.org/10.1080/15205436.2017.1362441

Mayrhofer, M., & Matthes, J. (2021). Laughing about a health risk? Alcohol in comedy series and its connection to humor. *Psychology of Popular Media, 10*(1), 59–73. https://doi.org/10.1037/ppm0000267

Mazmanian, M., Orlikowski, W. J., & Yates, J. (2013). The autonomy paradox: The implications of mobile email devices for knowledge professionals. *Organization Science 24*(5), 1337–1357. https://doi.org/10.1287/orsc.1120.0806

Mazur, A. (1987). Putting radon on the public risk agenda. *Science, Technology and Human Values, 12*(3/4), 86–93. https://www.jstor.org/stable/689387

Mbilinyi, L. F., Zegree, J., Roffman, R. A., Walker, D., Neighbors, C., & Edleson, J. (2008). Development of a marketing campaign to recruit non-adjudicated and untreated abusive men for a brief telephone intervention. *Journal of Family Violence, 23*(5), 343–351. https://doi.org/10.1007/s10896-008-9157-8

McCain, J. L., & Campbell, W. K. (2018). Narcissism and social media use: A meta-analytic review. *Psychology of Popular Media Culture, 7*(3), 308–327. https://doi.org/10.1037/ppm0000137

McCaul, K. D., Jacobson, K., & Martinson, B. (1998). The effects of state-wide media campaign on mammography screening. *Journal of Applied Social Psychology, 28*(6), 504–515. https://doi.org/10.1111/j.1559-1816.1998.tb01716.x

McCombs, M. E. (1992). Explorers and surveyors: Expanding strategies for agenda-setting research. *Journalism Quarterly, 69*(4), 813–824. https://doi.org/10.1177/107769909206900402

McCombs, M. (1999). Personal involvement with issues on the public agenda. *International Journal* of *Public Opinion Research, 11*(2), 152–168. https://doi.org/10.1093/ijpor/11.2.152

McCombs, M. E. (2004). *Setting the agenda: The mass media and public opinion.* Blackwell.

McCombs, M. (2014). *Setting the agenda: The mass media and public opinion* (2nd ed.). Polity Press.

McCombs, M. E., Lopez-Escobar, E., & Llamas, J. P. (2000). Setting the agenda of attributes in the 1996 Spanish general election. *Journal of Communication, 50*(2), 77–92. https://doi.org/10.1111/j.1460-2466.2000.tb02842.x

McCombs, M. E., & Shaw, D. L. (1972). The agenda-setting function of the mass media. *Public Opinion Quarterly, 36*(2), 176–187. https://www.jstor.org/stable/2747787

McCombs, M. E., & Shaw, D. L. (1993). The evolution of agenda-setting research: Twenty-five years in the marketplace of ideas. *Journal of Communication, 43*(2), 58–67. https://doi.org/10.1111/j.1460-2466.1993.tb01262.x

McCombs, M. E., Shaw, D. L., & Weaver, D. H. (2014). New directions in agenda-setting theory and research. *Mass Communication and Society, 17*(6), 781–802. https://doi.org/10.1080/15205436.2014.964871

McCombs, M., & Stroud, N. J. (2014). Psychology of agenda-setting effects: Mapping the paths of information processing. *Review of Communication Research, 2*(1), 68–92. https://doi.org/10.12840/issn.2255-4165.2014.02.01.003

McDaniel, B. T., & Coyne, S. M. (2016). "Technoference": The interference of technology in couple relationships and implications for women's personal and relational well-being. *Psychology of Popular Media Culture, 5*(1), 85–98. https://doi.org/10.1037/ppm0000065

McDivitt, D. (2006). Video games in education. https://davidmcdivitt.wordpress.com/

McDivitt, J. A., Zimicki, S., & Hornick, R. C. (1997). Explaining the impact of a communication campaign to change vaccination knowledge and coverage in the Philippines. *Health Communication, 9*(2), 95–118. https://doi.org/10.1207/s15327027hc0902_1

McGhee, P. E., & Frueh, T. (1980). Television viewing and the learning of sex-role stereotypes. *Sex Roles, 6,* 179–188. https://doi.org/10.1007/BF00287341

McGraw, K. M., & Ling, C. (2003). Media priming of presidential and group evaluations. *Political Communication, 20*(1), 23–40. https://doi.org/10.1080/10584600390172338

McGregor, S. C., & Mourão, R. R. (2017). Second screening Donald Trump: Conditional indirect effects on political participation. *Journal of Broadcasting & Electronic Media, 61*(2), 264–290. https://doi.org/10.1080/08838151.2017.1309418

McGuire, W. J. (1985). Attitudes and attitude change. In G. Lindzey & E. Aronson (Eds.), *Handbook of social psychology* (3rd ed., Vol. 2, pp. 43–65). Sage.

McGuire, W. J. (1989). Theoretical foundations of campaigns. In R. E. Rice & C. K. Atkin (Eds.), *Public communication campaigns* (2nd ed., pp. 43–65). Sage.

McGuire, W. J. (2013). McGuire's classic input-output framework for constructing persuasive messages. In R. E. Rice & C. K. Atkin (Eds.), *Public communication campaigns* (4th ed., pp. 133–143). Sage.

McKee, A., Byron, P., Litsou, K., & Ingham, R. (2020). An interdisciplinary definition of pornography: Results from a Global Delphi Panel. *Archives of Sexual Behavior, 49,* 1085–1091. https://doi.org/10.1007/s10508-019-01554-4

McKenna, K. Y. A., Green, A. S., & Gleason, M. E. J. (2002). Relationship formation on the internet: What's the big attraction? *Journal of Social Issues, 58*(1), 9–31. https://doi.org/10.1111/1540-4560.00246

McLaughlin, B., & Rodriguez, N. S. (2017). Identifying with a stereotype: The divergent effects of exposure to homosexual television characters. *Journal of Homosexuality, 64*(9), 1196–1213. https://doi.org/10.1080/00918369.2016.1242335

McLeod, J. M., Bybee, C. R., & Durall, J. A. (1979). The 1976 presidential debates and the equivalence of informed political participation. *Communication Research, 6*(4), 463–487. https://doi.org/10.1177/009365027900600404

McLeod, J. M., Daily, C., Guo, Z., Eveland, W. P., Bayer, J., Yang, S., & Wang, H. (1996). Community integration, local media use, and democratic processes. *Communication Research, 23*(2), 179–209. https://doi.org/10.1177/009365096023002002

McLeod, J. M., Kosicki, G. M., & McLeod, D. M. (1994). The expanding boundaries of political communication effects. In J. Bryant & D. Zillmann (Eds.), *Media effects: Advances in theory and research* (pp. 123–162). Lawrence Erlbaum Associates.

McLeod, J. M., & McDonald, D. G. (1985). Beyond simple exposure: Media orientations and their impact on political processes. *Communication Research, 12*(1), 3–33. https://doi.org/10.1177/009365085012001001

McQuail, D. (1972). *Towards a sociology of mass communications.* Collier-Macmillan. (Original work published 1969).

McQuail, D. (1979). The uses and gratifications approach: Past, troubles, and future. *Massacommunicatie, 2,* 73–89.

McQuail, D. (2010). *McQuail's mass communication theory* (6th ed.). Sage.

McQuail, D., Blumler, J. G., & Brown, J. R. (1972). The television audience: A revised perspective. In D. McQuail (Ed.), *Sociology of mass communications* (pp. 135–165). Penguin.

McQuail, D., & Windahl, S. (1993). *Communication models for the study of mass communications* (2nd ed.). Longman.

Meadows, A. (2019, April 2). *Netflix users collectively stream 164.8 million hours of video using nearly 500 million GB of data every day.* Soda. https://www.soda.com/news/netflix-users-stream-164-million-hours-per-day/

Medin, D., Ross, B., & Markman, A. (2001). *Cognitive psychology* (3rd ed.). Harcourt.

Meier, E. P., & Gray, J. (2014). Facebook photo activity associated with image disturbance in adolescent girls. *Cyberpsychology, Behavior, and Social Networking, 17*(4), 199–206. http://doi.org/10.1089/cyber.2013.0305

Meier, M. R., & Medjesky, C. A. (2018). *The Office* was asking for it: "That's what she said" as a joke cycle that perpetuates rape culture. *Communication and Critical/Cultural Studies, 15*(1), 2–17. https://doi.org/10.1080/14791420.2017.1394578

Meirick, P. C., Nisbett, G. S., Harvell-Bowman, L. A., Harrison, K. J., Jefferson, M. D., Kim, T.-S., & Pfau, M. W. (2018). To tell the truth: Ad watch coverage, ad tone, and the accuracy of political advertising. *Political Communication, 35*(3), 450–469. https://doi.org/10.1080/10584609.2017.1414089

Melkman, R., Tversky, B., & Baratz, D. (1981). Developmental trends in the use of perpetual and conceptual attributes in grouping, clustering and retrieval. *Journal of Experimental Child Psychology, 31*(3), 470–486. https://doi.org/10.1016/0022-0965(81)90031-x

Ménard, A. D., Weaver, A., & Cabrera, C. (2019). "There are certain rules that one must abide by": Predictors of mortality in slasher films. *Sexuality & Culture, 23*, 621–640. https://doi.org/10.1007/s12119-018-09583-2

Mendelberg, T. (1997). Executing Hortons: Racial crime in the 1988 presidential campaign. *Public Opinion Quarterly, 61*(1), 134–157. https://www.jstor.org/stable/2749515

Mendelsohn, H. (1963). Socio-psychological perspectives on the mass media and public anxiety. *Journalism Quarterly, 40*(4), 511–516. https://doi.org/10.1177/107769906304000403

Mendelsohn, H. (1973). Some reasons why information campaigns can succeed. *Public Opinion Quarterly, 37*(1), 50–61. https://doi.org/10.1086/268059

Mentzoni, R. A., Brunborg, G. S., Molde, H., Myrseth, H., Skouverøe, K. J. M., Hetland, J., & Pallesen, S. (2011). Problematic video game use: Estimated prevalence and associations with mental and physical health. *Cyberpsychology, Behavior, and Social Networking, 14*(10), 591–596. https://doi.org/10.1089/cyber.2010.0260

Messenger, J. C., & Gschwind, L. (2016). Three generations of telework: New ICTs and the (r)evolution from home office to virtual office. *New Technology, Work and Employment, 31*(3), 195–208. https://doi.org/10.1111/ntwe.12073

Messing, S., Jabon, M., & Plaut, E. (2015). Bias in the flesh: Skin complexion and stereotype consistency in political campaigns. *Public Opinion Quar-*

terly, 80(1), 44–65. https://doi.org/10.1093/poq/nfv046

Meta. (n.d.). *Company info.* https://about.facebook.com/company-info/

Meta. (2022, July 27). *Meta reports second quarter 2022 results.* https://s21.q4cdn.com/399680738/files/doc_financials/2022/q2/Meta-06.30.2022-Exhibit-99.1-Final.pdf

Miller, J. M., & Krosnick, J. A. (2000). News media impact on the ingredients of presidential evaluations: Politically knowledgeable citizens are guided by a trusted source. *American Journal of Political Science, 44*(2), 301–315. https://doi.org/10.2307/2669312

Miller, M. M., Andsager, J. L. & Riechert, B. P. (1998). Framing the candidates in presidential primaries: Issues and images in press releases and news coverage. *Journalism & Mass Communication Quarterly, 75*(2), 312–324. https://doi.org/10.1177/107769909807500207

Miller, M. M., & Reese, S. D. (1982). Media dependency as interaction: Effects of exposure and reliance on political activity and efficacy. *Communication Research, 9*(2), 227–248. https://doi.org/10.1177/009365082009002003

Miller, R., Parsons, K., & Lifer, D. (2010). Students and social networking sites: The posting paradox. *Behaviour & Information Technology, 29*(4), 377–382. https://doi.org/10.1080/01449290903042491

Milosevic, T. (2015). Cyberbullying in US mainstream media. *Journal of Children and Media, 9*(4), 492–509. https://doi.org/10.1080/17482798.2015.1089300

Mintzes B. (2012). Advertising of prescription-only medicines to the public: Does evidence of benefit counterbalance harm? *Annual Review of Public Health, 33*, 259–277. https://doi.org/10.1146/annurev-publhealth-031811-124540

Mitchell, A. (2018, December 3) *Americans still prefer watching to reading the news—And mostly still through television.* Pew Research Center. https://www.journalism.org/2018/12/03/americans-still-prefer-watching-to-reading-the-news-and-mostly-still-through-television/

Mitchell, K. J., Ybarra, M. L., Korchmaros, J. D., & Kosciw, J. G. (2014). Accessing sexual health information online: use, motivations and consequences for youth with different sexual orientations. *Health Education Research, 29*(1), 147–157. https://doi.org/10.1093/her/cyt071

Möller, I. & Krahé, B. (2009). Exposure to violent video games and aggression in German adolescents: A longitudinal analysis. *Aggressive Behavior, 35*(1), 75–89. https://doi.org/10.1002/ab.20290

Monahan, J. L., Shtrulis, I., & Givens, S. B. (2005). Priming welfare queens and other stereotypes: The transference of media images into interpersonal contexts. *Communication Research Reports,*

22(3), 199–205. https://doi.org/10.1080/00036810500207014

Mongeau, P. A. (1998). Fear-arousing persuasive messages: A meta-analysis revisited. In M. Allen & R. Preiss (Eds.), *Persuasion: Advances through meta-analysis*. Sage.

Monk, A., Carroll, J., Parker, S., & Blythe, M. (2004). Why are mobile phones annoying? *Behavior and Information Technology, 23*(1), 33–41. https://doi.org/10.1080/01449290310001638496

Monk-Turner, E., Heiserman, M., Johnson, C., Cotton, V., & Jackson, M. (2010). The portrayal of racial minorities on prime time television: A replication of the Mastro and Greenberg study a decade later. *Studies in Popular Culture, 32*(2), 101–114. http://www.jstor.org/stable/23416158

Moore, D. L., Hausknecht, D., & Thamodaran, K. (1986). Time compression, response opportunity, and persuasion. *Journal of Consumer Research, 13*(1), 85–99. https://doi.org/10.1086/209049

Moravec, P. L., Minas, R. K., & Dennis, A. R. (2019). Fake news on social media: People believe what they want to believe when it makes no sense at all. *MIS Quarterly, 43*(4), 1343–1360. https://doi.org/10.25300/MISQ/2019/15505

Morgan, M. (1983). Symbolic victimization and real world fear. *Human Communication Research, 9*(2), 146–157. https://doi.org/10.1111/j.1468-2958.1983.tb00689.x

Morgan, M. (1990). International cultivation analysis. In N. Signorielli & M. Morgan (Eds.), *Cultivation analysis: New directions in media effects research* (pp. 225–248). Sage.

Morgan, M., & Shanahan, J. (1995). *Democracy tango: Television, adolescents, and authoritarian tensions in Argentina.* Hampton Press.

Morgan, M., Shanahan, J., & Signorielli, N. (2009). Growing up with television: Cultivation processes. In J. Bryant & M. B. Oliver (Eds.), *Media effects: Advances in theory and research* (3rd ed., pp. 34–49). Routledge.

Morgan, M., Shanahan, J., & Signorelli, N. (2017). Cultivation theory: Idea, topical fields, and methodology. In P. Rössler (Ed.), *International encyclopedia of media effects* (Vol. 1, pp. 307–320). Wiley-Blackwell. https://doi.org/10.1002/9781118783764.wbieme0039

Morgan, M., & Signorielli, N. (1990). Cultivation analysis: Conceptualization and methodology. In N. Signorielli & M. Morgan (Eds.), *Cultivation analysis: New directions in media effects research* (pp. 13–34). Sage.

Morison, P., & Gardner, H. (1978). Dragons and dinosaurs: The child's capacity to differentiate fantasy from reality. *Child Development, 49*(3), 642–648. https://doi.org/10.2307/1128231

Mosher, D. L., & Maclan, P. (1994). College men and women respond to X-rated videos intended for male or female audiences: Gender and sexual scripts. *The Journal of Sex Research, 31*(2), 99–113. https://doi.org/10.1080/00224499409551736

Motion Picture Association of America. (2018). *G is for golden: The MPAA film ratings at 50.* https://www.motionpictures.org/research-docs/g-is-for-golden-the-mpaa-film-ratings-at-50/

Mott, F L. (1944). Newspapers in presidential campaigns. *Public Opinion Quarterly, 8*(3), 348–367. https://doi.org/10.1086/265694

Moy, P., Tewksbury, D., & Rinke, E. M. (2016). Agenda-setting, priming, and framing. In K. B. Jensen, R. T. Craig, J. D. Pooley, & E. W. Rothenbuhler (Eds.), *The international encyclopedia of communication theory and philosophy.* John Wiley & Sons, Inc. https://doi.org/10.1002/9781118766804.wbiect266

Moy, P., Xenos, M. A., & Hess, V. K. (2006). Priming effect of late-night comedy. *International Journal of Public Opinion Research, 18*(2), 198–210. https://doi.org/10.1093/ijpor/edh092

Moyer-Gusé, E., Chung, A. H., & Jain, P. (2011). Identification with characters and discussion of taboo topics after exposure to an entertainment narrative about sexual health. *Journal of Communication, 61*(3), 387–406. https://doi.org/10.1111/j.1460-2466.2011.01551.x

Muddiman, A., Stroud, N. J., & McCombs, M. (2014). Media fragmentation, attribute agenda setting, and political opinions about Iraq. *Journal of Broadcasting & Electronic Media, 58*(2), 215–233. https://doi.org/10.1080/08838151.2014.906433

Mulliken, L., & Bryant, J. A. (1999, May). *Effects of curriculum-based television programming on behavioral assessments of flexible thinking and structured and unstructured prosocial play behaviors* [Poster presentation]. International Communication Association 49th annual conference, San Francisco, CA, United States.

Mundorf, N., D'Alessio, D., Allen, M., & Emmers-Sommer, T. M. (2007). Effects of sexually explicit media. In R. W. Preiss, B. M. Gayle, N. Burrell, M. Allen, & J. Bryant (Eds.), *Mass media effects research: Advances through meta-analysis* (pp. 181–198). Lawrence Erlbaum Associates.

Mundt, M., Ross, K., & Burnett, C. M. (2018). Scaling social movements through social media: The case of Black Lives Matter. *Social Media + Society, 4*(4). https://doi.org/10.1177/2056305118807911

Murnen, S. K., & Stockton, M. (1997). Gender and self-reported sexual arousal in response to sexual stimuli: A meta-analytic review. *Sex Roles, 37*(3-4), 135–153 https://doi.org/10.1023/A:1025639609402

Murray, E., Lo, B., Pollack, L., Donelan, K., & Lee, K. (2004). Direct-to-consumer advertising: Public perceptions of its effects on health behaviors, health care, and the doctor-patient relationship.

Journal of the American Board of Family Practice, 17(1), 6–18. https://doi.org/10.3122/jabfm.17.1.6

Murray, J. P., Liotti, M., Ingmundson, P. T., Mayberg, H. S., Pu, Y., Zamarripa, F., et al. (2006). Children's brain activations while viewing televised violence revealed by MRI. *Media Psychology, 8*(1), 25–37. https://doi.org/10.1207/S1532785XMEP0801_3

Mutz, D., & Reeves, B. (2005). The new videomalaise: Effects of televised incivility on political trust. *American Political Science Review, 99*(1), 1–15. https://10.1017/S0003055405051452

Myers, L. J., LeWitt, R. B., Gallo, R. E., & Maselli, N. M. (2017). Baby FaceTime: Can toddlers learn from online video chat?. *Developmental Science, 20*(4), Article e12430. https://doi.org/10.1111/desc.12430

Myrick, J. (2020). Media effects and health. In M. B. Oliver, A. A. Raney, & J. Bryant (Eds.), *Media effects: Advances in theory and research* (4th ed., pp. 308–323). Routledge.

Nabi, R. L. (2020). Media and emotion. In M. B. Oliver, A. A. Raney, & J. Bryant (Eds.), *Media effects: Advances in theory and research* (4th ed., pp. 163–178). Routledge.

Nabi, R. L., & Clark, S. (2008). Exploring the limits of social cognitive theory: Why negatively reinforced behaviors on TV may be modeled anyway. *Journal of Communication, 58*(3), 407–427. https://doi.org/10.1111/j.1460-2466.2008.00392.x

Nabi, R. L., Stitt, C. R., Halford, J., & Finnerty, K. L. (2006). Emotional and cognitive predictors of the enjoyment and reality-based and fictional television programming: An elaboration of the uses and gratifications perspective. *Media Psychology, 8*(4), 421–447. https://doi.org/10.1207/s1532785xmep0804_5

Naigles, L. R., & Mayeux, L., (2001). Television as incidental language teacher. In D. G. Singer & J. L. Singer (Eds.), *Handbook of children and the media* (pp. 135–152). Sage.

Naimi, T. S., Ross, C. S., Siegel, M. B., DeJong, W., & Jernigan, D. H. (2016). Amount of televised alcohol advertising exposure and the quantity of alcohol consumed by youth. *Journal of Studies on Alcohol and Drugs, 77*(5), 723–729. https://doi.org/10.15288/jsad.2016.77.723

Nathanson, A. I. (1999). Identifying and explaining the relationship between parental mediation and children's aggression. *Communication Research, 26*(2), 124–143. https://doi.org/10.1177/009365099026002002

National Commission on the Causes and Prevention of Violence. (1969). *To establish justice, to insure domestic tranquility: Final report of the National Commission on the Causes and Prevention of Violence.* U.S. Government Printing Office. http://www.eisenhowerfoundation.org/docs/National%20Violence%20Commission.pdf

National Institute of Mental Health. (1982a). *Television and behavior: Ten years of scientific progress and implications for the eighties. Vol. 1: Summary report* (DHHS Publication No. ADM 82–1195). U.S. Government Printing Office. https://files.eric.ed.gov/fulltext/ED222186.pdf

National Institute of Mental Health. (1982b). Television and behavior: Ten years of scientific progress and implications for the eighties. In E. Wartella & D. C. Whitney (Eds.), *Mass communication review yearbook,* (Vol. 4, pp. 23–35). Sage.

National Institute on Alcohol Abuse and Alcoholism. (2021, May). *Alcohol facts and statistics.* https://www.niaaa.nih.gov/publications/brochures-and-fact-sheets/alcohol-facts-and-statistics

Nedelman, M. (2019, July 5). *Netflix to cut back on smoking after* Stranger Things *criticism.* CNN. https://www.cnn.com/2019/07/05/health/netflix-smoking-stranger-things/index.html

Nee, R. C., & De Maio, M. (2019). A "presidential look"? An analysis of gender framing in 2016 persuasive memes of Hillary Clinton. *Journal of Broadcasting & Electronic Media, 63*(2), 304–321. https://doi.org/10.1080/08838151.2019.1620561

Nelson, T. E., Clawson, R. A., & Oxley, Z. M. (1997). Media framing of civil liberties conflict and its effects on tolerance. *American Political Science Review, 91*(3), 567–583. https://doi.org/10.2307/2952075

Nelson, T. E., & Oxley, Z. M. (1999). Issue framing effects on belief importance and opinion. *The Journal of Politics, 61*(4), 1040–1067. https://doi.org/10.2307/2647553

Nelson, T. E., Oxley, Z. M., & Clawson, R. A. (1997). Toward a psychology of framing effects. *Political Behavior, 19*(3), 221–246. https://doi.org/10.1023/A:1024834831093

Nerone, J. (1994). *Violence against the press: Policing the public sphere in U.S. history.* Oxford University Press.

Neuman, W. R., Guggenheim, L., Jang, S. M., & Bae, S. Y. (2014). The dynamics of public attention: Agenda-setting theory meets big data. *Journal of Communication, 64*(2), 193–214. https://doi.org/10.1111/jcom.12088

Newman, M. Z. (2010). New media, young audiences and discourses of attention: From *Sesame Street* to "snack culture." *Media, Culture, & Society, 32*(4), 581–596. https://doi.org/10.1177/0163443710367693

Newsweek. (1999, 31 May). Fat-phobia in the Fijis: TV-thin is in. https://www.newsweek.com/fat-phobia-fijis-tv-thin-166624

Nicksic, N. E., Brosnan, P. G., Chowdhury, N., Barnes, A. J., & Cobb, C. O. (2019). "Think it. Mix it. Vape it.": A content analysis on e-cigarette radio advertisements. *Substance Use & Misuse, 54*(8), 1355–1364. https://doi.org/10.1080/10826084.2019.1581219

Nielsen. (2010). *U.S. teen mobile report card: Calling yesterday, texting today, using apps tomorrow.* https://www.nielsen.com/insights/2010/u-s-teen-mobile-report-calling-yesterday-texting-today-using-apps-tomorrow/

Nielsen. (2019a). *It's in the bag: Black consumers' path to purchase.* https://www.nielsen.com/wp-content/uploads/sites/3/2019/09/2019-african-american-DIS-report.pdf

Nielsen. (2019b). *La oportunidad Latinx: Cultural currency and the consumer journey.* https://www.nielsen.com/wp-content/uploads/sites/3/2019/09/nielsen-2019-latinx-DIS-report.pdf

Nielsen. (2019c). *The Nielsen total audience report: Q3 2018.* https://www.nielsen.com/insights/2019/the-nielsen-total-audience-report-q3-2018/

Nielsen. (2020a). *Being seen on screen: Diverse representation & inclusion on TV.* https://www.nielsen.com/us/en/insights/report/2020/being-seen-on-screen-diverse-representation-and-inclusion-on-tv/

Nielsen. (2020b). *Invisible no more: The rise of Native American power in media.* https://www.nielsen.com/us/en/insights/infographic/2020/invisible-no-more-the-rise-of-native-american-power-in-media/

Nielsen. (2020c). *Shattering stereotypes: How today's women over 50 are defining what's possible on-screen, at work and at home.* https://www.nielsen.com/wp-content/uploads/sites/3/2021/03/Women-50DIS-March-2021.pdf

Nisbet, M. C., Brossard, D., & Kroepsch, A. (2003). Framing science—The stem cell controversy in an age of press/politics. *The Harvard International Journal of Press/Politics, 8*(2), 36–70. https://doi.org/10.1177/1081180X02251047

Nisbet, M. C., & Huge, M. (2006). Attention cycles and frames in the plant biotechnology debate: Managing power and participation through the press/policy connection. *The Harvard International Journal of Press/Politics, 11*(2), 3–40. https://doi.org/10.1177/1081180X06286701

Nitz, J. C., Kuys, S., Isles, R., & Fu, S. (2010). Is the Wii Fit a new-generation tool for improving balance, health and well-being? A pilot study. *Climacteric, 13*(5), 487–491. https://doi.org/10.3109/13697130903395193

Noar, S. M. (2017). The transtheoretical model and stages of change in health and risk messaging. In R. L. Parrott (Ed.), *Oxford research encyclopedia of communication.* Oxford University Press. https://doi.org/10.1093/acrefore/9780190228613.013.324

Noar, S. M., Myrick, J. G., Zeitany, A., Kelley, D., Morales-Pico, B., & Thomas, N. E. (2015). Testing a social cognitive theory-based model of indoor tanning: Implications for skin cancer prevention messages. *Health Communication, 30*(2), 164–174. https://doi.org/10.1080/10410236.2014.974125

Noelle-Neumann, E. (1973). Return to the concept of powerful mass media. *Studies of Broadcasting, 9,* 67–112.

Noelle-Neumann, E. (1984). *Spiral of silence: Public opinion—Our social skin.* University of Chicago Press.

Noelle-Neumann, E., & Mathes, R. (1987). The "event as event" and the "event as news": The significance of "consonance" for media effects research. *European Journal of Communication, 2*(4), 391–414. https://doi.org/10.1177/0267323187002004002

Nomikos, M., Opton, E., Averill, J., & Lazarus, R. (1968). Surprise versus suspense in the production of stress reaction. *Journal of Personality and Social Psychology, 8*(2, Pt.1), 204–208. https://doi.org/10.1037/h0025274

Norman, D. A. (1983). Some observations on mental models. In D. Genter & A. L. Stevens (Eds.), *Mental models* (pp. 299–324). Lawrence Erlbaum Associates.

Norris, P. (2000). *A virtuous circle: Political communications in a post-industrial democracy.* Cambridge University Press.

Northup, T., & Dillman Carpentier, F. (2015). Michael Jordan, Michael Vick, or Michael who?: Activating stereotypes in a complex media environment. *Howard Journal of Communications, 26*(2), 132–152. https://doi.org/10.1080/10646175.2015.1011354

NPD Group. (2022, January 22). NPD video games topline: 2021 highlights [Video]. YouTube. https://www.youtube.com/watch?v=e-OQqiTXueI&t=13s

Nunez-Smith, M., Wolf, E., Huang, H. M., Chen, P. G., Lee, L., Emanuel, E. J., & Gross, C. P. (2010). Media exposure and tobacco, illicit drugs, and alcohol use among children and adolescents: A systematic review. *Substance Abuse, 31*(3), 174–192. https://doi.org/10.1080/08897077.2010.495648

Nyhan, B., & Reifler, J. (2012). Misinformation and fact-checking: Research findings from social science. https://cpb-us-e1.wpmucdn.com/sites.dartmouth.edu/dist/5/2293/files/2021/03/Misinformation_and_Fact-checking.pdf

Nyhan, B., & Reifler, J. (2015). The effect of fact-checking on elites: A field experiment on U.S. state legislators. *American Journal of Political Science, 59*(3), 628–640. https://doi.org/10.1111/ajps.12162

O'Brien, F. M. (1968). *The story of* The Sun. Greenwood Press.

O'Connell, D. (2018). #Selfie: Instagram and the United States Congress. *Social Media + Society, 4*(4). https://doi.org/10.1177/2056305118813373

Oddone-Paolucci, E., Genuis, M., & Violato, C. (2000). A meta-analysis on the published research on the effects of pornography. In C. Violato, E. Oddone-Paolucci, & M. Genuis (Eds.),

The changing family and child development (pp. 48–59). Ashgate Publishing.

Oeldorf-Hirsch, A. (2018). The role of engagement in learning from active and incidental news exposure on social media. *Mass Communication and Society, 21*(2), 225–247. https://doi.org/10.1080/15205436.2017.1384022

Oeldorf-Hirsch, A., & Sundar, S. S. (2016). Sharing and technological motivations for online photo sharing. *Journal of Broadcasting & Electronic Media, 60*(4), 624–642. https://doi.org/10.1080/08838151.2016.1234478

Ogden, C. L., Flegal, K. M., Carroll, M. D., & Johnson, C. L. (2002). Prevalence and trends of overweight among US children and adolescents, 1999–2000. *Journal of the American Medical Association, 288*(14), 1728–1732. https://doi.org/10.1001/jama.288.14.1728

O'Hara, R. E., Gibbons, F. X., Gerrard, M., Li, Z., & Sargent, J. D. (2012). Greater exposure to sexual content in popular movies predicts earlier sexual debut and increased sexual risk taking. *Psychological Science, 23*(9), 984–993. https://doi.org/10.1177/0956797611435529

O'Keefe, D. J. (2009). Theories of persuasion. In R. L. Nabi & M. B. Oliver (Eds.), *The SAGE handbook of media processes and effects* (pp. 269–282). Sage.

O'Keefe, G. J. (1985). "Taking a bite out of crime": The impact of a public information campaign. *Communication Research, 12*(2), 147–178. https://doi.org/10.1177/009365085012002001

Oliver, D. (2021, April 22). "Rutherford Falls" ushers in era of Native American representation on TV: "We've been ready." *USA Today.* https://www.usatoday.com/story/entertainment/tv/2021/04/22/native-american-representation-tv-celebrated-rutherford-falls-peacock/7210034002/

Oliver, M. B., Ramasubramanian, S., & Kim, J. (2007). Media and racism. In D. R. Roskos-Ewoldsen & J. Monahan (Eds.), *Communication and social cognition: Theories and methods* (pp. 273–292). Lawrence Erlbaum Associates.

Oliver, M. B., & Sanders, M. (2004) The appeal of horror and suspense. In S. Prince (Ed.), *The horror film* (pp. 242–260). Rutgers University Press. https://doi.org/10.36019/9780813542577-014

Olson, C. K. (2004). Media violence research and youth violence data: Why do they conflict? *Academic Psychiatry, 28*(2), 144–150. https://doi.org/10.1176/appi.ap.28.2.144

Omori, K., Zhang, Y. B., Allen, M., Ota, H., & Imamura, M. (2011). Japanese college students' media exposure to sexually explicit materials, perceptions of women, and sexually permissive attitudes. *Journal of Intercultural Communication Research, 40*(2), 93–110. https://doi.org/10.1080/17475759.2011.581031

Ortiz, R. R., & Brooks, M. E. (2014). Getting what they deserve? Consequences of sexual expression by central characters in five popular television teen dramas in the United States. *Journal of Children and Media, 8*(1), 40–53. https://doi.org/10.1080/17482798.2014.863477

Ortiz, R. R., & Thompson, B. (2017). Content effects: Pornography and sexually explicit content. In P. Rössler (Ed.), *International encyclopedia of media effects* (Vol. 1, pp. 246–257). Wiley-Blackwell. https://doi.org/10.1002/9781118783764.wbieme0122

Orton, W. (1927). News and opinion. *The American Journal of Sociology, 33*(2), 80–93. https://doi.org/10.1086/214335

Osborn, D. K., & Endsley, R. C. (1971). Emotional reactions of young children to TV violence. *Child Development, 42*(1), 321–331. https://doi.org/10.2307/1127086

Owens, J., Maxim, R., McGuinn, M., Nobile, C., Msall, M., & Alario, A. (1999). Television viewing habits and sleep disturbance in school children. *Pediatrics, 104*(3), e27. https://doi.org/10.1542/peds.104.3.e27

Ozanne, M., Cueva Navas, A., Mattila, A. S., & Van Hoof, H. B. (2017). An investigation into Facebook "liking" behavior: An exploratory study. *Social Media + Society, 3*(2). https://doi.org/10.1177/2056305117706785

Paasonen, S., Light, B., & Jarrett, K. (2019). The dick pic: Harassment, curation, and desire. *Social Media + Society, 5*(2). https://doi.org/10.1177/2056305119826126

Padon, A. A., Maloney, E. K., & Cappella, J. N. (2017). Youth-targeted e-cigarette marketing in the US. *Tobacco Regulatory Science, 3*(1), 95–101. https://doi.org/10.18001/TRS.3.1.9

Padon, A. A., Rimal, R. N., DeJong, W., Siegel, M., & Jernigan, D. (2018). Assessing youth-appealing content in alcohol advertisements: Application of a content appealing to youth (CAY) index. *Health Communication, 33*(2), 164–173. https://doi.org/10.1080/10410236.2016.1250331

Padon, A. A., Rimal, R. N., Siegel, M., DeJong, W., Naimi, T. S., & JernFigan, D. H. (2018b). Alcohol brand use of youth-appealing advertising and consumption by youth and adults. *Journal of Public Health Research, 7*(1), 1269. https://doi.org/10.4081/jphr.2018.1269

Paik, H., & Comstock, G. (1994). The effects of television violence on antisocial behavior: A meta-analysis. *Communication Research, 21*(4), 516–546. https://doi.org/10.1177/009365094021004004

Pain, P., & Chen, G. M. (2019). The president is in: Public opinion and the presidential use of Twitter. *Social Media + Society, 5*(2). https://doi.org/10.1177/2056305119855143

Palazzolo, K. E., & Roberto, A. J. (2011). Media representations of intimate partner violence and punishment preferences: Exploring the role of attributions and emotions. *Journal of Applied Communication Research, 39*(1), 1–18. https://doi.org/10.1080/00909882.2010.536843

Palen, L., Salzman, M., & Youngs, E. (2001). Discovery and integration of mobile communications in everyday life. *Personal and Ubiquitous Computing, 5*, 108–122. https://doi.org/10.1007/s007790170014

Palmgreen, P. (1984). Uses and gratifications: A theoretical perspective. *Annals of the International Communication Association, 8*(1: Communication Yearbook 8), 20–55. https://doi.org/10.1080/23808985.1984.11678570

Palmgreen, P., & Rayburn, J. D., II. (1982). Gratifications sought and media exposure: An expectancy value model. *Communication Research, 9*(4), 561–580. https://doi.org/10.1177/009365082009004004

Palmgreen, P., Wenner, L. A., & Rosengren, K. E. (1985). Uses and gratifications research: The past ten years. In K. E. Rosengren, L. A. Wenner, & P. Palmgreen (Eds.), *Media gratifications research: Current perspectives* (pp. 11–37). Sage.

Pan, Z., & Kosicki, G. M. (1997). Priming and media impact on the evaluations of the president's performance. *Communication Research, 24*(1), 3–30. https://doi.org/10.1177/009365097024001001

Panova, T., & Carbonell, X. (2018). Is smartphone addiction really an addiction? *Journal of Behavioral Addiction, 7*(2), 252–239. https://doi.org/10.1556/2006.7.2018.49

Pantic, M. (2020). Gratifications of digital media: What motivates users to consume live blogs. *Media Practice and Education, 21*(2), 148–163. https://doi.org/10.1080/25741136.2019.1608104

Papacharissi, Z. (2009). Uses and gratifications. In D. W. Stacks & M. B. Salwen (Eds.), *An integrated approach to communication theory and research* (2nd ed., pp. 137–152). Routledge.

Papyrina, V. (2019). The trade-off between quantity and quality of information in gender responses to advertising. *Journal of Promotion Management, 25*(1), 1–19. https://doi.org/10.1080/10496491.2018.1427652

Paragas, F. (2003). *Being mobile with the mobile: Cellular telephony and renegotiations of public transport as public sphere* [Paper Presentation]. Front Stage/Back Stage: Mobile Communication and the Renegotiation of the Social Sphere Conference, Grimstad, Norway.

Park, C. S., & Kay, B. K. (2019). Mediating roles of news curation and news elaboration in the relationship between social media use for news and political knowledge. *Journal of Broadcasting & Electronic Media, 63*(3), 455–473. https://doi.org/10.1080/08838151.2019.1653070

Park, J., Felix, K., & Lee, G. (2007). Implicit attitudes toward Arab-Muslims and the moderating effect of social information. *Basic and Applied Social Psychology, 29*(1), 35–45. https://doi.org/10.1080/01973530701330942

Park, N., & Lee. S. (2014). College students' motivations for Facebook use and psychological outcomes. *Journal of Broadcasting & Electronic Media, 58*(4), 601–620. https://doi.org/10.1080/08838151.2014.966355

Park, R. E. (1941). News and the power of the press. *The American Journal of Sociology, 47*(1), 1–11. https://doi.org/10.1086/218818

Parke, R., Berkowitz, L., & Leyens, J. (1977). Some effects of violent and nonviolent movies on the behavior of juvenile delinquents. *Advances in Experimental Social Psychology, 10*, 135–172. https://doi.org/10.1016/S0065-2601(08)60356-1

Parmelee, J. H. (2014). The agenda-building function of political tweets. *New Media & Society, 16*(3), 434–450. https://doi.org/10.1177/1461444813487955

Parmelee, J. H., & Roman, N. (2019). Insta-politicos: Motivations for following political leaders on Instagram. *Social Media & Society.* https://doi.org/10.1177/2056305119837662

Parrott, S., Hoewe, J., Fan, M., & Huffman, K. (2019). Portrayals of immigrants and refugees in U.S. news media: Visual framing and its effect on emotions and attitudes. *Journal of Broadcasting & Electronic Media, 63*(4), 677–697. https://doi.org/10.1080/08838151.2019.1681860

Pasnik, S., Moorthy, S., Llorente, C., Hupert, N., Dominguez, X., & Silander, M. (2015). *Supporting parent-child experiences with PEG+CAT early math concepts: Report to the CPB-PBS Ready to Learn Initiative.* Education Development Center and SRI International. http://cct.edc.org/sites/cct.edc.org/files/ms-resources/edc-sri-rtl-peg-math-study-report-2015.pdf

Pavlov, I. P. (1927/1960). *Conditioned reflexes* (G. V. Anrep, Trans.). Oxford University Press.

Pearce, L. J., & Field, A. P. (2016). The impact of "scary" TV and film on children's internalizing emotions: A meta-analysis. *Human Communication Research, 42*(1), 98–121. https://doi.org/10.1111/hcre.12069

Pearlin, L. I. (1959). Social and personal stress and escape television viewing. *Public Opinion Quarterly, 23*(2), 255–259. https://doi.org/10.1086/266870

Pechmann, C. (2001). A comparison of health communication models: Risk learning versus stereotype priming. *Media Psychology, 3*(2), 189–210. https://doi.org/10.1207/S1532785XMEP0302_04

Peck, E. Y. (1999). *Gender differences in film-induced fear as a function of type of emotion measure and stimulus content: A meta-analysis and a laboratory study* [Unpublished doctoral dissertation]. University of Wisconsin-Madison.

Peffley, M., Shields, T., & Williams, B. (1996). The intersection of race and crime in television news stories: An experimental study. *Political Communication, 13*(3), 309–327. https://doi.org/10.1080/10584609.1996.9963120

Pempek, T. A., Kirkorian, H. L., Anderson, D. R., Lund, A. F., Richards, J. E., & Stevens, M. (2010). Video comprehensibility and attention in very young children. *Developmental Psychology, 46*(5), 1283–1293. https://doi.org/10.1037/a0020614

Peña, J. F., Hancock, J. T., & Merola, N. A. (2009). The priming effects of avatars in virtual settings. *Communication Research, 36*(6), 838–856. https://doi.org/10.1177/0093650209346802

Peña, J. F., McGlone, M. S., & Sanchez, J. (2012). The cowl makes the monk: How avatar appearance and role labels affect cognition in virtual worlds. *Journal For Virtual Worlds Research, 5*(3), 1–16. https://doi.org/10.4101/jvwr.v5i3.6280

Peng, W., Lee, M., & Heeter, C. (2010). The effects of a serious game on role-taking and willingness to help. *Journal of Communication, 60*(4), 723–742. https://doi.org/10.1111/j.1460-2466.2010.01511.x

Peng, W., Liu, M., & Mou, Y. (2008). Do aggressive people play violent computer games in a more aggressive way? Individual difference and idiosyncratic game playing experience. *Cyberpsychology & Behavior, 11*(2), 157–161. https://doi.org/10.1089/cpb.2007.0026

Penn, W. (1938). *Some account of the province of Pennsylvania.* In J. R. Soderlund (Ed.), *William Penn and the founding of Pennsylvania, 1680–1684: A documentary history* (pp. 58–66). University of Pennsylvania Press. (Original work published 1681)

Perks, L. G., & Turner, J. S. (2019). Podcasts and productivity: A qualitative uses and gratifications study. *Mass Communication and Society, 22*(1), 96–116. https://doi.org/10.1080/15205436.2018.1490434

Perks, L. G., Turner, J. S., & Tollison, A. C. (2019). Podcast uses and gratifications scale development. *Journal of Broadcasting & Electronic Media, 63*(4), 617–634. https://doi.org/10.1080/08838151.2019.1688817

Pernicious literature. (1847, January). *United States Catholic Magazine and Monthly Review, 4,* 46–48.

Perry, D. K. (1996). *Theory & research in mass communication: Contexts and consequences.* Lawrence Erlbaum Associates.

Perse, E. M., & Rubin, A. M. (1990). Chronic loneliness and television use. *Journal of Broadcasting & Electronic Media, 34*(1), 37–53. https://doi.org/10.1080/08838159009386724

Peruta, A. & Powers, J. (2017). Look who's talking to our kids: Representations of race and gender in TV commercials on Nickelodeon. *International Journal of Communication, 11,* 1133–1148. https://ijoc.org/index.php/ijoc/article/view/5113/1962

Peter, J., & Valkenburg, P. M. (2006). Adolescents' exposure to sexually explicit online material and recreational attitudes toward sex. *Journal of Communication, 56*(4), 639–660. https://doi.org/10.1111/j.1460-2466.2006.00313.x

Peter, J., & Valkenburg, P. M. (2009). Adolescents' exposure to sexually explicit internet material and notions of women as sex objects: Assessing causality and underlying processes. *Journal of Communication, 59*(3), 407–433. https://doi.org/10.1111/j.1460-2466.2009.01422.x

Peter, J., & Valkenburg, P. M. (2011). The use of sexually explicit internet material and its antecedents: a longitudinal comparison of adolescents and adults. *Archives of sexual behavior, 40*(5), 1015–1025. https://doi.org/10.1007/s10508-010-9644-x

Peter, J., & Valkenburg, P. M. (2016). Adolescents and pornography: A review of 20 years of research. *Journal of Sex Research, 53*(4–5), 509–531. https://doi.org/10.1080/00224499.2016.1143441

Peters, P., & den Dulk, L. (2003). Cross-cultural differences in managers' support for home-based telework: A theoretical elaboration. *International Journal of Cross-Cultural Management, 3*(3), 329–346. https://doi.org/10.1177/1470595803003003005

Peterson, R. C., & Thurstone, L. L. (1933). *Motion pictures and the social attitudes of children.* Macmillan.

Peterson, R. T. (2007). Consumer magazine advertisement portrayal of models race in the US: An assessment. *Journal of Marketing Communications, 13*(3), 199–211. https://doi.org/10.1080/13527260601086488

Petrovic-Dzerdz, M. (2019). Gamifying online tests to promote retrieval-based learning. *The International Review of Research in Open and Distributed Learning, 20*(2), 25–42. https://doi.org/10.19173/irrodl.v20i2.3812

Petty, R. E., Briñol, P., & Priester, J. R. (2009). Mass media attitude change: Implications of the elaboration likelihood model of persuasion. In J. Bryant & M. B. Oliver (Eds.), *Media effects: Advances in theory and research* (3rd ed., pp. 125–164). Routledge.

Petty, R. E., Briñol, P., & Tormala, Z. L. (2002). Thought confidence as a determinant of persuasion: The self-validation hypothesis. *Journal of Personality and Social Psychology, 82*(5), 722–741. https://doi.org/10.1037/0022-3514.82.5.722

Petty, R. E., & Cacioppo, J. T. (1979). Issue-involvement can increase or decrease persuasion by enhancing message-relevant cognitive responses. *Journal of Personality and Social Psychology, 37*(10), 1915–1926. https://doi.org/10.1037/0022-3514.37.10.1915

Petty, R. E., & Cacioppo, J. T. (1981). *Attitudes and persuasion: Classic and contemporary approaches.* W. C. Brown.

Petty, R. E., & Cacioppo, J. T. (1986a). *Communication and persuasion: Central and peripheral routes to attitude change.* Springer/Verlag.

Petty, R. E., & Cacioppo, J. T. (1986b). The elaboration likelihood model of persuasion. In L. Berkowitz (Ed.), *Advances in experimental social psychology* (Vol. 19, pp. 123–205). Academic Press.

Petty, R. E., Cacioppo, J. T., & Goldman, R. (1981). Personal involvement as a determinant of argument-based persuasion. *Journal of Personality and Social Psychology, 41*(5), 847–855. https://doi.org/10.1037/0022-3514.41.5.847

Petty, R. E., Cacioppo, J. T., & Haugtvedt, C. (1992). Involvement and persuasion: An appreciative look at the Sherifs' contribution to the study of self-relevance and attitude change. In D. Granberg & G. Sarup (Eds.), *Social judgment and intergroup relations: Essays in honor of Muzafer Sherif* (pp. 147–174). Springer/Verlag.

Petty, R. E., Cacioppo, J. T., & Heesacker, M. (1981). Effects of rhetorical questions on persuasion: A cognitive response analysis. *Journal of Personality and Social Psychology, 40*(3), 432–440. https://doi.org/10.1037/0022-3514.40.3.432

Petty, R. E., Fazio, R. H., & Briñol, P. (Eds.). (2008). *Attitudes: Insights from the new implicit measures.* Psychology Press.

Petty, R. E., Gleicher, F. H., & Jarvis, B. (1993). Persuasion theory and AIDS prevention. In J. B. Pryor & G. Reeder (Eds.), *The social psychology of HIV infection* (pp. 155–182). Lawrence Erlbaum Associates.

Petty, R. E., Ostrom, T. M., & Brock, T. C. (Eds.). (1981). *Cognitive responses in persuasion.* Lawrence Erlbaum Associates.

Petty, R. E., & Priester, J. R. (1994). Mass media attitude change: Implications of the elaboration likelihood model of persuasion. In J. Bryant & D. Zillmann (Eds.), *Media effects: Advances in theory and research* (pp. 91–122). Lawrence Erlbaum Associates.

Petty, R. E., Schumann, D., Richman, S., & Strathman, A. (1993). Positive mood and persuasion: Different roles for affect under high and low elaboration conditions. *Journal of Personality and Social Psychology, 64*(1), 5–20. https://doi.org/10.1037/0022-3514.64.1.5

Petty, R. E., & Wegener, D. T. (1998). Matching versus mismatching attitude functions: Implications for the scrutiny of persuasive messages. *Personality and Social Psychology Bulletin, 24*(3), 227–240. https://doi.org/10.1177/0146167298243001

Petty, R. E., & Wegener, D. T. (1999). The elaboration likelihood model: Current status and controversies. In S. Chaiken & Y. Trope (Eds.), *Dual process theories in social psychology* (pp. 41–72). Guilford Press.

Petty, R. E., Wheeler, S. C., & Bizer, G. Y. (2000). Attitude functions and persuasion: An elaboration likelihood approach to matched versus mismatched messages. In G. R. Maio & J. M. Olson (Eds.), *Why we evaluate: Functions of attitudes* (pp. 133–162). Lawrence Erlbaum Associates.

Pew Research Center. (2015, April). *U.S. smartphone use in 2015.* https://www.pewresearch.org/internet/wp-content/uploads/sites/9/2015/03/PI_Smartphones_0401151.pdf

Pew Research Center. (2021a, April 7). *Internet/broadband fact sheet.* https://www.pewresearch.org/internet/fact-sheet/internet-broadband/#who-uses-the-internet

Pew Research Center. (2021b, April 7). *Mobile fact sheet.* https://www.pewresearch.org/internet/fact-sheet/mobile/

Pew Research Center. (2021c, April 7). *Social media fact sheet.* https://www.pewresearch.org/internet/fact-sheet/social-media/

Pfau, M., & Louden, A. (1994). Effectiveness of adwatch formats in deflecting political attack ads. *Communication Research, 21*(3), 325–341. https://doi.org/10.1177/009365094021003005

Phua, J., Jin, S. V., & Kim, J. (J.). (2017). Uses and gratifications of social networking sites for bridging and bonding social capital: A comparison of Facebook, Twitter, Instagram, and Snapchat. *Computers in Human Behavior, 72,* 115–122. https://doi.org/10.1016/j.chb.2017.02.041

Pickard, V. (2016). Media failures in the age of Trump. *The Political Economy of Communication, 4,* 118–122.

Pierce, J. P., & Gilpin, E. A. (2001). News media coverage of smoking and health is associated with changes in population rates of smoking cessation but not initiation. *Tobacco Control, 10*(2), 145–153. https://doi.org/10.1136/tc.10.2.145

Pingree, R. J., & Stoycheff, E. (2013). Differentiating cueing from reasoning in agenda-setting effects. *Journal of Communication, 63*(5), 852–872. https://doi.org/10.1111/jcom.12051

Pingree, S. (1983). Children's cognitive processing in constructing social reality. *Journalism Quarterly, 60*(3), 415–422. https://doi.org/10.1177/107769908306000304

Pingree, S., & Hawkins, R. P. (1981). U.S. programs on Australian television: The cultivation effect. *Journal of Communication, 31*(1), 97–105. https://doi.org/10.1111/j.1460-2466.1981.tb01209.x

Pinker, S. (2011). *The better angels of our nature: Why violence has declined.* Viking.

Piotrowski, J. T. (2014). Participatory cues and program familiarity predict young children's learning from educational television. *Media Psychology, 17*(3), 311–331. https://doi.org/10.1080/15213269.2014.932288

Piotrowski, J. T., & Fikkers, K. M. (2020). Media violence and aggression. In M. B. Oliver, A. A. Raney, & J. Bryant (Eds.), *Media effects: Advances in theory and research* (4th ed., pp. 211–226). Routledge.

Piper Sandler. (2021). *Taking stock with teens.* https://piper2.bluematrix.com/docs/pdf/3bad99c6-e44a-4424-8fb1-0e3adfcbd1d4.pdf?utm_source=newsletter&utm_medium=email&utm_campaign=newsletter_axiosam&stream=top

Pitoyo, M. D. (2019). Gamification based assessment: A test anxiety reduction through game elements in Quizizz platform. *International Journal of Education & Teaching, 6*(3), 456–471. https://iojet.org/index.php/IOJET/article/view/626

Ploughman, P. (1984). *The creation of newsworthy events: An analysis of newspaper coverage of the man-made disaster at Love Canal* (Unpublished doctoral dissertation). State University of New York at Buffalo.

Poe, E. A. (1902). Richard Adams Locke. In J. A. Harrison (Ed.), *The complete works of Edgar Allan Poe* (Vol. 15, pp. 126–137). Thomas Y. Crowell.

Poindexter, P. M., & Stroman, C. (1981). Blacks and television: A review of the research literature. *Journal of Broadcasting, 25*(2), 103–122. https://doi.org/10.1080/08838158109386436

Polansky, J. R., Driscoll, D., & Glantz, S. A. (2020). *Smoking in top-grossing US movies: 2019.* UCSF Center for Tobacco Control Research and Education. https://escholarship.org/uc/item/86q9w25v

Polanksy, J. R., & Glantz, S. A. (2020). *What is Hollywood hiding? How the entertainment industry downplays the danger to kids from smoking on screen.* UCSF Center for Tobacco Control Research and Education. https://escholarship.org/uc/item/3pw661mg

Poli, R. (2017). Internet addiction update: Diagnostic criteria, assessment and prevalence. *Neuropsychiatry, 7*(1), 4–8. https://doi.org/10.4172/Neuropsychiatry.1000171

Pollard, P. (1995). Pornography and sexual aggression. *Current Psychology: Developmental, Learning, Personality, Social, 14*(3), 200–221. https://doi.org/10.1007/BF02686908

Pool, I. De S. (Ed.). (1977). *The social impact of the telephone.* MIT Press.

Pornhub. (2019, December 11). *The 2019 year in review.* https://www.pornhub.com/insights/2019-year-in-review

Pornhub. (2021, April 8). *Pornhub tech review.* https://www.pornhub.com/insights/tech-review

Porpora, D. V., Nikolaev, A., & Hagemann, J. (2010). Abuse, torture, frames and the *Washington Post. Journal of Communication, 60*(2), 254–270. https://doi.org/10.1111/j.1460-2466.2010.01481.x

Postman, N. (1985). *Amusing ourselves to death.* Penguin.

Potard, C., Henry, A., Boudoukha, A.-H., Courtois, R., Laurent, A., & Lignier, B. (2019). Video game players' personality traits: An exploratory cluster approach to identifying gaming preferences. *Psychology of Popular Media, 9*(4), 499–512. https://doi.org/10.1037/ppm0000245

Potter, W. J. (1993). Cultivation theory and research: A conceptual critique. *Human Communication Research, 19*(4), 564–601. https://doi.org/10.1111/j.1468-2958.1993.tb00313.x

Potter, W. J. (1994). Cultivation theory and research: A methodological critique. *Journalism Mono-graphs, 147,* 1–34. https://www.aejmc.org/home/wp-content/uploads/2012/09/W.-James-Potter.Cultivation-Theory-and-Research.October-1994.pdf

Potter, W. J., & Warren, R. (1996). Considering policies to protect children from TV violence. *Journal of Communication, 46*(4), 116–138. https://doi.org/10.1111/j.1460-2466.1996.tb01509.x

Powell, J. A., Low, P., Griffiths, F. E., & Thorogood, J. (2005). A critical analysis of the literature on the internet and consumer health information. *Journal of Telemedicine and Telecare, 11* (Supplement 1), 41–43. https://doi.org/10.1258/1357633054461642

Powell, T. E., Boomgaarden, H. G., De Swert, K., & de Vreese, C. H. (2018). Video killed the news article? Comparing the multimodal framing effects in news videos and articles. *Journal of Broadcasting & Media, 62*(4), 578–596. https://doi.org/10.1080/08838151.2018.1483935

Power, J., Murphy, S., & Coover, G. (1996). Priming prejudice: How stereotypes and counterstereotypes influence attribution of responsibility and credibility among ingroups and outgroups. *Human Communication Research, 23*(1), 36–58. https://doi.org/10.1111/j.1468-2958.1996.tb00386.x

Prensky, M. (2001). *Digital game-based learning.* Paragon House.

Prescott, A. T., Sargent, J. D., & Hull, J. G. (2018). Metaanalysis of the relationship between violent video game play and physical aggression over time. *Proceedings of the National Academy of Sciences of the United States of America, 115*(40), 9882–9888. https://doi.org/10.1073/pnas.1611617114

Preston, M. I. (1941). Children's reactions to movie horrors and radio crime. *Journal of Pediatrics, 19,* 147–168. https://doi.org/10.1016/S0022-3476(41)80059-6

Price, V., & Tewksbury, D. (1997). News values and public opinion: A theoretical account of media priming and framing. In G. A. Barnett & F. J. Boster (Eds.), *Progress in communication sciences: Advances in persuasion* (Vol. 13, pp. 173–212). Ablex.

Price, V., Tewksbury, D., & Powers, E. (1997). Switching trains of thought: The impact of news frames on readers' cognitive responses. *Communication Research, 24*(5), 481–506. https://doi.org/10.1177/009365097024005002

Prieler, M. (2016). Gender stereotypes in Spanish- and English-language television advertisements in the United States. *Mass Communication & Society, 19*(3), 275–300. https://doi.org/10.1080/15205436.2015.1111386

Prince, D. L., Grace, C., Linebarger, D. L., Atkinson, R., & Huffman, J. D. (2001). Between the Lions *Mississippi literacy initiative: A final report to Mississippi Educational Television.* The Early Childhood Institute, Mississippi State University.

Prior, M. (2007). *Post-broadcast democracy: How media choice increases inequality in political involvement and polarizes elections.* Cambridge University Press.

Prochaska, J. O. (1994). Strong and weak principles for progressing from precontemplation to action on the basis of twelve problem behaviors. *Health Psychology, 13*(1), 47–51. https://doi.org/10.1037//0278-6133.13.1.47

Prochaska, J. O., Redding, C. A., & Evers, K. E. (2002). The transtheoretical model and stages of change. In K. Glanz, B. K. Rimmer, & F. M. Lewis (Eds.), *Health behavior and health education: Theory, research, and practice* (3rd ed., pp. 99–120). Jossey-Bass.

Prot, S., Anderson, C. A., Barlett, C. P., Coyne, S. M., & Saleem, M. (2017). Content effects: Violence in the media. In P. Rössler (Ed.), *International encyclopedia of media effects* (Vol. 1, pp. 257–276). Wiley-Blackwell. https://doi.org/10.1002/9781118783764.wbieme0121

Przybylski, A. K., Weinstein, N., & Murayama, K. (2017). Internet gaming disorder: Investigating the clinical relevance of a new phenomenon. *The American Journal of Psychiatry, 174*(3), 230–236. https://doi.org/10.1176/appi.ajp.2016.16020224

Pucci, L. G., Joseph, H. M., Jr., & Siegel, M. (1998). Outdoor tobacco advertising in six Boston neighborhoods: Evaluating youth exposure. *American Journal of Preventive Medicine, 15*(2), 155–159. https://doi.org/10.1016/s0749-3797(98)00034-8

Puckett, J. M., Petty, R. E., Cacioppo, J. T., & Fischer, D. L. (1983). The relative impact of age and attractiveness stereotypes on persuasion. *Journal of Gerontology, 38*(3), 340–343. https://doi.org/10.1093/geronj/38.3.340

Purvanova, R. K. (2014). Face-to-face versus virtual teams: What have we really learned? *The Psychologist-Manager Journal, 17*(1), 2–29. https://doi.org/10.1037/mgr0000009

Putnam, R. D. (2000). *Bowling alone.* Simon & Schuster.

Quackenbush, D. M., Strassberg, D. S., & Turner, C. W. (1995). Gender effects of romantic themes in erotica. *Archives of Sexual Behavior, 24*(1), 21–35. https://doi.org/10.1007/BF01541986

Quan-Haase, A., & Young, A. L. (2010). Uses and gratifications of social media: A comparison of Facebook and instant messaging. *Bulletin of Science, Technology & Society, 30*(5), 350–361. https://doi.org/10.1177/0270467610380009

Quick, B. L. (2009). The effects of viewing *Grey's Anatomy* on perceptions of doctors and patient satisfaction. *Journal of Broadcasting and Electronic Media, 53*(1), 38–55. https://doi.org/10.1080/08838150802643563

Quinn, D. (2019, September 2). Harry Potter books removed from Nashville school library on the advice of exorcists. *People.* https://people.com/books/harry-potter-books-removed-from-school-exorcists-advice/?fbclid=IwAR1nryWZYTLWcC4nWWf_m-QX5CgcEtGcKLIoiCwyBQUZs9sCSqiFFhh8Qzc

Rachman, S. (1966). Sexual fetishism: An experimental analogue. *Psychological Record, 16*(3), 293–296.

Rachman, S., & Hodgson, R. J. (1968). Experimentally-induced "sexual fetishism": Replication and development. *Psychological Record, 18*, 25–27. https://doi.org/10.1007/BF03393736

Rada, J. A., & Wulfemeyer, K. T. (2005). Color coded: Racial descriptors in television coverage of intercollegiate sports. *Journal of Broadcasting & Electronic Media, 49*(1), 65–85. https://doi.org/10.1207/s15506878jobem4901_5

Radicati Group. (2019). *Email statistics report, 2019–2023.* https://www.radicati.com/wp/wp-content/uploads/2018/12/Email-Statistics-Report-2019-2023-Executive-Summary.pdf

Ragas, M. W., & Tran, H. L. (2019). Peeling back the onion: Formative agenda building in business journalism. *International Journal of Communication, 13*, 4465–4486. https://ijoc.org/index.php/ijoc/article/view/11220

Ragas, M. W., Tran, H. L., & Martin, J. A. (2014). Media-induced or search-driven? A study of online agenda-setting effects during the BP oil disaster. *Journalism Studies, 15*(1), 48–63. https://doi.org/10.1080/1461670X.2013.793509

Rainie L., & Wellman, B. (2012). *Networked: The new social operating system.* MIT Press.

Rainie, L., & Zickuhr, K. (2015, August). Americans' views on mobile etiquette. Pew Research Center.

Ramasubramanian, S. (2010). Television viewing, racial attitudes, and policy preferences: Exploring the role of social identity and intergroup emotions in influencing support for affirmative action. *Communication Monographs, 77*(1), 102–120. https://doi.org/10.1080/03637750903514300

Ramasubramanian, S. (2011). The impact of stereotypical versus counterstereotypical media exemplars on racial attitudes, causal attributions, and support for affirmative action. *Communication Research, 38*(4), 497–516. https://doi.org/10.1177/0093650210384854

Ramasubramanian, S., Winfield, A., & Riewestahl, E. (2020). Positive stereotypes and counter-stereotypes: Examining their effects on prejudice reduction and favorable intergroup relations. In A. C. Billings & S. Parrott (Eds.), *Media stereotypes: From ageism to xenophobia* (pp. 257–276). Peter Lang.

Ramsey, L. R., & Horan, A. L. (2018). Picture this: Women's self-sexualization in photos on social media. *Personality and Individual Differences, 133*, 85–90. https://doi.org/10.1016/j.paid.2017.06.022

Ran, W., & Yamamoto, M. (2019). Media multitasking, second screening, and political knowledge: Task-relevant and task-irrelevant second screening during election news consumption. *Journal of Broadcasting & Electronic Media, 63*(1), 1–19. https://doi.org/10.1080/08838151.2019.1565659

Raney, A. A., & Bryant, J. (2020). Entertainment and enjoyment as media effect. In M. B. Oliver, A. A. Raney, & J. Bryant (Eds.), *Media effects: Advances in theory and research* (4th ed., pp. 324–341). Routledge.

Raney, A. A., Oliver, M. B., & Bartsch, A. (2020). Eudaimonia as media effect. In M. B. Oliver, A. A. Raney, & J. Bryant (Eds.), *Media effects: Advances in theory and research* (4th ed., pp. 258–274). Routledge.

Ranney, A. (1983). *Channels of power*. Basic Books.

Rasmussen, E. E., Shafer, A., Colwell, M. J., White, S., Punyanunt-Carter, N., Densley, R. L., & Wright, H. (2016). Relation between active mediation, exposure to *Daniel Tiger's Neighborhood*, and US preschoolers' social and emotional development. *Journal of Children and Media, 10*(4), 443–461. https://doi.org/10.1080/17482798.2016.1203806

Rasmussen, K. R., Millar, D., & Trenchuk, J. (2019). Relationships and infidelity in pornography: An analysis of pornography streaming websites. *Sexuality & Culture, 23* 571–584. https://doi.org/10.1007/s12119-018-9574-7

Rathnayake, C., & Winter, J. S. (2018). Carrying forward the uses and grats 2.0 agenda: An affordance-driven measure of social media uses and gratifications. *Journal of Broadcasting & Electronic Media, 62*(3), 371–389. https://doi.org/10.1080/08838151.2018.1451861

Ray, T. (2009, July 31). Hoover police charge two men in Facebook burglaries. *The Birmingham News.* https://www.al.com/hoover/2009/07/hoover_police_charge_two_men_i.html

Reese, S. D., & Danielian, L. H. (1989). Intermedia influence and the drug issue: Converging on cocaine. In P. J. Shoemaker (Ed.), *Communication campaigns about drugs: Government, media and the public* (pp. 29–45). Lawrence Erlbaum Associates.

Reese, S. D., & Shoemaker, P. J. (2016). A media sociology for the networked public sphere: The hierarchy of influences model. *Mass Communication and Society, 19*(4), 389–410. https://doi.org/10.1080/15205436.2016.1174268

Reid, L., & Vanden Bergh, B. (1980). Blacks in introductory ads. *Journalism Quarterly, 57*(3), 485–489. https://doi.org/10.1177/107769908005700318

Reimer, B., & Rosengren, K. E. (1990). Cultivated viewers and readers: A life-style perspective. In N. Signorielli & M. Morgan (Eds.), *Cultivation analysis: New directions in media effects research* (pp. 181–206). Sage.

Rhen, B. (2011, April 22). Critics target "School Shooter" video game. *Education Week.* https://www.edweek.org/leadership/critics-target-school-shooter-video-game/2011/04

Rice, M. L. (1984). The words of children's television. *Journal of Broadcasting, 28*(4), 445–461. https://doi.org/10.1080/08838158409386553

Rice, M. L., & Haight, P. L. (1986). "Motherese" of Mr. Rogers: A description of the dialogue of educational television programs. *Journal of Speech and Hearing Disorders, 51*(3), 282–287. https://doi.org/10.1044/jshd.5103.282

Rice, M. L., Huston, A. C., Truglio, R., & Wright, J. C. (1990). Words from *Sesame Street:* Learning vocabulary while viewing. *Developmental Psychology, 26*(3), 421–428. https://doi.org/10.1037/0012-1649.26.3.421

Rice, M. L., & Woodsmall, L. (1988). Lessons from television: Children's word learning when viewing. *Child Development, 59*(2), 420–429. https://doi.org/10.1111/j.1467-8624.1988.tb01477.x

Rice, R. E., & Atkin, C. K. (2000). *Public communication campaigns* (3rd ed.). Sage.

Rice, R. E., & Atkin, C. K. (2009). Public communication campaigns: Theoretical principles and practical applications. In J. Bryant & M. B. Oliver (Eds.), *Media effects: Advances in theory and research* (3rd ed., pp. 436–468). Routledge.

Richmond, S. (2010). Angry birds: Just what makes it so popular? *The Telegraph.* https://www.telegraph.co.uk/technology/apple/8192398/Angry-Birds-just-what-makes-it-so-popular.html

Riddle, K. (2010). Always on my mind: Exploring how frequent, recent, and vivid television portrayals are used in the formation of social reality judgments. *Media Psychology, 13*(2), 155–179. https://doi.org/10.1080/15213261003800140

Riddle, K., Cantor, J., Byrne, S., & Moyer-Gusé, E. (2012). "People killing people on the news": Young children's descriptions of frightening television news content. *Communication Quarterly, 60*(2), 278–294. https://doi.org/10.1080/01463373.2012.669340

Riddle, K., & De Simone, J. J. (2013). A Snooki effect? An exploration of the surveillance subgenre of reality TV and viewers' beliefs about the "real" real world. *Psychology of Popular Media Culture, 2*(4), 237–250. https://doi.org/10.1037/ppm0000005

Riddle, K., Peebles, A., Davis, C., Xu, F., & Schroeder, E. (2018). The addictive potential of television binge watching: Comparing intentional and unintentional binges. *Psychology of Popular Media Culture, 7*(4), 589–604. https://doi.org/10.1037/ppm0000167

Riddle, T. A., Turetsky, K. M., Bottesini, J. G., & Leach, C. W. (2020). "What's going on" in Ferguson? Online news frames of protest at the police killing of Michael Brown. *Group Processes*

& *Intergroup Relations, 23*(6), 882–901. https://doi.org/10.1177/1368430220917752

Riordan, M. A. (2017). Emojis as tools for emotion work: Communicating affect in text messages. *Journal of Language and Social Psychology, 36*(5), 1–19. https://doi.org/10.1177/0261927X17704238

Riordan, M. A., & Trichtinger, L. A. (2017). Overconfidence at the keyboard: Confidence and accuracy in interpreting affect in e-mail exchanges. *Human Communication Research, 43*(1), 1–24. https://doi.org/10.1111/hcre.12093

Ritterfield, U., Cody, M., & Vorderer, P. (Eds). (2009). *Serious games: Mechanisms and effects.* Routledge.

Rivadeneyra, R., Ward, L. M., & Gordon, M. (2007). Distorted reflections: Media exposure and Latino adolescents' conception of self. *Media Psychology, 9*(2), 261–290. https://doi.org/10.1080/15213260701285926

Robb, M. B., Richert, R. A., & Wartella, E. A. (2009). Just a talking book? Word learning from watching baby videos. *British Journal of Developmental Psychology, 27*(Pt 1), 27–45. https://doi.org/10.1348/026151008x320156

Roberts, D. F., & Christenson, P. G. (2000*). "Here's looking at you, kid": Alcohol, drugs and tobacco in entertainment media.* Kaiser Family Foundation. https://www.kff.org/other/report/heres-looking-at-you-kid-alcohol-tobacco/

Roberts, D. F., Foehr, U. G., & Rideout, V. (2005). *Generation M: Media in the lives of 8–18 Yr-olds.* Kaiser Family Foundation. https://www.kff.org/other/event/generation-m-media-in-the-lives-of/

Roche, S. P., Pickett, J. T., & Gertz, M. (2016). The scary world of online news? Internet news exposure and public attitudes toward crime and justice. *Journal of Quantitative Criminology, 32*, 215–236. https://doi.org/10.1007/s10940-015-9261-x

Rockman et al. (1996). *Evaluation of* Bill Nye the Science Guy: *Television series and outreach.* https://resources.informalscience.org/evaluation-bill-nye-science-guy-television-series-and-outreach

Rodenhizer, K., & Edwards, K. M. (2019). The impacts of sexual media exposure on adolescent and emerging adults' dating and sexual violence attitudes and behaviors: A critical review of the literature. *Trauma, Violence, & Abuse, 20*(4), 439–452. https://doi.org/10.1177/1524838017717745

Rodriguez-Garcia, A.-M., Moreno-Guerrero, A.-J., & Belmonte, J. L. (2020). Nomophobia: An individual's growing fear of being without a smartphone—A systematic literature review. *International Journal of Environmental Research and Public Health, 17*(580), 1–19. https://doi.org/10.3390/ijerph17020580

Rogers, E. M. (1983). *Diffusion of innovations* (3rd ed.). Free Press.

Rogers, E. M. (1994). *A history of communication study: A biographical approach.* Free Press.

Rogers, E. M., & Chaffee, S. H. (Eds.). (1997). *The beginnings of communication study in America: A personal memoir by Wilbur Schramm.* Sage.

Rogers, R. W. (1975). A protection motivation theory of fear appeals and attitude change. *Journal of Psychology, 91*(1), 93–114. https://doi.org/10.1080/00223980.1975.9915803

Rogers, R. W., & Prentice-Dunn, S. (1997). Protection motivation theory. In D. Gochman (Ed.), *Handbook of health behavior research: Personal and social determinants* (Vol. 1, pp. 113–132). Plenum.

Romer, D., Jamieson, K. H., & Aday, S. (2003). Television news and the cultivation of fear of crime. *Journal of Communication, 53*(1), 88–104. https://doi.org/10.1111/j.1460-2466.2003.tb03007.x

Roseberry, S., Hirsh-Pasek, K., & Golinkoff, R. M. (2014). Skype me! Socially contingent interactions help toddlers learn language. *Child Development, 85*(3), 956–970. https://doi.org/10.1111/cdev.12166

Rosenbaum, R. (1979, September). Gooseflesh. *Harpers.* https://harpers.org/archive/1979/09/gooseflesh/

Rosengren, K. E., & Windahl, S. (1972). Mass media consumption as a functional alternative. In D. McQuail (Ed.), *Sociology of mass communications* (pp. 166–194). Penguin.

Rosenthal, T. L., & Zimmerman, B. J. (1978). *Social learning and cognition.* Academic.

Roskos-Ewoldsen, B., Davies, J., & Roskos-Ewoldsen, D. (2004). Implications of the mental models approach for cultivation theory. *Communications, 29*, 345–363. https://doi.org/10.1515/comm.2004.022

Roskos-Ewoldsen, D. R. (1997). Attitude accessibility and persuasion: Review and a transactive model. In B. R. Burleson & A. W. Kunkel (Eds.), *Communication yearbook 20* (pp. 185–225). Sage.

Roskos-Ewoldsen, D. R., Klinger, M., & Roskos-Ewoldsen, B. (2007). Media priming. In R. W. Preiss, B. M. Gayle, N. Burrell, M. Allen, & J. Bryant (Eds.), *Mass media theories and processes: Advances through meta-analysis* (pp. 53–80). Lawrence Erlbaum Associates.

Roskos-Ewoldsen, D. R., Roskos-Ewoldsen, B., & Carpentier, F. D. (2009). Media priming: An updated synthesis. In J. Bryant & M. B. Oliver (Eds.), *Media effects: Advances in theory and research* (3rd ed., pp. 74–93). Routledge.

Ross, C. S., Maple, E., Siegel, M., DeJong, W., Naimi, T. S., Ostroff, J., Padon, A. A., Borzekowski, D. L., & Jernigan, D. H. (2014). The relationship between brand-specific alcohol advertising on television and brand-specific consumption among underage youth. *Alcoholism, Clinical and Experimental Research, 38*(8), 2234–2242. https://doi.org/10.1111/acer.12488

Ross, J., & Tomlinson, B. (2010). How games can redirect humanity's cognitive surplus for social good. *Computers in Entertainment, 8*(4), Article 25. https://doi.org/10.1145/1921141.1921145

Rothman, E. F., & Adhia, A. (2016). Adolescent pornography use and dating violence among a sample of primarily Black and Hispanic, urban-residing, underage youth. *Behavioral Science, 6*(1). https://doi.org/10.3390/bs6010001

Rothman, R. (2011, March). Video games take testing to the next level. *Education Digest, 76*(7), 4–8. https://eric.ed.gov/?id=EJ919044

Rounds, E. G., & Stutts, L. A. (2020). The impact of fitspiration content on body satisfaction and negative mood: An experimental study. *Psychology of Popular Media. 10*(2), 267–274. https://doi.org/10.1037/ppm0000288

Rousseau, A., & Eggermont, S. (2018). Television and preadolescents' objectified dating script: Consequences for self- and interpersonal objectification. *Mass Communication and Society, 21*(1), 71–93. https://doi.org/10.1080/15205436.2017.1341533

Rovio. (2019, December 3). *Annual report 2018.* Rovio Entertainment Corporation. https://investors.rovio.com/system/files/2019-12/rovio-annual-report-2018-pdf-1.pdf

Rubin, A. J. (2017, January 2). France lets workers turn off, tune out and live life. *The New York Times.* https://www.nytimes.com/2017/01/02/world/europe/france-work-email.html

Rubin, A. M. (1979). Television use by children and adolescents. *Human Communication Research, 5*(2), 109–120. https://doi.org/10.1111/j.1468-2958.1979.tb00626.x

Rubin, A. M. (1981). An examination of television viewing motives. *Communication Research, 8*(2), 141–165. https://doi.org/10.1177/009365028100800201

Rubin, A. M. (1984). Ritualized and instrumental television viewing. *Journal of Communication, 34*(3), 67–77. https://doi.org/10.1111/j.1460-2466.1984.tb02174.x

Rubin, A. M. (1986). Uses, gratifications, and media effects research. In J. Bryant & D. Zillmann (Eds.), *Perspectives on media effects* (pp. 281–301). Lawrence Erlbaum Associates.

Rubin, A. M. (1994). Media effects: A uses-and-gratifications perspective. In J. Bryant & D. Zillmann (Eds.), *Media effects: Advances in theory and research* (pp. 417–436). Lawrence Erlbaum Associates.

Rubin, A. M. (2002). The uses-and-gratifications perspective of media effects. In J. Bryant & D. Zillmann (Eds.), *Media effects: Advances in theory and research* (2nd ed., pp. 525–548). Lawrence Erlbaum Associates.

Rubin, A. M. (2009). Uses-and-gratifications perspective on media effects. In J. Bryant & M. B. Oliver (Eds.), *Media effects: Advances in theory and research* (3rd ed., pp. 165–184). Routledge.

Rubin, A. M., & Perse, E. M. (1987). Audience activity and television news gratifications. *Communication Research, 14*(1), 58–84. https://doi.org/10.1177/009365087014001004

Rubin, A. M., & Rubin, R. B. (1982). Contextual age and television use. *Human Communication Research, 8*(3), 228–244. https://doi.org/10.1111/j.1468-2958.1982.tb00666.x

Rubin, A. M., & Step, M. M. (2000). Impact of motivation, attraction, and parasocial interaction on talk radio listening. *Journal of Broadcasting & Electronic Media, 44*(4), 635–654. https://doi.org/10.1207/s15506878jobem4404_7

Rubin, A. M., & Windahl, S. (1986). The uses and dependency model of mass communication. *Critical Studies in Mass Communication, 3*(2), 184–199. https://doi.org/10.1080/15295039609366643

Rucker, D. D., & Petty, R. E. (2006). Increasing the effectiveness of communications to consumers: Recommendations based on the elaboration likelihood and attitude certainty perspectives. *Journal of Public Policy and Marketing, 25*(1), 39–52. https://doi.org/10.1509/jppm.25.1.39

Ruggiero, T. E. (2000). Uses and gratifications theory in the 21st century. *Mass Communication & Society, 3*(1), 3–27. https://doi.org/10.1207/S15327825MCS0301_02

Rust, L. W. (2001). *Summative evaluation of Dragon Tales: Final report.* Langbourne Rust Research. http://www.langrust.com/DragonTales%20FinalReportforDOE.htm

Ryan, E. (2010). *Dora the Explorer:* Empowering preschoolers, girls, and Latinas. *Journal of Broadcasting & Electronic Media, 54*(1), 54–68. https://doi.org/10.1080/08838150903550394

Ryan, E. L., & Hoerrner, K. L. (2004). Let your conscience be your guide: Smoking and drinking in Disney's animated classics. *Mass Communication & Society, 7*(3), 261–278. https://doi.org/10.1207/s15327825mcs0703_1

Ryding, F. C., & Kay, L. K. (2018). "Internet addiction": A conceptual minefield. *International Journal of Mental Health and Addiction, 16,* 225–232. https://doi.org/10.1007/s11469-017-9811-6

Saelens, B. E., Sallids, J. F., Nader, P. R., Broyles, S. L., Berry, C. C., & Taras, H. L. (2002). Home environmental influences on children's television watching from early to middle childhood. *Journal of Developmental and Behavioral Pediatrics, 23*(3), 127–132. https://doi.org/10.1097/00004703-200206000-00001

Sahly, A., Shao., C., & Kwon, K. H. (2019). Social media for political campaigns: An examination of Trump's and Clinton's frame building and its effect on audience engagement. *Social Media +*

Society, 5(2). https://doi.org/10.1177/
2056305119855141

Saito, S. (2007). Television and the cultivation of gender-role attitudes in Japan: Does television contribute to the maintenance of the status quo? Journal of Communication, 57(3), 511–531. https://doi.org/10.1111/j.1460-2466.2007.00355.x

Salomon, G., & Leigh, T. (1984). Predispositions about learning from, print and television. Journal of Communication, 34(2), 119–135. https://doi.org/10.1111/j.1460-2466.1984.tb02164.x

Sánchez-Martínez, M., & Otero, A. (2009). Factors associated with cell phone use in adolescents in the community of Madrid (Spain). Cyberpsychology and Behavior, 12(2), 131–137. https://doi.org/10.1089/cpb.2008.0164

Sandman, P. M. (1976). Medicine and mass communication: An agenda for physicians. Annals of Internal Medicine, 85(3), 378–383. https://doi.org/10.7326/0003-4819-85-3-378

Sandvine. (2018, October). The global internet phenomena report. https://www.sandvine.com/hubfs/downloads/phenomena/2018-phenomena-report.pdf

Sapolsky, B. S., Molitor, F., & Luque, S. (2003). Sex and violence in slasher films: Re-examining the assumptions. Journalism & Mass Communication Quarterly, 80(1), 28–38. https://doi.org/10.1177/107769900308000103

Sapolsky, B. S., & Zillmann, D. (1978). Experience and empathy: Affective reactions to witnessing childbirth. Journal of Social Psychology, 105(1), 131–144. https://doi.org/10.1080/00224545.1978.9924099

Sarafino, E. P. (1986). The fears of childhood: A guide to recognizing and reducing fearful states in children. Human Sciences Press.

Sarge, M. A., & Knobloch-Westerwick, S. (2013). Impacts of efficacy and exemplification in an online message about weight loss on weight management self-efficacy, satisfaction, and personal importance. Journal of Health Communication, 18(7), 827–844. https://doi.org/10.1080/10810730.2012.757392

Sargent, J. D. (2009). Comparing the effects of entertainment media and tobacco marketing on youth smoking. Tobacco Control, 18(1), 47–53. https://doi.org/10.1136/tc.2008.026153

Sargent, J. D., Beach, M. L., Adachi-Mejia, A. M., Gibson, J. J., Titus-Ernstoff, L. T., Carusi, C. P., Swain, S. D., Heatherton, T. F., & Dalton, M. A. (2005). Exposure to movie smoking: Its relation to smoking initiation among US adolescents. Pediatrics, 116(5), 1183–1191. https://doi.org/10.1542/peds.2005-0714

Sargent, J. D., Tanski, S., & Stoolmiller, M. (2012). Influence of motion picture rating on adolescent response to movie smoking. Pediatrics, 130(2), 228–236. https://doi.org/10.1542/peds.2011-1787

Sargent, J. D., Wills, T. A., Stoolmiller, M., Gibson, J., & Gibbons, F. X. (2006). Alcohol use in motion pictures and its relation with early-onset teen drinking. Journal of Studies on Alcohol, 67(1), 54–65. https://doi.org/10.15288/jsa.2006.67.54

Satici, S. A. (2019). Facebook addiction and subjective well-being: A study of the mediating role of shyness and loneliness. International Journal of Mental Health and Addiction, 17(1), 41–55. https://doi.org/10.1007/s11469-017-9862-8

Satici, S. A., & Uysal, R. (2015). Well-being and problematic Facebook use. Computers in Human Behavior, 49, 185–190. https://doi.org/10.1016/j.chb.2015.03.005

Savage, J. (2004). Does viewing violent media really cause criminal violence? A methodological review. Aggression & Violent Behavior, 10(1), 99–128.

Savage, J. (2008). The role of exposure to media violence in the etiology of violent behavior: A criminologist weighs in. American Behavioral Scientist, 51(8), 1123–1136.

Savage, J., & Yancey, C. (2008). The effects of media violence exposure on criminal aggression: A meta-analysis. Criminal Justice and Behavior, 35(6), 772–791. https://doi.org/10.1177/0093854808316487

Schachter, S., & Singer, J. (1962). Cognitive, social, and physiological determinants of emotional state. Psychological Review, 69(5), 379–399. https://doi.org/10.1037/h0046234

Schaefer, H. H., & Colgan, A. H. (1977). The effect of pornography on penile tumescence as a function of reinforcement and novelty. Behavior Therapy, 8(5), 938–946. https://doi.org/10.1016/S0005-7894(77)80163-9

Schaeffer, K. (2019, August 23). Most U.S. teens who use cellphones do it to pass time, connect with others, learn new things. Pew Research Center. https://www.pewresearch.org/fact-tank/2019/08/23/most-u-s-teens-who-use-cellphones-do-it-to-pass-time-connect-with-others-learn-new-things/

Schaffer, C. (2021, April 13). The FCC received over 1,000 complaints for Grammy's "WAP" performance. Rolling Stone. https://www.rollingstone.com/music/music-news/cardi-b-megan-thee-stallion-wap-performance-grammys-fcc-complaints-1155254/

Scharrer, E., & Blackburn, G. (2018a) Cultivating conceptions of masculinity: Television and perceptions of masculine gender role norms. Mass Communication and Society, 21(2), 149–177. https://doi.org/10.1080/15205436.2017.1406118

Scharrer, E., & Blackburn, G. (2018b). Is reality TV a bad girls club? Television use, docusoap reality television viewing, and the cultivation of the approval of aggression. Journalism & Mass Com-

munication Quarterly, 95(1), 235–257. https://doi.org/10.1177/1077699017706482

Scheufele, D. A. (1999). Framing as a theory of media effects. *Journal of Communication, 49*(1), 103–122. https://doi.org/10.1111/j.1460-2466.1999.tb02784.x

Scheufele, D. A. (2000). Agenda-setting, priming, and framing revisited: Another look at cognitive effects of political communication. *Mass Communication & Society, 3*(2–3), 297–316. https://doi.org/10.1207/S15327825MCS0323_07

Scheufele, D. A. (2004). Framing-effects approach: A theoretical and methodological critique. *Communications, 29,* 401–428. https://doi.org/10.1515/comm.2004.29.4.401

Scheufele, D. A., Hardy, B., Brossard, D., Waismel-Manor, I. S., & Nisbet, E. C. (2006). Democracy based on difference: Examining the links between structural heterogeneity, heterogeneity of discussion networks, and democratic citizenship. *Journal of Communication, 56*(4), 728–753. https://doi.org/10.1111/j.1460-2466.2006.00317.x

Scheufele, D. A., & Nisbet, M. C. (2007). Framing. In L. L. Kaid & C. Holz-Bacha (Eds.), *Encyclopedia of political communication* (pp. 254–257). Sage.

Scheufele, D. A., & Tewksbury, D. (2007). Framing, agenda setting, and priming: The evolution of three media effects models. *Journal of Communication, 57*(1), 9–20. https://doi.org/10.1111/j.0021-9916.2007.00326.x

Schlehofer, M. M., Thompson, S. C., Ting, S., Ostermann, S., Nierman, A., & Skenderian, J. (2010). Psychological predictors for college students' cell phone use while driving. *Accident Analysis & Prevention, 42*(4), 1107–1112. https://doi.org/10.1016/j.aap.2009.12.024

Schlinger, M. J., & Plummer, J. (1972). Advertising in black and white. *Journal of Marketing Research, 9*(2), 149–153. https://doi.org/10.1177/002224377200900205

Schmitt, K., & Anderson, D. R. (2002). Television and reality: Toddlers' use of information from video to guide behavior. *Media Psychology, 4*(1), 51–76. https://doi.org/10.1207/S1532785XMEP0401_03

Schneider, D. E. (2018). Unstructured personal use in the classroom and college student learning: A literature review. *Community College Enterprise, 24*(2), 10-20. https://home.schoolcraft.edu/cce/24.2.10-20.pdf

Scholastic Productions banks on best-sellers. (1997, July). *Broadcasting & Cable, 127*(31), 48.

Scholl, R. M., Pingree, R. J., Gotlieb, M. R., Veenstra, A. S., & Shah, D. V. (2016). Here's what you'll learn from this news story: Prior framing and learning reasons from news. *Electronic News, 10*(2), 71–86. https://doi.org/10.1177/1931243116650348

Schramm, W. (1954). How communication works. In W. Schramm (Ed.), *The processes and effects of mass communication* (pp. 3–26). University of Illinois Press.

Schramm, W. (1961). Untitled [Review of the book *The Effects of Mass Communication*, by J. T. Klapper]. *The Public Opinion Quarterly, 25*(2), 321–324. http://www.jstor.org/stable/2746716

Schramm, W. (1997). Carl Hovland: Experiments, attitudes, and communication. In S. H. Chaffee & E. M. Rogers (Eds.), *The beginnings of communication study in America: A personal memoir by Wilbur Schramm* (pp. 87–105). Sage.

Schramm, W., Lyle, J., & Parker, E. P. (1961). *Television in the lives of our children.* Stanford University Press.

Schug, J., Alt, N. P., Lu, P. S., Gosin, M., & Fay, J. L. (2017). Gendered race in mass media: Invisibility of Asian men and Black women in popular magazines. *Psychology of Popular Media Culture, 6*(3), 222–236. https://doi.org/10.1037/ppm0000096

Schultze-Krumbholz, A., Schultze, M., Zagorscak, P., Wölfer, R., & Scheithauer, H. (2016). Feeling cybervictims' pain—The effect of empathy training on cyberbullying. *Aggressive Behavior, 42*(2), 147–156. https://doi.org/10.1002/ab.21613

Schwalbe, C. B. (2013). Visually framing the invasion and occupation of Iraq in *TIME, Newsweek,* and *U.S. News & World Report. International Journal of Communication, 7,* 239–262. https://ijoc.org/index.php/ijoc/article/view/924/852

Schwalbe, C. B., Silcock, B. W., & Keith, S. (2008). Visual framing of the early weeks of the U.S.-led invasion of Iraq: Applying the master war narrative to electronic and print images. *Journal of Broadcasting & Electronic Media, 52*(3), 448–465. https://doi.org/10.1080/08838150802205702

Schwartz, A. B. (2015). *Broadcast hysteria: Orson Welles's* War of the Worlds *and the art of fake news.* Hill and Wang.

Schwartz, L. M., & Woloshin, S. (2019). Medical marketing in the United States, 1997–2016. *JAMA, 321*(1), 80–96. https://doi.org/10.1001/jama.2018.19320

Schwarz, N. (2015). *Metacognition.* In M. Mikulincer, P. R. Shaver, E. Borgida, & J. A. Bargh (Eds.), *APA handbooks in psychology. APA handbook of personality and social psychology, Vol. 1. Attitudes and social cognition* (pp. 203–229). American Psychological Association. https://doi.org/10.1037/14341-006

Sconce, J. (2000). *Haunted media: Electronic presence from telegraphy to television.* Duke University Press.

Scopelliti, M., Pacilli, M. G., & Aquino, A. (2021). TV news and COVID-19: Media influence on healthy behavior in public spaces. *International Journal of Environmental Research and Public Health, 18*(4), Article 1879. https://doi.org/10.3390/ijerph18041879

Scott, D. (1995). The effect of video games on feelings of aggression. *Journal of Psychology, 129,* 121–132. https://doi.org/10.1080/00223980.1995.9914952

Seabrook, E. M., Kern, M. L., & Rickard, N. S. (2016). Social networking sites, depression, and anxiety: A systematic review. *JMIR Mental Health, 3*(4), e50. https://doi.org/10.2196/mental.5842

Searles, K., & Smith, G. (2016). Who's the boss? Setting the agenda in a fragmented media environment. *International Journal of Communication, 10*(22), 2075–2095. https://ijoc.org/index.php/ijoc/article/view/4839

Seggar, J. F., Hafen, J., & Hannonen-Gladden, H. (1981). Television's portrayals of minorities and women in drama and comedy drama, 1971–1980. *Journal of Broadcasting, 25*(3), 277–288. https://doi.org/10.1080/08838158109386451

Selman, R. L., & Byrne, D. (1974). A structural analysis of levels of role-taking in middle childhood. *Child Development, 45,* 803–806.

Shadel, W. G., Martino, S. C., Setodji, C. M., Scharf, D. M., Kusuke, D., Sicker, A., & Gong, M. (2016). Hiding the tobacco power wall reduces cigarette smoking risk in adolescents: Using an experimental convenience store to assess tobacco regulatory options at retail point-of-sale. *Tobacco Control, 25*(6), 679–684. https://doi.org/10.1136/tobaccocontrol-2015-052529

Shafer, E. (2021, June 14). Lin-Manuel Miranda addresses lack of Afro-Latino representation in "In the Heights": "We fell short." *Variety.* https://variety.com/2021/film/news/lin-manuel-miranda-in-the-heights-afro-latino-representation-1234996523/?fbclid=IwAR0Db2JnX0S7RTp33jC_GcCVxbZtrG8H6yFzh28BMaAT72PzcGjpusFpq5E

Shah, D. V., McLeod, D. M., Kim, E., Lee, S-Y., Gotlieb, M. R., Ho, S., & Brevik, H. (2007). Political consumerism: How communication practices and consumption orientations drive "lifestyle politics." *The ANNALS of the American Academy of Political and Social Science, 611*(1), 217–235. https://doi.org/10.1177/0002716206298714

Shambare, R., Rugimbana, R., & Zhowa, T. (2012). Are mobile phones the 21st century addiction? *African Journal of Business Management, 6*(2), 573–577. https://10.5897/ajbm11.1940

Shanahan, J., & Morgan, M. (1999). *Television and its viewers: Cultivation theory and research.* Cambridge University Press.

Shannon, C., & Weaver, W. (1949). *The mathematical theory of communication.* University of Illinois Press.

Shapiro, J. S. (1999). Loneliness: Paradox or artifact? *American Psychologies, 54*(9), 782–783. https://doi.org/10.1037/0003-066X.54.9.782

Shaw, D., & McCombs, M. (Eds.) (1977). *The emergence of American political issues: The agenda setting function of the press.* West.

Shaw, D. L., & Weaver, D. H. (2014). Media agenda-setting and audience agenda-melding. In M. McCombs (Ed.), *Setting the agenda: The mass media and public opinion* (2nd ed., pp. 145–150). Polity Press.

Shearer, E. (2018, December 10). *Social media outpaces print newspapers in the U.S. as a news source.* Pew Research Center. https://www.pewresearch.org/fact-tank/2018/12/10/social-media-outpaces-print-newspapers-in-the-u-s-as-a-news-source/

Shearer, E., & Mitchell, A. (2021, May 7). *Broad agreement in U.S.—even among partisans—on which news outlets are part of the "mainstream media."* Pew Research Center. https://www.pewresearch.org/fact-tank/2021/05/07/broad-agreement-in-u-s-even-among-partisans-on-which-news-outlets-are-part-of-the-mainstream-media/

Shehata, A., & Strömbäck, J. (2013). Not (yet) a new era of minimal effects: A study of agenda setting at the aggregate and individual levels. *The International Journal of Press/Politics, 18*(2), 234–255. https://doi.org/10.1177/1940161212473831

Sheldon, P. (2008). Student favorite: Facebook and motives for its use. *Southwestern Mass Communication Journal,* Spring Issue, 39–53.

Sheldon, P., & Bryant K. (2016). Instagram: Motives for its use and relationship to narcissism and contextual age. *Computers in Human Behavior, 58,* 89–87. https://doi.org/10.1016/j.chb.2015.12.059

Shen, F. (2004). Effects of news frames and schemas on individuals' issue interpretations and attitudes. *Journalism & Mass Communication Quarterly, 81,* 400–416. https://doi.org/10.1177/10776990040810021

Shepard, W. J. (1909). Public opinion. *The American Journal of Sociology, 15*(1), 32–60. https://www.jstor.org/stable/2762619#metadata_info_tab_contents

Sherif, C. W., Sherif, M., & Nebergall, R. E. (1965). *Attitude and attitude change: The social judgment-involvement approach.* W. B. Saunders.

Sherif, M. (1967). *Social interaction: Processes and products.* Aldine.

Sherlock, M., & Wagstaff, D. L. (2019). Exploring the relationship between frequency of Instagram use, exposure to idealized images, and psychological well-being in women. *Psychology of Popular Media Culture, 8*(4), 482–490. https://doi.org/10.1037/ppm0000182

Sherman, B. L., & Dominick, J. R., (1986). Violence and sex in music videos: TV and rock 'n' roll. *Journal of Communication, 36*(1), 79–93. https://doi.org/10.1111/j.1460-2466.1986.tb03040.x

Sherry, J. L. (2001). The effects of violent video games on aggression: A meta-analysis. *Human Communication Research, 27*(3), 409–431. https://doi.org/10.1093/hcr/27.3.409

Sherry, J. L. (2004). Flow and media enjoyment. *Communication Theory, 14*(4), 328–347. https://doi.org/10.1111/j.1468-2885.2004.tb00318.x

Shih, C.-H. (2011). A standing location detector enabling people with developmental disabilities to control environmental stimulation through simple physical activities with Nintendo Wii balance boards. *Research in Developmental Disabilities, 32*(2), 699–704. https://doi.org/10.1016/j.ridd.2010.11.011

Shin, J., & Thorson, K. (2017). Partisan selective sharing: The biased diffusion of fact-checking messages on social media. *Journal of Communication, 67*(2), 233–255. https://doi.org/10.1111/jcom.12284

Shoemaker, P. J., & Reese, S. (1991). *Mediating the message: Theories of influence on mass media content.* Longman.

Shoemaker, P. J., & Reese, S. D. (1996). *Mediating the message* (2nd ed.). Longman.

Shoemaker, P. J., Wanta, W., & Leggett, D. (1989). Drug coverage and public opinion, 1972–1986. In P. Shoemaker (Ed.), *Communication campaigns about drugs: Government, media and the public* (pp. 67–80). Lawrence Erlbaum Associates.

Shor, E., & Golriz, G. (2019). Gender, race, and aggression in mainstream pornography. *Archives of Sexual Behavior, 48*(3), 739–751. https://doi.org/10.1007/s10508-018-1304-6

Shor, E., & Seida, K. (2019). "Harder and harder"? Is mainstream pornography becoming increasingly violent and do viewers prefer violent content? *Journal of Sex Research, 56*(1), 16–28. https://doi.org/10.1080/00224499.2018.1451476

Shor, E., & Seida, K. (2021). *Aggression in pornography: Myths and realities.* Routledge.

Shropshire, A. M., Brent-Hotchkiss, R., & Andrews, U. K. (2013). Mass media campaign impacts influenza vaccine obtainment of university students. *Journal of American College Health, 61*(8), 435–443. https://doi.org/10.1080/07448481.2013.830619

Shrum, L. J. (1995). Assessing the social influence of television: A social cognition perspective on cultivation effects. *Communication Research, 22*(4), 402–429. https://doi.org/10.1177/009365095022004002

Shrum, L. J. (1997). The role of source confusion in cultivation effects may depend on processing strategy: A comment on Mares (1996). *Human Communication Research, 24*(2), 349–358. https://doi.org/10.1111/j.1468-2958.1997.tb00418.x

Shrum, L. J. (1999). The relationship of television viewing with attitude strength and extremity: Implications for the cultivation effect. *Media Psychology, 1*(1), 3–25. https://doi.org/10.1207/s1532785xmep0101_2

Shrum, L. J. (2001). Processing strategy moderates the cultivation effect. *Human Communication Research, 27*(1), 94–120. https://doi.org/10.1093/hcr/27.1.94

Shrum, L. J. (2002). Media consumption and perceptions of social reality: Effects and underlying processes. In J. Bryant & D. Zillmann (Eds.), *Media effects: Advances in theory and research* (2nd ed., pp. 69–96). Lawrence Erlbaum Associates.

Shrum, L. J. (2004). The cognitive processes underlying cultivation effects are a function of whether the judgments are on-line or memory-based. *Communications, 29*(3), 327–344. https://doi.org/10.1515/comm.2004.021

Shrum, L. J. (2007). The implications of survey method for measuring cultivation effects. *Human Communication Research, 33*(1), 64–80. https://doi.org/10.1111/j.1468-2958.2007.00289.x

Shrum, L. J. (2009). Media consumption and perceptions of social reality: Effects and underlying process. In J. Bryant & M. B. Oliver (Eds.), *Media effects: Advances in theory and research* (3rd ed., pp. 50–73). Routledge.

Shrum, L. J. (2017). Cultivation theory: Effects and underlying processes. In P. Rössler (Ed.), *International encyclopedia of media effects* (Vol. 1, pp. 295–306). Wiley-Blackwell. https://doi.org/10.1002/9781118783764.wbieme0040

Shrum, L. J., Burroughs, J. E., & Rindfleisch, A. (2005). Television's cultivation of material values. *Journal of Consumer Research, 32*(3), 473–479. https://doi.org/10.1086/497559

Shrum, L. J., Lee, J., Burroughs, J. E., & Rindfleisch, A. (2011). An online process model of second-order cultivation effects: How television cultivates materialism and its consequences for life satisfaction. *Human Communication Research, 37*(1), 34–57. https://doi.org/10.1111/j.1468-2958.2010.01392.x

Shrum, L. J., Wyer, R. S., & O'Guinn, T. C. (1998). The effects of television consumption on social perceptions: The use of priming procedures to investigate psychological processes. *Journal of Consumer Research, 24*(4), 447–458. https://doi.org/10.1086/209520

Siegel, M., Johnson, R. M., Tyagi, K., Power, K., Lohsen, M. C., Ayers, A. J., & Jernigan, D. H. (2013). Alcohol brand references in U.S. popular music, 2009-2011. *Substance Use & Misuse, 48*(14), 1475–1484. https://doi.org/10.3109/10826084.2013.793716

Sifferlin, A. (2014, August 18). Here's how the ALS ice bucket challenge actually started. *TIME.* https://time.com/3136507/als-ice-bucket-challenge-started/

Signorielli, N. (1990). Television's mean and dangerous world: A continuation of the cultural indicators perspective. In N. Signorielli & M. Morgan

(Eds.), *Cultivation analysis: New directions in media effects research* (pp. 85–106). Sage.

Signorielli, N., & Bacue, A. (1999). Recognition and respect: A content analysis of primetime television characters across three decades. *Sex Roles, 40*(7-8), 527–544. https://doi.org/10.1023/A:1018883912900

Signorielli, N., & Morgan, M. (1996). Cultivation analysis: Research and practice. In M. B. Salwen & D. W. Stacks (Eds.), *An integrated approach to communication theory and research* (pp. 111–126). Lawrence Erlbaum Associates.

Sigurdsson, J. F., Gudjonsson, G. H., Bragason, A. V., Kirstjansdottir, E., & Sigfusdottir, I. D. (2006). The role of violent cognition in the relationship between personality and the involvement in violent films and computer games. *Personality and Individual Differences, 41*(2), 381–392. https://doi.org/10.1016/j.paid.2006.02.006

Silverman, A. (2020, August 21). *Indy 500 represents rare sports marketing opportunity for vaping brands.* Morning Consult. https://morningconsult.com/2020/08/21/indy-500-represents-rare-sports-marketing-opportunity-for-vaping-brands/#:~:text=While%20leagues%20such%20as%20the,to%20promote%20e%20cigarette%20brands

Silverman, C. (2016, November 16). *This analysis shows how viral fake election news stories outperformed real news on Facebook.* BuzzFeed News. https://www.buzzfeednews.com/article/craigsilverman/viral-fake-election-news-outperformed-real-news-on-facebook

Silverman, C., & Singer-Vine, J. (2016, December 6). *Most Americans who see fake news believe it, new survey says.* BuzzFeed News. https://www.buzzfeednews.com/article/craigsilverman/fake-news-survey

Simon, A., & Jerit, J. (2007). Toward a theory relating political discourse, media, and public opinion. *Journal of Communication, 57*(2), 254–271. https://doi.org/10.1111/j.1460-2466.2007.00342.x

Simons, D., & Silveira, W. R. (1994). Post-traumatic stress disorder in children after television programmes. *British Medical Journal, 308*(6925), 389–390. https://doi.org/10.1136/bmj.308.6925.389

Simonson, P., & Park, D. W. (2015a). Introduction: On the history of communication study. In P. Simonson & D. W. Park (Eds.), *The international history of communication study* (pp. 1–22). Routledge.

Simonson, P., & Park, D. W. (Eds.). (2015b). *The international history of communication study.* Routledge

Simpson, J. K. (2017). Appeal to fear in health care: Appropriate or inappropriate? *Chiropractic & Manual Therapies, 25*, Article 27. https://doi.org/10.1186/s12998-017-0157-8

Singer, J. L. (1975). *Daydreaming and fantasy.* Allen & Unwin.

Singer, J. L., & Singer, D. G. (1983). Implications of childhood television viewing for cognition, imagination, and emotion. In J. Bryant & D. R. Anderson (Eds.), *Children's understanding of television: Research on attention and comprehension* (pp. 265–295). Academic.

Singer, J. L., & Singer, D. G. (1994). Barney and Friends *as education and entertainment: Phase 2—Can children learn through preschool exposure to Barney and Friends?* Yale University Family Television Research and Consultation Center.

Singer, J. L., & Singer, D. G. (1995). Barney and Friends *as education and entertainment: Phase 3—A national study: Can children learn through preschool exposure to Barney and Friends?* Yale University Family Television Research and Consultation Center.

Singer, J. L., & Singer, D. G. (1998). Barney and Friends *as entertainment and education: Evaluating the quality and effectiveness of television series for preschool children.* In J. K. Asamen & G. L. Berry (Eds.), *Research paradigms, television, and social behavior* (pp. 305–367). Sage.

Singer, M. I., Slovak, K., Frierson, T., & York, P. (1998). Viewing preferences, symptoms of psychological trauma, and violent behaviors among children who watch television. *Journal of the American Academy of Child and Adolescent Psychiatry, 37*(10), 1041–1048. https://doi.org/10.1097/00004583-199810000-00014

Singhal, A., & Rogers, E. M. (1989). Pro-social television for development in India. In R. E. Rice & C. K. Atkin (Eds.), *Public communication campaigns* (pp. 331–350). Sage.

Sink, A., & Mastro, D. (2017). Depictions of gender on primetime television: A quantitative content analysis. *Mass Communication & Society, 20*(1), 3–22. https://doi.org/10.1080/15205436.2016.1212243

Sintchak, G., & Geer, J. (1975). A vaginal plethysymograph system. *Psychophysiology, 12*(1), 113–115. https://doi.org/10.1111/j.1469-8986.1975.tb03074.x

Slater, M. D. (1999). Integrating application of media effects, persuasion, and behavior change theories to communication campaigns: A stages-of-change framework. *Health Communication, 11*, 335–354.

Slater, M. D. (2007). Reinforcing spirals: The mutual influence of media selectivity and media effects and their impact on individual behavior and social identity. *Communication Theory, 17*(3), 281–303. https://doi.org/10.1111/j.1468-2885.2007.00296.x

Slater, M. D. (2017). Reinforcing spirals model. In P. Rössler (Ed.), *International encyclopedia of media effects* (Vol. 4, pp. 1709–1721). Wiley-Blackwell. https://doi.org/10.1002/9781118783764.wbieme0118

Slater, M. D., Henry, K. L., Swaim, R. C., & Anderson, L. L. (2003). Violent media content and aggressiveness in adolescents: A downward spiral model. *Communication Research, 30*(4), 713–736. https://doi.org/10.1207/S15327027HC1104_2

Slater, M. D., Henry, K. L., Swaim, R. C., & Cardador, J. M. (2004). Vulnerable teens, vulnerable times: How sensation seeking, alienation, and victimization moderate the violent media content–aggressiveness relation. *Communication Research, 31*(6), 642–668. https://doi.org/10.1177/0093650204269265

Sloan, W. D. (1998). The partisan press, 1783–1833. In W. D. Sloan (Ed.), *The age of mass communication* (pp. 119–146). Vision Press.

Smith, A. (2014, November 3). *Cell phones, social media and campaign 2014.* Pew Research Center. https://www.pewresearch.org/internet/2014/11/03/cell-phones-social-media-and-campaign-2014/

Smith, A., & Grant, A. (2020). *Differences in how Democrats and Republicans behave on Twitter.* Pew Research Center. https://www.pewresearch.org/politics/wp-content/uploads/sites/4/2020/10/PDL_10.15.20.twitter.dems_.reps_.fullreport.pdf

Smith, B. L., Lasswell, H. D., & Casey, R. D. (1946). *Propaganda, communication, and public opinion: A comprehensive reference guide.* Princeton University Press.

Smith, J. (1986). *A description of New England.* In P. O. Barbour (Ed.), *The complete works of Captain John Smith* (Vol. 1, pp. 323–361). The University of North Carolina Press. (Original work published 1616)

Smith, L. A., & Foxcroft, D. R. (2009). The effect of alcohol advertising, marketing and portrayal on drinking behaviour in young people: Systematic review of prospective cohort studies. *BMC Public Health, 9,* Article 51. https://doi.org/10.1186/1471-2458-9-51

Smith, L. W., Liu, B., Degenhardt, L., Richters, J., Patton, G., Wand, H., Cross, D., Hocking, J. S., Skinner, S. R., Cooper, S., Lumby, C., Kaldor, J. M., & Guy, R. (2016). Is sexual content in new media linked to sexual risk behaviour in young people? A systematic review and meta-analysis. *Sexual Health, 13*(6), 501–515. https://doi.org/10.1071/SH16037

Smith, S. L., Choueiti, M., & Pieper, K. (2016). *Inequality in 800 popular films: Examining portrayals of gender, race/ethnicity, LGBT, and disability from 2007–2015.* USC Annenberg School for Communication and Journalism. https://annenberg.usc.edu/sites/default/files/2017/04/10/MDSCI_Inequality_in_800_Films_FINAL.pdf

Smith, S. L., Choueiti, M., & Pieper, K. (2020). *Inequality in 1,300 popular films: Examining portrayals of gender, race/ethnicity, LGBTQ & disability from 2007 to 2019.* USC Annenberg Inclusion Initiative. https://assets.uscannenberg.org/docs/aii-inequality_1300_popular_films_09-08-2020.pdf

Smith, S. L., Choueiti, M., Prescott, A., & Pieper, K. (2012). *Gender roles & occupations: A look at character attributes and job-related aspirations in film and television.* Geena Davis Institute on Gender in Media. https://seejane.org/wp-content/uploads/full-study-gender-roles-and-occupations-v2.pdf

Smith, S. L., & Cook, C. A. (2008). *Gender stereotypes: An analysis of popular films and TV.* Geena Davis Institute on Gender in Media. https://seejane.org/wp-content/uploads/GDIGM_Gender_Stereotypes.pdf

Smith, S. L., & Granados, A. D. (2009). Content patterns and effects surrounding sex-role stereotyping on television and film. In J. Bryant & M. B. Oliver (Eds.), *Media effects: Advances in theory and research* (3rd ed., pp. 342–361). Routledge.

Smith, S. L., Pieper, K. M., Granados, A., & Choueiti, M. (2010). Assessing gender-related portrayals in top-grossing G-rated films. *Sex Roles, 62,* 774–786. https://doi.org/10.1007/s11199-009-9736-z

Snider, M. (2019, July 28). Teens rule at $30 million Fortnite World Cup, game gets a season 10 teaser. *USA Today.* https://www.usatoday.com/story/tech/gaming/2019/07/28/fortnite-world-cup-teens-win-millions-video-game-competition/1853236001/

Snow, D. A., & Benford, R. D. (1992). Master frames and cycles of protest. In A. D. Morris & C. McClurg Mueller (Eds.), *Frontiers in social movement theory* (pp. 133–155). Yale University Press.

Snyder, L. B., Anderson, K., & Young, D. (1989, May). *AIDS communication, risk, knowledge and behavior change: A preliminary investigation in Connecticut* [Paper presentation]. International Communication Association Conference, San Francisco, CA, United States.

Snyder, L. B., Hamilton, M. A., Mitchell, E. W., Kiwanuka-Tondo, J., Fleming-Milici, F., & Proctor, D. (2004). A meta-analysis of the effect of mediated health communication campaigns on behavior change in the United States. *Journal of Health Communication, 9* (Suppl 1), 71–96. https://doi.org/10.1080/10810730490271548

Soh, J. O. B., & Tan, B. C. Y. (2008). Mobile gaming. *Communications of the ACM, 51*(3), 35–39. https://doi.org/10.1145/1325555.1325563

Soley, L. (1983). The effect of black models on magazine ad readership. *Journalism Quarterly, 60*(4), 686–690. https://doi.org/10.1177/107769908306000415

Song, K. (2021, November 5). "Encanto" star John Leguizamo on why the film is so important: "I never thought I'd see this in my lifetime." *Variety.* https://variety.com/2021/scene/news/john-leguizamo-on-why-encanto-is-so-important-1235105235/?fbclid=IwAR2d_52knSA4tgECygbxx-3w9Pr8dOYq2YsFNP2MtziaDdfhWoaNZOXDcKI

Song, Y., & Gao, J. (2020). Does telework stress employees out? A study on working at home and subjective well-being for wage/salary workers. *Journal of Happiness Studies, 21,* 2649–2668. https://doi.org/10.1007/s10902-019-00196-6

Soomro, K. A., Zai, S. A. Y., & Hina, Q. A. (2019). Investigating the impact of university students' smartphone addiction on their satisfaction with classroom connectedness. *Education and Information Technologies, 24,* 3523–3535. https://doi.org/10.1007/s10639-019-09947-7

Sorokowski, P., Sorokowska, A., Oleszkiewicz, A., Frackowiak, T., Huk, A, & Pisanski, K. (2015). Selfie posting behaviors are associated with narcissism among men. *Personality and Individual Differences, 85,* 123–127. https://doi.org/10.1016/j.paid.2015.05.004

Sotirovic, M. (2003). How individuals explain social problems: The influences of media use. *Journal of Communication, 53*(1), 122–137. https://doi.org/10.1111/j.1460-2466.2003.tb03009.x

Sparks, D. A., Coughlin, L. M., & Chase, D. M. (2011). Did too much Wii cause your patient's injury? *The Journal of Family Practice, 60*(7), 404–409.

Sparks, G. G. (1986). Developmental differences in children's reports of fear induced by mass media. *Child Study Journal, 16*(1), 55–66.

Sparks, G. G., & Cantor, J. (1986). Developmental differences in fright responses to a television programme depicting a character transformation. *Journal of Broadcasting & Electronic Media, 30*(3), 309–323. https://doi.org/10.1080/08838158609386626

Sparks, G. G., Sherry, J., & Lubsen, G. (2005). The appeal of media violence in a full-length motion picture: An experimental investigation. *Communication Reports, 18*(1–2), 21–30. https://doi.org/10.1080/08934210500084198

Sparks, G. G., & Sparks, C. W. (2002). Effects of media violence. In J. Bryant & D. Zillmann (Eds.), *Media effects: Advances in theory and research* (2nd ed., pp. 269–285). Lawrence Erlbaum Associates.

Sparks, G. G., Sparks, C. W., & Sparks, E. A. (2009). Media violence. In J. Bryant & M. B. Oliver (Eds.), *Media effects: Advances in theory and research* (3rd ed., pp. 269–286). Routledge.

Speer, I. (2017). Reframing the Iraq war: Official sources, dramatic events, and changes in media framing. *Journal of Communication, 67*(2), 282–302. https://doi.org/10.1111/jcom.12289

Spradlin, A., Cuttler, C., Bunce, J. P., & Carrier, L. M. (2017). #Connected: Facebook may facilitate face-to-face relationships for introverts. *Psychology of Popular Media Culture, 8*(1), 34–80. https://doi.org/10.1037/ppm0000162

Stack, S. (2005). Suicide in the media: A quantitative review of studies based on non-fictional stories. *Suicide & Life-Threatening Behavior, 35*(2), 121–133. https://doi.org/10.1521/suli.35.2.121.62877

Stanmore, E., Stubbs, B., Vancampfort, D., de Bruin, E. D., & Firth, J. (2017). The effect of active video games on cognitive functioning in clinical and non-clinical populations: A meta-analysis of randomized controlled trials. *Neuroscience and Biobehavioral Reviews, 78,* 34–43. https://doi.org/10.1016/j.neubiorev.2017.04.011

Stein, J.-P., Krause, E., & Ohler, P. (2021). Every (Insta)gram counts? Applying cultivation theory to explore the effects of Instagram on young users' body image. *Psychology of Popular Media, 10*(1), 87–97. https://doi.org/10.1037/ppm0000268

Steinfield, C., Ellison, N. B., & Lampe, C. (2008). Social capital, self-esteem, and use of online social network sites: A longitudinal analysis. *Journal of Applied Developmental Psychology, 29*(6), 434–445. https://doi.org/10.1016/j.appdev.2008.07.002

Stempel, G. (1971). Visibility of blacks in news and news-picture magazines. *Journalism Quarterly, 48*(2), 337–339.

Stephenson, W. (1967). *The play theory of mass communication.* University of Chicago Press.

Stern, S., Livian, G., & Smith, R. E. (2020). A network perspective on intermedia agenda-setting. *Applied Network Science, 5*(31), Article 31. https://doi.org/10.1007/s41109-020-00272-4

Stern, S., & Mastro, D. E. (2004). Gender portrayals across the life span: A content analysis look at broadcast commercials. *Mass Communication & Society, 7*(2), 215–236. https://doi.org/10.1207/s15327825mcs0702_5

Stevens, E. M., & Garrett, K. P. (2016). Girls and sex: A content analysis of sexual health depictions in HBO's *Girls. Sexuality & Culture, 20,* 923–935. https://doi.org/10.1007/s12119-016-9365-y

Stever, G. S. (2017). Evolutionary theory and reactions to mass media: Understanding parasocial attachment. *Psychology of Popular Media Culture, 6*(2), 95–102. https://doi.org/10.1037/ppm0000116

Stieger, S. (2019). Facebook usage and life satisfaction. *Frontiers in Psychology, 10,* Article 2711. https://doi.org/10.3389/fpsyg.2019.02711

Stopera, D. (2020, February 19). *For everyone who's still scarred for life by the one scene in "Final Destination."* BuzzFeed. https://www.buzzfeed.com/daves4/wood-truck-final-destination

Stouffer, S. A. (1942). A sociologist looks at communications research. In D. Waples (Ed.), *Print, radio, and film in a democracy: Ten papers on the administration of mass communications in the public interest—Read before the Sixth Annual Institute of the Graduate Library School, The University of Chi-*

cago—*August 4–9, 1941* (pp. 133–146). University of Chicago Press.

Stoycheff, E., Pingree, R. J., Peifer, J. T., & Sui, M. (2018). Agenda cuing effects of news and social media. *Media Psychology, 21*(2), 182–201. https://doi.org/10.1080/15213269.2017.1311214

Strasburger, V., & Wilson, B. (2014). Television violence: 60 years of research. In D. Gentile (Ed.) *Media violence and children: A complete guide for parents and professionals* (2nd ed, pp.134–178). Praeger.

Strasburger, V. C., Wilson, B. J., & Jordan, A. B. (2009). *Children, adolescents, and the media* (2nd ed.). Sage.

Strizhakova, Y., & Krcmar, M. (2003, May). *Do we have access to our viewing motives? Assumptions in and extensions of uses and gratifications* [Paper presentation]. International Communication Association, San Diego, CA, United States.

Stroud, N. J. (2010). Polarization and partisan selective exposure. *Journal of Communication, 60*(3), 556–576. https://doi.org/10.1111/j.1460-2466.2010.01497.x

Strouse, G. A., & Ganea, P. A. (2017a). Parent–toddler behavior and language differ when reading electronic and print picture books. *Frontiers in Psychology, 8,* Article 677. https://doi.org/10.3389/fpsyg.2017.00677

Strouse, G. A., & Ganea, P. A. (2017b). Toddlers' word learning and transfer from electronic and print books. *Journal of Experimental Child Psychology, 156,* 129–142. https://doi.org/10.1016/j.jecp.2016.12.001

Stryker, J. E. (2003). Media and marijuana: A longitudinal analysis of news media effects on adolescents' marijuana use and related outcomes, 1977–1999. *Journal of Health Communication, 8*(4), 305–328. https://doi.org/10.1080/10810730305724

Subervi-Vélez, F. A., & Necochea, J. (1990). Television viewing and self-concept among Hispanic children—A pilot study. *Howard Journal of Communications, 2*(3), 315–329. https://doi.org/10.1080/10646179009359723

Sujon, Z., Viney, L., & Toker-Turnalar, E. (2018). Domesticating Facebook: The shift from compulsive connection to personal service platform. *Social Media + Society, 4*(4). https://doi.org/10.1177/2056305118803895

Suler, J. (2004). The online disinhibition effect. *CyberPsychology & Behavior, 7*(3), 321–326. https://doi.org/10.1089/1094931041291295

Sullivan, C. (2003). What's in a name? Definitions and conceptualizations of teleworking and home-working. *New Technology, Work & Employment, 18*(3), 158–165. https://doi.org/10.1111/1468-005X.00118

Sullivan, M. (2020, April 13). What it really means when Trump calls a story "fake news." *The Washington Post.* https://www.washingtonpost.com/lifestyle/media/what-it-really-means-when-trump-calls-a-story-fake-news/2020/04/13/56fbe2c0-7d8c-11ea-9040-68981f488eed_story.html

Sun, S., Rubin, A. M., & Haridakis, P. M. (2008). The role of motivation and media involvement in explaining internet dependency. *Journal of Broadcasting & Electronic Media, 52*(3), 408–431. https://doi.org/10.1080/08838150802205595

Sun, Y., Zhang, Y., Gwizdka, J., & Trace, C. B. (2019). Consumer evaluation of the quality of online health information: Systematic literature review of relevant criteria and indicators. *Journal of Medical Internet Research, 21*(5), Article e12522. https://doi.org/10.2196/12522

Sundar, S. S. (2008). The MAIN model: A heuristic approach to understanding technology effects on credibility. In M. J. Metzger & A. J. Flanagin (Eds.), *Digital media, youth, and credibility* (pp. 73–100). The MIT Press. https://www.issuelab.org/resources/875/875.pdf

Sundar, S. S., & Limperos, A. M. (2013). Uses and grats 2.0: New gratifications for new media. *Journal of Broadcasting & Electronic Media, 57,* 4, 504–525. https://doi.org/10.1080/08838151.2013.845827

Sundar, S. S., & Oh, J. (2020) Psychologiccal effects of interactive media technologies: A human-computer interaction (HCI) perspective. In M. B. Oliver, A. A. Raney, & J. Bryant (Eds.), *Media effects: Advances in theory and research* (4th ed., pp. 357–372). Routledge.

Sung, Y. H., Kang, E. Y., Lee, W.-N. (2018). Why do we indulge? Exploring motivations for binge watching. *Journal of Broadcasting & Electronic Media, 62*(3), 408–426. https://doi.org/10.1080/08838151.2018.1451851

Sutton, S. R. (1982). Fear-arousing communication: A critical examination of theory and research. In J. R. Eiser (Ed.), *Social psychology and behavioral medicine* (pp. 303–337). John Wiley.

Swanson, D. L. (1977). The uses and misuses of uses and gratifications. *Human Communication Research, 3*(3), 214–221. https://doi.org/10.1111/j.1468-2958.1977.tb00519.x

Swanson, D. L. (1979). Political communication research and the uses and gratifications model: A critique. *Communication Research, 6*(1), 37–53. https://doi.org/10.1177/009365027900600103

Swasy, J. L., & Munch, J. M. (1985). Examining the target of receiver elaborations: Rhetorical question effects on source processing and persuasion. *Journal of Consumer Research, 11*(4), 877–886. https://doi.org/10.1086/209023

Taber, C. S., Cann, D., & Kucsova, S. (2009). The motivated processing of political arguments. *Political Behavior, 31*(2), 137–155. https://doi.org/10.1007/s11109-008-9075-8

Taber, C. S., & Lodge, M. (2006). Motivated skepticism in the evaluation of political beliefs. *American Journal of Political Science, 50*(3), 755–769. https://doi.org/10.1111/j.1540-5907.2006.00214.x

Takacs, Z. K., Swart, E. K., & Bus, A. G. (2015). Benefits and pitfalls of multimedia and interactive features in technology-enhanced storybooks: A meta-analysis. *Review of Educational Research, 85*(4), 698–739. https://doi.org/10.3102/0034654314566989

Takeshita, T., & Mikami, S. (1995). How did mass media influence the voters' choice in the 1993 general election in Japan? *Keio Communication Review, 17,* 27–41.

Tamborini, R., & Weaver, J. B., III. (1996). Frightening entertainment: A historical perspective of fictional horror. In J. B. Weaver III & R. Tamborini (Eds.), *Horror films: Current research on audience preferences and reactions* (pp. 1–13). Lawrence Erlbaum Associates.

Tamborini, R., Zillmann, D., & Bryant, J. (1984). Fear and victimization: Exposure to television and perceptions of crime and fear. In R. N. Bostrum (Ed.), *Communication yearbook 8* (pp. 492–513). Sage.

Tan, A., Fujioka, Y., & Tan, G. (2000). Television use, stereotypes of African Americans and opinions on affirmative action: An effective model of policy reasoning. *Communication Monographs, 67*(4), 362–371. https://doi.org/10.1080/03637750009376517

Tandoc, E. C., Jr., Lim, Z. W., & Ling, R. (2018). Defining "fake news": A typology of scholarly definitions. *Digital Journalism, 6*(2), 137–153. https://doi.org/10.1080/21670811.2017.1360143

Tannebaum, M. (2018). College students' use of technology to communicate with romantic partners about sexual health issues. *Journal of American College Health, 66*(5), 393–400. https://doi.org/10.1080/07448481.2018.1440585

Tannenbaum, M. B., Hepler, J., Zimmerman, R. S., Saul, L., Jacobs, S., Wilson, K., & Albarracín, D. (2015). Appealing to fear: A meta-analysis of fear appeal effectiveness and theories. *Psychological Bulletin, 141*(6), 1178–1204. https://doi.org/10.1037/a0039729

Tannenbaum, P. H., & Zillmann, D. (1975). Emotional arousal in the facilitation of aggression through communication. In L. Berkowitz (Ed.), *Advances in experimental social psychology* (Vol. 8, pp. 149–192). Academic Press.

Taylor, C., & Stern, B. (1997). Asian-Americans: Television advertising and the "model minority" stereotype. *Journal of Advertising, 26*(2), 47–61. https://doi.org/10.1080/00913367.1997.10673522

Taylor, C. B., Winzelberg, A., & Celio, A. (2001). Use of interactive media to prevent eating disorders. In R. Striegel-Moor & L. Smolak (Eds.), *Eating disorders: New direction for research and practice* (pp. 255–270). APA.

Taylor, L. D. (2005). Effects of visual and verbal sexual television content and perceived realism on attitudes and beliefs. *The Journal of Sex Research, 42*(2), 130–137. https://doi.org/10.1080/00224490509552266

Taylor, L. D., Alexopoulos, C., & Ghaznavi, J. (2016). Touchy subjects: Sex in the workplace on broadcast, cable, and internet television. *Sex Roles: A Journal of Research, 75*(9–10), 476–489. https://doi.org/10.1007/s11199-016-0642-x

Taylor, M., & Gunby, K. (2016). Moving beyond the sound bite: Complicating the relationship between negative television news framing and in-depth reporting on activism. *Sociologial Forum, 31*(3), 577–598. https://doi.org/10.1111/socf.12264

Teevan, J. J., & Hartnagel, T. F. (1976). The effect of television violence on the perception of crime by adolescents. *Sociology and Social Research, 60,* 337–348.

Tefertiller, A., & Sheehan, K. (2019). TV in the streaming age: Motivations, behaviors, and satisfaction of post-network television. *Journal of Broadcasting & Electronic Media, 63*(4), 595–616. https://doi.org/10.1080/08838151.2019.1698233

Terlecki, M., Brown, J., Harner-Steciw, L., Irvin-Hannum, J., Marchetto-Ryan, N., Ruhl, L., & Wiggins, J. (2011). Sex differences and similarities in video game experience, preferences, and self-efficacy: Implications for the gaming industry. *Current Psychology, 30,* 22–33. https://doi.org/10.1007/s12144-010-9095-5

Tewksbury, D. (2020). Accessibility-applicability model. In J. Van den Bulck (Ed.), *The international encyclopedia of media psychology.* Wiley. https://doi.org/10.1002/9781119011071.iemp0231

Tewksbury, D., Jones, J., Peske, M., Raymond, A., & Vig, W. (2000). The interaction of news and advocate frames: Manipulating audience perceptions of a local public policy issue. *Journalism & Mass Communication Quarterly, 77*(4), 804–829. https://doi.org/10.1177/1077699000077004

Tewksbury, D., & Riles, J. M. (2018). Framing in an interactive news environment. In P. D'Angelo (Ed.), *Doing news framing analysis II: Empirical and theoretical perspectives* (2nd ed., pp. 137–162). Routledge.

Tewksbury, D., & Rittenburg, J. (2012). *News on the internet: Information and citizenship in the 21st century.* Oxford University Press.

Tewksbury, D., & Scheufele, D. A. (2009). News framing theory and research. In J. Bryant & M. B. Oliver (Eds.), *Media effects: Advances in theory and research* (3rd ed., pp. 17–33). Routledge.

Tewksbury, D., & Scheufele, D. A. (2020). News framing theory and research. In M. B. Oliver, A. A. Raney, & J. Bryant (Eds.), *Media effects: Advances in theory and research* (4th ed., pp. 51–68). Routledge.

Thayer, J. F., & Levenson, R. W. (1983). Effects of music on psychophysiological responses to a stressful film. *Psychomusicology: A Journal of Research in Music Cognition, 3*(1), 44–52. https://doi.org/10.1037/h0094256

The Effect of Television Violence on Children: What Policymakers Need to Know: Subcommittee on Telecommunications and the Internet, 108th Cong. (2004). (Testimony of Ronald M. Davis). https://www.govinfo.gov/content/pkg/CHRG-108hhrg96095/html/CHRG-108hhrg96095.htm

The Magic School Bus TV Project. (1997, March). *The Magic School Bus* research findings: Executive summary. https://www.osti.gov/servlets/purl/451251

Thomas, M. H., Horton, R. W., Lippincott, E. C., & Drabman, R. S. (1977). Desensitization to portrayals of real-life aggression as a function of exposure to television violence. *Journal of Personality and Social Psychology, 35*(6), 450–458. https://doi.org/10.1037/0022-3514.35.6.450

Thompson, D., & Filik, R. (2016). Sarcasm in written communication: Emoticons are efficient markers of intention. *Journal of Computer-Mediated Communication, 21*(2), 105–120. https://doi.org/10.1111/jcc4.12156

Thompson, K. M., & Yokota, E. (2001). Depiction of alcohol, tobacco, and other substances in G-rated animated films. *Pediatrics, 107*(6), 1369–1374. https://doi.org/10.1542/peds.107.6.1369

Thompson, S. (1998). Origins of advertising, 1600–1833. In W. D. Sloan (Ed.), *The age of mass communication* (pp. 81–95). Vision Press.

Thompson, S., & Bryant, J. (2000, June). *Debunking the media effects gospel: A reexamination of media effects research history and directions for researchers of the twenty-first century* [Paper presentation]. International Communication Association 50th Annual Conference, Acapulco, Mexico.

Thomson, S., Kluftinger, E., & Wentland, J. (2018). Are you fluent in sexual emoji? Exploring the use of emoji in romantic and sexual contexts. *The Canadian Journal of Human Sexuality, 27*(3), 226–234. https://doi.org/10.3138/cjhs.2018-0020

Thorson, E. (2016). Belief echoes: The persistent effects of corrected misinformation. *Political Communication, 33*(3), 460–480. https://doi.org/10.1080/10584609.2015.1102187

Tichenor, P. J., Donohue, G. A., & Olien, C. N. (1970). Mass media flow and differential growth of knowledge. *Public Opinion Quarterly, 34*(2), 159–170. https://doi.org/10.1086/267786

Tiggemann, M., & Zaccardo, M. (2015). "Exercise to be fit, not skinny": The effect of fitspiration imagery on women's body image. *Body Image, 15,* 61–67. https://doi.org/10.1016/j.bodyim.2015.06.003

Timmermans, E., Coenen, L., & Van den Bulck, J. (2019). The Bridget Jones effect: The relationship between exposure to romantic media contents and fear of being single among emerging adults. *Psychology of Popular Media Culture, 8*(2), 159–169. https://doi.org/10.1037/ppm0000175

Timmermans, E., & Van den Bulck, J. (2018). Casual sexual scripts on the screen: A quantitative content analysis. *Archives of Sexual Behavior, 47*(5), 1481–1496. https://doi.org/10.1007/s10508-018-1147-1

Tito, G. (2011a, February). Inside the sick mind of a *School Shooter* mod. *The Escapist.* https://www.escapistmagazine.com/news/view/108065-inside-the-sick-mind-of-a-school-shooter-mod

Tito, G. (2011b, March). ModDB shuts down *School Shooter* mod. *The Escapist.* http://www.escapistmagazine.com/news/view/108695-moddb-shuts-down-school-shooter-mod

Tiu, M., McCarthy, B., & Li, L. (2015). OddSquad: *Learning math with PBS KIDS transmedia content at school and home: A report to the CPB-PBS Ready to Learn Initiative.* WestEd. https://www.wested.org/wp-content/uploads/2016/11/1459805907resourceoddsquadlearningmathwithpbskidstransmediacontentatschoolandhome-3.pdf

Tokunaga, R. S., Wright, P. J., & Roskos, J. E. (2019). Pornography and impersonal sex. *Human Communication Research, 45*(1), 78–118. https://doi.org/10.1093/hcr/hqy014

Tormala, Z. L., Briñol, P., & Petty, R. E. (2006). When credibility attacks: The reverse impact of source credibility on persuasion. *Journal of Experimental Social Psychology, 42*(5), 684–691. https://doi.org/10.1016/j.jesp.2005.10.005

Towbin, M. A., Haddock, S. A., Zimmerman, T. S., Lund, L., & Tanner, L. R. (2003). Images of gender, race, age, and sexual orientation in Disney feature-length animated films. *Journal of Feminist Family Therapy: An International Forum, 15*(4), 19–44. https://doi.org/10.1300/J086v15n04_02

Towner, T., & Muñoz, C. L. (2020). Instagramming issues: Agenda setting during the 2016 presidential campaign. *Social Media + Society, 6*(3). https://doi.org/10.1177/2056305120940803

Tromholt, M. (2016). The Facebook experiment: Quitting Facebook leads to higher levels of well-being. *Cyberpsychology, Behavior, and Social Networking, 19*(11), 661–666. https://doi.org/10.1089/cyber.2016.0259

Troseth, G. L. (2003). Getting a clear picture: Young children's understanding of a televised image. *Developmental Science, 6*(3), 247–253. https://doi.org/10.1111/1467-7687.00280

Troseth, G. L. & DeLoache, D. S. (1998). The medium can obscure the message: Young children's understanding of video. *Child Development, 69*(4), 950–965. https://doi.org/10.2307/1132355

Trussler, M., & Soroka, S. (2014). Consumer demand for cynical and negative news frames. *The International Journal of Press/Politics, 19*(3), 360–379. https://doi.org/10.1177/1940161214524832

Truth Initiative (2017, February 6). *What do tobacco advertising restrictions look like today?* https://truthinitiative.org/research-resources/tobacco-industry-marketing/what-do-tobacco-advertising-restrictions-look-today

Truth Initiative. (2019). *While you were streaming: Smoking on demand.* https://truthinitiative.org/research-resources/tobacco-pop-culture/while-you-were-streaming-smoking-demand

Tsay-Vogel, M., Shanahan, J., & Signorielli, N. (2018). Social media cultivating perceptions of privacy: A 5-year analysis of privacy attitudes and self-disclosure behaviors among Facebook users. *New Media & Society, 20*(1), 141–161. https://doi.org/10.1177/1461444816660731

Tseng-Putterman, M. (2018, August 23). One way that *Crazy Rich Asians* is a step backward. *The Atlantic.* https://www.theatlantic.com/entertainment/archive/2018/08/asian-americas-great-gatsby-moment/568213/

Tsfati, Y., & Nir, L. (2017). Frames and reasoning: Two pathways from selective exposure to affective polarization. *International Journal of Communication, 11*(22), 301–322.

Tsfati, Y., Stroud, N. J., & Chotiner, A. (2014). Exposure to ideological news and perceived opinion climate: Testing the media effects component of spiral-of-silence in a fragmented media landscape. *The International Journal of Press/Politics, 19*(1), 3–23. https://doi.org/10.1177/1940161213508206

Tsfati, Y., & Walter, N. (2020). The world of news and politics. In M. B. Oliver, A. A. Raney, & J. Bryant (Eds.), *Media effects: Advances in theory and research* (4th ed., pp. 36–50). Routledge.

Tuchman, G. (1978). *Making news: A study in the construction of reality.* Free Press.

Tudor, A. (1989). *Monsters and mad scientists: A cultural history of the horror movie.* Blackwell.

Tukachinsky, R., Mastro, D., & Yarchi, M. (2015). Documenting portrayals of race/ethnicity on primetime television over a 20-year span and their association with national-level racial/ethnic attitudes. *Journal of Social Issues, 71*(1), 17–38. https://doi.org/10.1111/josi.12094

Tukachinsky, R., Mastro, D., & Yarchi, M. (2017). The effect of prime time television ethnic/racial stereotypes on Latino and Black Americans: A longitudinal national level study. *Journal of Broadcasting & Electronic Media, 61*(3), 538–556. https://doi.org/10.1080/08838151.2017.1344669

Turcotte, J., York, C., Irving, J., Scholl, R. M., & Pingree, R. J. (2015). News recommendations from social media opinion leaders: Effects on media trust and information seeking. *Journal of Computer-Mediated Communication, 20*(5), 520–535. https://doi.org/10.1111/jcc4.12127

Turner, C., & Berkowitz, L. (1972). Identification with film aggressor (covert role taking) and reactions to film violence. *Journal of Personality and Social Psychology, 21*(2), 256–264. https://doi.org/10.1037/h0032267

Turner, J. S. (2011). Sex and the spectacle of music videos: An examination of the portrayal of race and sexuality in music videos. *Sex Roles: A Journal of Research, 64*, 173–191. https://doi.org/10.1007/s11199-010-9766-6

Twenge, J. M., Martin, G. N., & Spitzberg, B. H. (2019). Trends in U.S. adolescents' media use, 1976–2016: The rise of digital media, the decline of TV, and the (near) demise of print. *Psychology of Popular Media, 8*(4), 329–345. https://doi.org/10.1037/ppm0000203

Tyler, T. R. (1980). The impact of directly and indirectly experienced events: The origin of crime-related judgments and behaviors. *Journal of Personality and Social Psychology, 39*(1), 13–28. https://doi.org/10.1037/0022-3514.39.1.13

Tyler, T. R. (1984). Assessing the risk of crime victimization and socially-transmitted information. *Journal of Social Issues, 40*(1), 27–38. https://doi.org/10.1111/j.1540-4560.1984.tb01080.x

Tyler, T. R., & Cook, F. L. (1984). The mass media and judgments of risk: Distinguishing impact on personal and societal level judgments. *Journal of Personality and Social Psychology, 47*(4), 693–708. https://doi.org/10.1037/0022-3514.47.4.693

Ugwu, R. (2020, September 9). The hashtag that changed the Oscars: An oral history. *The New York Times.* https://www.nytimes.com/2020/02/06/movies/oscarssowhite-history.html

Uhlmann, E., & Swanson, J. (2004). Exposure to violent video games increases automatic aggressiveness. *Journal of Adolescence, 27*(1), 41–52. https://doi.org/10.1016/j.adolescence.2003.10.004

U.S. Department of Commerce. (1993). *We the Americans: Blacks.* https://www.census.gov/prod/cen1990/wepeople/we-1.pdf

U.S. Department of Health and Human Services. (1994). *Preventing tobacco use among young people: Report of the Surgeon General.* https://www.cdc.gov/mmwr/pdf/rr/rr4304.pdf

U.S. Department of Health and Human Services. (2012). *Preventing tobacco use among youth and young adults: A report from the Surgeon General.* https://www.ncbi.nlm.nih.gov/books/NBK99237/

U.S. Food and Drug Administration. (2021, March 9). *Cigarette labeling and health warning requirements.* https://www.fda.gov/tobacco-products/labeling-and-warning-statements-tobacco-products/cigarette-labeling-and-health-warning-requirements

478   References

U.S. Surgeon General's Scientific Advisory Committee on Television and Social Behavior. (1971). *Television and growing up: The impact of televised violence* (DHEW publication No. HSM 72–9086). https://www.ojp.gov/pdffiles1/Digitization/147171NCJRS.pdf

Ustjanauskas, A. E., Harris, J. L., & Schwartz, M. B. (2014). Food and beverage advertising on children's web sites. *Pediatric Obesity, 9*(5), 362–372. https://doi.org/10.1111/j.2047-6310.2013.00185.x

Vaghettie, C. A. O., Monteiro-Junior, R. S., Finco, M. D., Reategui, E., & Silva da Costa Botelho, S. (2018). Exergames experience in physical education: A review, *Physical Culture and Sport. Studies and Research, 78*(1), 23–32. https://doi.org/10.2478/pcssr-2018-0010

Valentino, N. A. (1999). Crime news and the priming of racial attitudes during evaluations of the president. *Public Opinion Quarterly, 63*(3), 293–320. https://doi.org/10.1086/297722

Valentino, N. A., Beckmann, M. N., & Buhr, T. A. (2001). A spiral of cynicism for some: The contingent effects of campaign news frames on participation and confidence in government. *Political Communication, 18*(4), 347–367. https://doi.org/10.1080/10584600152647083

Valentino, N. A., Neuner, F. G., & Vandenbroek, L. M. (2018). The changing norms of racial political rhetoric and the end of racial priming. *The Journal of Politics, 80*(3), 757–771. https://doi.org/10.1086/694845

Valenzuela, S., Park, N., & Kee, K. F. (2009). Is there social capital in a social network site?: Facebook use and college students' life satisfaction, trust, and participation. *Journal of Computer-Mediated Communication, 14*(4), 875–901. https://doi.org/10.1111/j.1083-6101.2009.01474.x

Valenzuela, S., Puente, S., & Flores, P. M. (2017). Comparing disaster news on Twitter and television: An intermedia agenda setting perspective. *Journal of Broadcasting & Electronic Media, 61*(4), 615–637. https://doi.org/10.1080/08838151.2017.1344673

Valkenburg, P. M. (2017). Understanding self-effects in social media. *Human Communication Research, 43*(4), 477–490. https://doi.org/10.1111/hcre.12113

Valkenburg, P. M., Cantor, J., & Peeters, A. L. (2000). Fright reactions to television: A child survey. *Communication Research, 27*(1), 82–97. https://doi.org/10.1177/009365000027001004

Valkenburg, P. M., & Oliver, M. B. (2020) Media effects theories: An Overview. In M. B. Oliver, A. A. Raney, & J. Bryant (Eds.), *Media effects: Advances in theory and research* (4th ed., pp. 16–33).

Valkenburg, P. M., & Peter, J. (2013). The differential susceptibility to media effects model. *Journal of Communication, 62*(2), 221–243. https://doi.org/10.1111/jcom.12024

Valkenburg, P. M., Peter, J., & Walther, J. B. (2016). Media effects: Theory and research. *Annual Review of Psychology, 67*, 315–338.

Valkenburg, P. M., & Piotrowski, J. T. (2017). *Plugged in: How media attract and affect youth.* Yale University Press.

Vandenbosch, L., & van Oosten, J. M. F. (2017). The relationship between online pornography and the sexual objectification of women: The attenuating role of porn literacy education. *Journal of Communication, 67*(6), 1015–1036. https://doi.org/10.1111/jcom.12341

Van den Bulck, J. (2004). Media use and dreaming: The relationship among television viewing, computer game play, and nightmares or pleasant dreams. *Dreaming, 14*(1), 43–49. https://doi.org/10.1037/1053-0797.14.1.43

Van den Bulck, J., Çetin, Y., Terzi, Ö., & Bushman, B. J. (2016). Violence, sex, and dreams: Violent and sexual media content infiltrate our dreams at night. *Dreaming, 26*(4), 271–279. https://doi.org/10.1037/drm0000036

Van Dijk, T. A., & Kintsch, W. (1983). *Strategies of discourse comprehension.* Academic Press.

van Doorn, B. W. (2015). Pre- and post-welfare reform media portrayals of poverty in the United States: The continuing importance of race and ethnicity. *Politics & Policy, 43*(1), 142–162. https://doi.org/10.1111/polp.12107

Van Duyn, E., & Collier, J. (2018). Priming and fake news: The effects of elite discourse on evaluations of news media. *Mass Communication and Society, 22*, 29–48. https://doi.org/10.1080/15205436.2018.1511807

Van Gorp, B. (2007). The constructionist approach to framing: Bringing culture back in. *Journal of Communication, 57*(1), 60–78. https://doi.org/10.1111/j.1460-2466.2006.00329.x

Van Laethem, M., van Vianen, A. E. M., & Derks, D. (2018). Daily fluctuations in smartphone use, psychological detachment, and work engagement: The role of workplace telepressure. *Frontiers in Psychology, 9*, Article 1808. https://doi.org/10.3389/fpsyg.2018.01808

Vanman, E. J., Baker, R., & Tobin, S. J. (2018). The burden of online friends: The effects of giving up Facebook on stress and well-being. *The Journal of Social Psychology, 158*(4), 496–507. https://doi.org/10.1080/00224545.2018.1453467

van Oosten, J. M., Peter, J., & Boot, I. (2015). Exploring associations between exposure to sexy online self-presentations and adolescents' sexual attitudes and behavior. *Journal of Youth and Adolescence, 44*(5), 1078–1091. https://doi.org/10.1007/s10964-014-0194-8

van Rooij, A. J., & Prause, N. (2014). A critical review of "internet addiction" criteria with suggestions for the future. *Journal of Behavioral Addictions, 3*(4), 203–213. https://doi.org/10.1556/JBA.3.2014.4.1

Vargo, C. J. (2018). Fifty years of agenda-setting research: New directions and challenges for the theory. *The Agenda Setting Journal, 2*(2), 105–123. https://doi.org/10.1075/asj.18023.var

Vargo, C. J., Basilaia, E., & Shaw, D. L. (2015). Event versus issue: Twitter reflections of major news: A case study. In S. Cotton & L. Robinson (Eds.), *Studies in media and communications, vol. 9: Communication and information technologies annual* (pp. 215–239). Emerald Group. https://doi.org/10.1108/S2050-206020150000009009

Vargo, C. J., & Guo, L. (2017). Networks, big data, and intermedia agenda setting: An analysis of traditional, partisan, and emerging online U.S. news. *Journalism & Mass Communication Quarterly, 94*(4), 1031–1055. https://doi.org/10.1177/1077699016679976

Vargo, C. J., Guo, L., McCombs, M., & Shaw, D. L. (2014). Network issue agendas on Twitter during the 2012 U.S. presidential election. *Journal of Communication, 64*(2), 296–316. https://doi.org/10.1111/jcom.12089

Vega, R. P., Anderson, A. J., & Kaplan, S. A. (2015). A within-person examination of the effects of telework. *Journal of Business and Psychology, 30*(2), 313–323. https://doi.org/10.1007/s10869-014-9359-4

Velasquez, A., & LaRose, R. (2015). Social media for social change: Social media political efficacy and activism in student activist groups. *Journal of Broadcasting & Electronic Media, 59*(3), 456–474. https://doi.org/10.1080/08838151.2015.1054998

Velasquez, A., & Quenette, A. M. (2018). Facilitating social meidanad offline political enagagement during electoral cycles: Using social cognitive theory to explain political action among Hispanics and Latinos. *Mass Communication and Society, 21*(6), 763–784. https://doi.org/10.1080/15205436.2018.1484489

Velten, E. (1968). A laboratory task for the induction of mood states. *Behavior Research and Therapy, 6*(4), 473–482. https://doi.org/10.1016/0005-7967(68)90028-4

Verto Analytics. (2018). *Consumer behavior in 2018: Three trends to watch.* https://insights.vertoanalytics.com/Verto-Report-Trend-Forecast-2018.pdf

Vilela, A. M., & Nelson, M. R. (2016). Testing the selectivity hypothesis in cause-related marketing among Generation Y: [When] does gender matter for short- and long-term persuasion? *Journal of Marketing Communications, 22*(1), 18–35. https://doi.org/10.1080/13527266.2013.841272

Vogel, E. A., Rose, J. P., Roberts, L. R., & Eckles, K. (2014). Social comparison, social media, and self-esteem. *Psychology of Popular Media Culture, 3*(4), 206–222. https://doi.org/10.1037/ppm0000047

Vogel, J. J., Vogel, D. S., Cannon-Bowers, J., Bowers, C. A., Muse, K., & Wright, M. (2006). Computer gaming and interactive simulations for learning: A meta-analysis. *Journal of Educational Computing Research, 34*(3), 229–243. https://doi.org/10.2190/FLHV-K4WA-WPVQ-H0YM

von Salisch, M., Vogelgesang, J., Kristen, A., & Oppl, C. (2011). Preference for violent electronic games and aggressive behavior among children: The beginning of the downward spiral? *Media Psychology, 14*(3), 233–258. https://doi.org/10.1080/15213269.2011.596468

Vorderer, P. (2001). It's all entertainment—sure. But what exactly is entertainment? Communication research, media psychology, and the explanation of entertainment experiences. *Poetics, 29*(4–5), 247–261. https://doi.org/10.1016/S0304-422X(01)00037-7

Vorderer, P., & Bryant, J. (Eds.) (2006). *Playing video games: Motives, responses, and consequences.* Lawrence Erlbaum Associates.

Vorderer, P., & Hartmann, T. (2009). Entertainment and enjoyment as media effects. In J. Bryant & M. B. Oliver (Eds.), *Media effects: Advances in theory and research* (3rd ed., pp. 532–550). Routledge

Vorderer, P., Hefner, D., Reinecke, L., & Klimmt, C. (Eds.). (2018). *Permanently online, permanently connected: Living and communicating in a POPC world.* Routledge.

Vorderer, P., Park, D. W., & Lutz, S. (2020). A history of media effects research traditions. In M. B. Oliver, A. A. Raney, & J. Bryant (Eds.), *Media effects: Advances in theory and research* (4th ed., pp. 1–15). Routledge.

Wagner, S. (1985). *Comprehensive evaluation of the fourth season of 3-2-1 Contact.* Children's Television Workshop.

Wakefield, M. A., Loken, B., & Hornik, R. C. (2010). Use of mass media campaigns to change health behaviour. *Lancet, 376*(9748), 1261–1271. https://doi.org/10.1016/S0140-6736(10)60809-4

Walden, J. A. (2016). Integrating social media into the workplace: A study of shifting technology use repertoires. *Journal of Broadcasting & Electronic Media, 60*(2), 347–363. https://doi.org/10.1080/08838151.2016.1164163

Wall, W. D., & Simson, W. A. (1950). The emotional responses of adolescent groups to certain films. *British Journal of Educational Psychology, 20*(3), 153–163. https://doi.org/10.1111/j.2044-8279.1950.tb01653.x

Wallack, L. (1989). Mass communication and health promotion: A critical perspective. In R. E. Rice

& C. K. Atkin (Eds.), *Public communication campaigns* (2nd ed., pp. 353–367). Sage.

Walma van der Molen, J. H., & Bushman, B. J. (2008). Children's direct fright and worry reactions to violence in fiction and news television programs. *The Journal of Pediatrics, 153*(3), 420–424. https://doi.org/10.1016/j.jpeds.2008.03.036

Walsh-Childers, K. (1994a). Newspaper influence on health policy development: A case study investigation. *Newspaper Research Journal, 15*(3), 89–104. https://doi.org/10.1177/073953299401500308

Walsh-Childers, K. (1994b). "A death in the family": A case study of newspaper influence on health policy development. *Journalism Quarterly, 71*(4), 820–829. https://doi.org/10.1177/107769909407100406

Walsh-Childers, K., & Brown, J. D. (2009). Effects of media on personal and public health. In J. Bryant & M. B. Oliver (Eds.), *Media effects: Advances in theory and research* (3rd ed., pp. 469–489). Routledge.

Walt Disney Company. (2015). Smoking in movies. https://thewaltdisneycompany.com/app/uploads/Smoking-in-Movies.pdf

Walter, N., Cody, M. J., Xu, L. Z., & Murphy, S. T. (2018). A priest, a rabbi, and a minister walk into a bar: A meta-analysis of humor effects on persuasion. *Human Communication Research, 44*(4), 343–373. https://doi.org/10.1093/hcr/hqy005

Wang, T. L. (2000). Agenda-setting online: An experiment testing the effects of hyperlinks in online newspapers. *Southwestern Mass Communication Journal, 15*(2), 59–70.

Wang, T. W., Neff, L. J., Park-Lee, E., Ren, C., Cullen, K. A., & King, B. A. (2020). E-cigarette use among middle and high school students—United States, 2020. *Morbidity and Mortality Weekly Report, 69*(37), 1310–1312. http://doi.org/10.15585/mmwr.mm6937e1

Wang, Y., Monteiro, C., & Popkin, B. M. (2002). Trends of overweight and underweight in children and adolescents in the United States, Brazil, China, and Russia. *American Journal of Clinical Nutrition, 75*(6), 971–977. https://doi.org/10.1093/ajcn/75.6.971

Wanta, W. (1988). The effects of dominant photographs: An agenda-setting experiment. *Journalism Quarterly, 65*(1), 107–111. https://doi.org/10.1177/107769908806500114

Wanta, W., & Alkazemi, M. F. (2017). Agenda-setting: History and research tradition. In P. Rössler (Ed.), *International encyclopedia of media effects* (Vol. 1, pp. 12–25). Wiley-Blackwell. https://doi.org/10.1002/9781118783764.wbieme0030

Wanta, W., & Foote, J. (1994). The president-news media relationship: A time series analysis of agenda-setting. *Journal of Broadcasting & Electronic Media, 38*(4), 437–449. https://doi.org/10.1080/08838159409364277

Wanta, W., & Ghanem, S. (2000). Effects of agenda-setting. In J. Bryant & R. Carveth (Eds.), *Meta-analyses of media effects*. Lawrence Erlbaum Associates.

Wanta, W., Stephenson, M. A., Turk, J. V., & McCombs, M. E. (1989). How president's state of the union talk influenced news media agendas. *Journalism Quarterly, 66*(3), 537–541. https://doi.org/10.1177/107769908906600301

Waples, D. (1942a). Communications. *The American Journal of Sociology, 47*(6), 907–917. http://www.jstor.org/stable/2770096

Waples, D. (Ed.). (1942b). *Print, radio, and film in a democracy*. University of Chicago Press.

Waples, D., Berelson, B., & Bradshaw, F. R. (1940). *What reading does to people: A summary of evidence on the social effects of reading and a statement of problems for research*. University of Chicago Press.

Wartella, E. (1996). The history reconsidered. In E. E. Dennis & E. Wartella (Eds.), *American communication research—The remembered history* (pp. 169–180). Lawrence Erlbaum Associates.

Watt, J. G., Jr., & van den Berg, S. A. (1978). Time series analysis of alternative media effects theories. In R. D. Ruben (Ed.), *Communication yearbook 2* (pp. 215–224). Transaction Books.

Wawrzuta, D., Jaworski, M., Gotlib, J., & Panczyk, M. (2021). Characteristics of antivaccine messages on social media: Systematic review. *Journal of Medical Internet Research, 23*(6), Article e24564. https://doi.org/10.2196/24564

Weaver, A. J. (2011). A meta-analytical review of selective exposure to and the enjoyment of media violence. *Journal of Broadcasting & Electronic Media, 55*(2), 232–250. https://doi.org/10.1080/08838151.2011.570826

Weaver, A. J., Jenson, J. D., Martins, N., Hurley, R., & Wilson, B. J. (2011). Liking violence and action: An examination of gender differences in children's processing of animated content. *Media Psychology, 14*(1), 49–70. https://psycnet.apa.org/record/2011-05048-003

Weaver, D. H. (1977). Political issues and voter need for orientation. In D. L. Shaw & M. E. McCombs (Eds.), *The emergence of American political issues* (pp. 107–119). West.

Weaver, D. H. (2007). Thoughts on agenda setting, framing, and priming. *Journal of Communication, 57*(1), 142–147. https://doi.org/10.1111/j.1460-2466.2006.00333.x

Weaver, D. H., Graber, D. A., McCombs, M. E., & Eyal, C. H. (1981). *Media agenda-setting in a presidential election: Issues, images and interests*. Praeger.

Weaver, J. B., III, & Tamborini, R. (Eds.) (1996). *Horror films: Current research on audience preferences and reactions*. Lawrence Erlbaum Associates.

Weaver, J., & Wakshlag, J. (1986). Perceived vulnerability to crime, criminal victimization experience, and television viewing. *Journal of Broadcasting & Electronic Media, 30*(2), 141–158. https://doi.org/10.1080/08838158609386616

Webb, T., Martin, K., Afifi, A. A., & Kraus, J. (2010). Media literacy as a violence-prevention strategy: A pilot evaluation. *Health Promotion Practice, 11*(5), 714–722. https://doi.org/10.1177/1524839908328998

Weeks, B. E., Ardèvol-Abreu, A., & Gil de Zúñiga, H. (2017). Online influence? Social media use, opinion leadership, and political persuasion. *International Journal of Public Opinion Research, 29*(2), 214–239. https://doi.org/10.1093/ijpor/edv050

Weeks, B. E., Kim, D. H., Hahn, L. B., Diehl, T. H., & Kwak, N. (2019). Hostile media perceptions in the age of social media: Following politicians, emotions, and perceptions of media bias. *Journal of Broadcasting & Electronic Media, 63*(3), 374–392. https://doi.org/10.1080/08838151.2019.1653069

Weeks, K. R., Dixon, T. L., Tolbert, A. N., & Sevilla, M. (2020). Black stereotypes in the media: A continuing problem. In A. C. Billings & S. Parrott (Eds.), *Media stereotypes: From ageism to xenophobia* (pp. 93–111). Peter Lang.

Weinberger, M. (2016, September 3). This is what it's like to travel the world on a global Pokémon Go adventure. *Business Insider.* https://www.businessinsider.com/pokemon-go-nick-johnson-trip-2016-9

Weinstein, A. M. (2010). Computer and video game addiction—A comparison between game users and non-game users. *The American Journal of Drug and Alcohol Abuse, 36*(5), 268–276. https://doi.org/10.3109/00952990.2010.491879

Weiser, E. B., (2015). #Me: Narcissism and its facets as predictors of selfie-posting frequency. *Personality and Individual Differences, 86*, 477–481. https://doi.org/10.1016/j.paid.2015.07.007

Weiss, B. W., Katkin, E. S., & Rubin, B. M. (1968). Relationship between a factor analytically derived measure of a specific fear and performance after related fear induction. *Journal of Abnormal Psychology, 73*(5), 461–463. https://doi.org/10.1037/h0026153

Weld, H. P. (1912). An experimental study of musical enjoyment. *The American Journal of Psychology, 23*(2), 245–308. https://doi.org/10.2307/1412844

Wellman, A., Meitl, M. B., & Kinkade, P. (2021). Lady and the vamp: Roles, sexualization, and brutalization of women in slasher films. *Sexuality & Culture, 25*, 660–679. https://doi.org/10.1007/s12119-020-09788-4

Wells, C., Shah, D. V., Pevehouse, J. C., Yang, J., Pelled, A., Boehm, F., Lukito, J., Ghosh, S., &

Schmidt, J. L. (2016). How Trump drove coverage to the nomination: Hybrid media campaigning. *Political Communication, 33*(4), 669–676. https://doi.org/10.1080/10584609.2016.1224416

Wells, G., Horwitz, J., & Seetharaman, D. (2021, September 14). Facebook knows Instagram is toxic for teen girls, company documents show. *Wall Street Journal.* https://www.wsj.com/articles/facebook-knows-instagram-is-toxic-for-teen-girls-company-documents-show-11631620739?mod=hp_lead_pos7

Welsh, A. (2010). On the perils of living dangerously in the slasher horror film: Gender differences in the association between sexual activity and survival. *Sex Roles, 62*, 762–773. https://doi.org/10.1007/s11199-010-9762-x

Wertham, F. (1954). *Seduction of the innocent.* Rinehart.

West, D. (1993) *Air wars.* Congressional Quarterly Press.

Westley, B. H., & MacLean, M. (1957). A conceptual model for mass communication research. *Journalism Quarterly, 34*(1), 31–38. https://doi.org/10.1177/107769905703400103

Wetterneck, C. T., Burgess, A. J., Short, M. B., Smith, A. H., & Cervantes, M. E. (2012). The role of sexual compulsivity, impulsivity, and experiential avoidance in internet pornography use. *The Psychological Record, 62*(1), 3–18. https://doi.org/10.1007/BF03395783

Wheeler, S. C., Petty, R. E., & Bizer, G. Y. (2005). Self-schema matching and attitude change: Situation and dispositional determinants of message elaboration. *Journal of Consumer Research, 31*(4), 787–797. https://doi.org/10.1086/426613

Whitehead, C. (2014). *The nobel hustle: Poker, beef jerky and death.* Anchor Books.

Wicke, P., & Bolognesi, M. M. (2020). Framing COVID-19: How we conceptualize and discuss the pandemic on Twitter. *PLOS ONE, 15*(9), Article e0240010. https://doi.org/10.1371/journal.pone.0240010

Widyanto, L., & Griffiths, M. D. (2011). A psychometric comparison of the internet addiction test, the internet-related problem scale, and self-diagnosis. *Cyberpsychology, Behavior, and Social Networking, 14*(3), 141–149. https://doi.org/10.1089/cyber.2010.0151

Wiersma, B. A. (2001). *The gendered world of Disney: A content analysis of gender themes in full-length animated Disney feature films* [Doctoral dissertation, South Dakota State University]. Open PRAIRIE. https://openprairie.sdstate.edu/cgi/viewcontent.cgi?article=2925&context=etd

Williams, D. (2006). Virtual cultivation: Online worlds, offline perceptions. *Journal of Communication, 56*(1), 69–87. https://doi.org/10.1111/j.1460-2466.2006.00004.x

Williams, D., & Skoric, M. (2005). Internet fantasy violence: A test of aggression in an online game.

Communication Monographs, 72(2), 217–233. https://doi.org/10.1080/03637750500111781

Williams, R., & Slak-Valek, N. (2019). Pokémon Go is serious leisure that increases the touristic engagement, physical activity and sense of happiness of players. *Information Technology & Tourism, 21,* 515–533. https://doi.org/10.1007/s40558-019-00153-2

Williams, T. M. (1986). *The impact of television.* Academic.

Willis, M., Jozkowski, K. N., Canan, S. N., Rhoads, K. E., & Hunt, M. E. (2020). Models of sexual consent communication by film rating: A content analysis. *Sexuality & Culture, 24,* 1971–1986. https://doi.org/10.1007/s12119-020-09731-7

Willoughby, D., Evans, M. A., & Nowak, S. (2015). Do ABC eBooks boost engagement and learning in preschoolers? An experimental study comparing eBooks with paper ABC and storybook controls. *Computers & Education, 82,* 107–117. https://doi.org/10.1016/j.compedu.2014.11.008

Wilson, B. J. (1987). Reducing children's emotional reactions to mass media through rehearsed explanation and exposure to a replica of a fear object. *Human Communication Research, 14*(1), 3–26. https://doi.org/10.1111/j.1468-2958.1987.tb00119.x

Wilson, B. J. (1989). The effects of two control strategies on children's emotional reactions to a frightening movie scene. *Journal of Broadcasting & Electronic Media, 33*(4), 397–418.

Wilson, B. J., & Cantor, J. (1985). Developmental differences in empathy with a television protagonist's fear. *Journal of Experimental Child Psychology, 39*(2), 284–299. https://doi.org/10.1016/0022-0965(85)90042-6

Wilson, B. J., & Cantor, J. (1987). Reducing children's fear reactions to mass media: Effects of visual exposure and verbal explanation. In M. McLaughlin (Ed.), *Communication yearbook 10* (pp. 553–573). Sage.

Wilson, B. J., Hoffner, C., & Cantor, J. (1987). Children's perceptions of the effectiveness of techniques to reduce fear from mass media. *Journal of Applied Developmental Psychology, 8*(1), 39–52. https://doi.org/10.1016/0193-3973(87)90019-0

Wilson, B. J., Martins, N., & Marske, A. L. (2005). Children's and parents' fright reactions to kidnapping stories in the news. *Communication Monographs, 72*(1), 46–70. https://doi.org/10.1080/0363775052000342526

Wilson, C., & Gutierrez, F. (1995). *Race, multiculturalism, and the media: From mass to class communication.* Sage.

Wilson, T. D., Lindsey, S., & Schooler, T. Y. (2000). A model of dual attitudes. *Psychological Review, 107*(1), 101–126. https://doi.org/10.1037/0033-295X.107.1.101

Wimmer, R. D., & Dominick, J. R. (1994). *Mass media research: An introduction* (4th ed.). Wadsworth Publishing.

Winett, R. A., Leckliter, I. N., Chinn, D. E., Stahl, B. N., & Love, S. Q. (1985). The effects of television modeling on residential energy conservation. *Journal of Applied Behavior Analysis, 18*(1), 33–44. https://doi.org/10.1901/jaba.1985.18-33

Winn, M. (1977). *The plug-in drug.* Penguin.

Witte, K. (1992). Putting the fear back into fear appeals: The extended parallel process model. *Communication Monographs, 59*(4), 329–349. https://doi.org/10.1080/03637759209376276

Witte, K., & Allen, M. (2000). A meta-analysis of fear appeals: Implications for effective public health programs. *Health Education and Behavior, 27*(5), 591–615. https://doi.org/10.1177/109019810002700506

Wittenbrink, B., & Schwarz, N. (Eds.). (2007). *Implicit measures of attitudes.* Guilford Press.

Wober, J. M. (1978). Televised violence and paranoid perception: The view from Great Britain. *Public Opinion Quarterly, 42*(3), 315–321. https://doi.org/10.1086/268455

Woo, H.-J., & Dominick, J. R. (2001). Daytime television talk shows and the cultivation effect among U.S. and international students. *Journal of Broadcasting & Electronic Media, 45*(4), 598–614. https://doi.org/10.1207/s15506878jobem4504_4

Wood, J. M., & Duke, N. K. (1997). "Reading rainbow": A spectrum of strategies for promoting literacy. *Language Arts, 74*(2), 95–106. https://www.jstor.org/stable/41482846

Wood, R. (1984). An introduction to the American horror film. In B. K. Grant (Ed.), *Planks of reason: Essays on the horror film* (pp. 164–200). Scarecrow Press.

Wood, W., Wong, F. Y., & Chachere, J. G. (1991). Effects of media violence on viewers' aggression in unconstrained social interaction. *Psychological Bulletin, 109*(3), 371–383. https://doi.org/10.1037/0033-2909.109.3.371

Woodruff, S., Agro, A., Wildey, M., & Conway, T. (1995). Point-of-purchase tobacco advertising: Prevalence, correlates, and brief intervention. *Health Values, 19*(5), 56–62.

World Health Organization. (2018, September 14). *What is gaming disorder?* https://www.who.int/news-room/q-a-detail/gaming-disorder

World Internet Project. (2018). *World internet project: International report ninth edition.* USC Annenberg School Center for the Digital Future. https://www.digitalcenter.org/wp-content/uploads/2019/01/World-Internet-Project-report-2018.pdf

Worley, J. R., Rogers, S. N., & Kraemer, R. R. (2011). Metabolic responses to Wii Fit™ video games at different game levels. *Journal of Strength and Con-*

ditioning Research, 25(3), 689–693. https://doi.org/10.1519/JSC.0b013e318207eae9

Wortham, J. (2010). Angry birds, flocking to cell phones everywhere. *New York Times*. https://www.nytimes.com/2010/12/12/technology/12birds.html

Wouters, P., van Nimwegen, C., van Oostendorp, H., & van der Spek, E. D. (2013). A meta-analysis of the cognitive and motivational effects of serious games. *Journal of Educational Psychology, 105*(2), 249–265. https://doi.org/10.1037/a0031311

Wright, C. R. (1960). Functional analysis and mass communication. *Public Opinion Quarterly, 24*(4), 605–620. https://doi.org/10.1086/266976

Wright, J. C., & Huston, A. C. (1995). *Effects of educational TV viewing of lower income preschoolers on academic skills, school readiness, and school adjustment one to three years later: A report to the Children's Television Workshop*. Center for Research on the Influences of Television on Children, The University of Kansas.

Wright, J. C., Huston, A. C., Scantlin, R., & Kotler, J. (2001). The Early Window project: *Sesame Street* prepares children for school. In S. M. Fisch & R. T. Truglio (Eds.), *"G" is for "growing": Thirty years of research on children and* Sesame Street (pp. 97–114). Lawrence Erlbaum Associates.

Wright, J., St. Peters, M., & Huston, A. (1990). Family television use and its relation to children's cognitive skills and social behavior. In J. Bryant (Ed.), *Television and the American family* (pp. 227–251). Lawrence Erlbaum Associates.

Wright, P. J. (2011). Mass media effects on youth sexual behavior assessing the claim for causality. *Annals of the International Communication Association, 35*(1), 343–385. https://doi.org/10.1080/23808985.2011.11679121

Wright, P. J. (2013). Internet pornography exposure and women's attitude toward extramarital sex: An exploratory study. *Communication Studies, 64*(3), 315–336. https://doi.org/10.1080/10510974.2012.755643

Wright, P. J. (2018). Sex education, public opinion, and pornography: A conditional process analysis. *Journal of Health Communication, 23*(5), 495–502. https://doi.org/10.1080/10810730.2018.1472316

Wright, P. J. (2020a). Media and sexuality. In M. B. Oliver, A. A. Raney, & J. Bryant (Eds.), *Media effects: Advances in theory and research* (4th ed., pp. 227–242). Routledge.

Wright, P. J. (2020b). Pornography and sexual behavior: Do sexual attitudes mediate or confound? *Communication Research, 47*(3), 451–475. https://doi.org/10.1177/0093650218796363

Wright, P. J., & Arroyo, A. (2013). Internet pornography and U.S. women's sexual behavior: Results from a national sample. *Mass Communication and Society, 16*(5), 617–638. https://doi.org/10.1080/15205436.2012.754045

Wright, P. J., & Bae, S. (2013). Pornography consumption and attitudes toward homosexuality: A national longitudinal study. *Human Communication Research, 39*(4), 492–513. https://doi.org/10.1111/hcre.12009

Wright, P. J., & Bae, S. (2015). U.S. adults' pornography consumption and attitudes toward adolescents' access to birth control: A national panel study. *International Journal of Sexual Health, 27*(1), 69–82. https://doi.org/10.1080/19317611.2014.944294

Wright, P. J., Miezan, E., Sun, C., & Steffen, N. J. (2019). Relational monogamy, condomless sex, and perceptions of pornography as sexual information in an English sample. *Sex Health, 16*(1), 70–74. https://doi.org/10.1071/SH18050

Wright, P. J., Paul, B. Herbenick, D., & Tokunaga, R. S. (2021). Pornography and sexual dissatisfaction: The role of pornographic arousal, upward pornographic comparisons, and preference for pornographic masturbation. *Human Communication Research, 47*(2), 192–214. https://doi.org/10.1093/hcr/hqab001

Wright, P. J., & Randall, A. K. (2014). Pornography consumption, education, and support for same-sex marriage among adult U.S. males. *Communication Research, 41*(5), 665–689. https://doi.org/10.1177/0093650212471558

Wright, P. J., Randall, A. K., & Arroyo, A. (2013). Father-daughter communication about sex moderates the association between exposure to MTV's *16 and Pregnant / Teen Mom* and female students' pregnancy-risk behavior. *Sexuality & Culture, 17*, 50–66. https://doi.org/10.1007/s12119-012-9137-2

Wright, P. J., Sun, C., & Steffen, N. (2018). Pornography consumption, perceptions of pornography as sexual information, and condom use. *Journal of Sex & Marital Therapy, 44*(8), 800–805. https://doi.org/10.1080/0092623X.2018.1462278

Wright, P. J., Tokunaga, R. S., & Bae, S. (2014a). More than a dalliance? Pornography consumption and extramarital sex attitudes among married U.S. adults. *Psychology of Popular Media Culture, 3*(2), 97–109. https://doi.org/10.1037/ppm0000024

Wright, P. J., Tokunaga, R. S., & Bae, S. (2014b). Pornography consumption and US adults' attitudes toward gay individuals' civil liberties, moral judgments of homosexuality, and support for same-sex marriage: Mediating and moderating factors. *Communication Monographs, 81*(1), 79–107. https://doi.org/10.1080/03637751.2013.871048

Wright, P. J., Tokunaga, R. S., & Kraus, A. (2016a). Consumption of pornography, perceived peer norms, and condomless sex. *Health Communica-*

tion, 31(8), 954–963. https://doi.org/10.1080/10410236.2015.1022936

Wright, P. J., Tokunaga, R. S., & Kraus, A. (2016b). A meta-analysis of pornography consumption and actual acts of sexual aggression in general population studies. *Journal of Communication, 66*(1), 183–205. https://doi.org/10.1111/jcom.12201

Wroblewski, R., & Huston, A. C. (1987). Televised occupational stereotypes and their effects on early adolescents: Are they changing? *Journal of Early Adolescence, 7*(3), 283–297. https://doi.org/10.1177/0272431687073005

Wu, H. D., & Coleman, R. (2009). Advancing agenda-setting theory: The comparative strength and new contingent conditions of the two levels of agenda-setting effects. *Journalism & Mass Communication Quarterly, 86*(4), 775–789. https://doi.org/10.1177/107769900908600404

Wuang, Y.-P., Chiang, C.-S., Su, C.-Y., & Wang, C.-C. (2011). Effectiveness of virtual reality using Wii gaming technology in children with Down syndrome. *Research in Developmental Disabilities, 32*(1), 312–321. https://doi.org/10.1016/j.ridd.2010.10.002

Wyer, R. S., Jr. (2004). *Social comprehension and judgement: The role of situation models, narratives, and implicit theories.* Lawrence Earlbaum Associates.

Xie, G.-X., & Lee, M. J. (2008). Anticipated violence, arousal, and enjoyment of movies: Viewers' reactions to violent previews based on arousal-seeking tendency. *The Journal of Social Psychology, 148*(3), 277–292. https://doi.org/10.3200/SOCP.148.3.277-292

Xu, H., Zhang, Z., Wu, L., & Wang, C. J. (2019). The Cinderella complex: Word embeddings reveal gender stereotypes in movies and books. *PloS One, 14*(11), Article e0225385. https://doi.org/10.1371/journal.pone.0225385

Xu, Q. (2017). Dual process models of persuasion. In P. Rössler (Ed.), *International encyclopedia of media effects* (Vol. 1, pp. 418–430). Wiley-Blackwell. https://doi.org/10.1002/9781118783764.wbieme0074

Yang, C.-C., & Brown, B. B. (2013). Motives for using Facebook, patterns of Facebook activities, and late adolescents' social adjustment to college. *Journal of Youth and Adolescence, 42*(3), 403–416. https://doi.org/10.1007/s10964-012-9836-x

Yang., C.-C., & Brown, B. B. (2016). Online self-presentation on Facebook and self development during college transition. *Journal of Youth and Adolescence, 45,* 402–416. https://doi.org/10.1007/s10964-015-0385-y

Yang, H., Ramasubramanian, S., & Oliver, M. B. (2008). Cultivation effects on quality of life indicators: Exploring the effects of American television consumption on feelings of relative deprivation in South Korea and India. *Journal of*

Broadcasting & Electronic Media, 52(2), 247–267. https://doi.org/10.1080/08838150801992060

Yang, N., & Linz, D. (1990). Movie ratings and the content of adult videos: The sex-violence ratio. *Journal of Communication, 40*(2), 28–42. https://doi.org/10.1111/j.1460-2466.1990.tb02260.x

Yang, Y. (2020). Are you emoji savvy? Exploring nonverbal communication through emojis. *Communication Teacher, 34*(1), 2–7. https://doi.org/10.1080/17404622.2019.1593472

Yao, Q., Liu, Z., & Stephens, L. F. (2020). Exploring the dynamics in the environmental discourse: the longitudinal interaction among public opinion, presidential opinion, media coverage, policymaking in 3 decades and an integrated model of media effects. *Environment Systems and Decisions, 40,* 14–28. https://doi.org/10.1007/s10669-019-09746-y

Yarros, V. S. (1899). The press and public opinion. *The American Journal of Sociology, 5*(3), 372–382. https://doi.org/10.1086/210898

Ybarra, M. L., Strasburger, V. C., & Mitchell, K. J. (2014). Sexual media exposure, sexual behavior, and sexual violence victimization in adolescence. *Clinical Pediatrics, 53*(13), 1239–1247. https://doi.org/10.1177/0009922814538700

Young, D. G. (2013). Laughter, learning, or enlightenment? Viewing and avoidance motivations behind *The Daily Show* and *The Colbert Report. Journal of Broadcasting & Electronic Media, 57*(2), 153–169. https://doi.org/10.1080/08838151.2013.787080

Young, K. S. (1996). Psychology of computer use: XL. Addictive use of the internet: A case that breaks the stereotype. *Psychological Reports, 79*(3, Pt 1), 899–902. https://doi.org/10.2466/pr0.1996.79.3.899

YouTube. (n.d.) *YouTube for press.* https://www.youtube.com/about/press/

Yuen, E. K., Koterba, E. A., Stasio, M. J., Patrick, R. B., Gangi, C., Ash, P., Barakat, K., Greene, V., Hamilton, W., & Mansour, B. (2019). The effects of Facebook on mood in emerging adults. *Psychology of Popular Media Culture, 8*(3), 198–206. https://doi.org/10.1037/ppm0000178

Yzer, M. (2017). Theory of reasoned action and theory of planned behavior. In P. Rössler (Ed.), *International encyclopedia of media effects* (Vol. 4, pp. 1955–1962). Wiley-Blackwell. https://doi.org/10.1002/9781118783764.wbieme0075

Zajac, K., Ginley, M. K., Chang, R., & Petry, N. M. (2017). Treatments for internet gaming disorder and internet addiction: A systematic review. *Psychology of Addictive Behaviors, 31*(8), 979–994. https://doi.org/10.1037/adb0000315

Zaller, J. (1996). The myth of massive media impact revived: New support for a discredited idea. In D. C. Mutz, P. M. Sniderman, & R. A. Brody

(Eds.), *Political persuasion and attitude change* (pp. 17–78). University of Michigan Press.

Zeng, L. (2011). More than audio on the go: Uses and gratifications of MP3 players. *Communication Research Reports, 28*(1), 97–108. https://doi.org/10.1080/08824096.2011.541367

Zeng, S. (2020). The communication power of Chinese novel coronavirus pneumonia (COVID-19) news reports in light of the framing theory. *Theory and Practice in Language Studies, 10*(11), 1467–1470. https://doi.org/10.17507/tpls.1011.18

Zenith. (2021, May 24). *Business intelligence—Alcohol: Beer + spirits.* https://www.zenithmedia.com/insights/business-intelligence-alcohol-beer-spirits/

Zhang, G., Wu, L., Zhou, L., Lu, W., & Mao, C. (2016). Television watching and risk of childhood obesity: A meta-analysis. *European Journal of Public Health, 26*(1), 13–18. https://doi.org/10.1093/eurpub/ckv213

Zhang, L., & Min, Y. (2013). Effects of entertainment media framing on support for gay rights in China: Mechanisms of attribution and value framing. *Asian Journal of Communication, 23*(3), 248–267. https://doi.org/10.1080/01292986.2012.739187

Zhao, X. (2020). Health communication campaigns: A brief introduction and call for dialogue. *International Journal of Nursing Sciences, 7*(Suppl 1), S11–S15. https://doi.org/10.1016/j.ijnss.2020.04.009

Zhao, Y., & Zhang, J. (2017). Consumer health information seeking in social media: A literature review. *Health Information and Libraries Journal, 34*(4), 268–283. https://doi.org/10.1111/hir.12192

Zhong, B., Hardin, M., & Sun, T. (2011). Less effortful thinking leads to more social networking? The associations between the use of social network sites and personality traits. *Computers in Human Behavior, 27*(3), 1265–1271. https://doi.org/10.1016/j.chb.2011.01.008

Zhong, X., Zu, S., Sha, S., Tao, R., Zhao, C., & Yang, F. (2011). The effect of a family-based intervention model on internet-addicted Chinese adolescents. *Social Behavior and Personality: An International Journal, 39*(8), 1021–1034. https://doi.org/10.2224/sbp.2011.39.8.1021

Zhou, N., Cao, H., Li, X., Zhang, J., Yao, Y., Geng, X., Lin, X., Hou, S., Liu, F., Chen, X., & Fang, X. (2018). Internet addiction, problematic internet use, nonproblematic internet use among Chinese adolescents: Individual, parental, peer, and sociodemographic correlates. *Psychology of Addictive Behaviors, 32*(3), 365–372. https://doi.org/10.1037/adb0000358

Zhou, N., Cao, H, Liu, F., Wu, L., Liang, Y., Xu, J., Meng, H., Zang, N., Hao, R., An, Y. Ma, S., Fang, X., & Zhang, J. (2020). A four-wave, cross-lagged model of problematic internet use and mental health among Chinese college students: Disaggregation of within-person and between-person effects. *Developmental Psychology, 56*(5), 1009–1021. https://doi.org/10.1037/dev0000907

Zhou, S., Greer, A., & Finklea, B. W. (2010, April). *Discrimination, racist events, and their effects on behavioral and evaluative outcomes of movie posters with black and white protagonists* [Paper presentation]. Broadcast Education Association 55th Annual Meeting, Las Vegas, NV, United States.

Zill, N. (1977). *National survey of children: Summary of preliminary results.* Foundation for Child Development.

Zill, N. (2001). Does *Sesame Street* enhance school readiness? Evidence from a national survey of children. In S. M. Fisch & R. T. Truglio (Eds.), *"G" is for "growing": Thirty years of research on children and* Sesame Street (pp. 115–130). Lawrence Erlbaum Associates.

Zill, N., Davies, E., & Daly, M. (1994). *Viewing of* Sesame Street *by preschool children and its relationship to school readiness: Report prepared for the Children's Television Workshop.* Westat, Inc.

Zillmann, D. (1971). Excitation transfer in communication-mediated aggressive behavior. *Journal of Experimental Social Psychology, 7*(4), 419–434. https://doi.org/10.1016/0022-1031(71)90075-8

Zillmann, D. (1978). Attribution and misattribution of excitatory reactions. In J. H. Harvey, W. J. Ickes, & R. F. Kidd (Eds.), *New directions in attribution research* (Vol. 2, pp. 335–368). Lawrence Erlbaum Associates.

Zillmann, D. (1979). *Hostility and aggression.* Lawrence Erlbaum Associates.

Zillmann, D. (1980). Anatomy of suspense. In P. H. Tannenbaum (Ed.), *The entertainment functions of television* (pp. 133–163). Lawrence Erlbaum Associates.

Zillmann, D. (1982a). Television viewing and arousal. In D. Pearl, L. Bouthilet, & J. Lazar (Eds.), *Television and behavior: Ten years of scientific progress and implications for the eighties* (Vol. 2, pp. 53–67). U.S. Government Printing Office. https://files.eric.ed.gov/fulltext/ED228979.pdf

Zillmann, D. (1982b). Transfer of excitation in emotional behavior. In J. T. Cacioppo & R. E. Petty (Eds.), *Social psychophysiology.* Guilford Press.

Zillmann, D. (1988a). Cognition-excitation interdependencies in aggressive behavior. *Aggressive Behavior, 14*(1), 51–64. https://doi.org/10.1002/1098-2337(1988)14:1<51::AID-AB2480140107>3.0.CO;2-C

Zillmann, D. (1988b). Mood management through communication choices. *American Behavioral Scientist, 31*(3), 327–340. https://doi.org/10.1177/000276488031003005

Zillmann, D. (1991a). Empathy: Effect from bearing witness to the emotions of others. In J. Bryant & D. Zillmann (Eds.), *Responding to the screen: Recep-*

tion and reaction processes (pp. 135–167). Lawrence Erlbaum Associates.

Zillmann, D. (1991b). The logic of suspense and mystery. In J. Bryant & D. Zillmann (Eds.), *Responding to the screen: Reception and reaction processes* (pp. 281–303). Lawrence Erlbaum Associates.

Zillmann, D. (1996). Sequential dependencies in emotional experience and behavior. In R. D. Kavanaugh, B. Zimmerberg, & S. Fein (Eds.), *Emotion: Interdisciplinary perspectives* (pp. 243–272). Lawrence Erlbaum Associates.

Zillmann, D. (2000). Excitement. In A. E. Kazdin (Ed.), *Encyclopedia of psychology* (Vol. 3, pp. 283–285). American Psychological Association.

Zillmann, D., & Bryant, J. (1982). Pornography, sexual callousness, and the trivialization of rape. *Journal of Communication, 32*(4), 10–21. https://doi.org/10.1111/j.1460-2466.1982.tb02514.x

Zillmann, D., & Bryant, J. (1984). Effects of massive exposure to pornography. In N. M. Malamuth & E. Donnerstein (Eds.), *Pornography and sexual aggression* (pp. 115–138). Academic.

Zillmann, D., & Bryant, J. (1985). *Selective exposure to communication.* Lawrence Erlbaum Associates.

Zillmann, D., & Bryant, J. (1986). Shifting preferences in pornography consumption. *Communication Research, 13*(4), 560–578. https://doi.org/10.1177/009365086013004003

Zillmann, D., & Bryant, J. (1988). Pornography's impact on sexual satisfaction. *Journal of Applied Social Psychology, 18*(5), 438–453. https://doi.org/10.1111/j.1559-1816.1988.tb00027.x

Zillmann, D., Chen, L., Knobloch, S., & Callison, C. (2004). Effects of lead framing on selective exposure to internet news reports. *Communication Research, 31*(1), 58–81. https://doi.org/10.1177/0093650203260201

Zillmann, D., & Gibson, R. (1996). Evolution of the horror genre. In J. B. Weaver III & R. Tamborini (Eds.), *Horror films: Current research on audience preferences and reactions* (pp. 15–31). Lawrence Erlbaum Associates.

Zillmann, D., Hay, T. A., & Bryant, J. (1975). The effect of suspense and its resolution on the appreciation of dramatic presentations. *Journal of Research in Personality, 9*(4), 307–323. https://doi.org/10.1016/0092-6566(75)90005-7

Zillmann, D., Mody, B., & Cantor, J. (1974). Empathetic perception of emotional displays in films as a function of hedonic and excitatory state prior to exposure. *Journal of Research in Personality, 8*(4), 335–349. https://doi.org/10.1016/0092-6566(74)90025-7

Zillmann, D., & Weaver, J. B., III. (1999). Effects of prolonged exposure to gratuitous media violence on provoked and unprovoked hostile behavior. *Journal of Applied Social Psychology, 29*(1), 145–165. https://doi.org/10.1111/j.1559-1816.1999.tb01379.x

Zillmann, D., Weaver, J. B., Mundorf, N., & Aust, C. F. (1986). Effects of an opposite-gender companion's affect to horror on distress, delight, and attraction. *Journal of Personality and Social Psychology, 51*(3), 586–594. https://doi.org/10.1037/0022-3514.51.3.586

Zimmerman, A. G., & Ybarra, G. J. (2016). Online aggression: The influences of anonymity and social modeling. *Psychology of Popular Media Culture, 5*(2), 181–193. https://doi.org/10.1037/ppm0000038

Zimmerman, F. J., & Bell, J. F. (2010). Associations of television content type and obesity in children. *American Journal of Public Health, 100*(2), 334–340. https://doi.org/10.2105/AJPH.2008.155119

Zimmerman, F. J., Christakis, D. A., Meltzoff, A. N. (2007). Television and DVD/video viewing in children younger than 2 years. *Archives of Pediatrics and Adolescent Medicine, 161*(5), 473–479. https://doi.org/10.1001/archpedi.161.5.473

Zoglin, R. (1984, June 25). Gremlins in the rating system: Two hit films raise new concerns about protecting children. *TIME.* https://content.time.com/time/subscriber/article/0,33009,926639,00.html

Zuckerman, M. (1994). *Behavioral expressions and biosocial bases of sensation seeking.* Cambridge University Press.

Zwarun, L., & Farrar, K. M. (2005). Doing what they say, saying what they mean: Self-regulatory compliance and depictions of drinking in alcohol commercials in televised sports. *Mass Communication and Society, 8*(4), 347–371. https://doi.org/10.1207/s15327825mcs0804_4

Index